The Disciplines of Criticism

The Disciplines of Criticism

Essays in Literary Theory,
Interpretation, and History

Edited by
Peter Demetz,
Thomas Greene,
and Lowry Nelson, Jr.

NEW HAVEN AND LONDON, YALE UNIVERSITY PRESS, 1968

Copyright © 1968 by Yale University.
All rights reserved. This book may not be
reproduced, in whole or in part, in any form
(except by reviewers for the public press),
without written permission from the publishers.
Library of Congress catalog card number: 68-27751
Designed by Helen V. Buzyna,
set in Baskerville type,
and printed in the United States of America by
the Vail-Ballou Press, Inc., Binghamton, N.Y.
Distributed in Great Britain, Europe, Asia, and
Africa by Yale University Press Ltd., London; in
Canada by McGill University Press, Montreal; and
in Latin America by Centro Interamericano de Libros
Académicos, Mexico City.

For René Wellek
On the occasion of his sixty-fifth birthday
August 22, 1968

Foreword

The essays gathered in this volume have been written by colleagues, friends, and former students of René Wellek, to be presented to him on the occasion of his sixty-fifth birthday. The essays are concerned appropriately with all three of the major areas within the domain of literary study—history, analysis, and theory—areas which Mr. Wellek himself has discriminated and enriched. In the interest of structural clarity, the editors have grouped the contributions under these three headings, although some essays happily overflow the strict limits of the area assigned them. Separable in the abstract, the disciplines of criticism form a family whose practical felicity depends upon their perpetual remarriage.

It has been our hope, in the planning of this volume, to represent at once the range and the coherence of our distinguished colleague's own work. But despite the number of contributors, a kind of coherence has been easier to achieve than the full span of his interests. For most, perhaps all, of his contemporaries are fated to know his work fragmentarily. To read it all knowledgeably, including the translations, reviews, practical criticism, historical scholarship, discussions of aesthetics and the history of ideas, the history of criticism and criticism of criticism, ranging through all the modern literatures and from the Middle Ages to the most recent developments—to read it all with informed appreciation would be to approach the unique and strenuous scope of his own inclusive mind.

But despite its wealth, the writing of René Wellek has been informed by a few fixed principles, and among these perhaps the most persistent might be called the concern for definition. He has been interested literally in the history of definitions and curious to distinguish the complex meanings that entangle our contemporary critical vocabulary. But he has been equally concerned, whatever his subject, with definition in an ulterior sense—with scrupulous clarification and judicial exactness, with justice of praise and lucidity of interpretation. If the essayists gathered here have been successful, their work reflects his devotion to perspicuous thought and his double scorn for the blur of impressionism and the false precision of pedantry. That which their work cannot reflect is the kindness and warmth of its recipient, even if the respect with which they dedicate this volume is mingled with affectionate gratitude.

August 22, 1968

Contents

LITERARY HISTORY

Literary Theory

F. W. Bateson

Linguistics and
Literary Criticism

Il y a toujours un qui baise et un qui tend la joue. Mysteriously, in the curious flirtation now being conducted in our groves of academe between the specialists in linguistics and their opposite numbers in literature, the amorous advances have hitherto come exclusively from the linguists.[1] We literary critics and theorists, though naturally flattered by these attentions from our once hereditary enemies, have remained puzzled and more or less passive in the exchanges. Are the gentlemen's intentions *quite* as honorable as they profess them to be? Simpering coyly we have, it is true, occasionally allowed ourselves to be coaxed into a brief and embarrassed cooperation, but it has always been with a noticeable lack of enthusiasm. Perhaps, on the other hand, the whole thing is a colossal misunderstanding.

In this essay I propose to limit myself to the recent linguistic invasion of the once specifically literary area of style, though some of the seeds of doubt I hope to sow may prove to have a wider rele-

1. I have three recent works particularly in mind: *Style in Language,* ed. Thomas A. Sebeok (Cambridge, Mass., M.I.T. Press, 1960) ; *Linguistics and Style,* ed. John Spencer (London, Oxford University Press, 1964) ; *Essays on Style and Language,* ed. Roger Fowler (London, Routledge, 1966) . *Style in Language* incorporates papers originally read at a conference "to explore the possibility of finding a common basis for discussing and, hopefully, understanding, particularly among linguists, psychologists and literary critics, the characteristics of style in language" (Foreword, p. v). René Wellek contributed a closing statement, "From the Viewpoint of Literary Criticism," which includes a dictum on "the superstition of behaviourism" that may serve as epigraph to this paper: "It [behaviorism] denies the evidence of introspection and empathy, the two main sources of human and humane knowledge" (p. 409)

vance. If I have a methodological conclusion to offer it is, I am afraid, one of almost total skepticism. A linguist is certainly entitled to investigate works of literature for his own nonliterary purposes; what he must not expect, I suggest, is that criticism will derive any but the most marginal benefit from his findings. The premises and ideals of our respective disciplines—the linguist's of objective analytic description (analysis in order to describe), the critic's of intersubjective synthetic evaluation (synthesis in the service of value) —differ *toto caelo;* they cannot and should not be compromised.

The first question I am bound to ask therefore is whether "language," the apparent common denominator, has the same meaning for the linguist as for the literary critic. John Spencer for one, an English neo-grammarian who has recently edited a slim volume called *Linguistics and Style,* has no doubt about it. He begins his introduction as follows:

> Few literary scholars would suggest that literature can be satisfactorily studied without due attention to its medium, language. Nor would many linguists justify the investigation of literary language without guidance from those who devote themselves to the study of literature. There would, moreover, be a measure of agreement on both sides that the student of literature, whatever his particular interests, ought to be trained in the study of both language and literature. Yet, beneath this appearance of politeness and mutual esteem, discord and tension sometimes manifest themselves between what have become distinct disciplines.

That the "discord and tension" to which Mr. Spencer refers—and which R. H. Robins has also recently deplored as "a certain sense of rivalry and even at times of hostility expressed between literary pursuits and the study of language in linguistics today" [2]—may derive from a tendency of the two parties to force their own meaning of "language" on each other does not seem to have occurred to him. But the formula "language is the medium of literature"— which has a way of turning up whenever a linguist feels it necessary

2. *General Linguistics: An Introductory Survey* (London, Longmans, 1965), p. 368.

to justify his intrusion into literature—is an ambiguous one. After all, language is also the medium of conversation, of business, of scientific discourse, indeed of every aspect of human social intercourse. The immediate practical problem, however, is the kind and quantity of linguistic knowledge that is needed for the understanding and appreciation of, let us say, the plays of Shakespeare or the poems of Milton. If the literary student is a native of an English-speaking country, the quantity of additional linguistic knowledge that he will require can, I believe, easily be exaggerated.

The difference in historical premises is nicely, perhaps decisively, illustrated by the respective habits of linguist and critic whenever we read aloud or quote orally from any noncontemporary work of literature. A linguist will take it for granted, in classroom or lecture hall, that each phoneme in every word used by a Chaucer, Shakespeare, or Milton must be pronounced as far as possible just as it would have been by an educated Londoner of their time. To the critic, on the other hand, such detailed phonetic reconstructions appear an absurd affectation. The performance of one of Shakespeare's plays today as it was originally pronounced at the Globe is unthinkable to him, except as a philological curiosity. And the undoubted fact that Shakespeare himself would have considered the English used in a typical modern revival—or when quoted by a professor of English—to be grotesquely mispronounced does not worry the critic a bit.

The paradox that what is the "correct" pronunciation historically is not the "right" pronunciation critically is not affected by the notorious difficulty modern philologists find in agreeing upon exactly what vowel sounds Shakespeare and his actors employed. As long as English is a living language, the natural pronunciation of the works of Shakespeare and Milton—and indeed of any fifteenth- or sixteenth-century English writer (Chaucer is the borderline case)—will always be whatever English is current when they happen to be acted or read. The occasional exception in a rhyme or a pun only proves my general critical rule of continuous modernization.

An important theoretical principle is implicit in this paradox. It is right and natural for the native of an English-speaking country to pronounce the English literature of any period as if it had been written yesterday—whatever the historical evidence to the contrary may be—because English literature constitutes a cultural continuum. This is easily demonstrable. Thus it can never be an argument against the interpretation of this or that passage in Shakespeare that a usage is presupposed which did not exist in the English of Shakespeare's time. If the innovation was possible in later English it must also have been possible in Elizabethan English, because there is no essential discontinuity—apart from the introduction of certain new techniques and industries—between the culture of sixteenth-century England and that of later periods. Although the linguistic evidence will always be relevant, it cannot be the final determining literary factor in such cases. The determining literary factor is *stylistic effectiveness within the general cultural context.*

A simple example of this supra-linguistic principle is the Folio reading of *Macbeth,* II, ii, 63, "Making the Greene one, Red." To the obvious emendation, first proposed by Johnson, "Making the green, one red," C. J. Sisson has objected that "No contemporary instance has been cited of the use of *one* to mean 'totally' (however familiar it may seem today) and we may not without authority gloss *one red* as meaning *total gules.*" [3] He therefore retains the Folio's comma, explaining "the green one" as Neptune. This is certainly a grammatically possible sense; the objection to it is that it gives a bathetic anticlimax (even if we do not assume colloquial reduction of "one" in Sisson's sense to " 'un"—"green 'un") :

> Will all great Neptune's ocean wash this blood
> Clean from my hand? No, this my hand will rather
> The multitudinous seas incarnadine,
> Making the green one, red.

After the polysyllables of the previous line, the three final monosyllables must clearly all receive the maximum possible stress. To a literary critic the proposition is self-evident. That no contemporary instance of "one" in this emphatic sense is available

3. *New Readings in Shakespeare* (Cambridge, Cambridge University Press, 1956), II, 197.

is completely irrelevant. If Shakespeare can coin the verb "incarnadine" in the previous line, a license Sisson does not seem to object to, why may he not also extend the use of "one" to mean "totally"? Both usages were what may be called potential English, and the exact date when either became a formal part of the language has a merely antiquarian interest. What the critic is concerned with is the sentence's cultural significance in the continuum of English literature *from the viewpoint of the present*—not because the twentieth century can see more, or more clearly, than earlier centuries (losses have to be balanced against gains), but because an Englishman who happens to live in the twentieth century is committed to it willy-nilly. To become accessible to us critically, the literature of the past must in fact be translatable into the present tense. When confronted therefore with obsolete words or forms in it our only concern *as critics* is to know what they mean in modern English. The principle applies as much to a reader's own literature as to his reading of a foreign literature—such as that of the Romans or indeed, as I have argued elsewhere, the Anglo-Saxons. If we are to identify empathically with Hamlet, Macbeth, and the others, they must in effect become our contemporaries and so speak our English. Provided that object is obtained, however approximately and imperfectly, a cultural continuity is assured.

The hypothesis of a literary continuum—in the English case perhaps beginning about 1200 A.D. with works like *The Owl and the Nightingale* (in which language, prosody, style, and genre are essentially those familiar in later English poetry) —is a necessary one if the concept "English literature" is to have any substantial meaning. And we are then bound in logic, as I have implied, to concern ourselves principally, if not altogether, with those features of the English language that are *common* to the literature since 1200 or thereabouts.[4] The differences, in other words, must as far

4. *The Oxford English Dictionary* excludes Old English, except for purposes of etymological explanation, on two grounds: (i) the failure of so large a part of the O.E. vocabulary to survive after ca. 1150; (ii) the O.E. inflections would have meant a wholly different system of entry from that "adapted to the words which survived the twelfth century" ("General Explanations," 1933 ed., I, xxviii).

as possible be ignored—not because they do not exist but because this degree of anti-historicism is the price that has to be paid for the continuing vitality of an English literary tradition. (A parallel case would be the general implicit agreement, found within any linguistic area, to ignore for ordinary daily purposes of communication all but the grossest differences of class or regional dialect.)

The literary irrelevance that I have imputed in the preceding section to "diachronic" (historical) linguistics applies equally to "synchronic" linguistics, i.e. the detailed analysis of a language at any one period in its evolution. But the nature of the objection is different. The point that needs to be made depends, as it happens, on considerations invoked in a classic passage in that fountainhead of modern descriptive linguistics, Saussure's *Cours de linguistique générale* (Paris, 1916). It will be remembered that Saussure's point of theoretic departure—the distinction between *langue* (the language system) and *parole* (the language occasion)—was based on an analysis of the sequence of events implicit in "A" addressing a remark to "B." [5] The following diagram is a simplified summary of what Saussure called *le circuit de la parole*.

Psychological plane

An idea comes into "A" 's head.

The idea releases the appropriate "sound-image" associated with it (the idea is verbalized).

The "sound-image" detaches itself from the idea.

Physiological plane

"A" 's brain transmits the correlative nervous impulse to his vocal chords.

Physical plane

Certain sound waves pass from "A" 's lips to "B" 's ears.

["B" then repeats the processes undergone by "A" in an inverse order; i.e. whereas "A" 's contribution terminates on the physical plane, "B" 's begins on it, "B" then moving first to the physiological plane and ultimately to the psychological

5. "Place de la langue dans les faits de langage," pp. 27–32 of the 1955 ed.

plane, where "A" 's three processes are reenacted in the opposite order.]

It will be seen that "A" 's last stage, which is "B" 's first, is the only one common to them both. It is at this physical level that words, in the ordinary sense, are interchanged, but the conventional series of sounds emitted by "A" derive, of course, from "A" 's four earlier processes, just as they only "make sense" for "B" at the end of his four later processes. In the following diagram I have numbered the separate stages so as to make the full temporal sequence clear.

Psychological Plane

1. An idea enters "A" 's head.
2. "A" 's meaning is verbalized in linguistic "sound-images."
3. The "sound-images" detach themselves from the meaning.

9. "A" 's idea enters "B" 's head.
8. The "sound-images" release their conventional meanings.
7. The sounds are mentalized as linguistic "sound-images."

Physiological Plane

4. "A" 's brain transmits the appropriate nervous impulse to the vocal chords.

6. "B" 's ears transmit to his brain the appropriate impulses set in motion by "A" 's sounds.

Physical Plane

5. A series of conventional sound waves (the phonemes) are directed from "A" 's lips to "B" 's ears.

Saussure's details, some of which I may have oversimplified, need not detain us. For literary theory the point of particular interest is "B" 's exact repetition of "A" 's psychological, physiological, and physical processes *in an inverted order*. Whereas "A" proceeds from a psychological phase to a physical phase, "B" reverses the process and proceeds from the physical to the psychological. There is also a reversal of direction even on the same level. Thus on the physical plane, as the sound waves leave "A" 's mouth to impinge on "B" 's ears, "A" 'gives out' and "B" 'takes in.' It follows that even if communication is completely successful and "B" reproduces accurately at each phase the exact equivalent of what "A" has already contributed to *le circuit de la parole,* there is still this difference of direction. For "A" the sequence is toward

increasing externalization, for "B" toward increasing internalization. Saussure's analysis is, of course, incomplete. In the give-and-
take of everyday conversation, what "A" has to say to "B" is
counterbalanced by what "B" has to say to "A." Question begets
answer, as assertion begets either assent or contradiction. But once
the cycle of speech is inflated into what may be called the literary
cycle ("the *best* words in the *best* order"), and "A" becomes the
author and "B" the literary audience, the typical situation has
changed. The function of the author qua author is to externalize
all the time, just as the literary audience—once the curtain has
gone up or until the book is put down—is internalizing all the
time. Whether (i) the author is his own reader or reciter, or (ii)
a professional reader or reciter substitutes for him, or (iii) the
auditor becomes his own reader or reciter, either aloud or sotto
voce, does not affect this basic relationship. Even when we are
reading a work of literature to ourselves we are not doing it to
externalize a psychological condition of our own, as "A" or an
author "expresses" himself; on the contrary, our object is still
under normal circumstances simply to internalize somebody else's
externalizations. We are patients, not agents. The point becomes a
crucial one for literary theory when the terminal areas of the
linguistic or literary cycle are subjected to a rather different mode
of analysis from that of Saussure.

Since we are all readers I shall begin with "B" (who now
typifies the literary audience). "B," then, begins his book by reading the first sentence on page 1. The fact that a visual process is
superimposed on that of speech adds a further stage to the cycle of
communication but does not affect the direction of the series of
impulses; the writer is still externalizing, the reader still internalizing. Having identified the series of black marks at the top of
the block of printed matter as so many letters, and the separate
groups of letters as so many words, "B" is able to fill out mentally
what Saussure called *le signifiant* in front of his eyes with *le signifié,* a process that requires him to recognize the grammatical relationships between the words in his sentence as well as their separate meanings. At this point, if he is a competent performer, he
has "understood" the first sentence.

But what does "understanding" imply in this context? It is with this question that the distinction between speech, as it is normally practiced, and any form of literature, as the term is normally used, forces itself upon the theorist's attention. There are, no doubt, modes of speech which resemble literature in the silent acquiescence of "B" (but always "B" in a plural number) to sentence after sentence from "A." The preacher, the political orator, even the teller of a complicated story, or the narrator of an elaborate series of events, are all differentiated from the "A" of such typical speech phenomena as question and answer or assertion and counter-assertion. In these more elaborate situations the speaker becomes in effect indistinguishable from an author and the auditor from a theatrical spectator or the audience at a reading such as those Dickens used to give of his novels. "B" for once is now content to leave the role of externalization entirely to "A." Social custom does not allow or at least encourage him to answer back or challenge "A"—not at any rate until the speech is complete or the tale has reached its end. His only defenses against "A" 's eloquence are to walk out of the political meeting or to close his ears, physically or metaphorically, to what "A" is saying.

"A," however, in his role of prophet or entertainer, is always aware, consciously or unconsciously, of the possibility of "B" 's denial of *le circuit de la parole;* he has therefore developed his own counter-strategy, which is to *persuade* "B" to continue silent, interested, and attentive. The eloquence of the orator must now become so irresistible, the story must be told so amusingly or so excitingly, that "B" "cannot choose but hear." In other words, rhetoric is now added to speech. Unless rhetoric, in its most general sense, *is* added to speech, the prolongation of "A" 's role in the speech cycle will tend sooner or later to be resisted or refused by "B." A club bore cannot hold his audience, because his rhetoric is inferior or nonexistent, because he is innocent of the *ars dicendi.*

Literature is committed by the nature of its audience relationship to the superimposition upon speech of the specially heightened rhetoric that we call "style." Etymologically the word carries us back to the *stilus* of the scribe, just as "literature" itself implies a mode of speech recorded physically in *literae* inscribed by a *stilus.* In a written work, because a rereading or a reference back will elucidate the obscurities or ambiguities, the speech can be heightened, concentrated, elevated, coordinated. The speech rhythms in a poem have been specially regularized or diversified; the vocabulary is unusually varied or purified; certain unusual or artificial "figures" add color, balance, and subtlety to the word order; the subject matter has been sifted selectively; appropriate attitudes toward the audience and modes of presentation (the genres) have been distinguished and elaborated.

This, it will be agreed, is what literature looks like *ab extra*—to all of us, whether we are linguists or critics. It will be objected no doubt by a linguist that the traditional categories of prosody and stylistics are now being revised and reconstructed by descriptive linguistics with much more precise and up-to-date tools of external analysis. Why is it then, we retort, that so little of critical interest has so far emerged from modern linguistics? One answer, I suggest, stares us all in the face in the movements of *le circuit de la parole*. The linguist must always tend to refer the phenomena of style *back* to their constituents in language (stage 8 in Saussure's scheme in the second diagram above) rather than *forwards* to the post-linguistic or strictly psychological phase represented by Saussure's stage 9. Language after all is the linguist's business. But a realistic approach to the problems of style demands a two-way investigation—not only of the linguistic constituents of such devices as irony and metaphor, but also of their psychological origins and post-linguistic consequences. The essence of *le circuit de la parole,* as we have seen, is its temporal continuity: each phase in the series is being displaced at any one moment by its successor, as word follows word and sentence follows sentence. But, just as the separate letters of each word are immediately lost to sight in the reader's consciousness as he internalizes their total significance, so the separate words, phrases, clauses, and sentences disappear mentally once they translate themselves into the ideas or images that they symbolize. In Saussure's formula, "A" 's idea eventually enters "B" 's head, *le signifiant* having again become *le signifié.*

In the literary cycle, with the intervention of "style" between Saussure's stages 8 and 9, the process is more complicated. Reduced to its simplest linguistic terms, "style" can be described as a complex of verbal repetition, either overt or disguised. Thus meter is basically the abstraction from the verbal totality of certain syllable patterns which are then repeated; in an accentual system, for example, the "foot," consisting typically of any heavily stressed syllable preceded by any lightly stressed syllable (the iamb) , does not become a "line" unless it is repeated several times. Other modes or levels of repetition are equally familiar. A sonnet, for example, superimposes on the pattern of syllable recurrence the further pattern of its special rhyme scheme. In the area of figures of speech the repetition is usually a partial duplication. Thus in puns, ironies, and metaphors two things are being said at the same time which are in some respects identical, though in others blatantly discrepant or contradictory. A similar combination of identity and difference characterizes such other stylistic devices or categories as connotation, balance, ambiguity, and symbolism. I need not retraverse what is familiar ground.

A crucial point, however, tends to be overlooked in linguistic investigations into the various aspects of style, namely, the effect of such repetitions on Saussure's stage 9. As the separate words and sentences merge in the reader's consciousness into the verbal combinations or patterns that he has learned to associate with literature, *le signifié* changes its nature with *le signifiant*. The context of literary communication is different from that of speech in four respects: (i) "A" (the author) is invisible and "B" (the audience) cannot influence him or answer back in any effective way; (ii) "A" 's act of communication may often not be completed until "B" has spent many hours or days turning many pages; (iii) "A" 's communication is not meant to be confined to a single "B" but may sometimes have millions of readers, all responding to it in more or less the same way. But the real crux is the fourth difference, which might be described as the new sense of order and significance that the accumulated repetitions of style add to Saussure's stage 9.

In the literary cycle stage 9 can perhaps be called the Aesthetic Moment. As the actual words and stylistic devices recede from the reader's consciousness their place is taken by an illusion of actual experience, one in which the reader shares though without being actively involved in it. An aesthetic distance, as we say, separates the human situation which the reader appears to be contemplating from such a situation in real life. Lessing put it succinctly in Chapter xvii of his *Laocoön:*

> The poet wishes not only to be intelligible, his representations ought not only to be clear and perspicuous; with this the prose writer may be content. But the poet desires to make the ideas which he awakens in us so vivid, that from the rapidity with which they arise we believe ourselves to be really as conscious of his objects as if they were actually presented to our senses; and in this moment of illusion we cease to be conscious of the means—that is, of the words—which he employs for this purpose.[6]

We can now return to Saussure's stage 1. In *le circuit de la parole* "B" 's process of internalization repeated in an inverted order the phases—physical, physiological, and psychological—of "A" 's externalization. The idea that came into "A" 's head in stage 1 finally reached "B" 's head in stage 9. If we substitute the literary cycle for the speech cycle a similar relationship must be expected to hold. But if stage 9 is the reader's Aesthetic Moment, what are we to call stage 1? The author's Aesthetic Moment? The author's "moment of illusion"? If the parallel with stage 9 is valid, stage 1 in the literary cycle will at any rate be both pre-stylistic and pre-linguistic. Let us call it the Creative Moment, meaning by the term very much what Coleridge meant by the Imagination and Shelley by Inspiration.

The assumption that an author's progress toward composition follows the same pattern as a reader's toward the Aesthetic Moment but in an inverted order has an important theoretical consequence. It means that literary creation externalizes itself first as style and only secondarily as grammar or language. In style we are nearer to the working of the creative imagination than we are at the linguistic level. It follows that in interpreting literature's stylistic phenomena we shall be well advised to pay more attention to the causes of literary creation, the sources of a particular imaginative act and their correlatives in the reader's part of the cycle, than with the consequences in language.

6. Translation by Sir Robert Phillimore (London, 1874).

No doubt this advice will sound suspiciously vague and un-
practical, but the parallel between Saussure's *circuit de la parole*
and what I have called the literary cycle is once again reassuring.
It would not be difficult to discover why under certain circumstances a particular idea came into "A" 's head (he is passing a
shop with fresh strawberries displayed in the window) —or what
"B" 's reaction might be when he understood what "A" was saying
(the strawberries are five shillings a punnet). The simplest verbal
exchange operates in a social or cultural context which is no less
real for being tacitly taken for granted. And it will be agreed that
the reader's end of the literary cycle presents no special theoretical
difficulties. Stage 9 (the Aesthetic Moment) terminates with or
soon after the reading of the particular work of literature. But that
is not the end, as far as the particular work's particular reader is
concerned. As the experience released in the actual process of
reading loses its first imaginative freshness it will be followed by a
stage 10, which may be called the Emotional Response. (For Aristotle catharsis clearly occurred *after* the tragedy had reached its
end.) And a stage 11, that of the Critical Verdict, no doubt comes
later still, in most cases many hours or days later. By the time this
phase is reached the memory has had an opportunity to discard the
trivial and irrelevant elements from the original aesthetic experience, and the emotional consequences can also be seen in a perspective of similar reactions. It follows that when literary criticism
begins the originating linguistic stimulus is already very remote.

If the Saussurian formula of an inverted order is equally applicable to the author on this pre-linguistic level, we are presumably
left with a creative equivalent of the Critical Verdict as the ultimate origin of a work of literature. Perhaps this origin is some sort
of communal value judgment itching to express itself? And instead
of the Emotional Response of the reader do we posit an Emotional
Explosion within the author resulting from the general originating value judgment? I make these final equations with extreme
diffidence. The creative process begins below the level of consciousness, and hypotheses about its origins naturally resist adequate formulation and confirmation.

Nevertheless literary theory must insist that its concern with the
pre-linguistic in literary composition and the post-linguistic in the

reading of literature is legitimate and essential. To exclude these areas from the literary process, as modern descriptive linguistics is compelled to do, is unscientific as well as arbitrary. The literary cycle is as much a fact of experience as *le circuit de la parole.* Moreover—to reintroduce a concept that I have already applied to "diachronic" linguistics—both the circuit and the cycle must necessarily be experienced as continuous, if the terms are to have any meaning. In other words, for linguistic or literary communication to take place between them "A" and "B" must already be in preverbal contact as human beings. The sound waves directed from "A" 's lips to "B" 's ears presume an existing rapport between "A" and "B." I am not invoking any Jungian collective subconsciousness here but the elementary fact that "A" will not greet "B" unless some social bond already connects them. I do not say "How do you do?" to a complete stranger. There is therefore a *social* plane preceding Saussure's psychological plane that is as much a part of *parole* as of *langue.* And what is true of *le circuit de la parole* is equally true obviously of the literary cycle; authors do not write for a non-audience.

Because of its latent premise of discontinuity, linguistics, whether historical or descriptive, can contribute little to the critical study of literature. Some recent attempts to provide linguistic interpretations of poems by Donne, Hopkins, and Larkin have been dismal examples of ingenious irrelevance. Let us therefore follow Socrates' example with the poets, crowning these linguistic invaders of literature with garlands of wool and anointing them with myrrh—*and sending them away to another city.*

Cleanth Brooks

William Butler Yeats
as a Literary Critic

William Butler Yeats was obviously a brilliant literary critic. His
incidental comments on poets and poems are often exciting, sometimes profound. To be sure, Yeats was often cranky and perverse.
His *Oxford Book of Modern Verse* is a kind of monument to an
arbitrary taste. He had his blind sides; he could be unfair; he made
no bones about his prejudices and partialities. Yet it is a pleasure
to reread his prose and it is rewarding to do so. All of his writing
abounds in provocative comments, perceptive summations, revealing insights, often apparently tossed off as asides. Even *A Vision* is
rich in this kind of material: see, for example, his accounts of the
poets and artists used as illustrations of his twenty-six types of
men. Walt Whitman "makes catalogues of all that has moved him,
or amused his eye, that he may grow more poetical. Experience is
all-absorbing, subordinating observed fact, drowning even truth
itself, if truth is conceived of as something apart from impulse and
instinct." [1] Even the devoted Whitmanian will find it difficult to
cavil at this account of the basic stance of his hero though he
would want, of course, to claim for Whitman much more than
Yeats allows him here.

Yeats tells us that "in the poetry of Keats there is, though little
sexual passion, an exaggerated sensuousness that compels us to
remember the pepper on the tongue as though that were his
symbol. Thought is disappearing into image." [2] This is a one-
sided view, and the story that Keats put cayenne pepper into his
mouth in order to relish all the more the taste of cold claret has
apparently now been given up. Even so, Yeats has fastened on a

1. *A Vision* (London, Macmillan, 1937), p. 114.
2. Ibid., p. 134.

17

point worth exploring: he has noted the qualities in Keats's poetry that make the story of the pepper seem plausible. Yeats's account of Synge—he had known Synge personally—is brilliant. For Yeats, Synge was the artist who must discover his true vision not by striving for it—that, he must avoid—but by letting himself become absorbed in the technical problems of expression. He must "fill many notebooks, clap his ear to that hole in the ceiling," [3] listening to the talk of the Aran Island girls so that he may catch the exact cadence of their speech. He must not breathe his own spirit into the scene that he is describing, for that will simply blur and distort. As Yeats puts it in a beautifully precise figure: when Synge discovers his true art, he is like a man who "wipes his breath from the window-pane, and laughs in his delight at all the varied scene" [4] which the now transparent glass reveals to him.

Yeats's letters also are filled with insights of this sort. Byron is for him a "great English poet," though, he tells us, "one can hardly call him great except in purpose and manhood." [5] Doubtless Yeats was too severe on Poe and yet how much of what has been said later he anticipates in a letter written as early as 1899. There he confesses that Poe's

> fame always puzzles me. I have to acknowledge that even after one allows for the difficulties of a critic who speaks a foreign language, a writer who has had so much influence on Baudelaire and Villiers de L'Isle Adam has some great merit. I admire a few lyrics of his extremely and a few pages of his prose, chiefly in his critical essays, which are sometimes profound. The rest of him seems to me vulgar and commonplace and the Pit and the Pendulum and the Raven do not seem to me to have permanent literary value of any kind. Analyze the Raven and you find that its subject is a commonplace and its execution a rhythmical trick. [6]

Yeats always shows some antipathy toward Wordsworth and finds it difficult to be just to him. But how neatly—and up to a

3. Ibid., p. 166.
4. Ibid., p. 165.
5. *The Letters of W. B. Yeats,* ed. Allan Wade (New York, Macmillan, 1955), p. 710.
6. Ibid., p. 325.

point, I think, accurately—he assesses Wordsworth's characteristic weaknesses. He remarks in his "Anima Hominis" that Wordsworth, great poet "though he be, is so often flat and heavy partly because his moral sense, being a discipline he had not created, a mere obedience, has no theatrical element. This increases his popularity with the better kind of journalists and politicians who have written books." [7] Whatever the justice of this comment on Wordsworth, it at least tries to account for what the "two voices" theory merely describes; and it is at least a valid judgment on the typical nineteenth-century Wordsworthian.

The force and the truth of comments of this sort will be conceded by most readers—though most of us, of course, will want to make our own choices from Yeats's critical sallies and literary observations, discarding those that we feel are really outrageous, cherishing those that we feel have merit. But that Yeats's criticism attains to any real coherency and that it reveals any kind of systematic relationship among its parts will not be so readily granted.

I shall not claim that Yeats's criticism is entirely self-consistent or that it provides a complete view of poetry. But Yeats did value system, as his labors on *A Vision* show, and his basic conception of poetry and of the role of the poet does make a pattern. To work out this pattern in detail would be a project much too ambitious for this short essay. Mine is a more modest undertaking: to show that Yeats had a very clear notion of what poetry was and specifically that he conceived of it as providing a special kind of truth and therefore distinguished it, on the one hand, from mere self-expression and, on the other hand, from propaganda for a cause. (Yeats was throughout his life a man of causes, but he denied the title of poetry even to propaganda for causes that he thought were noble and in which as a man he deeply believed.)

Any account of Yeats's critical theory properly begins with his conception of the creative process. How a poet created was a matter of primary consequence to him, though as we shall presently see, his criticism did not remain fixated on it. Yeats's key concept is that "No mind can engender till divided into two." [8] Poetry is created through a dialectical process. But Yeats, in devel-

---

7. *Mythologies* (New York, Macmillan, 1959), p. 334.

8. *Autobiography* (London, Macmillan, 1961), p. 345. All subsequent page references to this volume will be found in parentheses in the text.

oping his celebrated notions of creation from an anti-self, had much more in mind than a compositional trick—a gimmick by which the poet could evade the superficial and topical aspects of his mind in order to get down to the layers beneath immediate consciousness. The dialectic through which the poem is produced gives its own impress to the poem. The tension developed in the play between opposites is built into the poem.

For Yeats, penetration into the depths of the mind was indeed necessary. He describes poetic genius as "a crisis that joins [the] buried self for certain moments to our trivial daily mind" (p. 272). Art is for him a special kind of knowledge, a revelation, and all revelation, he tells us, "is . . . from that age-long memoried self, that shapes the elaborate shell of the mollusc and the child in the womb, that teaches the birds to make their nest" (p. 272).

Stated less gaudily—translated into the terms of current depth psychology—this conception of the process of poetic composition is now commonplace, though we ought to remember that it was scarcely so when Yeats wrote his essay entitled "Hodos Chamelion- tos" in 1917. The difficulties encountered in peering into the depths of the self and the possibilities of self-deception in trying to do so are matters of which Yeats was fully aware. I shall return to them a little later. At this point, however, I want to stress his belief that the process of making a poem is not one of simple self- expression. Nor does it have anything to do with the manipulation of reality so as to secure something that the poet desires for him- self or for his society. Yeats is quite explicit on this point. In "The Tragic Generation," he puts the question:

> Does not all art come when a nature, that never ceases to judge itself, exhausts personal emotion in action or desire so completely that something impersonal, something that has nothing to do with action or desire, suddenly starts into its place, something which is as unforeseen, as completely or- ganized, even as unique, as the images that pass before the mind between sleeping and waking? (p. 332)

It is interesting to see how he applied this principle to the poetry of Shelley. Shelley had been the idol of the young Yeats; yet Yeats finally had to deny that Shelley had ever made this necessary severance of art from desire. In 1932 he wrote: "Shelley was not a mystic, his system of thought was constructed by his logical faculty to satisfy desire, not a symbolical revelation received after the suspension of all desire. He could neither say with Dante, 'His will is our peace,' nor with Finn in the Irish story, 'The best music is what happens.' " [9]

Yeats's poem "Ego Dominus Tuus" will show why he felt that the poet had to exclude from art personal emotion that was "unexhausted"—that is, emotion that was still alive and pushing toward expression in action or desire. In "Ego Dominus Tuus" [10] Yeats has, by the way, split his own mind into two in order to make his point. The poem is a debate between two antagonists, Hic and Ille—that is, "this one" and "that one," both of them presumably aspects of man's mind and specifically of Yeats's own mind.

Hic voices an expressive theory of art: the poet puts himself into his work, and the reader will expect to find the man who created the poem within the poem that he has created. Ille, however, denies that poetry is expressive—at least, that it is so in this simple fashion—and asserts that Dante, for example, created his poetry, not from what he was, but from all that he was not. Hic quite properly interprets this conflict between what a man is and what he is not as a "tragic war" and asks rather pointedly whether there are not at least some poets whose art comes, not out of such a conflict, but out of their love of life. Among the poets surely there are, Hic argues,

> Impulsive men that look for happiness
> And sing when they have found it.

Ille's answer categorically denies such a possibility. Those who are lovers of life and who have found their happiness in it do not sing at all, and Ille points out the reason: "those that love the world serve it in action." As happy, successful lovers of the world, they

9. *Essays and Introductions* (New York, Macmillan, 1961), pp. 421–22.
10. *The Collected Poems of W. B. Yeats* (New York, Macmillan, 1951), p. 158.

> Grow rich, popular and full of influence,
> And should they paint or write, still it is action:
> The struggle of the fly in marmalade.

(Yeats may be remembering here the rueful comment that Paul
Verlaine once made to him when, pointing to his bandaged leg, he
remarked that he knew Paris all too well. In fact Paris had
scorched his leg. He had lived in Paris "like a fly in a pot of
marmalade" [p. 341].)

In the lines that follow, Ille mentions two kinds of pseudo-
artists: the rhetorician (or, as we would more ordinarily call him
today, the propagandist) and the sentimentalist.

> The rhetorician would deceive his neighbours,
> The sentimentalist himself; while art
> Is but a vision of reality.

Whereas the rhetorician deliberately deceives his fellows, the
sentimentalist is self-deceived, the victim of his own illusions
about the world. Both kinds of deception are sharply set off from
the revelation of truth accomplished by authentic art.

Art, Yeats insists, "is *but* a vision of reality." I stress the adversa-
tive, for Yeats is here clearly emphasizing the sense of detachment
from action and from desire. Unlike the rhetorician and sentimentalist who involve themselves in the world and whose work is consciously or unconsciously a form of action, the artist stands back
from the world so that he may see it the more clearly.

The passage from "Ego Dominus Tuus" (written in December
1915) on which I have just been commenting obviously comes out
of the same matrix as Yeats's often-quoted remark that "We make
out of the quarrel with others, rhetoric, but of the quarrel with
ourselves, poetry" (written in February 1917).[11] It may seem odd
that a poet, and a great lyric poet at that, should think of poetry as
issuing from a quarrel of any sort. But if one is willing to grant any
validity to the notion that poetry issues from a quarrel, then surely
Yeats is right in making the relevant quarrel, not a contention
with others, but a deep-seated struggle within the self. For this
quarrel is part of a process of self-discovery and self-realization.

11. *Mythologies*, p. 331.

A vision of reality rather than a manipulation of reality—thus Yeats puts matters in his poem "Ego Dominus Tuus," but elsewhere in his writings he makes the distinction in somewhat different terms, as between truth and falsity. The genuine poet will be truthful in recording the defect, the ugliness, the evil that is to be found in reality. In one of his letters Yeats quotes Mabel Beardsley's statement that her brother Aubrey "hated the people who denied the existence of evil, and so being young he filled his pictures with evil. *He had a passion for reality* [italics mine]." [12] In his *Autobiography* Yeats ascribes this same passion to Dante and Villon, arguing that "had they cherished any species of optimism, they could have but found a false beauty." And again in his *Autobiography*, he writes that "Donne could be as metaphysical as he pleased, and yet never seemed unhuman and hysterical as Shelley often does, because he could be as physical as he pleased; and besides who will thirst for the metaphysical, who have a parched tongue, if we cannot recover the Vision of Evil" (p. 326). The apparent non sequitur—for what has the Vision of Evil to do with our thirst for the metaphysical?—disappears when we remember that Yeats considered the ability to discern evil to be an essential part of one's ability to apprehend reality.

The choice of Shelley as the antithesis of Donne is, by the way, a shrewd one. Shelley—at least the youthful Shelley—with his utopian optimism and his zeal to reform the world becomes in Yeats's notion "unhuman and hysterical." Because Donne knew the body and its limitations, clung to the body, refused to take off from the earth into ethereal skylark flights, and could not conceivably have apostrophized the skylark with the words *"Bird* thou never *wert"*—because of all this, Donne could be as metaphysical as he pleased.

One may sum up at this point by saying that Yeats's conception of poetry is closely linked to his conception of reality: the function of poetry is not to express man's desires or to change the world in which he lives, bringing it closer to his own desires, but to reveal reality. Yet so summary an account of Yeats's position leaves many loose ends to be tied up and many subsidiary questions to be answered. For instance, if the poet must create from his opposite—if

12. *Letters,* p. 575.

he must, as Yeats so often puts the matter, assume a mask and consciously play a part—may not such role-playing tempt the artist to
fall into insincerity and to become a rhetorician indeed? Or, to
notice a related problem, is there not a danger that Yeats's conception of art throws the poet too much back onto himself and thus
risks committing him to a morbid subjectivity? How does one
reconcile Yeats's stress upon meditation and solitude with his celebration of poets like Chaucer, who seemed to live in the sunlight
and to speak for a whole society? And how does one reconcile the
emphasis upon meditation with Yeats's own lifelong preoccupation with the unity of culture—with his praise of the robust spiritual health of some of the great civilizations of the past? Again,
what is the specific force of Yeats's reiterated attacks upon abstraction? Yeats constantly treats abstraction as the inveterate enemy
of art. Etymologically, abstraction is a *drawing away,* but in
Yeats's meaning of the term, a drawing away from what? In dis-
paraging an "external art," is not Yeats asking that the artist with-
draw from the world and thus condemning him to a form of
abstraction?

These are some of the possible self-contradictions that reveal
themselves when one reads Yeats's criticism. The reader has a right
to ask whether they can be reconciled with Yeats's basic position,
and if so, how; but he may at this point feel himself bemused by
abstractions of another sort, for few things are so difficult as abstract discussions of poetry. Can one produce concrete particulars,
illustrations of the genuine artist, the confused artist, and the
sham artist, as Yeats conceives them with reference to his rather
austere conception of art?

Yeats actually provides abundant illustrations. He had in
mind, for example, two specific artists when he wrote

> while art
> Is but a vision of reality

and continued with the lines

> What portion in the world can the artist have
> Who has awakened from the common dream
> But dissipation and despair?

The artists were Ernest Dowson and Lionel Johnson, as a passage in "Anima Hominis," written about the same time as "Ego Dominus Tuus," makes clear. In that essay Yeats observes that

> no fine poet, no matter how disordered his life, has ever, even in his mere life, had pleasure for his end. Johnson and Dowson . . . were *dissipated* men . . . and yet they had the gravity of men who had found life out and were *awakening from the dream.* . . . Nor has any poet I have read of or heard of or met with been a sentimentalist. The other self, the anti-self . . . comes but to those who are no longer deceived, whose passion is reality. [*italics mine*] [13]

Yeats constantly associates the artist with the hero and the saint. The hero and the saint also live their lives in terms of an anti-self, the hero modeling himself on some great figure of the past, the saint carrying out an *imitatio Christi;* but the material with which the hero and the saint work is their own flesh and blood whereas the material used by the poet is "paper or parchment." But the activity, Yeats insists, is an analogous one: he tells us that in "all great poetical styles there is saint or hero," even though, "when it is all over Dante can return to his chambering" [14]—in "Ego Dominus Tuus" we are told that though Dante found in his poetry "The most exalted lady loved by man," he was mocked by "Guido for his lecherous life"—and Shakespeare, after his great verse, can return "to his pottle-pot. [Dante and Shakespeare can do so because they] sought no impossible perfection [except when] they handled paper or parchment." [15]

In the capsule definition of art that we have quoted from "Ego Dominus Tuus," Yeats treats the rhetorician as a conscious manipulator and implies that he has an ulterior purpose: he means to "deceive his neighbours." But Yeats was well aware that in practice few literary rhetoricians were so clearly and consciously propagandistic as this. The typical case, both as to methods and motives, was far more complicated. A particular example will help make this point clear. Yeats says in so many words that Shelley

13. *Mythologies,* p. 331.
14. Ibid., p. 333.
15. Ibid.

lacked the vision of evil to which poets like Dante and Villon had
attained, and he is willing to associate Shelley with a naïve propa-
gandizing for vague utopias, but he is far from denying that
Shelley was a poet, and certainly he does not think that Shelley
consciously tried to gull his neighbors. Yeats does, on occasion,
chide Shelley for having dissipated his poetic energies in quarrels
with his neighbors, but that is a very different matter, though it
remains a sufficient indictment in view of Yeats's celebrated text
that it is out of our "quarrel with others" that we make "rhetoric,"
and only out of "the quarrel with ourselves" that we make poetry.

That celebrated text—the case of Shelley quite aside—is worth
a little elaboration. One is encouraged to quarrel with others if he
thinks that all problems are soluble and that only the stupidity or
the villainy of other men prevents our solving the world's problems. One is also encouraged to quarrel with others in proportion
as he knows himself imperfectly and is thus inclined to be too
easily impressed with his own virtue and his own good intentions.
Yet surely Yeats does not delude himself into thinking that self-
knowledge ever came easily, and he has acknowledged that his own
essential nature was in fact very much like Shelley's.[16] Yeats describes himself as by nature political, gregarious, quarrelsome, full
of schemes for the improvement of Irish culture and the liberation
of the Irish spirit, and not disposed to suffer gladly either the
knaves or fools who stood in the way of those schemes (see p.
171).

Most important of all, in Yeats's view of things, man is not a
completely free agent. He feels the pressure of his own time and it
imposes its limitations on him. Thus, when an artist fails to do
what Yeats believes authentic art demands, it is rarely simply a
matter of the artist's blindness or headstrong folly. One has to take
into account the nature of the time and the state of the civilization
in which the artist has been born. It was one of Yeats's deepest beliefs that some periods of a civilization had been propitious for the
arts and that others had not been.

16. Yeats regarded Shelley as a man of "Phase Seventeen" (see *A Vision*, p.
141), and there is abundant evidence that Yeats saw himself as belonging to
the same phase.

As we have already noted, Yeats wrote himself down as a man for whom unity of being was of supreme importance. The great ages for him were those in which a high degree of cultural unity was attained. The burden of his various accounts of literary history is the inevitable falling away from these periods of great and rich unity—the descent into mechanization, division, and abstraction.

In that brilliant little thumbnail sketch of English literature which Yeats borrowed from his friend William Magee ("John Eglinton") [17]—and improved upon—the history of English literature since the Middle Ages is described as essentially a movement from unity of culture to the isolation of the individual. Yeats arrives at our present day by imagining "Chaucer's personages" to have disengaged themselves from "Chaucer's crowd" through having forgot their "common goal and shrine," and after "sundry magnifications [to have become] each in turn the center of some Elizabethan play," and then, finally, through having split into their elements, to have "given birth to romantic poetry" (p. 193). When men experience a weakening of the common values that make them one people and when, as a consequence, they become more and more interested in themselves, they gain dramatic intensity; but as the process of disintegration goes on, eventually they become isolated monads, each man limited to his own subjective values and dreaming his own individual dream.

Yeats tells us in his *Autobiography* that he "thought that the enemy of [the desired cultural] unity was abstraction, meaning by abstraction not the distinction but the isolation of occupation, or class or faculty" (p. 190). But this process of isolation and specialization, of course, ultimately involves things far more deeply rooted in men's lives than even their occupations or their social classes. What occurs is an alteration in the very way in which men apprehend the world about them. In his attack on the mathematicians and the philosophers who begot the modern world, Yeats is not content to repeat the well-worn statement that Descartes had cut the throat of poetry. He writes that "Descartes, Locke, and

17. Thomas R. Whitaker, *Swan and Shadow* (Chapel Hill, University of North Carolina Press, 1964), p. 30.

Newton took away the world and gave us its excrement instead." [18]
Yeats made it the glory of Berkeley that he "restored the
world . . . . that only exists because it shines and sounds." [19] But
though Yeats in this passage hails Berkeley as a world-restorer, it is
plain from his other writings that he knew that the world had not
been restored and that for most men it remained simply the draff
and dregs of the complete and solid world of earlier ages.

The theme of cultural disintegration through growing abstraction is one to which Yeats returned again and again. One of his
more striking ways of locating the beginning of the mischief is his
remark that the "morning when Descartes discovered that he
could think better in his bed than out of it" (p. 192) was a significant day in our cultural history. Why in bed? Presumably because
Descartes discovered that thought could be divorced from action.
When thought is separated from action, including liturgical action, and from symbolism generally, it has become truly abstract
—and thus more efficient. Yeats sees very clearly the connection between such abstract thinking and the industrial revolution.
In one of his mocking short poems, John Locke becomes the new
Adam. The "garden" dies at the moment that God takes out of
Locke's side the new Eve, the spinning jenny, the first mass-
production machine.[20] Yeats says that, as a student of William
Morris, he had no difficulty in discovering that "machinery had
not separated from handicraft wholly for the world's good" (p.
192). The increasing specialization in a world that had undergone
an industrial revolution had grave social consequences as well.
Yeats notes that by Morris' time "the distinction of classes had
become their isolation" (p. 192).

To spell out the implied argument: as long as a culture does
share common values and makes its pilgrimage, like Chaucer's
Canterbury pilgrims, to a common shrine, men's ultimate values
do not have to be argued out afresh on every new occasion, and the
poet, rather than employing abstract arguments at all, can make
use of images. With the breakup of the culture, there are fewer

18. "Pages from a Diary in 1930," *Explorations* (New York, Macmillan,
1962), p. 325.
19. Ibid.
20. *Collected Poems,* p. 211.

and fewer values which can be taken for granted. Less and less can the poet rely on images and so will be tempted to establish his values by argument. Yeats is careful not to oversimplify: he does not deny that a kind of national unity is still possible in the modern world. He points out that even today a "powerful class by terror, rhetoric, and organized sentimentality may drive their people to war" (p. 195). This statement perhaps constitutes a prophecy of Nazism, but Yeats, of course, was making use of much more general terms of reference. The collocation of "terror, rhetoric, and organized sentimentality" is in itself interesting and throws a good deal of light on Yeats's conception of the artist's true role. The artist reveals reality; he does not try to manipulate men's passions. He does not try to win his reader by fraudulent argument or seduce him by playing on his affections or compel him by the threat of force.

If Yeats felt out of place in his own time, a fellow Irishman, George Bernard Shaw, seemed to him to be very much at home in it and certainly his affairs prospered in that world. Another contemporary Irishman, Oscar Wilde, was not at home in the contemporary world and, though full of literary talent and a brilliant conversationalist, he eventually came to disaster. Perhaps Yeats's comments on Wilde and Shaw can furnish specific illustrations of what he meant by such terms as "personality," "abstraction," and the "anti-self." They may also show why Yeats believed that the artist needed to assume a mask (with its implication of a histrionic role) and yet also believed that the artist needed solitude. His comments on Shaw and Wilde may also reveal his notion of the close relationship between the essential nature of the sentimentalist and the rhetorician and the sharp differences that separated both of them from the genuine poet.

Shaw obviously did not belong to "the tragic generation," those artists to whom the age denied a life in which body and mind, flesh and intellect, emotion and idea could be united in a symbol (pp. 291–95). In a brilliant phrase, Yeats remarks that Shaw was "quite content to exchange Narcissus and his Pool for the signal-box at a railway junction, where goods and travellers pass perpetually upon their logical glittering road" (p. 294). Yet in spite of Shaw's contempt for solitude and the complacency with which he adopted the "inorganic, logical straightness" of steel rails, Yeats was forced to admire his energy and his ability to cope with the Philistines. Yeats says that he "delighted in Shaw, the formidable man. He could hit my enemies and the enemies of all I loved, as I could never hit" (p. 283).

Shaw frankly used his writing to state, and to argue for, his ideas. Yeats refers to the "street-corner socialist eloquence" (p. 294) that Shaw had carried onto the stage. But one supposes that it was not so much Shaw's ideas that repelled Yeats as his notion that Pegasus should be put to the plow or turned into a dray horse. On this subject, Yeats could be downright savage. He declares that he could find not only in Shaw's "writing and his public speech," but even in "his clothes and in his stiff joints" (p. 294) the quality of a civilization that was abstract, mechanical, and therefore, for Yeats, brutal. Yeats once had a nightmare in which Shaw appeared as "a sewing machine, that clicked and shone, but the incredible thing was that the machine smiled, smiled perpetually" (p. 283).

Curiously enough, though Shaw, as a man who loved the world and served it in action, fits neatly Yeats's definition of the rhetorician, Yeats was unwilling to concede that Shaw possessed the art of rhetoric. On the contrary, Shaw had demonstrated, like his master Samuel Butler before him, "that it is possible to write with great effect without music, without style, either good or bad" (p. 283). (But perhaps no more is involved here than that "rhetorician" was for Yeats a term much more pejorative than "rhetoric," for Yeats conceded that even his beloved Elizabethans had rhetoric—by which he apparently meant nothing worse than an elaborate style, consciously embroidered. A rhetorician, on the other hand, was evidently something worse than a person who made use of rhetoric.)

Wilde, to Yeats, presented a much more complicated case than did Shaw, and as a person Wilde was much more interesting and attractive. The catastrophe that befell him apparently affected Yeats deeply. He devotes a great deal of space to it in his *Autobiography*. He had known the Wilde family, and its most brilliant member was evidently something of a hero to the younger man. Yet in spite of Yeats's high regard for Wilde's literary gifts, at the end he came to see Wilde as "essentially a man of action" (p.

285). Indeed, Yeats makes the remarkable assertion that Wilde would have been more important as soldier or politician, and that he was "a writer by perversity and accident" (p. 285).

Yeats never directly accuses Wilde of insincerity. He explains Wilde's misuse of his gifts in terms of his psychic make-up. He was, Yeats writes, of "the nineteenth Phase, as my symbolism has it" (p. 293). In the symbolism of *A Vision* the nineteenth phase is described as the "beginning of the artificial, the abstract, the fragmentary, and the dramatic," [21] and Wilde's degradation of his art into a means for action was fated and thus enforced—though not entirely so. According to *A Vision,* the true mask of Phase Nineteen is "conviction," but Phase Nineteen offers a false mask as well, and the false mask is "domination." [22] Yeats recalls Wilde's boast that he "who can dominate a London dinner-table can dominate the world" (p. 294). There is always more room for freedom of the will in Yeats's system than a casual acquaintance with it might suggest. Wilde's moon did not dictate the whole course of his life. It did not ensure that he would come to grief. His moon offered him a true mask as well as a false one.

Yet the pressures on Wilde were formidable. Yeats theorizes that Wilde felt a compulsion to

> project himself before the eyes of others, and, having great ambition, before some great crowd of eyes; but there [was] no longer any great crowd that [cared] for his true thought. [Consequently, he] must humor and cajole and pose, take worn-out stage situations, for he knows that he may be as romantic as he please, so long as he does not believe in his romance, and all that he may get their ears for a few strokes of contemptuous wit in which he does believe. (pp. 293–94)

So Yeats writes in his *Autobiography* and thus credits Wilde with a full awareness of his plight. In fact, Yeats says quite explicitly that Wilde "understood his weakness, true personality was impossible, for this is born in solitude" (p. 293). Wilde's failure was not, then, self-deception, the failure with which Yeats taxes the sentimentalist in "Ego Dominus Tuus."

The matter at issue here, of course, is not whether Yeats has

21 *A Vision,* p. 148.
22. Ibid., p. 147.

made a just estimate of Wilde's motives. His estimate of Wilde is important to my argument only insofar as it may tell us something about what Yeats considered the proper role of the poet to be. The fact that Yeats uses the phrase "true personality" (compare his reference to the "true" mask) implies that there is a sort that is false. True personality "is born in solitude." It comes out of the depths of a man or, to use Yeats's own phrasing, out of the dark well of the self. A man's true personality is not something that he adopts with a view to impressing others. Nor can it be remodeled to fit a particular situation or chosen with an eye to the appeal that it may have for a particular group.

It is evident that drama and the dramatic meant a great deal to Yeats. Yet his willingness to associate the dramatic (as he does in his account of Phase Nineteen) with the artificial, the abstract, and the fragmentary calls for clarification. In the first place one must note that the conscious adoption of a dramatic role—the assumption of a mask—is required of all men, not merely those who are poets or playwrights. In fact, in his "Estrangement" Yeats makes it a necessary condition of all "arduous full life" and of all "active virtue" as distinguished from "the passive acceptance of a current code." Yeats finds in "very active natures a tendency to pose." He tells us that one "notices this in [the characters described in] Plutarch's *Lives*" (p. 469). A conscious dramatization of life is therefore demanded, not merely of the artist and the poet, but of the man of action too. It is no accident that in the part of "The Tragic Generation" in which Yeats describes Wilde's psychic make-up as essentially that of a man of action, he should mention a statesman like Woodrow Wilson—he does so twice—and that he should suggest that Wilson's failure, like Wilde's, was occasioned by the fact that he too lived in a period of increasing fragmentation and abstraction.

The theatrical element, then, applies to the whole of life, and the exercise of it is not simply a means to produce a work of art. In fact, exercised in the wrong fashion and for the wrong ends, it may damage any work of art that is attempted. Yet it is essential to any vital work of art. It is in this general context that one is to place Yeats's characterization of Wordsworth's poetry as often "flat and heavy" because his "moral sense had no theatrical element" (p.

470) . But the proper use of this theatrical element is to discipline oneself in the modes of reality—not to initiate or control action, for, as we have already seen, in Yeats's austere view the kingdom of the artist is not of this world. Those who love the world and who serve it in action are not true artists.

In his "Anima Hominis" Yeats sets up a contrast between mirror and mask and tells us that the saint and the hero make themselves "overmastering, creative persons by turning from the mirror to meditation upon a mask." [23] Throughout Yeats's prose works there are references to what he regards as a false view of art which defines it as Stendhal did: a "mirror dawdling down a lane." [24] If the artist is content to mirror the world passively, he will reproduce mere mechanism. Yeats, by the way, connects this notion with what he calls the "mechanical philosophy of the eighteenth century" and supports his position here with Coleridge's judgment that such a philosophy had had the effect of turning "the human mind into the quick-silver at the back of a mirror" (p. 358) .

It may be useful here to come to Yeats's basic point in another way: Authentic poetry is a form of knowledge, and yet one can truly know only what one has himself made. It is on some such reasoning that Yeats can declare that "the world knows nothing because it has made nothing, we [that is, the artists] know everything because we have made everything." [25] Yeats must have held that when Shakespeare spoke of the poet's holding the mirror up to nature, he did less than justice to his own noble art, for elsewhere he writes, obviously with Shakespeare in mind, that the truly great literary artist "is Lear, Romeo, Oedipus, Tiresias; [Shakespeare] has stepped out of a play, and even the woman he loves is Rosalind, Cleopatra, never The Dark Lady. He is part of his own phantasmagoria and we adore him because nature has grown intelligible, and by so doing a part of our creative power." [26]

Yeats chides Shaw for so jauntily exchanging "Narcissus and his Pool for the signal-box at a railway junction," but the reader would be mistaken if he concluded that the pool of Narcissus is the

23. *Mythologies,* pp. 333–34.
24. *Essays,* p. 404.
25. Ibid., p. 510.
26. Ibid., p. 509.

proper alternative to the signal-box. Yeats did not account it so. Indeed, the setting up of such alternatives—objective logic against morbid subjectivity—is part of the process of abstraction that has split apart and parceled up the world. If the pool into which the poet stares turns out to be a mirror in which he regards his own features and forgets the world about him, then it is no better than that other mirror that dawdles down a lane. To become absorbed in one's own image would be simply another instance of the passivity against which Yeats inveighs. The pool of self that Yeats recommends has depths. It is neither the mirror of self-love nor, like that other shallow reflector, the "Utopian dream," which causes its bemused victims to "spread abstraction ever further till thought is but a film, and there is no dark depth any more, surface only" (p. 293). For the artist, mere subjectivity is not enough. Indeed, Yeats writes specifically of the withering despair that overwhelms the poet who has nothing but his own spiritual innards to feed upon. In his attack on such self-regarding subjectivity, Yeats, like Matthew Arnold before him, invokes Jonathan Swift's parable of the spider and the bee:

> Only where the mind partakes of a pure activity can art or life attain swiftness, volume, unity; that contemplation lost, we picture some slow-moving event, turn the mind's eye from everything else that we may experience to the full our own passivity, our personal tragedy; or like the spider in Swift's parable mistake for great possessions what we spin out of our guts and deride the bee that has nothing but its hum and its wings, its wax and its honey, its sweetness and light.[27]

More remarkable still is Yeats's assertion that his Irish ancestors "never accepted the anarchic subjectivity of the nineteenth century"![28] The context makes it plain that he is thinking here of the "romantic movement with its turbulent heroism, its self-assertion."[29] That movement, Yeats writes, is now over, but the reaction to it is a "new naturalism that leaves man helpless before

27. Ibid., p. 409.
28. Ibid., p. 407.
29. Ibid., p. 405.

the contents of his own mind." [30] In 1931, Yeats was willing to call down a plague on both movement and countermovement—on anarchic subjectivity and the naturalistic recoil from it. Never having accepted such subjectivity in the first place, he feels no need to react against it now. "Why," he asks, "should men's heads ache that never drank?" [31]

Yeats is thoroughly aware that the spider-like plight of the modern artist, forced to spin everything out of his guts, is novel in the history of Western man. Heretofore the poet has always had some "traditional doctrine to give [him] companionship with [his] fellows." Thus Arnold had his faith in "the best thought of his generation"; so with the other great Victorians: Browning had "his psychological curiosity, Tennyson, as before him Shelley and Wordsworth, moral values that were not [merely] aesthetic values" (p. 313). But to the poet today, the poet who has lost all intellectual unity with his fellows, Yeats asks, what "can the Christian confessor say?" What can the confessor say "to those who more and more must make all out of the privacy of their thought, calling up perpetual images of desire, for he cannot say, 'Cease to be artist, cease to be poet,' where the whole life is art and poetry, nor can he bid men leave the world, who suffer from the terrors that pass before shut eyes" (p. 314). This is one of Yeats's more somber comments upon poetry's having become all in all.

Thus, in spite of Yeats's insistence upon the importance of personality and in spite of his recognition of the poet's ineradicable subjectivity, the artist is no Narcissus. Contemplation, solitude, wrestling with the dark angel of one's anti-self, all of these were for Yeats ways of getting back to ultimate reality. Doubtless this is why certain concepts were very dear to him, concepts like that of a vast world memory through which individual minds could participate in the funded experience of all mankind and through which they could draw upon traditional wisdom. The trouble with Narcissus was that he did not quarrel with himself. Instead, he fell in love with himself—which for the poet, since it is only out of the "quarrel with ourselves" that he makes poetry, is disastrous.

30. Ibid.
31. Ibid., p. 407.

We may summarize as follows: Shaw, a man who was quite in tune with his own age, knew how to deal with it, how to please it, how to manipulate it, and how to use it for his own ends, but in doing so gave up poetry and perhaps art itself, and out of his quarrel with others made rhetoric, though a very effective rhetoric. Wilde, though he was not in accord with the age into which he was born, nevertheless did comply with it, for he was determined to dominate it and used his brilliant literary talent to that end. Like Wilde, Yeats too was out of tune with his own age, but he took another course. He eschewed rhetoric. He sought solitude and forged his poetry out of the quarrel with himself. Yeats, of course, does not spell out the contrast between himself and Wilde; he was above such self-congratulatory comparisons. But his own poetry implies clearly enough his notion of the proper course for the poet of our time—even of a highly subjective poet, a member of that same tragic generation to which he said Wilde belonged.

The tragedy of such poets had to be accepted as irremediable. Yeats came to see "the dream of my early manhood, that a modern nation can return to Unity of Culture, [was] false." It could be achieved in his day only "for some small circle of men and women." All the rest of us would have to wait until "the moon bring round its century" (p. 295). This is the view of the matter reflected in all of Yeats's later poetry: it is, of course, a basic theme of that poetry. The position taken here is not really very different from that of the protagonist at the end of *The Waste Land:* Yeats's idiom is different and his tone is different, and yet what he asserts in his own way is what the pilgrim at the end of Eliot's poem asserts:

> Shall I at least set my lands in order?
> These fragments have I shored against my ruins.

As the child of the romantic tradition, Yeats had to ask, as Wordsworth long before had had to ask, whether it was possible any longer to write poetry at all and, if it was, what manner of man the authentic poet would have to be. Yeats sees the poet as essentially a maker. He is not a poet in virtue of his possessing a certain kind of personality or a special sensitivity or because he is capable of passion. He is a poet by virtue of his ability to create poems. Even when Yeats talks, as he does from time to time, about the poet's turning his own life into a work of art, the dominant term in the analogy invoked is the art work, the structure formed, the lofty rhyme that has actually been built. The man who has made of his life a work of art is the man who has succeeded in giving to his own life the formed intelligibility, the unity and the stylization that one finds in a poem.

In a late essay, the "General Introduction for My Work," the introduction which Yeats wrote for the complete edition of his works that was never produced, he makes very clear this crucial distinction between the man and the artist. He tells us that though a "poet writes always of his personal life, in his finest work [he writes] out of its tragedy, whatever it may be, remorse, lost love, or mere loneliness." Then Yeats fixes the point in a decisive image. He remarks that the poet "is never the bundle of accident and incoherence that sits down to breakfast; he has been reborn as an idea, something intended, complete." [32] This new creature, the thing that has been reborn, incorporating in its own substance the disordered and incoherent fragments of its creator's life, is the poem, and the voice that speaks through this poem, because it is now truly articulate, is not for a moment to be confused with the voice of Willy Yeats, grumbling over the leader in the *Times* as he munches his toast.

William Wordsworth in his famous passage described poetry as the overflow of powerful emotions recollected in tranquillity. But Yeats, in a passage quoted on an earlier page of this essay, has gone far beyond any mere process of recollecting emotions. (Presumably Wordsworth as artist went beyond it too, but Yeats has taken the trouble here to spell out what he thinks occurs when recollection is deepened into meditation.) When the personal emotion of the man has been exhausted completely, "something that has nothing to do with action or desire, suddenly starts into its place, something which is as unforeseen, as completely organized, even as unique, as the images that pass before the mind between sleeping and waking" (p. 332).

The conception of art adumbrated here is again curiously like Eliot's: it is an impersonal art. It may be interesting to compare

32. Ibid., p. 509.

the two poets on this point. In an essay written in 1917, at just about the time that Yeats was writing "Ego Dominus Tuus" and "Anima Hominus," Eliot wrote: "Poetry is not a turning loose of emotion, but an escape from emotion; it is not the expression of personality, but an escape from personality. But, of course, only those who have personality and emotions know what it means to want to escape from these things." [33] A little later in the same essay, Eliot describes the kind of emotion that is significant for art. It is, he writes, an "emotion which has its life in the poem and not in the history of the poet. The emotion of art is impersonal. And the poet cannot reach this impersonality without surrendering himself wholly to the work to be done." [34] The passages are remarkably similar, and startlingly so when one remembers the differences in personality and in background of the poets who penned them.

In a letter that Yeats wrote to Sean O'Casey in 1938, he puts very forcibly his insistence on the total unity that any work of art must have. The immediate subject of the letter is a play, but what is said applies in full measure to poetry: "Dramatic action is a fire which must burn up everything but itself; there should be no room in a play for anything that does not belong to it. . . . Among the things that dramatic action must burn up are the author's opinions; while he is writing he has no business to know anything that is not a portion of that action." [35] In this letter Yeats also makes it very clear how the process of composition itself, when it is successful, discovers and authenticates the truth it embodies. (Incidentally, what Yeats says in this passage about the artist's anti-self—his Daimon—will be particularly helpful to those readers who are repelled by his more mystical descriptions of that ghostly entity.) Yeats goes on to ask O'Casey:

> Do you suppose for one moment that Shakespeare educated Hamlet and King Lear by telling them what he thought and believed? As I see it, Hamlet and Lear educated Shakespeare,

33. "Tradition and Individual Talent," *Selected Essays* (New York, Harcourt, Brace, 1950), pp. 10–11.

34. Ibid., p. 11.

35. *Letters,* p. 741.

and I have no doubt that in the process of that education [Shakespeare] found out that he was an altogether different man to what he thought himself, and had altogether different beliefs. A dramatist can help his characters to educate him by thinking and studying everything that gives them the language they are groping for through his hands and eyes, but the control must be theirs, and that is why the ancient philosophers thought a poet or dramatist Daimon-possessed.[36]

Yeats often used the adjective "cold" to describe the quality that he sought to attain in his own poetry. He tells us that he "once boasted, copying the phrase from a letter of [his] Father's, that [he] would write a poem 'cold and passionate as the dawn.' " [37] But the coldness of such art could never come from a numbed spirit and cold-stiffened fingers. The energy that produced poems that were cold and passionate as the dawn was best described as a kind of fire. So Yeats did describe it in the central passage of his "Poetry and Tradition."

The passage begins with an approving citation of Sainte-Beuve's remark that the only thing immortal in literature is style; and style, Yeats tells us, is "a still unexpended energy, after all that the argument or the story needs, a still unbroken pleasure after the immediate end has been accomplished—and builds this up into a most personal and wilful fire, transfiguring words and sounds and events." [38] But though Yeats calls it a "most personal" fire, the context makes it plain that the flame is applied strictly to anneal and glaze the work of art. In the sentence that follows, Yeats shifts his terms once more and now calls this unexpended energy a "playing of strength when the day's work is done, a secret between a craftsman and his craft, and is so inseparate in his nature that he has it most of all amid overwhelming emotion." [39] (In this last sentence Yeats may possibly be remembering Coleridge's celebrated definition of the imagination with its reference to "a more than usual state of emotion, with more than usual order." Yeats's general indebtedness to Coleridge is large, though most of his ex-

36. Ibid.
37. *Essays,* p. 523.
38. Ibid., p. 254.
39. Ibid.

plicit references to him come in the essays written in the 1930s.)

This "playing" of the craftsman's "strength" shows most "amid overwhelming emotion," and Yeats goes on to make a curious addition—"and in the face of death." [40] Though his next sentence hardly absolves him of syntactic confusion, it does make quite clear what he has in mind. It is not the dying artist who most of all manifests this graceful play of more-than-needful strength, but his characters, the characters that he has created, as they look into the face of death. The unconscious shift from artist to his characters is characteristic of Yeats, particularly the earlier Yeats. So also is his appeal to Shakespeare for illustrations of this tragic joy. "Shakespeare's persons, when the last darkness has gathered about them, speak out of an ecstasy that is one-half the self-surrender of sorrow, and one-half the last playing and mockery of the victorious sword before the defeated world." [41]

Style, as the play of unexpended artistic energy—as a fine excess, to borrow Keats's phrase—shows itself

> in the arrangements of events as in the words, and in the touch of extravagance, of irony, of surprise, which is set there after the desire of logic has been satisfied and all that is merely necessary established, and that leaves one, not in the circling necessity, but caught up in the freedom of self-delight. . . . This [self-delight, this] joy, because it must be always making and mastering, remains in the hands and in the tongue of the artist, but with his eyes he enters upon a submissive, sorrowful contemplation of the great irremediable things, and he is known from other men by making all he handles like himself, and yet by the unlikeness to himself of all that comes before him in a pure contemplation. [42]

What prompted the poem, what set the poet dreaming, may have been any of a hundred things—his enemy or his love or his political cause—but these incitations do not ultimately matter. The verses that he writes "may make his mistress famous as Helen or give a victory to his cause," but men will not honor him be-

40. Ibid.
41. Ibid.
42. Ibid., pp. 254–55.

cause he has been a devoted servant to his mistress or served well his cause. They will do so only because they "delight to honour and to remember all that have served contemplation." [43] As the passage continues, Yeats shifts once more from the artist himself to the characters that his imagination has created and, in particular, to Shakespeare's tragic characters. Yeats writes that "Timon of Athens contemplates his own end, and orders his tomb by the beached verge of the salt flood, and Cleopatra sets the asp to her bosom, and their words move us because their sorrow is not their own at tomb or asp, but for all men's fate." They are not obsessed with their own sorrow. They are not sentimental and self-regarding. The artist's "shaping joy has kept the sorrow pure, as it had kept it were the emotion love or hate, for the nobleness of the arts is in the mingling of contraries, the extremity of sorrow, the extremity of joy, perfection of personality, the perfection of its surrender, overflowing turbulent energy, and marmorean stillness." [44]

43. Ibid., p. 255.
44. Ibid.

Calvin S. Brown

Difficulty and Surface Value

Every profession has its own particular professional biases which are unconsciously shared by most of its practitioners, and the teaching of literature is no exception. This fact is the principal flaw in our cult of the expert, for though the expert knows more about his subject than the layman or the interested amateur, and though he must be consulted on technical matters and heard with respect, he can never be blindly trusted. It also means that the expert can sometimes learn from the amateur and even from the pure layman, if he can bring himself to listen to them and take them seriously. In our civilization it happens that most serious critics of literature are professional teachers, and hence the biases of the teachers of literature are conspicuously present in our literary criticism. There are doubtless a good many such biases, but the one which concerns us here has to do with the relationship between a writer and his potential audience.

All formal education is, by its very nature, based on artificially created situations, and the man who lives in universities is inclined to take their necessary artificialities for permanent characteristics of the world in general. The professor of literature knows that he can explain or condemn, analyze or eulogize a poet, but he seldom realizes where his unique power lies. *The professor of literature can deliver a captive audience* who cannot choose but hear, and the sanctions of grades, credits, and examinations mean that the author whom he favors needs no glittering eye to hold his hearers. The system does that for him. It is this fact of the academic world which leads professors of literature to emphasize the obligations of the reader to the poet and largely to ignore the obligations of the poet to the reader.

A typical illustration of this attitude can be found in an exegete's comment on Mallarmé's *Un Coup de dés.*

Un œuvre *est,* qu'elle plaise ou déplaise. Aussi est-il ridicule de contester la legitimité de sa forme, du moment qu'elle *est* et que personne n'y peut rien changer.

"Hérésie que ce Poème!" a-t-on dit, "œuvre hermétique s'il en fût!" Elle est comme elle est; il n'est pas en notre pouvoir de la modifier; telle nous devons donc la prendre et l'examiner.[1]

But why *should* we? We can never read every poem that exists, and we do not have to read any poem. If we are interested in taking a poem as it is and examining it, we can do so. If we are not interested, we can ignore it as it is or reject it after a brief glance or a first reading.

Strictly speaking, between the poet and the reader there is no obligation on either side. But the poet, by the very fact of publication, shows that he hopes to be read, and hence he cannot utterly ignore the requirements of his potential audience. Similarly, no one is under any moral obligation to read literature, and the great majority of the world's population never do. The literary world has its own code, however, and one of the principles is that a serious reader can ignore a book if he wants to, but once he picks it up he is supposed to give the author a sporting chance. As men, writer and reader owe each other nothing, but as writer and reader they can exist only in a state of symbiosis.

One of the most controversial problems in their relationship is the question of obscurity, which breaks down into a number of subordinate questions. What information can the poet expect from his reader? What intellectual ability? How much mental effort? Is it the poet's job to write so that the reader can understand him, or is it the reader's job to understand the poet no matter how he may choose to write? These and a host of similar questions have given rise to an extensive body of criticism, much of it partisan and acrimonious. The poets tend to demand more of the reader than the average reader is willing or able to give, and their attitudes vary from Ben Jonson's reasonable "Things, wrote with labour, deserve to be so read" to Blake's imperious "That

1. Claude Roulet, *Traité de poétique supérieure: Un Coup de dés . . .* (Neuchâtel, 1956), p. 28.

which can be made explicit to the Idiot is not worth my care." [2]
Some, like Sir Herbert Read, simply deny that poetry is rational
and insist that it may be felt or experienced, but never understood. This type of position is countered by Julien Benda's "On
pourrait dire que le littérateur désire l'applaudissement des
masses et méprise leur jugement" or, more aggressively, by the
petulant charges of deliberate humbuggery and fraud which Max
Eastman makes against difficult poets.[3] But Valéry praises Mallarmé for having created, in France, "la notion d'*auteur difficile.*" [4]
And so the battle rages, and has raged, off and on, since the days
of the Alexandrians.

I am not concerned with the general question of obscurity or
with the frequently sententious admonitions as to what the author
or his reader *should* do, but rather with a practical question of
what they *must* do if anything—be it ratiocination or experience
or sheer power—is to be communicated. And it must be conceded
that literary art of a high order has never had a really universal
mass appeal. Homer's art is an aristocratic one, and Thersites
could hardly have appreciated it even if it had not treated him
contemptuously. We are accustomed to imagine the whole male
populace of Athens listening with rapt enjoyment to the choral
odes of poetic tragedy, and a remarkable proportion of them probably did. But Aristophanes could suggest that if men had wings
they could fly out of the theater when bored by the choral odes,[5]
and the joke would have been pointless if love of tragic poetry had
really been as universal as we like to think. We may as well admit
at the outset that, though in the past the poet has often had more
listeners than he can now muster, he has always addressed a selected and somewhat restricted audience. He will therefore be able
to make considerable demands on his readers, unless he falls into

2. *Ben Jonson,* ed. Herford and Simpson, *8* (Oxford, 1947), 638; Blake's
quote from John Press, *The Chequer'd Shade: Reflections on Obscurity in
English Poetry* (London, 1958), p. 70. Hereafter cited as Press.

3. Julien Benda, *La France byzantine, ou le triomphe de la littérature
pure* (Paris, 1945), p. 218; Max Eastman, "The Cult of Unintelligibility,"
The Literary Mind (New York, 1931), pp. 57–78.

4. Paul Valéry, *Ecrits divers sur Stéphane Mallarmé* (Paris, 1950), p. 36.

5. *The Birds,* ll. 785–89.

the error of a great deal of "educational" television and, in a desperate effort to attract an audience that he can never win, drives away the audience that he could easily get. But there is a limit to these demands, and the poet who goes beyond it defeats himself.

This limit cannot be defined in terms of absolute difficulty or obscurity. The competent mind responds to the challenge of a good puzzle, and the cryptanalytic faculty can contribute to aesthetic enjoyment, though it does not always do so. A good example of its limitations is supplied by such puzzles as the "literary crypts" and the "double crostics" of our newspapers. In the former, a brief literary quotation, together with its author's name, is enciphered by a simple monalphabetic substitution which the reader must solve. In the latter, a somewhat longer passage is anagrammed into a set of words which are defined, with the transpositions of the letters indicated, so that one can work back and forth between the passage and the new words. These are good examples of the puzzle-solving faculty applied to making out the meaning of a literary passage, but having no aesthetic value or significance because the process of solution, though necessary for arriving at the final text, does not affect it. When the text is found, the puzzle is gone, and the process of finding the text, laborious though it may be, contributes nothing to the effect of the passage when found.

Yet it is widely recognized that the joy of puzzle-solving can be part of the appeal of poetry. Aldous Huxley comments that

> one of the pleasures we derive from poetry is precisely the crossword-puzzler's delight in working out a problem. For certain people the pleasure is peculiarly intense. I have known such people who, too highbrow to indulge in the arduous imbecility of crossword and acrostic, sought satisfaction for an imperious yearning in the sonnets of Mallarmé and the more eccentric verses of Gerard Hopkins.[6]

William Empson, telling why he annotated his poems in *The Gathering Storm,* explains what Huxley ignores, which is why the hermetic sonnets of Mallarmé are a very poor substitute for crossword puzzles as far as the appeal to the cryptanalytic faculty alone is concerned.

6. Press, p. 41.

> Partly they [the notes] are meant to be like answers to a cross-word puzzle; a sort of puzzle interest is part of the pleasure you are meant to get from the verse. . . . The fashion for obscure poetry . . . came in at about the same time as the fashion for crossword puzzles, and it seems to me that the revival of puzzle interest in poetry, an old-fashioned thing, has got a bad name merely by failing to know itself and refusing to publish the answers.[7]

Actually the solution of a genuine crossword puzzle or cryptogram verifies itself, and the successful puzzle worker never looks up the answer—only the one who gets stuck does that. But the solution of the difficult poem does not necessarily verify itself, in spite of the claims made by some exegetes. For example, Charles Maurras, replying to an interpretation of Mallarmé's "Hommage à Wagner," said: "Pardon, et la preuve que vous vous êtes trompé c'est que votre explication n'est ni logiquement ni textuellement irréfutable, et lorsqu'à travers l'indéchiffrable lacis des mots on a pu découvrir la véritable signification d'un poème de Mallarmé, celle-ci s'impose tellement par la clarté, par la vraiesemblance, que toute hésitation, toute discussion deviennent impossibles." [8] A glance at the flourishing industry of Mallarméan exegesis is enough to show that if this statement is true, then no one has yet hit on the true meaning of a number of Mallarmé's hermetic poems.

The puzzle-solving pleasure in literature is not an esoteric one limited to a handful of dedicated adepts. Mallarmé made a famous statement that to name an object destroys three-quarters of the pleasure, which properly consists of divining the object without having it named.[9] This sounds like a very rarefied doctrine indeed, but I have seen it verified by a miscellaneous audience that had no very high literary pretensions. During the Second World War I attended a public reading of Alice Duer Miller's *The White Cliffs*, a competent piece of topical poetic sentimentality which

7. Ibid.
8. Henri Mondor, *Vie de Mallarmé* (Paris, 1941), p. 475.
9. *Œuvres complètes de Stéphane Mallarmé*, ed. Henri Mondor and G. Jean-Aubry (Paris, Bibliothèque de la Pléiade, 1945), p. 869.

had no appeal for sophisticated poetic tastes. The poem contains a reference to "the smallest state in the U.S.A.," and when this point was reached, an audible whisper of "Rhode Island" rose like an exhalation from the whole audience. Here was a perfect justification of Mallarmé's comment. The audience was not really an intellectual one; it did not consist of habitual readers of poetry. The scrap of knowledge required of them was about as obvious and banal as any bit of information can be. Yet there was a definite pleasure in supplying the name of the object rather than having it given—and in whispering it to one's presumably less gifted companion.

This example (which is a condensed model of a great deal of the world of critical journals) serves to indicate one of the necessary conditions of puzzle-solving as a literary activity. In the cryptogram, the puzzle disappears when the solution is reached, but in the difficult poem puzzle and solution coexist in the reader's mind. If the poem must be studied and puzzled out to begin with, a subsequent reading performs the operation rapidly and easily; the solution is now *inherent in the poem itself* and is consequently a part of its aesthetic impact. This is probably what Hopkins was referring to when he wrote that "one of two kinds of clearness one should have—either the meaning of the text to be felt without effort as fast as one reads or else, if dark at first reading, when once made out *to explode.*" [10] The explosion results when the enigma and its solution are brought together in the reader's mind.

Another necessary condition of puzzle-solving as a literary activity would seem to be that the puzzle must have a solution. A long jumble of letters to be anagrammed at will is not a cryptogram, but a blank check to be filled in by one's ingenuity. This is why anagramming without any consistent pattern is such a favorite sport of literary cipher hunters: a little patience and a few archaic spellings or abbreviations can rearrange the letters of a passage to say whatever one wants said. For exactly the same reason, no one

10. Press, p. 204. The skaldic poetry of the Vikings, with its interlaced sentences, double kennings, and other ingenious complications, is an interesting case. All the conditions seem right for an explosion "when once made out," but the modern scholar usually gets only a fizzle. It would be interesting to know what happened in the minds of contemporary adepts of the cult.

tries to send a secret message so disguised—it is no message, but merely a challenge to the recipient's ingenuity and fantasy. The same principle would seem to apply to the puzzling aspect of the difficult poem, though this fact has been denied by some critics. The difficult poem may contain its deliberately contrived ambiguities and polysemantic devices, but these are all part of the answer and are simultaneously present. A poem which merely stimulates or irritates the reader's fantasy without in any way controlling its activity is the verbal equivalent of a dose of hashish or LSD, and these drugs are clearly not aesthetic objects.

Yet the claim has been made that a poem is impervious to reason. Sir Herbert Read takes this position in the final paragraph of his essay on "Obscurity in Poetry":

> It is a mistake, therefore, to ask a poet to explain his poems. That is to make the wrong approach to poetry, to knock at the wrong door. This emotional unity which is the *raison d'être* of every poem cannot be measured by the instruments of reason. Otherwise it would be simpler to express it in prose. The poem must be received directly, without questioning, and loved or hated. It has a necessary and eternal existence; it is impervious to reason, and if it has no discoverable meaning, it has immeasurable power. The poet has created in words an objective equivalence of his emotional experience: the words may not make sense; but they make the emotion—follow the contour of the thought—and reproduce, as nearly as possible, "the mind's internal echo of the imperfect sound." It was Rilke who said that "the poet is farther away from men than from things." That is perhaps why he seems so strange to us. But the things he approaches are eternal things, and because they endure in his words, his words grow familiar to men, until they are accepted without questioning, but always with fresh recognition.[11]

This is eloquently spoken, but is it true or is it, like the poems of which it speaks, a passage with no discoverable meaning but immeasurable power? A number of stubborn questions refuse to be exorcised. What is "the poem" of which Sir Herbert speaks? Is it

11. Read, *Collected Essays in Literary Criticism* (London, 1938), p. 100.

any and every poem? Every work of Lydgate and Shakespeare and
Milton and Edgar Guest? Do *The Rape of the Lock* and Gray's
Elegy have no discoverable meaning? Do all the poems in the Victorian keepsake albums have immeasurable power? Or, in the
statement, "if it has no discoverable meaning, it has immeasurable
power," does "if" mean "if and only if," so that "the poem" has
meaning *or* power, but not both? To answer that not all verses are
poems merely begs the question, for how is one to decide which
verses *are* poems when reason has been ruled out as irrelevant and
questioning has been forbidden? Actually, this position reduces
the reading of poetry to a form of irresponsible solipsistic impressionism and denies the possibility of literary criticism altogether.

Still, the approach is not wholly wrong. There *is* an element of
the irrational in the arts. There *are* effects which do not depend
on the reader's reason, though I would maintain (purely as a
matter of faith) that reason can explain how they are produced.
There are also poems where rational understanding is ultimately
necessary but is not the most pressing order of business.

> Il ne faut pas chercher à *comprendre* le sens des poëmes
> mallarméens avant de les *avoir aimés,* avant d'avoir passé par
> la période préliminaire ou l'on se contente de goûter leur
> beauté. Je suis en effet resté très longtemps à ignorer ce que
> signifiaient certaines pièces de Mallarmé, sans que cette ig-
> norance me troublât le moins du monde. Je savais que cette
> ignorance cesserait un jour et qu'elle ne cesserait que si, par
> une vaine curiosité, je ne cherchais pas à la détruire, en
> dépouillant prématurément ces textes lyriques de l'atmo-
> sphère de mystère que les rendait si attirants.[12]

Probably most readers have had such an experience. Certainly it is
a common one for a reader who was attracted to poetry in his
childhood to have the meaning of a familiar and beloved poem
—not necessarily a really difficult one—explode in his mind years
after his first reading of it.

This phenomenon brings me to my central point. The reception and eventual success of a poem is not a function of its difficulty or obscurity. Both difficult and easy poems have been both

12. Francis de Miomandre, *Mallarmé* (Paris, 1948), pp. 27–28.

accepted and rejected in every literature. What is required is that there be some easily accessible attraction, some value for the reader on the surface of the poem, to induce him to return to it and eventually to look deeper.

These surface values may be of many kinds. They may even be superficial values, though they are not necessarily so. They are not to be identified by their nature, but rather by their availability. They are simply any values which may (to repeat Hopkins) "be felt without effort as fast as one reads." One of the most obvious surface values is a good story. For most readers or spectators, *Oedipus* or *King Lear* is a gripping story at a first encounter, and this fact leads to the rereading which makes possible a grasp of more subtle values, such as the light-darkness and sight-blindness imagery which pervades both plays. (A reversal of the order of appreciation would be inconceivable. No reader could be first attracted by this play of imagery and thus led to reread the play and discover that it told a good story too.) But a surface value does not have to be a story or even any sort of meaning whatsoever. In the poetry of Swinburne, it is the sheer sensuous power of the sound. In a good deal of Poe, it is an eerie atmosphere. In the satire of Byron's *Don Juan* it is a flippant wit, and in that of Juvenal it is a bitter eloquence. These statements are necessarily oversimplifications, but I believe that they are sufficient to characterize those values which would immediately and almost effortlessly strike that time-honored myth, the intelligent general reader. And it is my contention that the poet who displays no such surface values cannot lure many readers not trapped in seminars to find any deeper values that he may offer.

If some poets, particularly the minor imitators of successful and fashionable "difficult" poets, are entirely unaware of this principle, it is probably because poetry has largely ceased to be publicly performed. A poet who must confront his hearers, see their bewilderment, watch them struggle and then stop listening if they find nothing worth the effort—a poet who fails visibly and publicly when he cannot hold his audience—learns facts of literary life which may never dawn on the isolated writer for little magazines. Dylan Thomas is an interesting case in point. When asked, "Is it ever fair deliberately to confuse the reader?" he replied: "No—it

is a deliberate avowal of your own inefficiency. It is impossible to be too clear. . . . I am trying for more clarity now. At first I thought it enough to leave an impression of sound and feeling and let the meaning seep in later, but since I've been giving these find it better to have more meaning at first reading." [13]
broadcasts and readings of other men's poetry as well as my own, I

Here Thomas not only admits the necessity for some surface value, but insists that that value must be *meaning*, in the ordinary sense of the word. "An impression of sound and feeling," he finds, will not hold an audience. It is possible to attract the child or the reader who (like the French critic quoted above) has an unusual sensitivity to language as sound and feeling without giving him a surface meaning, but the average intelligent reader probably requires one. Since it is impossible to isolate meaning from the total effect of a poem, it is sufficient here to note that some immediately accessible meaning (usually in conjunction with other poetic values) is likely to be the most effective lure for a poet to dangle before his audience.

This is especially true in long poems. Dante's *Commedia* and the second part of Goethe's *Faust* are far from light reading, and a lifetime of study will not exhaust their possibilities. Long before a reader has finished a first casual survey of either of these works, he has found serious and rewarding views on human life presented in appropriate and often splendid language. He also realizes that he has missed a great deal, and he is likely to return to the poem to broaden and deepen his understanding by further study. It is this combination of surface values with deeper levels of experience that produces the unforced reading and rereading on which a literary reputation ultimately depends. Without the surface values, a reader would probably never get through either work the first time, and without the promise of further values he would not return to it.

There are, of course, readers of the If-a-task-is-once-begun school who feel a sort of moral obligation to finish a book once they have started it. I know, for I am one of them. But this compulsion is a matter of puritanical conscience rather than literary judgment and is more likely to hurt the author of a book without surface values

13. Press, p. 91.

than to help him. The reader who casually drops an uninteresting book is usually willing to forgive and forget, but the one who doggedly plows through it develops a grudge against the author and warns other readers off.

In contrast to Dante and Goethe, we may take a difficult poem without surface values—or deeper ones, for that matter. To avoid the warfare of current partisanship, let it be a poem now largely forgotten but admired by its own clique and claque in its own day—the *Alexandra* of Lycophron. This work of some fifteen hundred lines, written in Greek in the third century before Christ, is the classical example of a wilfully difficult poem. It deals with the information given by a slave who has been set to eavesdrop on Cassandra and report her prophecies. (Alexandra is an alternative name for Cassandra, used here because it is little used elsewhere —as though a modern poet should insist on calling Odysseus "Laertides.") The slave has a few lines at the beginning and end, but the body of the poem consists of the ravings of the prophetess. Lycophron obviously selected this subject because prophecies are notoriously veiled and obscure. Cassandra covers a great deal of mythology and history, always under cover of indirect and recondite allusions. To make matters worse, there is bold experimentation with language in the form of ancient obscurities revived and new obscurities invented. Lycophron uses the trick of predicting in the poem things which have already happened at the time of his writing, but this does not help him. Dido's prophecy of the Punic Wars in the *Aeneid* is dramatically effective, and Cacciaguida's prediction of Dante's exile is Dante's first warning of his impending fate; but when the editor of Lycophron has completed his task of cryptanalysis his only reward is some bits of ancient legend and history that he has known for years. Lycophron's poem is simply unreadable, and even my puritan conscience has never been able to get me all the way through it. But a reader who demanded no surface values might waste years on it before he discovered that underneath its barren surface there lies a barren core.

Lycophron's poem is a notorious case, but by no means a unique one. There are plenty of difficult literary works, from before Lycophron to the literary magazines of 1970, which are not worth the effort they demand from the reader. "Il faudrait en quelque

sort—qu'on nous permette cette comparaison arithmétique—divi-
ser les résultats obtenus par les difficultés qu'il y avait à les
obtenir." [14] Sometimes such poems may be worthwhile to the
scholar on grounds irrelevant to the general reader. A good case in
point is Mallarmé's *Un Coup de dés*. This poem of 732 words has
given rise to a vast amount of commentary and exegesis, including
over half a dozen full-length books, representing almost every conceivable point of view. For reasons which need not detain us here,
I have worked through all of it carefully and have found the process interesting and worthwhile in respect to various problems of
literary history and theory. I have the greatest admiration for
Mallarmé's sincerity and his superhuman effort, but I must
confess—steeling myself against the favorite epithet of the cult,
"crétin"—that *as a poem* the work offers no rewards remotely
proportional to the effort of understanding it, though it belongs in
a class far above a monstrosity like the *Alexandra*. Nevertheless,
the fact that the reward is not sufficient for the effort brings the
two works together as illustrations of "the disproportion of means
to end" which a recent critic has pointed out as one characteristic
of a declining art.[15]

Sir Herbert Read certainly meant to include *Un Coup de dés* in
his description of "the poem." Did he include the *Alexandra* as
well? That, basically, is the problem facing the intelligent general
reader when he encounters an obscure or difficult poem. Is the
difficulty inherent in a serious literary effort—and, if so, is the
effort successful? Or is the obscurity the result of the author's in-
competence, or laziness, or affectation, or all three? Or, as in
Mallarmé's case, is it due to a gallant effort to achieve the impossible? The naïve reader, confronted with a difficult poem without surface values, throws up his hands and says, "I can't understand it"—
an admission which is usually intended as a condemnation of the
poet rather than a confession of the speaker's inadequacy. The more
sophisticated reader thinks (but seldom says), "I could doubtless
understand it if I made the effort, but I see no reason to believe
that the game is worth the candle." Since the great majority of

14. E. Noulet, *L'œuvre poétique de Stéphane Mallarmé* (Paris, 1940), p.
310.
15. Martin Cooper, *Ideas and Music* (London, 1965), p. 18.

"works of art" in all forms and all ages are bad, his skepticism has a firm statistical basis. Other considerations, such as established reputations or a love of puzzles, may modify this attitude, but it remains the healthy approach of a reader who is not caught in an academic captive audience.

The poet who offers a rich vein of buried gold has every right to expect his readers to dig for it, but only if he convinces the prospectors that the gold is actually there by leaving a few nuggets lying about on the surface.

Ralph Freedman

The Possibility of a
Theory of the Novel

The question posed in this essay is the critic's irritant. Is a theory
of the novel possible—a coherent theory that can serve as a practical guide and can justify tastes in accordance with a clearly drawn
literary ideology? Or do we expect of the novel what no theory of
literature can achieve? In a sense, these questions answer themselves. Clearly, there is no "total" theory, applicable everywhere,
although equally clearly theories lending structures to critical
methodologies are both needed and justified. Yet their limitations
are evident. Any poetic suggests a system of values which works
—at least generally and plausibly—primarily in the elucidation
of those literary forms it is chiefly designed to explain. It appears
most reliable when dealing with genres sufficiently coherent to
match the coherence of the theory. Poetry, both lyrical and epic,
or traditional forms of the drama belong in this category, because
their criticism proceeds from definite conventions which are historically conditioned.

Not so the novel, if we define that form as full-length narrative
prose to exclude such narrative types as the novella and the short
story, which follow prescribed traditions. But the novel—amorphous, multicolored, its different types having originated at the
most various points in time—cannot claim such coherence. It
poses a problem. The phrase *les problèmes du roman* signifies the
attempt of at least two centuries to come to terms with an intransi-
gent genre. At the same time, the accretion of philosophical and
literary probings has ushered in an increasing sophistication. The
novel has gained in seriousness; it has absorbed some of the implicit intellectual complexity which had been too often associated
chiefly with the lyric. Indeed, the very difficulties encountered in

the development of a coherent poetic for the novel may have contributed not only to a more profound conception of the genre by critics but also to a deeper understanding of the form by novelists themselves.

As in many literary forms, the novel's surface is deceptively simple, for it is based on story-telling—the expectations of narrative plots, identifications with characters, the enjoyment of descriptions of moods and scenes. It is different from most other genres, for in the novel we find few specific internal conventions or structural requirements, and its elements of plot, character, and scene can be fashioned and juxtaposed in an infinite number of ways. Yet this very looseness conceals the difficulties and opportunities in any attempt to develop coherent critical ideas. Part of the problem is historical: full-length narratives in prose have existed at various times without forming a continuous historical tradition, while individual types, like romances, *Bildungsromane,* novels of manners, even detective novels, have followed discernible lines of development. This situation has given rise to the practice of elevating one of these traditions, such as the *Bildungsroman* or the "social novel," to the "great tradition" of the novel and of applying standards appropriate to one type of prose fiction to the genre as a whole. Critics like Northrop Frye have established particular categories or "fictional modes" for all types of prose narrative (i.e. novel, romance, confession, satire), a useful scheme until the critic is faced with classifying the different kinds of a genre which remains mixed as well as complex and unwieldy.[1] Others again have simply despaired, conceding the impossibility of finding any but the most limited descriptions for a large form whose manifestations, despite all their diversity, have a great deal in common.

The other part of the difficulty remains formal. Since obvious poetic conventions—like epic structure, meter, or dramatic form—are absent, the problems of the novel are both more concealed and more evident. They are more concealed, because the apparent absence of any unifying form suggests that there may be no need whatever for formal conventions. But they are also more evident, because in the absence of any shield of conspicuous

1. *Anatomy of Criticism* (Princeton, Princeton University Press, 1957), pp. 303–14 passim.

formality they are more openly displayed. For the mirroring in one another of reality and artistic illusion, common to all literature, is reflected dramatically in the novel, i.e. in the language and in the universe of the novelist's creation. Prose exhibits more clearly than verse the tensions between the denotative pressures of language and internally directed aesthetic form. Similarly, the universe itself, whether wholly fantastic or meticulously "real," includes both the juxtapositions of life and art and the relationships between characters and their worlds. Since these various interactions turn particularly on the involvements of selves in worlds of people and things, and since prose language focuses on the display of these activities most dramatically, epistemological confrontations are revealed in the novel with particular clarity. Our exploration of the possibility of a theory of the novel will elucidate this facet of prose fiction, first on a historical, finally on a formal plane.

One of the perennial historical problems of the novel arises from the diversity of its points of origin. Its beginnings are as multitudinous as the number of its individual forms. Like a tree whose many roots reach down to different layers of soil, the novel's many strands reach to the most varied layers in time. *The Golden Ass,* as early as the second century, may suggest one landmark in history; the later romances evolving from classical and medieval epics, another. National as well as formal differences complicate the picture. The picaresque novel radiated as a fresh form from Renaissance Spain, though it was not without its roots in the romance; the realistic English novel, in its turn not without roots in the picaresque and in Elizabethan fiction, evolved in the late seventeenth century. French fiction of sensibility and manners, like Madame de Lafayette's, preceded and influenced the realistic English novel, although, since it was much more leisure class than middle class entertainment, it moved on a different if parallel course. By contrast, the German novel evolved an original form with Goethe and German Romanticism—a self-consciously aesthetic, intellectual form. Its origins were no different from those of other European novels—the picaresque (with Grimmelshausen's *Simplicissimus* as a model) and the novel of sensibil-

ity—but after Goethe it struck a fresh note, emphasizing history as
the novel's form, both collectively and individually in its unique
version of the *Bildungsroman*. Clearly, then, any comprehensive
perspective of the novel, *roman,* or *Roman* must take into account
the multiplicity of its points of origin and of the directions of its
development. Yet it has been a constant critical failure to take
these different historical layers into account, either by leveling
temporal and national differences unduly, or by distinguishing too
sharply between them. Two approaches may serve as examples:
the novel's reduction to a form of the epic and the sharp distinction between novel and romance as existentially separate forms.

The view of the novel as a species of the epic, often held
(though by no means exclusively) by German critics, appears, on
the surface, most plausible. The development of narrative, the
attempt to communicate man's struggle with the world around
him by fashioning his progress in schemes of time, points to a close
relationship between the genres. It also takes account of one
broad, continuous strand in the evolution of prose narrative from
ancient and medieval epics to many of the prose romances of the
Middle Ages and the Renaissance. In fact, as Fielding's remarks in
Tom Jones and in his preface to *Joseph Andrews* illustrate, the
model of the epic remains highly significant to the novel. It defines
relationships which have fashioned the most various forms from
the Middle Ages and the picaresque to our day—the hero's engagement, his search for fulfillment or order in his world. Thus,
Friedrich von Blanckenburg's *Theorie des Romans* (1795)
viewed the novel as emerging from an epic, which, in turn, had
been defined by the values of Greek citizenship (i.e. order and
civilization). The novel represents a less austere form as a result of
the decline of these values, the epic model having been turned
into a more subjective, perhaps also more arbitrary genre. German
romantic criticism sets out from a similar distinction. The epic
relates to the *Roman* as an objective versus a subjective form of
narration, reflecting, somewhat ambivalently, an analogous relationship between classical and romantic poetry. The novel, therefore, represents a step downward from the epic's austere objectivity, becoming a more flexible and more comprehensive form, yet
still reflecting a standard of historical narration. Its greater loose-

ness, according to Friedrich Schlegel's "Brief über den Roman" (1800), allows it to become a "total genre" which counteracts any dramatic flow of events.[2] The channeled course of the *Odyssey* or the *Aeneid* has widened into a seemingly boundless sea, as the hero's vision—in *Werther, Tristram Shandy,* or *Heinrich von Ofterdingen*—turns from the precise shapes of the external world to the less definite contours that describe the furniture of his mind.

Although this inward turning of the novel appears most conspicuously in eighteenth-century novels of sensibility, their predecessors, and their romantic successors, it has always been a defining characteristic of a form which, by its very nature, can tell a story from an external vantage point and at the same time invade the minds of its persons. This duality of an outer and an inner projection is indeed part of the novel's design, and its coherence as a form may lie in the juxtaposition of both these elements which the epic can combine only indirectly. If narration—i.e. sequence in time—is the quality novel and epic share, the novel's interior dimension compels a further, contrasting development. In a sense, it would be most tempting to view, with Emil Staiger, *pastness* (expansion in temporal depth) as an overall narrative characteristic. It points out the function of the novel as history—either in fantasy or in fact. Yet, as the narrative world is expanded from the engagements of men's minds (or wits) with external nature to their engagements with themselves, pastness must expand to include all other tenses as well, since consciousness detached from its objects exists in a present detached from time. In this way, the epic tendencies in the novel are transcended in precisely the manner which Friedrich Schlegel brilliantly foresaw and analyzed. Although both historical and mythical elements in prose fiction continue to reflect the epic, they must in the end be turned in on

2. "Der dramatische Zusammenhang der Geschichte macht den Roman im Gegenteil noch keineswegs zum Ganzen, zum Werk, wenn er es nicht durch die Beziehung der ganzen Komposition auf eine höhere Einheit, als jene Einheit des Buchstabens, über die er sich oft wegsetzt und wegsetzen darf, durch das Band der Ideen, durch einen geistigen Zentralpunkt wird" ("Brief über den Roman," cited from Friedrich Schlegel, *Sämmtliche Werke* [2nd ed. Wien, 1846], 5, 222).

themselves as past time is turned in on itself in the *Bilderbuch* (described as a *Roman*) which Heinrich von Ofterdingen views in the Hermit's cave.

Two contrasting treatments of the epic in modern novels may serve as examples. Joyce used the Homeric text in *Ulysses* to describe the pilgrimage of three minds as a modern transposition of the Odyssean triad. In doing so, he retained the movement of the epic quest, while at the same time dissolving it into states of consciousness. The structural movement of the novel is based on pastness (the day in Dublin), whereas the states of mind project a continuous presentness; their composite picture, made up of various levels of reality and consciousness simultaneously, creates contrasting movements and moments of stillness—a productive tension. By contrast, Broch's *Tod des Vergil* uses the *Aeneid* to reverse the epic situation. The hero, literally prone, is passively borne to his death. In his reveries, containing lines and quotations from the *Aeneid,* even in the epic tone of many of the passages, the juxtaposition of Virgil on his deathbed and the epic hero he created is constantly reinforced. Moreover, not only Aeneas but also the *Aeneid* as artifact functions crucially in the novel, as time flows toward the irrevocable end. Yet all these elements of the epic pattern are absorbed (literally as well as figuratively) by the timeless sea of Virgil's expanding mind which forms the concluding image. The epic method—and even the epic machinery—are used by the novel to be turned into a portrayal of consciousness moving toward its own dissolution.

If the epic model for the novel leads to its own transcendence, the famous distinction between novel and romance suggests similar tensions in relation to probability and fact. Although both are indigenous forms of prose narrative—each with its own history and tradition—the sharp and basic distinction between them is peculiarly English. This is so not only because critics writing in English, from Clara Reeve and Walpole to Hawthorne and Henry James, have belabored this distinction, but also because the self-conscious separation of the two forms presupposes the English realistic novel of the eighteenth and nineteenth centuries as an autonomous antithesis of the romance.

As a way of describing a special fictional type, allowing us to distinguish between realistic and improbable fiction, the term "novel" is, of course, in no way meaningless. Nor is it out of bounds to observe the critical bent among English critics who have focused on a peculiarly severe *disjunction* in their narrative tradition (sharper, perhaps, and more abrupt than in other European countries), which may well have begun with Defoe. Like German criticism and practice in the novel a century later, English fiction at the turn of the eighteenth century developed a new technique, utilizing available modes of narrative for the journalistic account and the novel of manners and adapting them for their purpose. Yet most critics have seen more in this development than descriptive terms for limited genres emerging from different points of origin.

The problems posed by this distinction may be illuminated by two examples. Ian Watt defined the novel through its "pervasive realism" and rejected any prose narrative written before Defoe as inadequate in these terms. Realism of texture, which, he allowed, occurred earlier, had to be matched with a probable plot. It is questionable, of course, whether the plot of *Simplicissimus*, cited by Watt, is really much more improbable than that of *Pamela* with its incredible stratagems.[3] The fact remains that realism of plot as well as of texture remains Watt's chief criterion for the novel in whose rise he is particularly interested. By contrast, Northrop Frye stands out as an important critic in the English tradition rejecting the parochial stipulation of the English strand of the novel as the only permissible narrative form and defining both novel and romance as legitimate subgenres of prose narrative. But, having taken this step, Frye obscured the issue by introducing rigid categories for each, thus suggesting a basic cleavage. He naturally imposed on the form of the romance his definition of it as a literary mode, introducing such terms as the "glow of subjective intensity," the "suggestion of allegory," the nearness to archetypal forms of expression, as distinct from the "novel" with its immediately accessible portrait of concrete reality. The characters in the romance, according to Frye, exist as elemental prototypes; they are conceived in a way more basic, more "revolutionary" than those of

3. *The Rise of the Novel* (Berkeley, University of California Press, 1965), p. 205.

the novel and are presumably less subject to social and psychological analysis.[4] Hence, even for a critic as generous as Northrop Frye, the romance is more than a particular historical phenomenon, as limited in its way as the comedy of manners, and becomes any form of prose narrative that transcends the task of mirroring life as it may be perceived by comparatively modern audiences.

Modern criticism in English, elaborating distinctions made by Hawthorne and Henry James, echoes in a varying chorus what Frye overtly states: that in addition to its high style and rhetoric, the typical romance re-creates experience symbolically. As Poe phrased it in discussing fancy and imagination: the higher truth is implied in the undercurrent of the fictional material.[5] Yet such a basic differentiation leaves open many questions, for, as descriptions of men's intercourse with their worlds, both forms fulfill rather similar functions, whether the universe they depict is contemporaneous and ostensibly true or mythical-fantastic and palpably false. From this point of view, a Gothic romance like *The Castle of Otranto* is not too different from *Tom Jones:* plot as formal design governs both works. And although *Wuthering Heights* is clearly quite different from *Pride and Prejudice,* it is questionable whether the genre of the romance or a symbolic or poetic use of some of its conventions can be held accountable for its powerful tone, its unrealistic atmosphere, its aura of passion. To clarify Emily Brontë's novel, an individual and formal rather than a generic distinction may be in order.

Once the terms "novel" and "romance" are applied to continental fiction and its own tradition of realism, they become even less clear. For example, Gustav Freytag's *Die Ahnen*—to choose a typical case rather than a work of high artistic merit—appears as a romance in the guise of a realistic novel. All of its elements reveal its dual nature: the ancient chronicle becomes historical fantasy

4. Frye, pp. 304–05. For a recent, broadly based study of narrative (including oral, classical, and medieval traditions), see Robert Scholes and Robert Kellogg, *The Nature of Narrative* (New York, Oxford University Press, 1966), in which the "novel" is assigned a place within a larger generic scheme of "narration."

5. Hawthorne, "Preface," *The House of the Seven Gables* (New York, Doubleday, n.d.), p. 5; Poe, "Fancy and Imagination," *The Complete Works of E. A. Poe* (New York, 1902), 7, 126–27.

disguised as fact; its archetypal heroes wander through the centuries yet always dressed up in period costumes as believable characters of fiction. At the same time, the novel merges easily with the form of the collective *Bildungsroman* (or even *Familienroman*) of the bourgeois tradition. Or, to choose a weightier example, Thomas Mann's *Doktor Faustus* remains basically a "novel," yet it absorbs an improbable mythical scheme (including even the supernatural machinery of the romance) into a chronicle of contemporary life and a portrait of recent history. In France, too, Gothic novels and historical romances do not seem to exist on a different level—structurally and existentially—from the realistic fiction with which we are familiar. On the other hand, there is no reason why typical romances, even allegories, should carry greater symbolic weight than novels like *Jude the Obscure.* Instead of separating genres or subgenres artificially and then accounting for exceptions by stipulating mixtures and compounds, it is simpler to view all of prose fiction as a unity and to trace particular strands to different origins, strands which would include not only the English novel of manners, or the post-medieval romance, or the Gothic novel, but also the medieval allegory, the German *Bildungsroman,* or the picaresque. Some of these strands may be closer to folk material or to classical epics, others may have modeled themselves on travelogues and journalistic descriptions of events, and others again suggest drawing-room comedies and even lyrical prose poetry, yet all, to varying degrees, seem to mirror life in aesthetically defined worlds (life as myth, as structures of ideas, as worlds of feeling or quotidian reality). Yet whether their basic direction is purely narrative and external, or symbolic and internal, depends on the *use* made in each work of its material and its available methods.

Of all the critical systems that have sought to clarify the nature of prose narrative, German romantic criticism seems to have come closest to such a comprehensive view of the genre. On the surface, it seems, the opposite may be the case. Friedrich Schlegel's "Brief über den Roman," a path-breaking essay on the theory of the novel, nevertheless sets out from premises as parochial as any we have encountered. His denunciation of the English novel (save Richardson's and Sterne's) and his excessive praise for Jean Paul's and Sterne's novels as well as for Rousseau's *Confessions* are limiting, to say the least. Yet, through the intellectual precision and comprehensiveness of his ideas, which became self-generating, Friedrich Schlegel created fresh concepts about the novel that neutralized the historical bent of narrative. These ideas affected the novel in one way, as Goethe's *Wilhelm Meister* had influenced it in another. Together, they may have created a further alternative to the European narrative tradition as crucial as had been Defoe's a century earlier.

At first glance, it may seem strange to select the German tradition as pivotal, since in the nineteenth century it was not German but English, French, and Russian fiction that had produced the most significant works in the genre. But German prose narrative, both in theory and practice, developed a new rationale from German Romanticism, new conceptions of time and reality. A comprehensive genre was projected, and works were produced which were beset by a passion for the simultaneous rendering of historical and internal realities, for a self-conscious use of narrative forms to re-create experience symbolically. In this way, German theory and practice of the novel affected the development of the European novel as a whole, while at the same time turning the important twentieth-century German novel in a unique direction.

Wilhelm Meister was a watershed, whatever its obvious shortcomings as narrative may have been. Although it was, of course, by no means the first novel of education, it exerted disproportionate power through the sheer pressure of Goethe's genius and reputation. Moreover, it seemed to express a peculiar bent in the novel which coincided with the metaphysical preoccupations of its later practitioners. It dramatized a constant involvement of the self with itself, its process of learning in time, its scope of experience in the realm of empirical space, its "learning," that is, its ascent toward a higher goal through which the temporal process is ultimately transcended. In *Wilhelm Meister* and in the realistic German *Bildungsromane* of the nineteenth century, novels like Keller's *Grüner Heinrich*, Stifter's *Nachsommer*, or even Sudermann's *Frau Sorge*, this transcendence occurred on a naturalistic level: success, mastery of a craft, or, possibly, ultimate destruction by a hostile environment. In novels like Novalis' *Heinrich von Ofter-*

dingen or Hölderlin's *Hyperion,* however, the goal is portrayed in its transcendental and symbolic qualities. Moreover, this form of the novel seemed to translate into more contemporary terms characteristics of two earlier forms of narrative, the allegorical romance and the picaresque. The hero wanders through time and space, his process of learning being mirrored in constantly changing relations between his thoughts and acts and the ideas and skills or goals to which he aspires. But he is also passive. Clearly, he is not a "doer," as even Tom Jones is a doer, but he is an agent whose world evolves through his imagination as he is modified in his growth. In the spirit of Friedrich Schlegel and Novalis, who reinterpreted Goethe's model in their spirit, the novel epitomizes "transcendental poetry." [6]

The *Bildungsroman,* even in this romantic conception, is, of course, not the only form that exemplified the German *Roman.* The romantic quest like Eichendorff's *Ahnung und Gegenwart,* elaborations of romantic *Novellen* like *Michael Kohlhaas,* or psychological romances in historical dress like the fiction of C. F. Meyer all suggest similar projections and cancellations of time through implicitly passive heroes. But it is the German version of the novel of education, the *Bildungsroman,* which suggests this trend most fully. Self and world mutually modify one another in the process of learning (an infinite process which seems to transpose Fichte's *Wechselwirkung* of self and non-self into literature) ; time and space, the usual determinants of narrative form, expand to include interior, aesthetic, even metaphysical dimensions. As a critical norm, this tendency represents an important impulse in nineteenth-century thought, bearing implications far beyond those suggested by the works themselves and affecting many other forms—like the novel of manners and the social novel—within the mainstream of European fiction.

Yet, despite their promise, these criteria remained marginal and incomplete because they applied to works sharing only partially in the general tradition of fiction. The problem is both semantic and aesthetic or formal. For one thing, terms like "sensibility" apply to specific French and English novels; they explain Jane Austen as

6. Friedrich von Hardenberg (Novalis), *Schriften,* ed. Paul Kluckhohn (Leipzig, Bibliographisches Institut, 1929), 2, 327.

well as Stendhal. But these same terms, when they are applied to
German novels of the period, require thorough redefinition.
Goethe's and Novalis' applications of sensibility turn this time-
honored notion in a different direction; it becomes enmeshed in
the "expanding mind" of Goethe's *Bildungsroman* and in Novalis'
metaphysical symbolism. Even in the hands of later writers like
Stifter, we noted, Goethe's form was used to modify the realistic
novel significantly. Hence, terms applied in English and French
contexts seem no longer pertinent even to German realistic novels.
We confront a fresh disjunction. But the problem is also formal.
Except where they were transmitted elsewhere and were further
refined, German conceptions of prose narrative remained relatively isolated. Where they occur outside Germany later in the
nineteenth and early in the twentieth century, they do so in a very
different, modified form. For example, we find clear traces of this
attitude in novels like *The Scarlet Letter*. Moreover, some of its
characteristics—the concentration on symbolic apprehension, or the
transcendence of the past through an awareness of the present, or
more specific conventions like plays of illusion—were absorbed
and refashioned in French novels. We find such elements both in
the earlier fiction of Nodier and Nerval and in the later experiments of Huysmans and Villiers de l'Isle Adam; we can discover it
even in much of Flaubert. But though these attitudes helped
create a special aura in nineteenth-century fiction and even helped
develop some fresh techniques, they were influential mostly in the
growth of an underground fiction, for the important novels of the
time expanded and enriched the realistic tradition of the novel
and followed narrative conventions far removed in tone and texture from any methods developed in the wake of German Romanticism. Hence these concepts in the novel, while interesting and
influential, could not of themselves furnish a coherent critical
scheme unless further refined. It therefore remains for us to determine the formal limits which govern any possibility of a theory of
the novel or any recognition of prose narrative as an autonomous
yet comprehensive genre.

We have so far focused on differences among several types of
narratives and critical approaches: the novel as epic, the novel and

romance, the German alternative. Other forms could have been chosen instead. Yet even this wide historical sample seems somehow inadequate, for while some possibilities seem more productive than others, none seem to respond fully to a comprehensive view of the novel.

A formal investigation of the genre forces us to retrace some of the steps we have taken historically. In our own linguistic environment, for example, the most important statements still reveal a tendency to regard the English realistic novel as typical of all fiction. They indicate a primary concern with the narrative and mimetic functions of the novel: point of view, verisimilitude, character, plot. Although unique for its time in its concentration on technique, Percy Lubbock's classic, *The Craft of Fiction,* focuses on the relationship between the novel's world and the writer's, reader's, and protagonist's point of view, cast in a narrative perspective.[7] The Jamesian emphasis on the discerning consciousness relates to the protagonist-author in a way not too different from Yorick's in *A Sentimental Journey.* These early writings have served as texts for those who have analyzed the novel as a formal construction (as Mark Schorer attempted to do in his influential essay, "Technique as Discovery"). Here too, with several important exceptions, Henry James' self-conscious and Faulkner's symbolic awareness were seen in an aesthetic context defined by the model of English fiction, i.e. the base of society and manners. Although pursuing an opposite course, R. S. Crane's famous essay on *Tom Jones,* identifying its plot with its form, arises from a bias in favor of the English form as the basic *logic* of narrative.[8] Wayne C. Booth's elaborate "rhetoric" of fiction expands this approach into a general scheme.[9] His constant emphasis on narrative requirements and his frequent reiteration of distinctions like "telling" and "showing," which by no means apply to all fictional forms, limit his work far more rigidly than was obviously intended. Indeed, two seemingly contradictory approaches in mod-

7. *The Craft of Fiction* (New York, Viking Press, 1957). See, for example, pp. 9–13.

8. "The Concept of Plot and the Plot of *Tom Jones,*" *Critics and Criticism* (Chicago, University of Chicago Press, 1952), pp. 616–47.

9. *The Rhetoric of Fiction* (Chicago, University of Chicago Press, 1961).

ern English and American criticism meet on this issue: the attempt to view the novel as an aesthetic re-creation of the world
analogous to that of a poem, and to define it as a naturalistic image
of man and world set within the scheme of narrative time. Except
for social and historical critics, only those following Freudian and
archetypal approaches have been able to evolve consistently a
wider perspective of the genre.

Despite the important difficulties we have observed, a critical
theory based on German Romanticism promises to open up the
genre to a wider perspective and to deal concretely with some of its
inherent problems. To be sure, later German critics, like Spiel-
hagen, developed rigid realistic standards, less generous and more
provincial even than other critics of their time, but the romantic
base of the German vision of the novel remained aesthetically
crucial. Even so "unromantic" a scholar as Georg Lukács could not
divorce his perspective entirely from the German romantic
scheme. His reasons were partly literary. A devoted classicist, he
worked within a literary tradition dominated by the Goethean
ideal, by the *Bildungsroman*, by a tendency to interpret reality
philosophically. However much he rejected the romantic world of
unreason, its ideological tensions were present to him even in
negation. But part of his vision naturally stems from his immer-
sion in the Hegelian and Marxist dialectic. Time and timelessness
were viewed by him in modified, structural terms. The novel
exists in both, duration and physical (as well as social) reality, in
time and space. To the extent that one cancels out or balances the
other, a pattern is created. Lukács' stringent realism is enriched by
his sense of tension between historical progression and a present-
tense social world.[10]

Whether history is counteracted by a solid physical or social
world, or whether it is absorbed into consciousness, a fruitful ap-

10. See, for example, the relationship between the ideology of the bourgeois revolution and the Napoleonic Age and the sense of history as "mass
experience." *The Historical Novel* (Boston, Beacon Press, 1962), pp. 24–25.
The tension described in this passage is, of course, present throughout in the
argument of Lukács' book, i.e. that the "classical historical novel" exists as
an index of the function of history and as a continuous state in man's consciousness of his present condition.

proach to the novel must eventually turn away from narrative requirements and expectations and concern itself with the novel's intrinsic function: to develop the tensions between an interior base (aesthetic, psychological, philosophical) and the external reference of the metaphoric structure it represents. As we have noted, Friedrich Schlegel's "Brief über den Roman" is pivotal, because it turns the novel from a historical movement into ahistorical art.

The originality of Friedrich Schlegel's essay, despite all of its shortcomings and parochialisms, lies in this substitution of new criteria for the traditional ones of external reality and chronological time. Interpreting both the fancy of the Spanish romance and the playful, internal logic of Sterne's novels philosophically, he introduced new conventions: the transcendental conception of sensibility, the "Arabesque," the notion of the novel as an all-encompassing genre. On the one hand, despite his denials, he retained a strong suggestion of historical relevance. Yet, on the other hand, any temporal meaning is caught in a spatial mirror: timeless consciousness and aesthetic freedom (in the sense of Kant and Schiller), humor and play. History, then, is dissolved by the infusion of the mind into the novel's material, to be replaced by the play of "significant, divine images," figures of fancy and fact (a gathering of Dante and Laura, Shakespeare and Cervantes, Sancho Panza and Don Quixote), all of them contemplated in quietude.[11] The stage of the novel's drama—the sequence of events or scenes—is refashioned in an imaginative space. History is absorbed into a fictional, an aesthetic, world.

Such a world, or cosmos, as Wellek and Warren have shown, remains a distinctive feature of all narrative.[12] It exists in juxtaposition with an external world which, if successful, can be dissolved into play. Other genres, of course, can also be defined in this way, but the novel is unique. It is not like the lyric, since it is specifically concerned with relationships, objects, and events outside itself, nor is it like the traditional drama, where all projections take place within the aesthetic limits of the stage. Instead, the novel functions through a continuity of past and present. The

11. "Brief über den Roman," p. 223.
12. *Theory of Literature* (3d ed. New York, Harcourt Brace, 1962), pp. 214–15.

relationships between its persons and the outside world are reversible, as perception is modified by objects and the novel's objects are, in turn, refashioned by their perceiver. For this reason, Friedrich Schlegel's dictum that the novel, as a "romantic book," is a universal genre has a special meaning. It is universal not only because it may comprise a variety of forms, but also because it functions from an Olympian perspective. Time and self can be interchangeable with their counterpoints, space and world. This proposition should be true of any novel, of Tom Jones' pilgrimage to prudence or of Tristram Shandy's variegated play. It should apply to Heinrich von Ofterdingen's search for the Blue Flower as well as to Henry James' *Ambassadors,* manipulating a finely chiseled world of manners and a self-reflecting, refined consciousness in mutual interaction.

Possibly a Kantian analogy may be appropriate, for more than any other genre, the novel projects an interpersonal mental structure in which its action takes place. It does so by seeming to be about real objects in the external world, and thus communicating knowledge, while being actually about fictional objects in an imaginary world, thus rendering them hypothetical. On the surface, neither James' Strether nor Broch's Virgil is hypothetical. The former lives and the latter dies in a seemingly real world, yet their relationships, in varying degrees of externality, always relate to an inner world projected by the novelist. The obvious point that neither Strether's nor Virgil's world exists in fact may seem negligible, but it may be significant for a general view of the novel's functioning. Each object presented to the mind of each of the two protagonists is possessed of a double nature, for it exists both in "real" space, in which Broch's Brindisi may be historically real, and in imaginary or aesthetic space—the space of the imagination—in which the actual novel unfolds.

The metaphor for the novel, more than for any other genre, is spatial, because its action unfolds literally in *places,* i.e., in a world where selves move and experience one another. Moreover, its illusion depends on the suggestion that the places be real, even if they be symbolic or fantastic. Secondly, the relations of people and objects depicted in this world are spatial, although the novel's fictional space may not always be continuous, but may be (as in

Tristram Shandy, for example) broken up into particular moments of awareness. For the novel always indicates distances between consciousness and objects which create space. In the lyric, the distance between self and other is practically eliminated as the world becomes part of the poet's consciousness. In the novel, distances between them widen and shorten at the novelist's discretion, for they basically exist as distinct entities, relating to one another, absorbing one another, to separate again. As we noted earlier, it appears to be a unique quality of the novel that its worlds exist both outside and within consciousness, both in past time and its transcendence or negation. Relations indicating distances vary in individual novels (*Great Expectations* and *The Waves*) and in different forms of the novel (*Werther* and *Pride and Prejudice*) .

The novel, then, is fashioned by a space, simultaneously "real" and aesthetic, in which its fundamental confrontation takes place: encounters of self and other mirroring the real confrontation in an actual world. Even when novels are panoramic and relatively exterior, like *Vanity Fair,* or historical displays of human interactions, like *Salammbô,* narrative time, the development of character, indeed, the entire stage business of the novel is concerned with this basic relationship. Selves constantly confront others in that classic pose which reproduces the basic pattern of the act of knowledge, as they train their discernment, their sensual apprehension, and their capacity to respond with feeling upon the world beyond their consciousness. Thus, in the largest perspective of the omniscient author, or in the narrowest compass of a single, experiencing persona, the novel's function remains that of investigating the self (in terms of its actual or imagined exterior relations) before rendering it aesthetic. For, by entering into the self with imaginative empathy, the novel is particularly well equipped to reflect vividly the images men have of themselves and their relationships with others, with their environment, with their historical condition.

The novel's involvement with the self, its relations with people and things, is accounted for by the special nature of the hero. We not only see him acting outside ourselves (as we do literally in the drama) , but we also see the world through his eyes and sense with extraordinary vividness his particular relations with the

world, either through perception or through a kind of physical
interaction that echoes the act of knowledge. Proust's famous image of the sliding walls is, of course, an example of perceptual confrontation. In the dim transition from wakefulness to dream, the
entire pageantry of Marcel's life is revealed to his inner eye. The
confrontation is internalized. Aschenbach's vision in *Tod in
Venedig* shows how an entire novella can be constructed from successive confrontations with objects viewed by the hero. Moreover,
after his tragedy has been developed through the impact of objects,
images, and figures on his perceiving mind, it is once more
symbolized externally after Aschenbach's death: the viewing
mind, detached, remains as a lone black camera, unmanned on the
beach. We experience a drama of perception while remaining in
the hero's mind, looking out. Indeed, in some novels, Kafka's
Prozess for example, we have no distinct impression of the way the
hero appears, although we see all persons appearing to him with
great clarity. The form, then, is not lyrical poetry, in which an
acute moment is cast in an image. Rather, it is focused on a living
and acting hero who is defined by his relations even as we penetrate his consciousness. Rooted in a milieu, acting from a particular social or historical perspective, he is a *man* whose experience
counts as an index of his relationships with a universe men pretend to control.

In this sense one may consider the novel as a particularly philosophical genre: not because it states philosophical propositions
(though it may also do that), but because even its most conventional forms constantly illustrate, dramatize, portray the interplay
of minds and objects as representations of the act of knowledge.
The recognition of this function of the novel has lent it its quality
of seriousness, or it has allowed us to see that any fiction—the
dying city in *La Peste,* Raskolnikov's personal conversion, even
the detached manipulation of objects in *Le Voyeur*—exists
through concrete relations which release inner experience and
allow it to be dramatized in the novel's space. Perhaps initially
formulated by Friedrich Schlegel, we now encounter this recognition again in modern criticism. Maurice Blanchot's "espace littéraire" can be narrowed to apply particularly to the novel as a

form that seeks its own transcendence even as it seems to be sufficient to itself.[13]

The relationships dominating the novel's form or "space"—re-
enacting the confrontation between self and other—are perhaps
most clearly exhibited, albeit in rudimentary form, in an early
model of modern fiction, the picaresque novel, which may well
serve as a *paradigm* for the novel as a whole.[14] This is not to suggest that all novels are picaresques or that all fiction reflects directly the picaresque method as a standard of criticism. Rather, to
the extent that the structure of the picaresque novel is fashioned
by the *picaro*'s constant engagements with the surrounding world,
its aesthetic space wholly enlivened by his adventures, it can be
viewed as a prototype. This function of the form as a paradigm is
clearly discernible in pure picaresques, like *Lazarillo de Tormes*
or *Simplicissimus*. It is brought out even more fully in a novel like
Don Quixote, where the relations inherent in the picaresque are
deliberately played upon and varied, and where illusory and real
universes are intricately mirrored in a subtle inversion of the
picaresque. For Don Quixote is the perennial victim of an environment he himself has created as an illusory as well as idealized
cosmos.

The picaresque, then, is a paradigm because its pattern presents
a space described entirely by interactions between heroes and their
antagonists, between selves and others. Although the *picaro* usually acts rather than reflects (sensually or intellectually), his
raison d'être is found in these relationships which suggest the confrontation between consciousness and its objects. Moreover, although he exists in time, i.e. in the temporal flow of the novel and
of the events in which he is engaged, he performs actions without a
structure or end beyond themselves. Hence the very time he uses
for his purpose becomes ultimately meaningless. He therefore

13. See *L'Espace littéraire* (Paris, Gallimard, 1955), pp. 20–22, 78 f. (on
Kafka), and passim.

14. This basic relationship, as noted on p. 60, also pertains to the epic,
but it does so in a different way. The epic is external and structured; the
picaresque enacts the adventures of an individual consciousness, its encounters existing outside a predetermined structure and outside time.

illustrates the German romantic view of the hero's function, the alternation between self and, as Fichte called it, the non-self, until both merge in infinity.

While his cancellation of time and his definition of fictional space through constant interaction illustrate a romantic view of the novel, the picaresque's internal structure also applies to seemingly remote forms, like the English realistic novel. For consecutive time is neither necessary nor antithetical to the novel's form. Defoe and others writing in England at the turn of the eighteenth century, faced with the need to treat reality factually and empirically, had to turn available methods, like the picaresque, to their use. As activities in which men were engaged in life were now directly mirrored in fiction, the novel became a brilliant attempt to show man's way of perceiving, clarifying, and controlling his world. In the picaresque, the protagonist's effort to control (or fail to control) his universe, and so to define himself, had been a subject of amusement. In the eighteenth century, however, notably in England, the idea of confrontation and control behind the picaresque, and, indeed, frequently the picaresque method itself, was also applied to such interests as commerce or marriage, the social world, the command of nature. In this sense, *Robinson Crusoe,* describing the effort of a man to overcome, clarify, and control his environment, can be seen as symptomatic. Although it is not picaresque in any technical sense, the novel's entire "space" is taken up by an oppressive environment which the rational man seeks to bend to his purpose, precisely as the world itself seeks to subdue him. In Defoe's novel the outcome is structured—intelligence wins—but a modern re-creation of its substance, William Golding's *Pincher Martin,* shows precisely the opposite end, dramatizing how structure must dissolve as intelligence is ultimately submerged in the irrational, hallucinatory ocean. Both novels illustrate the picaresque as a paradigm, even as they eschew its methods. Individual subgenres, like the novel of manners, or the *Bildungsroman,* or the historical romance, are organized in many different ways, but the confrontations implicit in the picaresque suggest that its form might serve as a general pattern to provide common ground for all types of fiction relevant to a theory of the novel. Whether the picaresque can perform so overwhelming a task and yet furnish useful critical tools on a practical level remains open to question.

The suggestion that the picaresque, in its most general outline, may be symptomatic of the novel's basic form involves the following assumptions: First, the novel's world is a structure or "space" composed of relations between heroes and their surrounding worlds, both human and nonhuman. Second, the hero's posture in facing his environment resembles the confrontation implicit in the act of knowledge with which most novels, in one form or another, are concerned. Third, the structure so created embodies the values mirrored in the work. In such a scheme, traditional terminology used in the criticism of fiction, like plot, character, point of view, and so on, would be subsumed under the larger concept of men's engagements with their worlds, of consciousness with its objects.

It remains a question whether the critic has gained in practical understanding of his genre, for the novel as a whole is still uncomfortably large, and individual books, precisely because of their length, yield to close analysis only with difficulty. Its subgenres are far more accessible through the individual methods devised for them by different critics, provided they are not made into standards for all fiction. Yet the general paradigm of the picaresque, the analogy between men's actions and the act of knowledge, and the recognition of the peculiarly dual nature of the novel as an internal and external genre do serve to clarify our understanding of the form's general impact and role as literature. It has shown, by means of the example of a very primitive form, the philosophical dimension of the novel, as the critic is permitted to turn away from an excessive preoccupation with narrative time to an understanding of the novel's "space": a cosmos enlivened by man's crucial activity, within and outside history, to define himself in relation to others and to be shaped by, even as he himself shapes, that terrifying reality outside, with which he must come to terms.

Helmut Hatzfeld

Comparative Literature as a Necessary Method

Some Theoretical Considerations

It seems to me that comparative literature for the time being has its main raison d'être as a method of critical control over the usual terms created by historians of single national literatures but meant to represent general periodizations. Comparative literature certainly is called upon to verify or modify such terms as they correspond to facts or to eliminate and replace them if they can be shown to be applicable only to one or the other of the national literatures in the Western world. Such a term, on the other hand, may well stand for a fact but cover only a marginal trend, not a period and its dominant features. The trend, however, may not have developed genetically but may have been imposed by cultural imposition (*Kulturlenkung, dirigisme*). Trends consciously created by an elite or by an outstanding individual for a sophisticated public may represent a deviation from the norm rather than the norm itself, from which they can not escape entirely, however. The new comparative method is also closely linked to the general shift from *Geistesgeschichte* to *Formgeschichte* in literary scholarship. Therefore contact with the history of art, "formal" by definition, from which many a literary term has also been borrowed, cannot be neglected either. On the contrary, since art history does not know national boundaries but is concerned with a general "language," it offers exactly the working pattern for comparative literature, aiming at common horizontal movements which affect at a certain moment of history the vertical constants of national artistic attitudes. The features of graphic artifacts projected into space are technically easier to observe, analyze, and discuss than the features of literary artifacts, which are not simultaneously perceptible as they extend in time. I think this was Oskar Walzel's discovery, despite all theoretical objection, that the literary critic has, so to speak, to project the literary artifacts, too, into space in order to distinguish their structures.

In the present essay, however, I am not steering the course for the comparison of the arts, although some comparatists consider this method important for our problem.[1] I use art history only as a scholarly branch methodologically comparable to but much more advanced than literary history. In art history there exists the necessity of interpreting pictures, which do not explain themselves as do literary works, the words of which (despite their structural and stylistic connotations within a literary artifact) never cease to preserve their lexical and denotational meanings, thus speaking directly to the reader. Therefore art historians know a more highly developed motif analysis, called iconography. Iconography within a historical continuum developed to a *Motivgeschichte*. This half-conceptual, half-formal discipline, transferred to literature, redeemed the latter from the unrefined *Stoffhuberei*. *Motivgeschichte* became a way to fix literary epochs according to dominating motifs, which helped to establish correct European literary periods since motifs predominant within a certain era notoriously transcend national and linguistic boundaries.

If I called the motifs semiformal, I meant that they are not simply *topoi* as to content but have in addition to their frequency a particular stylistic cast. This was, as one knows, the important correction Dámaso Alonso had to make on the theory of Ernst Robert Curtius.[2] The stylistic form of the motif is more important for deciding an epoch than the *topos* as such. From this fundamental distinction it seems rather clear that an epoch can be defined only by its style. Motif form and motif combination certainly are part and parcel of such a style. But what kind of style, evidently present in literature as well as in art? Certainly a cultural style, since the motivistic style is conditioned by cultural propensities.

Since Heinrich Wölfflin we know that, besides an ideologically

1. Mary Gaither, "Literature and the Arts," in P. Stallknecht and H. Frenz, eds., *Comparative Literature: Method and Perspective* (Carbondale, Southern Illinois University Press, 1961), pp. 153–70.

2. Dámaso Alonso, "Tradition or Polygenesis?" *MHRA*, 32 (1960), 17–34.

conditioned cultural style, there is also a structural style. Wölfflin's five principles of art history have been successfully extended to literary structures. He himself has proposed the transfer and sketched it for the epic, and it can be done for the novel and the lyrical poem as well. It certainly also may be done in the right way for the drama, although unfortunately the hasty and superficial attempts that have been made in this direction seem to disprove the transposition.

One may already be on safe ground for defining an epoch style and deriving from it a style epoch, if one considers a framework of choices, stylizations, and combinations of motifs, on the one hand, and the preference for a fundamental type of literary structure (tectonic or symphonic), on the other. The literary historian will not be satisfied, however, with discerning only a cultural and structural style. These styles are most important as links to the styles of nonliterary artifacts likewise typical for a time span. But the literary style itself means, of course, the syntactical and rhetorical style embedded exclusively in language. Here there are many deterrents and pitfalls which have been the causes of disagreement. The difficulty actually consists in discerning within the macro-structures of literary artifacts micro-structures or styles likewise conditioned by content, genre, and national and individual propensities and yet corresponding to the macro-structures. All these propensities again are kept in abeyance by traditional devices inherent in the different genres. The innovations themselves are limited to abstract or concrete preferences, verbal or nominal syntactical possibilities, modifications of imagery and rhythm, all of which coalesce into a distinguishable, time-conditioned synthesis. Here comparative literature as a method becomes a means of identifying the apparently diverse synthetic kaleidoscopes of different works from different countries as belonging together. The method was compared by Karl Vossler to one's surveying a whole landscape from an airplane without catching minor diversities in its parts, diversities that only could be distinguished from the window of a train. In a literary landscape there may be woods of exuberant metaphorical forms alongside meadows of humble, metonymical forms, *Schwellformen* and *Schrumpfformen,* but both are reducible to the same root. Both are the linguistic expression of an attitude which reflects in different micro-stylistic possibilities the same collective psychology and sociology. The comparability of the synthetic styles throughout the centuries raises the question of their meanings. At this point only does the history of literary art become a history of epochal ideas or *Geistesgeschichte* a posteriori, i.e. deducible from the forms. The spirit thus discovered within the forms rather than behind the structural and verbal style of the works has, like the style constellation itself, the character of historical uniqueness. This fact again, if a sound method is observed, excludes the application in a phenomenological sense of terms created for style combinations occurring at a particular moment of history. Any theory of recurring wave movements using the historically oriented terms is detrimental to historical insights.

Applications

With these ideas in mind and considering some publications which have appeared since Wellek's definitions of baroque, classicism and romanticism, I will reconsider the validity of these three collective literary styles or rather style epochs, if epochs they are. It seems to me they are only epochs if their style originates from particular circumstances in one country and spreads out from it to other countries, in a more or less accelerated tempo. The end of such a style epoch would be marked by transitional forms without particular concepts, forms which on their part eventuate in a new style coming from a new spirit.

Baroque

If the comparatist once has made the decision to borrow a term like "baroque" from the art historian, he has to take with it all the implications and analogies involved. If he judges the transfer meaningful, he has to follow all the refinement, improvement, and correction the art historian is constantly making with regard to his own material. While it is normal for the art historian as well as for the literary comparatist to cross national boundaries, each one in his own domain, it cannot be admitted as methodologically sound to compare, for instance, French or English literature with Italian baroque art. This is the blatant flaw of the otherwise very good and well-known books of Jean Rousset and Wylie Sypher.

Decades ago the art historian stopped talking about "late Renaissance" and "early baroque" and replaced these empty terms by a much better one, "mannerism," meaning a virtuosity in elongating, foreshortening, and destroying the classical Renaissance forms without giving them a new content. The majority of literary comparatists have ignored this most important change and thus confused the issue. But a connoisseur like A. M. Boase has shown that provocative, dramatic, heightening forms of virtuosity without a definable new Weltanschauung exactly characterize English literature between Lyly and Donne, French literature between D'Aubigné and Malherbe (including Jean de Sponde and Jean de La Ceppède, not confusing their religious tendency with "Protestant Baroque"), the Spanish literature of Góngora (1 would say from Garcilaso, at least from Herrera to Góngora), and the Italian literature between Tasso and Marini. On the whole Boase has logically severed a literary mannerism from a literary Baroque.[3] No doubt literary mannerism prevailed too long in the Western world to be only a generation style, as I for many years believed. It is now considered a period which shortens the baroque period itself to reasonable chronological proportions and, at least as far as France is concerned, cuts off exactly these post-Pléiade and "preclassical" authors whom the French critics would consider the true baroque authors. I have clarified the problem in my article "Mannerism Is Not Baroque."[4]

The baroque period was also prevented from trangressing the frontier between the seventeenth and the eighteenth centuries. Without the establishment of the baroque period by comparatism, one hardly can understand the book of Roger Laufer, who from an exclusively French viewpoint called his work with a commendable equation *Style Rococo, style des "Lumières,"*[5] an

3. A. M. Boase, "The Definition of Mannerism," *Actes du IIIe Congrès de l'Association Internationale de Littérature Comparée: 1961* ('S Gravenhage, Mouton, 1962), 143–55.

4. *L'Esprit Créateur, 6* (1966), 225–32.

5. Roger Laufer, *Style Rococo, Style des Lumières* (Paris, Corti, 1963).

equation I was bold enough to propose in 1938.[6] Laufer, however, not being a comparatist, obnubilates the point he wants to make by the absurd question, "Pourquoi notre classicisme est-il qualifié de 'baroque tardif!? Le rococo devient-il du baroque très tardif?" Instead of answering exactly with "of course," he says: "Nous prétendons seulement résoudre le paradoxe, encore communément accepté d'une pensée révolutionnaire exprimée dans un style académique." [7] Then he analyzes pertinently, nevertheless, *Les Lettres persanes, Manon Lescaut, L'Ingénu, Le Neveu de Rameau,* and *Les Liaisons dangereuses.* The wealth of his selections from enlightened erotic French literature, covering the entire eighteenth century, gives us the clue that it would be futile to look for a rococo period style in Italy (despite Goldoni), Spain (despite Gracián), England (despite Pope), or Germany (despite Wieland). Although Germany's "Zopfstil" would still be the closest guess, "any attempt to distinguish a Rococo period in German literature is doomed to failure." [8] In connection with our problem, however, this much can be said: the full rococo in France and the rump-rococo elsewhere mean a terminus ad quem for the baroque. So much has been clarified by the studies in mannerism and rococo that the European literary baroque is confined more or less to the seventeenth century.

The baroque thus envisaged has undeniable cultural, motivistic, structural, and micro-stylistic style features resulting from a good many analyzed works, the features of which can be and have been compared. The results, however, were and are resisted again and again, and this in a systematic method by the French critics who refuse to consider anything else but French literature for their wrong decision on concept and chronology of the baroque. One has only to look at the topics of the *"Journées internationales d'études du Baroque"* in Montauban (Sept. 26–28, 1963) to see that the identification of mannerism and baroque was simply a foregone conclusion. One has only to read the would-be *mise-au-*

---

6. Helmut Hatzfeld, "Rokoko als literarischer Epochenstil in Frankreich," *Studies in Philology, 35* (1938), 532–65.

7. Laufer, p. 36.

8. C. T. Carr, "Two words in Art History. II. Rococo," *Forum for Modern Language Studies: 1* (1965) 266–81, particularly 280.

point of J. Morel[9] to find the most banal definition of the baroque epoch, "un temps où le joyeux bilan de la Renaissance est remis en cause," and to see, however, the Counterreformation despite Bremond, despite Weisbach, excluded as a cause. For Morel, baroque may be defined by the existence of some exterior, thematically religious themes, like *La Semaine, Saint-Genêt,* and *Polyeucte;* he does not consider the existential interior "baroque" of Bossuet's *Oraisons funèbres,* delivered as the adequate *art de la parole* in an obvious baroque funeral setting and display, or the baroque of the drama of the soul of Pascal, or the baroque of the tragedy of Racine's *Phèdre,* all of which reflect the baroque theology of the difficult balance between Grace and Free Will, the Supernatural and the Natural. One finally has only to read the new edition of Henri Peyre's *Classicisme,* where baroque again is coupled with "Pré-classicisme," where it is stated that "la notion de baroque ne contribue que bien peu à en enrichir notre compréhension du classicisme français," i.e. "l'époque [sic] classique."[10]

Classicism

That the French baroque allegedly preceded classicism, not followed it, "as in other countries," is no problem for Peyre. He has also stated that the term "baroque" is unnecessary, misinterprets Spitzer's ingenious term *"baroque dompté,"* and reintroduces as almost equivalent Gide's ambiguous term *"romantisme dompté."* At this point I want to stress my leitmotif: comparative literature as a necessary method.

This method has proved that classicism is no epoch, in any country, unless one calls (following the oldest art historian) the period of the Italian Renaissance the period of classical art. The earliest Italian, renaissant, and humanistic type of classicism actually can be understood as a kind of national revival which identified a late medieval Italy with Rome and the Italians with the

9. J. Morel, "L'Intérêt méthodologique de la notion de baroque littéraire," *Australian Journal of French Studies, I* (1964), 11–22.

10. Henri Peyre, *Q'est-ce que le Classicisme?* (Paris, Nizet, 1965), pp. 76, 90.

Romans. And yet this Italian classicism is a dictation, a *Kulturlenkung* which has no existence *physei* but only *thesei*. Dante's Virgil imitation is foisted on medieval troubadour traditions; Boccaccio gives the French *fabliau* tradition a Ciceronian rhythmical icing; Petrarch's eagerness for ancient glory ends in a new Augustinian *contemptus mundi*, his Ovidian and Catullan love poetry in a *conscience dans le mal*; Ariosto indulges simply in art for art's sake. But all of them have a genuine patriotic relationship to the Latin tradition, which they believe to continue directly. The art historians therefore did not hesitate to speak about the art from Giotto to Michelangelo as classical art.

All the other neoclassicisms are more evident *dirigismes* and *Kulturlenkungen* of an existing style by an elite into something subdued, competing with the taste of the ancients at the zenith of their cultural periods. What the French elite developed throughout the seventeenth century is qualitatively and quantitatively the highest and most refined neoclassicism, but one cannot discuss this "classicism" at all if one neglects purposely the formal elements, the conscious and even rationalized link to antiquity, and the stress on the Aristotelian rules instead of the direct imitation of classical patterns, whatever may be the freedom of their application. But the rules as such are exactly the clue to all the baroque poetics and *artes rhetoricae*. Among the other classicisms which try not to lean on this French baroque classicism but to outdo it, the German "classicism" during full romanticism is the most serious parallel. However, the German type of a classical dirigism is so individualistic, practically staged by Goethe and perhaps Schiller exclusively, that there is not even a true collective elite behind it. But the attempt to refine the romantic trend for a short time within a small sector is of the same cultural dictation as the French attempt to refine the baroque trend. This is the unavoidable conclusion of the comparative, here again, necessary method. Considering the French classicism an epoch or a norm for any European neoclassicism is simply a wrong method. Does Germany, not having the French type of classicism, have no classicism at all? One cannot introduce French constant values reaching their peak in the seventeenth century as a criterion of classicism. But Peyre decrees, "Il n'y a donc pas, dans l'histoire littéraire de l'Allemagne, de classicisme, c'est-a-dire d'ensemble ayant poussé très avant l'étude de l'homme intérieur ou celle de l'homme en société." [11]

A more legitimate method would be to check the values of French and German classicism against the values of antiquity, and one would find with Carl Burckhardt a very similar scale of selected principles: order, tranquillity, moral measure, even bienséance, called by Goethe *Schicklichkeit*.[12] Another check would concern the behavior of classical painters, sculptors, and theoreticians who studied in Italy the art of the Renaissance and of antiquity. Then one would find that Poussin's concept of classicism deduced from his studies comes very close to Winckelmann's concept of "Edle Einfalt und stille Grösse." Actually Poussin, Racine, Winckelmann, and Goethe receive their taste from Italy and her Renaissance. The archeologist Ludwig Curtius has stated: "Der Klassizismus Winckelmanns und Goethes ist durch zeitliche Nähe, Zusammenhang der Kunst selbst und Tradition der Theorie mit der Renaissance viel enger verbunden als diese mit der Antike." [13] The main reason why the French "dictated" classicism was bound to impose itself and the German classicism was bound to evaporate lies in the fact that the first was helped by political power and the court of Versailles, while the second was not sponsored by a politically strong state (only by the tiny court of Weimar) with cultural aspirations.[14] The other reason is that the baroque concepts of duty, honor, and renunciation underlying French classicism were shared by the public (Racine's *Iphigénie*), and that romantic concepts like the healing of guilt and madness (Goethe's *Iphigenie*) were absolutely subjective and esoteric. There would be no Goethean *Iphigenia* without Frau von Stein.[15]

11. Ibid., p. 209.

12. Carl J. Burckhardt, "Zum Begriff des Klassischen in Frankreich und in der deutschen Humanität," *Concinnitas. Wölfflin Festschrift* (Basel, Schwabe, 1944), pp. 11–34.

13. L. Curtius, "Winckelmann und unser Jahrhundert," *Die Antike, 6* (1930), 16.

14. Walter Muschg, *Die deutsche Klassik, tragisch gesehen* (Mainz, Akademie der Wissenschaften und Literatur, 1952).

15. Fritz Strich, "Natur und Geist der deutschen Dichtung," *Die Ernte. Franz Muncker zu seinem 70. Geburtstag* (Halle, Niemeyer, 1926), pp. 3–29, esp. p. 11.

This fundamental difference between a successful and an unsuccessful cultural dirigism is the only reason why the whole world speaks about French classicism and only the Germans about German classicism. This semantic situation encourages the French to maintain that the generation style of an elite from 1660–1685 is an epoch and has nothing to do whatsoever with the baroque period, of which it is, however, not the successor but part and parcel.[16] On the other hand, the Germans are difficult to persuade not to sever their "classicism" from their romantic period, which practically starts with the Storm and Stress generation. They speak timidly about an inseparable "German classicism and romanticism (Fritz Strich, Franz Schultz) or, worse, "Goethezeit" or "Kultur des Idealismus" or "Deutsche Bewegung," thus making a comparative approach impossible. They are blocking comparative insights in the same manner as the French.

Romanticism

The Germans with their special terminology tend from the outset also to destroy the concept of a unified European romanticism and of a romantic period. That such a unified period exists for the Western world between 1760 and 1850 is, however, still widely admitted, and Mr. Wellek is the main champion of this idea. I agree that among the allegedly existing 11,396 definitions of romanticism,[17] his definition is a rather convincing one: "The same conception of poetry and . . . poetic imagination, the same conception of nature and its relation to man and basically the same style." [18] Going beyond "basically the same," however, I can see a

16. I am glad Mr. Wellek now shares my own oldest convictions: "French seventeenth century classicism will appear . . . clearly [sic] baroque . . . while English classicism seems most enlightened . . . it has affinities with what could be called rococo. German classicism even in its most self-consciously neoclassical stage, will appear to us as romantic" (René Wellek, "The Term and Concept of 'Classicism' in Literary History," in Earl R. Wasserman, ed., *Aspects of the Eighteenth Century* (Baltimore, Johns Hopkins Press, 1965), pp. 105–27, esp. pp. 126–27.

17. F. L. Lucas, *The Decline and Fall of the Romantic Ideal* (1948), quoted by Kurt Weinberg in *Preminger's Encyclopedia of Poetry and Poetics* (Princeton, 1965), p. 717.

18. René Wellek, "The Concept of Romanticism," in *Concepts of Criticism* (New Haven and London, Yale University Press, 1963), pp. 160–61.

common motivistic, cultural, and even literary style in English and German romanticism, though not in French. Therefore I once tried quite independently of Lovejoy (less radically, however) to oppose a German *Romantik* to a French *romantisme*.[19] I found that the characteristics of German romanticism, namely, the serious belief in the irrational, in poetic intuition and truth, the true nostalgia for a higher and a better life, the belief in meaningful myth and nature symbolism, are absolutely lacking in French romanticism. Such belief is replaced in France by the mystification of the *poeta-vates* concept, an erotic and spiritistic pseudo-metaphysics culminating in occultist attitudes, a cult of souvenir, a poetic materialism (René Bray), and a most banal humanitarian belief in progress. The style forms produced by these quite different attitudes are in German romanticism (and English likewise) dignified and highly lyrical, in French romanticism showy and rhetorical. Thus the approximation of substantial depth and superficial play in order to give some basis to the literary *magma* between Rousseau and the old Goethe seems to resist all suggestions of a primary and secondary romanticism, since the post-revolutionary French *romantisme* seems very little influenced by Germany despite the theoretical, ready-made "enthusiasm" of Mme. de Staël and the fairy-tale imitation of Nerval and Nodier, "pilot of romanticism." The latest attempt at stating similarities by Ole Koppang remains unsatisfactory.[20]

Thus one of the apparently most convincing unified periods fails to respond to the comparative questionnaire inquiring into the same motivistic, cultural, structural, and grammatico-rhetorical style. Even if there were no difference between depth and surface, genuine and playful symbolism, spontaneous and strained imagery, there remain two other stumbling blocks. The first is the cultural style of religious indifference in France versus the desperate cultural attempt of salvaging a serious new religion out of the slight German enlightenment, the idealistic philosophy, and the collision of liberal Protestantism with a secularized soci-

19. Helmut Hatzfeld, "Wesen und Gestaltelemente des französischen Romantisme," *Literaturwissenschaftliches Jahrbuch der Görresgesellschaft, 8* (1936), 216–73.

20. Ole Koppang, *Romantikk og Romantisme. En Samenlikning mellom Tysk og Fransk Romantikk* (Oslo, Akademisk Forlag, 1951).

ety. It is just this romanticism that appears strange to enlightened France, and the seriousness of this problem was recently brought to mind by John Herman Randall.[21] The second difficulty is the attempt at interpreting the "romantic" style as realism, which is impossible to find in German romanticism but which very easily may be discovered in Rousseau [22] and Chateaubriand, not to mention Vigny, Hugo, Stendhal, and Balzac. This latter view, which unified the nineteenth century at least in France instead of splitting it up, was the conviction of Karl Vossler. It is the conviction today of Wylie Sypher, who pleads for abolishing the whole concept of romanticism as a European style period.

Actually, by formally looking at romanticism with stress on grammatical style, one becomes clearly aware that the gulf between Romance and Germanic romanticism is unbridgeable. Romanticism remains for Sypher a trend, but not a style, and as such a *réalisme manqué*,[23] or, as I would say (more in harmony with Wellek's definition of realism and with the ideas of Auerbach), a *préréalisme*. In France and more so in Italy this definition would be fitting; Sypher believes, unconvincingly however, that England also could be included because this pseudo-realism is supposed to be the cultural expression of the general attitude associated with a rising positivism, lyrically draped pantheism, and therefore traceable in Keats and the "schizoid" Byron no less than in Lamartine. In Germany the nature philosophy, as Wellek has stressed, blocks positivism and realism. The implication of a classical trend within the romantic trend, leading to the ambiguous bastard unit "classicism AND romanticism," makes the discovery of a German romantic style in harmony with the rest of Europe more than difficult.

21. Marcel Brion, *L'Allemagne romantique* (Paris, Albin Michel, 1962), p. 8: "Dans le romantisme, le génie allemand se montre, plus qu'à aucun autre moment de son histoire éloigné du génie français, auquel la plupart de ces écrivains pourront parître étranges, et sans équivalent dans la littérature française." John H. Randall, "Romantic Reinterpretations of Religion," *Studies in Romanticism*, 2 (1963), 189–212.

22. One knows the remark of Irving Babbitt that, reading the *Confessions* of Rousseau, one finds on the same page Lamartine and Zola. *Rousseau and Romanticism* (Boston, Houghton Mifflin Co., 1919), p. 103.

23. Wylie Sypher, *Rococo to Cubism in Art and Literature* (New York, Random House, 1960).

The difficulties are so appalling that after the ravages created by Curtius and Hocke with the term "mannerism," Marianne Thalmann sees also in the German romanticism *sensu stricto* a rebirth of mannerism. She says:

> Manieristisch ist die Sehnsucht nach verlorenen Paradiesen, wie Novalis sie kennt, sind die deformierenden Grotesken E. T. A. Hoffmans mit ihren Vergrösserungen und Verkleinerungen, manieristisch sind die Klangspiele Brentanos, die Arabesken Ph.O.Runges. Davon hat schon Friedrich Schlegel gewusst, der Zacharias Werner, Adam Müller, Jean Paul "manieristisch" genannt hat.[24]

This "method" is illusive because Miss Thalmann discovers in one author a psychological motif which she posits in its vagueness already in the seventeenth century; in another writer she sees structural foreshortenings and amplifications which she compares to earlier painters like Mantegna or Pontormo; in a third one she picks out a single linguistic style element which may occur in isolation at all times and not only in mannerism; for a fourth author, who is more of a designer than a poet, she uses "arabesque" ambiguously; and in a fifth one she confuses manneristic and mannered.

Here the lack of method in mixing different types of style in an attempt to isolate the German romanticism has been exposed in order to justify what I have called a necessary method. The latter, comparative in principle, distinguishes in each and every text motivistic, cultural, structural, and microscopic literary style. A responsible method refers to art, not arbitrarily, but only when the aesthetic problem at issue can be seen more patently than in literature. This seldom is the case for romanticism.

Conclusion

By the comparative method only, I think, it was possible to establish baroque as a style epoch, to dethrone classicism as an epoch style (leaving it the role of an aristocratic *dirigisme* within

24. Marianne Thalmann, *Romantik und Manierismus* (Stuttgart, Kohlhammer, 1963), p. 20.

the baroque period as well as within other periods), and to shake
the pretension of romanticism as a European epoch style, in view
of its complex trends that resist anything more than a basic unifi-
cation. A method has consequences. The slight disagreement between Mr. Wellek and me on baroque and romanticism concerns
nuances and terminology and implies a groping for something
better. Our agreement that classicism cannot be either a French or
a German or a European (Friederich) epoch style may prove that
exact methods are imperative. Opposing them with national ideals
is a "kind of arrogance or rather ignorance . . . a defect in sensibility," and a blocking of the scholarly attempts to come as close as
possible to historical reality.[25]

25. C. E. Nelson, "Literature and 'littérature,' The Comparative Critic's
Problem of Definition," *Books Abroad* (Winter 1966), pp. 34–36, esp. p.
36.

Heinrich Henel

Metaphor and Meaning

In his essay "Semantik der kühnen Metapher," [1] Harald Weinrich is primarily concerned with a redefinition of the distinction between bold and feeble metaphors ("kühn" and "kraftlos" or "matt" are his words), but in the course of his argument he develops an entirely novel theory of metaphor in general. Briefly, his contention is that all metaphors bring together two contradictory terms or concepts (I am not sure which he means, and I do not think he is), that all metaphors are equally contradictory, and that they differ only in the degree to which the contradiction obtrudes upon the listener or reader. With these assertions Professor Weinrich wishes to remove metaphor from the domain of ontology and to assign it to that of logic, and he stresses the point by insisting that the *contradictio in adjecto* and the oxymoron are metaphors. That which is a contradiction to the logician is a metaphor to the student of literature. In fact, the *contradictio* is the boldest kind of metaphor, and the oxymoron the second boldest, because in them the contradiction is so conspicuous that it cannot be overlooked. Other metaphors obscure the contradiction more or less, and the feeblest metaphors are those in which it is least apparent.

The purpose of Mr. Weinrich's study is to establish a hierarchy of metaphors and thus a criterion for their aesthetic appreciation and evaluation: bold metaphors are good metaphors, and feeble metaphors are bad metaphors. However, his aesthetic theory depends on his general theory of metaphor, and it is the latter which I wish to question. The present essay will, therefore, be largely negative. It is a polemic against a point of view whose implications are so far-reaching that it deserves the closest scrutiny, and this

1. In *Deutsche Vierteljahrsschrift für Literaturwissenschaft und Geistesgeschichte, 37* (1963), 325–44. All subsequent references to this study are found in parentheses in the text.

polemic is all the more necessary because of Mr. Weinrich's great erudition and powers of persuasion. He presents a challenge which cannot be ignored: we must either discard our customary notions about metaphor and adopt his view or else refute his major premise.

Before embarking upon a detailed critique of Mr. Weinrich's assertions I should mention our areas of agreement. First, I share his view that metaphor should be distinguished from simile, that it is not, or not necessarily, based on analogy or likeness (*simili-tudo*). But I part company with him when, in effect, he replaces the *tertium commune* by searching for a governing term under which the two terms of the metaphor can be subsumed. Second, I join him in rejecting the belief "that the metaphors of language represent analogies, correspondences, and similarities which are given in the order of existence or in our thinking" (p. 337).[2] Metaphors cannot be explained by appealing to either ontology or psychology. But again I cannot follow him when, instead, he relates metaphor to logic. Finally, I applaud his emphasis on the importance of context for the functioning and interpretation of metaphor. However, Mr. Weinrich considers context only in deciding whether a metaphor is bold or not. Actually, the context often determines whether a word or phrase is a metaphor or a description, and it shows with what kind of metaphor we are dealing. For example, the line "Die Lilien sind weg, die Rosen sind dahin" might describe a garden in the fall, but the seventeenth-century poem[3] in which it occurs speaks of a woman who suffers from jaundice and whose cheeks have turned from white and pink to yellow. Again, the phrase "the sun of righteousness" might mean that righteousness is the sun ("the sun" is the metaphoric term, "righteousness" the proper term), but in Malachi 4:2 the whole phrase is the metaphoric term, and the context supplies "the Lord" as the proper term.[4]

A cardinal fault of Mr. Weinrich's essay is the inconsistency of his two definitions of metaphor. He says: "A metaphor—and this,

2. All translations of Weinrich's German text are mine.

3. *Die schöne Gelbsüchtige,* by an anonymous poet in the so-called *Neukirchsche Sammlung, 5* (Leipzig, 1710), pp. 8–10.

4. More about types of metaphors on pp. 108–13, below.

at bottom, is the only possible definition of metaphor—is a word in a context by which it is determined in such a way that it signifies something other than what it means" (p. 340). But he also says: "Every metaphor contains a contradiction between its two components [Glieder] and reveals it when it is taken literally" (p. 333), and he reduces this to the flat (and even more dangerous) assertion that "metaphor is a contradictory predication" (p. 337). To my mind, the former definition is acceptable, whereas the latter is not. If it is the essence of metaphor that the metaphoric term signifies something other than what it means, then surely it ceases to be a metaphor when the metaphoric term is taken literally. A metaphor is a metaphor precisely because it cannot be taken literally. Mr. Weinrich, it seems, wants to eat his cake and have it too. He is of course fully aware of the difference between literal and figurative language, but when it comes to metaphor he insists that it is to be taken both literally and figuratively. The contradiction which he construes exists only when the metaphoric term signifies what it means; it disappears when it signifies something other than what it means. Thus Mr. Weinrich's first (and true) definition of metaphor disproves his second definition, that "metaphor is a contradictory predication."

One of Mr. Weinrich's examples is the compound "Staatsschiff." Here is his comment:

> The ship of state—now is it a ship or not? The answer must always be: Yes and no. The state as a sociopolitical structure is of course not a ship, and yet it is a ship because the convention of figurative language wills it so. This is the contradiction which inheres *in every metaphor*. (p. 333)

It will be noted that Mr. Weinrich is not consistent in his use of the word "contradiction." In the definition he said that "every metaphor contains a contradiction between its two elements" (between "ship" and "state," in the present instance), whereas in analyzing his example he says that the contradiction is between two kinds of "state"—the state as a sociopolitical structure and the state to which the metaphoric compound refers. However, the assertion made in the analysis is no more tenable than that made in the definition. First of all, the ambiguity is not in the word

"state," but in the word "ship." When I say "The state is in
danger" or "The ship of state is about to founder," the word
"state" is used in exactly the same sense. In both cases I refer to
the state as a sociopolitical structure. But when I say "The ship is
about to founder" or "The ship of state is about to founder," the
word "ship" is used in two different senses—literally in the one
case, figuratively in the other. What Mr. Weinrich calls the contradiction is between the literal and figurative uses of the metaphoric
term, not between those of the proper term. Secondly—and this is
the important point—Mr. Weinrich fails to distinguish between
word and concept. The correct way to state the matter is to say
that the word "ship" designates more than one concept.[5] In literal
language, it designates a vessel or means of transportation borne
by water. In figurative language, it may designate an airborne con-
veyance ("Luftschiff") or almost anything a writer or poet wishes
it to designate. Since "Staatsschiff" is a conventional metaphor,
Mr. Weinrich is quite right in saying that it is convention which
wills the identity of "state" and "ship."

As soon as we realize that in discussing metaphor we are dealing
with words, not with concepts, all talk about contradiction becomes meaningless. Nobody claims that the various glosses which
follow an entry in the dictionary contradict each other. Nor was
the German author who wrote to the editor of the *Times Literary
Supplement* asking that his book be given "a little bewitching"
guilty of contradiction. He had looked up the word "Bespre-
chung" in the dictionary and was unlucky enough to pick "exor-
cism" or "bewitching" instead of "review." Metaphors, one might
say, are words used in senses not ordinarily listed in the dictionary.
At any rate, they are a semantic phenomenon and not a logical
one. It is the misfortune of Mr. Weinrich's essay that it departs
from the purpose announced in its title: instead of discussing the
semantics of metaphor, it discusses its logic.

The fault in Mr. Weinrich's analysis of "Staatsschiff" becomes
apparent in his shifting from the definite article to the indefinite.

5. Descriptive linguistics, which tries to get along without the notion of
"meaning," goes even further and says that there are as many different words
as there are referents of a word. These words would be homonyms, identical
in sound, but different in reference.

Of course the state is not a ship in the sense of "any ship" or "all ships," but it is the ship in the sense of "this ship," namely the ship to which the compound refers. That is to say, the metaphor implies the particularizing force which the definite article can have; it ceases to be a metaphor and becomes nonsense when it is taken to imply the generic force which the indefinite article can have.[6] "Ein Arbeiter ist seiner Speise wert" (Matt. 10:10) is not a metaphor: Christ tells his disciples that they are workers like any other workers. But "der alt' böse Feind" in Luther's *Ein' feste Burg ist unser Gott* can be a metaphor: it might out of context refer to a real enemy such as the pope, but the context shows that it refers to the devil.

Mr. Weinrich uses the word "contradiction" in a third sense. In addition to speaking of the contradiction between the two elements of a metaphor and that between the two meanings of one part of a metaphor he speaks of the contradiction between a metaphor and reality. He seems to think that there is no difference between these (alleged) contradictions or, at any rate, never stops to ask the question, but his reader must ask it to find out whether he can agree or not. Citing Rimbaud's "les parfums pourpres" Mr. Weinrich remarks that "scents are not in the order of reality red or colored in any other way," and he continues: "This metaphor contains a certain amount [!] of contradictoriness, and we love it because of this contradiction." Similarly with regard to "l'azur vert," "des vins bleus," and "la nuit verte": "All these examples are characterized by the fact that, according to the order of reality as we find it, the color does not fit [zukommt] the object in question or fits it only with difficulty." And of "schwarze Milch" and "les lèvres vertes" he says that these metaphors show a certain relation to reality as experienced by the senses (pp. 333, 334). What these examples show is not that there is a contradiction between

6. Christine Brooke-Rose, *A Grammar of Metaphor* (2d ed. London, 1965), discusses the particularizing force of the definite article on pp. 26–28 and the generic force of the indefinite article on pp. 37–38. While she is concerned with English usage and while German usage differs in some respects (e.g. in German the definite article is normally used with abstract nouns but has no particularizing effect), her observations apply to German as well as to English with regard to the matter in hand.

metaphor and reality, but that there is a difference between metaphor and description. Some of Mr. Weinrich's examples could be
descriptions. We have gotten used to green carnations produced
by dyeing and sold for St. Patrick's Day as well as to ladies dyeing
their hair platinum or violet and painting their lips an intense red
not found on lips "in the order of reality." So I suppose we are
braced against the day when vintners will grow blue wine and women sport green lips. Black milk can be obtained by adding a little
India ink (it could still be called milk), and blue horses or winged
horses (to cite examples also given by Mr. Weinrich) not only are
found on merry-go-rounds and in paintings but can also be real
horses who have stood still long enough to be painted blue or
fitted with wings. In description, black milk is no more contradictory than whitewall tires or the black snow so common in our
smog-ridden cities.

The reader's real task, then, is not to be conscious of a contradiction between metaphor and empirical experience, but to decide
whether he is faced with a description or a metaphor. The decision depends, of course, on the context in which the phrase is
found. Mr. Weinrich in explaining a poem by Paul Celan has no
difficulty in deciding that "schwarze Milch" is not "real milk" any
more than "die Milch der frommen Denkart" (Schiller's *Wilhelm
Tell*, l. 2573) or the milk of the biblical parable (presumably 1
Pet. 2:2, "Seid begierig nach der vernünftigen lautern Milch").
He even suggests that "black milk" simply means "melancholy,"
just as he reminds us that "winged horse" may mean "Pegasus"
(or "poetry") (p. 334). The point which Mr. Weinrich makes
here, albeit unwittingly, is that there is no contradiction between
real milk and metaphoric milk; they are simply different. Once
again the same word is used to denote two different concepts.
Thus the pleasure which Mr. Weinrich says we feel in grasping a
metaphor is not due to our more or less muted or muffled
("abgedämpft") awareness that it contradicts reality, but to our
realization of how versatile words are.

Mr. Weinrich's confusion of three kinds of contradictions (none
of which are contradictions) has made our demonstration that
metaphors are not contradictions somewhat complicated. It is
much easier to show the opposite, namely that the *contradictio in*

adjecto and the oxymoron are not metaphors. His example of a *contradictio* is the ancient one, "square circle." Now this phrase contains a contradiction only if both words are taken literally—in which case, according to Mr. Weinrich's first definition, it is not a metaphor. If both words are taken figuratively, the phrase becomes a metaphor for "contradiction" or "nonsense." This holds for all contradictions. Whatever their literal meaning, their figurative significance is always the same: "alkaline acid" understood as a metaphor signifies "contradiction" just as does "square circle." For our purpose, then, we may define contradictions as combinations of words which, if the context shows them to be metaphors, can be the metaphoric term for only one proper term, namely "contradiction." [7]

But what happens if the context shows that one part of the combination should be taken figuratively, the other literally? The English language has the expressions "a square deal" and "a square meal," where "square" is the metaphoric term for unstated proper terms like "fair" and "substantial." If in the combination "square circle" only the word "square" is taken figuratively, we get exactly the same kind of metaphor: "square" is now the metaphoric term for an unstated proper term such as "well drawn." This is not a common metaphor, but a poet could create it. It involves a significance of "square" which has not yet become an accepted meaning, i.e. it is not listed in the dictionary. But it will be listed if "square circle" in the sense just indicated should become common usage, just as the noun "a square" in the sense of a "non-beatnik" is defined as an "unsophisticate" or "philistine" in recent editions of American dictionaries. A "square deal" is, to use Mr. Weinrich's happy phrase, an ex-metaphor, whereas a "square circle" could be a living metaphor. However, my task is not to labor the well-known fact that an enormous number of metaphors have become part of everyday language and therefore are no longer felt to be metaphors, but to show that contradictions are

7. Contradictions are not often used as metaphors, but similar phrases are. Asking a person to "square the circle" is a common metaphor for asking him to perform the impossible. Thus, instead of telling a person not to talk nonsense, one might tell him not to talk about square circles or about alkaline acids.

not metaphors. This I hope to have done by demonstrating that
"square circle" is contradictory only when it is taken literally, and
that it is not contradictory when it is taken to be a metaphor of
either of the two types described.

The oxymoron, properly understood, is neither a *contradictio
in adjecto* nor a metaphor. Mr. Weinrich's examples are "concordia discors," "felix culpa," and "stulta sapientia." These
phrases can be taken literally—they are normally intended to be
taken literally—without exhibiting a contradiction. In ordinary
usage they are descriptions of specific cases or situations. For
example, "concordia discors" may refer to the relationship of
brothers or allies whose interests and inclinations coincide on the
whole, yet who quarrel a good deal. The not infrequent remarriage of divorced couples may be an even better case in point.
Or take the sentence, "In his foolish wisdom, he did nothing."
This may be interpreted as follows: "When in doubt, it is wise to
do nothing. In his particular situation, however, action (either
resistance or flight) would have saved him." Similarly 1 Corin-
thians 3:18–19: "Let no man deceive himself. If any man among
you seemeth to be wise in this world, let him become a fool, that
he may be wise. For the wisdom of this world is foolishness with
God. For it is written, He taketh the wise in their own craftiness."
Here the implied oxymoron "foolish wisdom" is resolved into a
double pun. Both "wise" and "foolish" bear two meanings at the
same time: worldly wisdom is folly with God, and worldly folly is
wisdom with God. Thus there is no contradiction between wisdom
and folly, but a confrontation of two kinds of wisdom and two
kinds of folly.

Just as contradictions can, straining ordinary usage, be understood as metaphors (but then are no longer contradictions), so
oxymora can, again straining ordinary usage, be understood as
contradictions (but then are no longer oxymora). "Foolish wisdom" is a contradiction if resolved into "Wisdom is foolish" and if
this sentence is understood to assert that "all wisdom is always and
necessarily foolish." However, no useful purpose is served by such
quibbles. We are fortunate to have the two terms *"contradictio in
adjecto"* and "oxymoron" to distinguish two different phenomena,
and we shall do well not to confuse them. Oxymora are soluble

paradoxes, whereas contradictions lose their contradictoriness only if the context turns them into metaphors.

That oxymora are metaphors seems to be proved to Mr. Weinrich by Rimbaud's "le paradis de tristesse," a phrase which he calls an oxymoron-metaphor. This is a particularly unfortunate coinage because it obscures rather than clarifies the linguistic phenomenon. "The bliss of sadness" (Goethe's "Wonne der Wehmut") is an oxymoron. Rimbaud took this oxymoron and replaced "bliss" by "paradise," thus combining oxymoron and metaphor—but not identifying them, as Mr. Weinrich's term oxymoron-metaphor and his explanation of it suggest. "Paradise" is the metaphoric term, but the proper term to which it refers is "bliss," not "sadness." The expression "He was in a cold fury" provides another example of the combination of oxymoron and metaphor. Fury normally shows in behavior. "Calm fury" is fury controlled, fury which does not show. This is an oxymoron. Now fury is metaphorically associated with heat (cf. "the heat of passion") so that "cold fury" combines the oxymoron "calm fury" with the metaphor "cold" in the sense of "calm."

Mr. Weinrich's only attempt to offer something approaching proof that *contradictiones,* oxymora, and metaphors are logically identical is found in the passages where he speaks of conceptual closeness and of governing terms (pp. 336, 338, 339). The two concepts in the contradiction "square circle," he says, can be subsumed under the governing term "geometric figure," those in the oxymora "foolish wisdom" and "concordia discors" under the terms "state of mind" and "social behavior," those in synaesthetic metaphors like "red scents" and "Farbton" under the term "sense impression," and those in metaphors like "courants de la lande" (cf. "welliges Land," "Wellenberge," "mountains of water") under the term "element"—"element" taken in the sense of the ancient doctrine of the four elements. Mr. Weinrich asserts that these governing terms offer themselves readily and convincingly and that this proves the conceptual closeness of the terms subsumed under them; and he concludes that metaphors of the two types mentioned (synaesthetic metaphors and metaphors relating to the four elements) reveal with particular clarity the contradiction inherent in all metaphors because of the conceptual closeness of their components. He calls such metaphors bold metaphors. Three objections must be made to his reasoning.

First, let us grant for the sake of argument that Mr. Weinrich's governing terms do indeed offer themselves readily and convincingly and that this fact proves the conceptual closeness of the subordinate terms. What has he gained? He has demonstrated (to his satisfaction, not mine) that a few types of metaphors are just as contradictory as *contradictiones in adjecto,* but he has also demonstrated by implication that the vast mass of metaphors are not contradictory in this sense. To be sure, he asserts that all metaphors are equally contradictory and that the two types he cites merely exhibit the contradiction more openly than other types. However, if no governing term can be found and if conceptual closeness cannot be discovered in the case of metaphors such as "the ship of state" or "a tissue of lies" or "dead-end street," then, by Mr. Weinrich's own reasoning, these metaphors cannot be analyzed in terms of logic and their components cannot be found to be either consistent or contradictory. Therefore, the practical result of his argument (if it were true) would be a split between metaphors which are amenable to logical analysis and others which are not [8]—and this, I venture to say, is the last thing Mr. Weinrich wishes to achieve.

Second, the notion of governing terms lets in by the back door the *tertium commune* to which Mr. Weinrich refuses admission in discussing what he calls the old theory of metaphor. It is best to quote him in the original at this point:

> Gerade bei den sehr kühnen Metaphern kleiner Bildspanne kommt uns ja mit dem Oberbegriff das gemeinsame Dritte am leichtesten in den Sinn. Am leichtesten bei den schulmässigen *contradictiones in adiecto.* Nichts ist leichter zu vergleichen als ein Kreis und ein Quadrat, die eine Fülle gemeinsamer Merkmale haben und aus diesem Grunde den Oberbegriff so leicht finden lassen. (p. 337)

8. Discussing Balzac's metaphor for the city of Paris, "steppes de pierre de taille," Weinrich (p. 340) suggests "landscape" as the governing term of "city" and "steppe." Nevertheless it remains true that for a vast number of metaphors no governing term can be found. For example, when Armin T. Wegner, in his poem *Die Weltstadt,* calls the metropolis a "flaming boiler"

The common third occurs to us together with the governing term, says Mr. Weinrich, and both are easily found because circle and square have a wealth of common characteristics and therefore are easy to compare. Are they not then merely different names for the same thing? If similarity and comparability lead to the governing term, is it not simply our old friend, the *tertium?* [9] The suspicion is confirmed when we consider some of Mr. Weinrich's other examples. "The light of truth," he says (p. 338), is a trivial metaphor because no *tertium* can be found which would not itself be a metaphor. Let us assume that "radiance" is the (metaphoric) *tertium:* could it not also be called the governing term, i.e. the name of the class of all things that shine? On the other hand, what common third or, for that matter, what governing term occurs to us readily in the case of "blue horse," "black milk," or "flowers that are chairs"—all of them counted among the bold metaphors by Mr. Weinrich? To cut the matter short, I contend that nothing is proved by the fact that a governing term can be found or cannot be found. If it can be found, it establishes a categorial relationship between the subordinate terms, but not their contradictoriness. If it cannot be found or found only with difficulty, the compound phrase may still be a metaphor. "Square circle" is a contradiction not because its components fall under the governing term "geometric figure," but because the definition of a circle includes roundness or non-squareness. On the other hand, "the light of truth" and "blue horse" are not contradictions, because the definitions of "truth" and "horse" neither include nor exclude their being radiant or blue.

Third, not only the *tertium comparationis,* but also ontology is let in by the back door. Mr. Weinrich's locutions that the governing term "presents itself easily" (p. 336) or is "readily at hand" (p. 338) imply that it preexists or is given in our minds—notions which he rightly rejects in discussing the old theory of metaphor

---

("Flammenkessel"), what governing term presents itself readily for either the two elements of the metaphor ("flame" and "boiler") or for the metaphor as a whole and its proper term, "metropolis"?

9. It is ironic that Mr. Weinrich on the same page rejects Aristotle's definition of metaphor as a sort of comparison and invokes similarity and comparability as proof of his contention that metaphors are contradictions.

(p. 337). His governing terms are not eternal verities, but names for classes which he himself is setting up or, at best, classes which might be set up by a scientist for his specific purposes of ordering and manipulating physical or psychological realities. They are not necessitated by those realities themselves. This is brought out very clearly by Mr. Weinrich's example of metaphors which bring together two or more of the four elements. To literary scholars like him and me the governing term "element" may present itself readily when we hear of "mountains of water," but not to chemists, who distinguish many more elements than four and define the term "element" quite differently from the ancients. The same is true of any classification, whether scientific or not. It arranges the data supplied by experience in ways which are found convenient or useful, but it is not authorized either ontologically or logically. It is in this sense that W. V. Quine, summarizing the work of modern logic since Russell, speaks of "the myth of mathematics" and "the myth of physics," explaining that "a platonistic ontology . . . is, from the point of view of a strictly physicalistic conceptual scheme, as much a myth as that physicalistic conceptual scheme itself is for phenomenalism." [10] Thus Mr. Weinrich in asserting that his governing terms present themselves easily is saying no more than that he has adopted certain conceptual schemes. Since these schemes are quite loose, they may suffice to bring out incompatibility, but not contradiction. The attribute "red" is incompatible with the noun "scents," but it does not contradict it.

There are two further passages in which Mr. Weinrich refers to logic, but these are so brief and vague that it is difficult to know what he means and hence difficult to argue with him. He seems to question Kant's teaching that *contradictiones in adjecto* are found only in analytic judgments, and he suggests that modern logic, if it could be persuaded to take notice of the phenomenon of metaphor, would support his contention that metaphors are contradictory predications (pp. 336, 337). Kant says that non-contradictoriness is a sine qua non of the truth of all judgments. With analytic judgments, it is in itself sufficient proof of their being true, whereas synthetic judgments need, in addition, empirical verifica-

10. Willard V. Quine, *From a Logical Point of View* (2d ed. Cambridge, Mass., 1964), p. 18.

tion.[11] Now if Kant's notion of analyticity is abandoned, *all* propositions need verification by reference to fact. According to this way of thinking, statements like "Some bodies lack extension" or "The circle is square" are not contradictory because the term "body," when analyzed, is found to contain the property of extension and the term "circle" the property of roundness; rather, they are false because no such bodies or squares can be found to exist. The only exceptions are propositions which wholly depend for their truth or untruth on purely logical particles such as "all," "no," "not," "un-," "if," and so on. For example, the statements "No unmarried man is married" and "No married man is married" are true or false by virtue of the particles "no" and "un-," irrespective of what "man" and "married" refer to.[12] This concept of contradictoriness is much narrower than Kant's. Mr. Weinrich goes the opposite way; he widens the concept of contradictoriness. He calls all propositions which are false, contradictory. And since metaphors, taken literally, are proved to be false by reference to fact, he says that they are contradictory predications.[13] But there is no system of logic which would support him.

As regards modern logic in general, I am told that some logicians uphold Kant's distinction between analytic and synthetic judgments, that others reject it, and that still others believe the difference between analytic and synthetic judgments to be gradual rather than absolute.[14] Assuming that Kant's radical critics are right, their conclusion cannot be applied to the problem of meta-

11. *Kritik der reinen Vernunft,* Elementarlehre, 2. Teil, 1. Abteilung, 2. Buch, 2. Hauptstück, 1. Abschnitt.

12. Quine, pp. 22 f.

13. Hans-Heinrich Lieb, "Was bezeichnet der herkömmliche Begriff 'Metapher'?" *Muttersprache,* 77 (1967), 50, says that a metaphor asserts an impossibility if all the words of the passage where it occurs mean what they ordinarily mean in the language in question. This formulation is closer to my view than to Weinrich's, but it does not cover all kinds of metaphor. "Impossible" means "unthinkable." That the state should literally be a ship, or words barbed, is indeed unthinkable. But it is not unthinkable that horses should be winged, or milk black.

14. Concerning modern logic I have enjoyed the advice of my colleagues Frederic B. Fitch (a logician) and Rulon Wells (a logician and linguist). I acknowledge their help gratefully but assume sole responsibility for what is said in this article.

phor without taking account of their argument. W. V. Quine, who is among them, restates Kant's definition of analyticity as follows: "A statement is analytic when it is true by virtue of meanings and independently of fact." [15] Again summarizing earlier work, he distinguishes between meaning and reference and shows that no statement is true by virtue of meanings, but is found to be true or false by examining its reference. For example, the statement "The Morning Star is the Evening Star" must be thought contradictory, hence false, if the meanings of "morning" and "evening" are considered, but it is true by virtue of its reference: astronomical observation has shown that both names refer to the same celestial object. The phrase "the Morning Star" is a singular term, i.e. it names an entity, but the argument is equally valid for general terms or predicates. For example, the statement "All men have ten fingers" cannot be verified by reflecting on the meanings of "men" and "ten" and "fingers" but is found to be false by virtue of its reference, namely when it is discovered that some men are born with fewer or more than ten fingers. Applying this thinking to the problem of metaphor, let us consider the statements "John is heartless" or "John has no guts." Mr. Weinrich would have us believe that these are contradictory predications because John actually does have a heart and guts. In the first place, the anatomical facts do not make the statement contradictory, but false. Moreover, the reference of the words "heart" and "guts" is not to John's body, but to his mind or character. To be sure, Mr. Weinrich says that metaphors merely "contain" a contradiction and that it is "revealed" only when the metaphor is taken literally. But this is precisely what he must not do if he wishes to base his argument on post-Kantian logic. To take "heartless" literally is to consider its meaning rather than its reference. There remains only the question of how we know what the reference is. The answer must be that the context tells. The assertion that a postmortem will show John to be heartless would be a tall story. Thus, unless we believe the speaker to be utterly ignorant or a liar, we must assume that he refers to John's character. A sentence such as "John is so heartless that he enjoys torturing cats" would leave no doubt

15. Quine, p. 21. For the sentences following in my text, see Quine, pp. 9, 21 f.

whatever. Similarly, the genitive link in "the ship of state" makes it impossible to think that "ship" refers to an object of wood or steel.

To put the matter as simply as possible: if it is the function of singular terms to name entities, a singular term used as a metaphor provides a new or uncommon name for an entity which is usually called by another name. And since names function irrespective of their meaning, it cannot be said that the common name and the metaphoric name contradict each other or that the metaphoric name contradicts the facts known about the entity to which it refers. Similarly, if general terms are true of a class of entities (as "black" is true of the class that includes such things as crows and certain kinds of ink and shoe polish), the metaphoric use of a general term enlarges the class of entities of which it is true ("black milk" adds "milk" to the class of which "black" is true). Again there can be no question of the metaphor "black" contradicting either "milk" or the non-metaphoric term "black." To think otherwise would be to assert that singular terms denote essences such as "Jackness" or "shipness," and general terms essences such as "blackness" and "heartlessness"—and these are assertions which modern logic denies.[16]

One more criticism must be made of Mr. Weinrich's essay. So far I have avoided his terms "image-giver" ("Bildspender") and "image-receiver" ("Bildempfänger")—terms which are basic to his conception of metaphor—because they confuse rather than clarify the subject. Indeed there is doubt about his understanding of the terms. In one place (pp. 326 f.) he identifies them with Hugo Friedrich's terms "Bild" and "Sache" (which correspond to my expressions "the metaphoric term" and "the proper term"),[17]

16. The purpose of the foregoing pages is merely to demonstrate the vacuity of Mr. Weinrich's claim that he is supported by modern logic. My article as a whole is not based on it, but on Kantian logic. For example, my appeal to dictionary meanings (above, pp. 96 and 99) and to definitions (p. 103) would not be permitted by Quine (see pp. 24–27). Whether or not metaphor can be dealt with successfully from a point of view such as Quine's, I am not competent to say.

17. The distinction between "Bild" and "Sache" is, of course, as old as thinking about metaphor itself. Miss Brooke-Rose (p. 9) criticizes I. A. Richards for having introduced the names "vehicle" and "tenor" because,

but throughout most of his essay he equates them with the two
components ("Glieder") of a metaphor (p. 333) —and these are
by no means always equivalent to "Bild" and "Sache." For example, in the metaphor "the ship of state" the first component
("ship") is the "Bild" or metaphoric term, and the second
("state") is the "Sache" or proper term; but in the metaphor "the
evening of life" the two components together are the "Bild,"
while the "Sache" is not stated and must be guessed: it is, of
course, "old age." It so happens that Mr. Weinrich's examples do
not include the type of metaphor which Christine Brooke-Rose
calls simple replacement. Had he thought of cases like Luther's
"der alt' böse Feind," he could not have missed that fact that this is
an image-giver which lacks an image-receiver—or, to use my language, that only the metaphoric term is given and that the proper
term ("the devil") must be supplied.

For the purpose of the present discussion, metaphors may be
divided into three types: [18]

---

she says, they emphasize the separateness of the metaphor and its referent.
The criticism seems hardly justified since it applies equally to her vocables
"the metaphoric term" and "the proper term" (which I have borrowed).
Richards, I believe, is just as aware of the new entity resulting from the
fusion of vehicle and tenor as is Miss Brooke-Rose—or indeed most writers
on the subject, including the present one. See René Wellek and Austin
Warren, *Theory of Literature* (New York, 1949), pp. 191 ff.

18. Many ways of classifying metaphors are possible and useful. My classification is designed to bring out the varying relationship of the two elements
of compound metaphors. It does not include simple replacements ("ass" for
"fool"), but these could be accommodated readily either by calling them
Type IV or by subdividing Type III into IIIa (simple replacements) and
IIIb (compound replacements). Verb metaphors largely elude classification
because they fuse with their context. Formally, they are simple replacements,
but many can also be understood as belonging to either Type I or Type II.
For example, "shrouded" replaces "hidden" in "The facts are shrouded in
mystery," and "barked at" replaces "attacked" in "Scipio was barked at by
Cato"; yet I have listed the first sentence as an example for Type I (because
mystery *is* the shroud), and the second as an example for Type II (because
"barking Cato" qualifies the noun). In the actual interpretation of literary
texts, verbs which personify their subject can pose real problems. With
abstract nouns ("The comparison lags"), the replacing function of the verb
is probably felt more strongly than its personifying force, whereas the opposite is true with concretes ("Wie lacht die Flur" in Goethe's *Mailied*).

I. Metaphors in which one component is the metaphoric term, the other the proper term. I shall call these appositional metaphors. Examples: the ship of state, the light of truth, the fire of love, Schiller's "Milch der frommen Denkart," Goethe's "der Dichtung Schleier" (*Zueignung*), the facts are shrouded in mystery.[19] In each of these examples, the metaphoric term and the proper term are placed side by side, and they are virtually identified: the state *is* the ship in question, love *is* the fire, gentleness *is* the milk, poetry *is* the veil, and mystery *is* the shroud. They might therefore also be called identical metaphors or tautological metaphors or open-secret metaphors or answered-riddle metaphors: the

---

E. R. Curtius (*Europäische Literatur und lateinisches Mittelalter* [Bern, 1948], p. 136) strikes a nice balance by saying of "pratum ridet" that "Man's laughter is 'transferred' to nature": the meadow remains a meadow but has the human capacity for smiling. This corresponds exactly to my definition of Type II metaphors.

Complex metaphors, i.e. metaphors within metaphors, are easily explained in terms of my typology. Shakespeare's "my salad days" (which I have borrowed from Brooke-Rose, p. 242) is listed below among the examples for Type II ("salad" for "green"), but the whole phrase also stands for "youth" (Type III). In Platen's "Salamandergefäss" (see p. 120, below), "salamander" is a simple replacement for "fire," while the compound as a whole is a Type I metaphor. See also "The Virgin Mary is the fountain of mercy" on p. 113, below.

While Brooke-Rose's classification is totally different and much more complex, I am indebted to some of her terminology and analyses. What I call Types I and III are clearly distinguished in her book, pp. 146–48. That the two elements of Type I metaphors are identical is said on her pp. 148 and 154, and that "the identifying compound is almost equivalent to apposition" on pp. 25, 147, and 170. Elsewhere she calls Type I the "Equated Type" (p. 209) and Type III the "Replacing Type" (p. 149). On the other hand, what she calls "Pure Attribution" (pp. 148, 160–64, 170) is a variant of Type I and not the same as my Type II (attributive metaphors). However, the chief characteristics of my Type II (that the metaphoric term replaces an unstated proper term and that it qualifies the accompanying noun) are brought out in her chapters on the metaphoric uses of compound nouns, verbs, and adjectives.

19. Here as throughout the study I have relied as much as possible on Weinrich's examples but have also borrowed from Brooke-Rose and have added many examples of my own. The mixture of languages in these examples needs no apology in a work dedicated to a distinguished comparatist.

riddle posed by the metaphoric term is in the same breath solved
by the addition of the proper term. I have called them appositional metaphors because apposition or vocative can be used to
express the same metaphoric relationship that is more commonly
expressed through a compound noun (especially in German) or
the genitive link: phrases like "the state, that ship" or "the ship,
our state" and "truth, oh light!" say the same as "the ship of state"
and "the light of truth." As will have been noted, this type of
metaphor usually binds together an abstract and a concrete. It is
the only type of metaphor where Mr. Weinrich's terminology is
appropriate: one of its components (e.g. "veil") is the image-
giver, the other (e.g. "poetry") the image-receiver.

II. Metaphors in which one component is the metaphoric term
and which do not state the proper term. I shall call these attributive metaphors. Examples: hatchet face, baby face, a computer
mind, Holzkopf (blockhead), Sackgasse (dead-end street), Kopfbahnhof (a station where the rails end and a train must back out
to continue on its trip), my salad days (Shakespeare), barbed
words, a cloudy thought, the shameless stone (Homer), Scipio was
barked at by Cato. Here the first component is an attribute of the
second, not another name for it. If it is a noun, it can be replaced
by an adjective: "a hatchet-like face," "ein kopfartiger Bahnhof."
Usually it designates a property of the second component, but it
can also designate quantity ("a mountain of debts" or "moun-
tainous debts"). Whereas the two components of Type I metaphors are congruous, the first component of Type II metaphors
limits or qualifies the second. The concept "poetry" is not limited
in the metaphor "the veil of poetry" (*all* poetry is thought of as a
veil), but face, head, and days in the examples just given are limited by their respective attributes: certain kinds of faces, heads,
and days are meant. Indeed the qualification can amount to a
change of meaning: the shameless stone is personified, and barking
Cato is turned into a dog. However, the important difference for
our purposes between appositional and attributive metaphors is
that the former name both the metaphoric and the proper term,
whereas the latter name only the metaphoric term and leave the
proper term to be guessed. "Hatchet" points to "sharp-featured,"

"barbed" to "hurtful," and "salad" to "green" (which in turn points to "youthful").

Now Mr. Weinrich calls "ship" the image-giver and "state" the image-receiver (with which I have no quarrel), but he also calls "hölzern" the image-giver and "Verstand" the image-receiver (p. 336)—and with this I do quarrel. It seems to me obvious—too obvious, indeed, to labor the point—that the relation of "ship" and "state" is not the same as that of "wooden" and "mind." "Wooden" (or in English "block") is not an image for "mind," but for the property of a certain kind of mind, namely for "slow-witted" or "unintelligent." It is the changing reference of Mr. Weinrich's terms "image-giver" and "image-receiver" which has led me to say that they confuse the issue and which makes it difficult to debate him on his own ground.

It should be added that certain metaphors can belong to either Type I or II. "The fire of love," which I have listed among the appositional metaphors, may also function as an attributive metaphor, namely if "fire" is the metaphoric term for "passion" and not another name for "love" itself. There is, after all, love which is not passionate, but gentle. Similarly with "a tissue of lies": "tissue" may be the metaphoric equivalent of "lies," or it may refer to the quantity and complex interrelation of the lies told. Other examples are "a torrent of words," "a flood of tears," and "the roses of her cheeks." Christine Brooke-Rose, who analyzes the last example, points out that "the roses" may either be the metaphoric term for the cheeks themselves or for attributes such as their pinkness, fragrance, and texture. She also explains that the uncertainty as to the type of metaphor intended is due to the ambiguity (in both English and German) of the noun compound and the genitive link.[20] In actual texts, poetry or prose, the uncertainty is often resolved by the context, but this is not necessarily the case.

III. Metaphors in which the two components together are the metaphoric term and which do not state the proper term. I shall call these replacing metaphors. Examples: Lebensabend (old age), Sorgenbrecher (wine), Flügelpferd (Pegasus or poetry),

20. Brooke-Rose, pp. 147 f. and 167 ff.

Schiff der Wüste (camel), shooting iron (handgun), firewater (liquor), the winged boy (Amor or love), living grave (prison or the body as the prison of the soul), Celan's schwarze Milch (melancholy). In ancient Germanic poetry this kind of metaphor is called a kenning. It may also be called metonymy, although this term is usually reserved for simple replacement ("sweat" for "work"). The two components are not congruous as in Type I nor does one qualify the other as in Type II; rather, they interact or interpenetrate each other so that a third idea emerges: firewater is neither fire nor water, but liquor. Mystery is still mystery when it is called a veil, and a station is still a station (although a station of a certain kind) when it is called a Kopfbahnhof; but the living grave is neither a grave nor alive: it is a prison.

Mr. Weinrich (p. 344) cites side by side the metaphors "Lebens-abend" and "Zeitenlauf," and he explains that in the latter "course" is the image-giver and "time" the image-receiver. That is to say, he interprets "Zeitenlauf" as a Type I metaphor. With this I agree (although "Zeitenlauf" becomes a Type II metaphor if the fact that time "runs" is considered merely one of its properties), but I do not agree with the implication—both here and through-out Mr. Weinrich's essay—that the two components of metaphors such as "Lebensabend" or "Flügelpferd" bear the same relation-ship as the components of "Zeitenlauf." "Evening" is not an alternative name for "life," nor is "wings" for "horse," so that the terms "image-giver" and "image-receiver" do not describe their relationship. Yet this is what Mr. Weinrich wants us to believe. In the same passage (p. 344) he identifies the image-receiver with "das Eigentliche" (the proper term), but surely "life" and "horse" are not "das Eigentliche" or "die Sache" to which "eve-ning" and "wings" refer. Rather, the two components of each of our examples together are the image-giver, and together they refer to an unstated "Eigentliches" or image-receiver—"old age" in the one case, "Pegasus" in the other.

What all this amounts to is that Mr. Weinrich fails to see that with Type II and III metaphors the proper term or image-receiver is unstated. When he says that all metaphors contain a contradic-tion, I am, therefore, not sure whether he means that the two stated terms (the components) are contradictory or that the image-giver and the image-receiver are contradictory. If he means the former, he has been refuted, I hope, by what has been said earlier. If he means the latter, he has been refuted expressly only with regard to Type I metaphors. However, I believe that my arguments are equally valid for the relation between a stated image-giver (whether simple as in Type II or compound as in Type III) and an unstated image-receiver.

It should be noted that some metaphors may belong to either Type II or III. "Black milk," which Mr. Weinrich interprets as "melancholy" (Type III), might also be used to suggest "bad milk" or "spoilt milk" (Type II). The metaphor would be understood because of the many analogous phrases existing in English. A "black deed" is wicked; a "black mood" is gloomy; a "black look" is hostile. Furthermore, Type I metaphors can be used as the metaphoric term of Type III metaphors. In the phrase, "The fountain of mercy," mercy *is* the fountain. But in the sentence "The Virgin Mary is the fountain of mercy" the phrase becomes the metaphoric term and the Virgin is the proper term. So also in the sentences "God is the sun of justice" and "You are the apple of my eye." As the last three examples show, context often decides which type of metaphor is intended.

If metaphors are not contradictory predications, what are they? In one of those passages in which, fortunately, Mr. Weinrich contradicts his main thesis, he says that metaphors "of themselves do not care much about right and wrong" and that "they have their own logic" (p. 332); in another such passage he says that metaphors "found analogies, create correspondences, and are demiurgic tools" (p. 338). We let it pass that Mr. Weinrich here asserts what elsewhere he denies, namely that metaphors are based on analogy (in my view, they can but need not be so based),[21] but underscore his verbs "to found" and "to create." Scents, he says in yet another passage, receive their red color from the poet's hand (p. 333). Putting this view into the language used in this essay we shall say that metaphors are names—new names. They duplicate

21. Except in intentionally obscure literature, the author wishes his metaphors to be understood and provides appropriate aids. He can do so by creating an analogy or, dispensing with analogy, by explaining the metaphor through its context—context taken in the broad sense defined below, pp. 117 f.

the original creation of language, not by producing new linguistic material, but by using the existing material in original and creative ways. They apply words to concepts which they do not ordinarily designate, or (which is the same thing looked at from the other end) they call concepts by names which they do not ordinarily bear.

There are two explanations of why this can be done, and they are not mutually exclusive. Philip Wheelright distinguishes between block language and fluid language.[22] Block language "ideally consists of terms defined and employed according to the law of identity." It is literal language in the sense that each term has only one referent. Fluid language, on the other hand, "has an indefinite number of possibilities in an indefinite number of respects: for instance, its terms can be plurisignative, they can undergo semantic variation according to context, the meanings can be presented in soft focus and can be suggested by indirection," and so on. Wheelright continues: "Language may be fluid to various degrees. Block language is therefore a limiting possibility of reduced fluid language; it occurs wherever the semantic fluidity is reduced to zero while the semantic function remains." Applying this distinction to the question of how metaphors are created, we obtain two different answers. In block language with its 1:1 correlation between word and referent there is substitution of one referent for another when a word is used metaphorically, whereas in fluid language there is merely a shifting of emphasis among two or more referents. Take "the flower" as a metaphor for an attractive young woman. For botanists and for persons with literal minds, "flower" is a vocabulary item of block language. It refers to the reproductive organ of plants. If such persons, indulging in a flight of fancy, use the word metaphorically, they substitute one referent for another. For most speakers of the language, however, the reference of "flower" is fluid. It refers to things which are fine and valued. No doubt they too use the word most often in referring to the flowers they grow in their garden or buy

22. Philip Wheelright, "Semantics and Ontology," in L. C. Knights and Basil Cottle, eds., *Metaphor and Symbol* (London, 1960), pp. 1–9, esp. pp. 3–4.

at the florist's, but they also use it easily in phrases such as "the finest flower of his mind," "the flowering of the Middle Ages," "the flower of the land lay dead on the battlefield," or indeed in referring to their neighbor's pretty daughter. Even those not reared in the Christian tradition do not have to relearn the language when they hear the old German Christmas carol, which says

> Das Röslein, das ich meine,
> Davon Jesaias sagt,
> Ist Maria die Reine,
> Die uns das Blümlein bracht

where the Virgin is the rose and Jesus the flower. These speakers, then, merely emphasize one referent, while none of the other possible referents is wholly ruled out.

In choosing so commonplace an example I have intentionally invited two objections: Is the botanical use of "flower" not the proper use, and are not all the other uses metaphorical? And have I not, throughout my argument, insisted on the difference between literal and figurative language, between the proper term and the metaphoric term? The answer to the first question is that of course the botanical use is the proper use—but only in block language. To explain this further I draw upon a lecture by Owen Barfield who argues (convincingly, I think) against the traditional view of how words change their meaning.[23] This view is that in the pristine stage of a word's development it has only one referent, that it has "born literalness"; that in a second stage it refers also to another referent so that there is concomitant meaning; that in a third stage the original referent is almost, but not quite, forgotten so that there is substituted meaning; and that in the final stage the original referent has vanished and only the new referent survives so that the word has "achieved literalness." Barfield's own view, on the contrary, is that words begin by being vague, i.e. capable of referring to more than one referent, and that literalness is always achieved through a process of narrowing or

23. Owen Barfield, "The Meaning of the Word 'Literal,'" ibid., pp. 48–57, esp. pp. 51–55.

selection. In other words, fluidity is the original and normal condition of language, and block language is a late and special development.

As for the second objection, I have simply accommodated myself to Mr. Weinrich so as to be able to debate with him. His proposition that metaphors are contradictory predications clearly presupposes the view that all language is block language. Block language is the language of lawgivers, lawyers, scientists, logicians— all those who strive for a maximum of literalness and a minimum of ambiguity. It is language which, as Wheelwright says, combines its terms "in such a way as to produce propositions obeying the law of non-contradiction." It is amusing, therefore, to hear Mr. Weinrich complain that "absolutely compelling examples of *contradictio* are, cunningly, always chosen from nomenclatures" (p. 336). There is no cunning because *contradictiones* can be found only in language whose terms are strictly limited and clearly defined.[24] However, the more important point is that Mr. Weinrich's bête noire, Aristotle, also thought of language as block language. This is why he said that the metaphorizing process—the process of "transference"—requires a mediator: the *tertium commune* mediates between the usual referent and the substituted referent of the metaphor. Mr. Weinrich's dissatisfaction with this theory must stem from the proverbial truth that all comparisons lag. He insists on the incompatibility of the literal and the meta-

24. Like contradiction, oxymoron and pun are found only in block language. The oxymoron says that in specific instances things mutually exclusive are not exclusive, or that what normally is true is not true: two persons can both agree and disagree, and wisdom, normally wise, can be foolish. To make its point, the oxymoron yields not one iota of the literalness of its two terms, but on the contrary depends on literalness for its effect. The pun, too, depends on literalness. (I have noticed that lawyers, whose business trains them to take words literally, are given to punning.) The punster contrasts two or more uses of a word without suggesting that there is a similarity among its several referents. The difference is that oxymora are meaningful, puns absurd. Puns amuse because it is felt to be absurd that the same concatenation of sounds should signal totally different things. And since one literal interpretation offers itself as readily as another, puns can go unnoticed. Metaphors, on the other hand, make us stumble if we are unobservant enough to take them literally. Only ex-metaphors or clichés can go unnoticed, because they have "achieved literalness."

phoric referent, and he chooses to call this incompatibility contradiction. In doing so, however, he has merely provided a reductio ad absurdum of an explanation of metaphor which, as Aristotle proposed it, is not a bad explanation if language is thought of as block language.

In fluid language words are plastic. They have a certain range of potential referents and adapt readily to varying contextual environments. Thus the process of metaphorizing is much less violent. Instead of substituted reference there is concomitant reference or, to use older terminology, instead of comparison there is association or even identification. It is this view which has given rise to various speculative theories which would link man's power of making metaphors to pre-rational modes of perception and thought ("mythisches Denken," Ernst Cassirer called them), such as those which brought about the totemistic systems or those which supposedly are found in children. Since in fluid language there is no literal use of words, metaphor becomes a matter of degree. It avails itself of the ambiguity inherent in any word and shifts the weight from the more common referent to a less common or uncommon one. Since this shift is not apparent in the word itself ("ship" suffers no change when it is used as a metaphor for the state), a metaphor, from this point of view, is a riddle.

Christine Brooke-Rose offers a disarmingly simple definition of metaphor: "In my study," she writes, "any identification of one thing with another, any replacement of the more usual word or phrase by another, is a metaphor." [25] Useful as this definition may be as a working hypothesis, it is also begging the question. How do we know that a given word replaces another? How do we know whether in a phrase only one word or several words are replacements? And how do we know what word or words have been replaced? Put differently, how do we know there is a riddle, and, if we know it, how do we know what kind of riddle it is, and how do we solve it? Of course Miss Brooke-Rose is aware of these difficulties, and she devotes her book to an analysis of the aids to their solution provided by grammar and syntax. Moreover, she realizes that often these aids are not enough so that meaning, context, and even outside knowledge must be drawn upon. Now all these fac-

25. Brooke-Rose, p. 17.

tors, from grammar at the one end to the cultural tradition at the other, may be called the context of a metaphor, so that a metaphor becomes insoluble only when the context in this widest sense fails us.[26] This happens most frequently in very modern poetry, where the reference of a metaphoric term is often nebulous, but it also occurs in earlier literature. There is practically no difficulty with Type I metaphors, where the metaphoric phrase includes both question and answer. There is more difficulty with Type II metaphors, but since one component of them is non-metaphoric and thus provides an immediate close context, the riddle is usually soluble. The greatest difficulty is presented by Type III metaphors and especially by those which, unlike the examples given earlier, consist not of a compound noun or a phrase, but of a single word. These simple replacements are not considered by Mr. Weinrich, and since I have also disregarded them in arguing with him, I shall draw my examples mostly from them in the remaining pages of this essay.

First, then, there is the question of how the listener or reader knows whether or not there is a metaphor, whether he is faced with description or metaphor. The answer is that he knows it when he stumbles—when what he thinks does not make sense, or when he is not sure what sense to make of what he hears or reads. I shall not waste time giving examples from difficult literature, where there are thousands, but I offer a simple example—an example, to be sure, which will trouble only an observant reader. One of Stefan George's most famous poems begins as follows:

> Der hügel wo wir wandeln liegt im schatten·
> Indess der drüben noch im lichte webt
> Der mond auf seinen zarten grünen matten
> Nur erst als kleine weisse wolke schwebt.

26. Weinrich (p. 340) says that a bold metaphor loses its boldness when it is explained by the context, when it is no longer a riddle. With this assertion he shifts his definition of boldness in metaphor. Up to this point, boldness was said to be due to an obtrusive contradictoriness; now it is said to be due to the metaphor's being unexplained or not understandable—a riddle. In this connection Weinrich (pp. 341 f.) mentions the possibility of metaphors supporting and thus explaining each other—a matter with which I deal differently in the concluding pages of this article.

The possessive in line 3 may refer back to either the distant hill or the moon: if to the hill, the meadows are real meadows; if to the moon, the meadows are a metaphor for (large) clouds of greenish hue from which the rising moon is just emerging, looking like a small white cloud. Both grammar and sense fail us in this instance: grammar permits both readings, and the sense is equally good. The context slightly favors the literal interpretation because the poem (it has two more stanzas) does not contain a single metaphor apart from the doubtful one under consideration. But if we think of George's poetry as a whole, the argument loses most of its force. For example, the poem following the one mentioned above in *Das Jahr der Seele* begins with the phrase "flammende wälder," and it is a metaphor for vineyards in the fall. If we go still farther afield, we come upon the lines

> Der Mond von einem Wolkenhügel
> Sah kläglich aus dem Duft hervor,

in Goethe's *Willkommen und Abschied,* and these in turn lead us back to his translation of Ossian's *The Songs of Selma:* "Stern der niedersinckenden Nacht! Schön ist dein Licht im Westen! Du hebest dein lockiges Haupt aus deiner Wolke: ruhig wandelst du über deinen Hügel." [27] Considering that George was an innovator who constantly built on tradition,[28] we may incline to the view that Goethe's poem, so very well known, was in the back of his mind when he wrote his own and that for this reason the metaphoric reading should be preferred. However, I do not argue this. What I argue is that the question of whether a word is used literally or metaphorically can be impossible to decide even when a poem is as straightforward as George's and when its tenor precludes the assumption of intentional ambiguity.

Second, there is the question of what kind of metaphor we are dealing with. That certain metaphors may belong to either Type

27. Heinrich Düntzer in his edition of Goethe's *Gedichte, 1,* 46 (Kürschner's *Deutsche National-Litteratur, 82*) suggests that Goethe's word "Wolkenhügel" was inspired by Ossian, but the passage in Ossian to which he refers is not nearly as close to Goethe as is the passage quoted above.

28. H. Stefan Schultz, *Studien zur Dichtung Stefan Georges* (Heidelberg, 1967), passim.

I or Type II, and others to either Type II or Type III, has been said earlier. George's "flammende wälder," just mentioned, might be a Type II metaphor referring to woods in the fall, but the context shows that the phrase includes *two* Type III metaphors placed side by side—"flaming" stands for leaves turned red, and "woods" for the mass of plants in a vineyard. Determining the type of metaphor intended can be vital for the understanding of a text; this is illustrated by one of the riddles which August von Platen liked to devise in his early years:

> Weder als Urne noch Krug, doch wahrt' es Asche der Toten
> Treu auf dem Holzstoss selbst, dies Salamandergefäss.

The solution of the riddle is given in the word "Salamandergefäss," but what does it signify? Erich Petzet, Platen's editor, thought it was a Type III metaphor and suggested "memory" as the proper term. However, he felt so unsure that he added two question marks, and indeed while the memory can be thought of as a container, it is difficult to see any likeness to fire (the salamander) —either to its heat or to the constantly changing shape of the flame. Following Petzet I, too, took "Salamandergefäss" at first as a compound replacing metaphor and toyed with the idea that it might refer to "the body." The body preserves the physical characteristics of one's ancestors, and it resembles the flame in the protean changes it undergoes in a lifetime. But it can hardly be said to be still loyal on the pyre: when it is consumed, the inherited features are destroyed. But what if "Salamandergefäss" is understood as a Type I metaphor? Then the salamander is itself the vessel, and the answer to the riddle is "fire." It is the fire of the funeral pile which preserves the ashes of the dead. This solution would be in keeping with Platen's pagan inclinations and with his admiration for the ancients. (Note the past tense "wahrt'.") Again, however, I do not argue that this is necessarily what Platen had in mind. Ideally, the "Salamandergefäss" should, like urn and amphora, both "contain" and "preserve" the ashes, but I cannot think of a solution which retains Platen's pun on "wahren." What I do argue is that the question of what type of metaphor is intended is as crucial as it can be elusive.

Finally, there is the question of what is replaced, what the proper term is. This question is so difficult, especially in the case of simple replacements, that even great poets often resort to the crude expedient of placing the proper term next to the metaphor, as Schiller does in *Wilhelm Tell* (ll. 1060–63) :

Melchthal:	Ich war zu Sarnen und besah die Burg.
Stauffacher:	Ihr wagtet euch bis in des Tigers Höhle?
Melchthal:	Ich war verkleidet dort in Pilgerstracht,
	Ich sah den Landvogt an der Tafel schwelgen.

Like Schiller, Friedrich von Logau uses two replacing metaphors side by side and, like him, finds himself obliged to supply the proper terms in this little poem:

> Die Mutter frisst das Kind;
> Dass dieser Stamm vergeh,
> Frisst ihn die Erd und Wind:
> Es regnet in den Schnee.

"Mother" and "child" have such a wide range of possible metaphoric reference that the answer must be indicated in the last line: Water is the mother, snow the child. Still, Logau's poem has charm, while the passage from *Wilhelm Tell* has not. It adds two further metaphors ("to eat," and "stem" in the sense of "race" or "kind"), and it gives the answer obliquely—thus exploiting the riddle character of metaphor for the creation of a real riddle and challenging the reader's ingenuity. The pleasure it affords is, however, not primarily intellectual. It suggests something of the mystery of the cognitive process and of the way in which this mystery is reflected in metaphoric language.

Poets have developed many devices with which to reveal the referents of their metaphors, and these might be arranged in an ascending scale of delicacy and difficulty. I shall skip them all except one, the last and most elegant way, the explanation of metaphor by metaphor. Here are the opening lines of a poem by Rilke:

> Jene Wirklichen, die ihrem Gleichen
> überall zu wachsen und zu wohnen
> gaben, fühlten an verwandten Zeichen
> Gleiche in den aufgelösten Reichen,

die der Gott, mit triefenden Tritonen,
überströmt bisweilen übersteigt.

The passage is a chain of riddles. Who are the Real Ones? Who are
their kin? What are the signs of kinship? What realms are dissolved? Who is the god? As the poem continues it concentrates on
the "kinsmen." They are named in metaphor after metaphor: they
are "the animal," different from the mute fishes, distantly disposed
toward human ways, "a troop," "the Warm Ones," "the Affectionate Ones," "the sailor's friend," and "the companion." This string
of mutually explanatory metaphors is so skillfully composed that
the explicit resolution in the title of the poem, *Dolphins,* is really
superfluous.[29] Indeed the metaphors are so suggestive that even
the metonymy with which the poem opens and which is never explained is elucidated by them: "Jene Wirklichen" must be the
Greeks. Not only here, but in many of his poems Rilke uses riddles
to resolve riddles, metaphors to explain metaphors, thus preserving an extraordinary fluidity of language while speaking of tangible things. The method is peculiarly apt in the present instance
because *Dolphins* speaks of "those realists," the Greeks, who were
also great makers of myths. But it is also the ultimate fulfillment
in literature of the nature of metaphor. It was Vico who said that
every metaphor is a short myth.

Lest it be thought that what Rilke does is merely a virtuoso performance, something suitable only for *l'art pour l'art* poetry or for
fanciful or playful verse, I offer a last example, August Stramm's
Patrouille:

> Die Steine feinden
> Fenster grinst Verrat
> Äste würgen
> Berge Sträucher blättern raschlig
> Gellen
> Tod.

29. Titles can explain otherwise obscure poems and can lend a symbolical
meaning to poems whose text alone would be taken literally. Among more
modern German poets, C. F. Meyer was apparently the first to use the technique frequently, and Rilke was very fond of it. Brooke-Rose (pp. 31 and 94
f.) notes examples from Blake and Yeats.

Rilke's metaphors are nouns or adjectives, Stramm's are verbs. The verb is more flexible than the noun; it adapts itself more easily to varying contexts, so that the fluidity is even greater here than in Rilke.[30] Yet, although the four statements which make up the poem are elliptical as well as metaphoric, they converge to create a concrete and unmistakable situation. Any one of them taken by itself is indefinite and could refer to any number of things, but they limit each other and thus yield the explanation which, as with Rilke, is explicitly given in the title. In its own way, this lean and stark poem is as great a masterpiece as is Rilke's more elaborate structure. Rilke uses his chain of metaphors to describe an early stage of civilization preceding rigid categorizing and the rigidity of block language. Stramm uses his to describe the total insecurity and fear of soldiers on patrol who penetrate deeply into enemy territory or no-man's-land. In their situation, objects are no longer objects; familiar modes of perception and inference are irrelevant; all things have only one significance: they have become metaphors for danger, death. In its latest stage, civilization has returned to the mythological condition.

30. Richard Brinkmann ("'Abstrakte' Lyrik im Expressionismus und die Möglichkeit symbolischer Aussage," in Hans Steffen, ed., *Der deutsche Expressionismus. Formen und Gestalten* [Göttingen, 1965], p. 102) says that one can hardly speak of metaphors in connection with this poem. What he probably means is that Stramm's language obliterates the distinction between literal meaning and figurative significance, that it is extremely fluid. If so, I differ from him in terminology only, not in substance. Brooke-Rose, p. 209, writes succinctly and penetratingly on the flexibility of verbs and its effect on their metaphoric use.

Harry Levin

Thematics and Criticism

A book which tried to simplify its problems by talking down to its readers was paraphrased by one of its critics in French: *"N'ayez pas peur, petits enfants; le sujet n'existe pas."* Possibly I could allay a well-grounded suspicion which may greet my title by pointing out that my subject has only very lately come into existence. But in a broader sense—the sense in which Monsieur Jourdain talked prose before he studied rhetoric—it has always existed, insofar as it is nothing more nor less than the subject matter of literature. Laymen have always recognized this, and amateurs practiced it whenever they wrote books about the women of Shakespeare or gave lectures illustrated with slides on the highways and byways of the Thomas Hardy country. On the other hand, men of letters single-mindedly devoted to craftsmanship have deprecated such an approach since Flaubert, who wanted to write a book without a subject and claimed that the rhythms of his sentences came to him before the words. Formalism has been a predominant trend, sharpening and narrowing the focus of our literary critics, ever since John Crowe Ransom published his manifesto, *The New Criticism,* twenty-five years ago. The contribution of René Wellek has been a connecting link between the earlier Slavic formalists and the American school, as well as between a strictly formalistic and a more broadly historical vantage point.

The comparative novelty of New Criticism, at least to us, and the common ground amid its diversity of approaches lay in its concentration upon the object as a work of art. That, in turn, had been a salutary reaction against an old-fashioned kind of scholarship which was so concerned with background, with externals of biography, history, sociology, that it all but ignored the foreground, the aesthetic texture of the works themselves. The leading critics of the nineteenth century could be psychologists like Sainte-

Beuve or moralists like Matthew Arnold, and there are distinguished continuators of those respective traditions, notably
Edmund Wilson and Lionel Trilling, who properly reach a much
wider and more general public today than their colleagues whose
concerns are more technical. We are also aware that the other half
of the world, the hemisphere that professes allegiance to Marxist
philosophy, regulates its criticism by ideological standards and
regards a critical formalist as a traitor to the working class.
Indeed there has been a heavily documented polemic by an East
German scholar, Robert Weimann, *"New Criticism" und die
Entwicklung bürgerlicher Litteraturwissenschaft* (Halle, 1962),
which views an undue concern with form as a symptom of bourgeois decadence. The self-limiting criterion of the New Critics, internal coherence, has been as extreme in its way as those
polar criteria which the Marxists derive from external conditions.

Yet there have been indications of late that some members of
the American school are allowing more leeway for the role of
personality and for the context of society. W. K. Wimsatt, its most
serious theoretician, has produced an impressive antiquarian
monograph on the portraits of Alexander Pope. Cleanth Brooks,
its most accomplished explicator of poetic texts, has brought out
an illuminating study of William Faulkner which explores the
highways and byways of Yoknapatawpha County. The open-
minded critic cannot afford to be too much of a purist, since literature has a habit—which he must follow—of absorbing so much
else, of involving itself in so many extraneous matters, of extending its purview farther and farther. Much of what interests readers
most is connected with what formalists might regard as literature's
impurities. A poem is a verbal artifact, yes, more obviously than
some of the freer forms; but its arrangement of signs and sounds is
likewise a network of associations and responses, communicating
implicit information and incidentally touching off value judgments. The programmatic survey of René Wellek and Austin
Warren, *Theory of Literature,* which has so widely and helpfully
influenced graduate studies since its publication in 1948, is sharply
subdivided between what it labels "intrinsic" (style and structure

and various formal devices) and what it considers "extrinsic" (the social, the psychological, and the philosophical aspects of literary art) .

This would seem to be turning inside out the old mechanical dichotomy between form and content, offering the inside position to factors that used to be looked upon as outer embellishments, mere decorations—all that Sainte-Beuve dismissed when he spoke of *"rhétorique."* The notion of content, of that which is contained, has its parallel in the German *Gehalt;* it presupposes form as a sort of container, a superficial holder for emotions or ideas, which constitute the substance to be imparted. But, as Plato suggested and Spenser affirmed, "soul is form and doth the body make." Hence form gets metamorphosed into content: "the medium," as Marshall McLuhan puts it, "is the message." One of our central terms, which we have had to borrow from the French, is "genre"; yet genre painting is the kind that subordinates the portrayal to what is portrayed; the picture itself counts for less than the anecdote it tells. When we speak of epistolary novels, we have a formal category in mind; but when we speak of Gothic novels, we seem to be dealing with subject matter. The novel's inherent dependence on the latter, its use or abuse as a convenient vehicle to convey a segment of actuality, has been recently underlined by the appearance of the so-called nonfiction novel—to say nothing of such self-contradictory compounds as the *anti-roman.* Fortunately the categories of modern fiction have found their Polonius in Wayne C. Booth, who can be as exacting over point of view as the neoclassicists were over decorum.

We continue to think of novels in terms of what they are about: a picaresque novel is about a picaroon, a rogue, and it exploits the opportunities that his misadventures present for a rambling survey of low life. But the very nature of that ramble, easygoing and loose as it may seem, is by no means formless. On the contrary, it incarnates a structural principle which has successfully adapted itself to the purposes of most of the major novelists at one time or another. Therefore the term "picaresque" implies not merely an anti-hero, with all his capacity for disillusionment, but a linear movement which is both episodic and comprehensive, which can linger by the wayside or take the highroad to town. By contrast, the epic presents a narration more formally composed, more implicated with such conventions as the invocation to the Muse, which can be traced back—through the studies of Milman Parry and Albert Lord—to the circumstances of oral delivery. Different epics narrate different stories; yet usually they contain certain analogous episodes which take on a functional significance, such as the journey to the underworld, the conclave of the gods, or the dalliance with a temptress—whether her name be Circe, Dido, Alcina, Armida, or Acrasia. Thus content gets metamorphosed into form; the selection and disposition of themes becomes an organic part of the artistic process; and Ben Shahn offered a usable hint to writers when he titled his lectures on painting *The Shape of Content*.

Our keyword "theme" may sound somewhat jejune, particularly to those who associate it with required compositions for Freshman English. The original Greco-Latin *"thema"* simply denoted a rhetorical proposition, the argument of a discourse, what in Jamesian parlance we now like to term the *"donnée."* It could be the topic chosen by the orator or assigned to the schoolboy; through the pedagogical influence of the Jesuits the term became equated with an academic exercise; and the French soon specialized it to mean a translation of a given passage into another language. The adjective "thematic" has generally had to do with meaning as distinguished from technique. Though his excogitations have done much to extend its possibilities, our critical anatomist Northrop Frye is quite conservative in his own definition. Thematic modes, as opposed to what he calls fictional modes, are dependent upon their conceptual interest; they are roughly equivalent to what Aristotle called *dianoia,* the thought of the poem. Stephen Gilman discriminates further, in his monograph on *La Celestina,* between thesis and theme, between the directive idea and the underlying "sense of life." Gradually, and rather charily, we have been approaching the sphere of thematology. If ever a word was set up to be knocked down, it is that forbidding expression, which no dictionary has yet been broad-minded enough to admit. Presumably it heralds a science of themes, although even a pioneering enthusiast might hesitate to describe himself as a thematologist or to attend a thematological congress. Perhaps its ablest pioneer was the Italian comparatist Arturo Graf, whose nineteenth-century monographs examined such phenomena as the Devil and the Earthly Paradise.

Thematology would seem to be a pseudoscientific approximation of the German *Stoffgeschichte*, literally the history of stuff or fabric—an underlying conception at once more solid and less pretentious. However, it came to stand for the less imaginative researches of Germanic philology, its plodding accumulations of medieval legend or oriental lore on its pedantic quest for sources and analogues. Wilhelm Dilthey assigned an important place in his poetics to the study of motifs, *Motivenlehre;* but all too many investigations bogged down at the level of source hunting, *Quellenforschung.* The method was severely condemned by Benedetto Croce, who felt that it was extra-literary because it established no inner relationship among the differing treatments of the same theme. It was viewed with something like a nationalistic suspicion by the official French exponents of comparative literature, Fernand Baldensperger, Paul Hazard, and Paul Van Tieghem. Latterly the Institut de Littérature Comparée at the Sorbonne, in delayed reaction to the changing methods of literary history (which it envisaged for so long as a chronicle of French authors traveling abroad or of foreign books translated into French), has begun to relax its pursuit of fortunes and influences and to concern itself more seriously with *thèmes et structures.* Meanwhile the masters of the twentieth-century novel had been enlarging and elevating the usages of the thematic.

Realizing that narrative is—like music—a temporal medium, and deeply preoccupied with time itself as a theme, they emulated Wagnerian *Leitmotiv* and worked out controlling designs through the repetition and recognition of identifying phrases. Literature may not have needed to borrow from music such effects as it had previously gained through the epithets and formulas of some of its earliest genres, but it could now orchestrate them with a complexity which was psychological as well as musical. Thomas Mann explicitly described the style and structure of his own writing as *"thematisch."* Marcel Proust expressed the modulating relations of his lovers in a "little phrase" from a sonata by his imaginary composer Vinteuil. James Joyce brought home the self-reproach of his young artist by intermittently echoing a monkish byword for remorse of conscience, "Agenbite of Inwit." Some of these techniques have been carried farther by the contemporary practitioners of *le nouveau roman*. Echoes, frequently in the guise of quotations from music and literature, play a strategic part in any attempt to recreate the stream of consciousness. Their resonance would be more clearly registered in a thematic index than in the dramatis personae. We seek guidance through Proust in Raoul Celly's *Répertoire des thèmes,* just as we look up Mozart's works in Köchel's catalogue. Here again there seems to be a tendency for a substantive element to turn into an instrumental device. The message (*pace* Mr. McLuhan) becomes the medium.

Psychology, too, has added a deeper dimension to the critical examination of themes. Not that the Freudians have contributed much beyond the reduction of everything to the same old sexual allegory, any more than the Frazerians have greatly enlightened us by imposing on every conceivable story the composite outlines of a blurred monomyth. By hypothesis, the Jungian archetypes are ungraspable in their fullest primordial force; but Maud Bodkin has traced their emergence through certain poetic patterns, such universals as Rebirth or Paradise/Hades. What is known as the Thematic Apperception Test confronts its beholder with a set of ambiguous pictures, which he is asked to interpret in his own fashion, thereby disclosing his personal configuration of traits. The originator, Dr. Henry A. Murray, who is a literary man as well as a clinical psychologist, has pointed out some of the implications of the test for the creation of literature in "Personality and Creative Imagination," a paper read to the English Institute and published in its *Annual* (1942). The situation of the writer is not subject to such controlled observation; yet culture provides him with a sequence of themes to which he responds according to his imaginative bent; and when we are fully aware of them and can trace their projection through the minds of other writers, we may then be in a position to gauge both the individual quality of that response and the functioning of the collective imagination.

When Tonio Kröger dedicates himself to his calling, in Thomas Mann's parable of the writer's vocation, he speculates: "I gaze into an unborn world of phantoms, which must be ordered and shaped; I look upon a swarm of shadows of human figures, who beckon me to conjure them up and redeem them." Without attempting to enter that private underworld, to catch its embryonic forms before they have been summoned from their matrix, or to accompany Faust on the subterranean stages of his exploratory descent, we still have some degree of conversance with those disembodied spirits through their transmigrations into literature. We can take stock of this stuff (to repeat a good Shakespearean word), we can gain a rough impression of the repertory, as it were, on the rudimentary plane of bibliographies, dictionaries, and handbooks. The *Bibliography of Comparative Literature* (Chapel Hill, 1950) is a well-meaning catchall which has probably outlived its usefulness. Initiated by Louis Betz (1897) and augmented by Werner Friederich, it was edited principally by Fernand Baldensperger (1904), whose schematic framework during many years virtually comprised a methodology for the field. The section headed "Literary Themes (Stoffgeschichte)" includes subsections covering "Fables and Fabliaux," "Legends," and "Literary Types," but only as "Generalities." Specific themes are listed alphabetically under "Individual Motifs" and categorically under "Collective Motifs."

Individual motifs include not only Hiawatha, Mary Magdalene, and Robert the Devil, let alone Chicago or Clocks and Bells, but also War and Peace subsumed in a single category, Love (though it laughs at locksmiths, it toes the line for bibliographers), and Humor—which Professor Frye would not be alone in regarding as a mode rather than a motif. Why are such broad abstractions not classed as collective motifs, if indeed they be motifs at all? That other heading proves to be even more of a taxonomic jumble. Under it we encounter the subheading "Characters and Types," which seems to overlap "American Types and Trends" on the one hand and "Ecclesiastical Characters and Localities" on the other. Evidently the problem is the logical one of discriminating substance from accident. There ought to be room for everyone under "Men, Women, Children"; yet, rather arbitrarily and narrowmindedly, there is a special compartment for "Foreigners, Bar-

barians, Gringos," while "Virtues, Vices, Crimes" are lumped
together with a truly ecumenical tolerance. The sole conclusion
we are led to is that the editors of our bibliography have not decided what they mean by a theme. It could be a geographical setting (the Alps), a cultural order (Chivalry), or a fundamental
idea (the Problem of Evil). Professor Friederich explains that certain lists are necessarily selective; manifestly Nature or Utopia
would warrant a bibliography by itself.

In defining their scope, the compilers of the *Dizionario let-
terario* published by Bompiani (Milan, 1947–50) were faced
with a much simpler task. Seven of their handsomely illustrated
volumes, after an introductory review of intellectual movements
(*"movimenti spirituali"*), deal with *opere,* the works themselves,
such as *Giuseppe Andrews* and *Signora Bovary*. To reread them
here in synopsis is like following the libretto of an opera. The
obstacle for the non-Italian reader is comparatively slight when he
must guess that Scott's *Heart of Midlothian* has been retitled *Le
Prigioni di Edimburgo;* it is somewhat more opaque when Whit-
tier's *Snowbound* figures as *I Prigioneri della neve,* so that we
must look them both up under the P's, although the later impris-
onment is purely metaphorical. The eighth tome of this fascinating work of reference has been reserved for *personaggi* from
Gilgamesh to Superman, and the modern figure is neither the hero
of Nietzsche nor the heroine of Shaw—neither a bird nor a
plane—but the prodigy of the comic strips. Such personages, as
Shakespeare could teach us if Clark Kent did not, have a way of
stepping out of their contexts and leading lives of their own. Some
characters, like those of the Commedia dell'Arte, exist independently of the many scenarios wherein they perform the same roles.
New Comedy often changed its scene, but never its cast. Errant
youths and heavy fathers, parasites and pandars, *et cetera,* were in-
variable with Plautus:

> haec urbs Epidamnus est, dum haec agitur fabula;
> quando alia agetur, alius fiet oppidum.
> sicut familiae quoque solent mutarier:
> modo hic habitat leno, modo adulescens, modo senex,
> pauper, mendicus, rex, parasitus, hariolus.

Literary characterization, as distinguished from allegorical personification, is most fully embodied in individuals rather than fixed types. Such individuals, however, may come to typify some of their outstanding characteristics: the idiosyncratic Don Quixote becomes the generalization "quixotic." Indeed we might assume that a theme is a genus, handed down through impersonal tradition, and that the author stamps his individuality on the species. The book that deals most directly with our subject—with the subject matter of literature thematically conceived—is the compact and up-to-date lexicon of Elisabeth Frenzel, *Stoffe der Weltliteratur* (Stuttgart, 1962). Herein the themes are presented as *Längschnitte*, longitudinal sections of literary history, printed under the names of their protagonists from Theodoric the Ostrogoth to Billy the Kid, with summaries of their successive incarnations in poems, plays, and books. The fact that Byron is represented and Homer is not reminds us of the increasing extent to which, over the centuries, poetry has become subjective and authors have confounded themselves with their characters. Though Venice is accorded a listing for the conspiracy that inspired Otway's *Venice Preserved* and one or two other writings (it was both the place and the subject for the 1955 congress of the International Comparative Literature Association), there is no entry for Rome—in spite of all the sentiments, ephemeral and eternal, which it has elicited from generations of poets and which have been recounted in Walter Rehm's *Europäische Romdichtung*.

Normally the assumption seems to be that a theme is identifiable by, if not completely interchangeable with, some particular hero. Such is the argument of Raymond Trousson, whose recent pamphlet bears the ballast of a triple title, *Un Problème de littérature comparée: les études de thèmes—essai de méthodologie* (Paris, 1965). In a substantial monograph, *Le Thème de Prométhée dans la littérature européenne* (Geneva, 1964), he has demonstrated how rewarding such a pursuit can be if its mythical protagonist holds as rich and varied a significance as Prometheus did for Aeschylus and Shelley, Tertullian and Shaftesbury, Hesiod and Gide. Another Belgian scholar, Robert Vivier, in *Frères du ciel* (Brussels, 1962), has broadened the issue by pursuing, rather more selectively and suggestively, the parallel and yet dissimilar flights of two classical prototypes for hubris, Icarus and Phaeton. M. Trousson would delimit a theme to a single figure, though he would pursue it through all its explicit phases. Yet Faust himself, ample and significant as his own manifestations have been, can also be treated as an extension of what E. M. Butler entitled *The Myth of the Magus*. (And the individualism of the romanticists can be universalized, as Ian Fletcher and his collaborators show in *Romantic Mythologies* [London, 1967].) M. Trousson's delimitation offers a practical alternative to the all-embracing categorization of Baldensperger and his disciples, and it receives some support from the influential handbook of Wolfgang Kayser, *Das Sprachliche Kunstwerk:* "Theme is always related to certain figures; it is more or less fixed in time and space."

But most of our thematologists would be interested in significant places as well as persons, not to mention ways of getting there, namely voyages. The *voyage imaginaire* is one of those genres determined by themes, and it ranges from fantasy to satire. Both are reflected, along with the ever-developing background of science, in Marjorie Nicolson's *Voyages to the Moon;* elsewhere, in *Mountain Gloom and Mountain Glory,* Miss Nicolson has shown how man's sense of infinitude has been affected by his fluctuating attitudes toward the landscape; while W. H. Auden, in *The Enchafèd Flood,* has focused his poetic insight on "The Romantic Iconography of the Sea." There seems to be a point, exemplified by Hardy and the naturalistic novelists, at which the setting of some works takes on a thematic aspect. In an epoch of unheroic modernity, when people must struggle with things, certain objects—notoriously the machine—have become crucial subjects: witness Leo Marx's instructive study of its impact on American writers, *The Machine in the Garden: Technology and the Pastoral Ideal in America* (New York, 1964). Frederick J. Hoffman has not flinched before the ultimate encounter of "Death and the Modern Imagination" in *The Mortal No* (Princeton, 1964). The meeting of lovers at dawn—surely one of the universals of culture—is the theme of *Eos,* a compilation latterly issued by experts working in some thirty languages. Sigmund Skard provided access to another branch of thematics in his bibliographical survey,

The Use of Color in Literature. A study just published by Robert Martin Adams, *Nil: Episodes in the Literary Conquest of Void during the Nineteenth Century,* addresses itself to the *ne plus ultra,* the theme of nothingness. At the other extreme, literary accounts of the creation and its consequences, as analogous to *Paradise Lost,* are catalogued, translated, and reprinted by Watson Kirkconnell in *The Celestial Cycle.*

Dr. Frenzel has increased our debt to her with a little manual, *Stoff-, Motiv-, und Symbolforschung* (Stuttgart, 1963). We can take the symbology for granted in this connection, since it involves interpretations of *Stoff* and *Motiv,* whether they be patristic or psychoanalytic, and ask her how she discriminates between those other two concepts. Very simply, albeit she is conscious of more complex and confusing definitions: themes are primary, the raw materials of the writer's craft, while motifs are the basic situations as he begins to shape them. If in our tentative gropings we turn to the Fine Arts, where criticism usually enjoys the benefits of more concrete perceptions, we find that usage diverges considerably. Motif seems to signify what is depicted—let us say a hillside in Provence—while theme means the manner of treatment, as it would differ between Cézanne and Van Gogh. So Erwin Panofsky's *Studies in Iconology* discusses the separation of themes and motifs during the Middle Ages and their reintegration during the Renaissance, which Jean Seznec illustrates by showing classical Virgins and Gothic nymphs in his *Survivance des dieux antiques.* Ernst Robert Curtius seems to come closer to the art historians than to his literary colleagues, when he pauses to define our terms in his essay on Hermann Hesse. *"Motiv"* is the objective factor for Curtius; it approximates the objective correlative of T. S. Eliot; it sets the plot in motion and holds it together. Whereas the *"Thema"* is the subjective component, the personal coloration, an endowment rather than a discovery, lyrical where the *Motiv* inclines to be epical or dramatic.

Note that Curtius, classicist that he was and Romance philologist, makes no use of *Stoff.* It is far from my purpose to quibble over terminology, even when some critics reverse the meaning that words have had for others, so long as their intentions are perfectly clear. The formulation works for Curtius as a distinction between subject and treatment, between what the artist draws out of the public domain and what he contributes out of the depths of his unique personality. To the concept of theme it adds a psychic charge which should be relevant in other connections. Its use of *Motiv* can be construed as a literary application of the module commonly used by the folklorists, which has its monument in Stith Thompson's *Motif-Index of Folk-Literature*. Therein some 40,000 tales, myths, fables, romances, jestbooks, exempla—the corpus of nonliterary fiction—are categorized under the twenty-six letters of the alphabet. Naturally the letter A stands for accounts of the Creation; not surprisingly D, which is the rubric for stories involving magic, brings in the largest quantity of entries. Now there is nothing magical about the number 26, and there is something arbitrary in any system of taxonomy when it is applied to the irreducible factors of human behavior. There are about 800 types of fairy tales in the classification of Antti Arne. More pertinently for us, his Finnish school, through its sustained endeavor to classify them, has been able to chart their migrations and metamorphoses.

Count Gozzi, the playwright, declared that there were just thirty-six plots for the stage—a declaration subsequently questioned by Schiller and confirmed by Goethe. A contemporary aesthetician, Etienne Souriau, has refined the analysis with his book, *Les 200,000 Situations dramatiques*. It does not very seriously matter how many there are; and, as potential spectators who would rather be surprised than bored, we really ought to prefer the larger figure. What matters are the natural ties that relate a twice-told tale to its archetypal source, the recognizable store of possibilities to which the world's fictions can be retraced, the continual recombination and ramification of traditional features to meet the onset of fresh experience. The universal custom of fabulation repeats itself in cross-cultural paradigms. How deeply the iceberg of culture itself subtends beneath the surface we have been coming to realize more and more. The sophisticated processes of a self-conscious literature do not differ as much as we used to think from the subliminal processes of folklore. The true cultural function of the nineteenth-century novel, as formulated by Mircea Eliade in *Images et symboles,* has been, "despite all its scientific, realistic, and social slogans," to comprise "the great reservoir of downgraded myths." What may seem detritus to a specialist in comparative religion, like Professor Eliade, may well seem refinement to a student of comparative literature. One man's notion of decadence is another's idea of progress. What matters, in such a circumstance, are the continuities.

The Sicilian storyteller Euhemerus has not left us much besides his name, which we invoke when admitting our predisposition to convert human beings into myths. Needless to add, this predisposition is dangerous, howbeit fundamental. The cause of enlightenment has been better served by the effort to demythologize. Friedrich Gundolf, whose thematic studies set the posthumous fame of Julius Caesar above the actuality of his historic career, ended by giving aid and comfort to one of the most heinous expressions of twentieth-century Caesarism, the imperial theme of Mussolini and Hitler. In our time we have watched history downgrading itself into legend. Nonetheless we must agree with Professor Eliade that mythopoeia continues from age to age, adapting itself to the exigencies of change for better and worse; and when the ancient demons go underground, their avatars are likely to reappear in the mass media. The most persistent continuity has been that of the classical pantheon. It was already scoffed at in the era of Lucian, yet the skeptical André Gide could take Theseus as the protagonist of his fictional testament. Iphigenia had as much vitality for Goethe as for Euripides; Antigone has been no less contemporaneous to Anouilh than to Sophocles; and the Agamemnon of William Alfred will not conclude the line that commenced with Aeschylus. The wanderings of Odysseus go far beyond Homer, as W. B. Stanford has retraced them in *The Ulysses Theme*. It follows that these protagonists must be polyvalent—that is to say, they embody values that vary from drama to drama and from period to period.

Myth is bound to be colored by the mythographers: consider the varying viewpoints of Hesiod, Ovid, Natalis Comes, Lemprière, Bulfinch, W. H. Roscher, Robert Graves. Those of us who were introduced to the Greeks by *Tanglewood Tales* may have grown up with unduly puritanical notions about them: Hawthorne's Hecate, for instance, when dazzled by the radiance of Phoebus, suggests that he ought to be wearing a black veil. Thanks to humanistic education, the retired Olympian gods and the un-employed Greek heroes have maintained their prestige in the West, though it has been challenged by their chthonic counter-parts from the Norse Valhalla. By the device of *figura,* which Erich Auerbach has done so much to illuminate, Christendom was en-abled to absorb Jewish prophets and even pagan demigods into its typology of saints. The Fathers of the Church reinterpreted epi-sodes from the Old Testament—and, in carefully selected cases, the classics—as prefigurations of the Gospels. But this did not ob-literate the sharp line between revealed truth and poetic fable. Milton was sternly criticized by more rigid classicists for compos-ing an epic about the Christian revelation, and for personifying Sin and Death allegorically, rather than drawing his cast of charac-ters from legend or romance. Dante intermingled mythical, legen-dary, and historical figures, but each of them was allotted an orthodox place in his afterworld. The point is that they all pre-existed somewhere in the racial memory; it would have been in-conceivable for him to invent a character.

Medieval literature drew upon a syncretic and secular mythol-ogy, epitomized by the canon of the Nine Worthies: "Three paynims, three Jews, and three Christian men." Equally triadic was the body of material that lay at the disposal of the romancers: the matter of France, the matter of Britain, and that of Rome the grand—still grand enough to include some relics of Greece and, above all, Troy. The utilization of those three matters in poetry was not limited to the countries they represented. King Arthur and his Knights served as heroes for Chrétien de Troyes and Hartmann von Aue; Charlemagne and his Paladins evolved the rallying cries for Italian heroic romance. Our understanding of Shakespeare is somewhat beclouded by a failure to appreciate his relation to his thematic material, to the stuff that dreams and dramas are made of. We are now ready to concede, on the internal evidence of what he managed to write, that he was a cultivated reader; we can conscientiously reread the British chronicles, the Greco-Roman biographies, and the Italianate *novelle* that fur-nished the eclectic grist for his unexampled mill; but we are still embarrassed by naïve presuppositions about artistic originality, or else intimidated by labored reductions of art to its sources and influences—whereas to see the problem as one of selection from the available narratives and adaptation to the dynamics of the theater is to gain insights into Shakespeare's dramaturgy. What he left out can be quite as meaningful, in this light, as what he concentrated upon or interpolated.

The marriage of the Ovidian enchantress Titania to the gnome king of Germanic lore, Oberon or Alberich, attended by the thoroughly English Puck or Robin Goodfellow, is a characteristic *discordia concors,* a harmony produced from the very disparity of its components. We may not award Shakespeare the palm when we remember what Homer and Chaucer did with the two plots he reworked in *Troilus and Cressida,* yet the conjunction raises some major critical questions. Corneille was attacked by the formalistic critics of his day, who invidiously compared *Le Cid* with models of neoclassical tragedy. A thematic criticism, by contrasting the play with Spain's national epic about the same hero, might have widened the whole aesthetic perspective. The extensive scrutiny that has been accorded to Shakespeare's imagery, when it has not been sidetracked by psychological or biographical curiosity, may afford further encouragement for thematics. An image may be too slight to constitute a theme; but, as a verbal and visual unit, it can carry a theme by association; and, in a cluster, it can help to organize that coordination of speech and action which fulfills the dramatic design. A case in point would be the sequence of images relating to horses and serpents, which are respectively associated with Antony and Cleopatra. Indeed the image has become so pervasive a part of our lives, and we are such an image-conscious society, that the economist Kenneth Boulding has proposed it as the nucleus of a new science—or, at any rate, a means of unifying the social sciences—to be known as Eiconics.

To be sure, it is the plastic arts that display the most tangible icons; and art history has developed a discipline for revealing the ideas that are symbolized in its painted or sculptured images. To follow Edgar Wind's interpretation of "The School of Athens" is to realize how vast a train of philosophical thought lies behind the sensuous brush strokes of a Raphael. In order to profit from the stimulating example of the iconologist, the would-be thematologist must be comparably well informed in the history of ideas. Here he may have learned some clarifying lessons from the philosopher-historian Arthur Lovejoy, whose work has conjoined so fruitfully with literary studies. Some of those key ideas, which he and his colleagues and students have signalized and tracked down, were diffused in the guise of literary themes, such as the attitude of primitivism so closely related to the pastoral mode. Lovejoy's Great Chain of Being itself might be viewed as a gigantic image, an unchanging outline for speculations which have altered with the intellectual climate, from the spiritual hierarchy of the Neoplatonists to the Darwinian struggle for existence. The theme is thus the avenue for a progression of ideas, whose entrance into literature it invites and facilitates. For those who like their great ideas made easy, authorities from the University of Chicago have fixed them at a definite number, derived them from a set of books they happen to sell, and indexed them in what is loudly advertised as a "Syntopicon."

Their enterprise, for all its self-promotion, has about it a quirk of medievalism. During the Middle Ages, when high culture was regulated by a Latin canon whose forms were static, when living authors were frankly derivative and readers depended heavily on excerpts, abridgments, and compendia, ideas tended to crystallize into set topics or commonplaces. Those *topoi,* as Curtius has magisterially demonstrated in *Europäische Literatur und lateinisches Mittelalter,* were links that ultimately transmitted the remote past of Greece and Rome to the awakening Europe of Dante's vision. A *topos* is a theme in the most expressly rhetorical sense: it may be a purple passage from an oration, a standardized description of a locality, or an elaborately protracted metaphor—such as the stock comparison of nature to a book, which is as old as the Phoenicians and as modern as Shakespeare. The rise of scientific empiricism would discourage such an analogy, just as the more naturalistic viewpoint of the Renaissance and subsequent epochs would foster an augmenting individualism, a mentality less receptive to the typical than to the original, more impatient with received ideas and prone to dismiss *topoi* as mere clichés. This does not mean that themes would not persist, but that they would take on more protean shapes. Charles Mauron pointed in a cyclic direction when he collected his interpretations of certain moderns under the title, *Des Métaphores obsédantes au mythe personnel* (Paris, 1963).

A personal myth, of course, is a contradiction in terms. In moving away from the traditional and the general, the cycle has moved toward the particular and the autobiographical, since when the writer rejects his inherited stock of subjects, he is forced back upon the innermost resources of the self. Then, half-consciously, his state of mind is projected through a series of obsessive metaphors, almost as if an artist were inscribing his signature. Along with the obsessions that have been transposed into myths by the artistry of French writers, in M. Mauron's account, we might adduce Poe's claustrophobia, Hawthorne's secret chambers, or Melville's feelings for blood brotherhood. English critics long have recognized the detection of fervors and recurrences as a way of bringing out a writer's distinctive pattern. When I tried to sketch a critical profile of Christopher Marlowe's shaping spirit, my poet—individualist though he was—led me back recurrently and fervidly to the classic myth of Icarus. The *"psychocritique"* of M. Mauron, which is based on subtle perception rather than amateur psychoanalysis, should be differentiated from such procrustean undertakings as J.-P. Wéber's *Domaines thématiques* (Paris, 1964). M. Wéber, after surveying an author through the totality of his work, reduces it rigidly to a single theme, e.g. a clock for Vigny. Jean-Pierre Richard has labeled this type of criticism with the unhappy adjective *"totalitaire,"* and Raymond Picard has polemicized against it in *Nouvelle critique ou nouvelle imposture* (Paris, 1965).

The most far-reaching effort to probe the poet's consciousness—if not to fathom the collective unconscious—has been the suggestive investigation of the late Gaston Bachelard. Professor Bachelard, the Sorbonne philosopher, shifted in mid-career from science to poetry in order to come to terms with *"l'imagination matérielle,"* with nothing less than the mind's direct response to the universe, with matter itself in its pristine reduction and the attempts of man's imagination to grasp it through the four elements: fire, water, air, earth. His introductory volume, *La Psychanalyse du feu,* is at once more and less than it claims to be. To be

precise, material things cannot be psychoanalyzed, nor is the
analyst trying to set his couch on fire; this is "a psychoanalysis of
subjective convictions relating to our awareness of the phenomena
of fire." Drawing upon mythology like Freud, Bachelard diagnoses
"the Prometheus complex" as "the Oedipus complex of intellectual life." Proceeding mainly by free association, and illustrating
richly by quotation from the more intuitive and surrealistic poets,
he has completed his elemental scheme with additional books on
l'eau, l'air, la terre, and the several kinds of revery that they respectively stimulate. A more discriminating and systematic inquiry is promised by Bernhard Blume's articles on islands and
rivers in German poetry. An overambitious venture, subjecting
the imaginative faculty to historical and even statistical analysis,
has been made by Jacques Bousquet in *Les Thèmes du rêve dans
la littérature romantique: essai sur la naissance et l'évolution des
images* (Paris, 1964).

To apprehend and characterize the mental landscapes of individual authors, to distinguish their lights and shades, their recognizable contours and sensory attributes, is the aim of an enlarging
school which has sometimes been adventurous enough to describe
its approach as phenomenological. Its most intrepid proponent,
Georges Poulet, with his *Etudes sur le temps humain,* perceptively
explored the sense of time in Proust and others less overtly immersed in it. With a companion study, *La Distance intérieure,*
Professor Poulet turned from the temporal to the spatial dimensions of literature. Mallarmé was his principal warrant there;
some of his other subjects seem less amenable to the sort of abstraction he strove to impose upon them. Isolated lines from
Marivaux ("I am lost, my head whirls, I know not where I am!")
may be quoted to lend a facile impression of metaphysical pathos
or existential vertigo. But in their contexts they express no more
than the age-old confusions of comedy, and can be vulgarly paralleled up and down the history of the stage. Jean-Pierre Richard
gets farther, in *Littérature et sensation,* because his measuring rod
is stylistics, not metaphysics. All close reading entails a certain
amount of impressionistic subjectivity, not less so when it looks at
interiors than when it looks at surfaces. When the reader is Vir-
ginia Woolf, commenting on the Brontës' love of red carpets, or

Proust, discerning Stendhal's fixation on heights, then the intuition is worth our while. But when J. Hillis Miller traverses "the inner space" of Yeats' or Eliot's poems, the result is a heavy-footed superimposition.

That, by stressing distance, duration, coloring, or tactile values, a critic actually penetrates to the interior of a writer's mind, alas, is merely another metaphor. Such concerns fill in our comprehension of the thematic texture; but, like those famous *nouveaux romans,* they leave us lonely in a world from which the humanity seems to have been abstracted. After all, it was the threatened disintegration of character that prompted modern novelists, in the wake of Joyce, to seek mythic prototypes. The prototype for Leopold Bloom is Ulysses; yet unofficially he seems to have more in common with the Wandering Jew; and there are moments when he would like to imagine himself as Mozart's Don Giovanni—who in turn, was one of more than 500 reincarnations of Don Juan Tenorio in song and story. (Actually, Bloom's operatic stand-in is less distinguished and more vulnerable: the jealous peasant Masetto.) Where the authorities disagree so completely, there is not much hope of reaching a consensus; but, so far as the disagreement is verbal, it may point the way to a critical redefinition. If there is any agreement that a theme should be identified with the name of a personage, then it may be said that the theme of Don Juan has occasioned some 500 variations. We are accustomed to evoke him as the very model of a single-minded amorist, and that impression is amply corroborated by Leporello's statistics in the opera. Yet no human personality is ever reducible to a single trait; even the Marquis de Sade occasionally had other matters than sex upon his mind.

Don Juan's original role, in the play by Tirso de Molina, was that of an all-round trickster, whose seductions were simply one of his many engaging tricks. His greatest part, in Molière's sinister comedy, was that of a sardonic iconoclast, a libertine in thought as well as love. The constant feature of his variable legend is the denouement, when the statue drags him down to hell. This is a fate which he shares with his northern contemporary, Faust, who paralleled his career in other spheres. However, the version of the Faust theme that we accept as the greatest, Goethe's, softened by the romantic cult of womanhood, overturns the somber Lutheran object lesson and replaces damnation by salvation. Thus a theme may veer from one extreme to the other. The infernal ending of both legends is classifiable as a motif; for if themes are linked to characters, motifs are segments of plot. The tale of Romeo and Juliet is one theme, and that of Pyramus and Thisbe another; but they share the same motif, the tryst in the tomb, which also has some relevance for Tristram and Iseult. When Shakespeare burlesqued Pyramus and Thisbe in *A Midsummer Night's Dream,* he retained the thematic story line while transforming the emotional charge. A comic theme may have a serious purport. The comedies about Amphitryon are so numerous that Giraudoux numbered his version 38, and the professional thematologists have multiplied that reckoning. An earlier, more fragmentary treatment, the Reformation interlude of *Jack Juggler,* exploits the confrontation of the twin Sosias, when Mercury assumes the body of Amphitryon's servant, to satirize the doctrine of transubstantiation.

Themes, like symbols then, are polysemous: that is, they can be endowed with different meanings in the face of differing situations. This is what makes an inquiry into their permutations an adventure in the history of ideas (see Don Cameron Allen on Noah or George K. Anderson on the Wandering Jew). Our knowledge can be enriched by finding out why certain themes have been chosen at certain periods (the Wagnerian resurrection of the *Nibelungenlied*) or in certain localities (the Virgilian linkage of Rome with Troy) or by certain authors—why should the saintly figure of Joan of Arc have impressed such skeptics as Mark Twain, Bernard Shaw, and Anatole France, while failing to win the sympathy of Shakespeare? Themes, like biological entities, seem to have their cycles, phases of growth, of heyday, and of decline, as with Troilus and Cressida. It is not surprising, in our latter day, that so many of them seem to have reached a state of exhaustion. Audiences get tired of hearing the same old names, and writers find it harder and harder to compete with their illustrious forerunners. But motifs seem inexhaustible. As long as man's aspirations and limitations are what they have been, his journey through life will be envisioned as an intercepted quest, like that of *Moby-Dick.* He will sooner or later find himself located somewhere, and place will be sublimated by dream. His ego will invoke its alter ego, its double or *Doppelgänger*, whether in reflection of the author's intimate bond with his protagonist or with his reader (*"mon semblable, mon frère"*) or by the sort of optical illusion that projects a fabric for our fantasies.

If a theme itself can be so concretely pinned down, particularized into a local habitation and a name, the speculative area of thematics remains much wider and more flexible: witness the timely study of Eugene H. Falk, *Types of Thematic Structure: The Nature and Function of Motifs in Gide, Camus, and Sartre* (Chicago, 1967). What is called thematism, in Bernard Weinberg's introduction, embraces much of what used to be set aside as having to do with the externals of literature. We are now willing to admit that a writer's choice of a subject is an aesthetic decision, that the conceptual outlook is a determining part of the structural pattern, that the message is somehow inherent in the medium. The scenery and the ideology are not less basic to the main design that the accepted constituents of plot and character. Ideas play their roles by appearing in the garb of images. Whatever the writer undertakes to describe, by the act of his description, becomes a contributing feature of the final arrangement. It emanates in large part from his powers of observation and his years of experience, but perhaps in larger part from a common store of associations and memories which—vast and varying as they are—tend nonetheless to assume familiar guises and to display recurrent characteristics. Criticism must teach itself to recognize them, to discriminate between their more and less creative embodiments, to place and relate them all within the continuous order of those things which men have imagined. Thereby we may come to understand what the imagination is, how it works, what it needs to work upon, how by selecting and arranging it modifies and transforms, how it enhances life by endowing it with meanings and with values.

Edgar Lohner

The Intrinsic Method:
Some Reconsiderations

It can be asserted without exaggeration that during the last thirty or forty years literary criticism has progressed in a new direction immediately apparent to any one familiar with the literary theories of this period. After the development of the French *explication de textes* and the theoretical studies of the Russian Formalists, a trend is to be observed in both Germany and America which manifests itself in an emphasis on the structure of a literary work of art as an autonomous entity. Intensive examination of individual works of literature has more and more become the basis of criticism. The analysis of each part of a literary work of art, of the relation of the parts to each other, and of their relation to the whole, has been employed to demonstrate the uniqueness of each work. The works of Oskar Walzel, Emil Staiger, and Wolfgang Kayser, as well as those of I. A. Richards and the New Critics, bear unmistakable testimony to this. Thus a healthy discontent revived interests which had been either neglected too long or relegated to a position of minor significance. Problems of literary form, theory, and practice suddenly occupied the center of the critic's attention.

Just as René Wellek and Austin Warren emphasized "that the study of literature should, first and foremost, concentrate on the actual works of art themselves," so also did Wolfgang Kayser in *Das sprachliche Kunstwerk,* when he wrote:

> Das subjektive Werk . . . ist der eigentliche Gegenstand der Wissenschaft von der Dichtung. Eine Forschungsweise, die ihm nicht voll und ganz gerecht wird, steht nicht im innersten Kreis der Wissenschaft.

And similarly in his preface:

> Ein neuer Abschnitt in der Geschichte der literarischen For-
> schung hat begonnen. Und die Erwartung scheint berechtigt,
> dass von dem wiedergewonnenen Zentrum der auf das Dicht-
> erisch-Sprachliche gerichteten Arbeit aus auch die Literatur-
> wissenschaft neue Masstäbe bekommen wird.[1]

But even before the methodological certainties of the nineteenth
and early twentieth centuries had been seriously questioned, and
before the new "formalistic" or "intrinsic" method had been
properly established, cries for a new approach were already to be
heard in Germany—and indeed not without justification. Hans
Schwerte referred to a crisis in literary scholarship.[2] Intrinsic
interpretation, in turn, was itself questioned; it was termed dubious, "die Gefahr unserer Zeit," and even "a type of affliction." [3]
Historical awareness, which had lately been ignored, was demanded once more.[4] The all too easy and impressionistic performance, elegant yet lacking methodological discipline, was
lamented. Critics spoke of "Nach- und Umdichten des Originals;" [5] indeed, of a *furor interpretandi*.[6] In fact, these objections

1. *Theory of Literature* (New York, 1949), p. 140; *Das Sprachliche
Kunstwerk* (2nd ed. Bern, 1951), p. 5.
2. Hans Schwerte, "Die problematische Kunst der Interpretation," *Die
Neue Furche, 30* (1959), 615; Clemens Heselhaus, "Auslegung und Er-
kenntnis. Zur Methode der Interpretationskunde und der Strukturanalyse
. . . ," in *Gestaltprobleme der Dichtung*, ed. Richard Alewyn et al. (Bern,
1957), p. 279.
3. Heselhaus, p. 260.
4. Friedrich Sengle, "Zur Einheit von Literaturgeschichte und Litera-
turkritik," *DVLG, 34* (1960), 327–37; also in *Ruperto-Carola, 12* (1960),
3–9.
5. Walter Muschg, *Die Zerstörung der deutschen Literatur* (Bern, 1956),
p. 98.
6. Schwerte, "Die problematische Kunst der Interpretation" and "Rück-
kehr zur Literaturgeschichte. Zur Methodik der Literaturwissenschaft und
des Deutschunterrichts," *Die Erlanger Universität, 11* (July 23, 1958); cf.
Erik Lunding, *Wege zur Kunstinterpretation*, Acta Jutlandica (Copenhagen,
Aarhus, 1953), p. 20; Benno von Wiese, "Geistesgeschichte oder Interpretation," *Festschrift für Friedrich Maurer* (Stuttgart, 1963), pp. 239–61;
Werner Ross, "Grenzen der Gedichtinterpretation," *Wirkendes Wort, 7*

became so persistent that it appeared as if one wished to abandon the genuinely valid achievements of the intrinsic method for one which had seen its glory in Dilthey's often misinterpreted accomplishments.

Almost the same arguments were to be heard in America with perhaps equal justification. "The signs that we are in for a change of weather, critically, are many," writes Hyatt Waggoner, mentioning the "revolt" against the New Critics by Robert Adams, Stanly Edgar Hyman, Philip Rahv, and others.[7] René Wellek, too, has indicated in various essays the shortcomings of the New Criticism. For him, its historical perspective is too limited; literary history is almost completely neglected; the possibilities raised by modern linguistics are left unexplored, "with the result that the study of style, diction and meter often remains dilettantish." Though often referred to in their practical criticism, aesthetics at the hands of the New Critics lacks any solid philosophical foundation. The "method" is applied all too often at random and without imagination.[8] The outstanding and very perceptive critic, Murray Krieger, though sympathetic to the intrinsic method, points repeatedly and convincingly to the "contextualist dilemma."[9] Less persuasive and predominantly of a polemic nature are the arguments of Walter Sutton.[10] Further emphasizing some aspects of the "basic art of misinterpretation," Richard M. Kain justifiably turns against what he terms "the new Cabalists," criticizing "the *insouciance* of William Empson's quest for ambiguities." Thus, he takes issue with G. Wilson Knight's interpretation of Shakespeare's sonnets and Quentin Anderson's analysis of Henry James'

(1956–57), 321–32; Horst Rüdiger, "Zwischen Interpretation und Geistesgeschichte," *Euphorion*, 57 (1963), 227–44.

7. "The Current Revolt Against the New Criticism," *Criticism*, *1–2* (1959–60), 211.

8. So, for instance, in "Trends of Twentieth-Century Criticism," *Concepts of Criticism* (New Haven, 1963), p. 359.

9. Cf. *The New Apologists for Poetry* (Minneapolis, 1956), esp. pp. 135–38; also "Contextualism Was Ambitious," *JAAC*, *21* (1962), 81–86.

10. "The Contextualist Dilemma—Or Fallacy?" *JAAC*, *17* (1958–59), 219–29; "Contextualist Theory and Criticism as a Social Act," *JAAC*, *19* (1961), 317–25; *Modern American Criticism* (Englewood Cliffs, 1963), pp. 98–151.

later novels. According to him the autotelism of art is an impossible goal.[11]

The arguments of the Neo-Aristotelians against the interpretative method of the New Critics are also well known. However, it quickly becomes apparent that the argumentation of the Chicago Critics is, though on a different level, no less formalistic than the method they so violently attack.[12] In addition to the Chicago group there are others who deny the new method: Douglas Bush, Robert Gorham Davis, Peter Viereck.[13] Viereck, for example, in his essay "Beyond Revolt: The Education of a Poet," is of the opinion that "aesthetic as well as ethical, psychological, and historical factors are inseparably fused together," and accordingly asks for "a return to . . . communication and ethical responsibility." [14]

In the face of so many new approaches to literature on the continent and in America, France surprisingly has remained conservative. Not only have the various aspects of the positivistic method been maintained there, as is demonstrated by the works of Gustave Lanson, Daniel Mornet, and Louis Cazamian, but the method of *explication de textes* has also remained essentially unchanged since Gustave Rudler's instructive work *L'Explication Française: Principes et Applications*.[15] This latter method has often condescendingly and inappropriately been considered only a useful pedagogical aid for the teaching of literary interpretation. It is surely

11. "The Limits of Literary Interpretation," *JAAC, 17* (1958–59), 214–18.

12. Cf. *Critics and Criticism, Ancient and Modern,* ed. Robert S. Crane (Chicago, 1952); see also Eliseo Vivas, "The Neo-Aristotelians of Chicago," *The Sewanee Review, 61* (1953), 139–149, reprinted in Vivas, *The Artistic Transaction and Essays on Theory in Literature* (Columbus, Ohio, 1963), pp. 243–59; William K. Wimsatt, Jr., "The Chicago Critics," *CL, 5* (1953), 50–74, reprinted in *The Verbal Icon* (Noonday Paperback, 1964), pp. 41–65; Edgar Lohner, "Die Neu-Aristoteliker in Chikago: Einige grundsätzliche Überlegungen zu Begriffen ihrer kritischen Theorie," *Lebendige Antike, Festschrift für Rudolf Sühnel* (Berlin, 1967), pp. 528–41.

13. "The New Criticism: Some Old-Fashioned Queries," *PMLA, 64* (1948–49), 13–21; "The New Criticism and the Democratic Tradition," *The American Scholar, 19* (1949–50), 9–19.

14. *The Arts in Revival* (Philadelphia, 1951), pp. 46, 45.

15. Paris, 1902.

much more than an instrument of instruction, even though it does, in a restricted sense, owe its existence to pedagogical efforts. It remains nevertheless a valuable tool of study, in spite of the fact that both the refusal to consider historical phenomena and the exclusive concentration on the text itself are more pronounced here than in any of the other intrinsic approaches. Explication, as Helmut Hatzfeld writes, "has been practiced since 1900 with progressively improved methods of approach." [16] To the best of my knowledge, there has never been any mention of "crisis" or "new" directions in the circles in which his method is practiced. The principles introduced in Gustave Rudler's work are still held to be valid today:

> Expliquer, c'est rendre compte d'un texte, c'est-à-dire le comprendre et le juger, dans son esprit et dans sa lettre, dans son ensemble, ses parties et son détail, intégralement.
>
> Soumission au texte; tel sera donc notre principe. . . . Ce qui intéresse dans l'explication, c'est le texte, vu sans doute à travers l'intelligence et la sensibilité du commentateur et réfracté par elles, mais c'est le texte.[17]

These and similar principles investigated at that time have also been maintained by Mario Roustan and the radical Belgian critic

16. *A Critical Biography of the New Stylistics, Applied to Romance Literatures 1900–1952,* (Chapel Hill, 1953), p. 2; however, in his *Initiation à l'explication de textes français* (p. 10) Hatzfeld stresses the historic aspect:
Si l'analyste n'est pas en même temps un historien, si ses analyses ne sont pas fondées sur une érudition historique, elles ne sont que le passe-temps d'amateur. L'analyse littéraire, il est vrai, est plutôt du domaine de la 'science littéraire' que de l'histoire. Cependant, pour que l'analyse soit en quelque sorte scientifique, vérifiable, objective, elle doit chercher la raison d'être des formes étudiées, en rapport avec le moment psychologique et culturel de leur création . . . . Il ne faut pas confondre cette étude historique avec un système "historiste," fondé sur la nécessité des influences: race, milieu, moment (Hippolyte Taine) et qui tend à s'abstenir d'un jugement de valeur. Le point de vue historique tend à comprendre correctement, expliquer la genèse d'un texte, mais réserve la liberté existentielle d'admettre ou rejeter les idées et la forme, ainsi que les valeurs esthétiques, morales, métaphysiques de l'œuvre, que seul pourrait négliger un pédant inhumain. L'analyse historique est une oeuvre ancillaire.

17. *L'Explication française* . . . (6th ed. Paris, 1930), p. 4.

Servais Étienne.[18] Well-known scholars such as Erich Auerbach, Leo Spitzer, Helmut Hatzfeld, Théophil Spoerri, and Amado Alonso made use of this approach, frequently with a more circumspect and refined sensibility than their French predecessors.[19] Instead of an approach deriving its impetus from the history of ideas and from the positivistic method, they helped develop a study of literature which is based upon close reading of the text, and which later evolved into stylistic interpretations.[20]

In Russia the theories of the Formalists were more or less tolerated by official Marxist criticism until about the middle of the twenties. At that time, however, crude and at times indiscriminately hostile attacks were launched against them, the first of which came from no one less than Lev Trockij, in his controversial book *Literature and Revolution*.[21] To be sure, he admitted grudgingly the validity of some of the achievements of the Formalists as far as the comprehension of poetry was concerned,[22] but

18. *Précis d'explication française* (Paris, 1911); *Défense de la Philologie* (Paris, 1933), esp. chap. 4, "La philologie opposée à la méthode historique," where Étienne tries to separate philology from the historical method.

19. Helmut Hatzfeld, *Einführung in die Interpretation neu-französischer Texte* (Munich, 1922), and *Initiation à l'explication de textes français* (Munich, 1957; 2nd ed., 1966), pp. 7–15. Erich Auerbach, *Introduction aux études de philologie romane* (Frankfurt, 1949); Leo Spitzer, "History of Ideas Versus Reading of Poetry," *The Sewanee Review, 6* (1940), 584–609, and *A Method of Interpreting Literature* (Northampton, 1949); see also, Giovanni Bruno, "Dell'interpretazione linguistica di alcune opere letterarie," *CN, 4–5* (1944–45), 157–62; Amado Alonso, "The Stylistic Interpretation of Literary Texts," *MLN* (1942), pp. 489–96; Théophil Spoerri, *Die Formwerdung des Menschen* (Berlin, 1938), esp. "Die stilkritische Methode."

20. "Dans l'ensemble l'analyse des textes me semble la méthode la plus saine et la plus fertile parmi les procédés d'investigation littéraire actuellement en usage, autant du point de vue pédagogique que pour les recherches scientifique" (Auerbach, p. 37).

21. See Victor Erlich, *Russian Formalism. History-Doctrine* (The Hague, 1955), esp. chap. 6, pp. 79–95; second revised edition (1965), pp. 99–117; Lev Trockij, "The Formalist School in Poetry and Marxism," *Literature and Revolution* (Moscow, 1923; New York, 1925), chap. 5; see also Erlich, pp. 100–04.

22. "The methods of Formalism, if confined within legitimate limits, may help to clarify the artistic and psychological peculiarities of literary form" (Trockij, p. 164).

he rejected the formalistic pursuits in general—their "arrogance and immaturity," their methodological sterility, philosophical heresy, and the decadent "escapism" of the Opojaz critics, which for him as well as Poljanskij and Lunačarskij produced only a preliminary stage of literary studies.

These attacks were launched not only from without, but also from within, thereby indicating a new development. Characteristically it was the erratic but brilliant Viktor Šklovskij who was the first to seek a compromise. In his study on Tolstoj's *War and Peace* (1928) he attempted to establish the mutual effect between "class" and genre in order to achieve a synthesis between the Formalist and the sociological approach.[23] Already as early as 1930, but especially at the beginning of the fifties, Šklovskij began to recant and not only to praise Marxist dialectics but also to show a highly favorable inclination for the prevailing doctrine of the Stalinist era.[24] Coupled with this outside pressure, Boris Ejxenbaum's and Jurij Tynjanov's gnawing doubts and growing dissatisfaction with the purely formalistic approach to literature marked the beginning of the end for the militant character of this movement.

By the thirties, owing partly to political circumstances and partly to the lack of inner direction, Russian Formalism had run its course. Ejxenbaum and Žirmunskij no longer concerned themselves with theoretical problems; others stopped writing altogether. Yet already working at that moment in Prague was Roman Jakobson, one of the most gifted and outstanding members of the movement. Together with scholars such as Jan Mukařovský, Dimitrij Čiževskij, René Wellek, and others belonging to the *Cercle Linguistique,* Jakobson developed a "structuralism" which viewed aesthetics not as an isolated fact but rather as a part of a dynamically integrated whole, in which all parts of language interact upon each other.[25] It was possible to ban the formalist

23. *Material i stil' v romane L. N. Tolstogo Vojna i mir* (Moscow, 1928).

24. Cf. Dimitrij Čiževskij, "Wiedergeburt des Formalismus? In welcher Art?," in *Immanente Ästhetik: Ästhetische Reflexion, Lyrik als Paradigma der Moderne,* ed. W. Iser (Munich, 1966), pp. 297–305.

25. *A Prague School Reader on Esthetics. Literary Structure and Style,* trans. and ed. Paul L. Garvin (Washington, D.C., 1955); see also Erlich, "Formalism Redefined," *Russian Formalism,* pp. 154–68.

activities in Russia and subsequently in the other Slavic countries; but as Victor Erlich writes, "many Formalist insights outlasted the totalitarian purge as they found a new lease on life in kindred movements on the other side of the 'Marxist-Leninist' iron curtain." [26]

These methods, with the exception of the *explication de textes*, appeared to be predominantly the result of the reaction which René Wellek calls the revolt against positivism: the reaction against the principles of causality; the mere accumulation of unrelated historical, biographical, and sociological details; in other words, against the consideration of literature as a document of cultural history and against "the whole underlying assumption that literature should be explained by the methods of the cultural sciences." [27] This holds good not only for the American but also for the Russian approach.[28]

26. Erlich, p. 274; see also Manfred Bierwisch, "Strukturalismus: Geschichte, Probleme und Methoden," *Kursbuch, 5* (1966), esp. pp. 86–151.

27. "The Revolt Against Positivism in Recent Literary Scholarship," reprinted in *Concepts of Criticism* (New Haven and London, 1963), pp. 256–81.

28. Cf. Norman Foerster, *American Criticism* (Boston and New York, 1928), pp. 223, 235, 259; W. Strell Holt, "The Idea of Scientific History in America," *Journal of the History of Ideas, 1* (1940), 361: "Most of the scholarly history written in the United States from 1875 to the present has been conceived in terms of objective facts. The value put on the facts as an end in themselves; the emphasis given to the establishment of facts; the fear of making any statements without a supporting document . . . the denial of any philosophy and theory of history in the prepossession that historians should, or could, be without prepossessions—all testify to the same conclusion"; Bernard Smith, *Forces in American Criticism* (New York, 1939); Norman Foerster et al., *Literary Scholarship: Its Aims and Methods* (Chapel Hill, 1941).

Viktor Zirmunskij, "Formprobleme in der russischen Literaturwissenschaft," *Zeitschrift für slavische Philologie, 1* (1942), 118; Erlich, chaps. 1 and 2; A. N. Voznesenskij, "Die Methodologie der russischen Literaturforschung in den Jahren 1910–1925," *Zeitschrift für slavische Philologie, 4* (1927), 145–62; Nina Gourfinkel, "Les nouvelles méthodes d'histoire littéraire en Russie," *Le Monde Slave, 6* (1929), 234, 263; *Russian Formalist Criticism: Four Essays,* trans. and with an Intro. by Lee T. Lemon and Marion J. Reiss (Lincoln, Nebr., 1965): "Until now, writes Roman Jakobson, literary historians have preferred to act like policemen, who, in order to

The expansion of the intrinsic method into Germany is, in addition, a reaction against a broad interdisciplinary trend called *Geistesgeschichte,* which, as an integrated study of all cultural phenomena, is therefore hard to delineate. Rudolf Unger views it as "eine spezifische Betrachtungsweise geistiger Dinge, die sich auf den idealen Oberbau der Kultursynthese richtet und das einzelne Geistesgebiet erfasst als Auswirkung des Gesamtgeistes der jeweiligen Kultureinheit." [29] This concept of 'Geistesgeschichte does not mean that the literary work has no significance whatsoever, but rather that it is not examined with respect to its inherent properties but to the manner in which it reflects both concepts and attitudes appropriate to its particular position in a given historical period. Thus the work is simply considered a link in the "great chain of being." The aesthetic structure of a given text, however, remains of secondary importance. In this fashion the work becomes too easily an excuse for extended excursions into all conceivable realms of cultural history. Since many a German critic who professes an adherence to the intrinsic method received his training in what is commonly designated the method of *Geistesgeschichte,* it is hardly surprising that some of the favored terms of that method, such as *Erlebnis, Geist,* and *Seele,* are still being used in the critical efforts of the German contextualists.

These are some of the historical phenomena preceding, and at the same time partly contributing, to the existence of the intrinsic method. With all respect to the ambitions and often diverse complex theories of the various critics belonging to the movements mentioned, one has also to recognize that there actually is no such thing as *the* school of the Russian Formalists, of the New Critics, nor is there a definite intrinsic method in German criticism. And yet, despite differences of criteria and details of argument, there is a common aesthetic ground which allows for critical appraisal of some of the essential assumptions on which these critics have based their arguments. What are their common aesthetic properties?

---

arrest one person, would confiscate everything in his apartment and, in addition, round up all the casual passers-by on the street" (*Novejšaja russkaya poezija* [Prague, 1921], p. 11) .

29. *Gesammelte Schriften I: Aufsätze zur Prinzipienlehre der Literaturgeschichte* (Berlin, 1920) , p. 190.

What did these critics actually achieve? And what were the theoretical deficiencies resulting in the stagnation of the intrinsic
method, a method which the Russian Formalists, the New Critics,
and the German scholars so valiantly approached and so fervently
embraced, and from which they have wrested partial, though not
completely satisfactory, answers? A more satisfactory or, for that
matter, even a new answer can hardly be claimed, however, until
an awareness and a clarification of the critical problem has been
supplied. Only then will it be possible to indicate a way out of the
methodological impasse in which the intrinsic method now finds
itself.

In general, the common feature of all these new critics is their
firm conviction about the uniqueness of literature, which is evident in their insistence on the unity and totality of the work of art.
For the literary work is no longer a written document containing forces and facts of an ideological nature. On the contrary,
it is a phenomenon manifesting its own peculiar independent significance and value. According to Roman Jakobson literary historians have used everything: "anthropology, psychology, politics,
philosophy. Instead of creating literary scholarship they have
created a conglomeration of home-spun disciplines. They seem to
have forgotten that their essays strayed into related disciplines,
into the history of philosophy, the history of culture, psychology,
etc., and that they could rightly use masterpieces of literature only
as secondary documents." [30] Consequently the representatives of
the new intrinsic method seek to comprehend the poetic work and
its qualities for their own sake. The proper object of the
study of literature is, as Professors Wellek and Warren state, the
literary work itself.[31] This new trend in criticism

> hat noch konsequenter als die Geistesgeschichte mit den Prin-
> zipien des Positivismus gebrochen, insofern sie nach Möglich-
> keit den Künstler und sein Werk von den Mächten des

30. *Novejšaja russkaya poezija,* p. 11, quoted from Lemon and Reiss, p.
107; cf. Heinz Otto Burger, *Gedicht und Gedanke* (Halle, 1942), p. 5; Erich
Auerbach, *Mimesis: Dargestellte Wirklichkeit in der abendländischen Literatur* (Bern, 1946), p. 488.
31. Wellek and Warren, p. 127; W. Kayser, *Die Vortragsreise: Studien zur
Literatur* (Bern, 1960), pp. 60, 61.

Raumes und der Zeit isoliert und die absolute Autonomie der Dichtung proklamiert.[32]

Accordingly from the beginnings in 1902 until the late fifties there is a plea, made with progressively greater emphasis, for a close analysis of a literary work of art in order to determine its artistic values. With equally strong insistence, and often with an uncritical reaction to "historicism," it has demanded that its self-sufficiency be recognized. Thus Roman Jakobson writes in 1921 that poetry is language in its aesthetic function, a remark which Jurij Tynjanov supplements when he asserts:

> The object of that branch of scholarship which claims to explore the nature of art should concern itself precisely with those things which distinguish art from other spheres of activity. Every work of art depends for its existence on a complex interrelationship of numerous factors. The task of the scholar is therefore to determine the specific nature of this interrelationship.[33]

In the same way, Viktor Žirmunskij asserts that "the material of poetry is neither images nor emotions but words. . . . Poetry is a verbal act."[34] Likewise Boris Ejxenbaum felt that the efforts of the Formalists were not directed toward the description of individual works, but toward the construction of a theory and history of literature as a self-contained discipline.[35] In his collection of essays, "About the Theory of Prose," Viktor Šklovskij states that he was concerned with the intrinsic principles of literature.[36] Still further, Ejxenbaum, quoting Jakobson, writes: "If literary scholarship is to become a discipline, then it must make the literary device its only champion, for the object of literary scholarship is

32. *Strömungen und Strebungen der modernen Literaturwissenschaft, Acta Jutlandica* (Copenhagen, Aarhus, 1952), p. 12.

33. *Modern Russian Poetry*, p. 5; quoted from Boris Ejxenbaum, *Aufsätze zur Theorie und Geschichte der Literatur* (Frankfurt/Main, 1965), p. 42 (translation my own).

34. "Zadači poètiki," *Voprosy teorii literatury* (Leningad, 1928), pp. 26–27, quoted from Erlich, p. 174.

35. "Vokrug voprosa o 'formalistax'" ("About the Problem of the 'Formalists'") in *Pečat' i revoljucija* (1924), pp. 5, 10.

36. *O teorii prozy* (Moscow, 1925), p. 6.

not literature but literariness, that is that which makes a given work a work of literature." [37] Literariness refers to the way and manner in which the poet uses his medium, language. In other words, it becomes obvious that the task envisioned by the Formalists was to define the differentia of literature and poetry, and this amounted basically to an attempted distinction between poetic language and other kinds of discourse. Literariness was not discovered in *Erlebnis,* nor in the soul of either the poet or the reader, but only in the work itself. Poetry was regarded as a unique mode of discourse, and one to be distinguished fundamentally from the practical speech of daily life, which was considered to be an amorphous mode of discourse. This distinction was not found in subject matter, i.e. the sphere of reality examined by the poet, but in the mode of presentation, which could be analyzed according to its component parts. The dichotomy of form and content was eliminated. In this respect, both Žirmunskij and Šklovskij attempted to prove the inextricable unity of the "how" and the "what":

> In literary art, the elements of so-called content have no independent existence and are not exempt from the general laws of aesthetic structure; they are a poetic "theme," an artistic "motif" or image, and in this capacity participate in the aesthetic effect to which the work of literature is geared.[38]

Metaphor and poetic image, for example, are only two eminent features which the poet has at his disposal, enabling him to construct a perceptible and compact poetic universe. Both Šklovskij and Jakobson refused to identify poetic language with imagery. For them literature consists of words and therefore is subject to the laws governing language:

> The distinctive feature of poetry lies in the fact that a word is perceived as a word and not merely a proxy for the denoted object or an outburst of an emotion, that words and

37. *Novejšaja russkaya poezija,* p. 11; Ejxenbaum, p. 14; cf. Manfred Kridl, "The Integral Method of Literary Scholarship: Thesis for Discussion," *CL, 3* (Winter 1951), p. 19; Lemon and Reiss, p. 107.

38. Quoted from Erlich, p. 186; Žirmunskij, *Voprosy teorii literatury,* pp. 20–22.

their arrangement, their meaning, their outward and inward form acquire weight and value of their own.[39]

Closely related to this predominant interest in the word is a similar interest in the interplay between phonetics and semantics. A functional type of speech is also realized in poetic language, all of whose components are subordinated to the same constructive principle in order to create a particular aesthetic effect. The device (*priëm*), understood as a conscious technique of "making" a literary work of art—of shaping its material (language) and of modifying its subject matter—became the key concept of the Russian Formalists. A literary work is the unity and sum total of artistic devices. Thus the art of making poetry, literary technology, and the specificity of the artistic object as such provided a much firmer ground on which to move critically than did the psychology and/or biography of the poet, or the often intangible realms of cultural history.[40]

Similar questions, though less systematically asked, were raised by German critics. Even before Oskar Walzel's *Wortkunst*, A. Kober, in the essay "Wesen und Methoden der Literaturwissenschaft," emphasizes that the fundamental task of literary scholarship is the examination of the literary work itself without regard to either author or environment.[41] Such a critical attitude indicated the direction which the intrinsic method was beginning to take in Germany. Despite certain divergences, Oskar Walzel, Fritz Strich, and Leo Spitzer—all strongly influenced by Sievers, Nohl, and Wölfflin—continued this trend which culminated in the influential works of Emil Staiger and Wolfgang Kayser.[42] Unlike

---

39. Erlich, p. 183.

40. Cf. ibid, pp. 171–91; see also Ejxenbaum, pp. 51–52; Lemon and Reiss, pp. 138–39.

41. *GRM,* 7 (1915–19), pp. 115, 116.

42. Oskar Walzel: "Analytische und synthetische Literaturbetrachtung," *GRM* (1910), pp. 257–74, 321–41, reprinted in *Das Wortkunstwerk* (Leipzig, 1926), pp. 3–35; cf. *Gehalt und Gestalt im Kunstwerk des Dichters* (Potsdam, 1923), pp. 182, 280, but "Stilprüfung bleibt unfruchtbar, solange sie nicht bis an das Letzte geht . . . Als letzte und schwerste Aufgabe stellt sich der Anspruch, die Geisteshaltung zu erkennen" (*Euphorion, 32* [1931], 451); Peter Salm, "The Literary Theories of Scherer, Walzel, and Staiger," Unpublished Ph.D. dissertation (Yale University, 1959), p. 85. Fritz Strich:

the numerous interpretative efforts which pay scant attention to
theoretical aspects,[43] the critical ideas of Staiger and Kayser
exemplify the basic procedure and tenets of this method. In this
context Staiger's fundamental concepts of poetics are of little interest since they reach well beyond the framework of the intrinsic
method.[44] They are placed entirely within an anthropological
and existential framework. "Die Poetik," Staiger writes, "ist ein
literaturwissenschaftlicher Beitrag zur philosophischen Anthro-
pologie. Sie zeigt, wie sich die Grundverfassung des Menschen,
die Zeit, in der Sprache und in den verschiedenen Stilmöglich-
keiten erfüllt." [45] There is, however, a rather strange dichotomy
in Staiger's theoretical considerations. On the one hand, he claims
that poetry and literature are a part of philosophical "anthropology," answering in their own way the question of what constitutes the nature of man. On the other hand, there is the sustained effort to do justice both to the essential qualities of a literary work of art and, at least implicitly, to the claim for its autonomy.[46]

"Der lyrische Stil des 17. Jahrhunderts," in *Abhandlungen zur deutschen
Literaturgeschichte,* Franz Muncker dargebracht (Munich, 1916), pp. 21–53.
Leo Spitzer: *Romanische Stil- und Literaturstudien* (2 vols. Marburg, 1931) ;
Stilstudien (2 vols. Munich, 1926, 1960) ; *Classical and Christian Ideas of
World Harmony* (Baltimore, 1963).

43. E.g. *Die deutsche Lyrik,* ed. Benno von Wiese (2 vols. Düsseldorf,
1956) ; Kurt May, "Zu Fragen der Interpretation," *DVLG, 33* (1959), 608–
30; Else Buddeberg, "Möglichkeiten und Grenzen philosophischer Interpretation von Dichtung," *Studium Generale, 7* (1954), 363–71; Paul Böckmann,
"Die Interpretation der literarischen Formensprache," *Formensprache*
(Darmstadt, 1966), 493–511. Much more valuable are Heinrich Lausberg's
Handbuch der literarischen Rhetorik (2 vols. Munich, 1960) and works such
as Wolfgang Babilas' *Tradition und Interpretation, Langue et Parole,* H.I.
(Munich, 1961).

44. Cf. *Grundbegriffe der Poetik* (Bern, 1946).

45. "Lyrik und lyrisch," *Der Deutschunterricht, 2* (1952), p. 12.

46. Thus, when he says in *Die Zeit als Einbildungskraft des Dichters*
(1939; 3rd ed., 1963), p. 11: "was den Literaturhistoriker angeht, ist das
Wort des Dichters, das Wort um seiner selbst willen, nichts was irgendwo
dahinter, darüber oder darunter liegt . . . dass wir begreifen, was uns
ergreift, das ist das eigentliche Ziel der Literaturwissenschaft." Cf. also Kurt
Müller-Vollmer, *Towards a Phenomenological Theory of Literature. A Study
of Wilhelm Dilthey's Poetik, SSGS,* I (The Hague, 1963), p. 40.

The interpretative method advocated by Staiger, somewhat loosely demonstrated in his essay "Das Problem der wissenschaft-lichen Interpretation von Dichtwerken," is primarily a creative act. Interpretation therefore must take its departure from the subjective impressions of the critic:

> Wenn . . . mein Entzücken richtig ist, so müssen alle Einzel-heiten, die ich an einem Gedicht bemerke, zu allen anderen Einzelheiten und damit zum Ganzen stimmen. Was ich über den Versbau sage, muss zu den Gedanken stimmen, der Gedanke zur Syntax und zum Motiv.[47]

Accordingly, Staiger proclaims the stylistic and structural harmony of all the individual elements in the work of art, the unity of the parts with the whole and the whole with the parts. In his critical procedure there is at the beginning an emotional confrontation with the work and at the end understanding. Emotion is the prerequisite for every interpretative act. It must first be questioned, however, whether an emotion is capable of providing a suitable foundation for a critical interpretation. To such objections there is no more response in Staiger's work than there is to questions of value and of the hierarchical order of literary works. In fact, he refuses to consider them.[48] Staiger's sensibility, which has given us many excellent interpretations, tends to outweigh the theoretical substantiation of his critical procedure. Kurt Müller-Vollmer has already referred to this lack of due relation when he writes that "Staiger fails to build a methodological bridge from his own literary analysis to philosophical anthropology. He does not say how the two are connected methodologically and in prac-

47. *Worte und Werke. Bruno Markwardt zum 60. Geburtstag* (Berlin, 1961), pp. 357, 358; see also Staiger's *Goethe* (Zürich, 1952–59), *3*, 478; "Alles echte Verstehen beginnt mit einer noch ganz unreflektierten Teil-habe an dem Rhythmus des Dichters, wir schwingen mit—im ersten Interesse, in wachsender Neigung und Liebe. Und nur indem wir weithin den Rhythmus in uns gewähren lassen, sind wir imstande, auch Bilder, Motive, Ideen im Geiste des Dichters zu würdigen und sein Werk als Kunstgebilde aufzunehmen."

48. *Die Grundbegriffe der Poetik* concludes, "Wom Wert einer Dichtung aber war bis jetzt ausdrücklich nicht die Rede. Eine Poetik, wie sie hier vorliegt, kann keine Wertung begründen" (p. 228).

tice." [49] Likewise, Wolfgang Kayser sought to understand the work of art through itself. More pointedly than ever before in German literary scholarship he emphasized the autonomy of the work of art, which has "Gegenständlichkeit eigener Art": "Eine Dichtung lebt und entsteht nicht als Abglanz von irgend etwas anderem, sondern als ein in sich geschlossenes sprachliches Gefüge." [50] Kayser repeatedly demands the definition of the creative and stylistic elements of poetry and an examination of the subject matter which is not derived from Weltanschauung or Zeitgeist, but from the structural representation of the work. Style, so he advocates, is more than the "how" in the form of language since the "what" is inextricably contained in language. Truth is "die einheitliche Perzeption, unter der eine dichterische Welt steht." [51] Even in his later work, *Die Vortragsreise,* Kayser exhibits this attitude:

> Im Fall der Werkinterpretation handelt es sich also darum, alle an der Gestaltung zur einheitlichen Gestalt beteiligten Formelemente in ihrer Wirksamkeit und in ihrem Zusammenwirken zu begreifen: von der äusseren Form, Klang, Rhythmus, Wort, Wortschatz, sprachlichen Figuren, Syntax, Geschehnissen, Motiven, Symbolen, Gestalten zu Ideen und Gehalt, Aufbau, Perspektive, Erzählweise, Atmosphäre . . . und was sich an Gestaltungsmitteln erfassen lässt.[52]

His attempt to define the mode of existence and the autonomy of the literary work of art is in this respect often reminiscent of the efforts of the Russian Formalists.

Similar expressions are to be found with the New Critics and, at the beginning of the fifties, with the Neo-Aristotelians in Chicago. The New Criticism as formalism, organicism, and literary analysis received its impetus from S. T. Coleridge, T. E. Hulme, T. S. Eliot, and I. A. Richards. Their insights and theories, especially those of the latter two, developed into the mainstream of what goes by the name of New Criticism. Both Eliot's theory of imagination, his concept of the creative act, his discussion of the objec-

49. Müller-Vollmer, p. 40.
50. Kayser, *Kunstwerk,* pp. 14, 5.
51. Ibid., pp. 57 ff., 83 ff., 101 ff., 154 ff., 271 ff., 331 ff.
52. *Die Vortragsreise,* p. 46.

tive correlative, and Richards' antithetic position stressing a thera-
peutic theory of poetry, his interest in the effect of poetry on the
mind and the soul of the reader, along with his valuable text-
analytical and semantic contributions,[53] led to a kind of formalistic literary criticism based predominantly on the nature and
function of words and language. The New Critics (J. C. Ransom,
Allan Tate, Cleanth Brooks, R. P. Warren, and others) take an
organic approach to poetry when they discuss the literary work of
art as an aesthetic object. Ransom calls for an ontological criticism
with epistemological overtones, envisioning a criticism which discusses the poem as an object possessing an autonomous, self-
contained mode of existence:

> I suggest that the differentia of poetry as a discourse is an
> ontological one. It treats an order of existence, a grade of
> objectivity, which cannot be treated in scientific discourse.
> . . . Poetry intends to recover the denser and more refractory
> original world which we know loosely through our percep-
> tions and memories. By this supposition it is a kind of knowl-
> edge which is radically or ontologically different.[54]

Hence the literary work is comprehended as an ontological structure, as "cognitive fact." The critic ought to regard the work as
nothing short of a desperate ontological or metaphysical ma-
neuver.[55]

Almost all the New Critics base their analyses of literary works
on two assumptions. First, that on the level of language a distinction must be made between science and poetry. Scientific language
possesses an unambiguously semantic function to the extent that
the sign and the object for which it stands have as close a one-to-
one relationship to each other as possible. In other words, it is, as
I. A. Richards said, referential in character. Poetic language is
quite another thing. It receives its sanction primarily from the
syntactic function and verbal complexities of language. The words
themselves and the context which they shape, and which in turn

53. Cf. *Principles of Literary Criticism* (London, 1925), esp. pp. 11–18,
107–33; *Practical Criticism* (New York, 1929).
54. *The New Criticism* (Norfolk, Conn., 1941), pp. 279–81.
55. *The World's Body* (New York, 1938), p. 347.

shapes them, lack the precise purposefulness of scientific discourse. Almost unanimously these critics assert that, while the words of a literary work of art considered individually may function referentially, the poetic structure of words considered intrinsically or contextually prevents the individual word from so functioning. Secondly, that the work of art is autonomous and has an independent existence. Thus, poetic discourse does not point anywhere but to itself. These assumptions determine the method and the goal of almost every interpretative effort. The formalist critic tries, as Cleanth Brooks points out, "to find a central point of reference from which he can focus upon the structure of the poem or the novel." [56] Ransom considers the central point of reference to be "structure" and "texture"; Cleanth Brooks, "irony" and "paradox"; and Tate, "extension" and "intension." [57] Thus the job of the critic is the description and the evaluation of a poetical work. It is primarily a question of uncovering the unity which is inherent in a work of art, and demonstrating to what extent the relationship of the various parts to each other contribute to the achievement of the whole. Form and content cannot be separated in a successful work. Form *is* meaning. Poetry is ultimately symbolic and metaphoric. Principles of criticism define those areas suitable for literary scholarship; however, they do not determine the method which would be obligatory for this scholarship.

It must now be obvious that I have no personal quarrel with the intrinsic method as such. In fact, I approve of the fundamental assumptions from which this method proceeds, namely, that the proper object of literary criticism is the work itself. The concern with the poem as artifact, as an object with its own structure and mode of existence, was largely responsible for a new and wholesome impetus to the study of literature. Undoubtedly these critics have added immensely to our knowledge of the many aspects of the poem and of the aesthetic process. They have advanced the

56. *Kenyon Review, 13* (1951), 75.

57. "Criticism as Pure Speculation," *The Intent of the Critic,* ed. D. A. Stauffer (Princeton, 1941), pp. 110–11; *The Well Wrought Urn: Studies in the Structure of Poetry* (New York, 1947), pp. 176–96, 226–38; "Tension in Poetry," *On the Limits of Poetry* (New York, 1948), pp. 75–90, 16–48, 115–28; also Robert Penn Warren, "Pure and Impure Poetry," *Kenyon Review,* 5 (1943), 228–54.

cause of literature to such an extent that Roman Ingarden's statement in 1927 no longer holds true today.

> In den literaturwissenschaftlichen Werken bedeutender Schriftsteller finden wir sogar gewöhnlich keine *klar gestellte* Frage nach dem Wesen des literarischen Werkes überhaupt, als ob es sich um eine allen bekannte und ganz unwichtige Angelegenheit handelte. Und wenn man auch hie und da diese Frage aufwirft, so ist sie von vorneherein mit verschiedenen, sachlich damit nicht zusammenhängenden Problemen und Voraussetzungen verwickelt, die ihre sachgemässe Beantwortung unmöglich machen. Während aber die zentrale Frage nicht gestellt wird, beschäftigt man sich eifrig mit verschiedenen speziellen Problemen die—so interessant sie an sich sind—sich nie restlos lösen lassen, wenn man über das Wesen des literarischen Werkes überhaupt im unklaren bleibt.[58]

And yet, despite the repeated assertion that the poem is, in a sense, an autotelic phenomenon, there are here still disturbing methodological and philosophical weaknesses, as is indicated by a general awareness of the ultimate failure of this approach. Some of its insufficiencies have often been mentioned: its lack of interest in either literary history or genre theory, for example; its inappropriateness for older poetry; and its inability to distinguish between value and evaluation. "Applied to drama," writes R. P. Blackmur in "A Burden for Critics," "it is as disfiguring as it is to the late seventeenth- and all the eighteenth-century poetry." [59] No doubt, some of these inadequacies partly account for the increasing dissatisfaction.

Perhaps most disconcerting is the failure to treat adequately the problems of value and also that of the hierarchical order among literary works. To my knowledge, virtually none of the critics adhering to the intrinsic method has ever examined thoroughly and systematically these two basic questions.[60] Particularly dis-

---

58. *Das literarische Kunstwerk* (3rd ed. Tübingen, 1965), pp. 1–3.

59. *Essays in Modern Literary Criticism,* ed. Ray B. West (New York and Toronto, 1952), p. 162.

60. "Ich erbitte Auskunft," writes Peter Demetz, "welche bedeutenden germanistischen Publikationen der letzten dreissig oder fünfzig Jahre darauf

turbing is the manifest uncertainty about the reality of a literary
work; in other words, its ontological status. Statements that the
work of art "leads an independent life," or that it lives "als solches
und in sich," and the fact that John Crowe Ransom pleads for an
ontological criticism, that Viktor Šklovskij tries to define "pure
form"—all this testifies to a willingness to come to terms with this
problem.[61] Unfortunately, however, these attempts lack a sound
philosophical basis. "It is very well to say," writes Kurt Müller-
Vollmer,

> that the work of art is "a whole system of signs" or *"das Gefüge
> einer Ganzheit"* consisting of various layers or "strata" extend-
> ing all the way from the "sound-stratum," the "units of mean-
> ing" in single expressions, to images and metaphors and finally
> to the "world" which is evoked in the reader or listener by the
> poem's "system of symbols". But can the reality of a work ac-
> tually be grasped by thus projecting it on to the one dimen-
> sional plane of such "intrinsic" analysis? Does the work of art
> represent such a closed and isolated "world of its own" which
> exists by virtue of its "poetic language"? Do not the "sym-
> bols" and "signs" which constitute the work point at some-
> thing that transcends the pure "giveness," the tangible struc-

erpicht gewesen wären, sich vor allem mit der Qualität der Literatur zu
beschäftigen, oder gar die Kühnheit besessen hätten, zwischen guten, mäs-
sigen und schlechten Werken der klassischen und romantischen Tradition zu
unterscheiden" (*Die Zeit* [Dec. 13, 1963]). Apart from Wolfgang Kayser's
superficial and inconclusive essay, "Literarische Wertung und Interpretation," *Der Deutschunterricht* (1952), pp. 13–27, there is only Hans Egon
Hass' significant study on "Das Problem der literarischen Wertung,"
Studium Generale, 12 (1959), 727–56, and just recently Wilhelm Emrich's
"Das Problem der Wertung und Rangordnung literarischer Werke," in *Geist
und Widergeist* (Frankfurt/Main, 1965), pp. 9–29; Eliseo Vivas, perhaps
more than any other modern American critic, with the exception of Murray
Krieger, offers us the most thorough and extensive discussion of the question
of value (see, for example, *Creation and Discovery. Essays in Criticism and
Aesthetics* [New York, 1955], pp. 81–82, 142–43, 195, 199, 201, 251, etc.); see
also Roman Ingarden's recent "Werte, Normen, und Strukturen nach René
Wellek," *DVLG, 40* (1966), 43–55, and his "Vorrede zur dritten Auflage,"
Das literarische Kunstwerk, pp. 19–204.

61. Wellek and Warren, p. 157; Kayser, *Kunstwerk,* p. 388; see Erlich,
chap. 5.

ture or *Gestalt* of the work? For how could we otherwise understand what the "units of meaning" in a literary work refer to? The answer which the "intrinsic" critic is ready to give, that these meanings mean nothing but the poetic world of the literary world itself, does not seem very satisfactory to us. For how can we understand a poetic world at all without relating it to the world which we know? [62]

Here the inadequacies of the intrinsic method are succinctly summarized. Murray Krieger, although more favorably inclined to the intrinsic method, has already elaborated a similar position.[63] In other words, the intrinsic method is based upon the assumption that the poetic complexities of words are self-contained and that these words, since they seem to derive meaning only from their use within the work, appear to exclude referential discourse. Therefore, the verbal structure is allegedly incapable of referring to anything beyond the realm of the work. This establishes of necessity, in the opinion of the majority of the intrinsic critics, the literary work's autonomy. However, if the verbal structure is not in any evident sense referential, if indeed it is actually autonomous and completely self-contained, how then can a literary work tell us something about the world? Furthermore, in view of the essentially referential character of language, how can any cognitive value be attributed to the work of art? Where is the reconciliation between the claim for autonomy and the cognitive value of the poem to be found? If, however, both words and language have referential character, which they must in order to establish any discourse whatsoever—be it poetic, scientific, or any other—in what way is poetry able to substantiate its claim to tell us something about the world which could not be learned from any other mode of discourse?

These are some of the essential questions which must be answered before the intrinsic method can recover its effectiveness, if indeed it can. If it is to be rescued from its stagnation, a body of principles must be formulated; the critic must start from an assumption which will be valid not only for the intrinsic method

62. Müller-Vollmer, pp. 80–81.
63. *The New Apologists for Poetry*, esp. pp. 3–30, 156–66, 182–201.

but for all critical endeavors. This, however, would mean that these principles should do full justice to each critical trend. They should, indeed they must, encompass definitively the truth which is contained in each critical method and exclude everything which is irrelevant to the proper study of literature. In such fashion a system could be established in which every critic would find those aspects reconfirmed which he had correctly perceived. In order to achieve this, the new efforts must assume a direction contrary to that in which the majority of critics, contentedly and complacently, are accustomed to move. These principles must be articulated in assertions which will prove to be irrefutable. The statements must be able to withstand the most exacting scrutiny by all those who are seriously concerned with literature as a discipline. This again would mean that the most general aspects to which literary criticism has adhered must now become the most particular. The most general in turn, which is to become the most particular, would be precisely the effort to come to terms with the ontological status of the literary work of art. It is absolutely necessary to clarify exactly what constitutes its mode of being.[64] This, it seems to me, is at present the most burning question. It can only be answered through the realization that the literary work of art exists essentially within the triad of poet, work, and reader. Such an assumption must be the starting point of any critical effort.

Since the literary work exists only within this ontological relationship, it is not an object like a chair (which will remain a chair whether one recognizes or makes use of it as such). The work forever remains essentially dependent upon its comprehension by a reader. Only through such an act of concretization (*Konkretisation* according to Roman Ingarden) does it become an aesthetic object.

64. René Wellek was one of the first scholars to recognize the necessity of providing the intrinsic approach with a theoretical basis. It is significant in this respect to note that the first chapter of that section of *Theory of Literature* devoted to the "intrinsic study of literature" is titled "The Mode of Existence of a Literary Work of Art." Wellek was also fully aware of the difficulties involved in this task: "To deal with matter properly we should have to settle such controversies as those of nominalism versus realism, mentalism versus behaviorism—in short, all the chief problems of epistemology" (p. 141).

This idea is not essentially new. The intrinsic critic, however, must be acutely aware of the undeniable fact that the poem exists only within this ontological framework with all its numerous and significant implications. The transcendental basis of this framework is the creative power of the imagination, which is surely the most mysterious of human activities. It yields the key to the understanding of a literary work, of its mode of existence, and perhaps of the creative process itself.

In view of his present dilemma the intrinsic critic must, if his method is to prevail, confront this basic ontological fact. He will have to ask himself again, indeed, far more thoroughly and systematically than ever, what distinguishes the mind of the poet and, correspondingly, that of his reader? What is the nature of the act which has its issue in the literary work of art, and what is the character of the process which results in our understanding of it? By this I do not mean to advocate a return to the outdated and rather irrelevant psychological and biographical studies of the past. Instead I would insist upon a new inquiry into the function of the poetic imagination a more complete appreciation of its significant role in the critical process. More clearly than ever before, one must reexamine the criteria which demonstrate just how independent the poetic imagination is from the laws of reality. Further, one must investigate in what manner and to what extent the knowledge conveyed by the poetic imagination can be differentiated from that provided by science, religion, or ethics.[65] The critic must ask himself, and again in a rigorously disciplined manner, just how the poet is able to articulate an experience through the faculty of imagination and in the medium of language. Only then can the critic pose the prime question: how is the artist able to create a unified structure, an articulated entity which conveys meaning that necessarily, owing to the inherent nature of language, reaches beyond the so-called autonomous body of the work itself. Any critic who today still pretends to approach the

65. See, for instance, Kurt Müller-Vollmer's able and penetrating interpretation in his book *Die Dichtungstheorie Wilhelm von Humboldts* (Stuttgart, 1967), where there is a most convincing analysis of Humboldt's concept of the imagination which, going beyond that of Goethe or the Schlegels, entails far-reaching consequences for modern poetic theories.

poem intrinsically without being aware of the linguistic problems involved will certainly fail to come to terms with the peculiar nature of the literary work of art. Its meaning cannot be grasped without reference to something which lies outside the work itself. The relations between the word in literature and its referent in the world of experience are actually much more complex than most critics have assumed. Discussions of the problems involved in this relationship have, for the most part, been sadly lacking in discipline. The often arbitrary distinction between poetic and scientific language, for instance; the differentiation between the aesthetic mode and other modes of discourse, however involved this differentiation might be; or the assertion that the literary work is so constructed as not to allow the mind of the reader to stray beyond its self-sufficient confines: all these critical positions seem to be too facile, and yet to be properly substantiated. Due to the very nature of language the literary work must, for its content, appeal beyond itself to relevant ontological meanings and values. Its aesthetic meaning necessarily derives from nonaesthetic sources.

Thus it is not only the functioning of the imagination but also, and perhaps most importantly, the problem of the nature of language which must be investigated anew. This investigation should undoubtedly take into consideration the latest achievements in the field of linguistics. All this, however, means that the problem of understanding, of hermeneutics, must also be reexamined. Textual analysis as developed by biblical exegesis, jurisprudence, and classical philology should now be clarified epistemologically. The question which a new hermeneutics would have to answer within the ontological frame of reference already mentioned is "how can a critic communicate, in terms that are universally valid, the result of an act of comprehension which can be realized only individually and subjectively?" This task raises still other fundamental problems: the question of communicable articulation of intellectual phenomena [*Objektivation des Geistes*], the question of meaningful forms in general and of poetic forms in particular. A literary theory which explores these problems must take into account the contributions other disciplines have recently made to the general study of hermeneutics.[66] It should also pay more attention to one of the most significant books of the last thirty years, Roman Ingarden's *Das literarische Kunstwerk,* a treatise which deals specifically with both the structure and the ontological status of the literary work of art.[67]

Such a more comprehensive concept of literary criticism, sketched here only tentatively, could perhaps produce a genuine and useful theoretical basis and quite possibly even an epistemology of language and literature, on the strength of which a formally respectable discipline of literature could be established. From such a concept there could be developed a critical method which would not be prohibitively dogmatic, and which in its flexibility would permit the exploration of the various aspects of the literary work itself. If one posits an honest wish for rational correction of judgment and a desire to arrive at a multidimensional understanding, then the complex problems occasioned by the particular relationship of poet-work-reader could be systematically examined in the light of their peculiar interdependence. This could then be done not from "without," as has been the practice, but from "within." Such a critical attitude could lead to a recognition of the true nature of aesthetic and, specifically, of linguistic and poetic phenomena. Any attempt to present a philosophical exposition of the intrinsic method has remained, with a few exceptions, either too contradictory or too vague. A clarification is urgently needed, a clarification which has as its point of departure a theory of understanding and considers the conditions under which the mind confronts reality. And, such a theory of understanding must con-

---

66. E.g. Hans-Georg Gadamer, *Wahrheit und Methode* (2nd ed. Tübingen, 1965); Emilio Betti, "Zur Grundlegung einer allgemeinen Auslegungslehre," *Festschrift für Ernst Rabel,* II (Tübingen, 1954), 79–168, *Teoria generale dell'interpretazione* (1955), and *Die Hermeneutik als allgemeine Methodik der Geisteswissenschaften, Philosophie und Geschichte,* 78/79 (Tübingen, 1962).

67. The work is almost unknown in both America and France; in Germany, where recently the third edition appeared, most critics and literary scholars know its content, indeed if at all, from Günther Müller's essay "Über die Seinsweise der Dichtung," *DVLG, 17* (1939), 137–53; an exception is Hans Egon Hass' "Das Problem der literarischen Wertung," pp. 727–56.

sist, phenomenologically, of a thorough analysis of the mind's fundamental modes of action and of the types of products through which it finds expression in the realm of literature. By preserving the "formalistic" achievements of the intrinsic method, while at the same time taking into consideration the hermeneutic achievements of the past and of the present, a viable critical method could be articulated. It would then no longer be necessary to make an apology for literature as a discipline.

Lowry Nelson, Jr.

The Fictive Reader and Literary Self-Reflexiveness

If it be taken as hypothesis that any work of literary art is in some way a communication—that is, making common or mutual an aesthetic experience—then not only the author's intentions and actual performance, not only the objective text to be interpreted and judged from age to age, but also the reader, to whom the communication is directed, can become in his individuality as well as commonality an accomplice or collaborator in the whole process. It is of course the reader's contractual duty in the very act of reading to assume provisionally a fictive role, not as outsider but as accomplice, communicant, collaborator, or willing suspender of disbelief. Coleridge's formulation here alluded to may seem merely negative or indulgent as a suspension of truth, reality, and common sense. Obviously one cannot wholly exist in a fictional world and cope with actual quotidian needs. Yet in accepting and evaluating an artistic communication the reader must dispose himself to the special and indeed prescriptive demands of a fictional world which in a truly aesthetic sense patterns his impulses deriving from his own experience of real life and also from his notions of what another real life might or could be. Given and having accepted his role, the reader must to some extent be drawn into the fiction as if it were true, as if it were entirely normative, as if it were for the time his full commitment. To what extent the suspension of disbelief is willing would depend naturally on experience, disposition, and what might be called aesthetic ambivalence, that is, the ability of mind to be actor and self-observer, participant and judge, at one and the same time.

We realize that the observer is himself observed in advance, that the reader is aware of being guided and manipulated by the text which he must both accept and eventually judge, that the fictionality could well, by analogy to real life, be otherwise; nonetheless, as readers we willingly enter into an imagined cosmos not properly as escapists or dupes but as provisional believers and hopeful collaborators; we enter into the world of the "as if," the simulacrum of reality, the self-aware questioners of what reality is.

It is still a puzzling question as to what Aristotle meant by "mimesis." We can, however, be quite sure that he was intrigued by the central question of what the relation could possibly be between story or myth and, on the other hand, exact truth or historicity. He must in fact have felt some of the same ambivalence, or even embarrassment, as his master Plato. Yet he did have the sort of mind to venture upon resolving dubieties into categories and syllogisms, as means of taxonomic observation and seeming certitude. One of his central conceptions is of course a dramatic involvement of the audience or readership in a "purgative" experience during the actual performance or, by analogy and extension, reading. Originally and properly the experience of ancient as well as modern drama was time-bound, both visual and aural, immediate in ways that are distinguishable from the experience of later poetry and narrative. In modern terms the *reader*, while experiencing in time, can return, dwell at leisure, skip, or otherwise manipulate the flow or sequence of discourse. He has then a certain control over the rate or flow of his own aesthetic experience, at least when reading printed texts. Horace, in his *Epistula ad Pisones*, comes closer to common modern assumptions that blur the distinction between spectator and reader, between dramatic and literary critic, though indeed the notion of the play as poem need not be programmatically rejected as irrelevant even to the current notion of the "living theater." If, in regard to the involvement of the literary communicant, Horace's criterion of applause be taken as a sign of artistic success or accomplishment, then of course a false democracy of approval by poll-count usurps the right of spectator and reader to argue the premises of their response and judgment. Involvement of the reader or spectator as accomplices or collaborators is essential in the curious situation of artistic communication. Any categorical notion of the "active" writer and the "passive" reader, conceived as entirely independent roles, would of course contravene the *contrat littéraire* between communicator and communicant, creator and collaborator, perpetrator and accomplice.

Such reflections are not essentially novel, in that essential novelty is rare in literary criticism. Yet one may argue that matters of systematic aesthetic constructions, with their play of emphasis and inventiveness in conceptualization, are at least relatively of the essence. In *Baroque Lyric Poetry* (New Haven, 1961) I have written of what I called the rhetorical situation: the interaction or collaboration of the speaker, the person or object addressed or presented, and the reader. By way of emphasis, if not novelty, I should like to stress the role of the reader as accomplice (literally after the fact) whose responses are written into the literary work itself which then becomes normative for any individual performance. Each work requires in its integrity what I would call by way of emphasis an *optimum* reader, initially well disposed, fully competent in "historical semantics," in the sense Leo Spitzer gave the phrase, and free from irrelevant associations of the sort I. A. Richards exposed and analyzed. These would be some of the basic qualifications of the optimum reader. His role is as ambivalent as that of a dramatic actor in being both performer aware of his real self and collaborator within the fiction. In seeming contrast to the fictive reader is the fact that in many works of literature one finds an inward-turning self-reflexiveness: the poem commenting on itself, first in the process of composition and then in the reading or performance of it. Yet one may argue that both the fictive role of the reader and the self-reflexiveness of the work have in common a playing with the reality of the fiction or, more strongly, the exposure of the fiction to the end, paradoxically, of reinforcing it.

Of the many ways in which the reader is granted his fictive role, perhaps the most elementary is the direct address to him, for instance by conventional dedication, as in Ariosto's apostrophe to Ippolito d'Este at the beginning of *Orlando Furioso* or Cervantes' Prologues to the "desocupado lector" in Part One and to the "lector ilustre" in Part Two. A further elementary and obvious means of reminding the reader of his role is direct mention of him within the fictional body of the work: here examples are numerous from Cervantes to Henry James. Fielding's *Tom Jones* is a particu-

larly rich instance. The novel is conceived as a direct dialogue
between narrator and reader as collaborators in observing actions
of the characters within the "true" fiction. Not only the inter-
calated chapters of discursive commentary and speculation, and
the occasional exposure of the puppets' strings, but also the direct
address to the reader ("my reader may please to remember") contribute to a fictional collaboration expressed in the first-person
singular and plural. Other, indeed many other, examples come
readily to mind.

Involvement of the reader in the fiction by such elementary
means can obviously serve to heighten the "truth" of the fiction
provided the fiction is skillful enough to draw the reader into his
fictive role and create for him a successful ambivalence between
his real and fictionally disposed self. One of the most effective uses,
on a more complex level, of the address to the reader is found in
the first of Baudelaire's *Les fleurs du mal,* "Au lecteur." As the
poem begins, and continuing almost to the end, we find no direct
address, only a pervasive reference to the first-person plural:

> La sottise, l'erreur, le péché, la lésine,
> Occupent nos esprits et travaillent nos corps,
> Et nous alimentons nos aimables remords,
> Comme les mendiants nourrissent leur vermine.

The reader is drawn into the poem at least provisionally and col-
laborates with it in an equilibrium of aesthetic ambivalence. Yet
in the second to the last stanza and the first two lines of the last he
is given, as it were, some respite: even though there is reference
immediately before to "la ménagerie infâme de nos vices," no
direct use of the first-person plural is made.

> Il en est un plus laid, plus méchant, plus immonde!
> Quoiqu'il ne pousse ni grands gestes ni grands cris,
> Il ferait volontiers de la terre un débris
> Et dans un bâillement avalerait le monde;

> C'est l'Ennui!—l'œil chargé d'un pleur involontaire,
> Il rêve d'échafauds en fumant son houka.

In the last two lines of the poem, however, something sudden, direct, and even shocking occurs: a frontal implication and accusation of the reader as accomplice, as exposed fellow sinner and sufferer:

> Tu le connais, lecteur, ce monstre délicat,
> —Hypocrite lecteur,—mon semblable,—mon frère!

It amounts almost to an unmasking of the reader's balanced ambivalence. The unexpected direct address in the intimate form of the second-person singular implicates him much more deeply in what has gone on before; his acquiescence, provisional until now, becomes a heightening of his involvement and an aesthetically necessary complicity with the speaker of the poem.

In such terms, as well as others, can be explained the force of those lines. That the last line should become for T. S. Eliot an Arnoldian "touchstone" in *The Waste Land* is not surprising. Still, the point must be emphasized that the line derives its force from the poem sequentially read or performed—in commoner terms, from the total context. Matthew Arnold's notion of the touchstone has of course been criticized before, most eloquently by Robert Penn Warren in his essay "Pure and Impure Poetry." Yet in defense of Arnold and certainly of Eliot one should perhaps assume that the single lines culled from this or that masterpiece are meant to evoke their total setting. Here it is the task of the reader to be or to make himself optimum. The allusions in the poetry of Eliot have provided a reading list for generations of readers who then can reread with more awareness and less bafflement and finally proceed to inherit their heritage and expect enriched futures in the future.

It is a descent from the eloquence, control, and "dramaticality" of Baudelaire's poem, yet as a further instance, perhaps a limiting one, of the role of the fictive reader it might be useful to consider a poem often derided, Wordsworth's "The Thorn." It is a work that was harshly treated not only by Francis Jeffrey in his essay "Crabbe's Poems" (1808), but also by Coleridge in Chapter XVII of *Biographia Literaria* (1817). Their strictures are of interest in this context. To quote Jeffrey, who is parodying Wordsworth's

somewhat defensive description of the speaker of his poem as a retired sea captain living on an annuity in "some village or country
town, of which he was not a native, or in which he had not been
accustomed to live": "Of this piece the reader will necessarily
form a very erroneous judgment unless he is apprised that it was
written by a pale man in a green coat—sitting cross-legged on an
oaken stool—with a scratch on his nose, and a spelling dictionary
on the table." Coleridge, giving qualified exception to the Nurse
in *Romeo and Juliet,* notes that "it is not possible to imitate truly
a dull and garrulous discourser, without repeating the effects of
dullness and garrulity." Yet he does go on to commend certain
passages of the poem, while compromising his commendation by
writing that with the exception of certain passages others "are felt
by many unprejudiced and unsophisticated hearts, as sudden and
unpleasant sinkings from the height to which the poet had previously lifted them, and to which he again re-elevates both himself
and his reader." Perhaps a casual passage in Dorothy Wordsworth's
Grasmere Journal (1801), though written of course after the
poem, can provide a general and mitigating clue. She attempts at
one point to reproduce the accent of a local native girl: "She says:
'ye may say what ye will, but there's naething like a gay auld man
for behaving weel to a young wife. Ye may laugh, but this wind
blows no [favour] and where there's no love there's no favour.'"
Are we not then confronted in "The Thorn" with an essentially
dialectal monologue produced in standard English form? Robert
Burns faced the artistic dilemma by resolving it both ways, by
standard and by dialectal spelling, as well as by both ways in the
same poem (e.g. "The Cotter's Saturday Night"). The problem of
the fictive reader, then, is to gauge his responsibility in reading or,
better, performing such poetry as "The Thorn."

It would be indeed troublesome to defend "The Thorn" as a
successful poem. Nonetheless, if granted its proper hearing by the
performing reader, it could undefensively be regarded as portraying the dramatically garrulous maundering of a simple man who,
like the Ancient Mariner, recites his obsessive experience. It is a
revealing contrast to attempt first to read the poem aloud in a
North Country accent and then in standard literate speech,
whether English or American. The latter rendition can easily

evoke derisory mirth and quick critical dismissal. But the former may well have the effect of reinforcing the reader's admiration for Wordsworth's artistic integrity even in so mediocre an example of his art. The third stanza may serve as a tryout:

> High on a mountain's highest ridge,
> Where oft the stormy winter gale
> Cuts like a scythe, while through the clouds
> It sweeps from vale to vale;
> Not five yards from the mountain path,
> This Thorn you on your left espy;
> And to the left, three yards beyond,
> You see a little muddy Pond
> Of water never dry;
> I've measured it from side to side:
> 'Tis three feet long, and two feet wide.

Though this is perhaps the most banal stanza of the poem, one might hope that a dialectal performance might help to quell the qualms not only of Wordsworth's admirers, but also of ready scoffers. It is not a matter of renouncing critical evaluation; it is a matter of fair and normative performance inherent in the text and justified historically. The author's imperfect intentions are not so much at stake as the imaginative and historically grounded awareness of the reader-performer who should be *optimus inter impares*. True, "The Thorn" is something of a limiting case, and any defense of it need not extend in principle to "The Idiot Boy" or to the tediously short and insipid "We are Seven." Yet the fictive reader's role surely demands first sympathetic and imaginative understanding, then "ambivalent" involvement, and finally the valid critical evaluation that is the reader's ultimate duty. A poem conceived as dramatic monologue should perhaps supply to the reader the sorts of direction common in musical compositions. There are very few among all who know the tune of the first aria in Handel's *Xerxes* (commonly known as the "Largo") who are also acquainted with the words and the condition of the king awakening from a Persian bout of drunkenness.

Special roles are assigned the fictive reader in the first-person novel and in the epistolary novel as well. To take the former first, let us assume that there is a gamut running from a novel like *The Brothers Karamazov* to *Lazarillo de Tormes*. It may come as a surprise to someone with a more or less distant recollection of his last reading of Dostoevsky's novel that it is, however faintly, cast as a first-person narrative. Yet in the very first sentence both the first-person singular and the first-person plural appear to the end of establishing the almost confessional veracity of the narrative about to unfold. The narrator thus identifies himself as a local witness of the notorious events that occurred in his native village: we are thus prepared for a full account from his point of observation. But soon the first-person observer dissolves into the narrative "we" of the omniscient narrator who is privileged to know what goes on in the secret minds of the characters he is creating: the single outside observer almost imperceptibly melts into the all-knowing narrator, only rarely to reemerge in his role as local witness, particularly, as it happens, at the trial where he is "realistically" able to describe the atmosphere, the jurymen, and the behavior of those in the courtroom audience and those called to the witness stand. He manages also, with no little embarrassment, to reveal to us the name of his village: Skotoprigonevsk, meaning something like a "stockyard." The first-person witness, then, is a latent resource whose usefulness is apparent and whose inconsistent presence is attenuated by the overwhelmingly vivid presentation of the omniscient narrator.

Still within the technique of the first-person novel we may consider toward the other end of the gamut *Lazarillo de Tormes*, that flawed but primordial exemplar of the picaresque novel. To begin with, there is the usual conventional or, most likely, parodistic prologue which ends in a supplicatory dedication to an unnamed man of wealth and of course a potential patron. What follows are seven chapters ("tratados") of unequal length and fictional merit. Though the novel is purportedly addressed to the hoped-for patron, it is of course the optimum reader who is called upon to allow himself to enter into the fiction presented as a confessional first-person narrative. The reader encounters a world of cruelty and uncertainty enhanced by squalid atmosphere and crude humor. Finally Lazarillo, whose vicissitudes could become so repetitive as to try the patience of the most willingly fictive reader, accepts the offer of the archpriest of San Salvador to marry one of his servant girls. Up to this point the autobiographical narrative has placed no particular strain on the reader's direct collaboration: everything has seemed straightforward and consistent in presentation. But then Lázaro, as he is now known, learns from "evil tongues" or "friends" that his wife has continued to frequent the house of the archpriest and that she had allegedly given birth three times before marrying him. Still he accepts the professions of innocence both from the archpriest and from his wife. If anyone thereafter should allude to the matter, he would say: "Look, if you're my friend, say nothing that would make me suffer, since I hold no one my friend who makes me suffer. . . . Why, I'll swear by the consecrated Host that she is as good a woman as lives within the gates of Toledo. Whoever would say anything else, I'll fight him to the death. And so they say nothing to me and I have peace in my house." What is the fictive reader, having faithfully followed the fictional veracity of the first-person narrator, to make of this? He is now on his own and left balancing the evidence as given and evaluated by his first-person fictional collaborator, who happens under the circumstances to be his only source.

Similar situations occur throughout the tradition of the picaresque novel. In the Simplicissimus cycle of Grimmelshausen most of the main characters are self-servers or dupes whose actions are presented either with authorial "objectivity" or with first-person self-defensiveness. It is often left to the knowing reader who is cast as a scamp drawn into the fiction to play his provisional role while, at the same time, reserving and accumulating his brief for an elusive final judgment. Daniel Defoe, in *Moll Flanders,* confronts the fictive reader with a first-person account of a life of crime (whoredom, theft, incest, and canny calculation) which ends, according to Moll, in marriage, respectability, and repentance. Having one witness, Moll herself, how are we to take this? Though it may seem a moot matter, I would suggest that Moll is again self-serving and self-defensive, that she enacts a parody of sincere confessionalism common enough in the Christian era, in particular in Defoe's own time and country, and that her affluent and agreeable settlement at the end represents a gilded conscience and self-satisfaction which cause the sympathetic reader, duped or ambivalently fictive, deep doubts concerning her veracity about herself and the validity of what might be called her final smugness. The fictive reader may seem to be left hanging in a limbo of irony created by the author behind the scenes and his first-person narrator who gives us all the surface *données*. Toward the end of the novel Moll, amid her protestations of repentance, declares: "I could fill a larger history than this with the evidences of this truth [that is, her husband's repentance], and but [*sic*] that I doubt that part of the story will not be equally diverting as the wicked part." It seems to me that here, as elsewhere in the novel, there exists a sort of contractual understanding between author and reader that transcends the self-knowledge of Moll and the fictional sincerity, as she nears the age of seventy, of her remorse. At all events, the fictive reader is cast in the role of wary rather than gullible witness and participant.

The fictive reader's role is even more complex in the epistolary novel. In Richardson's novels, Choderlos de Laclos' *Les Liaisons dangereuses,* and Smollett's *Humphrey Clinker*—to name a few notable examples—it is the reader who must weigh and adjudicate the motives and veracity of the fictional writer or writers of the letters. The result is a deep involvement of the reader as, so to say, reconstructive historian in accepting his commitment as fictive collaborator with the author. A particularly suggestive instance of the epistolary form of fiction is Goethe's *Die Leiden des jungen Werther*. About two-thirds of the novel consists of letters sent to Werther's intimate friend Wilhelm to whom he tells all: by the all-pervasive and unself-serving mode of sincerity and confidence the reader in his fictive role is bound to accept the veracity of Werther's sufferings. One might be tempted to say that distance lends sincerity, in the sense that Werther shows he has nothing to hide and everything, from is point of view, to confide. The essential theme of distance and fictional sincerity is asserted in the very first sentence of the epistolary part of the novel: "Wie froh bin ich, dass ich weg bin!" His letters to Wilhelm, as well as to Albert and Lotte, and also his intimate diary confirm the fictional necessity of the reader's accepting what is vouchsafed him as the authentic and unquestionable truth of the protagonist. It is a duty of the reader to learn and fictively embrace the code of feeling in any work of any age by the contractual exercise of his historical imagination—the reader being properly as much of a chameleon, in Keats' sense, as the author himself. Throughout *Werther* we are induced to dwell in a state of feeling memorably expressed in a passage alluding to a certain prince:

> Auch schätzt er meinen Verstand und meine Talente mehr als dies Herz, das doch mein einziger Stolz ist, das ganz allein die Quelle von allem ist, aller Kraft, aller Seligkeit und alles Elendes. Ach, was ich weiss, kann jeder wissen—mein Herz habe ich allein.

Besides its use of intense fictional sincerity, to which the fictive reader should contractually submit, the novel gains authenticity from the documentary mode of the last part. Werther has demonstrated his depth of feeling by committing suicide with the pistols lent by Albert and cleaned by Lotte for a purported hunting expedition. It could have been left at that. But Goethe had the genius to close with a section entitled "Der Herausgeber an den Leser," thus stressing the reader's role and the authenticity of the account. In the course of the last part of the novel the "editor" by his circumstantiality draws the willing fictive reader into a fictional credence or acquiescence, indeed an acceptance of the truth of the fiction. In startling contrast to the *Herzensausgiessungen* of Werther, the novel ends with a terse objective description of the burial in the manner of a newspaper dispatch:

> Um zwölf mittags starb er. Die Gegenwart des Amtmannes und seine Anstalten tuschten einen Auflauf. Nachts gegen elf liess er ihn an die Stätte begraben, die er sich erwählt hatte. Der Alte folgte der Leiche und die Söhne, Albert vermocht's nicht. Man fürchtete für Lottens Leben. Handwerker trugen ihn. Kein Geistlicher hat ihn begleitet.

Until the last "editorial" section the reader has been cast in the role of being his own editor or at least the master of his own collaborative surmises. It is in the last section that he finds himself "objectively" informed, corroborated, and ineluctably controlled in accepting the final fictional truth and his final fictive role.

In seeming contrast to the "active" role of the reader as directly and willingly involved in the literary work is the emphasis of some works, either pervasive or sporadic, on their inner self-awareness or self-reflexiveness. In the realistic novel of, say, Balzac, Flaubert, or Tolstoy, the reader is in some degree kept at a distance: he is more of a witness, along with the chronicler-narrator, than a directly "invited" participant or collaborator; at all events, his fictive involvement requires more strenuous efforts on his part to assess and play his role. I do not wish to suggest anything approaching an absolute contrast, but merely to suggest the important aesthetic difference between the confessional and conversational mode, on the one hand, and, on the other, the direct, seemingly impersonal or formal, presentation of fiction. In imaginative discourse, as distinct from "scientific" discourse, *impassibilité* is ultimately impossible. It is of course a matter of degree and coloring, but they are literarily of the essence. That the children of Mme. Aubain in "Un cœur simple" are named Paul and Virginie may be taken perhaps as a laggingly provincial and culturally pretentious allusion to Bernardin's sentimental novel; while naming the central character, the pathetic drudge, Félicité (a name within the bounds of common historical plausibility) must, however underplayed, involve the reader in her touchingly ironic fate. Flaubert cannot be accused here of coyness; he may even be commended for restraint or understatement.

Such tension for the fictive reader inheres in the role cast for him in the *Divine Comedy*. Here the rhetorical situation is extraordinarily complex. The Dante within the poem is both the individual and self-engrossed Christian pilgrim and also, at the same time, the representative wayfaring soul in search of certainty through extraordinary but exemplary revelation. At the very beginning of the introductory canto such meaningful ambivalence, the individual implicit in the general, the concrete circumstances implicit in the human condition, is set forth subtly by the use of a seemingly casual first-person plural adjective and by the concrete description of an actual first-person experience:

> Nel mezzo del cammin di nostra vita
> Mi ritrovai per una selva oscura . . .

The sudden appearance of Virgil, in the midst of "Dante's" danger of being devoured by the objectified beasts of his own sinfulness, and the further narrative of the unique *Bildung* of the Dante in the poem could have the effect of a rather distanced adventure tale in which the reader's involvement is rarely invited by direct appeal. Who else is there who has been offered such imagined or imaginative grace? Who else is there who has been granted such distinguished guides (Virgil, Beatrice, Piccarda, St. Bernard), and most portentously, who else is there who has been granted the special dispensation of traversing as a mortal all the regions of the afterlife? In his extraordinary pilgrim's progress, the Dante of the poem can allow himself a whole "personal" range from denunciation, human susceptibility, humble acquiescence, and joyous acceptance of a provisionally final revelation. Furthermore, the question of plausibility or fictional veracity is poised in as teetering an equilibrium as the reader finds himself, vacillating between his fictive role, along with his moral, anagogical, and allegorical belief. Here the fictive reader of any age or persuasion finds himself stretched along a gamut of literal acceptance (which, in orthodoxy, cannot always be accepted), interpretative or allegorical "truth" (which may lead to orthodox conviction), provisional acquiescence in the moral and religious relevance of the narrative, imaginative and critical acceptance of the poem after granting its premises, and finally, at the extreme, literal rejection of the unprovable pretensions of the narrative. It is here that the properly sympathetic, imaginative, aesthetically provisional, and self-enrolled fictive reader can hope to aspire to be the optimum reader. His task is demanding. He must, in the face of possible truth, fictively grant his willing suspension of disbelief; he must go beyond the fictional world of, say, Ariosto and somehow balance an awareness of the fiction and a willingness, or even desire, to believe in its ultimate truth in both imaginative and substantive senses.

On a direct and literal level the reader is often reminded of his role in varying intensities and in varying relations of the self-reflexiveness of the work: if instances were counted, whose evaluation would carry us to untoward length, the sum would be that direct address to the reader occurs five times in the *Inferno,* seven times in the *Purgatorio,* and four times in the *Paradiso,* notably large in a work of any age. Yet our conclusion may well be that Dante, as author, is managing to maintain an aesthetically peril- ous, though successful, balance between fictive involvement of the reader and artistically inward self-reflexiveness. There lies a cer- tain danger in such balance for the unhistorical fictive reader: he may willfully be tempted to rebel against the role cast for him by the text. Perhaps the surest test is the reading of the *Inferno.* The Dante in the poem reveals his own subjective susceptibilities: when he enters Hell and sees the uncompromising words "Lasciate ogni speranza voi che entrate," he says to Virgil, "Il senso lor m'è duro"; and when he hears Francesca's moving yet unrepentant words he, at the end of the canto, says, "E caddi come corpo morto cade." Indeed, we as readers sympathetically encounter, particu- larly in the *Inferno,* an uncertainty of fictive role, along with the fictional protagonist. Often when we think of Dante's Hell in retrospect we recall most vividly those figures who were great and unrepentant in being evil in a sense that is objective within the poem: those figures who have taken up a stance in spite of all, in- cluding God, and who, in a word or a gesture, express their ar- chetypal essence. We may think, for instance, of Francesca, of Farinata, of Guido da Montefeltro, of Ulysses. Perhaps, we might think provisionally, Dante succeeded all too well; perhaps we would rather dwell with the great sinners than with the righteous who may seem to lose their sharp identity in attuning their wills to God's. But we must reflect that it is easier to portray vice than virtue and that the fictive reader must stand responsibly on his own recognizance. Though vice may be, as the Baron de Charlus called it, a vicious circle, it still may seem to have the complicating movement and the charming devilishness that virtue may seem to lack. But after all, Dante is writing his notion of the afterlife with himself as provisional protagonist, and as he keeps reminding us in our own imaginary journey from Hell to Purgatory to Heaven, things are not the same beyond as they are here. Our imaginations as fictive readers are stretched almost beyond compass in being led to conceive in some way what it is like to exist in a state of not four dimensions (including time) but, as we would say in our paltry earthbound language, of either nullity or infinity of dimensions. As Dante writes in the first canto of the *Paradiso:*

> Trasumanar significar *per verba*
> non si porìa; però l' essemplo basti
> a cui esperïenza grazia serba.

Toward the end of the last *Cantica,* after the revelation of the Divine Vision, the reader is drawn in as collaborator with the speaker in a supremely inevitable failure to express the unexpressible. Dante's poem, with the masterful self-reflexiveness of his art, turns in upon itself and implicates, or literally enfolds, the reader. It is not only a poem about the writing of itself; it is a poem about the impossibility of its ever having been written.

It is Dante himself who, by his subject, means, and self-awareness, requires of a critic so intensely paradoxical a cryptic summation. Many other literary works can successfully maintain a viable balance between the role required of the fictive reader and their own self-reflexiveness: the "contract" between reader and work is astonishingly kept. It might be well, in lesser compass, to consider briefly a poem that has fascinated and teased the minds of countless readers, Coleridge's "Kubla Kahn." Written in irregular but persistent rhyme and in syllabic length ranging from six to eleven—from which it formally derives a sort of primitive, dithyrambic, or spontaneously authentic force—the poem has often seemed to readers an intriguing, perpetually "cliff-hanging" fragment. It was originally published with the title "Kubla Khan; or a Vision in a Dream" and was preceded by a circumstantial account of its composition "Of the Fragment of Kubla Khan." Here we are introduced to the famous or egregious "person or business from Porlock" who purportedly dispelled the remaining pregnant vapors of vision. It may seem presumptuous on my part and on the part of others before, but the poem, as we have it, can on arguable grounds be considered a whole, and indeed an impressive whole, which may serve as an instance of the tension, aesthetically productive, between fictive reader and self-reflexive work. In the first eleven lines the reader enters an exotic and mysterious setting in which the artifact of the "stately pleasure-dome" and the weirdly natural "sacred river" and "sunless sea" seem both to strain and assuage the reader's credulity almost simultaneously. In its wild course the "fountain" with the intermittent force of the river Alph unpredictably throws up "huge fragments vaulted like rebounding hail." For five miles the "sacred river" meandered through a normal landscape,

> Then reached the caverns measureless to man,
> And sank in tumult to a lifeless ocean:
> And 'mid this tumult Kubla heard from far
> Ancestral voices prophesying war!

By their very semblance of historicity and particular location ("In Xanadu . . . ," "Where Alph, the sacred river, ran . . ."), by their mingling of the familiarly natural and strangely artificial and unnatural, the first thirty-six lines of the poem engage the reader in his fictive and collaborative role. He may even have an inkling that the combination of natural and unnatural (or perhaps supernatural) succeeds in rendering the river potently symbolic. But symbolic of what? While holding Freud at bay and adverting proleptically to the latter part of the poem, I would suggest that the river in its "mazy motion" at least foreshadows a symbolic function as representing creative inspiration, that mysterious and gratuitous human experience sacred since the oracle at Delphi. What does Kubla Khan hear after decreeing his pleasure-dome but "Ancestral voices prophesying war"? Inspiration, prophecy, and poetry are in ancient terms barely separable. In "Kubla Khan" we have, I think, an imaginative presentation of the tradition of Antiquity in such matters, including the wellspring, the "mighty fountain," reinterpreted, especially in the last eighteen lines:

> A damsel with a dulcimer
> In a vision once I saw:
> It was an Abyssinian maid,
> And on her dulcimer she played,
> Singing of Mount Abora.
>   Could I revive within me
>   Her symphony and song,
>   To such a deep delight 'twould win me,
>   That with music loud and long,

> I would build that dome in air,
> That sunny dome! those caves of ice!
> And all who heard should see them there,
> And all should cry, Beware! Beware!
> His flashing eyes, his floating hair!
> Weave a circle round him thrice,
> And close your eyes with holy dread,
> For he on honey-dew hath fed,
> And drunk the milk of Paradise.

It might be asserted at first blush that these lines are discontinuous with the previous and longer part of the poem, a kind of break in rhetorical address and subject matter. But that I think is, pace Coleridge himself, a mistaken interpretation of a remarkably cohesive poem. True, there is something of a gap: a certain reflexive distancing supervenes, along with a direct first-person assertion of the speaker of the poem. The previous past narration gradually gives way to the conditional and then to the imperative mood. In the earlier part of the poem we are presented, not with a vision described as such, but with an "actuality," a *donnée,* described in historical "eyewitness" terms. In the latter and far shorter part of the poem the fictive reader is distanced as collaborative witness of what has gone on before, evoked in fictional frustration at the impossibility of poetically recreating "that sunny dome," "those caves of ice." He becomes sympathetically drawn into what may seem a hopeless effort of the imagination. But, almost paradoxically, has not that effort already succeeded in the earlier part of the poem? Has not the reader already been involved in what has already been accomplished? The poem, in the "truth" of its fiction, looks back upon itself and becomes thereby self-reflexive and complete. It is the fictive reader who is thus granted the imaginative task of successfully making a whole of the self-reflexive poem.

Here we have in "Kubla Khan" what may serve as a final, if not necessarily culminating, example of the particularly intimate aesthetic collaboration between speaker and reader, "script" and performer, author and audience. The sharpest point is, I hope, clear: first, that the literary work of art is a communication and that the communicant is thereby guided and controlled, though not co-

erced, by its totality. In the aesthetic experience of literature I
suggest that there exists a distinction between the fictional creation of the author and the implicit, nay obligatory, fictive or
participating role of the reader. I have in effect distinguished between "fictive" and "fictional" in an attempt to stress the reader's
double role as believer and agnostic and, on the other hand, the
author's double role as contriver and communicator. In the process the permutations and combinations of the acts of writing and
reading are wonderfully complicated and engrossingly complex.
We, if I may be permitted to involve my own reader, have traipsed
and trespassed through a galaxy of genres toward a hypothetical
conclusion: that the role of the reader is an intrinsic part of the
fiction of literature and that the fictive reader must provisionally
obey the contractual norms before rendering his incumbent verdict *in sede critica*. Every critic, by etymology and tradition, must
be judge according to his fullest knowledge and awareness. But
first of all he must be fictive participant, accomplice, collaborator,
and amicus curiae in the literary court—role which may render
him something of a hippogryph which, Ariosto assures us, is at
least half true.

That my examples, drawn from hither and yon, may give to
some readers the impression of a tourist among sacred and inviola-
ble sanctuaries does not weigh heavily on my sense of literature
and criticism, since *nihil litterarum alienum me puto*. I would
like, however, to stress my belief that general or theoretical
questions in literary criticism can be illustrated by our common
legacy without regard, in such a pursuit, to time, place, or language. Needless to say, time, place, and language are also and
equally, depending on the chosen context and emphasis, of the
essence. If my own reader looks back to my shifting terminology,
my rhetoric of critical ineffability, it may seem idiosyncratic,
perhaps even inevitable, to end up with a welter of words: accomplice, communicant, collaborator, real, fictive, fictional, self-
reflexive. Yet I plead the extenuating circumstance of nuance.
Such terms are not strictly synonymous since there are no true
synonyms; such terms may responsibly be used in an attempt to
express shades of meaning directed toward what we hope is actually there at a center which we may convincingly approximate

but never quite reach. The fictive reader and the self-reflexive work seem to be strangely parallel and, on occasion, even more strangely, to intersect. Is that not all emblematic in the word "mimesis"?

W. K. Wimsatt

Genesis: A Fallacy Revisited[1]

It would appear that literary studies, and especially theoretical studies, are subject to endless metamorphic cycles, and if they sometimes make progress, they can also suffer regress. Why not? Poems are, on one view, more or less imperfectly recorded acts of personal agents, and in literary study they are open to boundless speculation by further persons, whose activity, though sometimes partly scientific and historical, is always driven by an aim of individual intelligence. There is no theoretical or critical term set up for the purpose of clarifying or recommending a given perspective which is not susceptible of being seen and used in an opposite light. There is no rational and methodological concept, no attempted translucent universal, which is not capable of being transformed, and very quickly, into an opaque historical gimmick—as if some poems could be "beautiful" in some special Platonic sense (after a certain date), or as if symbolism had begun to appear in poetry about the time of Baudelaire or Mallarmé, just as blood began to circulate in human bodies about the time of William Harvey or dreams to have significance about the time of Freud. These reflections, verging on the melancholy, occur as I survey some recent writings on the critical problem of the artist's life story, his inspirations and his intentions, in relation to his work of art.

Whatever the truth in this debate, or the preferred side (if there is one, and I still think there is), it must be evident that

1. Two friends have specially contributed to this essay—Monroe Beardsley of course, who brought to my attention some of our critics in the journals and who read my early draft, and Donald Hirsch, whose differences from me, whether in conversation or in print (see below, p. 224), have the unusual character of being always illuminative. His essay of 1960 in *PMLA*, which I cite below and argue with (notes 18, 21, and 53), is one of the best on the subject which I now attempt to reapproach.

there are two antithetically opposed sides, and probably always will be, corresponding to two aspects of literature and to two kinds of persons who come to the study of literature. To speak broadly and to avoid the simplicity of one-word labels (or to defer the economy of such labels), let us say that an art work is something which emerges from the private, individual, dynamic, and intentionalistic realm of its maker's mind and personality; it is in a sense (and this is especially true of the verbal work of art) made of intentions or intentionalistic material. But at the same time, in the moment it emerges, it enters a public and in a certain clear sense an objective realm; it claims and gets attention from an audience; it invites and receives discussion, about its meaning and value, in an idiom of inter-subjectivity and conceptualization. If the art work has emerged at all from the artist's private world, it has emerged into some kind of universal world. The artist was not merely *trying* to do something worthy of notice in that world. He has done it. Artistic activity has produced a valued result. Some critics will wish to talk about just that result. Other critics, however, will not. These will be the critics who entertain an antithetic drive toward viewing the art work as mainly a token of its source, a manifestation of something behind it, that is, the consciousness or personality of the artist (or perhaps of the society in which he lived, or of himself as representative of that society). These critics, wishing to throb in unison with the mind of the artist, will wish to know all about that individual artist and as much as possible about his historic context. At the very least, they will wish to know not only the poem in question, but also all his other poems, his essays, letters, and diaries, his thoughts and feelings,[2] and not only those which occurred before the poem and might in any sense have caused it, but (in the more recent idiom) all those which came after it at any time and are thus a part of the whole personality of which the poem is an expression, the system of contexts of which it is a part.[3]

It was against a background of triumphantly prevalent genetic

2. I leave out his headaches and his gallstones, though there was a time when these too would have been important. For a rich and orderly assortment of artist's drives and motives, conscious and unconscious, during the creative process, see Monroe C. Beardsley, "On the Creation of Art," *JAAC*, 23 (Spring 1965), 291–304.

3. See below, p. 199, n. 14.

studies in various modes, and in an effort to give assistance in what seemed a badly needed program to rescue poems from the morass of their origins, that my friend Monroe Beardsley and I published in a *Dictionary of World Literature* (1944) an article entitled "Intention" and then, in response to a critique of that article, a further development of our argument in the *Sewanee Review* (1945), an essay entitled "The Intentional Fallacy." Mr. Beardsley followed these articles thirteen years later with some very lucid pages in his volume entitled *Aesthetics* (1958). It seemed to me then, and it still seems, that Mr. Beardsley and I succeeded in formulating a clear, reasonable, and viable statement of the thesis that the intention of a literary artist qua intention is neither a valid ground for arguing the presence of a quality or a meaning in a given instance of his literary work nor a valid criterion for judging the value of that work. "The objective critic's first question, when he is confronted with a new aesthetic object," says Mr. Beardsley in 1958, "is not, What is this supposed to be? but, What have we got here?"

As I have already noted, however, literary students who love the poem's genesis have no trouble in answering such arguments and returning to that luxuriant pasture. It is enough to assert that biography has such and such joys of discovery and communion, and thus biography *is* relevant to the study of the poem.[4] Or to say that the poet's life itself, or even the style of face he wears, is a work of art parallel to his produced art works, and hence the poet's life *is* a thing of great interest to the literary student.[5] Or that the intention of the artist, revealed in the title of a work or some simi-

---

4. See, for instance, Alfred Owen Aldridge, "Biography in the Interpretation of Poetry," *College English*, 25 (March 1964), 412–20: "I shall try to indicate a few reasons why biography serves to humanize poetry and therefore to heighten our enjoyment." "No purely esthetic criticism has ever stimulated the same public interest," the same "extraordinary sensation which has been caused by the recent announcement of A. L. Rowse's biographical study of Shakespeare—with its revelations" (p. 415). Or see John A. Meixner, "The Uses of Biography in Criticism," *College English*, 27 (November 1966), 108–13; or Carlos Baker, "Speaking of Books: The Relevance of a Writer's Life," *New York Times Book Review* (August 20, 1967), pp. 2, 31.

5. Leslie A. Fiedler, *No! In Thunder: Essays on Myth and Literature* (Boston, 1960), pp. 312–18.

lar adjacent index, is often a clue which the artist himself seems to
feel it prudent to supply to his public, or which the given viewer
of a work finds it very helpful to notice, and hence the intention of
the artist *is* sometimes "relevant" to the work.[6] One may even add
that in some instances, like that of Mr. Beardsley's invention, the
"cruller-shaped object of polished teak" said by the sculptor to
symbolize "Human Destiny," the plight of the artist who wishes to
convey that meaning will indeed be hopeless unless we grant him
the privilege of telling us what he wishes. And therefore his intention is indeed relevant and valid.[7] Or, a critic may prefer to talk,
not about the meaning of a poem, but about his own "responses"
to it, which may be "conditioned" by his knowledge of the author's intentions, as these create a kind of "field of force round the
work" or a "web of associations." If Housman says that he meant
no irony at all, that, it would appear, will settle the question for
this critic. If Eliot were to testify that he had never heard of
Andrew Marvell, that too would settle a question. Such a critic's
responses might apparently also be conditioned by his knowing
what Mr. Leavis thinks about a problem—though what this may
be, in the given instance, seems unhappily in doubt.[8]

The argument about intention is then, in a sense, hopelessly cir-
cular and reentering. There is no way to keep the simpler kinds of
intention-hunters from jumping on the vehicle of literary inquiry,
and nobody I suppose really wishes the power to legislate anything

6. William H. Capitan, "The Artist's Intention," *Revue Internationale de
Philosophie*, 68–69 (1964), 331–32. Cf. Joseph Margolis, *The Language of
Art & Art Criticism, Analytic Questions in Aesthetics* (Detroit, 1965), p. 99,
on stage directions and musical notations. Also see below, p. 212. Margolis is
a writer who cheerfully piles up examples that tell in favor of Wimsatt and
Beardsley and even quotes passages from them with which he cannot disagree and then with equal cheer somersaults to a guarded conclusion that
they "must be mistaken," that "intentional criticism has, to some extent at
least, a recognizable and not inappropriate place in the aesthetic examination of art" (p. 103).

7. Capitan, p. 332.

8. Dr. F. Cioffi, "Intention and Interpretation in Criticism" (from *Proceedings of the Aristotelian Society*, 1963–64), in *Collected Papers on
Aesthetics*, ed. Cyril Barrett, S.J. (Oxford, 1965), pp. 161–83, esp. 168,
170–71, 172, 174, 175, 179–81. See M. C. Beardsley's review of this volume,
with special attention to Cioffi, in *JAAC, 26* (Fall 1967), 144–46.

against them. But at the precise level of abstraction and definition at which Mr. Beardsley and I argued the question, I do not see that any notable revision is required, or even any very emphatic repetition. Let me try to make a useful reentry into the debate by first noticing a few related, parallel, or complementary terms and focuses of recent literary criticism, perhaps some of them obstructions to a right view of literary "intention."

The idea of poetic "impersonality" is, I believe, in the thinking of many students a close adjunct to, or required condition for, the kind of criticism which hopes to escape the "intentional fallacy." Much difficulty seems to arise here, however, and this has probably been promoted to a large extent by the writings early and late of a poet-critic who did as much as any other single authority to establish in English studies of the mid-century a climate favorable to objective inquiry—T. S. Eliot, of course. In a review of his posthumously collected essays, *To Criticize the Critic,* I have already discussed this matter in the perspective of his later career.[9] It will be sufficient here to look back for a moment at his seminal essay "Tradition and the Individual Talent" (published during the fall and early winter of 1919 in the last two numbers of *The Egoist, An Individualist Review*) . This celebrated early essay, despite its forceful suggestiveness, the smoothness and fullness of its definition of the poet's impersonality (or perhaps inevitably in achieving these qualities) , was a highly ambiguous statement. Therein, no doubt, consisted something of its pregnancy. In this essay Eliot as poet and critic is saying two things about three ideas (man, poet, and poem) and saying them simultaneously. He is saying that a poet ought to depersonalize his raw experience, transcend the immediacy of the suffering man. At the same time, he is saying that the reader ought to read the poem impersonally, as an achieved expression, not personally, with attendant inquiries into the sufferings, the motives, the confusions of the man behind the poem. The idea "poet" as Eliot employs it in this essay is sometimes the antithesis of "man" and sometimes the antithesis of "poem." "The more perfect the artist, the more completely separate in him will be the man who suffers and the mind which

9. *The Massachusetts Review,* 7 (Summer 1966) , 584–90.

creates." "Honest criticism and sensitive appreciation are directed not upon the poet but upon the poetry." The two meanings are inextricably interwoven in Eliot's rich and memorable sentences. But they are not one meaning, nor does either one entail the other. Eliot, at moments much later in his career, could be very clear about one half of his doctrine. "I prefer not to define, or to test, poetry by means of speculations about its origins; you cannot find a sure test for poetry, a test by which you may distinguish between poetry and mere good verse, by reference to its putative antecedents in the mind of the poet." [10] But this injunction against peeping into the poet's activity, if it is valid at all, must be equally valid whether that activity itself is, in the poet's own consciousness, personal or impersonal. In fact, the critical lesson is that from the poem itself we cannot really tell, and so far as we are critics interested in the poem itself, we do not care. Despite his double doctrine of impersonality, the notion of the poet has always been, for Eliot, deeply centered in that personal suffering man himself. "It is not in his personal emotions . . . that the poet is in any way remarkable or interesting. His particular emotions may be simple, crude, or flat." Poetry is an "escape" from personality. Yes, but of course "only those who have personality and emotions know what it means to want to escape from these things." [11]

The dubious notion of the poet's impersonal personality, deriving so pervasively in modern American criticism from the ideas of Eliot, has also been colored no doubt by Yeatsian occultist notions of the "self" and the "anti-self" or "mask" (the latter either "true" or "false") .[12] Which is the poet in a given poem expressing? His real self? A true mask? A false mask? A fascinating question—and a safe one, so long as the inquirer is aware that the area of his inquiry is at the moment biography, perhaps a very refined version of this art, but still biography. Perhaps it will be

10. *The Use of Poetry and the Use of Criticism* (London, 1933), p. 140.
11. All the words quoted are from *Tradition and the Individual Talent*.
12. See Richard Ellmann, *The Identity of Yeats* (New York, 1954) and *Yeats: The Man and the Masks* (New York, 1948). The article by A. O. Aldridge cited above confuses the poet's view and the critic's view throughout and refers to much literature which also does. In Slavic countries formalist critics during the 1920s defined a poem as "a deflection, not a reflection, of experience" (p. 412).

sufficient to say here, without a long excursion, that the thesis that biographical evidence does not establish meaning *in* poems is not the equivalent of a thesis that poems cannot contribute their own kind of meaning, and a very rich and subtle kind, to the writing of biography.[13] For whatever does get into a poem presumably is put there by the poet and reflects *something* in the poet's personality and life. It is for the biographer, in his particular insight and skill, to say what is reflected and in what relation to other things in the poet's life. Nowadays we are increasingly promised, or shown, the inner life of the author mainly on the evidence of the dialectic sequence of his works.[14] If anybody wishes to challenge this as sound biographical method (I at least have no specific wish to do so), it ought to be clear that he does not do so on the same principle as that on which a critic may refuse to decide the meaning or value of a poem on external auctorial testimony or other biographical evidence. Affirmation of a cause and affirmation of an effect are different in their entailments. If a poet sees red, he may well either write or not write a red poem. If he writes a red poem, it would seem to be a sound enough inference, though in some instances little more than a truism, that he has in some sense seen red.

Patrick Cruttwell, in a richly illustrated and nicely modulated essay of 1959, "Makers and Persons," [15] discriminates four degrees of "distance" between a "maker" (poet) and the "person" (man in whom the maker perforce quarries his stuff): (1) the degree or way of "simple transcript" (genuine or partly faked—Boswell, Pepys, Rousseau, Byron in letters and journals, Montaigne); (2) the "masked" way—"the making of a self which pretends not to be, but encourages the reader to think it is," the real person of the writer (Sterne-Shandy-Yorick, Conrad-Marlow); (3) the way of

13. "We ought to impute the thoughts and attitudes of the poem immediately to the dramatic *speaker,* and if to the author at all, only by an act of biographical inference" ("The Intentional Fallacy" [1945], paragraph 7).

14. See Leon Edel, *Literary Biography* (London, 1957); J. Hillis Miller, *The Disappearance of God, Five Nineteenth-Century Writers* (New York, 1965) —De Quincey, Browning, Emily Brontë, Arnold, Hopkins. But for Miller chronology is not important.

15. *The Hudson Review, 12* (Winter 1959–60), 487–507.

"mythologized" self-presentation—"transportation of the person
into symbolic figures, references" (The master of this obscure and
mysterious way is Mr. Eliot) ; (4) the "dramatized" way—here
"the distance is greatest between maker and person" (clearest in
actual stage drama—the Greeks, Shakespeare, "the ages of great
drama"). After presenting these distinctions, Mr. Cruttwell traces,
very interestingly and I believe correctly, the rise of the modern
cult of personality, the author as "exhibitionist," from about the
time of Boswell's *Johnson* (1791) through episodes in the career
of Byron and in Victorian literary biography. Modern poets themselves have sometimes protested against the invasion of their
privacy—in vain, and wrongly. The floodgates of the personal interest, once opened, cannot be forced back. Art betrays its creators,
and properly. They betray themselves, once the public and the
literary scholars have been put on the right track. In a closing
short section on problems for contemporary critics, Mr. Cruttwell
argues that it is time for critics to overcome any anti-biographical
inhibitions which may have been induced by the ideas of "Eliot,
Richards, Leavis and the Scrutineers" or by the "New Criticism"
in America. Let the critics now permit themselves a renewed and
healthy release in the satisfaction of the "curiosity" which poems
must in fact surely arouse in them. Who is the critic, after all, who
can say that his responses to poetry *are* pure? After we "have enjoyed" and have been "impressed" by a writer, by Wordsworth in
his Lucy poems, for instance, then we undertake the "microscopic
investigation." We want to know about Wordsworth's "incestuous
feelings for Dorothy" and what he "intended" Lucy to "stand
for." So, in spite of Mr. Cruttwell's effort to establish a *critical* direction for his essay, the argument swings round in fact to post-
critical interests, moving *from* the recognized and presumably
understood poem toward the "putative antecedents." Mr. Cruttwell has earlier noted that a certain "degeneration" in Sterne's
management of his Tristram and Yorick masks may be explained
by a parallel in Sterne's life. "His failure to hold his masks was a
symptom of his person's insincerity and weakness. . . . He slid
from one pose to the next, from bawdy to sobstuff and back again,
not through choice but through weakness" (p. 491). But Mr.
Cruttwell can also have his argument the opposite way, on a later

page (503), where he argues that Byron aspiring to escape from his true personality in *Childe Harold* wrote untruthfully and badly, but when he abandoned his aspiration to purity and simply "wrote out his mood as it came to him" in the "shameless self-parading of *Don Juan*," he "wrote at his best." The lesson of these two examples seems to be that the biographically oriented critic will find a correspondence between life and work an explanation of either goodness or badness in the work, as he happens to find the work itself good or bad. On another page (494), Mr. Cruttwell expatiates upon the futility of trying to find Eliot's personal or secret motive in the epigraph from Marston prefixed to *Burbank with a Baedeker*. Mr. Cruttwell is severe on Eliot for his two-faced stance of impersonal secretiveness yet constant invitation to the reader to speculate about personal reasons (in the absence of clear public ones). I think there is some justice in the complaint. I have dwelt long on Mr. Cruttwell's essay, however, not only because it seems to me probably the richest and most informative in the recent resurgence of biographically oriented "critical" arguments, but because in its own ambivalence or thwarted struggle to arrive at a "critical" direction, it is in fact a larger rewriting of Eliot's original and seminally confused essay of 1919.

A kind of critical metamorphosis to which I alluded in my opening paragraph is well illustrated in the recent history of the very useful term "persona" in American criticism. This term seems to have gained currency during the mid-century because it was a convenient way of referring to something *in the poem* which could be thought of as a counterpart of the *im*personality which was supposed either to reside in the author or, more accurately, to be a perspective adopted by the critic. This economical employment of the term "persona" (along with certain related or nearly equivalent terms such as "fiction," "ethos," "mask," or "muse") might be illustrated near its zenith in Maynard Mack's essay of 1951, "The Muse of Satire," [16] distinguishing three "voices" (the *vir bonus*, the *ingénu*, and the heroic public defender) in the persona or speaker of Pope's formal verse satire. All three of these voices were to be taken *by a critic* dramatically, not biographi-

16. *Yale Review, 41* (Autumn 1951), 80–92.

cally, rhetorically, not historically. Something like a sheer reversal from that kind of critical use of persona to a convenient reconfusion of questions about criticism and questions about biography may be witnessed in a very richly variegated essay of 1963 by Irvin Ehrenpreis, entitled "Personae." [17] An expression of grave concern that certain nameless "scholars" have been doing the wrong thing with persona (making it a "distinguishing property" or special kind of merit in Augustan poetry, rather than the universal and "inescapable part of language and communication" that it actually is) leads Mr. Ehrenpreis, not, as one might at first hope, to a purified image of the scholar-critic, but very quickly into an opposite sort of thing, an exceedingly dense involvement of poet and poem as man and mask, reality and "rhetorical pose." "One could never reveal the whole truth about oneself, even supposing that one knew it." "If there is any meaning in the concept of persona or mask, it must imply a difference between appearance and reality."

Like Mr. Cruttwell, whom we have cited above, and like most writers on W. B. Yeats, Mr. Ehrenpreis reminds us forcefully that, whatever the relation of persona to author, it is not a simple one either of likeness or of difference. Other recent writers, Maynard Mack in the essay already cited, and notably Wayne Booth in *The Rhetoric of Fiction* (1961),[18] have been stressing a somewhat

17. *Restoration and Eighteenth-Century Literature, Essays in Honor of Alan Dugald McKillop*, ed. Carroll Camden (Chicago, 1963), pp. 25–37.

18. See this large and interesting work passim, esp. Chap. 8, "Telling as Showing: Dramatized Narrators, Reliable and Unreliable." See too Allan Rodway and Brian Lee, "Coming to Terms," *Essays in Criticism, 14* (April 1964), 122; and E. D. Hirsch's very subtle and accurate distinction between "speaking subject" and "biographical person," as illustrated in the "secret awareness" of lying and the "truth-telling stance" ("Objective Interpretation," *PMLA, 75* [September 1960], 478–79). See also some good paragraphs on the theme of person and poet in Harry Berger, Jr., "Cadmus Unchanged," a review of *Selected Letters of Robert Frost*, in *Yale Review, 54* (Winter 1965), 277–82. For a range of examples and insights from a different area, see Victor Erlich, "The Concept of the Poet as a Problem of Poetics," *Poetics, Poetyka, Poetika* (The Hague, Mouton & Co., 192), pp. 707–17, and "Some Uses of Monologue in Prose Fiction: Narrative Manner and World View," *Stil- und Formprobleme in der Literatur* (Heidelberg, 1959), pp. 371–78.

different, if parallel, truth—that the relation of persona, internally, to other parts or aspects of the work, need not be simple. Persona is not in fact a sufficient conception for the *de*personalization of the poetic object as the critic attends to it. It is not as if the persona is always the simple focus for the expression of everything in the poem. Sometimes he betrays himself in contrast to some cooler or saner perspective. This is the kind of thing that happens obviously in a monodrama like Browning's *Soliloquy of a Spanish Cloister*, a miniature of the situation in a full-scale play or novel, where numerous personae contend within the ambit of an encircling and managing intelligence. Browning's *Soliloquy* is a steady sequence of not very delicate little antithetic jolts. "*Ave, Virgo!* Gr-r-r—you swine!" The ironies of Swift are a more plenary instance of such internal cunning. Mr. Ehrenpreis observes that in *A Modest Proposal* there are not two, but three mentalities or "styles"—that of the initially prominent "sensible projector" of the proposal, that of the "monster" looming behind him, and that of a directly speaking, bitter denunciator, all three of these, as we should expect in this essay, said to be styles of the author's own voice. (Here perhaps it is worth adding that while projector and monster are aspects of the same persona, the denouncer is part of a perspective, or, if one wishes, he is a second person, who has already manipulated the projector so as to reveal him as a monster.) But what I am trying to get back to here is the direction of argument. From the work to the author (when one wishes to be biographical) is not the same as from the author (outside the work) to the work. These directions remain opposites no matter how numerous and complicated a set of deflectors or baffles we set up between the two termini.

The fact is that we can, if we wish, learn with relative certainty from biographical evidence that some personae are close to or identical with the author and some are much different from him. Nobody would confuse the persona of Browning's *Soliloquy of a Spanish Cloister* with Browning himself. But almost everybody rushes to confuse the persona of Gray's *Elegy in a Country Churchyard* with Gray himself. In fact it can be shown on quite convincing biographical evidence that the melancholy poet who is the anonymous speaker of that poem is very close to the melan-

choly poet Thomas Gray—"me I; il Pensoroso." Nor is that correspondence, in biographical terms, an accident. The *Elegy* does
seem to come out of the historic person Thomas Gray much more
directly than many other poems come out of their authors. Nevertheless, the *Elegy* is not *about* the historic person Gray. The self-
contemplative speaker remains anonymous. The poem itself, if it
were anonymous, would be intact.

What, however, if the poem does happen to be a poem *about*
that historic person the author, about himself, his friends, and his
enemies? If the author of the *Epistle to Arbuthnot*, says Ehrenpreis, "were not the great poet of his age, if his relations with his
parents were not well known to have been as he testifies, if Atticus
and Sporus did not belong to public life, the force of the poem
would dwindle" (p. 32). Yet with increase of information, let us
notice, comes complexity—and doubt. The canny persona of
Pope's satire bears scarcely the same simple relation to the gardener of Twickenham as the melancholy churchyard speaker
seems to bear to the pensive fellow of the Cambridge college.
Three distinct voices are assigned by Mr. Mack to that satiric persona. In what variously shaded relations to the man who is both
behind the poem and the subject of the poem may be difficult to
say. Pope could be scheming and mean, as well as friendly and
noble. The main evidence for his piety to his father is in the
poem. Perhaps we do not inquire too rigorously whether he was
in fact so righteous, charitable, and simple as the poem would
make him. If he was not, still "his make-up of being so is in itself a
piece of greatness; and not to enjoy it is a piece of stupidity." [19]
Perhaps we enjoy it the more for its being in part make-up. And
we sense that this is so, or may well be so, in large part from internal
evidence, from the perspective or management of the whole witty
poem.

In accepting this kind of biographical claim, let us notice that it
is a particular kind of claim, not of intention but of subject matter. Pope's sincerity or insincerity, his virtue or his meanness, his
character and intention, as generators of the poem or as criteria of
its merit, do not really come into question. The poet and his

19. H. W. Garrod, *Poetry and the Criticism of Life* (Cambridge, Mass.,
1931), p. 83. Garrod refers to Arnold's "make-up" of being the greatest
English critic.

friends and enemies are present in the poem as historic figures, and furthermore as well-established historic figures in precisely the roles they play in the poem. Milton's sonnets 17, 22, and 23 and his other allusions to his blindness provide similar, easy, and unimpeachable examples. Here we enter the problem of the universality and significance of the protagonist—the stature of Samson the agonist compared to that of Hobson the carrier. Aristotle understood that it gives a certain kind of advantage if the man is important. After Milton and Pope, the world became increasingly convinced of the importance of every man. Still it is not true, it never has been true, that the simple meanings or wishes of any man, even of any important man, can generate or guarantee a significant poetic symbol.[20]

"It is not illusory appearances," says Ehrenpreis, "that the real person sets before us: it is the visible effluences, aspects, reflections—however indirect, of an inner being that cannot be defined apart from them. In order to understand any literary work, we must view it as a transaction between us and that inner being" (p. 31). "Only as a relationship between a real speaker and a real listener can meaning exist" (p. 37). Some years earlier, Father Walter Ong, in one of the best essays on the "personalist approach" that I know, *The Jinnee in the Well-Wrought Urn,* had written:

> Man's deepest orientation is personal. . . . Each work of art that bids for attention in an act of contemplation is a surrogate for a person. In proportion as the work of art is capable of being taken in full seriousness, it moves further and further along an asymptote to the curve of personality.[21]

20. See the excellent article, in effect about anonymous lyric personae, by Arthur K. Moore, "Lyric Voices and Ethical Proofs," *JAAC, 23* (Summer 1965), 429–39. "Lyrics are vouched for simply— . . . through intelligible relationships to activities, conditions, occasions, lives, ideologies, and states of consciousness into which interest enters" (pp. 429–30). See the same author's later "Lyric Personae and Prying Critics," *Southern Humanities Review, 1* (1967), 43–64.

21. *Essays in Criticism, 4* (July 1954), 315, 319. And see below, p. 224, n. 53, *langue* and *parole* as expounded by Hirsch, "Objective Interpretation," pp. 473–75.

Perhaps it does. Yet the argument against intentional reading
need not suppose, and does not suppose, that the monkeys in the
British Museum will in the foreseeable future, or in any future at
all, type out *Paradise Lost*.[22] "The words of a poem come out of a
head, not out of a hat," as we quoted long ago from E. E. Stoll.
James Thorpe has recently demonstrated how much some literary
works actually owe to editors and other agents of transmission and
even to such chance activity as that of a compositor, who may by
mistake introduce a word that conceivably is better than the
author's. Mr. Thorpe's philosophy of textual criticism says, however, that we should restore the author's own word, and I say the
same thing, though perhaps more simply on grounds of plain con-
venience than he wishes to. He believes that to accept the compositor's happy slip would be to put the aesthetic object not in the
realm of "art" (intended or designed work), but in that of the
now popularly received object made by "chance" (a spilled can of
paint, words selected by throwing dice, sounds of traffic recorded
at a busy intersection).[23] But it is possible and, as he shows, frequently is the fact that a designed work is the design of more than
one head. A second completes the work of the first. In this instance, it would be ourselves, the editors, who, in assessing and
adopting the accidental intrusion, were the very junior collaborators in the original author's designed and intended work.

In our frequent focus on the history of modern literature as outlined by Mr. Cruttwell, with its heavy personal underpainting, its
vigorous cult of personal authentication, let us not forget the massive foundations of the world's literature—the Book of Genesis,
the *Iliad*, the *Odyssey*, the works of Virgil, Dante, Chaucer,
Shakespeare—which survive for us either anonymously or with the
merest wisps or shadows of biography attached. These works, it is
to be assumed, no less than those of Milton, Johnson, Byron,
Keats, Yeats, or Joyce, speak to us with the "inner being" of "real
speakers," as "surrogates" for persons.

22. One of the monkeys employed in this experiment once got through
the whole poem all right, as far as the last word of the last book, but then
he slipped and wrote, instead of "day.," "lxdz.," and the whole version of
course had to be scrapped.

23. "The Aesthetics of Textual Criticism," *PMLA*, *80* (December 1965),
465–82, esp. 465–68, 475.

It may promote clarity if at this point we try to map the structure of the argument we are engaged in according to the following types of statement which are our subject matter:

1. Historical, biographical: Thomas Gray was a melancholy poet, and he planned or meant or was likely to mean certain things.
2. Historical, poetic: The speaker of Gray's *Elegy* is a melancholy poet; he uses certain words and images and means certain things.
3. Methodological, explicitly evaluative: The resemblance, or correspondence, between the poet Gray and either the speaker or the perspective of the *Elegy* makes it a good poem or shows that it is good.
4. Methodological, interpretive: The character, mind, or habitual meanings of the poet Gray are a valid guide (or the best guide) to the meaning of the *Elegy*.

This arrangement introduces one distinction on which I have so far not laid any emphasis, that between statements of type 3 and those of type 4. Statements of type 3 (the explicitly evaluative) are more ambitious than those of type 4 (the simply interpretive), but I use this order because those of type 3 are on the whole less plausible, and I wish to dispose of them first. In our articles of 1944 and 1945 Mr. Beardsley and I did not labor this distinction. In his *Aesthetics* of 1958 Mr. Beardsley has separated the two issues very cleanly, in fact by a space of 428 pages, with I think, considerable increase of clarity for the whole discussion. At the same time, it is my own view (and this will emerge more clearly as I go on) that an argument about instances of type 4 (the interpretive) will very often, or even characteristically, bring in considerations of value.

Let me proceed to notice and comment upon certain graded instances of argument, first some relating to statements of type 3 (a, b, c), then some relating to type 4 (a, b, c, d, e, f). There is some value in a chart or a guided tour of a field of argument even when the cartographer or guide has to confess that he looks on many of the stopping points as only of historic interest. The point of maximum live concern for our debate, and the one toward which I am working, let me confess in advance, is 4f.

(3a) The poet wrote his poem with the aim of making money, of winning a prize, of pleasing a mistress, of impressing an employer or patron—or for some opposite or more ideal sort of reason. His work was either a "free" work in Kant's sense, or not free. "He achieved a result commensurate with such aims. Therefore. . . ." Such reasonings concern what some writers on our problem take pains to distinguish as secondary or ulterior intentions of the artist. We ought to be able to see these as obviously outside any real critical question. In like manner, we should find no trouble in putting to one side the common artistic aim of creating a masterpiece—or perhaps of not creating a masterpiece, but just of turning out a potboiler—or of having a "lark." [24] "He intended only to appeal to popular sentiment; therefore we should not. . . ." (Or, to translate this kind of motive into the key of interpretive argument and thus get it out of the way: "We know that he thought of this as his masterpiece; therefore it. . . .")

(3b) The poem is or says what the poet himself was or thought or felt; it is hence good—or bad. We have been close to this framing of the argument in our whole discussion of persona. We have seen both kinds of conclusion (bad, for Sterne; good, for Byron) in Mr. Cruttwell's essay. This form of the argument runs very readily into talk about "sincerity" and "inspiration" and "authenticity," topics which Mr. Beardsley and I noted with some care in our essay of 1945. In his *Aesthetics* (p. 457) he lists "expression," "sincerity," and "intention" together, under the general head of the "genetic," but, rightly I believe, he sees "intention" as focusing most or all of what can be handled with any precision in this area.[25]

24. See Sidney Gendin's sensible short article, "The Artist's Intentions," *JAAC, 23* (Winter 1964) , 195.

25. Another term which Mr. Beardsley (pp. 457, 490–91) puts in this genetic group is "originality," which, like "skill" (see 3c below), is a merit which seems assignable more readily to the author than to his work. During the neoclassic age, in arguments comparing Homer and Virgil, the latter was sometimes said to have written doubtless the more perfect poem; the former got a good mark for originality. A 1966 Fairlane is a better automobile than a Model-T Ford, but not as original.

(3c) The poet had a specific aim or plan in mind; he managed (whether inspirationally or rationally) to carry this out in the poem; thus he is a successful artist; his work is good art. This is the "Spingarn-Croce-Carlyle-Goethe" theory named by H. L. Mencken. We alluded to this theory in our article of 1944, and it was defended by Ananda K. Coomaraswamy in his critique of that article.[26] A successfully planned and executed murder was for Mr. Coomaraswamy no less a work of art than a poem or painting. Mr. Beardsley makes the helpful suggestion that here we may indeed be likely to assign a kind of merit, but it should be understood as referring to the artist himself (who was "skillful" enough to do what he aimed at doing) rather than to the work—which may be murder, a robbery, a libel, a silly lampoon. It would scarcely be feasible to illustrate all the kinds of evidence (or supposed evidence) that may be adduced for an author's plan outside his poem. I do not know how many kinds there may be, each no doubt with somewhat special problems. Let me adduce a single example, representative I believe, if in part synthetic. Edgar Allan Poe's *Philosophy of Composition* professes to tell us how he proceeded in writing *The Raven*—a poem of a certain ideal length, presenting the most melancholy, moving, and poetic subject conceivable, the death of a beautiful woman, and making use of the most effective poetic device conceivable, a certain simple and sonorous refrain, repeated in various applications. There can be little question that *The Raven* does manifest Poe's professed intentions so far as they are specific and can be made manifest. But to argue (as some proponents of "intention" have seemed in general to argue) that, because we can here prove that the artist achieved his intentions, we know that *The Raven* is a good work of art would seem a fairly obvious kind of fatuity. A critical enterprise that would more seriously recommend itself would surely be the inquiry whether the proposed subject and technique were actually the most poetic conceivable. One kind of objection to such an argument from Poe's intention (or one explanation for giving it up) might be to say

26. See Beardsley, *Aesthetics* (1958), p. 489. Dr. Cioffi (p. 164) dismisses this form of the intentionalistic argument with great unconcern. He is no doubt largely unaware of the contexts of literary scholarship and criticism which framed our articles of 1944 and 1945. On "skill," cf. Gendin, p. 195.

that Poe's *Philosophy of Composition* is not a valid guide to his intention in the poem because it is an ex post facto invention and a tongue-in-cheek tour de force. Perhaps so. But here we catch ourselves moving from intention to intention—when does the witness mean what he says?—and we may be left with the generally not very satisfactory principle that an external statement of intention by an author has to be examined to see if it was written before the poem or after. So externality is invested with externality, and testimonies written before the poem might well have suffered by change of intention while the poem was being written.

Another sort of argument in favor of intention as a criterion of value might say: Well, what is meant is precisely the fullness of the executed plan as seen in the poem itself. We can see the author's *skill* precisely in this. To which we might retort: Yes, precisely. We see a value of fullness, richness, design in the poem itself. *From this* we infer an artist and a skillful artist, and not the other way round. We do not compare the poem with any blueprint of the author's mind.

Let us turn then and consider some phases of the intentionalistic argument relating to statements of type 4 in our plan, those of interpretation—the author's mind outside the poem as a key to his meaning inside the poem.

(4a) A few of the recent writers on the term "intention" have pointed out, as indeed Mr. Beardsley and I were careful to point out in 1944, that interpretations apparently based upon an author's "intention" often in fact refer to an intention as it is found in, or inferred from, the work itself.[27] Obviously the argument about intention (or about the author's intention outside the work) is not directed against such instances—unless in an incidental and general plea for clarity in the use of critical terms. Such arguments may extend to *conflicts* of intention, or shifts of design, in a given work. They may give rise to such notions as that of a "secret meaning" (or even an unconscious meaning) to be distinguished from an "overt meaning." "Milton was of the Devil's

27. See, for instance, John Kemp, "The Work of Art and the Artist's Intentions," *The British Journal of Aesthetics*, *4* (April 1964), 150–51; Capitan, pp. 324–26; and Gendin, p. 193.

party without knowing it." That is, Milton's *Paradise Lost,* in spite of certain contrary indications in it, on the whole makes Satan a hero. This argument can be enlarged by appeals to Milton's own rebellious personality, his political and religious prose writings. Yet it can be carried on too, and sufficiently, within the poem itself. Actually the poem itself seems to be the chief or only evidence which Blake, the author of the assertion just quoted, has in mind. Another classic instance is Tolstoy's judgment that Chekhov, in his story *Darling,* while trying to ridicule the womanliness of a woman, succeeded (like Balaam trying to curse the Israelites) only in pronouncing a blessing. Tolstoy had behind him a tradition of Russian book-reviewing which looked for covert and risky political meanings in nineteenth-century fiction.

(4b) In another variation of the same interpretive argument, the author's intention is sometimes said to have at least an "advisory" force.[28] This seems hardly a claim that ought to be debated. No doubt the author is likely to be a good guide. Yet it cannot be that on principle he is an infallible guide. As a commentator on his own works he enjoys no prescriptive, or creative, rights. If he says there is red in his poem, we will look carefully in the expectation of *finding* it.[29]

(4c) A somewhat similar sounding, but actually different, argument says that the intention of the artist (as learned in titles of works, epigraphs, and the like) may sometimes be said to fill in certain details or aspects of a work actually missing from the work but presumably needed for its understanding and appreciation.[30] In our article of 1945, Mr. Beardsley and I discussed something like this under the head of the modern poet's penchant for esoteric allusion, and we suggested that titles, epigraphs, and notes such as T. S. Eliot wrote for *The Waste Land,* were in fact loosely attached parts of poems or annexes of half-assimilated materials. As

---

28. Henry David Aiken, "The Aesthetic Relevance of Artists' Intentions," *The Journal of Philosophy,* 52 (24 November 1955), reprinted in *Problems in Aesthetics,* ed. Morris Weitz (New York, 1959), pp. 299–300. Cf Gendin, p. 194.

29. Kemp, p. 121, describes this situation very clearly.

30. Capitan, pp. 331–32.

such they seemed to raise some questions about the achieved integrity of the poems. The notes to *The Waste Land* are not a manifest virtue, rather something we accept and submit to being teased by, in view of the probable depths of the poem itself, and latterly in view of Mr. Eliot's reputation.[31] Taken literally, the argument seems to imply some deficiency in the work of art itself, some need of adjunct or aid. On the assumption that the work of art is on the whole, or basically, worthwhile, nobody would wish to rule out such help—any more than to deny a crutch to a lame man, or an extra stone to a sagging arch. Only note that the crutch must fit the man; the stone must fit the arch, and in fact the stone becomes part of the arch. These analogies seem closer to what is meant by such special invocations of artist's intentions than, say, the use of a strong glass to see a miniature painting or a strong light in a gallery. The glass and the light can find only what is already there.[32]

Certain external aids or annexes to poems, we have just assumed, do fit or are appropriate to the poems in question. More broadly, however, if we are to think of poems as having any built-in character or structure of their own at all, then the inquiry must run the risk of encountering inappropriately offered annexes, false clues, mistaken efforts of the energetic historian.

(4d) Certainly there are features of gross material or of structure in art works which not only do not call for the artist's intention to help their interpretation but will even strongly defy contradictory indications. If the artist makes a statue of granite, then it is granite, and an affidavit that he thought he was working in

---

31. See his extremely intentionalistic justification of these notes in a lecture on Dante in 1950: "I gave the references in my notes, in order to make the reader who recognizes the allusion, know that I meant him to recognize it, and know that he would have missed the point if he did not recognize it" (*To Criticize the Critic and Other Writings* [New York, 1965], p. 128).

32. The claim for artist's intentions as auxiliaries to works of art will no doubt mean somewhat different things for different kinds and instances of art. See, for instance, Beardsley, pp. 20–29; Capitan, pp. 327–33; Erwin Panofsky, "On Intentions," in *Problems in Aesthetics*, pp. 288–95, extracted from Panofsky's "History of Art as a Humanistic Discipline," in *The Meaning of the Humanities*, ed. T. M. Greene (Princeton, 1940).

marble or intended to work in marble or would rather have worked in marble will not make any difference.[33] The same principle will hold if the artist writes in English but happens to think he is writing in French. Or if he defies some code of classic rules, though he happens to think he is observing them, or vice versa. The former, or conservative, self-deception may be illustrated in Corneille's retrospective defense of *Le Cid*. The general principle for literary criticism was put precisely by Samuel Johnson in his *Preface to Shakespeare:* "Whether Shakespeare knew the unities and rejected them by design, or deviated from them by happy ignorance, it is, I think, impossible to decide and useless to inquire." [34]

(4e) Problems of local semantics may be more difficult. But even here, the more explicit the conflicting auctorial testimony, the more likely it is to seem comic in the degree of its externality and irrelevance. A member of the London Literary Club, Anthony Chamier, better known as a statesman than as a litterateur, once asked Oliver Goldsmith "What he meant by *slow,* the last word in the first line of 'The Traveller,' 'Remote, unfriended, melancholy, slow.' Did he mean tardiness of locomotion? Goldsmith, who would say something without consideration, answered 'Yes.' " But Samuel Johnson happened to be present and cut in, "No, Sir; you do not mean tardiness of locomotion; you mean, that sluggishness of mind which comes upon a man in solitude." "Chamier believed then" that Johnson "had written the line as much as if he had seen" Johnson write it.[35] It is worth adding that one editor of Goldsmith, Austin Dobson, has observed, "It is quite possible that Goldsmith meant no more than he said." [36] But an earlier commentator, John Forster, says: "Who can doubt that he also meant slowness of motion? The first point of the picture is *that.* The poet is moving slowly, his tardiness of gait measuring the heaviness of heart, the pensive spirit, the melancholy of which

33. See Beardsley, p. 20, on painting and sculpture, "the simplest descriptive level." Cf. Gendin, p. 194.
34. *Preface to Shakespeare* (1765) , paragraph 59.
35. Boswell, *Life of Johnson,* 9 April 1778.
36. *Poetical Works of Goldsmith* (Oxford, 1939) , p. 167.

it is the outward expression and sign." [37] The point of the present exposition is that Goldsmith, though undoubtedly in some sense closer to the generative intention of his own poem than the others, is not in virtue of that fact a better critic or interpreter. If Forster seems better than Dobson and better even than Johnson in this instance, the grounds of his judgment and ours must lie in the observable force and relevance of the word "slow" in the *context* of the first line of Goldsmith's pensive travelogue.

Mr. Beardsley has cited the nearly parallel instance of A. E. Housman's angry attempt to deny the irony at expense of state and church manifest in his poem for Queen Victoria's fiftieth anniversary. "Get you the sons your fathers got, And God will save the Queen." Here a statement made in retrospect and under provocation, a kind of profession of loyalty to a sovereign, stands in sharp contradiction not only to the cunning details of the poem in question but to the well-known skeptical and cynical cast of the poet's canon.

The two instances just adduced may seem a parody of the intentionalistic argument, but they are no more than a fair parody of that argument as often formulated. Simple, even extreme, examples have the advantage of revealing and clarifying principles.

A classic instance of an author's serious intention, antecedent to and simultaneous with the writing, yet doomed to defeat, is Chekhov's desire (revealed in his letters) to have his *Seagull* and *Cherry Orchard* produced as comedies—resulting only in Stanislavsky's successful and now well-established interpretation of them as tragedies—or at least as very cloudy "dramas." [38]

---

37. *Goldsmith* (London, 1848), *1, 369.*

38. Beardsley, p. 24; Margolis, pp. 97, 189; David Magarshack, *Chekhov the Dramatist* (New York, Hill and Wang, 1960), pp. 188–89, *The Seagull,* p. 273, *The Cherry Orchard.* "*The Seagull* is usually interpreted on the stage as a tragedy (a misinterpretation Stanislavsky was the first to impose on the play), and yet Chekhov always referred to it as a comedy" (p. 188). "Practically every producer . . . in spite of Chekhov's unmistakable intentions, regards the play as a tragedy" (p. 189). We are here concerned in part with nuances of local meaning, in part also with whole dramatic structure and import. The example of Chekhov might well have been adduced above under 4d.

Margolis, p. 96, quotes the instance, no doubt unusual in the annals of

(4f) But let us now refine (or complicate) the argument a little with an example from the other end of a scale of explicitness in auctorial testimony—where no single explicit statement is adduced, but where the author's life and canon or some parts of them are urged as a surrounding and controlling context for the poem or some details of it. In our article of 1945, Mr. Beardsley and I wrote: "The meaning of words is the history of words, and the biography of an author, his use of a word, and the associations which the word has for *him,* are part of the word's history and meaning." But a critic who is habitually concerned with this kind of evidence, we added, will in the long run produce a far different sort of comment from that of the critic who is mainly concerned with the public linguistic and cultural elements of the poem.

We are now seeking a maximum or crucial instance where a poet's private or personal and habitual meaning (as inferred from external documents) clearly clashes with what he managed to realize in the public materials (linguistic and cultural) of his poem. Such instances are no doubt difficult to find, because poets by and large do manage to say what they mean. There is a sense in which, even when their words are "peculiar" or catachrestic, poets remain the "servants" of their language rather than its "masters." [39] In order to show a clear instance of the sort of conflict we are interested in, it may be necessary for the expositor himself to drive both sides of an interpretive difference, the intentionalistic and the non-intentionalistic—and thus perhaps to expose himself to the opportunism of the captious. But the following may serve at least to define the issue. The materials are well known, but not the interpretive problem as I shall urge it. William Blake wrote in a sketchbook:

---

literature, of Melville's acknowledgment that Hawthorne had revealed to him allegorical meanings in *Moby Dick* which he himself had not specifically "meant."

39. Cf. T. S. Eliot, "What Dante Means to Me" (1950), in *To Criticize the Critic,* p. 133. The terms are Eliot's. Though he would concede that "some great English poets . . . were privileged by their genius to abuse the English language," yet the poets who have best served their language are the greatest, Virgil, Dante, Shakespeare.

An ancient Proverb

Remove away that blackning church
Remove away that marriage hearse
Remove away that man of blood
You'll quite remove the ancient curse [40]

These lines remained in the sketchbook, where they deserved to remain. They are a raw expression of certain soreheaded antinomian attitudes which are beyond doubt a part of Blake's biography at the period when he was writing the *Songs of Experience*. Blake also wrote in the same sketchbook a draft for his "song" *London,* which he worked over with much struggle, adding only as an afterthought, in several successive versions, the last black stanza.

I wander thro' each charter'd street,
Near where the charter'd Thames does flow,
And mark in every face I meet
Marks of weakness, marks of woe.

In every cry of every Man,
In every Infant's cry of fear,
In every voice, in every ban,
The mind-forg'd manacles I hear:

How the Chimney-sweeper's cry
Every black'ning Church appalls;
And the hapless Soldier's sigh
Runs in blood down Palace walls.

But most, thro' midnight streets I hear
How the youthful Harlot's curse
Blasts the new-born Infant's tear,
And blights with plagues the Marriage hearse.[41]

40. Number XXXV of the Rossetti manuscript, in Joseph H. Wicksteed, *Blake's Innocence and Experience* (London, 1928), after p. 256, p. 261, and facing p. 285; cf. *Poetry and Prose of William Blake,* ed. Geoffrey Keynes (London, 1932), p. 96.

41. Keynes, p. 75; Wicksteed, after p. 244, and p. 252.

The concluding phrase repeats that of the second line of the *Ancient Proverb* and creates a crux on which I wish to focus. This dark city poem is about human "weakness" and "woe" as they may be observed in certain (uncertain) visual and auditory betrayals ("marks" and "cries") and in certain (uncertain) imputed human causes (charters, bans, mind-forged manacles). The word "ban" as it is used in the second stanza of the poem no doubt includes many kinds of legal or official yells, proclamations, summonses, prohibitions, curses—no doubt even marriage bans. At this point let us consult one of the best informed and most soberly reliable of recent Blake critics.

> The one thing needful in achieving this transformation [of the human spirit] is the removal of the mind-forged manacles of the institutional tyrannies—marriage, the church, and the king.
>
> "Every ban" . . . is a multiple clank of the awful trinity of king, priest, and marriage.
>
> It is the marriage hearse that breeds youthful (and thus potentially innocent) harlots, by creating the necessity for prostitution. If there were no marriage, there would be no ungratified desires, and therefore no harlots. Thus it is ultimately the marriage hearse itself and not the youthful harlot which breeds the pestilence that blights the marriage hearse.[42]

Mr. E. D. Hirsch, as I have said, is well informed about Blake and reliable, and I believe he gives us an accurate reading of a sort of intention which Blake probably did entertain, a phase at least of Blake's habitual mind as it may be supposed to stand at some distance behind the poem. Mr. Hirsch gives us a good and learned instance of the new cryptography in Blake reading. "If there were no marriage, there would be no ungratified desires, and therefore no harlots." One thing, however, which perhaps he does not notice, or perhaps does not worry about, is that these ideas are silly. (Why wouldn't there be *many* ungratified desires, as many at least as there were losers in stag combats, or wooers rejected, or pursuers

42. E. D. Hirsch, Jr., *Innocence and Experience: An Introduction to Blake* (New Haven, 1964), pp. 263–65.

eluded, or matings frustrated? and *many* harlots? and *many* whore-masters?) An admirer of Blake the poet might well be content to leave these ideas, if he could, on a back shelf in the doctrinaire part of Blake's mind. What if we actually do find them or manage to put them in the poem? Won't this make the poem silly? And, since interpretation and evaluation are at the very least closely related, won't we be in danger of reading the poem as a pretty bad poem? And isn't this poem, in fact, supposed to be a masterpiece, "one of the best city poems ever written"? Isn't it, in fact, a masterpiece? It will be worthwhile to look closely at the difference between the last stanza of the engraved poem *London* and the crude second line of *An ancient Proverb,* which stayed in the sketchbook. Blake's struggle with *London* was in part a struggle to make the last line of the last stanza viable. The tough fact was that the word "marriage" in the history of English usage and culture was not the name of an evil. ("Let me not to the marriage of true minds admit impediments.") It was the name of a sacred institution and a first principle of stability for nearly every important value in a whole religiously and ethically oriented civilization and culture. The explosive force of the two violently juxtaposed terms at the end of the last line of *London* is a poetic fact. But this was not to be achieved by the easy way of simple supposition or assertion (though that may be a rationale which very well suits the aims of the biographical critic or cryptographer). Here the angry conscience of William Blake the doctrinaire prophet and activist clashed violently with the more tactful and skillful conscience of William Blake the poet, master and servant of the English language.[43] The latter conscience, apparently after a hard struggle, won and (perhaps without Blake's being fully aware of what happened—who knows?) saved him from engraving a poem with a lame, perhaps even silly and ruinous, last line. Let us imagine that some inquisitor of school curricula, reading Mr. Hirsch's gloss on *London,* were to file a protest against corrupting the minds of

43. The evidence of the Rossetti manuscript supports the biographical dimension which I introduce for the sake of dialogue with the biographically minded. The distinction between the doctrinaire man and the subtle poem would remain even if the poetic achievement had cost Blake no trouble at all.

schoolchildren by the required study of this depraved poem. One sort of answer, from the defenders of the English curriculum, might be that it was good for children to hear all views and to be exposed to a liberal assault upon the mores in which home, church, and state were trying to educate them. But another answer that surely would not be long delayed would be to the effect that Blake's *London* in fact says no such thing. True, the English teacher or the school principal would say, the poem stresses charters and mind-forged manacles, but circumstances, real and symbolic (the cry of sweeps, the decay of churches, the blood of soldiers), are adduced to give specific topical color to the imputations. We are dealing with very concretely colored instances. And in the last stanza it is potently suggested that there is a very real and evil antecedent cause why the marriage bed turns to a hearse. For an initiate reading of the last stanza, consult the career of an eighteenth-century Londoner like James Boswell or Charles Hanbury Williams.

In sum, a critic who says that the "poem" means that "if there were no marriage, there would be no ungratified desires," ought to show that this meaning actually operates in the poem or is generated by it—and is not merely a concealed or balked idea entertained by the author as revolutionary person. I myself think the poem is better than that meaning, and to judge from the contexts where the poem has often appeared and from earlier critiques, it would seem that most readers have also thought so.

> Yet even these [blackened churches and blood-stained palace walls] are less terrible than the hideous perversion of the fairest joy on earth, voiced in the midnight cry of the young harlot. Love itself and the beauty of marriage and birth are stained by this most cruel misery of all.[44]

I have set up this discussion of the poem as a frame of reference within which a student may be able to see the direction in which his own mind moves in search of evidence for the meaning and

44. Wicksteed, p. 190. "I do not doubt that he continued to accept marriage at its face value even after his mind had learnt to entertain the revolutionary suggestions of the rationalistic and antinomian circles he came to mingle in" (p. 215).

value of a poem. When he can really see the difference between the directions and the results, then let him decide.

Mr. Hirsch's method of reading *London* is not an isolated instance, though his clarity in realizing what he is doing and his frankness in admitting it may be unusual. A new mode in historical studies, which I would describe as a kind of attempted Vista-Vision intentionalism, searches reasons for inferring an author's intention not only in the whole canon of his own works and life record, early and late, but in motifs selected from anywhere in the intellectual ambient of his era. Let me cite a remarkable instance of this new mode in Paul de Man's essay of 1956, "Keats and Hölderlin." [45] Here, with the pursuit of the poet as philosopher-hero in full cry and the method of theme and analogy rampant, we bring Keats's *Endymion* into line with his own later *Hyperion* and with Hölderlin's novel *Hyperion* by the simple if eloquently disguised method of arguing that throughout the poem Keats failed to say what he meant. His interest in another kind of meaning was just too much for him. Keats should have been writing, or he wished to be writing, about a very serious subject, the "eccentric road" of man's repetitive search for recovery of "unity of being." But he wrote actually about love (erotic love) . "No wonder it becomes difficult to keep apart the passages in which love is an actual experience, among others, from those in which it is a symbol for something else. But only at the expense of this effort [i.e. violence] can *Endymion* be given a thematic coherence which Keats's *Hyperion* amply substantiates" (p. 36) . We proceed to a reading of *Endymion* which makes its point only at the expense of finding the imagery "incongruous," "confusing," "bizarre," "stifled," "awkward" (pp. 37–38) —in short, utterly ineffectual (or inexpressive) and hence unpoetic. This is Keats's *Endymion*. "A thing of beauty is a joy for ever."

Some of our critics have argued that Mr. Beardsley and I have examined the term "intention" in too restricted and too simply mentalistic a sense (intention in the mind of the artist) ; at the same time they have adduced statements by us that show that we do not in fact object to certain broader invocations of "intention"

45. *Comparative Literature, 8* (Winter 1956) , 28–45, esp. 36–38.

(in effect, "intention" as present and verifiable "intent" in works of art themselves). And they have praised other writers, or themselves, for taking the term "intention" in a broader (or at least other) and more "generous" sense.[46] One writer has pointed out that we selected an example which showed what we meant and tended to support our argument, and thus he considers our example "tendentious." [47] It is difficult to see how such arguments are better than obscurantist devices of one-upmanship. We took "intention" in a specific or limited sense, because it was just the difference between this sense and the broader (or other) sense that we believed to be often obscured in critical argument, with consequent concealed dilution of, or escape from, objective criticism. At the same time, we tried to make the idea of "intention" a focal point (and I still believe it was a well-chosen focal point) for a cluster of genetically oriented ideas (inspiration, expression, authenticity, sincerity, purpose, and the like). What might seem at first glance a merely verbal and ambiguous cluster turns out on acquaintance to be a dynamic pattern that is well treated with as much unity of vision as possible. It is my opinion that as criteria for criticism these ideas stand or fall together.

Both in our essay of 1945 and in our earlier dictionary article, Mr. Beardsley and I argued "that the design or intention of the author is neither available nor desirable as a standard for judging the success of a work of literary art." A recent writer on the same theme has accused Mr. Beardsley of having, in 1958, weakened this thesis by asserting merely that the "specific intention" of the artist outside the work is "practically never available"—thus, it would appear, making the question only empirical and forfeiting its "theoretical" and "philosophical" status.[48] What we meant in 1945, and what in effect I think we managed to say, was that the closest one could ever get to the artist's intending or meaning mind, outside his work, would be still short of his *effective* intention or *operative* mind as it appears in the work itself and can be

46. Margolis, pp. 103 and 189, citing Isabel Hungerland, "The Concept of Intention in Art Criticism," *Journal of Philosophy,* 52 (24 November 1955), 733–42, and other sources.
47. Dr. Cioffi, p. 167.
48. Margolis, p. 103, quoting Beardsley, p. 490.

read from the work. Such is the concrete and fully answerable character of words as aesthetic medium.[49] The intention outside the poem is always subject to the corroboration of the poem itself. No better evidence, in the nature of things, can be adduced than the poem itself. This observation seems to me less needed in meeting the directly evaluative form of the argument (see above, pp. 207–10) than in meeting the interpretive form which we have just been considering. The statement in our essay of 1945 should certainly have read: "The design or intention of the author is neither available nor desirable as a standard for judging either the meaning or the value of a work of literary art."

We have never said that the way of the objective critic could be smooth, easy, or perfect. Still we have tried to delineate one of the principles by which this critic will have to discipline his efforts unless he wishes to surrender to the flux, the gossip, the muddle and the "motley" for which philosophers like Dr. Cioffi, Professor Aldridge, and Mr. Cruttwell seem so earnestly to yearn.

It is true that verbal compositions do not subsist metaphysically, by or in themselves, as visual words on paper. The difference between "inside" the poem and "outside" the poem (to which some of our critics object[50]) is not like the difference between the printed words and the margin of the page. But neither are verbal compositions merely passing acts or moments of the human spirit, sounds heard then or now but not again. The words have their

49. One of our critics, Emilio Roma III, seems to grasp this principle firmly enough and to accept it. ("The Scope of the Intentional Fallacy," *The Monist*, 50 [April 1966], 250–65, esp. 250–51, 256, 265). It is perhaps his main reason for recognizing a sort of "minimal" and "pitifully easy" meaning in our notion of the "intentional fallacy." But he believes that a distinction between what the speaker means and what the "sentence" means, urged very explicitly by Mr. Beardsley in 1958, is not to be found in our essay of 1945. Mr. Roma writes with the air (e.g. p. 254) of painfully spelling out what we said. "Style," he says, "is treated [by us] as though it had nothing whatsoever to do with content" (p. 265). To me at least, and I think to Mr. Beardsley, this can come only as a matter of surprise. How much of what we have written, in the essay of 1945 and elsewhere, is really understood by Mr. Roma?

50. Roma, pp. 251–52, 258, 262; Cioffi, pp. 167, 170 (on excluding "illicit sources" of interpretation). The word "motley" in our text just above is from Cioffi, pp. 176, 183, taken by him "probably" from Wittgenstein.

peculiar existence in their meaning, and that derives from and is determined by their context or their history. The study of poems in their public contexts of language and culture sees them in a spread-out and universalized relation to those contexts. It is a study of pattern and ideal and is the only study which is capable of discriminating between the cogently organized artistic structure (both concrete and universal) and the mere particularities of personal moments, accidental and nonce meanings. What kind of unity or entity is the most valid object of literary study? Roughly, there are three possible answers: the Age, the Author, the Work. Various kinds of interest in race, milieu, and moment (so familiar to academic literary criticism for more than two centuries) come under the first head. Studies of literary genre come here when they get out of hand, and also the more extreme instances of deference to the historical audience.[51] One kind of ultimate metaphysician in favor of the author may be found in Benedetto Croce, who hardly believes in the literary work at all, certainly not in works of any length, but sees the whole duty of the critic as the pursuit of the "poetical motive," the "poetic personality" which he can find anthologically here and there in writers like Goethe, Corneille, and Dante. A newer sort of canonical historicist, as we have seen, makes the idolatrous assumption that a given author's mind or vision during his whole career is necessarily a coherent whole or a dialectic development, as good an entity as, or better than, any one of his works. For the objective critic of literary works, an author has as much unity as he can demonstrate in any given work or in a part of a work. The whole for which the critic looks is the coherently expressive structure, large or small. The poet's canon and life are "the most essential part of the context of the poem"[52] only to the extent that the poet is talking to himself. The words

51. This may involve what Mr. E. D. Hirsch calls the "fallacy of the homogeneous past." "The homogeneous critic assumes that everybody in a given cultural milieu shares the same basic attitudes and beliefs. He is content to speak of the Greek Mind, the Medieval Mind, the Victorian Mind" ("Criticism versus Historicism," mimeograph of a paper read at the meeting of the Modern Language Association, December 1963).

52. Hyatt H. Waggoner, in *What To Say About a Poem*, *CEA Chapbook*, by W. K. Wimsatt, Jr., and others, ed. Donald A. Sears (College English Association, 1963), pp. 22, 32.

which the poet writes in a given passage depend for their meaning in one sense on the personal context and the author's intention (his word as *parole*), but they depend also, in a sense more important to the critic, on the wider context of the language (his words as *langue*) and culture.[53] Otherwise they would never, here and now, there and then, make sense to anybody but the author himself. Authors characteristically graduate from earlier, naïve stages and write masterpieces. Characteristically also they write later weaker works. To appreciate *Lear* and *Hamlet* it is not necessary to take into account *A Comedy of Errors* or *Timon of Athens* (or such parts of the latter as Shakespeare wrote) or even *The Tempest*. The search for the author's generative intention as context of the poem is a search for a temporal moment which must, as the author and the poem live on, recede and ever recede into the forgotten, as all moments do. Poems, on this theory of their

53. See Mr. Hirsch's exposition of Saussure's distinction ("Objective Interpretation," pp. 473–75), where *langue,* the "system of linguistic possibilities shared by a speech community," "contains words and sentence-forming principles, but it contains no sentences." A poem or any other verbal text containing sentences cannot then simply "represent a segment of *langue*" (as modern literary theorists are said to hold) but must be a *parole,* "a particular, selective actualization from *langue,*" a determinate individual expression. "Only individuals utter *paroles,*" and "a *parole* of the speech community is non-existent." "Meaning requires a meaner." When we come to the difficulty of the "bungled text," the "freshman essay," the malapropism (which, let me add, is the basic difficulty of poem and purpose made large and unavoidable), we solve it by saying that the author's text, failing to "represent the *parole* he desired to convey," "represents no *parole* at all." But such an intuitionist and absolute (or Crocean) conclusion does not sit well in the abstractive and scientific premises (of *langue* and *parole*) with which we have begun. If we are going to have "words" and "principles" conceived as prior to *parole,* we must face the possibility of their being badly put together. A "house" put together of ill-matched cardboard prefabrications would not be no house at all, or nothing, but simply a bad house.

Mr. Hirsch's *Validity in Interpretation* (New Haven, Yale University Press, 1967), which urges his views in greater detail and usefully reprints his essay of 1960, appeared only some time after I had completed the present essay. Mr. Beardsley, in an essay entitled "Textual Meaning and Authorial Meaning," has written what I consider a shrewd critique of the book, scheduled to appear in a symposium in *Genre, 1,* No. 2 (June 1968), a new quarterly issued from the University of Illinois at Chicago Circle.

meaning, must always steadily grow less and less correctly known and knowable; they must dwindle in meaning and being toward a vanishing point. The best known and most valuable poem must be that written but a moment ago—and its best or only possible audience must be the author. But poems we know are not really like that. The most self-assured authors publish their works and hang upon public recognition. Shakespeare has more meaning and value now than he had in his own day. There is a sense in which even Homer, though we construe his language with pain and are not sure how many persons he was, has more meaning and is more valuable today than ever before.

Literary Interpretation

Victor Erlich

The Masks of Nikolaj Gogol

To say that Gogol is one of the most controversial major figures in Russian literature is to offer one of the few noncontroversial statements that can be legitimately made about this baffling writer. Both during his lifetime and after his death, Gogol often was a center of what he himself called in a letter to a friend a "whirlwind of misunderstandings." Though the magnitude of Gogol's achievement is clearly not at issue, we are still far from agreeing as to the nature of his genius, as to the meaning of his bizarre art and his still weirder life.

No student of Gogol needs to be reminded of the fact that the haunting, uncanny quality of his prose finds a striking counterpart in the well-advertised strangeness of the man behind it. "Queer," "strange," "enigmatic"—adjectives such as these abound in the eyewitness testimony. "What an intelligent, queer, and sick creature!" exclaims Turgenev.[1] S. Aksakov, sympathetic and bewildered, speaks of the "unintelligible strangeness of his spirit." [2] A. O. Rosset writes to his sister, A. O. Smirnova, who in Gogol's later years seems to have been his closest friend and confidante: "Gogol was one of the most undeciphered (nerazgadannykh) men I knew." [3] "Enigma" is the key term in Vjazemskij's poetic epitaph: "You who have flitted past us as a willful enigma." "Your life was an enigma, so today is your death." [4] Interestingly enough, Gogol seemed to share some of this bafflement. In a letter to Zhukovskij

1. I. Turgenev, *Literary Reminiscences and Autobiographical Fragments* (New York, Farrar, Straus and Cudahy, 1958), p. 161.

2. S. Aksakov, *Istorija moego znakomstva s Gogolem* (1854) (Moscow, Izd. Akademii Nauk SSSR, 1960), p. 17.

3. Quoted from N. P. Barsukov, *Zhizn' i trudy M. P. Pogodina*, (St. Petersburg, 1888–1911), *11*, 547.

4. P. A. Vjazemskij, "Gogol" (1853), *Polnoe sobranie sochinenij*, (St. Petersburg, 1887), *11*, 10–11.

written in 1842 he looks to Part II of *Dead Souls* as a moment of spiritual clarification or breakthrough which, at long last, will offer a solution to the "riddle of my existence." [5]

Doubtless, Gogol was an unhappy, anxiety-ridden, and profoundly disturbed man. Though it is clearly much too late for psychiatric help, it may not be too late for an illuminating retrospective diagnosis. The fact of the matter is that the extant attempts to assess Gogol's personality in psychiatric terms have been of limited value.

The fiftieth anniversary of Gogol's death, which occasioned a spate of memoirs and of critical or biographical reevaluations, featured at least three post-factum diagnoses. The most thoughtful and plausible of them, N. Bazhenov's "Gogol's Illness and Death," describes Gogol as a depressive, most likely a manic-depressive.[6] In a more ambitious and wide-ranging disquisition, drawing on both biographical and literary evidence, Dr. V. Chizh urges the view of Gogol as an all-around psychotic, complete with paranoia, delusions of grandeur, premature senility which presumably set in at the age of thirty, and a plethora of other symptoms.[7] Some of Chizh's hypotheses may be valid, but he clearly weakens his case by what could be charitably termed ideological parochialism. At some point, Gogol's "reactionary" views are adduced as incontrovertible proof of his psychosis—a reasoning which assumes a more organic relationship between liberalism and sanity than can be conclusively demonstrated. The third psychiatrist, Dr. G. Troshin,[8] pronounced Chizh ludicrously wrong and gave Gogol, perhaps a bit too hastily, a clean bill of mental health. His symptoms, such as they were, were adjudged purely somatic. Gogol's life, to Troshin, is a "tug-of-war between physical frailty and genius." A layman may find all this just a bit confusing, though he will do well to remember that the above controversy represents a very early stage in the development of Russian psychiatry.

5. N. V. Gogol, *Sobranie sochinenij*, (Moscow, 1953) , *6*, 336.

6. N. Bazhenov, "Bolezn' i smert' Gogolja," *Russkaja mysl'*, (1902), *1*, 132–49; 2, 52–71.

7. V. Chizh, "Bolezn' N. V. Gogolja," *Voprosy filosofii i psikhologii*, 2–5 (1903) , 1 (1904) .

8. G. Troshin, "Genij i zdorov'e N. V. Gogolja," *Voprosy filosofii i psikhologii* (1905) , *1*, 37–85; 2, 187–249; *3*, 333–83.

More recent attempts to approach Gogol's personality and work in depth-psychological terms have been somewhat more provocative. I am not referring here primarily to the specific sexual symbolism which can be so easily read into some of the Gogol plots or incidents. (Few Freudians—and indeed not too many non-Freudians—will resist the temptation to invoke castration anxiety in connection with "The Nose" or to think of phallic symbols while contemplating Ivan Fedorovich Shponka's burlesque dream.[9]) I have, rather, in mind the ingenious and partly convincing discussions of Gogol's "retreat from love," [10] of the manifold ways in which his vaunted fear of sex infiltrates his writings, now through the theme of destructive passion that burns its victim to ashes ("Viy") or makes him betray his primary loyalties ("Taras Bulba"), now through his blindingly, unbelievably dazzling women who, be they witches or goddesses, are objects of awestruck worship rather than of quenchable desire.

It occurs to me that the problem of a possible connection between Gogol's weird personality and his grotesque art is susceptible to yet another treatment. Two general propositions suggest themselves at this point: First, an attempt to establish a link, however tenuous, between the core of the writer's personality and the nature of his craft can be a more rewarding and critical procedure than a search for possible psychic roots of theme or incident. Second, whatever one's estimate of the strengths and weaknesses of the Freudian vision, it stands to reason that standard psychoanalytic concepts are not always the most appropriate guide through the thickets of an artist's self. More specifically, it is my contention that, while the "Freudian" concern with Gogol's warped sexuality may help illuminate certain emphases in his work, in our efforts to pin down what Aksakov has called the unintelligible strangeness of Gogol's spirit we are liable to get more

9. Some will recall that this pathetically timid squire dreams of being pulled by a rope up a belfry which, very much to his surprise, turns out to be his formidable aunt. To make things even more disturbing, it is his wife who does the pulling.

10. Cf. the provocative paper by Hugh McLean, "Gogol's Retreat from Love: Toward an Interpretation of *Mirgorod*," *American Contributions to the Fourth International Congress of Slavicists* (The Hague, Mouton and Co., 1958), pp. 225–44.

assistance from existential psychology than from straightforward psychiatry or orthodox psychoanalysis. The view of the human psyche which lays special stress on such dichotomies as the real self versus the false, unauthentic self, which pays special attention to the devices of concealment and impersonation employed by a peculiarly frail ego as protection against the encroachments of feared reality,[11] is likely to shed significant light on the strange case of Nikolaj Gogol.

A careful reading of Gogol's copious correspondence—a revealing if not altogether attractive body of evidence—is bound to make us wary of hasty diagnoses and tempting simplifications. Thus, it would be misleading to describe Gogol without qualifications as a lonely, withdrawn man, in a word, an "isolate." There is ample evidence that he had a strong need for friendship and intimacy, that he was capable of cordiality and solicitude, that he often took an active, sometimes in fact overactive, interest in his fellow humans. Yet it is also a matter of record—and a fact richly attested to by Gogol's correspondence—that most of his contemporaries who tried to be his friends often found him tantalizingly elusive, devious, and distrustful, that even those closest to him kept complaining of not being able to reach him, of not knowing what made him tick. Aksakov, whose warm and sensitive memoir was quoted above, speaks of "the long and painful story of an incomplete understanding between Gogol and the people who were closest to him . . . who thought themselves his friends." "Not until Gogol's death," he avers, "was their faith in his sincerity absolute or unquestioning." [12]

---

11. For an important statement of this position, see R. D. Laing, *The Divided Self: A Study of Sanity and Madness* (London, Tavistock Publications, 1960). Some of Laing's formulations seem remarkably opposite. One of his test cases is described thus: "His ideal was never to give himself away to others . . . . His personality was not true self-expression, but was largely a series of impersonations" (p. 74). At a later stage, Laing's discussion of the "false-self system" contains the following passage: "Anxiety creeps back more intensely than ever. The unrealness of perception . . . extends to feelings of deadness of the shared world as a whole, to the body, in fact, to all that is and infiltrates even to the true self. Everything becomes suffused with nothingness" (p. 152).

12. Aksakov, p. 110.

If anything, this was an understatement. The Moscow editor and historian, N. P. Pogodin, a coarser and more impetuous man than Aksakov, flatly accused Gogol of insincerity in a moment of exasperation. The same charge, couched this time in political terms, was hurled at Gogol a few years later by Belinskij in his famous diatribe. Will this grave accusation stand up under closer scrutiny? I do not think so. The notion of the late Gogol's ideological hypocrisy was already challenged by Chernyshevskij who had as much reason to resent the tenor of *Selected Passages from a Correspondence with Friends* as did Belinskij. How about personal relations? It seems to me that the tragic flaw here was not insincerity but a strange lack of spontaneity, not pretending to feelings which one did not have, but an inability to "project" directly, to find a straightforward, humanly credible vehicle for feelings which one did experience, a failure to achieve emotional communication with others and, I suspect, with oneself. Gogol alludes to this crippling defect in a revealing letter to Shevyrëv: "I never could speak frankly about myself . . . but let me assure you: everything down to the last movement will yet be revealed. There is much that I have not been able to say, not because I don't want to say it, but I can't say it because I have not yet found the words with which to say it." [13]

In fact, as one wades through the volumes of Gogol's copious correspondence, a paradoxical fact seems to emerge: The more vital the emotion which the writer is trying to convey, the more stilted, ponderous, "dead" the mode of expression. Nearly every time Gogol tries to "open up," to unburden himself, a kind of stylistic rigor mortis sets in. A would-be confession freezes into a cliché which undercuts credibility and blocks the hoped-for response. An intimate chat is nipped in the bud as it degenerates into a stodgy harangue, a sanctimonious homily.

This is apparent already in Gogol's peculiarly "unchildish" Nezhin letters.[14] A schoolboy of nearly sixteen, he reacts to the

13. Quoted from "N. V. Gogol, Pis'ma k druz'jam," *Russkaja starina* (St. Petersburg, 1875), *14*, 118.

14. The point was made by a perceptive student of Gogol, V. V. Kallash, in *N. V. Gogol v vospominanijakh sovremennikov i perepiske* (Moscow, 1924).

news about his father's death in a stilted and rhetorical letter.[15] Nearly twenty years later he attempts to lay his soul bare to S. Aksakov, Pogodin, and Shevyrëv.[16] A characteristic failure of communication ensues. Writing from abroad, Gogol makes a genuine attempt to take his Moscow friends into his confidence, to convey to them the nature of his moral crisis and prevail upon them to serve as his spiritual executors. What emerges instead is a tedious sermon and a pedantic, overbearing, tactless set of instructions which baffles and antagonizes his would-be confidants.

Finally, there is that crowning "misunderstanding," the debacle of *Selected Passages*. When, in an unprecedented act of moral exhibitionism, Gogol proceeded to share with the Russian reading public his hunger for salvation, his desperate reaching toward true Christian faith, he did not merely shock and horrify his erstwhile radical admirers; he also alienated most of his conservative readers, not so much by the tenor of his preaching, as by its governessy, lifeless ponderousness. Only in a few passages of this strange and much-abused book does live emotion break through the crust of sanctimonious rhetoric. When this happens, the feeling more often than not is one of anguish, of moral panic: "I am terrified, countrymen!"

Apollon Grigoriev, who in his less turgid moments could be very perceptive indeed, contributes a telling, if somewhat cryptic, phrase: "Gogol was an altogether manufactured [*sdelannyj*] man." [17] Unfortunately, Grigoriev failed to amplify his tantalizing dictum. It is tempting to assume that he meant something akin to what was suggested here—notably that Gogol was a thoroughly unspontaneous man who barricaded himself behind a set of con-

15. On April 23, 1825, Gogol writes to his mother: "Do not worry, dearest mummy! I endured this blow with the firmness of a true Christian. True, I was at first terribly shaken by this news . . . I even wanted to take my life, but God has prevented me from this; and toward the evening, I detected in myself only sadness . . . which finally turned into a light, barely noticeable melancholy mixed with a feeling of awe toward our Maker . . . I bless you, my holy faith. Only in you do I find a source of comfort and consolation" (*Sochinenija N. V. Gogolja* [St. Petersburg, 1915,] *9*, 9).

16. See especially Gogol's letter to Shevyrëv, February 28, 1843 (ibid., pp. 178–87).

17. A. Grigoriev, "I. S. Turgenev i ego dejatelnost' po povodu 'Dvorjanskogo gnezda'" (1859), ibid., *1*, 328.

trivances, that out of an irrational fear of premature exposure, of rebuff and ridicule, he tended to hide his pathologically vulnerable self behind a screen of rhetoric, a crust of "moral make-up" (Kallash),[18] and thus, ironically, to ensure the very misrepresentation which he was so anxious to prevent.

Is it permissible, at this point, to leap from "Wahrheit" to "Dichtung," from the man's style of life to the style of his fiction? I believe it is, provided that we do not lose track of the fact that art as distinguished from "life" thrives on artifice and that we treat the link between the two realms as a mutually illuminating analogy rather than a one-way causal relationship. Clearly, the basis for the analogy—such as it is—is the motif of the mask. Gogol's adeptness at producing an illusion of oral narration, at mimicking the phraseological and intonational mannerisms of a "folksy" speaker, has been often commented on. Yet the "orality" here is part of a larger phenomenon—the tendency to speak in somebody else's voice, the strategy of indirection and impersonation.

It all starts, we will recall, with the garrulous beekeeper Rudyj Pan'ko in *Evenings on a Farm near Dikanka*—a rustic old-timer, a chatty, rambling storyteller who, incidentally, obtrudes himself upon the story only intermittently. In Gogol's Ukrainian goblin tales, Pan'ko had a definite function to perform. His folksiness, his dialect helped authenticate the proceedings by lending an additional regional flavor to the pseudo-folkloristic *Kunstmärchen*. Yet Gogol's proclivity for hiding behind a lowbrow narrator survived this particular motivation. The voice of a "local yokel," be he a naïve villager, a small-town gossip, or a chronically befuddled St. Petersburg dweller, is heard in the moronic raptures of the narrator of "Ivan Ivanovich and Ivan Nikiforovich,"[19] the inane meanderings toward the end of "The Nose,"[20] in the misplaced

18. V. V. Kallash, ed. *N. V. Gogol v vospominanijakh sovremennikov i perepiske* (Moscow, 1924), p. 8.

19. "What a glorious coat Ivan Ivanovich has! A most splendid coat! And the astrakhan! Hang it all, such an astrakhan! . . . Ivan Ivanovich is such a wonderful man!" (*Mirgorod* [New York, Noonday Press, 1962], p. 221).

20. "To think of such an affair happening in the northern capital of our vast empire! As we consider all the angles of this affair, we see that there is much in it that is improbable. . . . Yet, even considering these things, there is something in this whole business. Whatever you may say, such things do happen in this world: seldom, to be sure, but they do happen."

hyperboles of the description of the governor's ball in *Dead Souls*,[21] and, last but certainly not least, in that masterpiece of inarticulateness, of hemming and hawing, of timid, status-conscious stammering which is the narrative texture of "The Overcoat."

Now there is nothing uniquely or even characteristically Gogolian about the very presence of a narrator mediating between the author and his audience. This is a frequent and time-honored literary device. What is more pertinent is the cat-and-mouse game which Gogol tends to play here with the point of view, the "now you see it, now you don't" quality of the narrative manner. As Viktor Vinogradov aptly pointed out, Gogol's prose is a verbal crazy quilt, a bizarre mosaic of various modes of discourse—literary, rhetorical, and colloquial—which fails to project a psychologically coherent image of the narrator.[22] To put it somewhat differently, it is a dizzying succession of interlocking and mutually cancelling verbal masks.

"The Story of How Ivan Ivanovich Quarrelled with Ivan Nikiforovich" is a good case in point. It will not quite do to say simply that the tale is told by a babbling fool whose glaring inadequacy is shown up, in the final passage, by the much-quoted authorian sigh, "It's a tedious world, gentlemen!" Seen at closer range, the narrative texture of "The Two Ivans" proves to encompass at least three disparate modes. The comic oral narration of a provincial chatterbox who raves about Ivan Ivanovich's "glorious coat" and his alleged refinement and laments the rift between two "ornaments of Mirgorod" yields, be it for a short time, to a thoroughly literary mode as the narrator introduces, in a mock-heroic vein, the theme of Ivan Ivanovich's nocturnal sabotage.

> "Oh, if I were a painter, I would have depicted the charm of that night wondrously well! I would have depicted the whole

21. "There was no end of tastefulness about their attire: the muslins, satins, and tulles were of such fashionable pastel shades that one could not even give their names, to such a degree had the refinement of taste attained!" (*Dead Souls* [New York and Toronto, Rinehart and Co., 1948], p. 188).

22. Cf. V. Vinogradov, *Etjudy o stile Gogolja* (Leningrad, 1926), p. 150.

of Mirgorod asleep; how the countless stars were looking steadily down upon the sleeping town; how the palpable stillness was broken by the everlasting barking of dogs . . . I would depict the black shadow of a bat across the white road flitting as it settled on the white chimneys of the houses. . . . But I could hardly have depicted Ivan Ivanovich as he went out that night with a saw in his hand. Oh, how many different emotions were written on his face!" [23]

In the next chapter, the first voice is heard again, rhapsodizing the "wonderful city of Mirgorod" and the "splendid puddle" in the middle of the city square. These eulogies are mercilessly undercut in the last movement of the story as a third voice, that of a despondent outsider ("Five years ago I was passing through the town of Mirgorod . . .") delivers itself of a melancholy indictment of Mirgorod and the tedious world which it epitomizes.

So frequent and abrupt are the shifts in the point of view and the narrative tone that at times it becomes difficult to say who is telling the story. Nor is it any easier to answer the question, who in this polyphonic universe speaks for Nikolaj Gogol? Certainly not the brilliantly mimicked and shrewdly debunked parochial jerk. But is it the author's voice we hear in the lyrical effusions, the upward flights of eloquence such as, "Do you know the Ukrainian night?" or "And art thou, my Russia, soaring along even like a spirited, never-to-be-out-distanced troika?" Perhaps. But I would prefer to speak here about a persona rather than a personality—a romantic poet, wacky, exuberant, dreamy, grandiloquent, now rapturous, now wistful, forever lovestruck by the beauty of a never-never land, forever intoxicated with the "music"—the cacophonies, the cadences, the sonorities—of the Russian language.

For in this lifeless, stagnant universe, language is the only active protagonist, the only dynamic force, both as a great impersonator of dismal reality and as a major avenue of escape from it. Where comic "sound gestures" [24] and inspired clowning reign supreme,

23. Cf. *Mirgorod,* p. 241.

24. See the brilliant essay by Boris Eikhenbaum, "How Gogol's 'The Overcoat' Was Made," *Skvoz' literaturu, Voprosy poètiki, 4* (Leningrad, 1924).

as they do in "Ivan Fedorovich Shponka and His Aunt," in "The Two Ivans," and, above all, in "The Overcoat," language effectively mimics and enacts its subject. The dislocation of speech —the logical incoherence, the orgy of non sequiturs—serves as a verbal epitome of the subhuman inanity or absurdity of the universe portrayed. Conversely, when in the triumphant finale of Part I of *Dead Souls*, Chichikov's troika and his grotesquely morbid schemes disappear into the "smoke and thunder" of Gogol's rolling eloquence, one can speak of a poetic sleight of hand whereby the dismal subject dissolves into, and is superseded by, dazzling verbal magic.

Here, it seems to me, lies the major difference between Gogol's "life" and his "work." In both realms, the motif of impersonation, the strategy of concealment was paramount. Yet what for the man seems to have been a crucial flaw was for the artist a source of strength, richness, and infinite variety, an element of freedom rather than of constraint. This, I submit, is not surprising, for poetry, in the broader sense of the word, is self-transcendence as well as self-expression or, to modify T. S. Eliot, an escape from, as well as a stylized vehicle for, personal emotions. (In art, "escape" and "escapism" are not necessarily pejorative terms.) For the man that Gogol apparently was, a flight into cliché was self-defeating or more exactly a source as well as an acknowledgment of defeat, of a failure in dealing with his fellow humans. For Gogol the writer, the verbal mask was part and parcel of an intricate and exhilarating verbal play—a play with the manifold possibilities of the Russian literary idiom which this Ukrainian provincial, whose Russian grammar was not exactly flawless, enriched and enlivened beyond measure.

"Was unsterblich im Gesang soll leben, muss im Leben untergehn," says Schiller. Gogol's fate illustrates this dictum in a very special way. I do not wish to pretend to know what finally killed this strange, tortured man, what triggered his death which looks so much like a slow suicide. It is widely assumed that he broke down under the burden of some superhuman moral effort, of a desperate straining toward an epiphany, a Word that would "break the evil spell" (Remizov). Might we not speculate a bit further and suggest that Gogol may have been throttled by his mask, worn down by his futile attempt to break through what R. D. Laing has called the "false-self system," so as to overcome the emotional numbness and establish a meaningful dialogue with others and with his walled-off "real self"?

The man died in anguish and pain. The music of his prose, born from the anguish yet soaring beyond it, will endure as long as the Russian language.

Thomas Greene

The Flexibility of the Self
in Renaissance Literature

The noblest of philosophies for sale, the
most distinguished; who'll buy? Who
wants to be more than man? Who
wants to apprehend the music of the
spheres and to be born again?
                              Lucian

It is by no means clear that the term "Renaissance" retains much
usefulness for the literary critic. Our use of the term today still
derives primarily from the work of certain nineteenth-century
historians—chiefly Michelet and Burckhardt—despite the buffetings their formulations have received over the last hundred years,
buffetings mostly from the hands of other professional historians.
It is significant that we owe our fullest account of the term's history not to such a literary scholar as René Wellek, from whom we
have learned so much about other period concepts, but to still
another historian, Wallace Ferguson.[1] The literary scholar may
well feel that this term belongs to the broader field of general history; he may also feel, with some justification, that the beginning
and end of the period are impossible to demarcate, that the movement changes profoundly as it moves northward, that it seems to
end in one country before blossoming in another, that its character is confused by the Reformation, that its characteristic literary
forms are chaotically various—in short, that the "period," if it is
one, is too amorphous and unwieldy to help the literary scholar
understand his material. Some of these factors may indeed have

---

1. Wallace K. Ferguson, *The Renaissance in Historical Thought: Five
Centuries of Interpretation* (Boston, 1948).

contributed to the lull which has lately overtaken the historians' great wandering anarchic battle over the definition of the Renaissance—a lull more probably symptomatic of despair than of unanimity.

Yet despite these discouraging considerations the term and concept may yet be salvageable for the literary as well as the general historian. One may point, at any rate, to several recent studies by Comparatists which use the Renaissance as a delimiting concept in fresh and seminal ways.[2] The debate which has raged so long may prove to be salutary if it helps us to understand what kinds of unity or continuity are likely to be found and, on the other hand, what kinds of symmetry stem from the deceptively synthetic intelligence of a Burckhardt or his epigones. The real lines of continuity, I submit, are less likely to depend on patterns of agreement than disagreement. We may learn less from what a given age believed or thought it believed unanimously than from its quarrels, its tensions, or the half-conscious uneasiness that blurs its unanimity. Here the literary scholar has a clear role to play in tracing lines of intellectual, linguistic, social, and critical dialectic. In the discussion that follows I shall try to disentangle one very knotted pattern of disagreement. But the matter is so vast that my notes can amount at best only to a ghostly paradigm.

To define the issue, a convenient point of departure will be the so-called *Oration on the Dignity of Man* by Pico della Mirandola. At the opening of that document Pico relates a fable about the creation, wherein God assigns every creature his proper place and proper nature. When He has finished, He misses a creature who will ponder and love and marvel at the greatness of the work, and so He creates man, whose nature is indeterminate, who has no fixed abode or form or function, but can assume any nature or function within the vast spectrum of the universe. "We have made thee," God says to Adam,

> neither of heaven nor of earth, neither mortal nor immortal, so that with freedom of choice and with honor, as though the

2. Walter Kaiser, *Praisers of Folly* (Cambridge, Mass., 1963); Joseph A. Mazzeo, *Renaissance and Revolution* (New York, 1966); A. B. Giamatti, *The Earthly Paradise and the Renaissance Epic* (Princeton, 1966); Rosalie Colie, *Paradoxia Epidemica* (Princeton, 1966).

maker and molder of thyself, thou mayest fashion thyself in whatever shape thou shalt prefer. Thou shalt have the power to degenerate into the lower forms of life, which are brutish. Thou shalt have the power, out of thy soul's judgment, to be reborn into the higher forms, which are divine.[3]

Thus, writes Pico, man may choose to fashion (*effingere*) himself as a plant, or a brute, or an angel; moreover, he continues in a supreme burst of heretical optimism, man can if he chooses make himself one with the Godhead Itself.

I suppose there has never been—perhaps there could not be—a more extravagant assertion of human freedom, particularly of the freedom to select one's destiny, to mold and transform the self. It is the conception of a very young man, instructed less by human experience than by books and ideas. It could never be the conception of a novelist, whose equipment must include a practical awareness of all those inhibitions to freedom imposed by society and character and the human condition. But Pico's exhilarating fable is nonetheless representative of a certain strain of Renaissance Humanist enthusiasm. And it entitles us to ask to what degree the men of the Renaissance actually accepted and felt the ultimate freedom that Pico asserted, or anything like that freedom. If it is agreed that he, in his ardent optimism, went beyond his age in positing the flexibility of the self, one may still inquire how flexible the self does in fact appear in works of Renaissance literature, what capacities for change it allows, and what techniques, if any, it reveals for the willed metamorphosis of the personality. Did the Renaissance believe in renascence? The answers are enlighteningly inconsistent.

Before considering some of those answers, it would be well to note the several ways Pico's thought violated the letter and spirit of medieval thought. First of all, the doctrine of man's indeterminate nature conflicted with the doctrine common to Aristotle and the Scholastics which held human nature to be unalterably fixed. It conflicted as well with medieval doctrines of personality or of

3. Trans. Elizabeth Livermore Forbes, in *The Renaissance Philosophy of Man,* ed. Ernst Cassirer, Paul Oskar Kristeller, and John Herman Randall, Jr. (Chicago, 1948), p. 225. For the idea of indeterminacy, see also in the same volume Vives' *Fable About Man,* pp. 387–93, esp. p. 390.

haecceitas, doctrines which attribute an unalterable *thisness* to each separate creature, a thisness which the individual is unable to modify. Pico would appear equally to deny the Aristotelian-Scholastic conception of *habitus,* a term which we must translate imperfectly as "habit." A *habitus* according to Aquinas is an acquired disposition inhering in a man which enables him to act in accordance with his nature; every virtue, every art is a *habitus,* and although acquired rather than innate, it is *difficile mobilis,* slowly built up and slowly if ever lost, so that Maritain can speak of its "intransigeance." [4] Such a conception obviously sets very narrow limits to any hypothetical metamorphosis within the human consciousness, and in particular it protects a virtuous character from sudden, involuntary descent into viciousness. As for the vicious character who has fallen into sin, medieval thinkers stipulated an even greater rigidity; in that case, the individual is impotent to recreate by himself the order he has destroyed by his sin and so must depend upon grace for restoration. Here Scholastic thought went well beyond Aristotle in stressing the sinner's incapacity for self-improvement, as Saint Bonaventure himself pointed out:

> The Greek philosophers did not know that sin is an affront to the divine majesty, nor yet that it deprives our faculties of their power. They asserted therefore, that in the performance of just acts a man might restore that justice which . . . he had lost. . . . But Catholics . . . know well that sin offends God. . . . And they concluded . . . that if free will is to be saved from slavery to sin, grace is altogether necessary. [5]

For Saint Bonaventure, as for most Scholastic thinkers, the will to reform, the will to conversion, remains helpless so long as it remains unaided by God.

All of these doctrines clearly militate against that total freedom of self-determination asserted by Pico. When we turn to medieval literature, the variety and abundance of texts render generaliza-

---

4. Jacques Maritain, *Art and Scholasticism,* trans. J. F. Scanlan (New York, 1954), p. 9.

5. Quoted by Maritain in *The Spirit of Medieval Philosophy* (New York, 1940), pp. 340–41.

tion much more difficult, and yet here also, by and large, we encounter a nearly equal rigidity in the actual representations of
human personality. Here as in theology there is a sharply limited
belief in man's capacity to alter and especially to alter himself at
will. For the literary imagination, the doctrinal conceptions of the
personality probably counted for less than sociological factors,
such as the social immobility imposed by feudalism, the small extent and prestige of formal education, and a view of personality
which depended heavily on the social role which a man was called
upon to play. If we think of the *chansons de geste* or the *Roman
de la Rose* or *The Canterbury Tales,* we think of any number of
presences who make themselves felt as varied and colorful and
forceful personalities, but we do not think of them for the most
part as volatile, evolutionary, fashioned or capable of fashioning.
We think of them rather as four-square, metaphysically immov-
able, defined by occupation and estate and a complex of given
traits. Or if in a few characters of the finest medieval writers, in
the Roland of the *Chanson* or the Troilus of Chaucer, we sense a
development, a softening of the rigidity, that development is
never a product of human design.[6]

This relative inflexibility of medieval character by no means
disappears from such a masterpiece of the early Renaissance as
Boccaccio's *Decameron,* where part of the pleasure depends on the
satisfaction of the reader's expectations regarding the various characters' conduct. The younger Boccaccio had attempted in the
Ameto to write the account of a moral transformation, not without echoes of Dante, but the wooden and unconvincing triviality
of this work shows how uncongenial he found the theme. This
awkwardness also weakens the one story of the *Decameron* which
attempts to describe a profound alteration of a personality, the
first story of the fifth day. In this famous story the stupid and
clownish hero, Cimone, is transformed by love into an accomplished and polished gentleman. "In assai brieve spazio di tempo
non solamente le prime lettere apparò, ma valorosissimo tra'

6. None of these generalizations can be adequately applied to Dante. I
have attempted to discuss elsewhere the theme of rigidity and change in the
Comedy at the length it deserves. See Thomas Greene, "Dramas of Selfhood
in the Comedy," in *From Time to Eternity,* ed. Thomas Bergin (New
Haven, 1967).

filosofanti divenne." But Cimone's subsequent conduct betrays the ruffian rather than the philosopher, and we are left only with Boccaccio's word for the depth of the change. This story remains in any case isolated within the collection. If the great majority of the stories alter anything at all, they tend to alter degrees of awareness or knowledge on the part of a given individual, an awareness which in turn may affect little networks of human relationships within a small knot of people. The novella indeed is ill adapted as a form to record a convincing alteration of character, and Boccaccio's successors in the genre were to portray, if anything, characters still more rigid than his own. The truly significant step was taken, albeit unwittingly, by his friend and idol.

The radical stasis of the medieval personality was first explicitly challenged by Petrarch who, gazing steadily upon himself, found an altogether different state of affairs. The egoism of Petrarch was so monumental and so acute that it was an event in European intellectual history. What troubled Petrarch about himself was precisely the *lack* of continuity in his tangled passions, the distractions of his cluttered motives, the fatal complexity as he called it in the *Secretum*, "varietas mortifera," [7] which obstructs the path of lucid thought in its journey to the highest Good. The passages in the *Secretum* wherein he complains of that diversity are too eloquent, frequent, and vivid to be anything but genuine, and the complaint is repeated again and again elsewhere in both secular and religious contexts, above all in the *Canzoniere* and in the correspondence. Indeed the most famous of the letters, the account of the ascent of Mount Ventoux, concludes unforgettably with a prayer for salvation from spiritual instability: "Pray to God," writes Petrarch to Dionigi da Borgo San Sepolcro, "that my thoughts may find rest at last, my thoughts so long restless and fleeting, tossed without purpose about and about, that they turn now to the one good, the true, the secure, the abiding." [8] We note the significant progression of those adjectives as they move from the high to the highest value: "ad unum, bonum, verum, certum, *stabile*."

7. Francesco Petrarca, *Prose*, ed. G. Martelletti and others (Milan, 1955), p. 66.
8. Trans. Hans Nachod, in *The Renaissance Philosophy of Man*, p. 46.

In placing such strenuous emphasis on his, and all men's, psychic discontinuities, Petrarch was of course echoing the psychology of his interlocutor in the *Secretum* dialogues—Saint Augustine himself. Doubtless it was Augustine's passionate restlessness and anxious disquietudes which first attracted the poet to the saint and which render them both so recognizably, so intimately modern. In effect, Petrarch's new emphasis constituted a reversion from an Aristotelian-Thomist psychology to an older, Platonic-Augustinian psychology. But for Petrarch the spiritual kinship involved inevitably a bitter taint of reproach, since for all his vacillation Augustine had won through to a triumphant reordering of the self, a conversion, a transformation. There is a pathos in Petrarch's lifelong wait for that decisive event, in his growing fear, his growing realization that the miracle of will and grace was not to be vouchsafed him. And insofar as his psychology came to focus on the soul's instability without any opening to the divine, he recalls not so much Augustine as those pagan moralists who had earlier recognized the volatility of passion. He recalls the voice of Horace inquiring of the nature of man, "Quo teneam voltus mutantem Protea nodo?" [9] the Horace who cried out in exasperation at himself:

> quid, mea cum pugnat sententia secum,
> quod petiit spernit, repetit quod nuper omisit,
> aestuat et vitae disconvenit ordine toto,
> diruit, aedificat, mutat quadrata rotundis? [10]

Petrarch's discontent often assumes such classical rhetoric. Yet despite such anticipations in Horace and Augustine and many others, his "varietas mortifera" contained an element that was essentially new and of great importance, an element not so much in his thought—he may well have been incapable of articulating

9. "With what knot can I hold this Proteus whose face is ever changing?" Horace, *Epistles*, I, 1, l. 90 (translation mine).

10. "What, when my judgment is at strife with itself, scorns what it craved, asks again for what it lately cast aside; when it shifts like a tide, and in the whole system of life is out of joint, pulling down, building up, and changing square to round!" *Epistles*, I, 1, ll. 97–100. In Horace, *Satires, Epistles and Ars Poetica*, trans. H. Rushton Fairclough (Cambridge, Mass., and London, Loeb Classical Library, 1966).

it—as in the achievement of the life he lived. Petrarch's life, for all its vanities and comedies, was so striking to his contemporaries and immediate posterity precisely because of its *creative* "varietas." By this I do not refer only to the variety of the books he wrote with their several styles and modes and genres. That variety is impressive enough, but it is subsumed by the variety of the roles Petrarch improvised successfully upon the stage of European politics and letters. For most of these roles there were precedents, but he recast them all, informing each with the flair and intensity of his dramatic imagination: the role of the secular *recluse* in the Vaucluse, the solitary, walker, reader, nature-lover, gardener; the role of the *lover*, who shifted single-handed the conventional focus of interest from a mythical lady to a half-recognizable suitor; the role of the *scholar-philologist*, who ceaselessly sought manuscripts, had them copied, studied them, quoted, popularized, collected them in a library; the role of the *poet-laureate*, who brought a new stature and dignity to the writing of poetry; and thus the role of the *public voice*, who celebrated, admonished, warned, and encouraged popes, emperors, and despots; the role of the *Christian*, reverent, wavering, impatient, fascinated by the analysis of his self-accusations; the role of the *friend*, whose correspondence was to be one of his best books, who rediscovered the human, moral, literary dimensions of friendship and made it a cultural force; and lastly, the role of the *wanderer*, forever exiled and peripatetic, contented with no role, no book, no place, no pose, moving on ever wearily and dramatizing his weariness. The multiplicity of Petrarch's existences was so meaningful because other men did not share the weariness and saw only the astounding richness, the multiplication of possibilities. Petrarch achieved, simply by living as fully as he did, a freedom which to him was terrible in its confusing and distracting disorder, but a freedom which remained and still remains to us a token of his greatness.

The new flexibility embodied by Petrarch represented an implicit challenge to medieval habits of thought and thus was doubtless of negative historical importance. It did not, however, greatly influence the "psychology" of the succeeding two hundred years. Petrarch's flexibility was by no means Pico's. Pico conceived essentially of a *vertical* scale along which men might move upward and downward—upward toward the angel, downward toward the brute. Petrarch's scale is *lateral;* he demonstrated how rich a human life could be at a single rung of the metaphysical ladder. In his own eyes the horizontal diversity impeded the vertical mobility. Despite his example, the important scale throughout the fifteenth century remained the vertical, although the Humanist writers of the Quattrocento conceived of that scale in terms Ciceronian rather than Christian. That is to say, they conceived of individual development upward to an ideal as the result of basically secular training, education, formation, rather than in terms of Augustinian conversion or the Thomistic *habitus* of virtue. The finished product of such training fell somewhat short of the angelic or the saintly, but it represented nonetheless an achievement of intellectual poise and dignity and clarity, of linguistic mastery, and of moral insight, based upon a slow, methodical, carefully designed curriculum of humane study.[11]

"Homines non nascuntur, sed finguntur," Erasmus wrote—men are fashioned rather than born—a formula which might be taken as the motto of the Humanist revolution. The metaphor of fashioning implies that a man's nature is essentially formless, like wax, essentially neutral, and not, let us note in passing, tainted with original depravity. Education in Humanist thought is the seal imprinted on the soft wax of consciousness. Already at the beginning of the fifteenth century the Humanist Vergerius speaks of the advantageous suppleness of young boys' minds, and he urges parents to begin the molding of their sons before that suppleness is lost, "while the minds of the young are quick and their age flexible."

Dum faciles animi iuvenum, dum mobilis aetas. [12]

That line is from a passage in the *Georgics* where Vergil is speaking of breaking in young bulls, and Vergerius of course quotes it without irony. The instructive and symptomatic word in the line is "mobilis." If it had been reassuring to medieval men that habits were *difficile mobilis,* resistant to change, now it is that very pli-

11. This Humanist ideal to be sure owed something to Petrarch in his roles as scholar and bibliophile. But the debt should not be exaggerated; Petrarch hated the very idea of schoolmastering.

12. *Georgics,* III, 165, quoted by Vergerius in *De Ingenuis Moribus,* ed. A. Gnesotto, in *Atti e Memorie della Reale Accademia di Scienze, Lettere, ed Arti in Padova,* N.S., *34* (1918), p. 113.

ability which the Humanist seizes on, which indeed justifies his pedagogical existence. During the generations following Vergerius, the basically optimistic belief in human pliability grew. For the first time in a millennium, man saw himself as basically malleable, without quite acknowledging that his belief threatened to involve him in the Pelagian heresy, the heresy with which Humanism characteristically and commonly flirted.

The Humanist faith in the fashioning of the self led to the rebirth of a genre which was to become one of the most popular and typical of the Renaissance. It seems to have no name; I shall call it the *institute*. The Renaissance was not a fertile age in the invention of new genres, but it was immensely creative in recapturing and extending the potentialities of those genres which it inherited. The Renaissance institute was inspired by such works as Plato's *Republic,* Cicero's *De Oratore,* and Quintilian's *Institutiones Oratoriae,* ideal portraits of a society or institution or occupation. The Renaissance produced innumerable institutes; there is space here to recall at least the most familiar: the portraits of an ideal society (More and Bacon), of a family (Alberti), a prince (Pontano and Machiavelli), a courtier (Castiglione), a magistrate (Elyot), a gentleman (Della Casa and Spenser, in their very different versions), a schoolmaster (Ascham), a poet (Minturno and any number of other authors of *artes poeticae*), a lover (Ficino, Bembo, Leone Ebreo, and so on). Even such devotional works as Erasmus' *Enchiridion* tended during this period to assume the character of the institute. Works like these might have been calculated to inhibit the vertical as well as horizontal flexibility of the individual by fixing him in a given role much as medieval society did. And yet on the whole the institutes did not do this.

The reason why they did not, it seems to me, is that so many men of the Renaissance, particularly the Italian Renaissance, tended to confuse "formation" (education, discipline, pedagogy in its broadest sense) with "transformation." "Transformation" means here the surpassing of natural human limitations, undoing the constraints of the incomplete, the contingent, and the mortal.[13] Once the Humanist mind discovered—or thought it dis-

13. I believe that I owe these terms to Professor John Freccero of Cornell University.

covered—the receptivity of the mind to fashioning, it was very difficult to determine where the upper limits of the fashioning process intervened. It was difficult to know when the ideal of individual development approached the superhuman, the impossible, the divine. Once one begins to dream of ever more noble forms to imprint on the wax of consciousness, one begins to forget the limitations of that wax. Or rather, taken in by the metaphor, one forgets the stubborn consistency of the mind which renders the analogy inexact. Many (though by no means all) authors of institutes found themselves extending the development toward their hypothetical ideal beyond the limits of the human.

The impulse to transformation found support from the renewed interest of certain Renaissance thinkers in magic and hermetic philosophy. It is no accident that Pico's *Oration* combines the aspiration to the Godhead we have already noticed with a defense of magic: "As the farmer weds his elms to vines, even so does the *magus* wed earth to heaven, that is, he weds lower things to the endowments and powers of higher things." [14] It is an easy step for the magus from the role of high priest at that wedding, the controller of divine as well as earthly, to actual participation in the divine. This is a step which Pico himself certainly wanted to take. Although it would be dangerous to overestimate the heady fascination of the so-called Hermes Trismegistus, we have recently had an impressive scholarly survey of the wide range of his influence.[15] Doubtless there were many whom that influence did not seduce directly but whom, in a diffused form, it rendered more sympathetic to less heretical versions of human transcendence.

The really astonishing aspect of the *Oration* is the reliance Pico places on a pedagogical curriculum to elevate him to the Godhead. The curriculum was divided into four disciplines always listed in ascending order: ethics, dialectic, natural philosophy, and theology. Of course we have just seen that these disciplines were not so innocuous in the hands of Pico as they might have been for Vergerius; in addition to magic and the hermetic teachings, they somehow involved the Cabala, Orphic mysteries, and Zoroastrianism along with the orthodox content of Christian Humanism.

14. *Renaissance Philosophy of Man*, p. 249.
15. Frances Yates, *Giordano Bruno and the Hermetic Tradition* (Chicago, 1964).

Nonetheless the four disciplines remained for Pico bodies of knowledge to be mastered, while at the same time they became steps on the ladder which led to the divine. And on each step, with each new discipline, a man made himself radically new. The fashioning of the pupil by the pedagogue was replaced by the reflexive fashioning of the individual's own mind and soul. Humanist formation first assisted in, then gave way to, metaphysical transformation.

In the paragraphs that follow I shall argue that some roughly analogous process, less audaciously formulated, can be traced in several important and representative books of the sixteenth century. Necessarily, in an argument of this kind, the analogies must be rough and hastily sketched. If something like a pattern can be suggested, we shall then need to glance at a few of the individuals and movements that attacked the flexibility of the self with growing success through the course of the century.

In the *Utopia* of Thomas More, the movement from formation to transformation concerns a community rather than an individual and yet remains essentially unchanged. For again in More the dream of a social alternative, the dream of a newly fashioned society, leads to the dream of a new human being, an altered human condition—all the more easily perhaps in this book which masquerades as a jeu d'esprit, a fantasy which nobody has to take seriously. The distinction between the social novelty and the human novelty is bridged, somewhat naïvely, with what Professor Hexter calls More's environmentalism, that is to say, his faith that institutions determine human nature. The naïveté emerges very clearly in those passages purporting to explain why certain fundamental human vices do not afflict the Utopians, as in the comment that greed "can have no place in the Utopian scheme of things." [16] The scheme of things, the precise economic arrangements, control the moral nature of man. More goes on to cite with apparent approval the Utopian belief that men are naturally drawn to virtue, that virtue consists in living according to nature, that evil is nothing but "perverse habit." More, like Pico, overestimated the flexibility of the human creature and, in the zeal of forming a

16. *The Complete Works of Saint Thomas More*, vol. 4, *Utopia*, ed. Edward Surtz, S.J., and J. H. Hexter (New Haven and London, 1965), p. 139.

community, transformed the soul. He is not, to be sure, equally naïve everywhere in his book, and the very regimentation of Utopian life testifies to More's nervousness about perverse habits. But in the last analysis he did regard the dull harmony of the Utopian system as possible and preferable to the freer, more colorful inequities of Europe. He called for a world where reason overcomes habit, even if monotonously, in preference to a world where pride overcomes grace, even if dramatically. In the most serious of literary jokes, he held out the feasibility of a humorless New Jerusalem, with sharply limited moral choice, without love, without injustice, without hierarchy, without tragedy. By assuming so much human mobility, he produced the Immobile State.

The situation in such a work as the *Cortegiano* of Castiglione is much more delicate—not surprisingly, in view of the resonant subtleties and dialectical obliquities within that beautiful book. One such subtlety lies in the way the conversation derives part of its precious elegance from the context of mutability which encloses it. The tone of the author's prefaces is consistently elegiac, and we are led increasingly to *look back* at the conversation, back from a present emptied of the speakers and of their rare harmony. There is plenty here to remind us of the contingent, the incomplete, and the mortal, and in the portrait of the courtier himself, there is nothing extravagantly superhuman about that gracious and calculating urbanity.[17] Throughout its first three books, at least, Castiglione's institute makes few gestures toward the upper limits of humanity. But Book Four, composed some years after the others, does of course violate these limits, and in two quite different areas. The first is political. The discussion which occupies most of the book begins by stressing the prince's need for moral guidance, for discreet molding on the part of the courtier. But the discussion ends with a grandiloquent celebration of the perfect prince, supreme in his wisdom and independent of any external counsel. The prince may become, writes Castiglione, an image of

17. In his prefatory epistle the author guards himself against the imputation of asking too much of imperfect human nature: "Se . . . non potran conseguir quella perfezion, qual che ella si sia, ch'io mi son sforzato d'esprimere, colui que più se le avvicinarà sarà il più perfetto." *Il Cortegiano*, ed. Bruno Maier (Turin, U.T.E.T., 1955), pp. 76–77.

God Himself, "by Whose grace he will attain the heroic virtue that will bring him to surpass the limits of humanity and be called a demigod rather than a mortal man." [18] Rhetoric like this betrays less the habit of courtly flattery than the terrible need, within the Italian court, for a governor of character and skill. It is succeeded in turn by the still fuller rhetoric and noble aspiration of Bembo's discourse, which leaves the contingent and the mortal far behind as it rises at last to the banquet of angels and union with God. So eloquent, so perfervid, so grandiose that vision is, and so irrelevant! Emilia Pia bends forward to pluck the speaker gently by the sleeve and wakes us all from the intoxicating dream. It is marvelous but it is really about nothing at all. In that society of physical and spiritual uncertainty, of violence and skepticism, Castiglione drifted away from his worldly faith in the fashioning of a polished, flawless, successful self, drifted like so many of his contemporaries into a touchingly baseless vision of exaltation.

Something of the same drift is detectable in one of the greatest, most difficult, and most complex of Renaissance books—Rabelais' *Gargantua and Pantagruel.* Here I must oversimplify even more cruelly than elsewhere, but in general one can say that the first two books of Rabelais, like the first three of Castiglione, dramatize a moral view more or less closed to human transcendence. They place heavy stress on the body, its pleasures, its needs, and its filth; upon the perversity, stupidity, and greed of a great many people; upon the comical paradoxicality of moral questions; and, in the figure of Panurge, upon a kind of roguish folk-hero whose pranks and whose wit savor of a very earthbound society. But the first book also represents magnificently the metamorphosis of the hero under a program of Humanist and physical discipline, a metamorphosis which never exceeds in theory the limits of the properly human. (In practice, I suppose, we would all of us crumble under the regime of a Ponocrates.) Even the abbey of Thélème, unlike More's Utopia, presupposes the rigid exclusion of those morally unfit for admission. Put another way, my argument implies that the gigantic scale of certain episodes in Rabelais does not violate the earthly, human, and Humanist focus. This is,

18. Baldassare Castiglione, *The Book of the Courtier,* trans. Charles S. Singleton (Garden City, N.Y., 1959), p. 306.

however, less true of the last three books. There the value of formal education and study tends to disappear, and somewhat different values take its place, values which lend themselves more easily, even if ambiguously, to transcendental interpretations. In the third book, for example, one must deal with Panurge's discourse in praise of borrowing and lending, a discourse whose outrageous implications on the practical level do not quite cancel out its vision of human and cosmic harmony on the symbolic level. Or one must deal with the magical plant, the *pantagruelion,* symbol of the Rabelaisian spirit of courage and joy, whose virtues are so marvelous that the gods in heaven fear lest, with its aid, man rise to emulate them—once again with a seriousness not altogether veiled by the facetious tone. Finally, at the end of Book Five (which Rabelais must have sketched out even if he did not live to write it), Pantagruel and his friends encounter at the oracle of the *dive bouteille* a series of hermetic rituals designed to transform and regenerate them. The monosyllabic advice of the oracle— "Trinch!"—receives a hermetic interpretation: by drinking one becomes divine. "De vin divin on devient." It is clear that more than mere liquid is involved. Rabelais' epic of formation has turned into an epic of transformation, without of course ever drying up the robust comedy which complicates and toughens his thought.

Thus in Pico consciously, in More, Castiglione, and Rabelais more insidiously, the vertical flexibility of man becomes virtually a structural principle. It would be easy to trace still other analogous versions of the same upward movement in a number of sixteenth-century writers. One might note for example in the *Paraclesis* of Erasmus the progression from study to morality to spiritual metamorphosis. The metamorphosis in this case is an orthodox Christian conversion, but it is movingly presented as the result of reading a book, Erasmus' new edition of the New Testament. Nothing is more typical of the Christian Humanist in Erasmus than his faith in the moral fashioning of the self through sacred study, a fashioning which leads directly to transformation: "Let us all, therefore, with our whole heart covet this literature, let us embrace it, let us continually occupy ourselves with it, let us fondly kiss it, at length let us die in its embrace, *let us be transformed in it,* since indeed studies are transmuted into morals" (italics mine) .[19] Or in a very different kind of work, the great Petrarchan love sequence, *Délie,* by Maurice Scève, one could study the way the conventional rituals and disciplines of the love relationship are transmuted into a quite distinct experience: an initiation into higher reality, a participation in eternity, a metamorphosis of the poet through his discovery of himself and of virtue, of the anguish of loneliness and the ecstasy of communion. Or at the end of the century, in the thought of Giordano Bruno, one could study the curious way in which a materialistic metaphysics gets confused with a strained Neoplatonism until, in such a work as the *Eroici Furori,* the materialism falls away and the poet is left gasping with enthusiasm in strenuous, cerebral, cosmic isolation. Or one could follow, in the drama of Christopher Marlowe, how a Doctor Faustus, "glutted new with learning's golden gifts," comes to scorn them and conclude that "a sound magician is a mighty god." All of these figures, each in his peculiar way and with peculiar qualifications, embody a hope for human transcendence.

As the century wore on, the belief in the capacity of the self for fashioning was increasingly modified or challenged by alternate views, and we may follow the complex conflicts of thought and feeling through the end of the century by tracing the challenges to Humanist optimism. The most powerful challenge arose of course from the Protestant Reformation and its aftermath. When Erasmus, after years of delay, misunderstanding, and vacillation, finally allowed himself to be badgered into attacking Luther, he chose significantly the freedom of the will as his point of attack; and Luther, understanding perfectly the central importance of that issue, joined the combat with vigor. It was clear to both men that without freedom the entire Humanist enterprise was meaningless. Whatever we may feel today about the relative persuasiveness of the two tracts, it was Erasmus' position that had to give ground steadily on the continent during the following decades. The mellow irony, the enlightened and affirmative skepticism of Erasmus were virtually overwhelmed in a blood-dimmed tide of

19. Desiderius Erasmus, *Christian Humanism and the Reformation: Selected Writings,* ed. John C. Olin (New York, Evanston, and London, 1965) , p. 105.

religious enmity, seeming in its gentle patience to lack all conviction where so many were full of passionate intensity.

In the Catholic camp, the Erasmian ideal of Humanist formation, of gradual and quiet discipline, was transformed by the Counter-Reformation into the quasi-military exercises of Saint Ignatius. Ignatius and his followers seized upon the concept of fashioning through discipline and altered it brilliantly for their own purposes. The transformation they envisaged as the end of their discipline was to a new, hard, resolute, unwavering dedication to God's will as interpreted by His Church. The individual will was screwed up to an unnatural pitch and placed at the service of a directing intelligence outside itself. Other currents of the Counter-Reformation rejected intellectual discipline altogether in the name of a swirling baroque emotionalism or mysticism or fideism, with such literary results as the facile conversions in Tasso of characters like Rinaldo and Armida. Among the great Reformers, on the other hand, the will was theoretically denied *any* autonomy and above all denied the autonomy of choosing a destiny. The predestinarianism of Luther and Calvin really represented a return to the Augustinian miracle of conversion through grace, a miracle which the individual accepts but does not initiate. Thus both major parties to the religious quarrel basically rejected the Humanist path of willed metamorphosis through intellectual discipline.

The path was rejected as well by a number of secular sixteenth-century writers who were to enjoy considerable influence. The first of these was Machiavelli. Machiavelli, like More, was interested in changing political states rather than in changing men, but we can nonetheless discern the tendencies of his thought in this regard. For him, the vertical flexibility of man is very limited, and such as it is, leads downward to the brute rather than upward to the angel. *The Prince* indeed is the one institute that comes to mind lacking a belief in fashioning and in metaphysical freedom. The successful despot of the book's title cannot be formed by slow, controlled discipline. Machiavelli cannot do that for him; all he can do is to alert the prince to the rules of power politics and the changeless nature of man as Machiavelli has observed them operating throughout history. The end product of Machiavelli's instruction will not be a better man or greater or more polished or even wiser in the full sense of the word; he will simply be warier, better armed with precept and cunning. The crucial process for Machiavelli is not metamorphosis; it is rather the endless, inconclusive struggle between fortune and human resourcefulness. In various contexts Machiavelli is more and less optimistic about the chances for that resourcefulness, his famous *virtù*, but he does make it clear that *tactical* flexibility is the great weapon if one is to hope for consistent success. Tactical flexibility is a kind of horizontal flexibility, the capacity to change one's style, one's strategy, one's mode of procedure, with the flux of events. "He is happy whose mode of procedure accords with the needs of the times. . . . If one could change one's nature with time and circumstances, fortune would never change." [20] "Se si mutasse di natura con li tempi e con le cose, non si muterebbe fortuna." The verb tense is conditional: "fortune would never change." The implication, if not downright contrary to fact, is ruefully skeptical. Men do not, perhaps cannot, change their nature with circumstance, and so their fortunes do almost always change, and for the worse.

One might deduce similar implications from the *Orlando Furioso* of Machiavelli's contemporary, Ariosto. One episode, to be sure, pays lip service to an authorized and perfunctory morality. This is the episode of Logistilla, the personification of reason, of whom it is said:

> Ella t'insegnerà studii piú grati
> Che suoni, danze, odori, bagni, e cibi;
> Ma come i pensier tuoi meglio formati
> Poggin piú ad alto che per l'aria i nibi.[21]

Logistilla will instruct the hero Ruggiero how his thoughts may reach higher into the air than kites can fly, thoughts which shall now be better framed—"meglio formati"—than when he pursued sensual pleasures. Here briefly the sky seems to open, to permit something like human transcendence, but we know from the rest of the poem how deceptive that opening truly is. For when, in a

20. Niccolò Machiavelli, *The Prince and the Discourses* (New York, Modern Library, 1950), p. 93.
21. Canto 10, stanza 47.

later canto, the comic figure of Astolfo ascends to the sphere of the moon, he discovers only a limbo of futility. The futility of hope underlies all the unreal glamor and imaginary achievement of *Orlando Furioso;* futility is the wellspring of its irony and tinges with sadness all its gossamer comedy. The very miraculousness of Orlando's cure (or Rinaldo's) demonstrates that no earthly cure for hope and love exists within this landscape of fools. Ariosto permits perhaps our closest approach to his moral vision in his description of an enchanted castle where everybody pursues fanatically his heart's desire, the mirage of his beloved, tantalizingly near but elusive. The gates of that castle are open but no one ever departs. The rational will is gulled and passion imposes its own rigidity, the imprisoning walls of obsession.

Machiavelli and Ariosto represent already a stage of disillusionment in the rapid decline of Italian Renaissance optimism. In the north, this stage was long delayed and partially avoided. As the century wore on, however, with all its interplay of shifting currents, intellectual and literary fashions, movements and countermovements, the aging Humanist ideal of willed metamorphosis was increasingly eroded. But it did not, in the end, receive its deathblow from a doctrine of rigidity but rather from the other direction, from a doctrine of total inconsistency. It was Montaigne who dwelt so persuasively and acutely and passionately on the inconstancy of our conduct, "l'inconstance de nos actions," the inconstancy of a creature without firm knowledge or firm will or firm perception, vacillating, unpredictable, and motley-colored. Montaigne's man cannot transform himself vertically because his velleities upward fluctuate and flicker; he cannot develop himself laterally because his lateral driftings and evasions never cease. We return to something like the problem of Petrarch, but in Montaigne the anguish fades away. The *Apologie de Raimond Sebond* concludes with an attack upon a remark of Seneca: "Man is a vile and abject thing if he does not rise above humanity." Montaigne replies that the idea is absurd:

Car de faire la poignée plus grande que le poing, la brassée plus grande que le bras, et d'esperer enjamber plus que de l'estandue de nos jambes, cela est impossible et monstrueux.

> Ny que l'homme se monte au dessus de soy et de l'humanité:
> car il ne peut voir que de ses yeux, ny saisir que de ses
> prises.[22]

Impossible and monstrous! That is Montaigne's verdict on any metamorphosis willed by man. But in Montaigne the renewed circumscription of human potentialities is attended with a growing acceptance of limitation. The serenity of his last essays is so firm because it is achieved without straining upward to the suprahuman, the impossible and monstrous, or what he himself calls elsewhere the *extravagant*.

In Montaigne there disappears as well one of the basic instruments of Humanist education—the belief in rhetoric, the pursuit of formally disciplined language, the cult of the word. "C'est un bel et grand agencement sans doubte que le Grec et Latin, mais on l'achepte trop cher." "Que notre disciple soit bien pourveu de choses, les parolles ne suivront que trop." "Il ne dira pas tant sa leçon, comme il la fera." [23] The attitude was not altogether new, but in the *Essais* it acquired a new authority. The seventeenth century, influenced by such thinkers as Montaigne and Bacon and Comenius, would see the Ciceronian wedding of eloquence and wisdom weakened by an increasing distrust of the word. Thus the thought of Montaigne denied the possibility of both formation and transformation as the preceding century had conceived them. The influence of his book served to clear away, for better or worse, a great deal that was crucial to that century and raised fresh issues in turn which were to preoccupy the century that followed him.

The rise and fall of a Humanist anthropology upon the European continent found only a vague analogy in England. If the English Renaissance was also concerned with the metamorphosis of the self, it fixed much firmer upper limits to human potentiality than did the continent. In spite of More, sixteenth-century England was seldom Utopian; it retained by and large a healthy skepticism toward human transcendence; and it remembered more

---

22. Montaigne, *Essais,* ed. Albert Thibaudet (Paris, Editions de la Pléiade, 1940), p. 592.

23. Ibid., pp. 184, 179–80, 179.

steadily than the continent the orthodox doctrine of original depravity. One reason for this circumstance may be that the Reformation reached English shores earlier than the full glow of the Renaissance. In any case the conflict between anthropologies in England was to remain considerably narrower than, say, the conflict between a Pico and a Machiavelli. Thus even Christopher Marlowe, whose hero dreamt of godhead through magic, hedged the dream about with tragic irony and in the end sent the aspiring Faustus screaming off to hell.

This instinctive conservatism is notable in all the main Elizabethan genres. The best sonneteers, eschewing the Neoplatonism of a Scève or Du Bellay, followed the lead of Wyatt in bringing a wry Anglo-Saxon irony to the Petrarchan convention. *Astrophel and Stella,* like "They flee from me" and the best of Drayton's *Idea,* might be said to record a metamorphosis manqué. The Humanists themselves, from an early figure like Roger Ascham to the much greater genius at the century's end, Ben Jonson, show a striking refusal to transcend the formation of literary discipline. The best of Elizabethan novelists, Thomas Nashe, was obsessed with sin and damnation; his best-known book, *The Unfortunate Traveler,* concludes with the briefest and least convincing of conversions because, I suspect, Nashe could not really bring himself to believe in a genuine conversion. His true belief is probably better represented by his inspired defense of Robert Greene: "Debt and deadly sin who is not subject to? With any *notorious* crime I never knew him tainted." [24]

A comparable sense of human limitation confines the achievements of the heroes of Spenser's *Faerie Queene.* Spenser's poem is described at the outset as an epic of fashioning: "The general end . . . is to fashion a gentleman or noble person in virtuous and gentle discipline." That sentence sounds Erasmian; it sounds as though Spenser believed that *homines non nascuntur, sed finguntur,* and the stress placed on discipline renders it all the more Humanist. But the letter to Raleigh does not in fact reflect faithfully Spenser's conception of human flexibility, and it has to

24. Thomas Nashe, *Selected Works,* ed. Stanley Wells (London, 1964), p. 279.

be confronted with other, very different pronouncements within the poem. For the opposite pole of Spenser's thought, we might turn to a well-known passage in Book Two:

> And is there care in heaven? and is there love
> In heavenly spirits to these creatures bace,
> That may compassion of their evils move?
> There is: else much more wretched were the cace
> Of men, then beasts. (II.8.1)

Without heavenly compassion, man's estate would be more miserable than the beasts'. There is little room here for poetic or pedagogic fashioning, and throughout the poem Spenser seems to waver in his hopes for our capacity to choose our destinies. The first book of *The Faerie Queene* describes very fully and subtly a Christian transformation, but a transformation much more dependent on grace than on will. The remaining books, in varying degrees, always stop short of a definitive metamorphosis. Just as in Book One Red Cross glimpses the New Jerusalem he cannot enter, so in the later books the hero is always tantalized by the momentary vision of completeness: Guyon by the angel, Britomart by the vision of Isis and Osiris, Scudamour by the vision of Concord, Calidore by the vision of the Graces. In the "Mutability Cantos" there is no hero but there is a vision of Nature, before she in turn yields to the poet's own weary cry for the Sabbaoth God and for the last day's fulfillment. Within the poem itself, there is little fulfillment; there are many betrothals but few marriages, many victories but few enduring triumphs. The process of fashioning is frustrated by the inconsistency of the clay amid the quicksand of history.

Renaissance speculation on the theme of flexibility reaches a natural end point with the plays of Shakespeare, dramatizing as they do the painful difficulty of moral ascent and the happy success of lateral resourcefulness. Shakespeare is not at all concerned with the discipline of Humanist formation and is too shrewd to dream, with Marlowe, of miraculous transformations. His theater is a theater of horizontal maneuverings and adaptations, and so ushers in the modern era we still inhabit. One way to explore the question in Shakespeare's comedies is to ask why only likable girls engage in transvestism. Julia (*Two Gentlemen of Verona*), Portia, Rosalind, Celia, Viola, Imogen, all prove their resourcefulness, their suppleness, their courageous willingness to change roles by changing clothes and sexes, just as Isabella acquires a new flexibility when she takes off her nun's habit, and just as Helena has to don a pilgrim's cloak to win back her husband. One of the first comedies, *Love's Labor's Lost*, makes game of men who are maladroit at shifting roles and disguises, and so throughout most of the rest, the palm goes to the quicksilver wit, the alert, the volatile, the adroit improviser, the *débrouillard*—not only the Puck and the Autolycus but the Petruchio, the Maria (*Twelfth Night*), the Rosalind, the Prince Hal. The tragedies, on the other hand, dramatize typically a stubborn rigidity, heroically or blindly tardy in its adaptations, dooming the protagonist to an agonizing and belated evolution upward toward tragic wisdom. All of the tragic heroes are too stiff to adjust, obstinately and massively embedded in roles which no longer fit. In Machiavelli's terms, they cannot accord their natures with circumstance, and so their fortunes disintegrate. Coriolanus is too rigid to play the politician, or Lear the abdicated king; Richard cannot adapt to revolt, or Hamlet to tyrannicide, or Romeo to the mature restraints of marriage; Brutus muddles his unbecoming role as conspirator, and Antony, once his Roman uniform is off, can scarcely choose the identity that fits him. Even Macbeth never learns to carry off the murderous role in which his wife has cast him. Heroically and perversely obtuse, each of the tragic protagonists is altered and enlightened beyond his will by the anguish of events. Only in the last play, *The Tempest*, does Shakespeare remove from the human sphere the responsibility for metamorphosis and assign it to magic, to the supernatural, to Mercy:

> My ending is despair
> Unless I be relieved by prayer
> Which pierces so, that it assaults
> Mercy itself, and frees all faults.

Here, almost uniquely in Shakespeare, the scale is vertical and the agency transcendent.

It is very unlikely that Shakespeare was conscious of rejecting an age. It is much more likely that Cervantes *was* so conscious. Whatever his awareness, Cervantes wrote the most powerful of all attacks upon the transforming imagination, most powerful probably because most sympathetic. The knight of La Mancha is so lovable a caricature because his ridigity is so pure, and his will for a world made new so movingly inflexible. But he is already *old* in 1605: he belongs to a past that is suddenly seen to be decayed. With the intuitive recognition across the continent that Don Quixote's hope was tragically anachronistic, an age was over. Europe was left with the resignation of the earthbound, and with the novel, which teaches through disillusionment. The blurring of man's upper limits had gradually yielded to a humbling lucidity, and the modern age was free to play, like Don Juan and Scapin, with the wealth and the ennui of our fixed condition.

Thomas R. Hart

The Literary Criticism of Mário de Andrade

The most important current in Brazilian literature in the first half of the twentieth century was the Modernist movement of the twenties, which first attracted widespread attention as a result of the *Semana de Arte Moderna* held in São Paulo in February 1922. Just who conceived the idea of the *Semana* is not clear; it seems to have arisen spontaneously out of the conversations of a group of young poets and painters. Mário de Andrade denied the idea was his, yet it is surely fair to say that no one played a more significant role than he in the early history of Modernism.[1] The most important literary work of the movement's first phase is his book of poems, *Paulicéia desvairada;*[2] its most comprehensive theoretical statement is his long essay, *A escrava que não é Isaura.*[3]

Written in December 1920, the poems of *Paulicéia desvairada* were widely known in São Paulo literary circles even before Mário read some of them at the second evening program of the *Semana de Arte Moderna*, a reading repeatedly interrupted by whistles and catcalls from the audience. They were not published until July 1922, a half-year after the *Semana*, and were preceded by a "prefácio interessantíssimo," written, according to Mário, at the

1. *Aspectos da literatura brasileira* (São Paulo, n.d.), in the series *Obras completas de Mário de Andrade,* published by Livraria Martins. Hereafter cited as *Aspectos.*

2. São Paulo, Casa Mayença, 1922. The title page of the first edition reads *Paulicea,* not *Paulicéia;* this is also the spelling used by Mário in his letters to Manuel Bandeira. The poems, but not the preface, are included in Mário's *Poesias* (São Paulo, Livraria Martins, 1941). Hereafter cited as *Paulicéia.*

3. São Paulo, 1925. My citations are to the reprint in *Obra imatura* (São Paulo, 1960) in the *Obras completas.* Hereafter cited as *Escrava.*

insistence of some friends and one enemy ("por insistência de amigos e dum inimigo") .[4] The "enemy" was the publisher and short-story writer, Monteiro Lobato, who insisted, as a condition for publishing the book, that Mário write a preface explaining his aims; Monteiro Lobato, however, finally decided not to publish it.[5] Many points touched on in the preface to *Paulicéia* are more fully developed in *A escrava que não é Isaura*. Written in April and May 1922, shortly after the *Semana de Arte Moderna,* the little book was not published until January 1925. In a note at the end dated November 1924, Mário speaks of the "lamentable position" of "those who write books in Brazil and lack money to have them published immediately, at least a certain kind of books which try to break new ground and a certain kind of writers who are quite unconcerned with posterity and with vanity." [6] Some of his own views, he declares, have been considerably modified since he wrote the book, an assertion which has led the Brazilian critic Jamil Almansur Haddad, in a perceptive study of Mário's poetics, to disregard *Escrava* on the ground that it represents a stage of Mário's thought which he had abandoned even before the work

4. Ibid., p. 297. I have adopted the practice, followed in René Wellek's *History of Modern Criticism,* of giving all quotations in the text in English; the translations from Mário's writings are my own. The original Portuguese will be found in the footnotes, except for an occasional short phrase, as here. In quoting from Mário's works, I have retained his own somewhat inconsistent spelling and accentuation; cf. Manuel Bandeira's preface to *Cartas de Mário de Andrade a Manuel Bandeira* (Rio de Janeiro, Organização Simões, 1958) , pp. 6–7, and Mário's own remarks in *Aspectos,* p. 6.

5. Fernando Góes, "História da *Paulicéia desvairada,*" *Revista do Arquivo Municipal* [São Paulo], Ano XII, *106* (janeiro-fevereiro, 1946) , 98, 101. A few points presented in the preface to *Paulicéia* are anticipated in a series of seven articles. "Mestres do passado," published in the São Paulo newspaper *Journal do Comércio* in August and September 1921 and in another article, "Futurista?!," which appeared there in July of the same year. They have been reprinted by Mário de Silva Brito, *História do modernismo brasileiro, I: Antecedents da Semana de Arte Moderna, segunda edição revisada* (Rio de Janeiro, Editôra Civilização Brasileira, 1964) , pp. 254–309 and 234–38.

6. *Escrava,* p. 297: "Reconheça-se que é lamentável a posição dos que escrevem livros no Brasil e não têm dinheiro para publica-los imediatamente. Ao menos certa casta de livros que lidam tentativas e para certa raça de escritores que não dão á eternidade e á vaidade a mínima importancia."

was published.[7] Mário himself compares the book to a photograph taken in April 1922 and insists that "the main lines have remained intact." [8] Indeed, it is possible to argue that "the main lines" will be retained throughout the rest of his career, a period of only twenty years, cut short by his death at the age of fifty-one in February 1945.

The ideas presented in the preface to *Paulicéia* and in *Escrava* are fundamentally the same—not surprisingly, since the two essays were written at almost the same time—and it will be convenient to consider them together. The tone, too, is more or less the same, sometimes frankly intended to shock the bourgeois reader or even to insult him openly, sometimes pleading for understanding—a note Mário may have borrowed from Apollinaire's poem "La jolie rousse," a brief quotation from which comes at the very end of the twenty pages of appendixes printed at the end of *Escrava*. Both essays make lavish use of capital letters, italics, and occasional very short paragraphs composed of a single phrase or even a single word. The language, while often violent, is not slangy or even colloquial, nor is it self-consciously Brazilian. In *Paulicéia,* Mário repeatedly calls into question the seriousness of his own writing: "Besides, it's very hard to tell in this stuff where I leave off joking and begin to talk seriously. Even I can't tell." [9] Near the end of the preface he insists that "this whole preface, with all the wild theories there are in it, isn't worth a damn. When I wrote *Paulicéia desvairada,* I didn't think about any of this stuff." And, a moment later, "And that's the end of the 'Hallucination' school of poetry. In my next book I'll found another." [10] In *Escrava*, his tone is more serious, though still far from solemn. There are

7. "A poética de Mário de Andrade," *Revista do Arquivo Municipal* [São Paulo], Ano XII, *106* (janeiro-fevereiro, 1946) , 119.

8. *Escrava*, p. 297: "Não se esqueçam de que é uma fotografia tirada em Abril de 1922. A mudança também não é tão grande assim. As linhas matrizes se conservam."

9. *Paulicéia*, p. 8: "Aliás muito difícil nesta prosa saber onde termina a *blague,* onde principia a seriedade. Nem eu sei."

10. Ibid., p. 38: "Mas todo êste prefácio, com todo o disparate de teorias que contém, não vale coisíssima nenhuma. Quando escrevi 'Paulicea Desvairada' não pensei em nada disto"; p. 39: "E está acabada a escola poética 'Desvairismo'. Próximo livro fundarei outra."

other, perhaps more important, differences. The preface to *Pau-licéia* is an introduction to Mário's own poetry, at once a manifesto and an apology. *Escrava,* on the other hand, is concerned with Mário's creative work only secondarily and by implication. It is a manifesto combined with an annotated anthology of works by French, Italian, and Brazilian poets, two of the latter, incidentally, represented by poems in French; significantly, none of Mário's own poems is included. It is, in short, exactly what its subtitle proclaims it to be, a lecture on some tendencies of modernist poetry, "discurso sobre algumas tendéncias da poesia modernista." [11]

Few of the ideas in either essay could have seemed shocking, or even very new, to anyone familiar with the debates over the new poetry which had been going on in France and Italy for more than a decade. That the Modernists could arouse so much incomprehension and hostility in São Paulo has much less to do with their ideas than with the prevailing climate of opinion in the city, and especially with the fact that the new ideas were introduced all at once rather than emerging gradually in the course of a prolonged public debate.[12] Both the incomprehension and the hostility were nevertheless very real. The *Semana de Arte Moderna,* which marked the first public appearance of the Modernists as a group, was a *succès de scandale* in the most literal sense: in some São Paulo families, the *Semana* was considered a flagrant breach of morality, not to be mentioned in the presence of children or women. Mário himself recalled, years later, the difficult position in which he had found himself among the members of his own family and even before the *Semana* itself.[13] It is perhaps partly for this reason that he takes such pains in both essays to insist that his revolutionary ideas are confined to the realm of aesthetics and do

11. It will be noted that Mário does not use the term "Modernist" to refer to the group of Brazilian poets we now call by this name; he uses it rather to refer to contemporary poets in general, or at any rate to those who share a particular aesthetic orientation. In the preface to *Paulicéia,* he had used *"futurista"* in the same way, as a label for an international movement in poetry, rather than limiting it to Marinetti and his followers.

12. Cf. Mário's own remarks on the reasons why the Modernist movement began in São Paulo rather than in Rio de Janeiro and on its reception there (*Aspectos,* pp. 236–37).

13. Ibid., pp. 233–34.

not touch on morality or religion: "My demands? Liberty. I use it; I don't abuse it. I know how to keep it under control in my philosophical and religious truths; because philosophical and religious truths aren't conventional like Art, they're truths. I don't go that far!" [14] Even within the realm of aesthetics, Mário insists that he is not presenting Truth itself but only his own version of Truth: "Christ said: 'I am the truth.' And he was right. I always say: 'I am my Truth.' And I'm right, too. The Truth of Christ is immutable and divine. Mine is human, aesthetic, and transitory." [15]

I should not want, however, to suggest that Mário is here only making a concession to spare the feelings of his family and friends. On the one hand, there is abundant evidence that he was a practicing Catholic who took his religion very seriously; on the other, a distinction between nature and art is at the very center of his aesthetic theories. The distinction is precisely that art, unlike nature, is not concerned with eternal values but with ever-changing conventions. The essential quality of art at any moment is its newness, its difference from everything that has preceded it.[16] Artistic beauty is thus quite different from natural beauty:

The beautiful in art is arbitrary, conventional, transitory—a question of fashion. The beautiful in nature is unchanging, objective, natural—it has whatever permanence nature has. Art doesn't succeed in reproducing nature, nor is this its aim. All the great artists . . . have distorted nature. From which I infer that the beautiful in art will be artistic and subjective in proportion to its distance from natural beauty.[17]

14. *Paulicéia,* p. 22: "Minhas reivindicações? Liberdade. Uso dela; não abuso. Sei embridá-la nas minhas verdades filosóficas e religiosas; porquê verdades filosóficas, religiosas, não são convencionais como a Arte, são verdades. Tanto não abuso!"

15. *Escrava,* p. 201: "Cristo dizia: 'Sou a Verdade.' E tinha razão. Digo sempre: 'Sou a minha verdade.' E tenho razão. A Verdade de Cristo é imutável e divina. A minha é humana, estética e tranzitória."

16. Ibid., p. 238, n. 3.

17. *Paulicéia,* p. 18: "Belo da arte: arbitrário, convencional, transitório—questão de moda. Belo da natureza: imútavel, objectivo, natural—tem a eternidade que a natureza tiver. Arte não consegue reproduzir natureza, nem êste é seu fim. Todos os grandes artistas . . . foram deformadores da natureza. Donde infiro que o belo artístico será tanto mais artístico, tanto mais subjectivo quanto mais se afastar do belo natural."

The artist must not take nature for his model: "Let us flee nature! Only thus can art escape the ridiculous weakness of color photography." [18] And again, still more succinctly, in *Escrava:* "The poet doesn't photograph: he creates."[19]

Poetry resides, not in the poet's subject matter, which may be ugly or merely commonplace, but in his treatment of it. The poet, moreover, does not choose his subject matter. He simply takes whatever his subconscious offers him:

> The lyrical impulse is free; it doesn't depend on us, nor on our intelligence. It can spring from a bunch of onions as easily as from a lost love. . . . Inspiration may be called forth by a sunset and by a Matarazzi factory chimney, by the divine body of a Nize and by the divine body of a Cadillac. All subjects are *alive.* There is no such thing as a subject poetic in itself.[20]

Since the subconscious takes its materials from the external world, the poet, if he is true to himself, must also deal with that world. It is for this reason that true poets have always been Modernists:

> The Modernists haven't forced themselves to take sports, machinery, eloquence, and exaggeration as the [underlying] principle of all lyricism. Not at all. Like true poets in all periods, like Homer, like Virgil, like Dante, they sing the epoch in which they live. And it's just because they follow the old poets that the Modernists are so new.[21]

18. Ibid., pp. 19–20: "Fujamos da natureza! Só assim a arte não se ressentirá da ridícula fraqueza da fotografia . . . colorida." The ellipsis is Mário's.

19. *Escrava,* p. 237: "O poeta não fotografa: cria." Mário's views on this point recall those of Baudelaire; cf. René Wellek, *A History of Modern Criticism, 4* (New Haven and London, 1965), 439 ff.

20. Ibid., p. 208: "A impulsão lírica é livre, independe de nós, independe da nossa inteligéncia. Pode nascer de uma réstea de cebolas como de um amor perdido. . . . A inspiração surge provocada por um crepúsculo como por uma chaminé matarazziana, pelo corpo divino de uma Nize, como pelo corpo divino de uma Cadillac. Todos os assuntos são *vitais.* Não há temas poéticos."

21. Ibid., p. 224: "Os poetas modernistas não *se impuseram* esportes, maquinarias, eloquencias e exageros como principio de todo lirismo. Oh

But the poet's job is not done when he has transcribed the message sent him by his subconscious: "It is inspiration which is subconscious, not creation. In all creation there is an effort of will. . . . *Lyricism* isn't the same thing as *poetry*." [22] In the preface to *Paulicéia*, Mário gives this account of his own method of composition: "When I feel the lyrical impulse I write down, without thinking, everything my unconscious shouts to me. I think later: not only to correct, but also to justify, what I've written. That's the reason for this 'Very Interesting Preface.' " [23] Later in the preface he restates the same proposition as a definition of poetry in general, in a formula borrowed from the French poet Paul Dermée, "Lyricism + Art = Poetry":

> Art, which, added to lyricism, gives poetry, doesn't consist of holding back the mad race of the lyrical moment in order to warn it about the stones and barbed-wire fences along the road. Let it stumble, fall, hurt itself! Art is a matter of weeding out, later on, annoying repetitions, bits of romantic sentimentality, unnecessary or inexpressive details.[24]

The same idea is developed at much greater length in *Escrava* and with still more stress on the poet's conscious control of his material in the interest of making his work intelligible to his readers. For Dermée's formula, Mário now substitutes his own revision, intended to stress the importance for the artist's work of the medium he had chosen: "Pure lyricism + [self-] criticism + lan-

---

não! Como os verdadeiros poetas de todos os tempos, como Homero, como Vergílio, como Dante, o que cantam é a época em que vivem. E é por seguirem os velhos poetas que os poetas modernistas são tão novos."

22. *Ibid.*, p. 243: "A inspiração é que é subconsciente, não a criação. Em toda criação dá-se um esfôrço de vontade. . . . Lirismo não é *poesia.*"

23. *Paulicéia*, p. 8: "Quando sinto a impulsão lírica escrevo sem pensar tudo o que meu inconsciente me grita. Penso depois: não só para corrigir, como para justificar o que escrevi. D'ai a razão dêste Prefácio Interessantíssimo."

24. *Ibid.*, pp. 15–16: "Arte, que, somada a Lirismo, dá Poesia não consiste em prejudicar a dôida carreira do estado lírico para avisa-lo das pedras e cercas de arame do caminho. Deixe que tropece, cáia e se fira. Arte é mondar mais tarde o poema de repetições fastientas, de sentimentalidades románticas, de pormenores inúteis ou inexpressivos."

guage = poetry," though he adds, somewhat inconsistently, that
"some men are poets who have written only prose—or never
written anything at all. D'Annunzio's finest poem is the Fiume
adventure." [25] But this seems to be a momentary slip; in the rest
of the essay, Mário returns again and again to his view of the poet
as a conscious craftsman (though one whose materials are given
him by his subconscious). He defines the work of art as "a machine for producing emotions" and refers in a footnote to Poe's
essay "The Philosophy of Composition"; a few pages later he
defines a poet as "one who has achieved what he set out to do." [26]

The poet has an obligation to make his meaning clear, though
Mário recognizes that what is clear for one reader may not be clear
for another: "Hermeticism must be resisted without quarter. But I
don't mean by that that poems have to be so plain that a yokel
from Xiririca can understand them as well as a cultivated man
who is familiar with psychology, aesthetics, and the historical development of poetry." [27] The poet, then, has obligations to the
reader, but the reader has some obligations of his own:

> [Georges] Ribot has said somewhere that inspiration is a tele-
> gram in code sent by the unconscious to be translated by the
> consciousness. That conscious activity may be divided be-
> tween the poet and the reader. Thus the poet doesn't coldly
> strip the lyrical moment and break it into little pieces: he
> generously grants the reader the glory of collaborating in his
> poems.[28]

25. *Escrava,* p. 205: "Lirismo puro + Crítica = Palavra = Poesia"; p.
206: "São poetas homens que só escreveram prosa ou . . . jamais escreveram
coisa nenhuma. O mais belo poema de D'Annunzio é a aventura de Fiume."
The ellipsis is Mário's.

26. Ibid., p. 258: "uma máquina de produzir comoções"; p. 270: "E é na
verdade um Poeta, isto é, conseguiu o que pretendia."

27. Ibid., p. 244: "É preciso pois combater sem quartel o hermeticismo.
Não quero porém significar com isso que os poemas devam ser tão chãos que
o caipira de Xiririca possa compreende-los tanto como o civilizado que
conheça psicologia, estética e a evolução histórica da poesia."

28. *Paulicéia,* p. 31: "Ribot disse algures que inspiraçao é telegrama
cifrado transmitido pela actividade inconsciente á actividade consciente que
o traduz. Essa actividade consciente pode ser repartida entre poeta e leitor.
Assim aquele nao escorcha e esmiuça friamente o momento lírico; e
bondosamente concede ao leitor a glória de colaborar nos poemas."

Mário returns to the same analogy in *Escrava:* "It is the reader who must raise himself to the level of the poet's sensibility, not the poet who must stoop to the level of the reader's sensibility. It's up to him [the reader] to translate the telegram!" [29]

The reader's collaboration becomes particularly crucial in the case of much modern poetry because of its use of juxtaposition: the poem offers a disconcerting series of apparently unrelated elements unconnected by logical transitions which would guide him in establishing a meaningful relationship among them. In the preface to *Paulicéia* Mário calls this type of verse "harmonic": "If . . . we place words one after another without joining them together in any way, then these words, by the very fact that they don't follow each other intellectually or grammatically, will be superposed one upon another, so that we shall have the sensation of hearing, not melodies, but harmonies." [30] As an example of harmonic verse, Mário cites a line which might be an extraordinarily condensed and evocative account of the settlement of his native state of São Paulo:

> "Ecstasies . . . Struggles . . . Arrows . . . Songs . . . To Settle [a new land]! . . ." These words aren't joined together. . . . Each one is a separate phrase, an elliptical sentence, reduced to a telegraphic minimum. If I say the word "ecstasies," since it doesn't form part of a phrase (a melody), it calls attention to its isolation and keeps on vibrating, waiting for a phrase that will give it a meaning and that DOES NOT COME. "Struggles" doesn't make any sort of conclusion for "ecstasies"; and, by the same token, without making us forget the first word, it keeps on vibrating together with it. The other words do the same thing.[31]

29. *Escrava*, p. 209: "É o leitor que se deve elevar á sensibilidade do poeta, não é o poeta que se deve baixar á sensibilidade do leitor. Pois êste que traduza o telegrama!"

30. *Paulicéia*, p. 24: "[Si] fizermos que se sigam palavras sem ligação imediata entre si: estas palavras, pelo facto mesmo de se não seguirem intellectual, gramaticalmente, se sobrepõem umas ás outras, para a nossa sensação, formando, não mais melodias, mas harmonias."

31. Ibid., pp. 24–25: " 'Arroubos . . . Lutas . . . Setas . . . Cantigas . . . Povoar! . . .' Estas palavras não se ligam. . . . Cada uma é frase, período elíptico, reduzido ao mínimo telegráfico. Si pronuncio 'Arroubos,' como não

In a footnote, Mário declares that he had discovered the theory for himself and discussed it with his friends six or eight months before learning that the same pheonomenon had been discussed by the French critic Jean Epstein in the review *Esprit nouveau* under the name *"simultanisme."* [32] In *Escrava,* he presents the same theory at much greater length and gives it a new name, "polyphonism." This time his claim to originality is limited to the name itself and, by implication, to the presentation of the phenomenon in terms of an analogy with music, though he is careful to repeat and to amplify his assertion in *Paulicéia* that the analogy is to be understood only in a figurative sense.[33] Now he is anxious to invoke the authority of European poets and critics: "I give the name 'polyphonism' to the Simultaneity of the French, with Epstein as their spokesman, the Simultanism of Fernand Divoire, the Synchronism of Marcello-Fabri." [34] Polyphonism, however, is not to be equated with simultaneity in the ordinary sense of two or more things which happen at the same time. It demands a deliberate effort of analysis, a "vontade de análise," and the intention, on the artist's part, of creating a unified total effect.[35]

Mário does not present polyphonism as a program for future poets: "I have no pretensions to creating anything at all. 'Poly-

---

faz parte de frase (melodia), a palavra chama a atenção para seu insulamento e fica vibrando, *á espera duma frase que lhe faça adquirir significado e QUE NÃO VEM.* 'Lutas' não dá conclusão alguma a 'Arroubos'; e, nas mesmas condições, não fazendo esquecer a primeira palavra, fica vibrando com ela. As outras vozes fazem o mesmo."

32. Ibid., p. 30, n. 1. Cf. *Escrava,* p. 256, where Mário insists that "at that time," that is, when he wrote the preface to *Paulicéia,* he was unfamiliar with the work of Epstein and Fernand Divoire, and that he had been unable to obtain any reliable information about the "synchronism" of Marcello-Fabri, though he says he was acquainted with the theories of Soffici, "which don't satisfy me," and those of the Cubist and Futurist painters.

33. *Escrava,* pp. 256, 268; *Paulicéia,* pp. 26–27. It is worth remarking that Mário was a professional musician, who taught for a number of years at the São Paulo Conservatory, and that he wrote extensively on musicological subjects, including a history of Brazilian music.

34. *Escrava,* p. 226: "Denomino Polifonismo a Simultaneidade dos franceses, com Epstein por cartaz, o Simultaneismo de Fernando Divoire, o Sincronismo de Marcelo Fabri."

35. Ibid., p. 268.

phonism' is the theoretical formulation of certain techniques employed every day by certain modernist poets." [36] It is not even something entirely new, or rather its effect is not wholly different from that of older, more traditional poetry: "In all the arts of time, there could not be understanding without the sum of successive acts of memory, each relating to a single isolated sensation. Even in an old-fashioned sonnet, it is the complex total, final sensation produced by this sum, which determines the emotional effect of the work." [37] The difference is that in traditional poetry ideas are presented one at a time and the logical connections between them spelled out by the poet, while in Modernist poetry the elements are simply juxtaposed, with the relations between them left to be filled in by the reader. Yet "left" is not quite the right word; the connections may remain implicit, but the poet must take care to see that they are present. Here, as always, Mario holds fast to his premise that *"the poet doesn't photograph the subconscious";* [38] every poem must be subjected to revision to ensure its ability to stand alone, independent of the more or less accidental circumstances of its composition.

The value of *Escrava* does not lie in the originality of its insights into the distinctive qualities of twentieth-century poetry. Mário's basic thesis that poetry consists of inspiration plus craftsmanship underlies most twentieth-century thought on the subject, uniting poets as far apart as Paul Valéry and André Breton. The former is quite willing to admit the existence of inspiration, though he tends to minimize its importance; the latter confesses that no Surrealist poem is wholly a product of the subconscious.[39] The

36. Ibid., p. 256: "Não tenho a pretenção de criar coisa nenhuma. Polifonismo é a teorização de certos processos empregados quotidianamente por alguns poetas modernistas."

37. Ibid., p. 269: "Em todas as artes do tempo sem a soma total de actos successivos de memória (relativo cada um a cada sensação insulada) não poderia haver compreensão. Mesmo num soneto passadista é a sensação complexa total final provindo dessa soma, que determina o valor emotivo da obra."

38. Ibid., p. 242: *"O poeta não fotografa o subconsciente."* The italics are Mário's.

39. Cf. the excellent treatment of this point in Robert Gibson's anthology, *Modern French Poets on Poetry* (Cambridge, 1961), pp. 235–59; the passage

real importance of *Escrava* is its revelation of the mind of the
young poet-critic at a crucial point in his development and its role
as a transmitter of the new European theories of poetry, and of the
poetry itself, to the younger Brazilian writers of the twenties; the
latter reason alone would be more than enough to give Mário an
honored place among those intermediaries whose activities have
traditionally attracted the attention of students of comparative
literature.

   Mário's essay on Brazilian Modernization holds a special place
among his writings. Originally a lecture celebrating the twentieth
anniversary of the *Semana de Arte Moderna,* it was first published
separately as a book and then incorporated in the second edition
of his collection of essays, *Aspectos da literatura brasileira.* It is
both a fascinating autobiographical document and an important
source for the history of Modernism written by one of its central
figures, but it has relatively little to say about the aesthetic theories with which we are primarily concerned. It is not that Mário
repudiates the ideas presented in his earlier essays; what he rejects
is the refusal of the Modernists, and especially his own refusal, to
play an active role in attempting to solve the social and political
problems of the day. The end of the essay, in particular, is a frank
confession of guilt, in which Mário invites his former comrades to
join.[40] He recognizes that the aims of the movement were not, in
practice, identical with those he had proclaimed in the preface to
Paulicéia and in *Escrava.* He now sees Modernism as essentially
destructive, an accusation he had taken great pains to refute in his
earlier essays.[41] Although he had insisted there that the artist's
matter has no bearing on the value of his work, he now introduces
an important distinction: subject matter is irrelevant to the
"aesthetic intelligence" itself, but this intelligence is manifested in
art, which is concerned with the needs of society, and, as such, has
"a pragmatic human function which is of greater importance than

---

from Valéry referred to in the text is on p. 248, that from Breton on p.
239.

   40. *Aspectos,* p. 252.
   41. See, for example, *Escrava,* pp. 223, 246, and 274.

the hedonistic creating of beauty." [42] He is now convinced that the Modernists' preoccupation with aesthetic problems was by no means as disinterested and idealistic as it had appeared to them at the time: "With a few unconvincing exceptions, we were victims of our pleasure in life and of the merrymaking with which we destroyed our virility. If we transformed everything about ourselves, there is one thing we forgot to transform: our attitude of self-seeking toward contemporary life. And this was the most important thing!" The Modernists, he concludes, "should not serve as an example to anyone. But we can serve as a lesson. Man is passing through a wholly political phase. . . . Refusals to take part and eternal values can wait till later." [43]

The whole essay offers an excellent example of the tone of moral seriousness and personal involvement characteristic of Mário's later essays and in striking contrast to the flippancy, though not the intensity, of the preface to *Paulicéia* and of *Escrava*. In its concern with the social value of art and the writer's duty to take part in the social and political struggles of his time, it is typical of Mário's mature critical writing.

Both the preface to *Paulicéia* and *Escrava* represent attempts to make European culture, specifically contemporary European poetry, more widely known and accepted in Brazil. Indeed, one is tempted to say that it is precisely this preoccupation with Europe—which Mário never visited—that links his work with that of a great many other writers in both Spanish and Portuguese

42. *Aspectos*, p. 252: "O assunto não tem a menor importância para a inteligência estética. . . . Mas a inteligência estética se manifesta por intermédio de uma expressão interessada da sociedade, que é a arte. Esta é que tem uma função humana, imediatista e maior que a criação hedonística da beleza."

43. Ibid., p. 252: "Fomos, com algumas excepções nada convincentes, vítimas do nosso prazer da vida e da festança em que nos desvirilizamos. Si tudo mudávamos em nós, uma coisa nos esquecemos de mudar: a atitude interessada diante da vida contemporânea. E isto era o principal!"; p. 255: "Os modernistas da Semana de Arte Moderna não devemos servir de exemplo a ninguém. Mas podemos servir de lição. O homem atravessa uma fase integralmente política da humanidade. . . . Os abstencionismos e os valores eternos podem ficar pra depois."

America. In *Escrava,* Mário boasts of his familiarity with European culture, his firm belief that he is a citizen of the world. At the same time he insists that this does not make him any less Brazilian, offering as proof his willingness to stay in Brazil and do what he can to help his country enter into the life of the contemporary world—though one must not fail to note his ironical tone when he says that he accepts his wretched position in Brazil so that his country "may one day come to understand that the telegraph, the steamship, the telephone, and the Fox Movietone News exist, and that SIMULTANEITY EXISTS." [44]

The later essays, on the other hand, deal exclusively with Brazilian topics.[45] They have been collected in two volumes of Mário's *Obras completas, Aspectos da literatura brasileira,* which contains a dozen essays written between 1931 and 1943, and in *O empalhador de passarinho,* a collection of shorter occasional pieces (mostly reviews of recent books), first published between 1939 and 1944. Not all the essays are primarily concerned with literature. That on Tristão de Ataíde, in *Aspectos,* aside from a few brief remarks on the latter's literary criticism, is given over to a refutation, based on Mário's extensive knowledge of Brazilian folklore and popular traditions, of Tristão's assertion that Brazilian culture is essentially Catholic; the essay "Elegia de abril" in the same volume is a series of reflections on the role of the intellectual in Brazilian society. I shall limit my discussion to two essays on nineteenth-century novelists, both included in *Aspectos da literatura brasileira*—that on Manuel Antônio de Almeida and that on Machado de Assis.

The essay on Almeida, first published in 1940 as the introduction to an edition of his novel *Memórias de um sargento de milícias,* is a good example of Mário's mature criticism. It is obvious that he finds Almeida an attractive subject, partly, no doubt, because of the latter's interest in folklore (pp. 130–31). At the same time, Mário is careful to point out that Almeida did not see

44. *Escrava,* p. 266: "para que . . . venha a compreender um dia que o telégrafo, o vapor, o telefonio, o Fox-Jornal existem e que *A SIMULTANEIDADE EXISTE."*

45. The brief article on the Chilean poetess Gabriela Mistral in *O Empalhador de passarinho* is only an apparent exception, since its immediate cause was the rumor, later confirmed, that she was to become her country's ambassador to Brazil.

the beauty of the folk traditions he describes with such precision, adding that "from his material difficulties, the poverty he knew as a child, the artist retained no pity for the poor, no charitable understanding of lowly suffering and of humble people." [46] This is, of course, fundamentally moral criticism, as is Mário's charge that Almeida was too much an aristocrat to interest himself in the problems of the poor, even too much a coward to take an active part in trying to better their situation (p. 137). The harshness of Mário's judgment on this point, as so often in the later essays, is surely not unrelated to the fact that the flaws he points out in the authors he studies are those which troubled him in his ceaseless examination of his own actions and of his motives for them. Here, for example, one senses a connection between Mário's appraisal of Almeida and his increasing sensitivity, in the last years of his life, to the charge that he, like some of the other Modernists, had refused to play an active part in the struggle to create more equitable social and political conditions in Brazil. It is hardly an exaggeration to say that Mário accuses Almeida of the same error he saw in his own conduct, his failure to love his fellowmen, his sense that he had been a victim of his own individualism, "vítima do meu individualismo": "I've come, in my declining years, to the conviction that I've lacked humanity. My sense of my own superiority has hurt me." [47]

Mário praises the naturalness and precision of Almeida's style; his language, like his treatment of folk traditions, offers material of great value to historians of Brazilian society. Mário notes Almeida's ironic play with the sentimental exaggerations of the romantics but denies that the book should be considered either realistic or naturalistic. Almeida takes neither himself nor his subject so seriously; he has no interest in social reform. His book belongs to the tradition of the picaresque novel or, more inclusively, to that of the comic adventure novel which begins with Apuleius and Petronius. Despite its wealth of accurate historical informa-

46. *Aspectos,* p. 139: "Das suas angústias materiais, da infância pobre, o artista não guardou nenhuma piedade pela pobreza, nenhuma compreensão carinhosa do sofrimento baixo e dos humildes."

47. Ibid., p. 252: "Chego no declínio da vida à convicção de que faltou humanidade em mim. Meu aristocracismo me puniu."

tion, it is not a portrait from life, but a caricature; Mário remains firmly convinced that "the artist doesn't photograph: he creates."

Mário begins his essay on Machado de Assis with a question to the reader: "Do you love Machado?" [48] The implication is clearly that he fears the answer will be "No," and this is indeed Mário's own answer. One can admire an author without loving him, and this is the case with Machado; Mário finds him unattractive as a man, though he can derive great aesthetic pleasure from his work. The work, moreover, has a moral value, that morality of technique, "a moralidade da técnica," to which Mário refers so often, with an insistence that surely comes in part from his feeling that the Modernists, with their stress on freedom from formal constraints, had encouraged slovenliness and amateurishness in a generation of Brazilian writers. But the perfection of Machado's style, though it is a triumph of dedication, of conscious effort, is also a kind of double betrayal, both a refusal on Machado's part to reveal himself as he really was and a denial of the essential nature of art by equating it with conscious calculation. One recalls Mário's definition of poetry in the preface to *Paulicéia* and in *Escrava;* Machado, he is saying in effect, is so preoccupied with technique that he leaves no room for lyricism. His victory, moreover, is incomplete: "He was unable to conquer his own unhappiness." [49] Unable to escape the limitations of a world-view shaped by his own misfortunes, Machado saw them as the universal lot of mankind.

Although Mário praises Machado for his probity both as a public official and as a private citizen, he suggests that the security Machado fought so hard to achieve was bought at the price of estrangement from the real problems of his time. Machado refused to concern himself with social and political questions; as a result the world of his novels is quite different from the real world in which he lived, and still more different from our own modern world. Here one may feel that Mário's attack on Machado springs in part from his dissatisfaction with the lack of social involvement in the work of the Modernists; the essay was written in 1939 when he was coming increasingly to feel the absence of social commit-

48. Ibid., p. 89: "Eu pergunto, leitor, pra que respondas ao segredo da tua consciência; amas Machado de Assis? . . . E esta inquietação me melancoliza."

49. Ibid., p. 105: "Não soube vencer a própria infelicidade."

ment in his own earlier work as a grave moral error. In the same way, it is possible to see Mário's rejection of Machado's pessimism as a counterpart to his harsh judgment of his own earlier writings on the ground that they represent the views of a man devoted solely to pleasure and to the cultivation of his own mind, unaware that for most men, certainly for most Brazilians, the struggle for mere existence makes such a pursuit of pleasure inconceivable.[50]

In the preface to *Aspectos da literatura brasileira,* Mário expresses his hope that his readers will recognize in the essays collected there "not the aim of meting out justice, which I consider petty in the art of criticism, but a passionate effort to love and understand." [51] Such a view must not, however, be taken to mean that value judgments have no place in criticism. To speak of justice implies adherence to an impersonal standard, whereas criticism, for Mário, means the examination of one's own disciplined responses. It is the product not merely of understanding and love, but of the will to understand and love something which at first may seem meaningless or repugnant to us. Criticism, in short, is a record of the critic's search for a vantage point from which the writers he studies can be shown to have a positive value *for him.* Mário would surely have endorsed Baudelaire's view that "[the use of] *I,* rightly considered impertinent in many cases, implies nevertheless a great modesty; it confines the writer within the strictest limits of sincerity. By reducing his task, it makes it easier." [52] Criticism is thus always essentially moral criticism: it involves both an attempt to understand and judge the writer as he is revealed by his work and a constant reappraisal by the critic of his own tastes and values; it is perfectly understandable that Mário's

50. Ibid., pp. 253–54.

51. Ibid., p. 5: "não o propósito de distribuir justiça, que considero mesquinho na arte de crítica, mas o esforço apaixonado de amar e compreender."

52. *Baudelaire as a Literary Critic,* trans. and ed. Lois Boe Hyslop and Francis E. Hyslop, Jr. (University Park, Pa., 1964), p. 11; the quotation is from *L'art romantique,* ed. Jacques Crépet (Paris, Louis Conard, 1925), p. 199: "Ce *Je,* accusé justement d'impertinence dans beaucoup de cas, implique cependant une grande modestie; il enferme l'écrivain dans les limites les plus strictes de la sincérité. En réduisant sa tâche, il la rend plus facile."

criticism of other writers should reflect so often his uneasiness about the social usefulness of his own work and, ultimately, the moral value of his life.

Mário's role in the creation of Modernism was by no means limited to his critical writing; his own fiction and poetry were of far more importance. Nor was his role limited to his published works; he was a tireless correspondent whose letters to a great number of other writers or would-be writers, many of them not personally known to him, did much to further the spread of Modernist ideas throughout Brazil.[53] His letters to the Brazilian poet Manuel Bandeira are of particular importance, for they are our best source for studying the development of Mário's thought on the problems of creating a distinctively Brazilian literary language.[54]

Any poet might claim that his goal is to "donner un sens plus pur aux mots de la tribu," but for the writer who undertakes to create a new literary language, and not just his own personal style, this means a concern with problems of grammar which need not worry the writer in the more established literary traditions; it may mean, for instance, in the case of Brazilian Portuguese, something as simple as deciding whether to place object pronouns before or after the verb. When the writer must use a dialect of a language which already has an established literary tradition in another country—when, in other words, he is an ex-colonial, as any Latin-American writer must be—his problems, both practical and psychological, become still more complex.

Mário was proud of his knowledge of Portuguese. In a letter of 1925 to Manuel Bandeira, he declares that "I've studied Portuguese and I'm aware of my mistakes. At least of the great majority of them." [55] In another, written ten years later, he says: "It's

53. Antônio Cândido, "Mário de Andrade," *Revista do Arquivo Municipal* [São Paulo], Ano XII, *106* (janeiro-fevereiro, 1946), 69–70.

54. Mário de Andrade, *Cartas . . . a Manuel Bandeira,* prefácio e notas de Manuel Bandeira (Rio de Janeiro, Organização Simões, 1958). Hereafter cited as *Cartas.*

55. Ibid., p. 96: "Estudei o português e estou consciente dos meus erros em português. Ao menos da grande maioria dêles."

funny, but I have a secret desire to speak Portuguese well and to write it correctly." [56] In a newspaper article reprinted in *O empalhador de passarinho,* he insists that the writer must be thoroughly familiar with the literary language in its traditional form, even though he may choose to depart from its prescriptions: "only someone who knows the rules has a right to break them. Only then does a mistake cease to be a mistake and become a matter of going beyond the established conventions, which have been made useless by the new demands of a new form of expression." [57] This is one more instance of Mário's insistence that art necessarily contains a large measure of craftsmanship, a note he had stressed from his earliest writings on poetry and one he came increasingly to feel had not been sufficiently understood by his contemporaries; in his lecture on the Modernist movement he remarks sadly that "today, with respect to the general level of the literary language, our position is worse than it was a hundred years ago." [58] Already in 1929, in a letter to Bandeira, he reveals misgivings about his own role in creating a new Brazilian language: "I even recognize that a dash of cold water on the Brazilianizing mania won't do any harm. I'm very much to blame for all that has happened and if I'd dreamed the fashion would catch on in such a big way I would certainly have been more moderate." [59]

Though Mário insists that the writer must know the literary language, he realizes that this very knowledge makes his task more difficult: "At every moment I find myself using needless Lusitanisms [forms or idioms characteristic of European Portuguese]. It's only natural. Remember that I've been writing Portuguese for 32

56. Ibid., p. 349: "É engraçado, mas eu trago . . . um desejinho secreto de falar bem o português e escrevê-lo sem êrro."

57. *O empalhador de passarinho* (São Paulo, Livraria Martins, [1955]), p. 215: "Só tem direito de errar quem conhece o certo. Só então o êrro deixa de o ser, pra se tornar um ir além das convenções, tornadas inúteis pelas exigências novas de uma nova expressão."

58. *Aspectos,* pp. 244–45: "Hoje, como normalidade de língua culta e escrita, estamos em situação inferior à de cem anos atràs."

59. *Cartas,* p. 221: "Até reconheço que um bocado de agua fria na fervura brasileiristica não fará mal. Eu tenho muita culpa de tudo o que sucedeu e si tivesse imaginado que a moda ficava tamanha de certo que havia de ser mais moderado."

years. . . . Rome wasn't built in a day. They're my new barba-
risms" [60] To write Brazilian is very different from speaking it: it
demands a conscious effort, which Mário aptly calls one of translation. In a letter of 1925 to Bandeira he speaks of the early book of
poems *Losango Cáqui,* "which I translated completely into Brazilian." In another, he says: "Here's that poem I wrote a year ago.
I've spent a year, off and on, in correcting it. . . . Finally I've
Brazilianized the whole thing." [61]

Mário was perfectly aware that the writer's problem could not
be solved simply by urging him to write as he speaks. In his long
letter of 1925 to Manuel Bandeira, he offers a remarkable perspective of the problems of the writer who must make use of what
Mário calls "a language which is not yet a language," *língua que
ainda não é língua.* He rejects Bandeira's accusation that he is
writing, not Brazilian, but the dialect of São Paulo: "A grave injustice. I'm not writing *paulista.* On the contrary. Rather, in the
Brazilian language I'm writing now, I combine terms from both
North and South." And, a little further on: "It's a question of a
learned systematization and not a photograph of popular speech.
. . . And that systematization must inevitably be a personal
one. . . . I don't want to think my Brazilian—*the style I've
adopted*—will be the Brazilian language of tomorrow. I don't have
that pretension, I swear it. Besides, if I didn't systematize in that
way, I would be a folksy writer and I want to be a cultivated and
literary one." [62] Fifteen years later, in an essay, he says much the
same thing:

60. Ibid., p. 89: "A toda hora me escapam ainda lusitanismos substituiveis.
É natural. Se lembre que faz 32 anos que escrevo português. . . . Roma não
se fez num dia. São os meus novos vícios-de-linguagem."

61. Ibid., p. 87: "no Losango Caqui que traduzi inteirinho pro brasileiro";
p. 65: "Ai vai êsse poema escrito faz um ano. Com intermitencias, franca-
mente, levei um ano corrigindo. . . . Por último abrasileirei o cujo."

62. Ibid., p. 86: "Você diz por exemplo que eu em vez de escrever
brasileiro estou escrevendo paulista. Injustiça grave . . . Não estou escrevendo paulista, não. Ao contrário. Tanto que fundo na minha linguagem
brasileira de agora termos do norte e do sul"; p. 87: "Se trata de sistematização culta e não fotografia do popular. . . . Agora: essa sistematização tem de ser fatalmente pessoal. . . . Nao quero imaginar que o meu
brasileiro—*o estilo que adotei*—venha a ser o brasileiro de amanhã. Não

The standard language, especially when it is used for literary purposes, is a living language, too. Indeed, it's the only living language which reconciles within itself all the partial forms [i.e. the regional, social, and professional dialects] of a language. And of other languages. . . . If, in São Paulo, talking with my sister who's a *paulista,* I should ask her to go into the *camarinha* [bedroom] and get my slippers, I would be as much an anarchist and a pedant as if I spoke to her in the style of Camões. But as an artist, I insist on my right to use *"camarinha"* in my short story or in my poem, whether for the sake of regionalism, or that of picturesqueness and comedy, or simply that of sonority and rhythm. And the use of the word may nevertheless be a simple and very useful fact of personal psychology. I've traveled through the Northeast, there I've slept in lots of *camarinhas,* there I've used the word to make myself more readily understood, there I've dreamed, there I've had illusions, there I've suffered. So the word may spring up within me, a flower of my own garden. And I, as an artist, have the right to express myself by means of it.[63]

This notion of the literary language as the sum of the possibilities offered by its various specialized forms recalls that offered by

tenho essa pretenção, juro. Por outro lado si eu não fizesse essa sistematização eu seria um escritor sentimentalmente popular e quero ser um escritor culto e literário."

63. *O empalhador de passarinho,* p. 215: "A linguagem culta, especialmente quando artística, é também uma língua viva. É mesmo a única língua viva que congraça em sua entidade tôdas as linguagens parciais de uma língua. E das outras. . . . Si em São Paulo, falando com minha mana paulista, eu lhe peço que vá na 'camarinha' buscar meus chinelos, eu estarei tão anarquista e pedante como si lhe falasse no estilo de Camões. Mas como artista, eu quero o meu direito de empregar 'camarinha' no meu conto ou na minha poesia, seja pra efeitos de regionalismo, seja pra efeitos de pitoresco ou de comicidade, ou seja mesmo para efeitos de sonoridade ou de ritmo. E ainda o emprêgo da palavra pode ser um simples e utilíssimo fato de psicologia pessoal. Viajei pelo Nordeste, lá dormi em muitas camarinhas, lá empreguei a palavra pra me fazer mais imediatamente compreendido, lá sonhei, lá me iludi, lá sofri. A palavra pode pois surgir em mim sem necessidade estilística nenhuma, flor do meu próprio jardim. E eu, como artista, tenho o direito de me expressar com ela."

Dante in *De vulgari eloquentia,* and indeed Dante's name often
appears in Mário's remarks on language and style. Mário, however,
is careful to insist that his own role is not that of Dante but the
humbler one of those poets of the *dolce stil novo* who prepared the
way for him: "Dante didn't just spring up all by himself. Before
him, a lot of poets had begun to write in the vernacular and they
prepared the way for Dante." [64] But the fate of writers who prepare the way for those who will come after them is to be superseded. In the letters to Bandeira, Mário returns again and again to
the theme that his linguistic experiments will be no more than a
passing phase, though a necessary one. They demand a deliberate
sacrifice, which Mário willingly accepts. In a letter of November 8,
1924, he declares that "I am ready to sacrifice myself. It's necessary
to give courage to those poor fellows who still don't have the
courage to write Brazilian." [65] Again, in 1925, he speaks of "the
Messianic element in my struggle, sacrificing my works, writing
them in a language which is not yet a language." [66]

This sacrifice is twofold. In the first place, it means giving up
the place one might have had in posterity, a consideration Mário
repeatedly declares is of no concern to him: "I don't attach the
slightest importance to fame or to posterity. I've none of that kind
of vanity." And again: "It isn't my destiny to survive. . . . What
do I care about being praised in 1985?" [67] He insists that it is not
really a question of sacrifice, but simply of accepting his own
limitations: "I said I'm sacrificing myself. But that isn't quite true.
I've only given up, sensibly, a pretension I mustn't have: to be
famous and have a place in the histories [of literature] as an
important writer. . . . I'm convinced my destiny is to be transitory. That neither saddens me nor makes me proud. It's just a

64. *Cartas,* p. 33: "Dante não surgiu sòzinho. Antes dêle uma porção de
poetas começaram a escrever em língua vulgar e *prepararam* Dante."
65. Ibid.: "Estou disposto a me sacrificar. É preciso dar coragem a essa
gentinha que ainda não tem coragem de escrever brasileiro."
66. Ibid., p. 86: "A parte messiânica do meu esfôrço, a sacrificar minhas
obras, escrevendo-as em língua que ainda não é língua."
67. Ibid., p. 85: "Não dou prá celebridade e eternização do meu nome a
mínima importância. Não tenho nenhuma vaidade nêsse sentido"; p. 54:
"Meu destino não é ficar. . . . Que me importa ser louvado em 1985?"

fact." [68] On this point, Mário is perhaps speaking with something less than perfect candor; one recalls the remark of his good friend Bandeira that "certain aspects of his powerful personality are even difficult to classify; are we to call them virtues or defects? For example, his pride, which was immense, but frequently expressed itself in forms of apparent humility, forms which intrigued Mário himself." [69]

But there is another, though not unrelated, sense in which the sacrifice must have been very real: Mário's realization that for what we may call polemical reasons his writings could not take the form he himself would have preferred to give them. In a letter of 1929 to Bandeira, he declares that his style is now less self-consciously Brazilian "simply because there's no longer any reason to exaggerate," *simplesmente porque já não há mais razão pra forçar a nota.* "You know I either told you or wrote you that I was experimenting and that I had no intention of continuing to exaggerate in that way." [70] Such a conception of the task at hand implies rejecting those means of expression which are not themselves arms in the war to create a Brazilian language: "You understand, Manuel, I've impoverished my means of expression. I've got no doubts about that. I've impoverished them deliberately. There is a phrase of Machado [de Assis] which constantly throbs in my memory: 'Something must be sacrificed.' " [71] But this, in turn, goes

68. *Ibid.*, p. 34: "Disse que me sacrifico. Nem isso é bem verdade. Apenas desisti razoàvelmente duma pretensão que não posso ter: ser célebre e ficar nas Histórias, como escritor de grande valor. . . . Meu distino, estou convencido disso, é ser transitório. Isso não me entristece nem me orgulha. É."

69. *Ibid.*, p. 5: "Certos aspectos de sua personalidade poderosa são mesmo difíceis de classificar: como qualidade ou como defeito? O seu orgulho, por exemplo, que era imenso, mas freqüentemente se exprimia em formas de aparente humildade, que a êle próprio intrigavam." Cf. Antônio Cândido, pp. 70–71.

70. *Ibid.*, p. 220: "Você sabe que ou falei ou escrevi pra você que eu estava experimentando e não pretendia continuar no forçamento de brasileirismos em que estava.

71. *Ibid.*, p. 90: "Você compreende, Manuel, eu empobreci os meus meios de expressão. Nao faço dúvida nisso. Empobreci-os conscientemente. Tem uma frase do Machado que me bate sempre na memória. 'Alguma coisa é preciso sacrificar.' "

counter to one of Mário's most deeply held convictions about the nature of literary creation, that it is a spontaneous revelation of the unconscious. The polemical aim of his attempt to create a distinctively Brazilian style, coupled with the many decisions on minute points of grammar inherent in the attempt itself, meant that he could not give free rein to his creative powers: "My naturalness now is affectation because the problem preoccupies me at every moment and therefore distorts my natural style. I am in a period of transition. I am creating a new natural style. For the time being, it looks like a great affectation." [72] Four years later, in 1929, he insists that this phase has already passed: "As for what you call willful and premeditated [in my style], I've examined my conscience and I know it's not that at all. It's just a new habit I've picked up. . . . My pronouns and Brazilianisms . . . pour forth now like water from a spring with no special effort on my part." [73]

Yet the danger was real, and the damage done to Mário's work remains, as even very sympathetic critics have conceded.[74] It is the judgment which Mário himself extended to the other Modernists: "The Modernist movement was essentially destructive. Even destructive of ourselves, because the pragmatism of our experiments always weakened our freedom to create." [75] To weaken, however, is not the same as to destroy. The Modernist movement gave to Brazilian literature much that is of lasting value and surely the writings of Mário de Andrade are not the least of its gifts.

72. Ibid., p. 88: "A minha naturalidade agora é a afectação porque o problema está me preocupando a todo instante e por isso me desvirtua o modo natural. Estou em época de tranzição. Estou criando um novo modo natural. Por enquanto se vê nisso muita afectação."

73. Ibid., p. 220: "O que você chama de acintoso e de proposital [no meu estilo], ponho a mão na consciencia e sei que não é. Apenas é um novo hábito adquirido. . . . Meus pronomes e brasileirismos . . . saem hoje como agua que brota sem nenhuma preocupação mais."

74. For example, Mário Neme, "Linguagem de Mário de Andrade," *Revista do Arquivo Municipal* [São Paulo], Ano XII, *106* (janeiro-fevereiro, 1946), pp. 110–13.

75. *Aspects*, p. 240: "O movimento modernista foi essencialmente destruidor. Até destruidor de nós mesmos, porque o pragmatismo das pesquisas sempre enfraqueceu a liberdade de criação."

Geoffrey H. Hartman

Romantic Poetry and the Genius Loci

*Reason suffered a few demons still to lin-
ger, which she chose to retain under the
guidance of poetry.*
                    Thomas Warton

It is no longer necessary to protect the Romantic poets from the
charge of neoprimitivism. But it may be timely to consider them
as fulfilling, in addition to criticizing, the Enlightenment. Their
concern with the darker graces of poetry, with the realities of myth
and the relation of the poetic and the religious genius, did not
mean an unscrutinized use of archaic beliefs. On the contrary, the
struggle of the Romantic poets with romance is a moving, intense,
and endless one. They knew light must be fought with light, and
that the great intellectual movement which preceded them, and in
which they continued to participate, could not be reversed. Between the time of Gray and that of Wordsworth—the epoch here
considered—the fate of poetry seemed to depend on poetry's
revaluation of its founding superstitions. I would like to study
one of the most persistent of these, the belief in Spirit of Place, in
a *Genius loci*.[1]

1. For the most convenient summary of the belief, see Andrew Tooke,
The Pantheon of the Heathen Gods (1st ed., 1698), Pt. V, chap. 2, "The
Genii." Also, tendentious but important, Blake's *The Marriage of Heaven
and Hell* (1793), "The ancient Poets animated all sensible objects with
Gods or Geniuses" and so on. A late but absolutely conventional statement,
representing the most common form of the belief, is found in T. L. Peacock,
The Genius of the Thames (1810), in his note on "the tutelary spirits, that
formerly animated the scenes of nature." For the Genius idea as it enters
English literature, the following may be consulted: E. C. Knowlton, "The
Genii of Spenser," *SP 25* (1928), 439–56; D. T. Starnes, "The Figure of
Genius in the Renaissance," *Studies in the Renaissance, 11* (1964), 234–44;
and C. S. Lewis, "Genius and Genius," in *Studies in Medieval and Renais-*

Returning from Italy in 1741, Gray revisited the monastery of
the Grande Chartreuse and inscribed in its album an Alcaic Ode
composed in memory of his stay two years earlier. I quote from the
opening invocation:

> O Tu severi Religio loci,
> Quocunque gaudes nomine (non leve
> Nativa nam certe fluenta
> Numen habet, veteresque sylvas;
> Praesentiorem et conspicimus Deum
> Per invias rupes . . . .)
> Salve vocanti rite, fesso et
> Da placidam juveni quietem.[2]

In length, subject, and tone, the poem is a genuine Inscription.[3] It
is addressed to the Spirit of the Place, except that the poet writes
"Religio loci" for Genius loci [4] to avoid the least hint of superstition and to suggest that the religion is not his but "of the
place," although more universal than the particular name might

sance Literature (New York, 1966), pp. 169–74. The latter contains an
exceptionally clear distinction between Genius *sive Natura* and Genius as
alter ego. No study exists on the fortunes of the belief beyond the Renaissance, but Maynard Mack has shown its purified yet amazing hold on Pope
in "A Poet in His Landscape: Pope at Twickenham," *From Sensibility to
Romanticism,* eds. Frederick W. Hilles and H. Bloom (Oxford, 1965), pp.
3–29, esp. 10–12 and 19–21. For German thought and literature there is the
splendid entry on "Genie" in *Deutsches Wörterbuch,* by Jakob and Wilhelm
Grimm and others.

2. "O Thou, Religion of this stern place, or whatever name pleases Thee
(for surely no negligible divinity rules these native streams and ancient
forests; and surely we behold God more present amid pathless steeps . . .)
hail to Thee! And if I invoke Thee correctly, grant to a weary youth quiet
and repose." For a complete text and translation, see *The Complete Poems
of Thomas Gray,* eds. H. W. Starr and J. R. Hendrickson (Oxford, Claren-
don, 1966), p. 151.

3. On Inscriptions as a genre, cf. the author's "Wordsworth, Inscriptions,
and Romantic Nature Poetry," in *From Sensibility to Romanticism,* pp.
389–413.

4. Eighteenth-century translations of the ode bring this out. "O Thou, the
Genius of this Wild Retreat" Edmund Cartwright, *Poems* (London, 1786),
p. 64. "Oh, Genius of this hallow'd place," *European Magazine, 19* (1791),
285.

suggest ("Quocunque gaudes nomine") .[5] He who pays this ritual tribute ("Salve vocanti rite") is a stranger yet respects, and asks the favor of, the divinity of the region.

In this early poem Gray's attitude toward the Genius loci is circumspect. Since it is also a Latin poem, where more liberty might be taken, the scruple is doubly remarkable. Gray seems to abandon such scruples, if we believe Dr. Johnson—*The Bard* incurs the latter's wrath for indulging in "the puerilities of obsolete mythology." Yet Gray remains the most careful of poets: in his devotional poetry and his few epitaphs there is no trace of what the Protestant Enlightenment called "Superstition"—mythological ideas associated with paganism or the Counter-Reformation. A neoclassic decorum makes them resemble, like the Alcaic Ode, Universal Prayers. The pagan element, moreover, in such poems as *The Bard,* is clearly a virtuoso development of the personification style common to Gray's time.

Dr. Johnson has, nevertheless, a sure instinct for the problematic. The problem is not myth as such (pagan or Christian) but the bolder vision of poetry it implies. The presence of myth is a sign of poetry's higher destiny, of its link to inspiration and prophecy. Gray's early style avoids more than pagan fictions; it avoids the prophetic—the "speaking out." *He never spoke out* was Arnold's verdict on him. It is part of the decorum of the Alcaic Ode that it mutes the epiphany of the Genius loci. Only the odes reprehended by Dr. Johnson began to speak out and to acknowledge the connection of poetry and vision. According to Gray's Nordic and Pindaric odes, true poetry means heroic poetry, high deeds in high style, prophecies and dooms. *The Bard* is one long and ferocious "speaking out."

Yet even in Gray's boldest poems there is a reluctance to rouse the English lyre from its torpor. If the *Progress of Poesy,* echoing the Psalms, starts with the opposite impulse—"Awake, Aeolian lyre, awake" [6]—and ends on a note heralding Blake—"O! Lyre

---

5. A very old liturgical formula; see E. Norden, *Agnostos Theos* (Berlin, 1913), pp. 143 ff. Cf. Milton's varying of the place name for the seat of inspiration, *Paradise Lost* I.6–12. The formula, as Milton and Gray use it, modifies the idea of Christianity as a "Religio loci" or "local religion."

6. Gray himself footnotes the echo to David's Psalms in the 1768 edition. But "Aeolian," as he adds in the note, comes from Pindar.

divine, what daring Spirit/ Wakes thee now?"—the question reveals the doubt. Can England be the home of a strong-spirited
poetry? It promised to be in the time of Shakespeare, Milton, and
(even) Dryden. The Muses, having left Greece for Latium, follow
the progress of liberty and seek Albion next (II.3) . But the end of
that epoch seems already at hand. Gray refuses to engage in a reversal of the destiny of poetry in the Enlightenment. In *The
Descent of Odin,* it is, characteristically, the prophetess' unwillingness to speak which dominates the visionary interview:

> Now my weary lips I close:
> Leave me, leave me to repose.

Now the existence of a Genius loci (the "rising Genius" as he
was sometimes called) is intrinsically related to vision and prophecy: to determining the destiny of an individual or a nation.[7] We
continue to sense this in the Alcaic Ode, which expresses a charged
if transient moment of encounter, one that made Gray aware of "a
road not taken." In comparison, however, with his letters ("Not a
precipice, not a torrent, not a cliff, but is pregnant with religion
and poetry") and the poetry of Wordsworth and Shelley which it
anticipates, Gray's ode is but a formal tribute to the divine Presence working through nature ("Praesentiorem conspicimus
Deum") . It will need Wordsworth to truly acknowledge the

7. See, inter alia, Virgil, *Aeneid* VII.31 ff.; Spenser, *Faerie Queene,* II.xii.
47–48; Milton, *On the Morning of Christ's Nativity,* xix ff. (where the
"parting Genius" is linked to the cessation of the oracles) ; Thomson,
Liberty, IV (esp. the episode of the "Genius of the Deep") ; Hölderlin,
Patmos and *Hymne an den Genius Griechenlands;* Shelley, *The Daemon of
the World;* Carlyle, *Sartor Resartus,* "It was his guiding Genius (Dämon)
that inspired him; he must go forth and meet his Destiny" (Bk. II, chap. 5) .
A Genius, of course, is not inevitably "local": Socrates has his familiar
daimon, comparable to a guardian angel, and the examples cited above from
Spenser and Shelley show Genius as demiurge or god of nature. Yet the
place associated with the appearance of such a Genius is felt to be sacred;
the Genius is often held to be *ingenium,* or so closely associated with birth
(a "natale comes qui temperat astrum" as Horace says) that time and place
become charged with significance (fatal or fated births are what mythical
stories elaborate) ; and calling Shakespeare "Sweet Swan of Avon" suggests
that the birth of a genius (in the ordinary sense) consecrates the place of
which he becomes the Genius loci.

visibilia of the region, and to undergo, through their hold on his memory, something like a conversion.[8] A second ode of Gray's, *On a Distant Prospect of Eton College,* will confirm this muting of the figure and visionary implications of the "rising Genius."

In the Eton Ode, with its evocation of overarching presences, "Ye distant spires, ye antique towers . . . Henry's holy Shade," spirit of place again confronts the poet. As in Wordsworth, moreover, the idea of place blends with that of time: what confronts the poet's consciousness is best rendered by "prospect" in the modern sense of the word. Unlike Wordsworth, however, Gray withdraws from envisioning a future that restores a lost happiness. The past is a "distant prospect," and the future, at least the future within the proper realm of speculation, is not open. It is characterized for all men by the same fatality: manhood and the pains of manhood. Vision therefore is but the knowledge of suffering, and there is no point in disturbing those without it. "Why should they know their fate," the poet asks of the "little victims" that play in the shadow of Eton (their Eden).

The inutility of vision is curiously illustrated by the ode's one explicit instance of Genius loci personification. Gray's address to the towers, hills, and fields culminates in an invocation to Father Thames, who is asked to identify this new generation of children at play:

> Say, Father THAMES, for thou hast seen
> Full many a sprightly race
> Disporting on thy margent green
> The paths of pleasure trace,
> Who foremost now delight to cleave
> With pliant arm thy glassy wave?

8. See *The Prelude,* Bk. VI. The lines referring specifically to the region of the Grande Chartreuse (see also n. 11, below) celebrate the theophanic qualities of the place (the "imaginative impulse" from forests, cliffs, and floods that allow us "to look with bodily eyes, and be consoled") and are like a descant on the plainchant of Gray's ode. Shelley's *Mont Blanc* moves, spiritually, in another direction but is not unaware of the "Praesentiorem conspicimus Deum" tradition or of the habit of entering inscriptions in the Albums of the neighborhood. Cf. Harold Bloom, *Shelley's Mythmaking* (New Haven, 1959), pp. 11 ff.

Dr. Johnson remarks tartly that "Father Thames has no better means of knowing than [Gray] himself." Yet Father Thames is presented as a guardian genius of the place and is also therefore its historian: like the Muse in epic poetry, he could tell, having seen the generations as they pass.[9] Homer, moreover, used the device to number the warriors before Troy, and Gray expects us to understand his development of the topos, which brings into one picture children at play and soldiers fated to die. But the ultimate pathos is that as a guardian or "father" spirit the Thames should be able to protect the children from the ambush in wait, those murderous allegorical abstractions which replace the nature personification in the poem's latter half:

> Lo, in the vale of years beneath
> A griesly troop are seen,
> The painful family of Death . . . .

Yet Father Thames is eloquently mute; there is no formal prosopopeia; the invocation is purely rhetorical and does not expect an answer. An inauthentic figure of speech becomes an authentic figure of silence.

The muteness of the Genius loci is even more significant in the light of tradition. In his turn toward pathos and away from the sublime or prophetic occasion, Gray extends (as is his wont) a literary commonplace. Father Thames appears at the end of Pope's *Windsor Forest* dressed like Virgil's Father Tiber, and like him a prophetic *deus ipse loci*.[10] When his prophecy threatens to overflow the decorum of a georgic poem, Pope intervenes ("Here cease thy Flight") and repeats Virgil's famous apology ("Enough for me, that to the listening Swains/ First in these Fields I sung the Sylvan Strains," cf. *Georgics* IV.563 ff.) . This would be sufficient to establish a precedent, but the formal tension between higher and lower styles had a greater English master than Pope.

The conclusion of *Windsor Forest* recalls the "uncouth Swain"

9. A "genius" is commonly employed for the historian's function: Francis Coventry in *Penshurst* (1750, see below) addresses the "Genius of Penshurst" for the same purpose, and Milton had introduced the "Genius of the Wood" into *Arcades* as a similar kind of authority.

10. *Aeneid* VII.31 ff., and n. 7, above.

of Milton's *Lycidas,* and in that poem also the prophetic threatens to transgress the pastoral mode. Milton's progress of mourners reaches a first climax with the appearance of Camus, the river god and genius of Cambridge, who speaks but a single line: "Ah! Who hath reft . . . my dearest pledge?" The real climax, the prophetic admonition or "dread voice," is reserved for a Christian tutelary spirit—St. Peter. His words, as if already heralding the Apocalypse, "shrink" the streams that murmur through Milton's Sicilian elegy. Yet Milton allows the pastoral mode to reestablish itself and keeps the incident of his friend's death from forcing him prematurely into the visionary's role.

Camus or St. Peter? Milton's "long chosing" ends on the side of the latter, with the Judeo-Christian rather than Greek tradition. The relative muteness of Camus (which may be compared with the real muteness of Gray's Father Thames) and the impotence of the invoked troop of nature spirits anticipate this choice. Yet Milton is a divided person. His lines in the Nativity Ode on the "parting Genius" left their imprint on almost every major poet of the following century.[11] The idea of English poetry is associated for him with the idea of a nature poetry transformed from the classics, and at the highest level with Spenserian romance.[12] When, in *Lycidas,* he asks the Sicilian Muse to "call the Vales, and bid them hither cast/ Their Bells and Flowrets of a thousand hues," the "hither" is England—English poetry as well as the resting place of the dead

11. "It is usually thought that by Pope's time the Nymphs have departed, leaving no addresses; but this judgment is not altogether correct: the 'Genius' Milton sees 'parting,' Pope sees persisting as a 'Genius of the Place,' who continues to embody that intuition of a mysterious life in things which for another two hundred years his descendants will also embody, in a succession of changing forms, from ancient mariner and old leech-gatherer to scholar gypsy, Mr. Apollinax, and the cartoons of Charles Addams" (Maynard Mack, "Pope at Twickenham," p. 10). For direct allusions to the "parting Genius," see, e. g., Thomas Warton, Ode VII ("Sent to a Friend on His Leaving a Favorite Village in Hampshire") and James Beattie, *The Minstrel,* II.xlviii. When Wordsworth visits the Grande Chartreuse and fears that the French Revolution will dispossess this natural temple, he imagines voices of lament and admonition coming from nature: "are they by the parting Genius sent / Unheard till now and to be heard no more?" (*The Prelude,* eds. E. de Selincourt and H. Darbishire [Oxford, 1959], p. 556).

12. The marriage of the Thames and the Medway (*Faerie Queene* IV.xi) could have been a prototype for Milton's procession of rivers in *Lycidas.*

poet whom he promotes to be the "Genius of the shore." He wants
an English genius for an English place. "Remembrance oft shall
haunt the shore" is Collins' extension of the classical conceit in his
lament on "Druid" Thomson.

English tradition in the seventeenth and eighteenth centuries
concentrates on how to create a native poetry which would express
the special destiny of the nation. The poetical genius should reflect the Genius loci, the spirit of England's religion, history, and
countryside. From Milton through Thomson, Gray, Collins, and
the Romantics, the idea of a Progress of Poetry from Greece or the
Holy Land to Britain is essential:

> The Muses, still with freedom found,
> Shall to thy happy coast repair . . . .[13]

Blake is "English Blake"; and Keats's *Hyperion,* like Wordsworth's *Prelude,* is still under the influence of this largest of Enlightenment clichés: the migration of the spirit of poetry and of
liberty from East to West.[14]

13. Thomson, "Rule, Britannia!" *The Masque of Alfred* (1740).

14. For Blake, see Northrop Frye, *Fearful Symmetry,* pp. 172–77, and my
"Blake and the 'Progress of Poesy'" in the *Festschrift* for Foster Damon
(Brown University Press, forthcoming). For Keats, E. B. Hungerford, *The
Shores of Darkness* (1941), and R. H. Griffith, "The Progress Pieces of the
Eighteenth Century," *Texas Review,* 5 (1920), 218–29, esp. 227 f. The
opening of *The Prelude,* where Wordsworth discusses the epic subjects he
had considered, also reflects the link between the progress of poetry and
liberty. For the earlier history of the concept, see Irwin Primer, "The Progress
Piece in the English Literature of the Seventeenth and Eighteenth Centuries"
(Unpublished Ph.D. dissertation, Yale University, 1960); A. L. Williams,
Pope's Dunciad (Baton Rouge, 1955), pp. 42–48; J. Hagstrum, *The Sister
Arts* (Chicago, 1958), pp. 301–06; and René Wellek, *The Rise of English
Literary History* (1941 and 1965), chap. 3. Wellek shows that the idea is
fundamental to the beginnings of English literary historiography but full of
variations and contradictions. What remains constant is the growing importance of the idea of a "genius of the age" or "genius of place," as of various
"climate" theories; the close, but not unchallenged, association of liberty and
letters; and the description of a "Genius of the East" from which, in the case
of Warton's *History,* all strongly figurative and imaginative conceptions are
supposed to be derived via an East-West movement. For a second "Progress"
theory, on a North-South axis, see Thor J. Beck, *Northern Antiquities in
French Learning and Literature* (New York, 1934).

The spiritual map of eighteenth-century England is, of course, a complicated one and should not be simplified. It seems certain, however, that the Protestant Enlightenment—the powerful combination of an intellectual and a religious movement—incited a new and prophetic consciousness in the vocation it wished to demystify: the vocation of poetry. I do not mean, by this consciousness, certain enthusiasms peculiar to the Age of Reason—nationalistic georgics on English agriculture, commerce, science, and liberty. Your sage and serious poet was concerned with something different, which forced him into despair or prophetic hope. Could poetry outlive the Enlightenment, when it was perfectly clear that the great works of the past had been based on "Superstition"? The thought that a new poetry might be founded, peculiarly English, which would be great *and* enlightened, enchanting *and* rational, inspires the hope that culminates in Romanticism.

The Elizabethan Age had already pointed to this synthesis of imagination and reason.[15] Between the time of Milton and Gray, however, a formula arose which anticipated the new poetry more completely. It suggested that the daemonic, or more than rational, energy of imagination might be tempered by its settlement in Britain, its naturalization, as it were, on British soil. This conversion of the demon meant that the poetical genius would coincide with the Genius loci of England; and this meant, in practice, a meditation on English landscape as alma mater—where landscape is storied England, its legends, history, and rural-reflective spirit. The poem becomes, in a sense, a seduction of the poetical genius by the Genius loci: the latter invites—subtly compels—the former to live within via media charms.[16]

The formula is strongest in "local poetry," which took the scheme of *Cooper's Hill* and added to it a Miltonic observer, melancholy or carefree or vacillating in mood. It is also seen in the Pleasures of Imagination poem, where a moody poet finds "what will suffice" (dark or joyful) in a nature he half-creates. In many of these poems there is a tension between the high Miltonic mode

15. Wellek, *Rise of English Literary History*, esp. pp. 192 ff.
16. P. S. Wood in "Native Elements in English Neo-Classicism," *MP*, *24* (1926), 201–08, describes the political aspects encouraging a similar ideal.

and the vernacular, because the aim is to create a new middle or georgic style which would reflect this accommodation of the visionary temperament to an English milieu. Thomson's *Seasons* are therefore especially important: they attempt a direct cultural translation of the *Georgics*. The brilliant yet simple idea of changing Virgil's didactic fourfold into a seasonal fourfold allowed a varied if still cultic celebration of the English countryside. Season and weathers, not pagan gods, are now the presiding deities of the natural cycle. Thomson's popularization of these *dii minores* opened the way for some of the finest "Romantic" odes from Collins to Keats.

Looking back once more to the Eton Ode—this subtlest of Prospect poems—we see that the formula merges with an ultimate issue: who the genius or tutelary power of human progress may be. The ode is about the human condition, not about poetry—but it is also about poetry's role in aiding the human condition. Gray makes us aware of the exposed nature of man and questions whether *any* tuition can ultimately be of use. He puts in doubt the visionary hopes of both science (learning) and art. Though he evokes an English landscape shadowed by ancient and protective presences—at Eton, "grateful Science still adores/Her Henry's Holy Shade"—he suggests that these protectors, these Genii loci, are powerless. There is, for instance, that "progress" of lazar-house spooks (ll. 61–90) compared to which that other "progress" of science is spectral. Poetry fares no better. Coleridge, in the Dejection Ode, accepts his exclusion from joy by thinking of the joy of others, but Gray thinks of his absence of bliss as the portion of man and as something poetry cannot alter. This is made very clear by what happens to the ode's ritualism. Though Gray addresses the "shades" of Eton three times, the near anacoluthon of the first stanza and the fact that the opening invocations do not culminate in formal petition subvert the ritual structure and prepare for the muted question to Father Thames. Does not this impotence of the ritual form reflect on visionary poetry as a whole? The poet, like the other shades, seems a mere ghost in the landscape, a guardian genius unable to help:

> Alas, regardless of their doom
> The little victims play!

It is not that he has no vision (if hindsight is vision), but vision cannot avail and engenders at best pathos and dramatic irony.

If Gray, then, does not attempt to reverse the fate of poetry, it is not because he accepts the thesis that it is doomed by the Enlightenment or some other progress. His position may be termed religious: man is too radically exposed to find shelter anywhere but in "The bosom of his Father and his God." The advancement of learning does not ensure, and the recession of poetry does not prejudice, salvation. Yet Gray's attitude, though religious, is also historically self-conscious. That man is naked may be a religious and universal truth, but that science and poetry are of little avail is not equally true of all ages. Gray suggests, as is well-known, that poetry played a more authentic role in the previous century. He declares that the fire that was holy in Shakespeare and Milton is now in eclipse or a questionable flame. So pronounced is his modesty toward himself and his age that he opposes "greatness" to "goodness" and leaves Genius, including the poetical genius, in doubt of its justification.[17] It is no longer death to hide one's talent. This recessiveness, this almost theological self-incrimination, harmonizes easily with the neoclassical thesis we have been discussing: that the age demands something other than Genius—in fact, an accommodation of Genius to the Genius loci. Collins will give the thesis a stormier, but also more hopeful, embodiment. We turn to him, and initially to the *Ode to Evening*.

Mr. Wimsatt's essay on Romantic nature imagery discerned a problem of structure where many readers had tended simply to approve or condemn. In certain Romantic poems we find landscape playing a dual role: the poet represents it as animated both by its own and by a transcendent spirit. "We have a double personification conjured from one nature, one landscape, in a wedding that approximates fusion."[18] Collins' *Ode to Evening* provokes a similar question: "Is Evening a divine person who governs the scene or is she immanent in the scene itself?"[19]

17. See the ending of *The Progress of Poesy*, and *Stanzas to Mr. Bentley*.
18. W. K. Wimsatt, Jr., "The Structure of Romantic Nature Imagery" (1949), republished in *The Verbal Icon* and elsewhere.
19. Martin Price, *To the Palace of Wisdom* (New York, 1964), pp. 375–76.

The answer is that Evening has a double nature modeled on
that of the Genius loci. As spirit of place, she is both spirit and
place. She is also, as the poem makes clear, a divine guide ("Now
teach me," "Then lead me") and a wisdom figure who outlives
temporal change (ll. 41 ff.). Collins' Evening is virtually the
guide, guardian, and nurse of the poet's moral being. These functions belonged preeminently to the Genius loci.

Yet, as Mr. Wimsatt points out, referring to Ruskin, the Greek
gods of nature were depicted as distinct from their element ("This
something, this great Water Spirit, I must not confuse with the
waves, which are only its body") and from the viewer's mind (that
"curious web of hesitating sentiment, pathetic fallacy, and wandering fancy").[20] Milton's Camus and Pope's and Gray's Father
Thames are such distinct persons, decorated sometimes with the
symbols of their state, yet separate and confronting powers—in
Gray less so than in Pope or Milton. And in Collins the "curious
web" weaving together person and element is complete; the theme
of weaving may even enter directly through the imagery and the
poem's winding progress. If Collins is inspired by the ancient concept of the Genius loci, he is differently inspired. The problem of
understanding a new type of poetry remains, though we may have
found what is common to both types, what is restructured.

The new poetry projects a sacred marriage: that of the poet's
genius with the Genius loci. To invoke the ghost in the landscape
is only preparatory to a deeper, ceremonial merging of the poet's
spirit and spirit of place—hence the new structure of fusion.
Poetry is to be attuned with this place and this time. Teach me to
sing to you with your own music, says Collins. Let mine be thine,
and thine mine. The "musing slow," which almost deprives the
main connectives ("now," "when," "then") of temporality and
delays the formal petition, emphasizes a calm extension of poetical
thought which suits the stealing stillness of the spirit invoked. The
delicate Spenserian syntax and the weaving in-and-out of the
measured verse evoke a dance like that of the Hours, a ritual as

20. See "Modern Painters," chap. 13 in *Of Classical Landscape*. Ruskin's
positive Hellenism on this point should be compared with Coleridge's attack,
in the name of Hebrew poetry, on Greek "godkins" and "godesslings." Cf.
M. H. Abrams, *The Mirror and The Lamp* (1953), X.v.

well as temporal progress which draws (like a marriage procession) a "gradual dusky veil" around the scene. The poem's probable source in conventional odes to an Evening star, which guides lover to beloved in the dangerous dark,[21] may also help to induce this prothalamic effect.[22]

A literalist might object that Evening is not a spirit of place. He would be wrong: Collins' Evening is distinctly Occidental in its gradual advent. Evening is a regent ("Thy Springs," "Thy darkening Vale"), and the region governed is less a specific country than the West, the *Abendland*. It is the Westering of the Spirit which is hailed and which in the *Ode to Peace* issues explicitly in a sacred marriage: "Come to grace thy western Isle. . . . With Him [British Honor] for ever wed!"

But the literalist is right insofar as Collins has conflated the Genius loci notion with that of the Spirit of the Age. Collins is evoking, in the exact sense of calling forth, the possibility of a Hesperidean Muse—inspired by the archaic *numen* of nature poetry yet genuinely expressive of the ideals of polite society. In the coda, therefore (the obscurest part of an intricate poem), the four seasons may represent passions transformed into Fancy, Friendship, Science, and Peace by the civilizing influence of the Evening Muse.

That the *Ode to Evening* foresees a "holier reign" in which an Eastern genius is wedded to a Western region is also shown by subtle amalgams. Eastern, we should recall, can imply both Asiatic and Attic. Thus when we read, near the beginning of the ode, of the "bright-hair'd Sun" that "Sits in yon western Tent," we recognize an allusion to the biblical verse depicting the sun as a "bridegroom coming out of his chamber," but with a 180° westerly conversion of scene and mood.[23] When, similarly, toward the end of

21. *To the Evening Star* was a well-known "idyllium" attributed to Moschus. It was often translated and imitated in the eighteenth century, although the examples I know are later than Collins' ode. Cf. Spenser's *Epithalamion*, ll. 282 ff.

22. When Collins ends his first invocation with "I hail / Thy genial lov'd Return," the stock word "genial" may mean "congenial" or may refer us to its original derivation from the Genius who guards and fructifies the marriage bed. Cf. Spenser, *Epithalamion*, ll. 398 ff.

23. Psalm 19:5–6; cf. Milton, *On the Morning of Christ's Nativity*, xxvi.

the opening strophes, we read of Evening's "Dewy Fingers," we recognize the Homeric "rosy finger'd dawn," again westernized. The capstone evidence, however, comes from a poem directly on the subject of poetry. In the *Ode on the Poetical Character* the beautiful if extravagant image of Milton's "Ev'ning Ear" contrasts with that of the "rich-hair'd Youth of Morn" to suggest once more this westering movement, but which by Collins' time is feared to have lost contact with the source. The final scene is upon us, an alienation of poetic power; the "gradual dusky veil" seems to have "curtain'd close . . . from ev'ry future View" Milton's and Spenser's visionary landscapes.

Thus an alliance of the poetical genius with a Western or English climate remains doubtful. The Elizabethans, and Milton as the last in that tradition, may have achieved it; and the *Ode to Evening* tries to summon the hope once more. Wordsworth still talks of Milton's "Union of Tenderness and Imagination," as Collins at one point praises Shakespeare's "beauteous Union" of "*Tuscan* Fancy, and *Athenian* Strength." [24] Yet in his first publication, the *Persian Eclogues* (1742), Collins admits that in Oriental poetry "There is an Elegancy and Wildness of Thought which recommends all their Composition; and our Geniuses are as much too cold for the Entertainment of such Sentiments, as our Climate is for their Fruits and Spices." His next publication, the *Verses to Sir Thomas Hanmer* (1743), expresses an admiration for Shakespeare somewhat in conflict with the Enlightenment scheme of the gradual improvement of the arts:

> Each rising Art by slow Gradation moves,
> Toil builds on Toil, and Age on Age improves.
> The Muse alone unequal dealt her Rage,
> And grac'd with noblest Pomp her earliest Stage.

The *Ode to Fear* explicitly recognizes poetic power as *daimonic* and addresses Fear as a genie in the primitive classical (and Oriental) sense: [25]

24. See Lamb's report in *The Letters of Charles Lamb,* ed. Lucas (London, 1935), I.246; and Collins' *Verses to Sir Thomas Hanmer,* l. 60.

25. "In the *Odes* of William Collins the 'Thou' seems to me always a type of daemon, most obviously so in the *Ode to Fear*" (Angus Fletcher, *Allegory,*

> Dark Pow'r, with shudd'ring meek submitted Thought
> Be mine, to read the Visions old,
> Which thy awak'ning Bards have told.

Even the *Ode to Evening*, that late prothalamion which celebrates "gentlest Influence" and delays by its intricate turns the decline into darkness, contains a moment where a glint of the demon appears:

> Then let me rove some wild and heathy Scene,
> Or find some Ruin 'midst its dreary Dells,
>   Whose Walls more awful nod
>   By thy religious Gleams.[26]

Collins rarely breaks through to the new poetry. His personifications are divinities, principalities, Blake's later "giant forms," which seduce or compel our imagination. He returns to an archaizing mode, like so many of the poets succeeding him: Smart, Macpherson, Chatterton, Blake, even Coleridge. The Genius of Poetry becomes a genie once more, a compelling psychic force that works its own salvation in a man, and often as an adversary to accepted values. The poetry now written believes in a formula it violates—the progressivist's formula, which envisaged a domestication of the "daemon of poetry" [27] on British soil. The Ossianic songs, for example, are the genie idea gone wild, dead warriors or dead memories rising up everywhere from spots associated with them, compulsive myths in ghostly converse with the faltering identity of belated poets. A Macpherson spirit is a Collins-type daemonic abstraction with a Gaelic habitation and name.

The Theory of a Symbolic Mode [Ithaca, 1964], p. 51, n. 51.) Fletcher's seminal book shows the daemonic basis of allegory and personification. His first chapter, "The Daemonic Agent," is especially relevant to the present study. For the ritual sources of personification in Collins, cf. Kurt Schlüter, *Die Englische Ode* (Bonn, 1964) , chap. 6; for the progress of "horror-personification" in the eighteenth century, see P. M. Spacks, *The Insistence of Horror* (Cambridge, Mass., 1962) .

26. Collins later changes this stanza, perhaps to remove the darker suggestion.

27. "This man is the very Daemon of poetry, or he has lighted on a treasure hid for ages" (Gray on Macpherson, to T. Warton, July 1760) .

Yet the daemon odes of Collins remain within the sophisticated tradition of the Sublime Ode. Caught in the middle, their personifications are "forcible *and* picturesque," [28] the first term pointing to the daemonic and the second to the sophisticating element. So in eighteenth-century poetic theory there is a constant vacillation between the Longinian sublime, which emphasizes "ravish't ears" and "ravish't eyes," and the pathetic or picturesque, which is indebted to Milton's *L'Allegro* and *Il Penseroso,* poems that begin by dismissing the daemonic machinery of the sublime style, while raising from it (like a free-ranging butterfly out of its spooky cocoon) new and airy personifications.

Collins does teach us, however, that the generic subject of the Sublime Ode (as distinct from that of individual poems) is the Poetical Character: its fate in an Age of Reason. The odes are generally addressed to invited powers and, like the gothic novel, raise the ghosts they shudder at. Their histrionic, sometimes hysterical, character stems from the fact that they are indeed theatrical machines, evoking a power of vision they fear to use. Collins, like a sorcerer's apprentice, is close to being overpowered by the spirit he summons:

> Ah *Fear!* Ah frantic *Fear!*
> I see, I see Thee near.
> I know thy hurried Step, thy haggard Eye!
> Like Thee I start, like Thee disorder'd fly . . . .

We easily recognize this as a displaced or heightened mode of ritual identification.[29] But that is the point: where there is ritual there should be a divinity and a votary, and Collins had the courage to invoke those "Divine Emotions" which art must raise but the Enlightenment wished to repress.

Toward the latter half of the eighteenth century the main options before the ambitious, non-satirical poet were the sublime ode

28. My italics. Said by Collins of Cooper and cited by A. S. P. Woodhouse, "Collins and the Creative Imagination," *Studies in English by Members of the University College* (Toronto, 1931), p. 100, n. 20.

29. Collins is not unwittily adapting Horace's "Si vis me flere." If you want me to be terrified, you yourself must show terror. His two odes on fear and pity treat of the "tragic" emotions, those closest to sacred or ritualistic drama and hence most closely concerned with *participation*.

and local poetry. As in Gray's ode and even Collins', or such poems as Thomas Warton's "On the Approach of Summer" (Ode XII) , the two types could mingle. What helped lyric and narrative genres to combine was the formula of the poet guided by the Genius loci. In many poems the mythological assumptions are felt only in the ritual syntax, that sublimated compulsion which aids the narrative line: lead me, teach me, guide my steps, let me be thine. A *leading Genius* of this kind is never far away; the only question is its relation to the poet's mind, its benignant or demonic influence. Francis Coventry's *Penshurst,* a topographical poem from the middle of the century,[30] shows the formula in its explicit form.

The poet begins with an address to the Genius loci:

> Genius of Penshurst old!
> Who saw'st the birth of each immortal oak,

begs permission to enter the sacred realm:

> O suffer me with sober tread
> To enter on thy holy shade;

recalls the spirit of liberty which is part of the spirit of the place:

> Here thoughtful-walking Liberty
> Remembers Britons once were free
>
> · · ·
>
> Ere yet their *Lares* they forsook,
> And lost the genuine British look,

recalls the spirit of poetry, Genius and Fancy merging in this poet-haunted domain:

> Come, friendly Genius! lead me round
> Thy sylvan haunts and magic ground;
> Point every spot of hill or dale,
> And tell me, as we tread the vale,
> "Here mighty Dudley once wou'd rove . . .
> . . . There looser Waller . . .
> . . . And Philip. . . ."

30. First published, 1750. Also in Dodley's *Collection,* IV.50 ff., from which I print my text.

and reaches its rapturous climax as we approach the seat of inspiration, the Dodonian oak planted the day Sidney was born:

> Hark! I hear the echoes call,
> Hark! the rushing waters fall;
> Lead me to the green retreats,
> Guide me to the Muses' seats
>
> . . .
>
> What Genius points to yonder oak?
> What rapture does my soul provoke?

Some two hundred verses later, having toured house and garden, Coventry ends with a last salute to the genial soil, mother of heroes and poets, which (we now learn) has been the place of his first poetic attempt, these very lines.

Wordsworth will also begin with a local poem—"The Vale of Esthwaite" (ca. 1787). It was encouraged, moreover, by a school exercise, written at Hawkshead, which has some interest as a clear if commonplace expression of the Enlightenment theory of history. Thinking about the founding of his school, Wordsworth sees the "Power of EDUCATION" rising to eulogize the joint reign of Protestantism and Science:

> Science with joy saw Superstition fly
> Before the lustre of Religion's eye;
> With rapture she beheld Britannia smile,
> Clapp'd her strong wings, and sought the cheerful isle.[31]

Superstition will reappear, with other demon personifications, in "The Vale of Esthwaite." It is clear that Wordsworth wished to see Esthwaite as a home for the enlightened imagination. Yet apocalyptic and superstitious fancies lead him astray: he enters a ghostly "world of shades" influenced by the imagery of Collins' *Ode to Fear*. The spirit of the valley, its true Genius loci, is undetermined; it vacillates between benign and demonic; and the poet appears as a quester in search of a leading Genius—his own identity. Which of the nature spirits haunting the valley is *his* guide?

---

31. *The Poetical Works of William Wordsworth*, ed. E. de Selincourt, *1* (Oxford, 1940), 260.

The early manuscripts of what was to be *The Prelude* reflect the same dilemma:

> Yes there are genii which when they would form
> [A favor'd spirit] open out the clouds
> As with the touch of lightning seeking him
> With gentle visitation. Others use
> [Less homely?] interference ministry
> Of grosser kind & of their school was I [32]

But the identity crisis is perhaps that of poetry itself. Words-worth would not be so centrally concerned with the character of his leading Genius unless prompted by the hope that an enlightened poetry—the union of poetical genius with English spirit of place—was possible. This hope, this union, is the very "consummation" for which his poetry aims to be the "spousal verse." The metaphor of a holy marriage is explicit in the Prospectus of his ambitions prefixed to the 1814 *Excursion* but which originally climaxed his greatest local poem, "Home at Grasmere." Wed the human mind to nature, and you will find paradise "A simple produce of the common day." The spirit is sufficed, the need for fictions dispelled, the burden of the mystery lifted. This is the *Wordsworthian* Enlightenment.

32. *The Prelude*, eds. de Selincourt and Darbishire, p. 638. Cf. Akenside's "Genii" in the opening of *The Pleasures of Imagination* (1744):
> Be present, all ye Genii, who conduct
> The wandering footsteps of the youthful bard,
> New to your springs and shades; who touch his ear
> With finer sounds; who heighten to his eye
> The bloom of Nature, and before him turn
> The gayest, happiest attitude of things. (I.25–30)

But Akenside's use of the word still echoes pictorial tradition, where "genii" are often the attendant or subordinate spirits (occasionally *putti*) surrounding the main figure. Thomson, in *Liberty* (1735), can use the word in its original sense of tutelary spirits ("earth, forsook/ By her best Genii, lay to Demons foul,/ And unchain'd Furies, an abandon'd prey") and in its extended, pictorial sense ("The native Genii, round her [Britain] radiant smiled"). When Lessing, in *Wie die Alten den Tod gebildet,* calls the winged boy holding a torch upside down a "Genius," he blends these senses. It is exceedingly hard, in eighteenth-century poetry, and even at times in Shelley's poetry, to distinguish a picturesque from a mythopoeic conception.

Thus Wordsworth refuses to renew archaic modes. An unghostly poetry is born, a true vernacular, "words that speak of nothing more than what we are." He never abandons the idea that England can provide a homecoming for the poetical spirit: his poems remain an encounter with English spirit of place. Yet the difference between Wordsworth and the archaizing poets is not as absolute as it seems. At the end of *Vala,* Blake describes the moment of apocalypse, when Mystery is finally consumed. "Where is the Spectre of Prophecy? where is the delusive Phantom?/Departed. . . . The dark Religions are departed & Sweet Science reigns." This is as triumphant a statement as the Enlightenment ever produced. Blake is ready to disenchant himself, like Prospero at the end of *The Tempest,* and even to suggest a parallel between all prophecy (his included) and the "parting Genius" exorcized by Milton. In Blake as in Wordsworth vision plots the end of vision: it desires to be consummated by realities.

What difference is there, then, between the two poets? It is a difference in their response to a common problem: if poetry is Oriental in spirit, and the genius of the West is on the side of Enlightenment, how can poetry survive? Blake and Wordsworth agree on one thing: they reject the halfway house of neoclassical style, its temperate Orientalism, its endless delicate compromises between demands of reason and imagination. But while Blake adopts and seeks to rationalize an aggressively Eastern style (his poetry is a veritable Battle of the Genii), Wordsworth creates a new and distinctly Hesperidean mode—deeply reflective, journeying constantly to the sources of consciousness. There are no ghosts, no giant forms, no genii in the mature Wordsworth. He is haunted by a "Presence which is not to be put by," but it is a ghost without a ghost's shape, not a specter but an intensely local and numinous self-awareness. The spirit of poetry survives in both Wordsworth and Blake, wherever

> The very sunshine spread upon the dust
> Is beautiful,

or where

> The Sky is an immortal Tent builded by the Sons of Los.

East and West (or South and North) are not necessarily points on a map. The Romantics, indeed, as distinct from the generation that goes from Gray and Collins to Blake, tend to consider the Westering of the Spirit less a geographical event than a development within the individual consciousness. Theirs is mainly a spiritual topography. Blake is a complex intermediate figure who transforms the previous generation's mythology of history into a systematic topography of the human imagination. "Albion" and "Jerusalem" are converging states of the soul. But the form of his complex machinery—of "Albion," "Jersusalem," and similar representations—is not clear without reference to the historical vision that inspired poets from Gray to Wordsworth: the union, as in the Renaissance, but even more intense and conscious, of the prophetic East and the "western isle," of the Poetical Genius and England's Genius loci.

The history of English literature since the Renaissance suggests a continuous process of demystification. Thomas Warton observed of the Reformation that "Truth propagates Truth, and the mantle of mystery was removed not only from religion but from literature." [33] This is a statement both Blake and Wordsworth could support. There may be lapses or relapses, but they do not affect the "great stream of tendency."

Whether literature, to be demystified, must also be demythologized, has never been resolved, however. And with respect to myth and personification, there have clearly been several Enlightenments: the first an era of "civilized superstition," [34] which began with the Elizabethans but which the Augustans refined and Gray's scruples still attest to; and the Wordsworthian Enlightenment, which attempts an unghostly and entirely "Western" kind of visionariness. For Wordsworth personification may be trivial but it is not innocent: Collins had restored the psychological and ritual link between it and the daemonic Persona.

A third kind of demystification is easy to mistake for mystification, because it works from within a revival of Romance and of the daemonic Persona. Blake is its great exponent, but Coleridge took its part in the original plan of *Lyrical Ballads* ("my endeavours

33. *History of English Poetry* (1774–81), sec. LXI.
34. Ibid.

should be directed to persons and characters supernatural, or at least romantic") ,[35] while Shelley and Keats develop it mainly from Elizabethan sources. Its meaning is best approached through a short synopsis of the original concept of personification, which Collins helped to revive.

The Persona, in Roman times, was the mask worn by actors; but we know that similar masks were used in initiation ceremonies to represent gods or heroes or deified father spirits. There is evidence that divine masks of this kind were set in the fields as tutelary objects of worship; hence, perhaps, a link to pastoral poetry and the theme of the tomb in the fields. There existed, moreover, ancestral masks called *imagines,* which were kept in the home as a guardian influence and were used to impersonate ancestors at funeral rites. Thus personification is at least distantly related to the ritual assumption of god or ancestor via his mask.[36]

How much weight the Persona has shed when we consider the current use of the term! Of the Enlightenments so far described, the first trivialized it by the extensive use of personification-allegory for picturesque ends; while the second, or Wordsworthian Enlightenment, sent it underground. For examples of the heavy Persona we must return to the Renaissance. The revival of antiquity included a passion for masque, masquerade, pageant, emblem, and *imagines.*[37] Lyric poetry was not unaffected by this: it ab-

35. *Biographia Literaria* (1817) , chap. 14.

36. C. Kerenyi in "Man and Mask" (*Spiritual Disciplines, Papers from the Eranos Yearbooks, 4* [1960]) brings evidence for masks worshipped in wood and field and describes the masks as "creating a relation between the living and the dead" and in many cases an "encounter" with a father archetype. "The human face—otherwise the vehicle of individual features, the features of a 'personality,' as this unique entity is named by a shift in meaning of the Latin word for mask, *persona*—is here the form in which the universal and collective are manifested." For the *imagines maiorum* and their role in funeral ceremonies, see Polybius, *History,* 6.35.5. (Scipio, in the famous dream recorded by Cicero and preserved via Macrobius' *Commentary,* recognizes his father Africanus by the latter's likeness to the *imago* in the house.) Cf. F. M. Cornford, *From Religion to Philosophy* (1912), pp. 106–08, and Jane Harrison, *Themis* (1912) , chap. 8, for the relation between father archetype and local daemon.

37. Cf. Warton's description of the mythomania of the Elizabethan Age in sec. LXI of the *History.* For France, see Jean Rousset, *La Litterature de l'âge baroque en France* (Paris, 1954) .

sorbed such operatic features as ritual exordiums, allegorical persons, processional structure, and pictorialism. Not until Romantic poetry, and then chiefly in Wordsworth, do the longer forms of lyric poetry overcome this operatic style. In other countries, France for example, it takes even longer to "purify the words of the tribe." We think of the rhetorical inflation of a Victor Hugo, the *classicisme noir* of a Baudelaire, and the influence of Wagner. When, in the most original poetry of the 1850s, Nerval's "Il Desdichado" begins,

> Je suis le Ténébreux, le Veuf, l'Inconsolé,
> Le Prince d'Acquitaine à la tour abolie

we still feel as if an actor had stepped forward and begun his aria. The person who speaks is in costume, with his heraldic lute that bears "le soleil noir de la mélancolie."

In Wordsworth, an exceedingly undramatic poet, the problem of Persona arises only surreptitiously. Daemonic confrontations take place as usurpations, as waylayings—great moments which the poet records but which do not alter his purpose. One such waylaying is Imagination "rising up" to halt the mental traveler of 1804, the poet in the process of completing his autobiography (*Prelude* VI.525). Imagination here is exactly like genie or kelpie confusing the wanderer in some lonely place. A second self rises up, challenging the basis of his poem and the very project of his life.[38]

The marriage of genius and Genius loci (of imagination and nature) remains, therefore, precarious. A daemonic agent—bardic, prophetic, ancestral—is never far away. A central incident in "The Vale of Esthwaite" reveals this spectral figure, "on one branded arm he bore / What seem'd the poet's harp of yore," who leads the fledgling poet into "Helvellyn's inmost womb" where he is initiated.[39] *Tintern Abbey*, the perfect instance of a meditation on English landscape as alma mater, still shows Wordsworth's mind moving toward a ghostly figure, that of the Hermit. The most striking appearance of the Persona, however, is in *Resolution and Independence*, where that "oldest man . . . that ever wore gray hairs" materializes suddenly in the landscape. Here is another

38. For an extended discussion of the incident, see my *Wordsworth's Poetry, 1787–1814* (New Haven, 1964), pp. 39–48.
39. *The Poetical Works of William Wordsworth, 1*, 277–78.

Father Thames, an ancestral figure, virtually prophetic, the genius of the place, and even associated with waters. "His voice to me was like a stream / Scarce heard." That Wordsworth seems to have drawn, consciously or not, on biblical rather than classical sources, makes no difference. The situation is that of visionary encounter.[40]

What modern literary theory tends to call an *epiphany* involves a confrontation with a second self in the form of Genius loci or Persona. There is a djinee in every well-wrought urn.[41] Ironically enough, these concepts of Genius and Persona have practically disappeared because of the very success of the Wordsworthian Enlightenment. We no longer require a Romance or Eastern mode to express visionary encounters. Wordsworth writes Westerns only. Compared to *Resolution and Independence*, Coleridge's *Ancient Mariner* is Eastern: an open vision of daemonic agency centering imaginatively and morally on the Genius loci. The Mariner in his ancientness is the admonitory Persona; the world he describes is daemonic; his drama is that of "Compulsion," of a journey in which the self is kidnapped by various genii and made to suffer a number of spectral confrontations; the crime is basically one against the Genius loci; [42] and the punishment, a homeless voyaging, fits the crime. This account by no means exhausts even the grosser structure of the poem but does suggest its inner relation to the contrary poetics of *Resolution and Independence*.

Yet just as Wordsworth effects a rhetorical and spiritual purification, so the *Ancient Mariner* is a light and winged thing com-

---

40. Cf. *Wordsworth's Poetry*, pp. 202–03 and 272–73. A remark of Kerenyi's is intriguing: "The Greeks had many legends concerning the father role of the river gods; in the marriage rite the river god preceded the bridegroom. Ultimately, the . . . mask became that of Father Oceanos himself, the Homeric 'source of all things' " (ibid.).

41. I borrow this phrase from the title of an essay by W. J. Ong (see *The Barbarian Within* [New York, 1962]).

42. Coleridge's gloss at the end of Part V identifies it as a wrong done to the Polar Spirit, who is a daemon of the earth or middle air. Wordsworth apparently suggested the nature of the crime. "Suppose . . . you represent him as having killed one of these birds on entering the South Sea, and that the tutelary Spirits of those regions take upon them to avenge the crime" (*The Poetical Works of William Wordsworth, 1, 361*).

pared to Spenser's "Faerie" which already volatilized heavier medieval machines. A further essay on "The Discrimination of Enlightenments" would be needed to show the *play* (in Huizinga's sense) of allegorical Romance in the poetry of Shelley, Keats, and Blake.[43] Not, perhaps, until Wallace Stevens does the Wordsworthian tradition triumph over its rival mode. Even so, it may be doubted that poetry in the allegorical or mythological mode is a thing of the past. That would be making the mistake of the Age of Reason all over again. There is, for instance, a purely internal deepening of the spirit which forces poets to make contact with transcended forms. Keats's *Hyperion,* with its two generations of gods, heavier and lighter, seems to mimic directly the Progress of Poetry we have traced. Yet Apollo, the new god, moves with alarming speed from the dawn of indolent sensation to the overpowering second dawn of prophecy. The epoch of a new sensibility, in which the *burden* of the mystery is lifted, lasts no longer than the morning dew.[44] The poet wrestles once more with what Yeats will call the mask, the anti-self, the body of fate.

In fact, whenever the question of Persona arises in a radical way, whenever self-choosing, self-identification, becomes a more than personal, indeed a prophetic decision—which happens when the poet feels himself alien to the genius of country or age and destined to assume an adversary role—poetry renews itself by its contact with what may seem to be archaic forces. Such a turn of events is clear in the poetry of Blake, Shelley, and Byron. They could not, like Wordsworth, equate the England of their day with the Spirit of liberty. That Spirit, having migrated from East to West, must blow, if at all, from the West: the French Revolution, in its original form, was often thought to be an extension of British ideas of freedom.[45] "Be thou, Spirit fierce / My spirit" is Shelley's prayer to a West Wind that rouses both Mediterranean and Atlantic.

---

43. One of the services rendered by Harold Bloom's *The Visionary Company* (1961) is to reaffirm this "dialectical" aspect of Romantic myth-making in England. In Germany, of course, "Romantic irony" is an explicit concept.

44. *Hyperion,* III.31 ff.

45. Cf. M. H. Abrams, "English Romanticism: The Spirit of the Age," in *Romanticism Reconsidered,* ed. N. Frye (New York, 1963).

Shelley in self-exile and Blake as an inner émigré were forced back on an ancient religious theme with revolutionary implications: the Oriental "heavy" allegory of a War in Heaven.

This is the very theme Milton had revived and Wordsworth had passed by "unalarmed" [46]—which he had silenced, in fact, by his bloodless purge of the gods. We need only compare *The Prelude* with Blake's *Milton* to see how differently they "redeem" England's great champion of liberty and prophetic poetry. For Wordsworth as for Keats, Milton is part of a "grand march of intellect" and contributes to that humanization of the mind (the true subject of the *Prelude*) which frees poetry from his kind of divine machinery. For Blake, however, Milton is limited not by the historical horizon of his age but, like every man, by his attitude toward the power in him. *Paradise Lost* and the Bible are the great Testaments of a human imagination afraid to be human: instead of expanding into the form of man, it shrinks back into the mystery of religion. Blake's War in Heaven is a *human* war—a war in the human breast to reunite Albion, the Genius of England, with the Poetic Genius, the "eternal all-protecting Divine Humanity" [47] which a priestly religion had usurped. The prophetic spirit of Blake's poetry is therefore a measure of the extent to which his native country is already being recalled to itself:

> I will not cease from Mental Fight,
> Nor shall my Sword sleep in my hand:
> Till we have built Jerusalem,
> In England's green & pleasant Land.

46. Prospectus to the 1814 *Excursion, Poetical Works of William Wordsworth, 5,* 4–5.
47. *Milton* I, Pl. 14.

Robert Louis Jackson

Chance and Design
in *Anna Karenina*

In Chapter 18, Part One, of *Anna Karenina,* some seventy pages from the beginning of the novel, Tolstoy introduces Anna to the reader for the first time in person. The scene is a Moscow railroad station. Stepan Oblonsky is there to meet his sister Anna who is arriving from Petersburg; Vronsky, to meet his mother who is arriving on the same train. All four meet, exchange amenities, and prepare to leave the station; momentarily, a disturbing incident draws their attention: a railroad guard has been crushed by one of the cars. After a brief delay (Vronsky leaves some money for the guard's family) , the group departs.

Chance seems to rule this occasion: Vronsky and Oblonsky, though acquainted, have met by chance at the station. Anna, it turns out, had been entrusted by her husband to Vronsky's mother at the Petersburg station and they have made the trip together. Vronsky's meeting with Anna, then, is fortuitous. The death of the guard, apparently, also is an accident.

A view of the surface, or visible structure, of this chapter reflects the unplanned or "natural" character of the action: people alight from a train and greet other people; bits of conversation seem to advance in a kind of meandering movement—in short, build up a sense of the ritualistic, yet banal and basically unstructured character of most meetings and departures at railroad stations. The dramatic incident—the death of the guard, which takes up the final portion of this slight chapter—explodes the sense of the casual and ordinary; it provides a momentary focus of attention for the characters. Yet its sudden and alarming intrusion into the casual routine serves only to increase our feeling of the unplanned in Chapter 18. Our impression of the unplanned, however, is pre-

cisely an impression: on closer analysis it gives way to a sense of
organized movement and design. The action, seen from the artist's
point of view, is coherent and saturated with content.

The unifying element in the chapter, indeed its axis, must be
sought in Anna. She is the primary focus of the artist's attention;
her embryonic relationship with Vronsky constitutes the motive
force for the inner action of the chapter. In this action Anna's
character is free to attract, magnetize, and, in this sense, introduce
"order" in the field of personalities around her; but in this action,
also, character is revealed as a determined shape, as an embodiment of an already existing fate. We may define Tolstoy's purpose
in Chapter 18, then, as twofold: to disclose those elements of character in Anna which are her fate, and to capture that moment
when, under the impact of character and the changes brought
about through encounter, the elements of chance group themselves into coherent design. To present this whole action, without
allowing its inner dynamics to obtrude upon, or overwhelm, the
"natural" and free flow of surface action—here is the real art of
Tolstoy.

At the opening of Chapter 18, Vronsky steps up to the door of a
train compartment and stops in order to make way for a lady who
is coming out. He glances "at the exterior of this lady" who obviously belongs to the upper classes, begs her pardon, and is about to
enter the carriage when he feels the need to have another look at
her, "not because she was very beautiful, not because of the elegance and modest grace which were evident in her whole person,
but because there was something particularly caressing and tender
in the expression of her lovely face when she passed him."

Not so much exterior beauty or elegance as a certain compelling
interior richness of being, a refined sensuousness defines Anna.
Tolstoy's emphasis here is carried over into the crucial characterization of Anna as seen through Vronsky. Anna turns to look at
Vronsky and her dark eyes rest momentarily upon him in a
friendly, attentive manner. She then turns to the approaching
crowd as if in search of someone.

> In that brief glance Vronsky had time to notice a restrained
> animation which played over her face. . . . It was as though

her nature were so brimming over with an abundance of
something that against her will it expressed itself now in a
radiant look, now in a smile. She deliberately shrouded the
light in her eyes, but it gleamed against her will in a barely
perceptible smile.

Tolstoy has drawn Vronsky—and the reader—into the interior
of Anna's being. He now calls attention to the welling up from it
of a vital life force: animation (*ozhivlenie*) —a key word used
three times in Chapter 18 in descriptions of Anna. But it is "restrained animation"; it is held back by "will," and yet it makes
itself felt "against her will." Precisely this force of energy, this
vitality, this almost animal animation is a distinguishing mark of
Anna. At the moment Vronsky meets Anna, these opposite forces
of animation and restraint ("will") are in delicate equilibrium; at
the end of the chapter, when Anna leaves the station, that equilibrium has been lost.

Contradiction, conflict, tension between opposite elements,
then, is evident in Anna's nature from the outset; it also enters
into her social perspective. Tolstoy brings this out obliquely in the
scene under discussion. Vronsky, after exchanging glances with
Anna, steps into the train, greets his mother, and, while talking
with her, overhears a conversation of a woman (Anna) with a
man outside the door.

> "All the same [*vsë-taki*], I do not agree with you," said the
> voice of the woman.
> "That's the Petersburg way of looking at it, Madame."
> "Not the Petersburg way, but simply a woman's way."
> "Well, anyway, permit me to kiss your hand."

These are the first words uttered by Anna in the novel. We do
not know the subject of dispute, but this makes it possible for the
words to produce a more general impression upon us. Almost the
first word, *vsë-taki,* superbly establishes that singular quality of
contrariety which will define, in a sense, Anna's whole stance before society; *vsë-taki* (all the same, nonetheless, however that may
be) is a word which implies some kind of concession, perhaps, in
the sphere of logic, but thereupon indicates clearly a stubborn
adherence to one's own point of view in spite of logic or of con-

vincing counter-argument.[1] The little colloquy we have quoted serves also to raise the problem content of Anna's nature to a general intellectual and social level—the level of action of the novel as a whole. What emerges from the colloquy is the image of a woman of tenacious viewpoint, one who rejects identification, significantly, with a "Petersburg" outlook, but who firmly embraces the "woman's" point of view. The polarity here of Petersburg and the "woman's" point of view anticipates the major confrontation of Anna in the novel.

Assertiveness, decisiveness, the readiness to take the lead—these are essential qualities of Anna, and they are manifested throughout her relationship with Vronsky. Tolstoy at the very first appearance of Anna in the novel signals these qualities. Vronsky introduces himself to Anna: "You probably don't remember me." "On the contrary," Anna replies.

> "I should have recognized you—your mother and I, it seems, talked of nothing but you the whole journey," she said, at last allowing the animation that sought release to express itself in a smile. "But still no sign of my brother."
>
> "Do go and call out for him, Alesha," said the old Countess.
>
> Vronsky went out onto the platform and shouted: "Oblonsky! here!"
>
> But Madame Karenina did not wait for her brother and, as soon as she caught sight of him she stepped down from the

1. Tolstoy's use of the word "vsë-taki" recalls another occasion on which he uses this word to give expression to a sense of deep contradiction or disjunction in consciousness. In *War and Peace*, on the eve of the Battle of Austerlitz, Prince Andrey dreams of his happy moment of glory, of his "Toulon" (Vol. One, Pt. Three, Sec. xii). Tolstoy presents his consciousness as a dialectic of voices—one dreaming of glory, the others reminding him of the price: death, wounds, suffering. But the initial voice stubbornly insists that it would give everything for a moment of glory, for triumph over people, for people's love, the people out there. And as Andrey reflects, some good-hearted banter between two peasant-soldiers outside drifts into his consciousness. This bit of small talk, in its simplicity and humanity, clearly strikes at the egoism and vanity of Andrey's aspirations. The implicit challenge of this small talk is recognized but rebuffed. Andrey's reflections conclude: "Yet all the same [*I vsë-taki*] I love and value only a triumph over them all, I value this mysterious power and glory which now swirls about me in this mist."

train with a resolute step. And, as soon as her brother reached her she flung her left arm around the neck of her brother, with a movement that struck Vronsky by its resoluteness and grace, and drawing him quickly to her warmly kissed him. Vronsky could not take his eyes off her and, without knowing why, smiled. But recollecting that his mother was waiting for him, he went back again into the train.

Animation,[2] decisiveness, directness—these qualities of character in Anna are expressed in her physical actions and being as well. What is equally striking in this episode, however, is Tolstoy's emphasis upon Anna's independence. Her readiness to initiate action, significantly, contrasts with the merely responsive action of Vronsky. He steps out onto the platform in response to his mother's request; Anna, on the other hand, "did not wait for her brother." Further, it is in this passage that Tolstoy calls attention to a pattern in Vronsky's relationship with his mother. The final line in the passage cited—"But recollecting that his mother was waiting for him, he went back again into the train"—is the first embodiment, however slight, of a motif sounded at the conclusion of Chapter 17, Part One: the purely external obeisance and respect Vronsky accords his mother.[3]

This motif, which Tolstoy weaves into the very texture of the most casual actions of Vronsky,[4] forms a brilliant yet eminently natural prelude to the exchange between Vronsky and his mother on *"le parfait amour."* Vronsky's mother lets fall a veiled hint apropos of the value of a liaison with a woman like Anna, coupling

2. From "restrained" animation to animation finally released in a smile, Tolstoy moves (in Chap. 29, Pt. One) to the "irrepressible joy and animation" which shows on Anna's face when she meets Vronsky during the train trip back to St. Petersburg.

3. "In his heart he did not respect his mother and, though not acknowledging this to himself, did not love her; but in accordance with the ideas of his set and of his education, he could not imagine any other relations to his mother than those dutiful and respectful to the highest degree, and the more externally dutiful and respectful he was, the less he respected and loved her at heart."

4. It is noteworthy that on three different occasions in Chap. 18, Vronsky's contemplation of Anna is interrupted by a shift of attention to his mother.

it with an indirect disapproval of his courting of Kitty. Though Vronsky is irritated by his mother's remarks he in fact does break off his courtship of Kitty and strikes up an affair (though not in the cynical spirit of his mother) with Anna. The motif of Vronsky's curious social attachment to his mother's person rises to the surface once again in the exchange which follows between Anna and Vronsky's mother on the question of getting along without their sons. Vronsky's mother tells Anna not to worry about her son: "You cannot expect never to be parted"—a remark, of course, that would be better directed to herself and her own obvious concern over Vronsky's apparent interest in Kitty.

The final episode of the chapter serves to bring into sharper relief the characters of Anna and Vronsky. Anna and her brother, as well as Vronsky and his mother, prepare to leave the station when they learn of the guard's accident. Vronsky and Oblonsky follow the crowd to find out about the accident. They return:

> Oblonsky and Vronsky had both seen the disfigured corpse. Oblonsky, plainly, was suffering. His face was distorted and he seemed ready to burst into tears.
>
> "Oh, what a horror! Oh, Anna, if you had seen it! Oh, what a horror!" he kept repeating.
>
> Vronsky was silent and his handsome face was serious, but perfectly tranquil.
>
> "Ah, if you had seen it, Countess," said Stepan Arkadich. "And his wife is here. It was awful to see her. She threw herself on the body. They say that he supported a huge family. There's the horror of it all!"
>
> "Can't something be done for her," Anna said in an agitated whisper.
>
> Vronsky looked at her and immediately left the train.
>
> "I'll be right back, Maman," he added, looking around in the doorway.

The passage lightly but deftly discloses something essential to the character of all participants. "Oblonsky, plainly, was suffering. His face was distorted and he seemed ready to burst into tears." There are no profundities to Oblonsky, yet his reaction is typical of his open, good-hearted, and somewhat two-dimensional nature.

His emotions are near the surface and are easily—if not permanently—touched. Anna's "agitated whisper" and her immediate practical concern for the wife of the guard reveal both the depths of her responsiveness to human misfortune and the generosity of her nature. Both Oblonsky's and Anna's reactions have a direct verbal and even physical character. In striking contrast, Vronsky is silent and his handsome face, though serious, "perfectly tranquil."

Is there a dimension of human experience closed to Vronsky, this eminently decent and honorable gentleman? Unquestionably there is. What is involved here is a certain shallowness, broadly cultural, perhaps, and not one of basic intelligence; even more, a certain unconscious yet organic egoism which prevents him from communicating, or empathizing, with the full depth of feeling of another. The only moment when Vronksy's face will definitely lose its physical composure—a tranquillity which seems to define his limitations—is in his final appearance, after Anna's suicide, at a railroad station. Kozdnyshev scans the "obviously suffering face of Vronsky." Is Vronsky responding, here, to the tragedy of Anna? Has Anna's action finally broken through the composure of his face and being? It is difficult to answer this question with a yes or a no. It is of paramount significance, however, that Tolstoy observes of Vronsky on this occasion that "a gnawing toothache . . . impeded his speech." Tolstoy's own point of view is clear. He has lowered the plane of Vronsky's suffering—yet not arbitrarily, not maliciously, but fully in accord with the essential nature of Vronsky.

Anna questions whether something could not be done for the family of the guard. "Vronsky looked at her and immediately left the train." But the glance here is not one of common sentiment; it is only a glance of recognition of Anna's request. Vronsky does not share Anna's deep response to the disaster, and he will never understand or reach Anna at that deeper level on which her question was formulated. He will never really succeed in communicating with her. And this is one of the essential elements, of course, in the tragedy of Anna.

Vronsky, gentleman that he is, goes off to fulfill Anna's request, but man that he is, he characteristically leaves the money with an official without indicating that it should be used for the family of the deceased guard. As he leaves to fulfill his duty, he remarks: "I'll be right back, Maman." In a sense, Vronsky's whole relationship with Anna opens on a note of his mother's approval and ends with a return to mother. How important Tolstoy viewed the motif of Vronsky's concern for his mother may be judged alone by the reemergence of this motif in full force at the moment of Vronsky's final break with Anna:

> "It's a matter of complete indifference to me what your mother thinks and how she wants to marry you off," she said, putting down the cup with a trembling hand.
>
> "But we're not talking about that."
>
> "No, precisely about that. And let me assure you that I have no interest in a heartless woman—whether she be an old lady or not, your mother or somebody else—and I don't want to have anything to do with her."
>
> "Anna, I beg you not to speak disrespectfully of my mother."
>
> "A woman whose heart does not tell her wherein lies the happiness and honor of her son—such a woman has no heart."
>
> "I repeat my request that you do not speak disrespectfully about my mother, whom I respect," he said, raising his voice and looking at her severely. . . .
>
> "You don't love your mother. Those are all words, words, words!" she said looking at him with hate. (Chapter 25, Part Seven)

The theme of respect for his mother, in short, the problem of comme il faut behavior and morality, points to a permanent concern of Tolstoy: the disjunction between form and content (and the atrophy of the latter) in the aristocratic, Petersburg world. Vronsky's unwillingness and inability to come to terms with this hypocrisy in his relations with his mother points to the permanent ambiguity that marks his attitude toward Anna's rebellion, on the one hand, and society on the other. It is because Anna, both in her essential nature and her actions, refuses to tolerate this disjunction of form and content, this rule of hypocrisy and facade, because she

insists on full integrity in choice and action, that she pays the price
of "vengeance." "You're very much a whole man [*tsel'nyj che-
lovek*]," Oblonsky remarks on one occasion to Levin. "It's your
virtue and your shortcoming." The same words, of course, may be
applied to Anna.

At their last meeting, Vronsky fails to measure the depth of
Anna's anxiety and despair and goes away thinking: " 'I've tried
everything . . . only one thing remains, to pay no attention,' and
he began to get ready to go to the city and then to his mother's
again, to get her signature to the power of attorney." Do we not
find here, perhaps, the solution to the enigma of Vronsky's composure at the scene of the accident? In the face of an event or situation that does not yield to rational endeavor, or of one that is
beyond the reach of one's feelings, *to pay no attention?*

The conclusion of Chapter 18, centering on Anna's reaction to
the accident of the guard, provides a brilliant psychological climax
to the chapter. Anna gets into the carriage, her lips trembling,
barely restraining her tears. Her brother asks her what is the
matter.

> "It's a bad omen," she said.
> "What nonsense!" said Stepan Arkadich. "You've come,
> that's the main thing. You can't imagine how I count on
> you."
> "And have you known Vronsky for a long time?" she asked.
> "Yes. You know we hope that he will marry Kitty."
> "Really?" Anna said quietly. "Well, now let's talk about
> you," she added, shaking her head as though she wanted phys-
> ically to drive away something extraneous, oppressive.

How are we to interpret Anna's remark, "It's a bad omen"? Of
central importance in any analysis of it is the fact that it is evoked
in the context of her meeting with Vronsky. A major preoccupation of Tolstoy throughout Chapter 18 is to record the mutual
interest of Vronsky and Anna in its embryonic, at first almost unconscious phases. This interest, which first manifests itself almost
entirely in terms of basic physical instinct, then rises to the conscious game of "coquetry," suddenly is recognized for what it is by
Anna ("she, obviously, did not want to continue in this tone")

and suppressed, driven underground, only to reappear again, almost involuntarily, in another seemingly irrelevant context. Anna's remark, "Have you known Vronsky long?" at the time of the accident suddenly makes us aware that the appearance of Vronsky has destroyed the internal equilibrium that seems to have been manifest in the tension of animation and restraint. The impact of the accident in the context of her encounter with Vronsky has aroused in her a disturbing and pessimistic awareness of her own situation. The thoughts that Anna wishes almost physically to drive away are, of course, not at all "extraneous" to her nature, but of its very essence. Oblonsky's twice-repeated remark at this juncture that he is counting on Anna (*nadejus' na tebja, vsja nadezhda na tebja*) to resolve his marital difficulties, have—in retrospect—a tragic irony to them.

It is obvious that Anna's remark, "it's a bad omen," is drawn from the permanent depths of her nature. It reflects a feature of her personality which the reader often notes: what Dolly calls Anna's "too gloomy" way of looking at things, or what Princess Betsy suggests is Anna's "tendency to look at things too much in a tragic light." There is even a kind of Greek fatality to the character and outlook of Anna. Restlessly, actively, almost physically, she seeks out and creates her own reality, or realm, to play out her drama. The play of chance—such play as we noted at the outset of our essay—is more of an illusion than reality. For such a type as Anna, moreover, the opportunity of chance only provides a consciously or unconsciously anticipated opening;[5] for such a person (Lermontov explored a very extreme example of this type in Pechorin) chance is *fate*. Anna's comment, "it's a bad omen," is of course a perfect illustration of this active, willed transformation into fateful actuality of one of those infinite and endlessly drifting bits of chance that reality has in continual reserve.

Oblonsky, for his part, responds to Anna's comment on the level

5. No doubt, too, many combinations or circumstances would have led to a break or crisis in Anna's life, provided an opening gambit to the fulfillment of her nature. Moreover, all the "chance" elements we have noted are very far from being *pure* chance. Consider the closely interknit family and social relations of all the characters involved: the encounter between Vronsky and Anna could easily occur again in other circumstances. And, in fact, Tolstoy lets us know that Vronsky and Anna actually have met *before* this occasion.

of his own ache—the domestic drama which brings Anna to Moscow. He finds it ridiculous to see in the accident of the guard a "bad omen" for the resolution of his problems. His response, "what nonsense!" reflects more than just the sober approach of the reasonable man to an admittedly quite subjective and, outwardly at least, superstitious reaction; it serves also to distinguish for us, albeit in a rudimentary and preliminary way, the ordinary consciousness from the one with tragic potential. Tolstoy's instructive juxtaposition of Anna and Oblonsky in this interchange, of course, is part of his whole contrast between Anna's tragic drama and Oblonsky's bourgeois domestic drama, or melodrama.

Chapter 18, then, may be regarded as constituting in microcosm the action of the novel as a whole as it pertains to Anna. The movement of the chapter from the buoyant, physically animated, and emotionally surcharged Anna, who steps down from the train, to the emotionally distraught, inward Anna of the chapter's conclusion paraphrases the fall of Anna in the novel at large; it lays the psychological and social groundwork for her real suicide toward the end of the novel. At the end of Chapter 18 the purity of Anna's animation has been compromised and the tragic interiority of her nature revealed; by the end of the novel Anna's "tendency to look at things too much in a tragic light" has become a pathological phenomenon enveloping her entire world view in darkness.

The principle of realism guiding Tolstoy in this chapter, as elsewhere in his work, is one which Chekhov will develop to the highest point of perfection: the view that our casual everyday appearance, behavior, conversation—in short, our everyday "character" and confrontations—contain, reflect, anticipate the larger shape of our destiny.[6] An old notion, of course (and one expressed by Heraclitus: "A man's character is his fate"), but one rarely embodied in art with consummate artistic mastery. Much of what

---

6. Chekhov summed up this principle of realism in these words: "Let everything on the stage be just as complex and at the same time just as simple as in life. People dine, merely dine, but at that moment their happiness is being made or their life is being smashed" ("Vospominanija D. Gorodetskogo," *Birzhevye vedomosti* [1904], No. 364).

will be recognized as the typical behavior and action of both Anna and Vronsky is discernible in embryonic form in this opening phase of their relationship.

The beauty of the chapter lies in Tolstoy's ability to maintain a primary focus upon the "natural" movement of surface action, of ordinary and casual encounter and conversation, while at the same time revealing in this seemingly routine material the texture of a dynamic reality rapidly acquiring design and shape. The themes of Anna and also, to some extent, those of Vronsky culminate in the episode of the accident. Here we have an explosion which momentarily smashes the "natural" calm of everyday life and behavior and brings to the surface the full, usually hidden, content of reality: in a single stroke Tolstoy reveals the tragic outlines of the future. The significance of the chapter as it pertains to Anna is summed up in its final episode: the death of the guard signals the birth of the tragic Anna.

The problem of the accident of the guard, indeed, Tolstoy's whole choice of the railroad station as a stage to introduce Anna, deserves some discussion. The fact that the image of the guard recurs to Anna and that she ultimately commits suicide in the same fashion as the guard only points to Tolstoy's vital preoccupation with the psychological motivation of Anna's suicide. But why, specifically, the death of a railroad guard, why a railroad station? Here Tolstoy's concern is not only with the dramatic and psychological potential of his material (this potential, after all, could be found elsewhere) but also with its *social* content and implications. The accident of the guard is a symbol and an embodiment—in Tolstoy's novelistic world view—not of some irrational, metaphysical factor in existence that may at any moment strike us down, but of the rational disorder of modern social and economic existence. It is of cardinal significance that two or three of the most traumatic moments of Anna's existence are played out in interaction with the harsh and discordant rhythms of the railroad. The iron railroad, or jarring train, as a symbol of dislocation of life, as an embodiment of new forces ruthlessly destroying the old patterns of patriarchal existence, becomes in *Anna Karenina* (as it does later, in a more didactic way, in *The Kreutzer Sonata*) a kind of symbol for the disorders of individual and family existence.

The accident of the guard is for Tolstoy not an occurrence of chance (except in the sense that it happens today and not tomorrow, to this guard and not to that one) ; it emerges, as a concrete possibility, from the actuality of a modern capitalist existence, that "external civilization" [7] which increasingly alienates man from the products of his labor, from the sense of "usefulness" of his labor, and from those organic harmonies of man and labor which Tolstoy extols in his famous collective mowing scene in *Anna Karenina*. (When Levin asks that "we try to think of labor not in the European way," not as "abstract man *power,* but as the *Russian peasant* with his instincts," he is appealing also for a rational humanization of the labor process, a return to the "useful" labor of a patriarchal, agricultural existence.) Anna's suicide, likewise, is the final result of an alienation which for Tolstoy is rooted socially in the same dislocations and contradictions that the railroads bring to Russian life, dislocations which somehow acquire a unique and terrifying embodiment (in all its abstraction and senselessness and brutality) in the accident or suicide of the guard.[8]

The shrieking chaos, the blinding play of lights and shadows, the choking sensations, the madly fluctuating temperatures and weird visual imagery of the night train back to St. Petersburg—to take another illustration of the same problem in *Anna Karenina*—not only accompanies but defines, one might almost say

7. Levin's phrase in *Anna Karenina*. See Chap. 25, Pt. Five, where he enumerates the features of this "European" civilization carried over into Russia: "in particular the means of communications, the railroad, which brought about centralization in the cities, the growth of luxury and as a result—to the detriment of agriculture—the development of industry, the credit system with its concomitant—speculation on the Stock Market."

8. Tolstoy, it should be noted, is somewhat ambiguous on this point. As omniscient author he writes: "The guard, either because he was drunk or too muffled up against the bitter cold, had not heard the train shunting back and had been crushed." The bystanders, however, have a different impression: " 'What? What? Where? Threw himself under—was crushed,' passers-by were heard saying." The notion of the suicide of the guard, therefore, is planted—rightly or wrongly—in Anna's mind (a psychological detail that neatly enters into the general motivation of her suicide) .

induces, Anna's annihilating moral crisis at that moment. "Then something screeched and clattered in a fearful way, as though somebody were being torn to pieces." The rending of her moral consciousness—for on this train trip, in fact, she breaks through the moral barrier—is significantly accompanied by a sense of upheaval and distortion throughout her being and by a terrifying sense of self-alienation: "And what am I doing here? Am I myself or somebody else?" We have an anticipation here of that total psychological and social alienation that Anna experiences in the period just before her suicide.

Of course, as we have noted, Anna's tragedy is firmly rooted in her own peculiar nature: her decision to commit suicide, as well as her choice of a particular form of suicide, may and must be explained in terms of her nature and of her unique personal history in which chance plays a role (though a minimal one). In short, there had to be a particular person of the nature of Anna Karenina and a particular combination of personal circumstances for there to have been a tragedy of the kind we have in this novel. But it is no less true that the Anna we know is inseparable from the problem content of the Russian society in which she lives; her rebellion, indeed the specific character of that rebellion, is in large part determined by the society which is the object of her rebellion.

In the light of these considerations, Chapter 18 emerges as one of the most important and decisive ones in the novel. Here we have both "complication" and denouement. For the death of the guard and the death of Anna in the stupendous social perspective of Tolstoy are neither mutually detached phenomena nor accidents of chance, but—the one inert, the other conscious—inelectable phenomena of a society, like the obsessed Ahab, rushing toward catastrophe on iron rails.

In the final summation, one recognizes a distinct parallel and ultimate convergence in the lines of personal, that is, psychological, and also social motivation or fatality in Anna Karenina. It is precisely the convergence and organic unity of these lines that provides the tragedy of Anna with its depth, its amplitude, in the final analysis, its grandeur. Yet in positing the overwhelming elements of psychological and social fatality we do not deny the indispensable elements of freedom in Anna's tragedy. This freedom lies in the conscious choice of a tragic destiny. This will to meet one's destiny (which for the novelist Tolstoy is always concrete, social, historical) is a will to reach out and exemplify one's personal fate through an exploration of the limits of one's reality. A character exercises his enormous potential of freedom—and there are moments of critical choice—when he chooses to explore these limits, whether out of a sense of a lofty ideal, a sense of personal injustice, or a feeling of incompleteness. Such a character, on the subjective plane, tests his freedom and discovers his inherent fatality. But objectively such a character rises above the purely individual and pedestrian precisely because his discovered fate embodies more of the *necessity* of social existence. Anna, of course, is revealed in this unique, tragic perspective, one which, through its total illumination of reality, seems to transcend fatality itself.

Not without reason did Dostoevsky refer to Tolstoy as a "god of art."

Herman Meyer

On the Spirit of Verse

A delightful numbskull, this Monsieur Jourdain, Molière's *bourgeois gentilhomme,* who has to be lectured by his philosophy master on the difference between prose and verse and then exclaims in amazement, "Par moi foi, il y a plus de quarante ans que je dis de la prose, sans que j'en susse rien." The theater audience laughs heartily, secure in the sense of its own superiority and discernment. Yet one is entitled to ask how many of the spectators might one day truthfully admit: "Here I have been listening to plays in verse for more than forty years and never noticed a thing." The number is probably considerable. Certainly it is a well-known fact that blank verse—which is used in the great majority of the verse plays performed today—hardly impresses itself on the average spectator's ear, if at all; this applies equally to Shakespeare, Goethe, Schiller, or Kleist. Indifference toward verse form receives support from the actors, who, with the encouragement of the director, do their utmost to speak their roles "naturally"; this means that they try to blur over the specific qualities of the verse. The director in turn can cite the authority of noted theoreticians of verse who expressly approve the actors' practice of running their lines together into prose because that contributes to a natural speech style. When one considers this state of affairs, it does not seem surprising that the inquiry into the exact nature of verse in general and specific kinds of verses lies beyond the horizon of popular awareness.

Literary scholarship is but poorly equipped to provide clarification on this problem. Within its own ranks a curious situation prevails as to awareness of the mode of existence and inherent value of verse. In fact, the study of versification occupies a subordinate position in literary scholarship, and an isolated one as well. Verse study has been evolving more and more into an esoteric discipline with methods, a vocabulary, and a conceptual apparatus which are becoming increasingly difficult for the un-initiated to gain access. At the same time, even the initiates com-plain that this discipline has not really succeeded in working out a uniform terminology and a sound methodological basis for its en-deavors. Thus one need not wonder that the "science" of verse sheds little brightness outside its own confines. Indeed, one notices that it makes a pathetically small contribution to the total inter-pretation of poetic works. The bridge from one discipline to the other is narrow and precarious.[1]

Thus we will be following barely trodden paths across the wilderness as we turn to a problem which time and again con-fronts the interpreter of poetry: what is the inherent spirit of our metrical and strophic forms? "Spirit" should not be taken here to suggest something mysterious or lofty. We are not chasing after some metaphysical ghost which pursues its sinister ways in the realm of poetry; rather we are interested in whether specific metric and stanzaic patterns possess a fixed expressive character. Our observations and reflections will concern themselves both with the types of metrical line and with the strophic forms; the latter can be considered provisionally as the organic extension of the former.

Poetic material seems somehow to resist questioning of this sort. To be sure, we can say of a given work that its language expresses a definite character and that its metrical or strophic form is in har-mony with that character. But in most cases we come away empty-handed when we ask after the character of a verse form seen by itself, separate from the work; we lack to a great extent valid cri-teria for objectifying our subjective impression. Therefore the in-quirer should consider detours and look for certain marginal

1. The relatively rare cases in which prosody and interpretation are suc-cessfully combined and lead to significant results are all the more gratifying. Examples are Wolfgang Binder, "Hölderlins Odenstrophe," *Hölderlin Jahr-buch* (1952), pp. 85–110; Emil Staiger, "Goethes antike Versmasse," *Die Kunst der Interpretation* (Zürich, 1955), pp. 115–31; Wolfgang Kayser, "Goethes Dichtungen in Stanzen," *Doitsu Bungaku* (Die deutsche Litera-tur), Die japanische Gesellschaft für Germanistik, *2* (May 1959), 1–16; Alfred Kelletat, "Zum Problem der antiken Metren im Deutschen," *Der Deutschunterricht, 16* (1964), 50–85.

phenomena and unusual constellations of meters and strophes which, precisely because of their exceptional character, provide insights which would be difficult to obtain by normal means. Beggars cannot be choosers: let us be permitted, therefore, to go into some rather weird poetic phenomena, not out of any reprehensible pleasure in oddities for themselves, but for the sake of increasing our understanding. I have chosen rather disparate materials to discuss. Uniting them is the methodological approach suggested by the questions we have posed.

It can prove illuminating for our inquiry when a poet chooses a stanzaic form previously used by another poet and gives it a new application. I once tried to examine a few significant examples to see what conclusions about the innate character of stanzaic patterns arise out of this particular phenomenon in the history of verse. It became evident that we are in great danger of mistakenly attributing to a given strophic scheme a predisposition to the expression of a definite poetic content. Utmost caution is called for if we are postulating a specific expressive power (in the sense of content) for stanzaic patterns.

The patterns have a more or less marked profile or personality. It is true that those forms with a more distinctive physiognomy tend, in the process of historical evolution, to become associated with a certain poetic content or even a definite theme. As a clear example of such an association I discussed the history of the four-line iambic strophe (with alternation of five and two stresses) which Goethe used for his poem "Nähe des Geliebten." [2] Ever since this strophic form first appeared in Ewald von Kleist's "Lied eines Lappländers" (1757), the theme of longing for the distant beloved has remained attached to it. We would be wrong, however, to see a generally valid law of poetical history in the affinity of a distinctive form for fixed thematic material. The following example to the contrary may therefore be appropriate here.

In 1896 young Hofmannsthal composed his "Lebenslied." This is the first of the four stanzas:

2. "Vom Leben der Strophe in neuerer deutscher Lyrik," *Deutsche Viertel-jahrsschrift für Literaturwissenschaft und Geistesgeschichte,* 25 (1951), 436–73. Reprinted in *Zarte Empirie* (Stuttgart, 1963), pp. 113–59.

Den Erben lass verschwenden
An Adler, Lamm und Pfau
Das Salböl aus den Händen
Der toten alten Frau!
Die Toten, die entgleiten,
Die Wipfel in dem Weiten—
Ihm sind sie wie das Schreiten
Der Tänzerinnen wert!

None of Hofmannsthal's poems has been such a challenge to the critics as this one. Several studies have been devoted to it, and most recently a thorough monograph even appeared in book form.[3] There is general agreement as to the cryptic character of what the poem says, but opinions diverge on how the secret should be unveiled, if at all. The critics also agree in their high evaluation of the rhythmic and musical qualities of the poem. Only in passing have they concerned themselves with the stanzaic form, which in its great artistry so obviously contributes to the poem's fascination. Its features are determined above all by the difference between the two parts of the strophe. Of the eight lines in iambic trimeter, the first four are linked by alternating rhyme; by itself that would hardly be remarkable, a simple *Volkslied*—like form. But then the group of three lines joined by a common feminine rhyme has a highly suggestive dynamic which is dammed up by the final unrhymed line. This combination of lilting movement and solid rounding-off produces a delicate and balanced structure with strong individuality.

As far as I know, it has always been tacitly assumed that Hofmannsthal was the creator of this stanzaic form. In fact he borrowed it from Keats, whose poems he had early come to admire. The poem in question is "Stanzas," [4] the first strophe of which runs like this:

3. Marianne Schultz-Hector, "Hugo von Hofmannsthals 'Lebenslied,' " *Akzente*, 2 (1955), 85–95; Paul Gerhard Klussmann, "Hugo von Hofmannsthals 'Lebenslied,' " *Zeitschrift für deutsche Philologie*, 82 (1963), 192–210; Richard Exner, *Hugo von Hofmannsthals "Lebenslied," eine Studie* (Heidelberg, 1964), 151 pp.

4. Hofmannsthal owned *The Poetical Works of Keats* published by Frederick Warne and Co. (London and New York, 1892). See Michael Hamburger, "Hofmannsthals Bibliothek," *Euphorion*, 55 (1961), 50. The

> In a drear-nighted December,
> Too happy, happy tree!
> Thy branches ne'er remember
> Their green felicity;
> The north cannot undo them
> With a sleepy whistle through them
> Nor frozen thawings glue them
> From budding at the prime.

We can easily understand that this wonderfully lilting and sonorous poem put Hofmannsthal under its spell precisely through the enchanting quality of its highly structured strophic form.[5] Adoption of the form must have been at once a great stimulus and a real challenge to him.

Our third example is a classic of modern Dutch poetry and equals both its predecessors in terms of significant beauty: Martinus Nijhoff's "Satyr en Christofoor" (from the volume *Vormen*, 1924). In the first stanza of this poem, which portrays in ballad style a legendary happening, the satyr asks St. Christopher to entrust the child Jesus to him:

> "Ach, Christofoor, vertrouwder
> In 't water dan op 't land,
> Til het kindje van je schoudcr,
> Geef zijn handje me in de hand:
> Ik wijs het in de bosschen
> De bronnen en de mossen,
> De vogels en de vossen,
> De slang, den haas en 't hert."

---

poem "Stanzas (from the *Literary Gazette,* 1829)" appears in this edition on p. 281, printed in such a way that the internal structure of the stanza is indicated by differing degrees of indentation. We have followed this printed form in our quotation. Michael Hamburger had the goodness to provide me with the short list which Hofmannsthal (probably in later life) made of the poems he found important in this edition. "Stanzas," however, is not included.

5. A small but clearly audible difference should be pointed out. Keats links his three strophes by having the last lines, unrhymed within the strophe, rhyme with each other. Neither Hofmannsthal nor Nijhoff (see below) adopted this practice.

"Oh, Christopher, more at home
In water than on land,
Lift the child from your shoulder,
Put its little hand in mine.
In the woods I'll show him
The springs and mosses,
The birds and foxes,
The snake, the hare and the deer."

In a conversation shortly before his death, Nijhoff pointed out to me the poem's relationship to poetical tradition. He was familiar with the two previous poems by Keats and Hofmannsthal and admired them highly.[6] I remember from our talk that he thought of the adopted stanzaic form as a lovely melody to which he had written a new text.

The musical comparison seems to me to touch on something essential. These three poems do strike us as being very closely related in their ethereal, festive spirit. Yet if one looks for obvious thematic correspondences, one is disappointed. The stanzaic form they share plainly has a powerful "spirit" of its own, but in a purely formal sense. The stanza can be freely joined to widely differing contents without becoming tied to them. Singing sweetly like a lark, it soars above the dark terrestrial remains of theme and content matter.

In our search for the spirit of verse we now enter a winding sidepath, but perhaps it will lead to some fine vantage points. We turn to the rather rare phenomenon of a verse form's being made the main theme or at least a major theme of the poem in which it occurs; the form thus explicitly mirrors itself in the poem. What heuristic value does this particular kind of poetry-of-poetry have for our understanding of verse form?

First let us mention in passing a few well-known and obvious examples. Schiller made the distich the theme of a distich which compares the hexameter line to the rising jet of water from a foun-

6. The connection has already been alluded to by Simon Vestdijk in his volume of essays *De glanzende kiemcel* (3d ed. Amsterdam, 1964), although he does not mention the Keats and Hofmannsthal poems by name.

tain, the pentameter line to the falling one. The poem defines its own form. Poets are known to be fond of using the sonnet to define itself. August Wilhelm Schlegel has a sonnet in which the octave describes with virtuosity, but rather pedantically, the technical recipe for the sonnet, while the sextet tries to conjure up its poetical essence. It is characteristic that the personified sonnet steps forward and proclaims itself in the first person singular:

> Den werd' ich nie mit meinen Zeilen kränzen,
> Dem eitle Spielerei mein Wesen dünket,
> Und Eigensinn die künstlichen Gesetze.
> Doch, wem in mir geheimer Zauber winket,
> Dem leih' ich Hoheit, Füll' in engen Grenzen,
> Und reines Ebenmass der Gegensätze.

Goethe responded in two sonnets, first with ironic reservations, then with an affirmative attitude. The second of Goethe's sonnets ("Natur und Kunst, sie scheinen sich zu fliehen") goes beyond the limited topic and launches into a general doctrine of art and morality, while keeping sonnet form as the immediate subject:

> Wer Grosses will, muss sich zusammenraffen.
> In der Beschränkung zeigt sich erst der Meister,
> Und das Gesetz nur kann uns Freiheit geben.

The most ingratiating example of poetological reflection within a poem occurs in Mörike, however; this aspect of his poetry has, by the way, hardly been noticed. Miles removed from any doctrinaire pedantry, he makes the theme of prosody an element of his carefree, serene poetic play, which seems so guileless and ingenuous but is at bottom extremely artful. In contrast to the defining poems mentioned above, Mörike's craftily conceal the theme of poetic form. Just compare Schlegel's recipe poem with the enchanting sweetness of Mörike's sonnet "Am Walde."

> Am Waldsaum kann ich lange Nachmittage,
> Dem Kuckuck horchend, in dem Grase liegen;
> Er scheint das Tal gemächlich einzuwiegen
> Im friedevollen Gleichklang seiner Klage.
>
> Da ist mir wohl, und meine schlimmste Plage,
> Den Fratzen der Gesellschaft mich zu fügen,

Hier wird sie mich doch endlich nicht bekriegen,
Wo ich auf eigne Weise mich behage.

Und wenn die feinen Leute nur erst dächten,
Wie schön Poeten ihre Zeit verschwenden,
Sie würden mich zuletzt noch gar beneiden.

Denn des Sonetts gedrängte Kränze flechten
Sich wie von selber unter meinen Händen,
Indes die Augen in der Ferne weiden.

At first sight the poetological element seems a minor addition, confined to the closing lines. The sonnet form is not defined but only briefly evoked in the words "des Sonetts gedrängte Kränze." On closer examination, however, the formulation turns out to apply to the whole poem. It not only summarizes the fictional *hic et nunc* of the concrete situation—the poet lying at the edge of the forest—but one can go so far as to say that the poem which comes into being seemingly of itself is the very sonnet beginning "Am Waldsaum kann ich." For all the poem's apparent looseness, the poet really is plaiting "gedrängte Kränze"; the reader need only observe the lucid structure and especially the rich sound texture to be convinced. The poem has come full circle: in its end is its beginning. Instead of offering a theoretical explication of the poetic essence of the sonnet, the poem offers itself as an exemplary realization of the form.

Just as the sonnet form enters into the theme of the poem "Am Walde," the elegiac meter—alternating lines of hexameter and pentameter—is the theme of Mörike's humorous idyll "Häusliche Szene." In this poem the form's self-commentary is much more evident; the playful element predominates, and the theme has been transmuted with vigor into a fictitious plot. This *Biedermeier* genre piece deals with the harmless subject of a marital quarrel—rendered in dialogue—over a husband's peculiar hobby of experimenting with vinegar production. The good *Hausfrau* finds this annoying. The elegiac meter must adapt itself to a charming, half-parodistic domestication, as the very beginning shows:

"Schläfst du schon, Rike?"—"Noch nicht."—"Sag! hast du
    denn heut die Kukumern

> Eingemacht?"—"Ja."—"Und wieviel nahmst du mir Essig
>   dazu?"—
> "Nicht zwei völlige Mass."—"Wie? fast zwei Mass? Und von
>   welchem
> Krug? von dem kleinern doch nicht, links vor dem Fenster
>   am Hof?"—
> "Freilich."—"Verwünscht! So darf ich die Probe nun noch
>   einmal machen,
> Eben indem ich gehofft, schon das Ergebnis zu sehn!"

The clever young woman acts friendly and ready to make concessions, but her husband's bumbling annoyance refuses to be
soothed; rather it increases steadily for eighty lines. When he has
used up all his arguments on vinegar, he finds a new bone of contention that is of special interest for us. He changes the subject—as
so often happens in marital quarrels—from the substance of the
discussion to its form, which in this case naturally means the
metrical form.

> "Heut, wie ich merke, gefällst du dir sehr, mir in Versen zu
>   trumpfen."—
> "Waren es Verse denn nicht, was du gesprochen bisher?"—
> "Eine Schwäche des Mannes vom Fach, darfst du sie
>   missbrauchen?"—
> "Unwillkürlich, wie du, red' ich elegisches Mass."—
> "Mühsam übt' ich dir's ein, harmlose Gespräche zu
>   würzen."—
> "Freilich im bitteren Ernst nimmt es sich wunderlich aus."—

The husband forbids his wife to use metrical speech, but to no
avail. He tries angrily to put an end to the conversation:

> "Ei, dir scheint es bequem, nur das Wort noch, das letzte, zu
>   haben:
> Hab's! Ich schwöre, von mir hast du das letzte gehört!"—

But the woman, or Mörike, hits upon an inspired punch line:

> "Meinetwegen, so mag ein Hexameter einmal allein stehn!"

A hexameter in an elegiac poem without a subsequent pentameter—that is a sheer impossibility for our ears as well as for those

of the henpecked preceptor. The jet of water has spurted up and failed to return to earth: that goes as much against the basic law of gravity as against our most elemental aesthetic sense. The incomplete ending gapes like an open wound. Fortunately the poet does not leave us hanging with the unresolved dissonance. After leaving her husband in suspense for a while, the woman takes pity and rounds out the distich with a line of pentameter, whereupon nothing stands in the way of a happy ending.

To gain her victory, the woman makes use of the inherent power of this particular verse form; the hexameter and the pentameter lines necessarily and indivisibly belong together. This was what Schiller was referring to in his distich on the distich and what the gifted elegiac poet Mörike knew intimately from experience. By translating this essential trait of the elegiac meter into dramatic action, he demonstrates it before our very eyes.

A man's character asserts itself in its confrontation with the world and with the adversities it experiences. Something similar can be said of verse forms. They reveal part of their character by the way they behave when they are shaken or plucked at or placed in uncongenial surroundings. Thus such cases deserve our close attention.

This kind of difficult and therefore significant situation can easily arise when a poet works a text fragment from another poet into his own work. Emil Staiger once demonstrated sensitively that such borrowings are often subtly distorted and transposed into quite a different personal style.[7] He gives the instructive example of Brentano's fairy tale "Radlauf erzählt seine Reise nach dem Starenberg." Here Brentano, without batting an eyelash, suddenly incorporates the first stanza of Goethe's "Harfnerlied" into his own song cycle. He renders the strophe this way:

> Wer nie sein Brot in Tränen ass,
> Wer nie die kummervollen Nächte
> Weinend auf seinem Bette sass,
> Der kennt euch nicht, ihr himmlischen Mächte.

7. Emil Staiger, "Entstellte Zitate," *Die Kunst der Interpretation* (Zürich, 1955), pp. 161–79.

Brentano has changed something, whether consciously or unconsciously we do not know, but that does not make much difference. Goethe had written: "Auf seinem Bette weinend sass." [8] Placing "weinend" first, where it clashes with the meter, produces an emotional *rubato* effect, a sort of suppressed sobbing which is foreign to Goethe's sterner use of language in this poem. We agree with Staiger that this change in the rhythm is an essential element of the distortion, but the change does not stop at rhythm. Hand in hand with the rhythmic variation goes a syntactical reversal. Placed at the beginning, "weinend" receives the main stress and gives a different emphasis to the sense of the line.

The purpose of our inquiry will be better served by cases of borrowing in which, despite absolutely "correct" quoting, the passage undergoes a distortion of its rhythm simply by being dislocated. This may seem almost inconceivable, but we can cite several such cases.

One of Klopstock's most lovely poems is the ode "Die frühen Gräber," in which eighteenth-century churchyard poetry achieves an unusual purity. As is well known, Klopstock not only used the traditional classical meters of the ode but also created new ones which, in the proper spirit of the ode, he applied as rigidly as the ancient ones: an established meter is maintained exactly in every stanza of the poem. To Klopstock the abstract metrical pattern possessed its own poetic reality, a sacrosanct substance. Not for nothing did he have the metrical patterns printed carefully above his poems. Characteristic for his poetry is the harmonious combination of rigid metrical exactitude with a hovering delicacy of the verbal construct. This is abundantly clear in the ode we are discussing, the first stanza of which reads:

> Willkommen, o silberner Mond,
> Schöner, stiller Gefährt der Nacht!
> Du entfliehst? Eile nicht, bleib, Gedankenfreund!
> Sehet, er bleibt, das Gewölk wallte nur hin.

About thirty years later Johann Heinrich Voss writes his idyll in hexameters—"Luise" (1795). Voss is one of the most skillful and

---

8. We will not go into another of Brentano's changes, not mentioned by Staiger, i.e. that of "mit Tränen" to "in Tränen."

learned metrical experts of his day, and his idyll proves it. With true virtuosity he blends different literary texts, especially songs and biblical passages, into his hexameters. The integration is often successful in terms of content and mood as well; the quotations merge completely with the warm, intimate atmosphere which makes this pastoral poetry so entrancing. Sometimes, of course, Voss has to modify the wording in the quotations to make it fit his meter, but that was not necessary in the following interesting passage. In one passage Voss gives a charming description of the pastor of Grünau's rural repast with his family in the pleasant North German landscape. As evening comes and the damp night air begins to rise, the venerable pastor speaks:

> Töchterchen, folge dem Rath, und verhülle dich. Besser ist
>   besser;
> Hüpft dir auch in den Pulsen das achtzehnjährige Blut noch
> Jugendlich. Schaue, da hängt des Neumonds werdende Sichel
> Duftig. Wohlan! Willkommen, o silberner Mond: ihm
>   gesungen!
> Frischer Gesang giebt Muth auch dem Zärtlinge; schreienden
>   Kindern
> Naht im Gesange der Schlaf; mit Gesang schlug Luther den
>   Teufel!

We are certainly not playing the *advocatus diaboli* when we note that the quotation has a remarkably comic effect; the reader cannot suppress a smile. We sense that Klopstock's line has been deformed and injured somehow, even though it is quoted correctly. The ode expressed pure solitude; it forfeits some of its poignancy when sung as a simple expression of contentment and good fellowship.[9] But the ode's form suffers an equally significant injury when it is incorporated into the line of hexameter. The problem is not metrical, for Klopstock's pattern ($\smile - - \smile \smile - \smile \smile -$) fits perfectly into the pattern of our hexameter ($- \smile \smile - \smile - \smile \smile - \smile \smile - \smile \smile \smile$). The rhythm of the line undergoes a great transformation, however. The line loses entirely its restrained fluidity, its reflective

9. What we have said remains valid even if we consider that the pastor may have been thinking of Klopstock's ode in a musical setting, for instance, the well-known one by Gluck.

lingering, its gradual dying away, for it must adapt itself for better or worse to the more vigorous step of the hexameter. In addition, the line from the ode has been forced into a completely alien, imperative context between two hortatory exclamations ("Wohlan!" and "gesungen!"). The hexameter insists in a lordly way on the rights due its robust nature, while the line from the ode must pay the high price of self-estrangement in order to fit into the new surroundings.

These observations are founded on our auditory and emotional impressions and may be subjective. Can we somehow give them an objective basis? I am well aware of the ontological difference between a poem in itself and its reproduction in speech, but I was interested to see whether a phonetic analysis of the spoken pattern of our poem would provide a technical corroboration of our earlier results. Three suitable persons were found to speak the texts and record them on an oscillograph in a phonetics laboratory. With all three, the recordings showed considerable differences in speaking time, loudness, and pitch between the Klopstock line in its original context and the line in the context of the Voss poem. It was almost more interesting to find that the differences with all three speakers lay in the same direction, so that a general tendency emerged in spite of individual nuances.

All three speakers recited the verse faster as a quotation than in the ode, apparently because of the force of the hexameter. In the hexameter, the pause of about half a second after "Willkommen" and the longer pause of about one second at the end of the line were lost entirely. But apart from that the hexameter generally speeded up the tempo. Two of the three speakers read the quoted line in half the time required for the original! The differences in volume were equally marked. In the hexameter line the accents were much stronger, with the result that the average volume was at least doubled. Regarding pitch, the most noticeable feature of all three test recordings was that the falling melody of the line from the ode was forced upward at the end by being placed in the hexameter context; probably the exclamatory character of the hexameter played its part.

The question arises as to whether the poet intended the comic effect produced by distortion of the rhythm. I tend to think it was

unintentional, although one would certainly have a right to suspect that a clever versifier like Voss was aware of the divergence in
tone and was merely following a private whim. Try as one will,
however, one cannot discover within the poem a clear function
for the whimsical effect. Here we find the difference from the concluding case we are about to discuss.

As an old man Theodor Fontane suffered considerably from the
daily grind, from the cold narrow-mindedness of the unartistic
petty bourgeois in all walks of life. Sometimes melancholy, sometimes sharp and biting, he stubbornly resists in his late poems the
dreary monotony and the oppressive mendacity of his bourgeois
surroundings. His self-defense is all the more genuine because he
does not take recourse to easy pathos; instead, he levelheadedly
searches for the sources of comfort which will enable him to tolerate life and maintain his inner sense of superiority. The famous
serenity of Fontane's Olympian detachment has a strangely restric-
tive function; he gives solace in small doses, but it gains thereby in
effectiveness.

Fontane creates a unique picture of comfort and encouragement
in his short verse tale "Fritz Katzfuss," one of his loveliest late
poems. His blank verse has been toned down to sound prosaic and
almost careless. Within the German poetic tradition, this means
that the *Klassik*'s favorite verse form has been wantonly deprived
of its elevated character. Fontane's domesticated blank verse is free
of noticeable rhythmic tensions; it proceeds evenly with fairly infrequent, mild changes of tone. One remarks that the iambic feet
rattle with particular monotony when Fontane takes a close look
at the microcosm he is describing and enumerates its prosaic ways:
the mimicking, carefully measured-out, half-parodistic impression
produced by the flat rhythm is unmistakable. One need only look
at the opening lines:

> Fritz Katzfuss war ein siebzehnjähr'ger Junge,
> Rothaarig, sommersprossig, etwas faul,
> Und stand in Lehre bei der Witwe Marzahn,
> Die geizig war und einen Laden hatte,
> Drin Hering, Schlackwurst, Datteln, Schweizerkäse,
> Samt Pumpernickel, Lachs und Apfelsinen

> Ein friedlich Dasein miteinander führten.
> Und auf der hohen, etwas schmalen Leiter,
> Mit ihren halb schon weggetretnen Sprossen,
> Sprang unser Katzfuss, wenn die Mädchen kamen
> Und Soda, Waschblau, Griess, Korinthen wollten,
> Geschäftig hin und her.

Within this narrow world the young assistant moves back and forth with a calm, unchanging smile, the sign of his inner superiority. He does his work even-temperedly and more or less satisfactorily; the only annoying thing is that he takes much too long whenever he is sent to fetch anything from the attic or the cellar. One day the proprietress of the shop discovers what keeps him so long, and thus we are let in on the secret source of comfort and strength which enables the boy to put up with his oppressed form of existence. Without his noticing, something falls out of his pocket:

> Die Witwe Marzahn aber
> Schlich sich heran und nahm ein Buch (das war es)
> Vom Boden auf und sah hinein: "Gedichte.
> Gedichte, erster Teil, von Wolfgang Goethe."
> Zerlesen war's und schlecht und abgestossen
> Und Zeichen eingelegt: ein Endchen Strippe,
> Briefmarkenränder, und als dritt' und letztes
> (Zu glauben kaum) ein Streifen Schlackwurstpelle,
> Die Seiten links und rechts befleckt, befettet,
> Und oben stand, nun was? stand "Mignonlieder",
> Und Witwe Marzahn las: "Dahin, dahin
> Möcht' ich mit dir, o mein Geliebter, ziehn."—
> Nun war es klar. Um so was träg und langsam,
> Um Goethe, Verse, Mignon.

Something extraordinary happens to the lines quoted from Goethe. We sense that they are deformed by the way the outraged petty soul of the widow Marzahn receives them. Simply by reading the lines she kills them, although not a single letter is harmed. What rhythmic manipulation does Fontane use to achieve this macabre effect? Let us recall briefly what we know of the miracle Goethe performed in the Mignon stanza. To be sure, the basic meter of the stanza is iambic pentameter; there we must give the widow Marzahn credit. But this basic meter encounters opposition, and it is this tension between two meters that gives the song its agitated rhythm. In each of the three strophes the second, third, and fourth lines stay closest to the normal pattern of the iambic pentameter, although even in them a strong tendency to dipodic tetrameter can be felt. But the trochaic beginning of the first and last line is in open contrast to iambic pentameter; here, too, we find the tendency to dipodic tetrameter. When one has felt one's way into the dipodic rhythm of the poem, the last line reads: "Möcht ich mit dir,/ o mein Geliebter, ziehn!" What happens in Fontane's context and under the pressure of his flat, smoothed-down blank verse? We can almost see it before us: the widow Marzahn coldly and unfeelingly spells out Mignon's cry of longing as if it were a want ad in the local paper; she reads the line in the dry iambic trot which suits her withered soul.

The distortion is strictly functional, directly related to the central meaning of the poem, for which it provides a palpable intensification. Exiled to the world of blueing and sausages, the line from Mignon's song offers a compressed statement of the contradiction in the existence of a poetic shopboy in a paltry, unpoetic environment. At the end of the poem Fontane leaves no doubt that this discrepancy mirrors a painful part of his own experience:

> Wie dir die Lehrzeit hinging bei Frau Marzahn,
> Ging mir das *Leben* hin. Ein Band von Goethe
> Blieb mir bis heut mein bestes Wehr und Waffen,
> Und wenn die Witwe Marzahn mich gepeinigt
> Und dumme Dinger, die nach Waschblau kamen,
> Mich langsam fanden, kicherten und lachten—,
> Ich lächelte, grad' so wie *du* gelächelt,
> Fritz Katzfuss, du mein Ideal, mein Vorbild.
> Der Band von Goethe gab mir Kraft und Leben,
> Vielleicht auch Dünkel. . . . All genau dasselbe,
> Nur andres Haar und—keine Sommersprossen.

In short: a lyrical line collides with an unsuitable environment, and the resulting small rhythmic incongruity acquires the dignity of an existential symbol. We have approached the problem of the spirit of verse from three completely different angles. The results were as varied as the paths leading to them, yet all the results point toward a common center. Hofmannsthal borrows a stanzaic form; Mörike's idyll provides a mirror for its own verse scheme; Voss and Fontane quote verbatim but vary the rhythm: what we could perceive through all these media, though in different ways and to different degrees, is the autonomous power of the metrical forms involved and affected—ultimately the *vis superba formae.*

Translated by Krishna Winston

Stephen G. Nichols, Jr.

Toward an Aesthetic of the Provençal *Canso*

The *canso* has never lacked partisans willing to assert its primacy as the progenitor of the modern love lyric. C. S. Lewis and Eugène Vinaver in England, E. R. Curtius in Germany, Reto Bezzola in Switzerland, Jean Frappier in France, and a host of others have asserted that the troubadours were the first to give lyrical expression to the sorrow and passion of love.[1] Even a recent attacker of the claim, Peter Dronke, who feels that "this received opinion, this belief in a wholly new conception of love, is false" and that "Poetry of the courtly experience has always existed, and is not confined to a 'courtly class,' " nonetheless recognizes that the troubadours offer the earliest and most extensive example of vernacular love poetry in the modern period.[2]

Despite the general recognition of its importance, the canso has not shared in the intensive study enjoyed by poetry in our time. Specifically, there has been little rigorous theoretical discussion of the aesthetic of this important genre.[3] Insofar as it has been con-

---

1. C. S. Lewis, *The Allegory of Love* (1936); E. R. Curtius, *European Literature and the Latin Middle Ages* (New York, 1953); R. Bezzola, *Les Origines et la formation de la littérature courtoise en occident* (Paris, 1944–63); Jean Frappier, *La poésie lyrique en France aux xiie et xiiie siècles* (Paris, n.d.); Eugène Vinaver, "A la recherche d'une poétique médiévale," *CCM*, 2 (1959), 13.

2. Peter Dronke, *Medieval Latin and the Rise of the European Love-Lyric* (Oxford, 1965), *1*, 2, 46.

3. This is not the case, however, for the northern love lyric, the *chanson courtoise*. One thinks immediately, to name only two recent works consecrated to the study of the chanson courtoise, of Roger Dragonetti's *La Technique poétique des trouvères dans la chanson courtoise* (Bruges, De Tempel, 1960) and Daniel Poirion's *Le Poète et le prince, L'evolution du*

349

sidered at all, the canso has been the concern of two principal
groups: the formalists on the one hand, and the musicologists on
the other. Rare indeed have been such balanced studies as that of
Professor Margaret Switten, who demonstrates in her article on
the language and music of Peirol's cansos that the music of the
troubadour corresponds intimately to the poetry with which it was
written.[4] More typical have been claims to the effect that the
Provençal lyric is "above all a poetry of rhyme where the sound
patterns created in a poem almost take precedence over the total
meaning to be conveyed by the words."[5] In his article "D'une
poésie formelle en France au moyen âge," Robert Guiette makes
even more sweeping claims for the formalist view. Speaking of the
chanson courtoise, he says that "l'individualité éclate non dans le
contenu idéologique, mais dans la création des formes." The
poetry must be found in the "object," in the formal element of the
poem for "le style est tout et l'argument idéologique n'est qu'un
matériau."[6] Eugène Vinaver also pleads the formalist cause when
he elaborates Guiette's statement with the words:

> Est-ce parce que nous sommes trop peu sensibles à la pure
> activité poétique, à celle qui refuse de confondre *essence* et
> *donée,* que nous entrons si mal dans la connaissance d'un tel
> art? Là où se situent les éléments créateurs, nous ne voyons
> que 'faiblesses'; et nous allons jusqu'à chercher dans l' "excès
> de formalisme" les raisons de la décadence du genre, comme
> si ce formalisme, c'est-à-dire l'instinct et la science formelle,
> ne constituait pas, au contraire, le principe même de sa vital-
> ité. La donnée, le thème d'un poème lyrique courtois n'en est
> jamais que le prétexte: c'est l'oeuvre formelle qui est le véri-

---

lyricisme courtois de Guillaume de Machaut à Charles d'Orléans (Paris,
Presses Universitaires de France, 1965).

4. "Text and Melody in Peirol's *Cansos,*" *PMLA, 76* (1961), 325.

5. S. G. Nichols, Jr., et al., *The Songs of Bernart de Ventadorn* (Chapel
Hill, University of North Carolina Press, 1962), p. 16.

6. *Revue des sciences humaines, 54* (1949), 64, 66. Cf. also Guiette's
formulation of the attitude of the poets toward their work: "[ils] ne s'in-
quiètent pas d'un aveu, mais d'une chanson. Le jeu qui les sollicite est celui
de la *composition:* mise en place des éléments connus, élaboration d'un
ensemble verbal définitif" (p. 64).

table "sujet," c'est elle qui met en valeur le terme élu par la tradition, le situe dans la phrase, dans la strophe, comme elle situe la phrase mélodique dans le contexte musical.[7]

We certainly recognize in these various statements an implicit tone of apology. Vinaver especially pleads for recognition of the canso in the south and the *chanson courtoise* in the north as poetry worthy of comparison with the best if only it is properly understood. The net result of both kinds of argument—the formalist and the musical—however, is to admit that the love lyric of *langue d'oc* and *langue d'oïl* was a poetry devoid of significant meaning, at least as conveyed by the words. In vain Vinaver asserts that it is "de la succession, de l'ordre et du rapport d'éléments sonores organisés en texte chanté que jaillit enfin un accent qui émeut: l'aveu, non d'un événement, mais d'une pensée poétique, non d'un amour vécu, mais d'un amour lui-même émané d'un état d'âme."[8]

Such a poetic vision, even as Vinaver describes it, involves emotion *and* idea; it is a poetically meaningful statement achieved in the only way possible—by utilizing words as signs as well as sounds. And yet, it is precisely on the devaluation of the individual word as sign that Vinaver, Guiette, and others would base their defense of medieval lyric! Such a devaluation of *parole,* in the Saussurian sense, may be understandable as a means of dealing with the complex problem of convention, but it is unnecessary. There is no reason why we should not be able to recognize the importance of the individual word without running the risk of minimizing the role of formal convention or without compromis-

7. Vinaver, p. 13. The formalists are not the only ones to have subjected the canso to a one-sided scrutiny. Musicologists and their supporters have long claimed that the artistic value of the canso lay not in its poetry properly speaking, but in the melody. In the words of Jean Frappier: "Dans la poésie des troubadours et des trouvères, la mélodie suggérait et le vers expliquaient [sic], un peu prosaïquement parfois, discrètement aussi. C'est que la musique est impérieuse et *ne s'accommode vraiment que d'une poésie peu chargée de pensée ou de sentiment;* elle tend à s'assurer la meilleure part. C'est elle surtout, on peut le croire, qui traduisait l'émotion intime du troubadour ou de trouvère, le plus pur de son inspiration et l'ineffable" (p. 4; italics mine).

8. Vinaver, p. 13.

ing the importance of melody. To do so, however, one must renounce any attempt to formulate a general theory of medieval
literature from the lyric. We must cease to apologize for the canso
and begin to look at it at least initially as a poetic form with its
own aesthetic tradition.

So far, we have spoken of the canso as though it were a fixed
form with minor internal variations, somewhat on the nature of
the sonnet, the sestina, the villanelle, the rondeau, and so on. One
of the striking features of the canso, and one which must be taken
into account in any phenomenology of the genre, is its formal
diversity. Rhyme scheme, stanza linking, verse length, stanza
length, number of rhymes per stanza, kinds of rhyme (isolated,
feminine, masculine, grammatical, internal, fixed-word rhymes,
shifting-word rhymes, unrhymed refrain words), and the number
of stanzas all are subject to variation within broad limits. No fixed
form for the canso existed nor—and in this the formalists are quite
correct—was one considered desirable. By the same token, formal
simplicity was eschewed.[9]

Varied as these formal resources may be, even a cursory analysis
reveals their common function, the construction and elaboration
of the individual stanza. In any stanzaic form of poetry, the individual stanza will have a certain importance as a unit of construction. In most cases, however, the individual stanza is clearly subordinate to the whole. With the other stanzas, it constitutes a
definite pattern whose meaning and purpose become apparent
only as the whole poem is experienced. This is not so of the canso.
Taking into account only the formal elements of a *cobla*, one finds
it to have an amazing autonomy.

Consider, for example, the first stanza of Raimbaut d'Aurenga's
"Cars, douz e fenhz del bederesc" (Pattison I).

9. Walter T. Pattison observes that the simplest form of the canso would
be a poem "in *coblas singulars* (individually rhymed stanzas) with a small
number of verses and all lines of the same length. Since it would have only
one or two easy rhymes, there would be no question of complicated stanza
pattern or exceptional categories of rhyme. *No existing poem meets every
one of these requirements*" (*The Life and Works of the Troubadour
Raimbaut d'Orange* [Minneapolis, 1952], p. 48; italics mine).

Cars, douz e fenhz del bederesc
M'es sos bas chanz, per cui m'aerc;
C'ab joi s'espan viu e noire
El tems que.lh grill pres del siure
Chantan el mur jos lo caire;
Que.s compassa e s'escaira
Sa vos, qu'a plus leu de siura
E ja uns non s'i aderga
Mas grils e la bedersca.

[Precious, sweet, imagined and thus exhalting is the wren's soft song to me; it feeds on joy, grows and spreads through the evening when crickets, near the cork-oaks, sing in the wall, under the stone; true and finished (literally: a builder's metaphor using verbal forms of the compass and square) their voices, lighter than cork, and none ought to exhalt himself so high, but the cricket and the (female) wren.]

Composed of nine octosyllabic lines, the stanza has nine different rhymes, eight of which are related. The relationship of these eight rhymes provides the structural unity that makes the stanza a poem in microcosm. The rhyme scheme progresses to the center of the stanza, introducing new rhymes through line five. Line six introduces a grammatical rhyme that plays on line five, line seven plays on line four, line eight on line two ("noire," line 3, is the isolated rhyme of the stanza), and finally, "bederesca," line nine, echoes the masculine "bederesc" of line one. The near-perfect chiasmus of the rhyme scheme (abcde, $\epsilon\delta\beta a$), based as it is upon grammatical rhyme, ensures a corresponding order in the content of the cobla. Thus the stanza begins by evoking the quality and emotion of the wren's song, passes to that of the cricket, then completes the circle by joining the two in a kind of musical epiphany in the final line. Clearly this stanza is a closed world: subsequent stanzas will be joined to the first by juxtaposition rather than logical development.

There is no question but that the self-sufficiency of the above stanza is facilitated by the use of *coblas unissonans,* thereby allowing each cobla to have its own set of rhymes. Nevertheless, if we take a canso with a more intricate stanzaic pattern, the image of the self-sufficient stanza changes very little. In Bernart de Ventadorn's "Lo tems vai e ven e vire," [10] we find *coblas doblas* in which the stanzas are linked in pairs by the repetition of the same rhymes in the same place in each pair of stanzas. In effect, the poem is made up of four pairs of stanzas, each pair representing, at least formally, the self-contained unit represented by the individual stanza in the first example. Taking a still more intricate pattern, that of the *coblas redondas,* we find that the stanzas do reveal some formal interaction in as much as the final rhyme of a stanza becomes the initial rhyme of the following stanza. Once again, however, the relationship is limited to contiguous stanzas.[11]

If confirmation be needed as to the overriding formal importance of the cobla in the construction of the canso, we need only turn to the *chanson courtoise,* a genre directly inspired by the canso. The work of Dragonetti, Maillard, Poirion, and Reaney, among others, has demonstrated conclusively that the stanza is the heart of the *chanson.* Dragonetti points out that, as early as Dante's *De vulgari eloquentia,* the stanza, called by Dante "*stantia*" (house, chamber), was recognized as concentrating in itself all the creative elements of the song: "Puisque la chanson est définie par l'ensemble de ses strophes, c'est que la strophe forme véritablement l'âme; Dante l'appelle *stantia,* une 'chambre,' parce qu'en effet elle est l'endroit *où tout l'art se concentre.*" [12]

By itself, the formal evidence regarding the importance of the stanza is hardly sufficient to reveal the focal point of the poetic

10. Appel/Nichols 30. References to Bernart's poems are to the order and numbering established by Appel in his edition (*Bernart von Ventadorn, Seine Lieder,* Halle a S., Niemeyer Verlag, 1915) and retained by my collaborators and myself in ours (n. 5).

11. In Bernart de Ventadorn's "Tant ai mo cor ple de joya (Appel/Nichols 44), the initial effect is that of an endless chain. In fact, the chain is deliberately broken by the omission in each stanza of the key rhyme from the preceding stanza. In its place, a new rhyme is introduced which will figure as the key rhyme in the following stanza, only to be abandoned in its turn. In effect, one cannot even speak of "stanza pairs," but once again, of self-contained units, each different from the preceding and the following.

12. Dante, *De Vulgari Eloquentia,* ed. Marigo, II, IX, 2; La "stantia" est la cobla provençale. Dragonetti, p. 382.

experience in a canso. Nevertheless, such evidence at least provides us with a starting point. While formal elements are hardly the whole show, they are certainly a part of the poetic experience. If we now examine the emotions and ideas of some representative cansos and find that they too may best be apprehended in terms of individual stanzas or stanza sequences, we shall then have a real basis for critical understanding and evaluation. Specifically, we shall need to distinguish different kinds of poetic experience and differing degrees of success in stating the experience.

For the purposes of demonstration, let us take three poets, relatively close chronologically, but stylistically diverse—Bernart de Ventadorn (ca. 1150–80), Raimbaut d'Aurenga (ca. 1161–73), and Arnaut Daniel (ca. 1180 1210). I would suggest that we can find in their work three distinct kinds of experience and that these three kinds of experience represent by and large the major varieties of canso expression from Guillaume IX to the coming of the *dolce stil nuovo*.[13]

The first variety might well be called that of direct involvement with the poet's emotional experience, an emotional experience which takes its meaning from its closeness to life or nature. Bernart de Ventadorn has often been praised for the "sincerity" of his poems. If we examine the five or so that stand out as really first-rate from the forty-odd preserved, we find that in each case they are those in which we actually "feel" the poem's meaning as well as "understand" it. Or we might say that we *sense* its meaning in the first instance, only later realizing the extent of its intellectual implications. In every instance, the intellectual resonances proceed from the emotional experience. In undertaking such a poem, the poet seeks to portray the experience of love in terms of its intenser emotions. It is definition by direct involvement—at least that is the fiction. The poem will fail if the poet cannot make us believe the emotional experience is the shaping principle of the speaker's existence as represented by the poem.

13. It should be borne in mind that the poems discussed will be representative of particular varieties of poetic experience; I do not mean to suggest that all of a poet's work approximates the same experience. The value of the critical categories developed here depends on their appropriateness for the entire corpus of the Provençal love lyric.

Taking three of Bernart's songs which deal, at least initially,
with the same conceit, the conceit of winter welcomed as though it
were summer or winter transformed by love, we find that canso 25,
"lancan vei la folha," stands out from canso 26, "lancan vei parmi
la landa," and canso 37, "can la frej'aura venta," precisely because
Bernart succeeds in making of the love experience ostensibly
portrayed a means to understand the speaker and his existence.
Here is the first stanza:

> Lancan vei la folha
> jos dels arbres chazer,
>   cui que pes ni dolha,
> a me deu bo saber.
>   No crezatz qu'eu volha
> flor ni folha vezer,
>   car vas me s'orgolha
> so qu'eu plus volh aver.
>   Cor ai que m'en tolha
> mas no.n ai ges poder,
>   c'ades cuit m'acolha
> on plus m'en dezesper.   (ll. 1–12, Appel's ed.)

[Whomever else it may pain or grieve, it should please me to
see the leaves fall from the trees. Do not believe that I am interested in seeing flowers or leaves: the one I want most to
have is haughty to me. I have a mind to leave her, but can't
muster the strength because even in despair, I continue to
believe that she will accept me.]

The stanza postulates a psychological opposition between autumn and summer. Whereas spring is anticipatory, autumn is
melancholy and nostalgic.[14] One thinks of the nostalgia of the old
for youth; the dying, about to be plunged into the "froides ténè-
bres," for life; or the poor for summer, when life was easier than it

14. As Baudelaire so perfectly expressed in his "Chant d'Automne,"
> Bientôt nous plongerons dans les froides ténèbres;
> Adieu, vive clarté de nos étés trops courts!
> J'entends déjà tomber avec des chocs funèbres
> Le bois retentissant sur le pavé des cours.

will be during the "morte saison/ que les loups se vivent de vent."

In all cases, there is regret for the benevolent relationship with nature that winter will soon destroy. Man laments because he is out of phase with nature and will suffer for it. He would be delighted "flor e folha vezer" because the coming spring implied in such a sight would herald a reestablishment of the benevolent relationship. Even as man laments the coming of autumn, then, there is at least the distant comfort of a specific, endurable term to the suffering. Provided he survives the winter, he may look forward to spring and summer; the rapport between man and nature, if harsh, at least follows certain fixed laws.

Against this background of primordial simplicity exists another relationship, equally primordial, but much less simple. It is the relationship of man to woman, the poet to his mistress. The implication in "lancan vei la folha" is that the love relationship, which should be a part of the natural order, is out of phase with it. Worse still, once out of phase with nature, there is no certainty that the resultant suffering will end or that there will be a return to the natural order.

It is not simply that winter is something other to the poet than to "ordinary" people. Bernart insists that the "morte saison" his speaker professes to welcome as an analogue to his own winter of discontent is something infinitely worse for him than for others. For them, winter is only a physical experience, while for the speaker it is a gauge against which to measure the death of his own spirit. Even so, the evocation of physical winter hardly suffices to express the extent of the waste land within himself. When he observes, "No crezatz qu'eu volha/ flor ni folha vezer," we only begin to understand the scope of his despair. Returning spring, the sustaining hope of those who face the physical winter, would only render the speaker's state more painful. Winter is at once the measure of his suffering *and* a consoling disguise. At least in winter, he can *appear* to be in harmony with the natural world (a theme he will elaborate at the end of stanza three), although we know that he is no more in harmony with it than he is with himself.

Only in the last lines of the stanza does the persona bring the image of desolation to its fullest development. There we find the deceptively quiet admission:

> Cor ai que m'en tolha
> mas no.n ai ges poder,
> c'ades cuit m'acolha
> on plus m'en dezesper.

The lover stands bereft of the conventional forms of consolation available to those whose suffering is part of the natural order. The latter have the comfort of knowing that their condition is not of their own making and that consequently there is little to be done but endure. For the speaker, on the contrary, there is the terrible knowledge that his suffering is *self-willed*. He alone bears the responsibility for his condition; he alone could, yet cannot, alter it. He cannot even comfort himself with the thought that the hope which keeps him in this self-imposed thralldom is well-founded. He knows that it is false, a fabrication of his own imagination. The authenticity of the speaker's suffering cannot be questioned when we witness his readiness to admit his responsibility for it.

If we compare this stanza to another using the same conceit, we may see exactly how important the role of authentic experience, as projected in the language of the individual stanza, is in making a meaningful statement of a conventional conceit. The light rhythm and graceful sound of canso 37, "can la frej'aura venta," cannot help but please at first reading.

> Can la frej'aura venta
> deves vostre päis,
> vejaire m'es qu'eu senta
> un ven de paradis
> per amor de la genta
> vas cui eu sui aclis,
> on ai meza m'ententa
> e mo coratg' assis,
> car de totas partis
> per leis, tan m'atalenta   (ll. 1–10)

[When the cold wind blows from your land, I seem to feel a wind from paradise because of love for a gentle lady, toward

whom I am drawn and in whom I have placed my understanding and my feeling. I break with all women on her
account, so greatly does she please me.]

The meaning of the stanza depends on the single conceit of lines
one through four. In stating that the bitter wind transforms itself
into a paradisal zephyr because it blows from the *domna*'s land,
the speaker makes a profound claim about the way his love affects
the physical nature of the universe. He claims to have reached a
transcendent state beyond self-awareness, a state beyond purely
physical relationships to the here and now. To support this claim,
one would expect the speaker to show us, as he did in the earlier
poem, not simply the external physical state, but the inner vision,
the altered perspective induced by the new experience. This seems
to be what he intends at the beginning of the stanza, but we expect
an intensification of the emotional impact of the first conceit, a
sounding of its emotional center. Above all, we await the revelation it presages.

As it happens, we find none of these things. The claims are
made, but the means to realize them are not forthcoming. Unlike
"lancan vei la folha," where the speaker epitomizes his alienation
from the natural order in telling strokes, each evoking a distinct
aspect of the situation, the whole culminating in a profound discovery of self, here we find only the initial claim regarding the
wind's metamorphosis, followed by three poetically inconsequen-
tial statements. We have to do, then, with a conventional conceit,
sufficient to make a pleasing song, but insufficient to make a poem
on the order of "lancan vei la folha." [15]

15. Lest it be thought that the more authentic experience of "lancan vei
la folha" obtains at the expense of formal excellence, let us note that its
stanza pattern is more complex than "can la frej'aura venta." The latter has
a stanza composed of ten six-syllable lines rhymed "a,b,a,b,a,b" down to the
final quatrain where, as so frequently happens in Provençal poetry, the
impending close is signaled by a slight rearrangement in the pattern ("a,b,
b,a"). "Lancan vei la folha," on the other hand, is more ambitious. The
stanza consists of six five-syllable, a rhyme verses, and six six-syllable, b
rhyme verses. The twelve lines thus alternate meter and rhyme. In both
cansos, the a rhymes are feminine, the b rhymes masculine, but "lancan vei
la folha" links the formal couplet division to the sense—each feminine a
rhyme line is a thesis whose antithesis follows in the b rhyme. In this way,
Bernart assures a continued development of meaning throughout the stanza.

How do subsequent stanzas of "lancan vei la folha" bear out the experiences of the first? The second and third dwell upon the larger implications of the themes of will and fate. The speaker admits the mutability of worldly happiness and the essential baseness of false hope, but because he lives in disharmony with himself, he cannot act upon his knowledge. The two stanzas do not vitiate the achievement of the first, but neither do they match it. Only in the fourth stanza do we again find a shaping process at work that acts upon and surpasses the meaning of the first stanza.

As in the first, the focus in stanza four falls, not on the manifestation of the speaker's unhappiness, but upon the effective causes. Again we find that concentration of energies striving to cut through the welter of externals to reach a deeper understanding of the life forces:

> Als no.n sai que dire
> mas mout fatz gran folor
> car am ni dezire
> del mon la belazor.
>   Be deuri'aucire
> qui anc fetz mirador,
>   can be m'o cossire,
> no.n ai guerrer peyor.
>   Ja.l jorn qu'ela.s mire
> ni pens de sa valor,
>   no serai jauzire
> de leis ni de s'amor.   (ll.37–48)

[I can say nothing but this that I act with very great folly in loving and desiring the most beautiful lady in the world. I should certainly kill whoever contrived the mirror. In fact, when I think about it, I have no worse enemy. Surely, on the day when she looks at herself in the mirror and thinks of her worth, I shall enjoy neither her nor her love.]

If the first stanza betrayed painful resignation to an intolerable situation, this betrays nervous apprehension. The speaker fears an event which has not yet taken place, but which has suddenly become fatally imminent. Bernart goes so far as to present the event as a certainty, and it is this that gives us pause. Surely the certainty is misplaced? Not the future, but the past must have been the moment when the *domna* looked into her mirror to discover her beauty. The moment seen by the speaker as drawing inexorably closer should have taken place before the creation of the poem.

This is precisely what could not have happened, for only now is the mirror in question coming into existence. The poem alone, not a mute looking glass, has the power to hold up to the woman the knowledge of her beauty. Indeed, the poem not only asserts her beauty but confirms it by revealing the effects of that fatal attractiveness on the speaker. To modify slightly an assertion of Mikel Dufrenne's, we may say that to declare beauty is not merely to draw attention to a preexisting state, but to create beauty itself by naming it. "To name something discloses a veritable new world." [16] If this be so, then the speaker himself is that "guerrer peyor," that worst enemy who made the mirror; he himself has raised the lady to that state of exaltation where communion with a second person, a lover full of flattering attention and *Angst,* becomes unnecessary. There is thus a triple meaning realized in the stanza: The woman of the poem attains a degree of exaltation where relationship with another is superfluous; the persona recognizes that he alone bears the responsibility for the elevation; and finally, he recognizes—and forces the *domna* to recognize—that a continuation of the relationship on the old footing will be impossible.

The speaker's intuition in this stanza concerns a premise basic to his roles as poet and lover. The anguish permeating the stanza results from his understanding that the vocation of poet must destroy that of lover. In creating the image that will henceforth be the woman, there will be ever less room for possible gratification of the lover's desire. The poetic vocation does not seek to gratify but to objectify. The poetic experience of the stanza is authentic because it is based, not on the frustration of an *affaire de cœur* about which we know very little, but upon a dilemma created and realized within the stanza itself. The persona's anguish is predicated upon a dawning realization that one part of the man will

16. *Language and Philosophy* (Bloomington, 1963), p. 83.

destroy another; it is a destruction of self, planned, willed, and executed by the self.

> No.n ai guerrer peyor.
> no serai jauzire
> de leis ni de s'amor.[17]

[I have no worse enemy (than myself), for I shall never enjoy either her or her love.]

Emotionally and meaningfully, "lancan vei la folha" reaches a conclusion at the close of stanza four. The movement from the first to the fourth stanzas could not again be matched within the canso. Indeed, we saw that even among the first four stanzas only the first and fourth exhibited the direct involvement with life that is the hallmark of this first variety of canso expression at its best. We shall have to postpone discussing the implications of this observation until the evidence from Raimbaut d'Aurenga and Arnaut Daniel has been assessed. We might simply note at this

17. The genius of Bernart's achievement in this stanza may be more appreciated when we recall that the mirror conceit which became a standard image in medieval narrative and lyric poetry was quite different from that used here. Canso 43, the famous "Can vei la lauzeta mover," uses the "standard" form of the mirror conceit:

> Anc non agui de me poder
> ni no fui meus de l'or' en sai
> que.m laiset en sos olhs vezer
> en un miralh que mout me plai.
> miralhs, pus me mirei en te,
> m'an mort li sospir de preon,
> c'aissi.m.perdei com perdet se
> lo bels Narcisus en la fon.   (ll. 17-24)

[Never have I had control of myself, or could even call my soul my own, since the hour when she let me gaze into her eyes: into that mirror which so pleases me. Mirror, since I mirrored myself in you, deep sighs have been killing me. I have lost myself just as the handsome Narcissus lost himself in the fountain.]

Based upon the Narcissus analogy, the image does not force either the speaker or the woman to see themselves reflected in the poem. We have simply to do with a conventional symbol of submission. The woman's eyes as mirror symbolize the submissive optic of the lover rather than the creative perspective of the poet.

time that the manuscript tradition confirms the apparent decline in quality of stanzas subsequent to the fourth.[18]

Turning to Raimbaut d'Aurenga, we find quite a different kind of poetic experience in his canso "Ara.m so del tot conquis" (Pattison XXIX). This canso does not attempt a direct involvement with a speaker's emotional existence in the manner of Bernart's poem. For Raimbaut, the poem is a moment of total immobility, stasis, a sculpture carved from the bedrock of language. Words are used to fix, for all time, a tableau which should be contemplated rather than lived through. Far from being a direct confrontation by the speaker of his own existence, the poem serves to mediate between the two. Raimbaut's speaker has no desire to risk the kind of self-destruction recounted in "lancan vei la folha"; on the contrary, he conceives of the poem as a means of preventing just so disastrous an action.

It would be difficult to claim that formalism and emotional content are incompatible. We can say, however, that highly formalized poetry on the order of "Ara.m so del tot conquis" chooses to emphasize aspects of the love experience other than the emotional conflicts seen in Bernart's poem. This may be explained in part by Guiette's observation that formal poetry tends to make of the poem an object distinct from the poet-lover's emotional existence.[19] Instead of remaining on the periphery of the reader's consciousness, formal elements constitute an important part of this lyrical experience.

18. Eleven of the eighteen manuscripts in which the song has been preserved give stanzas one to four in sequence. Several more would prolong the climax by inserting Appel's stanza five before stanza four. One manuscript hastens the climax by omitting the third stanza, while a final manuscript concludes the song after the fourth stanza. The agreement on the first four or five stanzas breaks down entirely when it comes to ordering the later ones. Stanzas six through eight may be wholly or partly omitted or else presented in a variety of orders. Clearly, even the scribes felt the later stanzas to be lacking in the impact of the first four.

19. "J'imagine que tout en étant imprégné du sentiment général de l'œuvre, ce que son chant met en relief, c'est la structure organique de la mélodie et de chacune de ses parties. . . . Dans ces conditions, la composition du texte n'a pas à s'embarrasser de logique rationnelle ou même sentimentale ou psychologique: l'ordre esthétique prime tout" (Guiette, pp. 64–65).

Composed in the rare and difficult *coblas ternas,* Raimbaut's poem has a complex formal structure indeed. Coblas ternas require the poet to compose a canso of three sets of stanzas, three stanzas to a set. Each set must be distinguished by a rhyme pattern or rhyme words elaborated in each stanza, but completed only with the third.[20] In "Ara.m so del tot conquis," the formal pattern depends upon the shifting of three key rhymes in each sequence. When the pattern has gone full cycle, a new set is begun. In other words, the rhyme scheme of the first stanza is "a,b,a c,d,c,d." The second stanza then leads off with the b rhyme, relegating the a rhyme to the role played by the d rhyme in the preceding stanza: "b,d,b c,a,c,a." The third and final stanza of the sequence honors the d rhyme: "d,a,d c,b,c,b." Stanzas four to six and seven to nine repeat the sequence. In this way, we find three basic sets of stanza rhymes for the whole poem. Stanzas one, four, and seven share the first set; two, five, and eight, the second; and three, six, and nine, the third. One might think that the limitation thus imposed on the rhyme scheme would simplify the poet's task inasmuch as the poem would require fewer types of rhymes. Were the same rhyme words repeated, this might well be the case. As it happens, the limitation of rhymes actually renders the poet's task more difficult, since, with one exception (the a rhyme "ris" in lines 3 and 43) , not a single rhyme word is repeated in the three sequences. In short, Raimbaut had to find fifteen a rhymes, fifteen b rhymes, eighteen c rhymes, and fifteen d rhymes and then distribute them in the rather complicated manner required by the coblas ternas.

It is obvious, therefore, that Raimbaut could hardly have composed his canso without giving a great deal of attention, indeed the lion's share, to the formal composition. If we turn now to the content of the song, we may understand his motives in choosing so rigid a structure.

> Ara.m so del tot conquis
> si que de pauc me sove
> c'oblidat n'ai gaug e ris

20. For Pattison's assessment of the rarity and difficulty of Raimbaut's undertaking in this poem, see his introduction, p. 48.

> e plor e dol e feunia;
>> e no.i faz semblan trop bel,
>> ni crei—tant ai manentia—
>>> que res, mas Dieus, me capdel.   (ll. 1–7)

[I am so utterly overcome that I remember little, for I have forgotten joy and laughter, tears, and grief and sadness. I do not show too fine a countenance, neither do I believe—such riches have I—that any force but God's governs me.]

The stanza pictures the poet in a state of immobility, a state in which life forces are arrested, as the metabolism of the mystic slows during a profound religious experience. Beyond self, the speaker abandons himself to a great, external force.

Reiterating the image of immobilization, stanza two observes further that the exalted state cannot be attained or apprehended by rational thought or other acts of the will:

> Car ges per mon sen no cre
> ni per prec ni per gragel,
> qu'eu poges aver per re
> Ni conquerer tal amia   (ll. 8–11)

[Never through my wit, or prayers or threats do I think that I might have or conquer such a friend . . .]

In stanza three, the immobility is still prominent, but the complete suspension of energies seen in the first stanza gives way to active contemplation of the causes for his good fortune. The sequence concludes with the observation that the state of bliss is a reward for good conduct. Under the circumstances, we may equate good conduct with inaction.

The second sequence, stanzas four to six, raises the fear of betrayal. The greatest threat is not that the *domna* may be betrayed by another, but that the persona himself will give way to his hitherto suppressed emotions and make an indiscreet revelation. In other words, if he emerges from the state of inactivity, he might be forced to reveal the woman's excellence, thereby setting in motion the inexorable forces that destroyed the poet-lover in Bernart's poem.

The third and final sequence returns to the theme of joy through inaction. Raimbaut is talking about purely contemplative joys, since he specifically speaks of the exaltation experienced in hearing *someone else* speak of the *domna:*

> qu'esser cug em paradis
> can de midons, c'aixi.m lia
> que vas autra no.m apel
> auzi parlar ses folia,
> sol c'om de leis me favel.   (ll. 45–49)

[For I am in paradise when I hear someone speak seemingly of my lady—who binds me so closely that I do not address myself to other women—provided he talks *to me* about her.]

But perhaps the ultimate value of such a love comes from the transcendence of self that it fosters. One's own value as a being depends on the value of the higher good:

> c'ans que.l fos aclis
> no sai per que ren valia,
> mas pel be c'ar n'ai, m'es vis.   (ll. 54–56)

[I do not understand how I could have been worth anything before I loved her, but (my worth) is now apparent to me from the good I have from her.]

The meaning could hardly be clearer. Like the lover's, the poet's vocation is a contemplative one. He does not risk betraying the *domna* or himself by indecorous action, poetic or otherwise. Accordingly, the poems of this experience must be precisely controlled in form and content. Like abstract sculpture or geometric design, they may be inspired by nature but are removed from it.

When advising the actors who were to assist him in the famous YWHA premiere of *Under Milk Wood,* Dylan Thomas gave them just one injunction: "Love the words." Arnaut Daniel would have understood Thomas perfectly, for in his poetry we find a third variety of experience, based upon the poet's awareness of the power of individual words to control the texture and color of a poetic image. He recognizes that different or rare forms of substantives and adjectives, for example, "Roines," "Rosiers" for

"Rozers," "messoigna" for "mensonja," "aigonencs" for "aguilencs," "ramencs," and so on, can alter our perspective of the thing named.[21] Equally sensitive is his recognition of the verb as the most immediate means of communicating experience and its consequent prominence in his poetry. As a result of these and other linguistic devices, Arnaut's language reveals an ingenious fusing of metaphor and symbol that gives a gnomic quality to his verse. Love is seen as a means to knowledge of the world, and the love poet as a sage, wise in the ways of man and nature. In effect, Arnaut's metaphoric language creates a bridge between the everyday, natural world and the world of love.

We see just how his predicative metaphors unite the two worlds in a stanza like the following:

> En cest sonet coind' e leri
> fauc motz e capuig e doli,
> que serant verai e cert
> qan n'aurai passat la lima
> q'Amors marves plan' e daura
> mon chantar, que de liei mou
> qui pretz manten e governa.   (ll. 1–7, Toja X)

[To this gracious and gay tune, I shall set the words that I am stripping and trimming; and they will be true and plumb when I finish filing them; for Love now polishes and gilds my song which is inspired by her who protects and controls merit.]

Sublimely indifferent to possible incongruity, Arnaut takes us into a medieval carpenter's shop. He himself is not the master carpenter, but a journeyman in the service of the masterbuilder,

21. Mikel Dufrenne has commented on this phenomenon in *Le Poétique* and in *Language and Philosophy*, but W. H. Auden recounts an anecdote illustrating the same effect when he says of his youthful enthusiasm for geological terms: "I now realize that I had read the technological prose of my favorite books in a peculiar way. A word like *pyrites*, for example, was for me, not simply an indicative sign, it was the Proper Name of a Sacred Being, so that, when I heard an aunt pronounce it *pirrits*, I was shocked. Her pronunciation was more than wrong, it was ugly. Ignorance was impiety" (*The Dyer's Hand* [New York, 1962], p. 34) .

Love. Just as the master carpenter and his workmen were subject to the control of a guild, whose governors ensured the quality (and price) of the work produced by the guild members, so the woman is both the inspiration and the guarantor for the work produced by the laborers in Love's workshop. With the exception of the final allusion to the guild, the metaphoric transference of the stanza depends entirely on the predicative expressions Arnaut takes from the carpenter's vocabulary: *capuig* (*capuzar*), *doli* (*dolar*), *plana* (*planar*), *daura* (*daurar*), *passar la lima*.

Arnaut's borrowings from the vocabulary of the everyday world are by no means uniquely urban in orientation. Popular knowledge from the surrounding countryside figures prominently in his similes and metaphors. When he says, in "Sols sui qui sai lo sobrafan qe.m sortz,"

> que ies Rozers, per aiga qe l'engrois
> non a tal briu c'al cor plus larga dotz
>
> (ll. 26–27, Toja XV)

[for even the Rhone, swelled by its floods, has not so great a force as that greater torrent in my heart]

he knows that the Rhone, even in its normal stage, is the fastest flowing river in Europe. At flood stage, it can carry away the sturdiest of bridges and frequently did during the Middle Ages. As a symbol for rampaging water, with all the horror and fascination man sees in it, the Rhone could hardly have been a more appropriate example.

Leaving the river for the fields, we find Arnaut drawing upon his observation of flowers in "Ans qe.l cim reston de branchas"

> e.m di que flors no.il semble de viola
> qui.s camia leu, sitot nonca s'iverna,
> anz per s'amor sia laurs o genebres.
>
> (ll. 12–14, Toja XVI)

[and (Love) said to me that for her (the domna's) sake, I should not be like the violet, which fades quickly, even before winter comes, but for love of her, I should be like the laurel or the broomplant.]

The import of the simile goes beyond the obvious comparison of the quickly wilted flower, the violet, to the enduring evergreens, the laurel and the broom. Arnaut's figure shows a familiarity with all the phases of the plants in question. The yellow flowers of the broom inspired others besides Arnaut, notably Wordsworth in *To Joanna,* " 'Twas that delightful season when the broom, full-flowered . . . Along the copses runs in veins of gold." The laurel too has a memorable bloom as well as the evergreen leaves so aptly described in Johnson's edition of Gerard's *Herball* (1633) : "The laurel is now got into many of our choice English gardens where it is well respected for the beauty of the leaves and their lasting or continuall greenesse." Both plants are particularly well-suited to symbolize enduring love: brilliant in its first flowering, but equally beautiful and robust once the bloom has passed.

As we might surmise from these examples, Arnaut's metaphoric harmonizing of the worlds of love and life goes far beyond simple ornamentation. Looking briefly at "Lancan son passat li giure," we see how Arnaut uses the technique to make both stanza and meaning. The theme of the song is the knowledge of the human condition to be learned from the treachery and deceit associated with love. The state of love, the lover, the *domna,* and Love himself are discussed in successive stanzas with detachment and humor. Above all, one is struck by the immediacy of the vignettes. This effect obtains in part from Arnaut's mastery of oblique understatement. Sketching with unelaborated phrases, he leaves it to the reader to fill in details and draw conclusions. When he wishes to say that "the greatest men are befuddled by love, although they have drunk nothing intoxicating," we find only the terse:

> totz lo plus soms en va hiure
> ses muiol e ses retomba.
>
> (ll. 17–18, Toja IV)

[Even the most eminent go drunk from it, without goblet or stein.]

In the same stanza, Love is directly addressed as *gignos,* "trickster," and described as "stealing (from the lover) even the hair he wears on his head"

> cui ill, gignos', en cel sembla
> la crin qe.il pend a la coma.   (ll. 19–20)

[for he, trickster, steals from him the scalp which he hangs
from his own mane.]

The seduction responsible for the befuddlement of lines 17–18
becomes in Arnaut's compressed style:

> e plus pres li brui de l'auzil
> on plus gentet s'en desloigna;
> e.l fols cre miells d'una moigna
> car a simple cor e gentil.
>
> (ll. 21–24)

[and nearer still, the murmuring in the ear where the honest
ones take their leave, but the fool believes more faithfully
than a nun, for he has a simple and an honest heart.]

Perhaps the most striking metaphor of the faulty perspective in-
curred by lovers is the two-part one found in the fifth stanza. In
the first part, we find the delightfully ambiguous *adynaton* noted
by Curtius in *European Literature and the Latin Middle Ages:* [22]

> qui Amor sec, per tal.s liure:
> cogul tenga per colomba
>
> (ll. 33–34)

[Whoever follows Love, delivers himself to these fates: he will
mistake the cuckoo for the dove]

Curtius points out that the line is a symbol of the "havoc wrought
in the lover's mind by false love" (he mistakenly attributes the
havoc to the poet's mind), but he might also have observed the
satirical aptness of the birds chosen. The cuckoo, of course, is the
symbol of the cuckold, so that whoever chooses love, according to
Arnaut, chooses cuckoldom instead of the peace (dove) he thinks
to gain.

The second part of the metaphor may betray an autobiographical note:

22. (New York, 1953), p. 97 n.

s'ill o ditz ni ver li sembla,
fassa.il plan del Puoi de Doma,

(ll. 35–36)

[With nothing but words and verses, it will seem to him that he has made a plain from the mountain of Doma.]

Arnaut not only mocks the secret illusion of every writer that he may somehow change the face of the world but asserts that the love poet's delusions are wilder than other writers, since he thinks he can move mountains with his pen.

Reading through the stanzas, one is impressed by the calmness of the poet in the face of so much folly. Neither bitterness nor reforming zeal seem his motivation. Instead, he appears to be recording as deliberately as possible the steps leading to the logical decision of the final stanza:

Ben conosc ses art d'escriure
que es plan o que es comba

. . .

per que ieu loing son seignoril.

(ll. 41–42, 48)

[I am perfectly able to tell a plain from a mountain without the help of poetry . . . wherefore I quit Love's realm.]

The stanzas record the poet's sentimental education—the passage from idealism and illusion to knowledge and experience.

Whereas the self-knowledge of Bernart's speaker revealed the tragic vocation of the poet, Arnaut's stresses the universal role of the poet as educator. Each of his stanzas is formed around one or two lines of pithy observation, proverbial in character and thus imparting a tone of folk wisdom. It is the aptness of this folk wisdom that give his poems their gnomic quality.

What precisely have we learned from the foregoing that may be of value in understanding the Provençal lyric as a whole? Are the three types of lyrical experience described really representative? And even if they are, of what use are the descriptive categories?

There should be little disagreement on the prevalence of the first kind of lyrical experience. Far and away the most common troubadour reaction to love, the poem claiming the speaker's total emotional involvement has such currency that it has been taken on more than one occasion as representing the whole canso tradition. The second type of poem, the poem as object of contemplation, may well require further discussion. Unlike the first, it does not attempt to portray love in terms of its intenser emotions, nor does it maintain the fiction that we are not reading a poem, that we are really witnessing an action where the words are deeds and the statements, accomplished fact. On the contrary, the second type draws attention to the poem as artifact. The claim may be made indirectly, by means of complex formal structures coupled with a content on the order of Raimbaut's poem ("Ara.m so del tot conquis"), or by means of direct statements like Bernart de Ventadorn's "Chantars no pot gaire valer" and "Ab joi mou lo vers e'l comens."

Perhaps the most famous example of the contemplative canso is Jaufre Rudel's "Lancan li jorn son lonc en mai." As the very first of its type, Jaufre's poem does much to explain the existence of a lyrical form that serves not, as one might expect, to bring the *domna* into more intimate contact with the lover-poet, but to preserve the love reverie that intimacy would surely destroy. While the persona of "Lancan li jorn" struggles to possess the *domna,* the poem's structure uncompromisingly insists upon the distance that must separate them by repeating, at the end of the second and fourth lines of each stanza, *amor de lonh, alberc de lonh, lonh, tan m'es lonh, amor de lonh,* and so on. Since the structure is fixed, it is the speaker who must bend himself to the idea of distance as a necessary precondition of the joy and pain of contemplative love:

> car nulhs autres joys tan no.m play
> cum jauzimens d'amor de lonh.
> Mas so qu'ieu vuelh, m'es atahis.

(ll. 45–47)

[for no other joy is as dear to me as rejoicing in my far-off love. But my desire is my pain.] 23

23. A more superficial but nonetheless striking use of form to stress the contemplative role of the poetic vocation may be found in Raimbaut de

What I have called the gnomic poem, a form in which the speaker demonstrates the self-knowledge gained from the love experience and then turns to larger concerns of life, naturally has a relatively rare incidence in the lyric tradition. Nevertheless, there is no reason to assume from its relative rarity that the type is an anomaly in the medieval love lyric. On the contrary, as the antithesis of the ecstatic lyric, its presence in the tradition is as natural as its absence would be inexplicable. By nature an analytic kind of poem serving to reduce the significance of love as a way of life, the gnomic canso is a poem of reaction, even renunciation. Like the others, it is a true, if less frequently celebrated, aspect of the ever-changing experience of love.

Although Arnaut's "Lancan son passat li giure" was noticcably free from emotion, either joy or sorrow, many of the gnomic poems are colored by overtones of nostalgia or regret. For this reason, it might well be profitable to broaden the definition to include certain of the *planh,* especially those like Cercamon's "Lo plaing comenz iradamen," where the speaker's experience with a changing world is the subject of the poem. On the whole, though, the effectiveness of the gnomic canso depends upon its dispassionate, almost detached analytical movement. A *planh* on the order of Bertran de Born's lament on the death of Richard the Lionheart, "Si tuit li dol e.lh plor e.lh marrimen," could hardly be termed "dispassionate"; if ever a troubadour strove to prove his speaker's total emotional involvement with the subject of his canso it was Bertran in this lament. Such poems would more accurately be considered under the first category.

The range of the gnomic poem might better be illustrated by returning to its origin in William IX's "Pos de chantar m'es pres talantz." Here we find the first instance in the troubadour lyric of

---

Vaqueiras' polyglot lyric, "Eras quan vey verdeyar." Just as Raimbaut d'Aurenga fixes his happy accord with the *domna* in "Ara.m so del tot conquis," so Raimbaut de Vaqueiras wishes to show the unnatural disaccord worked by his *domma's* fickleness, the better to contemplate his despair. Music, words, language are set awry as each successive stanza utilizes a different language: "Per qu'ieu fauc dezacordar/Los motz, e.ls sos e.ls lenguatges" (ll. 7–8). Another manifestation of the inversion of natural order, the song treats the topic contemplatively rather than in the manner of Bernart's "lancan vei la folha."

a disabused lover's sobering assessment of the real state of human affairs. The assessment clearly depends upon the persona's intimate experience with the limited, selfish vision of young love, and yet the memory is not bitter, but realistic. From William IX to Arnaut Daniel, the gnomic poem plays its part whenever a troubadour seems moved to expand his vision.

In his course on lyric poetry of the twelfth and thirteenth centuries given at the Sorbonne, Jean Frappier felt obliged to renounce a comprehensive view of the canso because "elle serait condmanée à n'être guère qu'une simple nomenclature." [24] Frappier's embarrassment has been shared by many who have thought only in terms of extrinsic or partial classifications. But this need not be so. Intrinsic classifications such as those proposed here provide a unified view of the tradition as a whole while enabling us to study individual poems in a meaningful context. On the one hand, the categories allow us to see that the canso, as a poetic tradition, possessed abundant creative resources to explore the whole range of love experience. They permit us to say with certainty that these resources were present from the beginning and continued to be imaginatively exploited. On the other hand, our understanding of the resources of the tradition as a whole allows us to appreciate more fully and evaluate more surely the individual canso. Each view complements and controls the other; neither may be complete in itself. Finally, it may be of some comfort to know that the kind of synthesis here suggested approximates the creative process of the troubadours themselves, who, without sacrificing their own individuality, were supremely aware of the work of their predecessors and contemporaries.

24. Frappier, p. 103.

Eléonore M. Zimmermann

"Vision" in Poetry

The oldest meaning of "vision," according to the *Oxford Universal Dictionary,* is "something which is apparently seen otherwise than by ordinary sight, especially an appearance of a prophetical or mystical character, or having the nature of revelation." "Vision" can also be a mental concept of a distinct and vivid kind, and finally "A thing actually seen, an object of sight." Thus we find that the term "vision" can be applied both to the function of seeing and the thing seen, and that the latter can be either "real" or "imaginary."

When speaking of the "vision" in a poem (or of a poet's "vision," since the term, according to the definitions just quoted, can be used in either sense), I shall take advantage of these ambiguities. But "vision" shall mean first of all that which can be "visualized," which has the elements, if not the composition, of "a thing actually seen" or which *could be* "actually seen." Of course what we may perceive in a poem has its origin in the poet's mind, and in that sense "vision," however concrete its components, is also a "mental concept." Moreover, from a psychological point of view, each "picture" drawn by the poet obviously has its origin partly in what he has actually seen—due to external circumstances and determined by his talent for observation—and partly in his will, or refusal, to see or to show. But when placing ourselves in a literary perspective, we cannot and should not base our reaction to a poem on speculations about the poet's mind and the "reality" which surrounded him. In order to speak of his "vision," therefore, I am taking as a starting point that which the poet has created for us to see, which emerged from the fusion of these external and personal elements.

In lyrical poetry—and this is the only kind of poetry which I shall be considering here—the poet's vision can be found both in

straight descriptive passages and in metaphors; I shall not separate
the two in my discussion.

Twentieth-century criticism has been deeply involved in the
study of the meaning of poetry, or perhaps we should say of the
intellectual dimension of poems. Much critical effort has been
spent on the definition and classification of various types of
metaphors, on attempts to discover the secret of their poetic validity. Another major area of poetic studies has been sound patterns,
which have been analyzed recently with the help of statistics and
at times with computers. This has led to much more sweeping
conclusions than were possible previously.[1]

I do not want to deny the validity of either of these approaches
or to question their importance. Lyrical poetry has its origin in
song and will touch us by the magical echo which certain sounds
allied with certain representations awaken in us. We also owe a
great debt to the critics who have revived the interest in metaphors. They have shown the reader how to penetrate the surface of
a poem and explore multiple layers of meaning. Yet, possibly as a
result, many readers now tend to leave the poem's surface too
quickly. When a modern critic announces he will discuss the
"images" of a poem, one finds that ninety percent of the time he is
not referring to the picture which might be conjured up in a
reader's mind, but to the poet's use of metaphorical speech.[2] Thus,
stress upon one level of meaning has led to the neglect of another.
An exclusive involvement with metaphors can present all the
dangers of rushing to a translation: one might say that the word is
transformed too quickly into a sign of something else, is *replaced*
by one of its meanings.

Yet, as in a foreign language, the immediate and apparent level
is not always easily accessible to those who have not learned to look

1. Thus Guy Michaud has found what he believes are the constant and
secret set of correspondences between sounds and emotions in some poets'
work (*Connaissance de la littérature, L'œuvre et ses techniques* [Paris, Nizet,
1957]).

2. Hermann Pongs (*Das Bild in der Dichtung* [2 vols. Marburg, 1927–
39]) discusses image almost exclusively as metaphor in his two volumes. For a
more recent and better known example, see John Ciardi, "The Image and
the Poem," *How Does a Poem Mean?* (Boston, Houghton Mifflin, 1960), pp.
900 ff.

at it. I want to suggest that we must train ourselves again to stop at what should be most obvious, to swim on the surface as well as dive below it. In considering the surface elements of a poem, I have chosen to discuss vision, because visual images are more frequent than any other in poetry. One could examine allusions to sounds, smells, and tactile impressions in a similar way.

Vision as a critical approach will of course be more enlightening with some poets than with others (although it is in fact less limited than one might think at first). However, a critical tool is not invalidated because it is not universally applicable.

It has been said that an attempt to imagine each visual image the poet proposes may destroy the poem, that certain metaphors are so worn that they have lost their sensuous content.[3] That is certainly true in many cases and only serves to emphasize that vision must, as all critical tools, be used with discrimination. A good example of an empty metaphor would be the comparison of a rose to a girl, the most worn courtly cliché from the Middle Ages to the late seventeenth century. When an anonymous English poet of that time writes, "The rose and lilies in your cheek/Flourish, and no more ripeness seek," the images are best left as words alone, or a strange surrealistic picture will emerge in the reader's mind. However, when we read

> Comme on voit sur la branche, au mois de mai, la rose
> En sa belle jeunesse, en sa première fleur

if we do not make an effort to "see" the first line, the whole poem is the poorer for it. The second line could encourage us to feel that the poem is abstract, that the rose has lost its flower nature and simply stands for "youth." Perhaps the first line will attract our attention only because of its harmony, yet it also discloses one aspect of Ronsard's vision. By the simple words "sur la branche," the rose gains concreteness: it returns to its context in nature. It is

3. This argument has been brought forth mostly in the discussion of the theory of "pure visibility," to which I am not referring here. Cf. René Wellek and Austin Warren, "The Nature of Literature," in *Theory of Literature* (New York, Harcourt, Brace & Co., 1962); and B. Croce, "La Teoria dell'arte come pura visibilità," in *Nuovi Saggi di Estetica* (Bari, Laterza, 1926).

also placed, and that placing is meaningful: as the rose detaches itself from its natural background, so the word "rose" is set apart in the line, so Marie, in her short life, attracted everyone's attention amid lesser beauties. The abstractness of the second line, then, becomes a transition which brings out the *tertium comparationis* and, by softening the impact of the image, allows it to blend with the evocation of the young girl.

Sur la Mort de Marie

Comme on voit sur la branche, au mois de mai, la rose
En sa belle jeunesse, en sa première fleur,
Rendre le ciel jaloux de sa vive couleur,
Quand l'Aube de ses pleurs au point du jour l'arrose;

La Grâce dans sa feuille et l'Amour se repose,
Embaumant les jardins et les arbres d'odeur;
Mais, battue ou de pluie ou d'excessive ardeur,
Languissante elle meurt, feuille à feuille déclose.

Ainsi, en ta première et jeune nouveauté
Quand la terre et le ciel honoraient ta beauté,
La Parque t'a tuée, et cendre tu reposes.

Pour obsèques reçois mes larmes et mes pleurs;
Ce vase plein de lait, ce panier plein de fleurs,
Afin que vif ou mort ton corps ne soit que roses.

The eighth line of the sonnet is as remarkable for its harmony as the first. Its charm is further enhanced by our awareness of its concrete meaning:

Languissante elle meurt, feuille à feuille déclose.

No other flower dies in this beautiful way: most of them become colorless, shrivel, or curl up. The rose alone loses its leaves one after the other. Once more, we are made aware of the uniqueness of Marie in life and death. The image goes much beyond the "languissante," and this adjective, applied to the rose instead of the young girl, is wonderfully fresh while serving as a link between the two since it maintains its "human" quality.

The general movement of the poem shows that Ronsard meant us to "see" the rose here. He wants to dwell on grace and beauty, not on the horrors of death, and hides the feeble "meurt" in the middle of the line to replace it by a lovely image, the climax of the two quatrains. Thus a poet has, by his appeal to our visual imagination, given life and tension to the most worn metaphor.

It has been repeatedly claimed that nothing could be said about visual images because they were too subjective.[4] Indeed, if the readers were asked to illustrate a poem, each one would probably use different lines and different colors. When they read "my house," some, for lack of further indication, will see it large, and some small, some out of wood, and others out of brick. It may have a flat or a pointed roof, green shutters or a columned portico. But these matters are, finally, irrelevant. All we can conclude from them is that words are not pictures, and that each person has his own associations. We should be allowed to speak of the vision of a poet without being called upon to make a drawing, just as we may speak of the harmony of his verse without being asked to write a corresponding song. Painting and music are different arts. If we borrow their vocabulary at times to speak of poetry, we should be aware that the meaning of the vocabulary changes to adapt itself to a new medium.

We should first focus on the poet's carefully chosen language before we let ourselves be carried away by our own private associations. The opening line of "Sur la Mort de Marie" may, and probably will, conjure up in most readers' minds the vision of a red rose on a dark branch. The fact remains that Ronsard does not mention "red." "Sa vive couleur," in the third line of the sonnet, confirms the impression given by the first line: Intensity and contrast play a large role in Ronsard's vision. However, if we had only this poem by which to reconstruct his vision, we could not say anything about his sense of color.

How, then, can we speak in a reasonably objective way of a poem's vision? Our most immediate reaction often concerns its clarity or lack of clarity. To verify the validity of this impression, and to establish how the poet achieved it, one might first of all re-

4. Cf. I. A. Richards, *Principles of Literary Criticism* (New York, Harcourt, Brace & Co., 1955), pp. 122 ff.

flect on his handling of space: is it vast or narrow, circumscribed or open? Is the placing of objects clearly indicated? How is one object related to another? A second set of criteria with which to consider the vision created in a poem might center around the "object" itself: A sense of clarity can stem from focusing on a few objects or, if many are enumerated, from grouping them logically so that the inner eye does not have to move frantically from one to the other. The relationship of the verse to the description is also important in this connection: if one verse as a unit corresponds to a single descriptive stroke, if there are no enjambments, and if the rhythm stresses the main words, the object will tend to stand out more clearly. Finally one can examine the description as such, determine whether it is general or detailed, and whether the details are salient features or come to be a source of confusion: whether the emphasis lies on forms; on contours, and if so what contours; or on colors, and if so what kinds of colors.

No great poet's vision ever is truly vague. A poet may have other more important frames of reference than vision, or he may be unimaginative about it; but the use of language as a precise tool, which is the condition of his greatness, precludes vagueness in his vision. Such eighteenth-century landscape poets as Ossian and Saint-Lambert, whose modes of vision are vague and confused, are minor or very minor poets. Therefore when in the work of a major poet the first impression of a poem's vision is one of vagueness, it is important to find the exact origin of that impression in order to understand to what extent the poet may have erased precise contours for a special effect: is an unusual visual effect intended; is the outer world replaced by an inner world of emotions; is the object made to melt into its metaphorical meaning?

I have chosen three passages from very different poets in an attempt to illustrate how the criteria just suggested might serve to define the vision of a poem, to help us read on that level, and to lead to certain conclusions about the poet's aesthetics. One passage is from a poet praised for his clarity, two from poets who are often accused of vagueness. Two are presented as straight descriptions; one is expressly metaphorical. It so happens that all three poets lived in the late eighteenth and early nineteenth centuries. The prevailing concern with nature, both in a concrete and an abstract sense, might lead one to assume that description plays an important part in the writing of this time. Indeed, an analysis of vision might be less meaningful for writers of the seventeenth and early eighteenth centuries. But it is not only rewarding in the following decades. We have discussed the vision of Ronsard; one could do the same for many poets of the post-romantic or the modern era. However, in considering three authors who lived roughly at the same period, one is dealing with a general frame of reference— that which is not personal, but inherent to the world they lived in—which is somewhat similar. This makes the juxtaposition of their visions more revealing.

The importance of the eye in Goethe has often been commented upon. Lynkeus, the watchman, the pure eye, pronounces some of the most memorable lines in *Faust II*, the work which Goethe finished only a few months before he died. It is the privilege of one of the two Lynkeuses first to see Helena, pure Beauty, and to be dazzled by her whom only the spirit can see, to intuit her true being by confusing her with the Sun, which is her symbol in the drama. In the last act, it is Lynkeus again who sings a hymn to vision, which turns into a hymn to the harmony of the universe and the joy of living. The function of vision, and therefore its nature, varies a great deal in the course of Goethe's life, concurrently with the shift in his aesthetic conceptions, but the gift of seeing is so basic to his nature that it always manifests itself in some form. "Auf dem See," one of Goethe's best known poems, was written at the end of what critics tend to call Goethe's first period of creativity, his "Storm and Stress."

> Und frische Nahrung, neues Blut
> Saug' ich aus freier Welt;
> Wie ist Natur so hold und gut,
> Die mich am Busen hält!
> Die Welle wieget unsern Kahn
> Im Rudertakt hinauf,
> Und Berge, wolkig himmelan,
> Begegnen unserm Lauf.

Aug', mein Aug', was sinkst du nieder?
Goldne Träume, kommt ihr wieder?
Weg, du Traum, so gold du bist:
Hier auch Lieb' und Leben ist.

Auf der Welle blinken
Tausend schwebende Sterne,
Weiche Nebel trinken
Rings die türmende Ferne;
Morgenwind umflügelt
Die beschattete Bucht,
Und im See bespiegelt
Sich die reifende Frucht.

One could devote pages to the rhythm of this poem as it changes to render admirably the three moments of the mood depicted: a burst of energy, a forced cheerfulness at first, with two alternating meters, as though in hesitation; then melancholy, forcing its way to the surface from the depths to which it was confined; and finally a perfect balance, as a regular rhythm comes to prevail. I shall not attempt to give a complete reading of these lines here and shall limit myself to examining the vision they express.

Vision's function is essential: at the center of the poem we find a reproachful invocation to the eye which is closing itself to the outer world so that the inner world may take over. The eye responds to the call of the will, and the last stanza is full of visual impressions.

In the first stanza the words are abstract, and the rousing rhythm dominates. It would certainly be a mistake to visualize "die mich am Busen hält," which is only there to indicate the maternal side of Nature, completing the suggestion of the first and mainly of the second lines (Goethe had first written 'Ich saug' an meiner Nabelschnur," translating this mother-son relationship into a much clearer picture, so clear that it draws too much of our attention). "Die Welle wieget unsern Kahn," because of its alliterations (the "w" whose meaning is determined by "wieget"), its regular alternations of vowels ("e" under stress in "Welle" and "i" under stress in "wieget" dominate and form the pattern "i e ǝ, i ǝ"), and because of the following line ("im Rudertakt"), car-

ries more rhythmical than visual meaning. Thus only the last two
lines conjure up a picture in our minds. The "Berge" are not described (are the mountains high or low, round or pointed, in a
chain or isolated?), nor are they really situated in space. We can
assume that they are in front of the poet, but this is subordinated
to the feeling of movement in the verb "begegnen."

Thus there has been no description so far, no panorama, no
clear contours, no colors. And yet there is no feeling of visual confusion. The impression of clearness comes from the order of the
lines: here as in the last, more descriptive stanza, two lines are
given to each element in the landscape, and the sequences suggest
that the eye rises from the lake to the surrounding heights. The
mountains, on the other hand, although not described, are qualified by two words which capture our whole attention, and because
they are so specific, so seemingly "realistic," and correspond to the
movement of the eye, they give us the impression that we have
read a description: "wolkig himmelan." [5]

The "sinking" of the eye in the second stanza, after it has followed the outline of the mountains to their cloudy tops, is all the
more dramatic. Goethe is always sparing of color. We see here,
however, why he has avoided it in the first stanza. The "gold"
twice repeated in the middle stanza stands out all the more in contrast. So much so, in fact, that one is unaware of the vagueness of
"Traum" which it qualifies, and that this undescribed dream has
almost more concreteness than the surrounding "real" world.
Again an effect of clarity is achieved without precision, and the
state of mind is perfectly characterized through it: the inner
"vision" of the poet may lack contours, but its presence at that
moment outweighs all the outer eye could see. The strength of this
presence is expressed in the visual metaphor, "gold," which dominates the visual design of the whole poem.

In the last stanza one visual impression follows closely upon
another, and each is conveyed and concluded in two lines. We
accept the stars (or are they reflections of the sun on the water?),
the mist, the shadows in the bay, and the mirrored fruit because
each image is so compelling that in reading it the previous one dis-

5. In his first version, Goethe had written "wolkenangetan," which is less
precise and does not include the movement of the eye we have stressed.

appears. One may have been familiar with the poem for years before questioning the compatibility of these successive pictures and realizing, possibly with some regret, what may be their "realistic" correspondence: although every image is so "present" as to seem static, between the first and the last line of the stanza time has passed, space relationships, never described, have changed. Possibly night has been replaced by day; the numerous, uncertainly blinking reflections in the center of the lake have been replaced by that of the fruit, which can only be seen from the shore; the poet has touched land. We are left with the last image, that of the ripening fruit, which is so immediate in spite of the indeterminate quality of the noun that the intermittently sparkling lights and the remoteness of the mist-hidden mountains have indeed vanished into the background, and maybe even the gold of the dream has finally found its counterweight and lost its force by yielding to the present, to the here and now announced in the last line of the second stanza.

Thus we see that at this moment of Goethe's development the individual images in which his vision expresses itself have an immediate and compelling appeal which discourages questioning, which only puts the mind of the reader into a state similar to that of the poet without ever telling him what that state is. The vision's force, the impression of clarity it gives, does not stem, as one might expect, from placing in space or in time, from detailed or systematic description, from an abundance of color. The objects mentioned are not even seen directly: they are shrouded in mist, reflected in the water. Yet neither the fog nor the mirroring attacks their reality. It is as though the early Goethe already felt what was later to become an important theme of his work, what he was to state most clearly in "Zueignung." There it is Truth which cannot be looked at directly, but only in reflection. At the beginning of the poem the poet, full of courage after a pleasant sleep, ascends a mountain and greets the reborn nature around him. But his sight is soon obscured by clouds. "Wahrheit," when he finally perceives her, is a blinding light, but she changes the clouds around her into a light veil which does not hide but refreshes and hands the poet "der Dichtung Schleier," the veil of poetry. In a similar way, at the beginning of *Faust II*, Faust awakens after a regenerating sleep, rejoices in the newborn nature around him, looks up toward the sun, but is blinded. He can only see it in the spray of the waterfall, a multicolored rainbow. But although absolute truth, absolute beauty, every pure goal of our endeavors may be blinding to mortal eyes, the veil of poetry which allows us to look at it is not a veil of vagueness. It reveals more than it hides.

In "Auf dem See" we can see the artist at work. The impression of clarity he creates is linked to the controlled presentation of one impression after the other, with no hurried accumulation. Each image begins and ends with the individual line. Each has its center, one simple element (star, mist, bay, fruit), rendered unforgettable, unique, not by its descriptive, external correspondence, by some unusual perception which would qualify it, but by Goethe's endless inventiveness with language which leads him to create ever-new words or word combinations. "Weiche Nebel trinken/Rings die türmende Ferne": each of these words is a miracle. Yet Goethe is aware enough of the outside world so that the creation through language does not become a game in itself but adheres to a possible reality. The "rings" reminds us of the vast circle of the lake, the "türmende" transforms the mountains into fortresses, slightly threatening, while the "Ferne" assigns them some place within the panorama and takes away something of their concreteness, as does the suddenly tactile "Nebel" (Goethe had first only written "liebe" instead of "weiche"), which "drinks" them. Thus the everyday gains a remarkable freshness which, in the context of this particular poem, it needs to be able to compete with the inner world of dreams.

It may be unfair to quote Lamartine after Goethe, and it is probably not the wisest thing to do if one wanted to rehabilitate the French romantic poet. "Auf dem See" might bring to one's mind "Le Lac," but the elements which I should like to stress are more clearly recognizable in the first of the *Méditations poétiques,* in "L'Isolement." As in "Auf dem See" the situation of the poet would allow him to see a wide landscape from a distant point of view. The effect achieved is of course entirely different; the visions of the two poets, their ways of expressing themselves, have nothing in common. I quote the first three of the thirteen stanzas:

Souvent sur la montagne, à l'ombre du vieux chêne,
Au coucher du soleil, tristement je m'assieds;
Je promène au hasard mes regards sur la plaine,
Dont le tableau changeant se déroule à mes pieds.

Ici, gronde le fleuve aux vagues écumantes;
Il serpente, et s'enfonce en un lointain obscur;
Là, le lac immobile étend ses eaux dormantes
Où l'étoile du soir se lève dans l'azur.

Au sommet de ces monts couronnés de bois sombres,
Le crépuscule encor jette un dernier rayon;
Et le char vaporeux de la reine des ombres
Monte, et blanchit déjà les bords de l'horizon.

While everyone praises Goethe for the clarity of his vision, Lamartine was first admired, then scoffed at—after many poor imitators had bored a generation of readers—for the vagueness of his. The mood which a poem like "L'Isolement" is intended to create is certainly one of melancholy, a kind of psychological vagueness: "tristement" and "je promène au hasard" point to it, as well as the indefiniteness in time expressed by the opening "Souvent," and the associations of "à l'ombre du vieux chêne" and "au coucher du soleil." Nonetheless, what is most striking in the whole picture is its precision and clarity. In spite of the "char vaporeux de la reine des ombres," Lamartine is far removed from French eighteenth-century idyllic "nature" poetry.

The dominant feature is Lamartine's sense of space. We are presented with a wide, generous panorama. We may not be told whether the mountains are east or west, but that is the only confirmation of "je promène au hasard mes regards." On the whole Lamartine defines with great precision all relationships, following the slow wandering of the eye.

The first two lines place the poet: "La montagne," "au coucher du soleil" supply the perspective, the time and the light; the "vieux chêne" and "je m'assieds" may indicate the mood of the discouraged poet, but they also complete the sketch of his situation in space. Lamartine does not like to float. In "Le Lac" he sits "sur cette pierre," near rocks which hang over the water. The indications are schematic and may serve the function of making us focus on the poet, but they are not at all vague. The use of the definite article with the substantive—as in "la montagne" and "le vieux chêne"—completes the impression of the precise-indefinite: the reader can ask no questions about this mountain, this oak tree which he does not know, since it is treated as though he did. The point of view is entirely the poet's, for whom no other mountain exists just then.

From the mountain he looks down into the plain, first close by ("ici"), then, following the river, further away ("lointain" and "Là"), and then to the sky, at the top of the mountains which have become silhouettes, and still higher.

The panorama does not present us with anything exotic or picturesque, and the vocabulary, in strong contrast to Goethe's, is equally devoid of all originality. Anything outstanding would seem jarring and destroy the mood of indifference that Lamartine wishes to create here. Therefore if his vision is successfully conveyed, it is only because of the way it is structured. Lamartine gives us a systematic if incomplete description according to a rhetorical rhythm which makes us accept it more readily. He uses his lines in a way comparable to that of Goethe: two unrhymed lines complete one image, while almost each individual line could also be taken separately. The overall structure of these three stanzas, however, is dependent on a rhetorical use of pairs of opposites: adverbs, "ici" and "là," or nouns and adjectives, montagne-plaine; écumante, vague-immobile, dormante; sombre-rayon. Thus here again Lamartine avoids anything unexpected, disturbing. His lack of color works in the same direction.

Lamartine does not—like Verlaine, for instance, the other great French poet mistakenly celebrated for his "vagueness"—destroy the picture he traces so convincingly by a choice of adjectives and verbs which dissolve the nouns. The outline remains clear. Only in the later stanzas of the poem, as the attention shifts to the dominant emotional theme, does it get more and more sketchy, as a seemingly indiscriminate accumulation of nouns fills the ever-growing space:

6

De colline en colline en vain portant ma vue,
Du sud à l'aquilon, de l'aurore au couchant,
Je parcours tous les points de l'immense étendue,
Et je dis: Nulle part le bonheur ne m'attend.

7

Que me font ces vallons, ces palais, ces chaumières?
Vains objets dont pour moi le charme est envolé;
Fleuves, rochers, forêts, solitudes si chères,
Un seul être vous manque, et tout est dépeuplé.

8

Que le tour du soleil ou commence ou s'achève,
D'un œil indifférent je le suis dans son cours;

The famous key-line of the poem, the last line of the seventh stanza, explains the vision: nature is emotionally empty; it is a skeleton. Its very clearness is not assurance of reality, but sign of death. That which was a solace to Goethe, which he created to combat inner misgivings, paralyzes Lamartine:

5

Mais à ces doux tableaux mon âme indifférente
N'éprouve devant eux ni charme, ni transports,

As in the passage of Wordsworth which I shall discuss below, the clearness of the universe seems to be a threat. The poet's salvation lies in flight and in denying the reality of the visible world of whose limitation he is aware:

10

Mais peut-être au-delà des bornes de sa sphère,
Lieux où le vrai soleil éclaire d'autres cieux,
Si je pouvais laisser ma dépouille à la terre,
Ce que j'ai tant rêvé paraîtrait à mes yeux?

Lamartine does not, like Goethe, flee the indeterminateness of dream. Indeed, that which he seeks lacks contours and name, and it is not to be expressed by vision alone:

12

Que ne puis-je, porté sur le char de l'aurore,
Vague objet de mes voeux, m'élancer jusqu'à toi;

11

Là, je m'enivrerais à la source où j'aspire,
Là, je retrouverais et l'espoir et l'amour,
Et ce bien idéal que toute âme désire,
Et qui n'a pas de nom au terrestre séjour!

Thus we see that *vagueness* is indeed inherent to Lamartine's poetry of that time. However, it does not belong to his vision of the world, but seems rather the negative side of it, born of his flight from a frightening clarity. A careful reading of the early Lamartine makes it possible to come without too much surprise to the later works of the poet: his relationship to the clarity of his perception will change, not his basic vision. It is not a completely different man who writes *Jocelyn* with its multiplicity of precise observations, or *La Chute d'un ange,* with its sweeping yet well-structured panoramic "visions"—with the stress on the mystical meaning of the word—where we often recognize the very elements which dominate in the early poems: large dark trees contrasting with a brilliant moon.

The situation is both similar and different in Wordsworth's poetry, where the flight from outer reality penetrates the vision itself. Wordsworth uses the word "vision" so much that it is difficult to set aside his definitions of it, with all the problems they involve, in order to maintain the one which has been used in these pages. That his power to see changed over the years, that the outside world darkened around him while a world of private meanings took over, is the great theme of his later poetry. But again I shall discuss not what he saw but what he makes us see, and that only at one moment of his aesthetic development.

The passage I have chosen is from the fourth book of *The Prelude.* It is presented as a simile and is, in fact, in more ways than Wordsworth states, a metaphor for the whole poem.

As one who hangs down-bending from the side
Of a slow-moving boat, upon the breast
Of a still water, solacing himself
With such discoveries as his eye can make
Beneath him in the bottom of the deep,
Sees many beauteous sights—weeds, fishes, flowers,
Grots, pebbles, roots of trees, and fancies more,
Yet often is perplexed, and cannot part
The shadow from the substance, rocks and sky,
Mountains and clouds, reflected in the depth
Of the clear flood, from things which there abide
In their true dwelling; now is crossed by gleam
Of his own image, by a sunbeam now,
And wavering motions sent he knows not whence,
Impediments that make his task more sweet;
Such pleasant office have we long pursued
Incumbent o'er the surface of past time
With like success, nor often have appeared
Shapes fairer or less doubtfully discerned
Than these to which the Tale, indulgent Friend!
Would now direct thy notice.

This passage illustrates not only a searching for the past but, as in all of *The Prelude,* a questioning of reality. It is most revealing when we become aware that the reality which is looked for is put out of reach by the poet, since the seeing eye is separated from it through the glass of the water, while a more directly graspable reality—that of rocks and mountains—is perceived only as a hindrance to the perception of the pebbles in the stream. Of course the water is time, and none of us can touch the past. Yet in a wider context we can say that we are witnessing here the way in which the poet dissolves all objects by putting a screen between them and himself—a screen composed of what surrounds him, which will enrich or reduce them (his attitude is ambiguous) —and by finally rejecting them and replacing them by their meaning, a movement in direct contrast to that which we found in Goethe.

Although we are again on a body of water, this passage does not present us with a wide panorama of what surrounds it. The picture seems at first glance to be contained in a carefully defined frame, and the frame is small. In the first lines a person, seen as an external object, is hanging down the side of a boat; at the end he is mentioned again as a reflection, having thus become unreal himself, the object of his sight but, perhaps not unlike Narcissus, also impeding his own perception. From the first his eye is turned "beneath him" and thus the wide sweep of the horizon is excluded. When the sky and the mountains penetrate the picture, they are reduced to its scale. Yet, and this too is characteristic of the whole picture and of Wordsworth's vision in general, the frame does not completely close around the picture. The boat is not static but "slow-moving," and the viewer cannot completely control what he sees or even his own perspective. He is himself carried by the water which through its reflections determines his vision of the universe, by a motion "sent he knows not whence," the motion which other writings of Wordsworth have taught us to recognize as the link of the individual to the cosmic.

Within that frame—clear and indeterminate, narrow and finally dissolved—we have a picture which presents the same characteristics. Wordsworth sees and draws with precision, but in order to transcend the object which he presents quite vividly, he erases its contours; he does this through the structure of the sentence, since we are dealing with words and not with lines on canvas. If we let our visual imagination take precedence, the individual elements of the picture arise clearly, and the succession of events is easy to reconstruct. We look down into the water and see fish, roots, and pebbles, then the outside world, sky and mountains, reflected on the surface of the water, obscure its depths. The sentence thereafter becomes involved, and Wordsworth tries artificially to make the sequence seem obvious by repeating the adverb "now," "now" as a link, when he adds more disturbing reflections to his picture: a sunbeam, the mirror image of the onlooker. Reflections and the deep are then obscured by the rippling water. Goethe and Lamartine, intent on conveying an easily graspable picture, present individual elements, one by one, defined, then juxtaposed. Wordsworth, in contrast, accumulates them first, then merges them within one long sentence.

Thus to our inner eye there appears a series of flashes, clear, but instantly dissolved. "Weeds, fishes, flowers,/Grots, pebbles, roots of trees"—these insights into the deep are not allowed to impose themselves too strongly upon our minds. They form approximately one line out of a fifteen-line sentence, and the two verses in which they are embedded begin before the enumeration and go on beyond. The first of these two verses weakens them in advance by the flat introductory: "many beauteous sights," with its conventional adjective and adverb. They fade completely at the closing of the second verse into the formless shapes which the poet "fancies." Another flash, two lines further down, is treated with a similar technique. "Rocks and sky,/Mountains and clouds" forms and enjambment. Before the visual impression is even mentioned, it is destroyed by its being questioned—through the nature of the question ("Shadow or substance") as much as through its abstractness, which addresses itself to our mind when our vision should be called upon. The end of the second line has the same effect since we are made aware that these strangely illogically presented elements are "reflected," that we therefore only get a secondary vision of them. While Lamartine, to facilitate our re-creation of the picture he sketched in the opening lines of his poem, used our expectations, Wordsworth, after this flash of description, upsets them completely: we are used to thinking of rocks and sky as "reality" and we find, as we read on, if we had not yet understood it, that they are phantoms which actually get in the way of our perception of the "reality" as it is posited in the poem, the reality under the water. Two more lines bring us a last flash, in a more literal sense of the word this time: a "gleam" and "sunbeam," soon drowned in a general motion.

The visual impressions, then, are not born of long patient descriptions, although in the first enumeration at least we become aware of Wordsworth's knowledge of concrete things and a concrete vocabulary, of his possible interest in details which, at other periods of his creation, he has exploited at length, as in "The Old Cumberland Beggar." Here in *The Prelude* objects are out of context and impress themselves upon the mind by the suddenness of their appearance and their disappearance. This abrupt, at times seemingly traumatic quality of Wordsworth's perception of reality is indeed characteristic of much of his poetry: thus the daffodils in

"I wandered lonely as a cloud" are seen "all at once"; the shepherd of Book VIII of *The Prelude* appears among the hills "suddenly," "in size a Giant," "his form hath flashed upon" the boy; and of course, in the famous night boating scene of Book I, the threatening black peak unexpectedly "upreared its head."

I have used the word "flash" to express the suddenness and shortness of the perception and, in its more literal sense, for the perception of light. "Gleam," usually contrasted with a "shadow," is a key word in Wordsworth's visual vocabulary, and again and again we find the momentary perception to be one of light. The most memorable example of this may be in the beautiful skating scene of Book I of *The Prelude*, when the boy leaves his companions "To cut across the reflex of a star/That fled, and, flying still before me, gleamed/Upon the grassy plains." The gleam is here, as is frequently the case elsewhere, seen as a reflection.

This quotation emphasizes another aspect of Wordsworth's vision: it is often linked to motion. At times it is the aggressive motion of the boy, often leaving a telltale streak behind him, as in the skating and the night boating scenes of Book I. Then again it comes to blend with the motion of the universe as in "A slumber did my spirit seal" or in the last lines of the skating scene, or as it seems to do in the passage I have examined in this essay: the passing flashes dissolve before something larger and more mysterious.

Thus we see that in Wordsworth the impression of clearness is destroyed not so much to create a certain mood or to create a symbol—for in a symbol the image and its meaning can coexist; when one focuses on the vision revealed in the passage I quoted, it becomes evident that Wordsworth attacks the object from all sides, isolating it, reducing it, changing its expected significance in an attempt to absorb it into lasting meaning. Perhaps Wordsworth hoped thus to reduce the threatening quality, the shocking, dazzling concreteness of the contingent detail which imposed itself on him with special force, carrying its temporality in its very concreteness.

I have tried to offer here, by theory and illustration, some criteria which could be used for the study of a poet's vision, and to suggest that it may be undertaken with as much objectivity as that afforded by any critical method. I hope to have shown that such a method may be revealing. In a true work of art there is no ornamentation independent of the basic meaning. A great poet has, or tries to create, one coherent inner universe of which his visual imagery is but a part. To this he constantly refers. Each metaphor, each description, is but a fragment of that universe. An awareness of a given poet's vision, while it may increase our enjoyment of the poem's sensuous surface, should also provide us with one means of access to the core of his world. But in order that this may be done fully, a poet's vision should be studied in the wider context of his whole work. I have found, in making such a study elsewhere,[6] that it confirmed the value of vision as a critical tool. Since the structure of the poet's inner world is rarely static, it is most rewarding to go further than I have been able to do in this limited space and, by following closely the *evolution* of his vision, to try and reach a deeper understanding of his general aesthetic development.

6. Cf. Chap. 10, "Le Paysage," *Magies de Verlaine* (Paris, José Corti, 1967). Some time after completing this essay, I came across André Joussain's *Le Pittoresque dans le lyrisme et dans l'épopée, L'esthétique de Victor Hugo* (Paris, Boivin, 1920), who applies a similar point of view to a very interesting study of another poet's evolution.

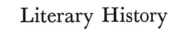

Literary History

Peter Demetz

Balzac and the Zoologists:
A Concept of the Type

Few theoretical statements of the mid-nineteenth century are less
coherent and more seminal than Honoré de Balzac's "Avant-
Propos" (1842) to his *Comédie Humaine;* only Walter Scott's
review (1815) of Jane Austen's *Emma,*[1] which finally divorces the
romance from the novel, may perhaps compete with its final if
momentary joining of two disparate views of narrative prose.
Driven by the modern novelist's hunger for a total re-creation of
the social world, Balzac poses the abiding question of which
method would enable him to cope with the broad drama of society
in an all-inclusive work of art. His answer centers on the concept
of the "personnage typique" or "le type"; and, adding intensity to
a discussion symptomatic of contemporary criticism in France,
Germany, and Russia, he defines and combines concepts that will
continue to confuse his disciples far into the following century.
The trouble is, I believe, that Balzac employs his term in a double
sense, which reflects conflicting strains of thought as well as opposing methods of interpreting character in the novel; and little has
been gained by ignoring ambivalence or asserting, as Georg
Lukács has, that Balzac elaborates only one concept of the type
when he actually treats two. I am not alone[2] in believing that in
his theoretical statement (as well as in his self-interpretation)
Balzac comes close to juxtaposing a traditional, or "romantic,"
concept with a scientific, or "realistic," concept of the type; and
while being aware of the heritage alive in the romantic concept, I
should like to concentrate on sketching briefly the semantic history of the scientific concept of the type, its emergence within a

1. *Quarterly Review, 14* (1815–16), 188–201.
2. Cf. Pierre Laubriet, *L'intelligence de l'art chez Balzac* (Paris, 1961).

397

cluster of related ideas informing Balzac's theory and self-interpretation, and its functional survival in the thought of some of Balzac's disciples who chose to call themselves realists. It is a moot question whether Balzac was a romantic or a realist, but those of his followers who professed to be *réalistes* certainly preferred to fasten their thought to his scientific rather than to his romantic concept of the type.

Of course, the term "type" has a long history of morphological connotations (Aristotle) as well as massive theological referents, few of which are of immediate relevance in my context. With grateful acknowledgment to the pioneering scholarly analyses of Erich Auerbach [3] and René Wellek [4] I suggest that the term (as ubiquitous as "symbol") was first lifted from its organological context into theological speculations concerning past event and future fulfillment by the Church Fathers and later more or less secularized and seized upon both by literary criticism and the biological sciences: the metaphysical aura inherited from theology can still be felt very strongly in the literary speculations of A. W. Schlegel, Charles Nodier (who, according to René Wellek,[5] transmitted the romantic definition of the term to France), and Victor Hugo, who always thrives on terms charged with prophetic meaning. Again, I should like to leave the question of the romantic *embranchement,* suggested by René Wellek and others,[6] in abeyance and turn instead to the semantic developments of the term within a modern scientific context in which the pre-theological, i.e. morphological, connotations were resolutely restored. The new secularization of the term by the scientists implies a return to the Greek sources.

During the second half of the eighteenth century, the French natural sciences increasingly considered "prototype" and "type" as useful terminological instruments in discussing central issues of

3. Cf. "Figura," in *Scenes from the Drama of European Literature* (New York, 1959), pp. 11–76. Also in *Neue Dantestudien* (Istanbul, 1944), pp. 11–71.

4. Cf. "The Concept of Realism in Literary Scholarship," in *Concepts of Criticism* (New Haven, 1963), pp. 222–25.

5. Ibid., p. 243.

6. Ibid., pp. 242–44; Peter Demetz, *Marx, Engels und die Dichter* (Stuttgart, 1959), pp. 178–79.

comparative anatomy and zoology; and if Balzac later employed the terms within an extended scientific framework, he almost inevitably took sides with one group of scientists rather than with another. The scientific term initially had to compete with a fairly wide range of technical equivalents (*dessein, plan, souche, patron*), but its Greek origins particularly recommended it to the educated mind coping with the essential problem of ordering the richness of living forms according to a few structures, if not according to a single all-informing pattern. Yet for almost half a century the natural sciences used the term hesitantly, with or without the prefix; and even the most cursory examination of the semantic development suggests something of important opinions and continuing ideological transformations.

Buffon's *Histoire naturelle, générale et particulière* (first volume, 1749) offers a good view of prevailing mid-eighteenth-century beliefs concerning the totality of organized terrestrial life. Buffon was a philosophical nominalist who cautiously admitted the potential usefulness of supra-individual concepts of order; to him (as to Flaubert) the individual horse or lion was the "real" thing and all "genres, ordres et classes" [7] merely a necessary evil because the scientist had to organize the overabundance of his experience. But Buffon could not close his eyes to "la plus grande merveille" [8] of succession and procreation; each species continued generating its proper form, and even the nominalist had to accept "cette espèce d'une unité toujours subsistante," [9] which in turn suggested "l'idée d'un premier dessein sur lequel tout semble avoir été conçu." [10] It was Goethe who almost eighty years later (1831) approvingly quoted Buffon's famous formulation as "eine ursprüngliche und allgemeine Vorzeichnung, die man sehr weit verfolgen kann." [11] In his own contribution to the fourth volume of the *Histoire naturelle*, Buffon's close collaborator, Louis Daubenton, considerably added to the terminological variety; apart from speaking about the "moule intérieur" (from which

7. G. L. L., Comte de Buffon, *Histoire naturelle* (Paris, 1750–53), *1*, 38.
8. *Œuvres complètes de Buffon* (Paris, 1774–79), *3*, 377.
9. Ibid.
10. G. L. L., Comte de Buffon, *4*, 381.
11. *Goethes Werke* (Hamburg, 1955), *13*, 230.

Shaftesbury's and Goethe's *inner form* may well derive), he hinted
at a "prototype générale"[12] according to which, in the animal
realm, the individual of each kind (*espèce*) had been modeled.
Daubenton's term reappears in Germany in Johann Gottfried
Herder's *Ideen zu einer Philosophie der Geschichte der Menschheit* (1784), occasionally based on a close reading of the *Histoire naturelle;*[13] in an early sketch as well as in the more moderate revised version Herder speaks, with a varying degree of
emphasis, of "eine Hauptform" or "Ein Prototyp,"[14] which seems
to precede the formation of universal existence. Herder does not
in the least hesitate to expand the boundaries of the term; and
while Daubenton merely suggested that specific patterns were
visible in the shaping of differing groups of animals, Herder postu-
lated, at least in his early text, one central and primeval image informing all creation, mineral, vegetable, and animal alike: "wo
die Bildung anfängt, von der Schneeflocke und dem Crystall
(ohne Zweifel noch tiefer) durch alle Gebilde der Pflanzen und
Fische hinauf, scheint ihr immer nur ein- und derselbe Prototyp
vorzuliegen."[15] In the later version, he expresses his visionary
idea more moderately and reasserts something of the variety of
organic life:

> nun ist unläugbar, dass bei aller Verschiedenheit der le-
> bendigen Erdwesen überall eine gewisse Einförmigkeit des
> Baues, und gleichsam Eine Hauptform zu herrschen scheine,
> die in der reichsten Verschiedenheit wechselt. Der ähnliche
> Knochenbau der Landthiere fällt in die Augen . . . selbst
> die vornehmsten Glieder derselben sind nach Einem Prototyp
> gebildet, und gleichsam nur unendlich variiert.[16]

12. G. L. L., Comte de Buffon, *4*, 215. Buffon prefers to use the term
"premier dessein" instead of "prototype générale" (p. 379).

13. Cf. the extremely learned monograph by Hermann Bräuning-Oktavio,
"Vom Zwischenkieferknochen zur Idee des Typus: Goethe als Naturforscher
in den Jahren 1780–1786," in *Nova Acta Leopoldina*, N.F. *18*, No. 126
(Leipzig, J. A. Barth, 1956).

14. E.g. J. G. Herder, *Ideen zu einer Philosophie der Geschichte der
Menschheit* (Leipzig, Riga, 1785), *1*, 101.

15. J. G. Herder, *Ideen zu einer Philosophie der Geschichte der Menschheit*, ed. B. Suphan (Berlin, 1887), *13*, 66.

16. Ibid. (Note a₁.)

These divergencies indicate that differing areas of meaning corresponded to the term "prototype" in the later eighteenth century;
cautious "singularists" like Daubenton (to use Goethe's later
terminology) believed that a limited number of organic forms
emerged from a close view of nature, while more philosophically
inclined "universalists" like Herder (anticipating the doings of
the Hegelian *Weltgeist*) were ready to reduce the overwhelming
richness of being to one fundamental and awe-inspiring form; it
was unavoidable that, within a generation, French scientists and
German *Naturphilosophen* parted ways.

I suspect that the young French zoologist Felix Vic d'Azyr
(1748–94) was among the first to feel some qualms about the
implications of the term "prototype." Vic d'Azyr occasionally
leaned toward the universalist side (his later adversaries even
made him responsible for the deplorable deviations of German
Naturphilosophie),[17] but more often than not he pragmatically
concerned himself with the structural analogies of certain organs
in different groups of animals and suggested that there possibly
persisted an essential and resilient form throughout individual
variation. In his *Mémoire sur les Rapports qui se trouvent entre
les usages et la structure de quatre extrémités dans l'Homme et
dans les Quadrupèdes*,[18] presented to the French Royal Academy
(1774) and highly praised by Condorcet, Vic d'Azyr cautiously
formulated a tentative proposal avoiding assertive generalizations:

> si les parties qui diffèrent le plus en apparence, se res-
> sembloient au fond, ne pourroit-on pas en conclure, avec plus
> de certitude, qu'il n'y a qu'un ensemble, qu'une forme essen-
> tielle, et que l'on reconnoît, par-tout cette fécondité de la
> Nature, qui semble avoir imprimé à tous les êtres deux ca-
> ractères nullement contradictoires, celui de la constance dans
> le type, et de la variété dans les modifications?[19]

17. Georges Cuvier, *Histoire des Sciences Naturelles,* ed. G. Magdeleine de
Saint-Agy (Paris, 1841–45), *4,* 299–300. Volumes 4 and 5 were actually
written by the editor.

18. In *Histoire (et Mémoires) de l'Académie Royale des Sciences* (1774),
pp. 254–70. [Later printed in Vic d'Azyr, *Œuvres* (Paris, 1805), *4,* 315–91.]

19. Ibid., p. 254.

It is in this central passage of Vic d'Azyr's *Mémoire* that the term "type" (rather than "prototype") again acquired its morphological relevance; from then on it successfully counteracted, in France as well as in Germany, the older "prototype" all too heavily charged with ontological meaning concentrated in the prefix.

It is difficult to say whether Goethe's friend Johann Heinrich Merck independently shared Felix Vic d'Azyr's views or (as I believe) [20] closely studied, as many other intellectuals in Germany did, Vic d'Azyr's successive writings; while expertly discussing the organization of whales in the *Hessische Beiträge zur Gelehrsamkeit und Kunst* (1786), Merck looked back upon seventeenth-century anatomical research and, perhaps employing Vic d'Azyr's terminology, remarked: "die vergleichende Anatomie war damals in ihrer Kindheit, also darf man nicht erwarten, dass man nach gewissen Prinzipien die so weit von einander abgehenden Gestalten der Tiere aller Art auf einen gewissen Typus hätte zurückführen sollen." [21] Goethe developed his scientific terminology slowly and probingly. In an early stage of his studies he hinted at a *harmonia naturae* (1784), enthusiastically praised, in his correspondence with Frau von Stein, nature's "wesentliche Form," and only in his "Versuch über die Gestalt der Tiere" (1790) used the term "Typus" (as had Merck in 1786) to denote a general structure informing all organic creation.[22] Goethe retained "Typus" in his later comparative studies of nature and became an astute and critical observer of French terminological developments: he was neither the first to discover the *os intermaxillare* (as German popular criticism still assumes) nor to employ his favorite term, but the author of *Faust II* has other achievements to his credit.

The French zoologist Etienne Geoffroy St.-Hilaire, always praised by Goethe and sometimes by Balzac, opposed the discrete observations of an unphilosophical science and was, from his early years in the Royal Ornithological Cabinet, intent upon grasping and articulating relationships, analogies, correspondences, the to-

20. The supporting evidence has been convincingly presented by Hermann Bräuning-Oktavio, pp. 10–26.

21. Bräuning-Oktavio, p. 125.

22. Cf. Bräuning-Oktavio's exhaustive study, esp. pp. 10–26.

tality of creation. More resolutely than anyone else in his generation he seized upon the universalist suggestions of Buffon, Daubenton, and Vic d'Azyr and arrived at an incisive view of the
structural unity of all animal life which his enemies, above all
Cuvier, readily identified with the poetic dreams of German
Naturphilosophie. In his polemics, Cuvier did not acknowledge
that Geoffrey St.-Hilaire had condemned the "ardeur indiscrète"
of the Germans, disparaged Schelling's "ambition sans calculs et
sans freins," [23] and declared, as if he were a literary realist, that he
preferred to be "l'historien de ce qui est." [24] I think Geoffroy St.-
Hilaire manages to balance a fundamental universalist view of the
organic world with the strong singularist inclinations of the working scientist: he believes in an essential pattern which nature has
followed in creating life, but the great general form has been modified by the pressures of the environment; to the overall pattern
corresponds (because of the continued transformation caused by
time and "world") a number of particular forms determining the
organization of analogous organs or entire groups of animals. I
suspect that Geoffroy St.-Hilaire tries to separate these differing
principles by his terminology. Speaking about the central form of
organic creation he alluded in his earlier writings, e.g. in his
Mémoire sur les rapports naturels des Magnis (1795), to a "plan
unique" [25] but later preferred his favorite term "l'unité de
composition," [26] which articulated his essential tenets to contemporary observers including Balzac, who quoted it in the "Avant-
Propos." [27] Goethe disparaged the term because he thought it had
too many mechanistic implications: "unité du type würde die
Sache schon näher auf den rechten Weg geleitet haben, und dieser
lag so nahe, indem sie [die Franzosen] das Wort type im Kontext
der Rede wohl zu brauchen wissen [1831]." [28] Curiously enough,
Geoffroy St.-Hilaire (as if he had heeded Goethe's criticism) did

23. *Fragment sur la nature* (Paris, 1828), p. 12.
24. *Histoire naturelle des mammifères* (Paris, 1834), p. 8.
25. I quote from the excellent study of Edmond Perrier, *La Philosophie
Zoologique avant Darwin* (Paris, 1884), p. 93.
26. *Philosophie anatomique* (Paris, 1818), *38.*
27. *La Comédie Humaine,* ed. Pléiade (Paris, 1956), *1, 3.*
28. *Goethes Werke, 13,* 247.

occasionally substitute, in his *Histoire naturelle des mammifères* (1834), a new formulation, namely "le type primordial," [29] for the usual "unité de composition," and I am inclined to assume that he reserves the terms "plan unique" or "unité de composition" for the universal form and usually employs "type" to denote particular patterns or specific structures. He may speak of a "type" according to which all birds are shaped [30] or one which characterizes all animals whose marrow has been enclosed by a sheath of bone; [31] occasionally, he even speaks of a "type secondaire" [32] in order to demonstrate that these subordinate forms are not identical with the awe-inspiring "unité de composition." But Geoffroy St.-Hilaire differs from his predecessors by his profound awareness of time as a massive force that alters and modifies forms of life; his view is "historical" even though history, to him, may imply geological ages rather than human centuries. It is time or rather a continuous process of modification which related the universal image (plan unique, unité de composition, or type primordial) to the particular forms (types or types secondaires), and by way of trying to arrive at a basic formula of his terminology I am inclined to suggest that, in his universe, expanding history separates if not alienates the paramount form, or the type primordial, from the particular pattern, or the secondary types. It looks like Platonism tempered by laboratory experience.

These semantic and conceptual developments tend to confirm my belief that Balzac's "Avant-Propos" implies an early and important encounter of the natural sciences and literary theory. In a certain sense "naturalism" begins right there. Balzac rehashed some of Geoffroy St.-Hilaire's ideas and came close to lifting certain formulations from the scientist's writings almost word for word. By employing the term "type" in a zoological context, he inevitably took sides with the universalist tradition defined by

29. *Histoire naturelle des mammifères,* p. 12.

30. *Principes de Philosophie Zoologique* (Paris, 1830), p. 84.

31. *Philosophie anatomique, 15.*

32. Cf. "Considerations sur les pièces de la tête osseuse des animaux vertébrés, et particulièrement sur celles du crâne des oiseaux," *Annales du Musée d'histoire naturelle de Paris, 10* (1807), 360.

Buffon, Daubenton, and Vic d'Azyr and isolated himself—at least in the "Avant-Propos"—from those who followed the classifying rage of Linné and Cuvier; like "le grand Goethe" [33] whom he quoted as his major witness, Balzac—was more interested in a view of totality rather than in a neat catalog. The very choice of terminology betrayed an undercurrent of opposition to Cuvier and his allies, who merely admitted the four forms of *animalia—vertebrata, mollusca, articulata,* and *radiata*—and believed that they were "perpetuées depuis l'origine des choses" [34] and neatly subdivided into classes, orders, and families. In discussing the zoological "type" Balzac deals with a term which Cuvier disparaged as far too philosophical. Cuvier relegated it, in his *Le règne animal distribué d'après son organisation* (1817), to an amusing footnote concerning sketches of orangutans in successive zoological handbooks.[35] To Cuvier, it seems, the term "type" implied the meaning of "first illustration" and thus belonged to printer's language rather than to scientific discourse. Perhaps I should add that a symptomatic point of the literary polemics in the "Avant-Propos," namely the critique of Walter Scott's deficiencies, obliquely relates to Balzac's scientific preferences and his opposition to Cuvier. Of course, Balzac's scientific ideas and literary concepts seem but two different ways of articulating a few fundamental if not obsessive insights. While he praised the richness of Scott's world, Balzac deplored that Scott had found his manner of writing by trial and error rather than by a "système"; unfortunately, Balzac added, Scott "n'avait pas songé à relier ses compositions l'un à l'autre de manière à coordonner une histoire complète." [36] Balzac implies, to my mind, that Scott had created a rich but compartmentalized universe in the mode of Cuvier; he did not, as did Buffon or Geoffroy St.-Hilaire, succeed in creating a totality by linking image to image (this was thus Balzac's task). Scott offered "compositions" rather than an "unité de composition," and it was precisely here that Balzac and his later followers wanted to differ from

33. Balzac, *Comédie Humaine, 1,* 4.

34. Georges Cuvier, *Le règne animal distribué d'après son organisation* (Paris, 1817), *1,* 19, 65–66.

35. Ibid., p. 102.

36. *Comédie Humaine, 1,* 6.

literary tradition: the *Comédie Humaine* was to do Buffon's job for human society, and Zola's *Les Rougon-Macquart,* with its subtitle *(Histoire naturelle et sociale . . .)* equally reminiscent of the sciences, was to describe the total growth as well as the total depravation of at least one paradigmatic family.

Balzac, however, struggled with the question of the types more than ten years before he decided to articulate the problem in partly scientific terms. In the early thirties he still felt more inclined to employ abstract and epigrammatic formulations which, I suspect, he also imposed on his loyal friends. In his letter of October 26, 1834, addressed to Mme. Hanska, Balzac elaborated on the theoretical assumptions which were to govern his developing work. Although he establishes a neat antithesis unrelated to his chaotic practice, his formulation does illuminate the double relevance of his characters: "dans les *Études de Mœurs* sont les *individualités* typisées; dans les *Études Philosophiques* sont les *types* individualisés." [37] Felix Davin's famous introduction to the fourth edition of the *Études Philosophiques* (dated December 6, 1834, but published later) merely confirms Balzac's plans; Davin suggests an identical distinction between the typified individuals in the *Moral Studies* and the individualized types in the *Philosophical Studies* and adds a useful set of examples: the perfume merchant César Birotteau summarizes a large class of similarly successful bourgeois who emerge from the Revolution while Père Grandet, "un avare qui semble être l'avarice tout entière," comes close to being "un personnage allégorique." [38]

In the "Avant-Propos" Balzac's scientific loyalties fully inform his concern with the representative character which he, in the true fashion of his age, considers decisive for the writer's ability to cope with the total "history of the human heart." The masters of the past, above all Walter Scott, who raised the secondary genre of the historical novel to philosophical excellence, created one or two "personnages typiques," but Balzac feels that the new writer has to present at least two or three thousand figures which constitute

37. *Lettres à l'Etrangère,* ed. Calman-Lévy (Paris, 1899), *1,* 205.
38. Charles de Louvenjoul, *Histoire des œuvres de Honoré de Balzac* (Paris, 1886), pp. 194–207.

"la somme des types"[39] of each generation; Karl Ferdinand Gutzkow, Balzac's most intelligent German disciple, modestly echoes his teacher's demands by saying that the reader of his own nine-volume social novel *Die Ritter vom Geiste* (1850) has to cope with at least one hundred major figures in order to become aware of what happens to the millions of people behind them.[40] I think it is difficult to ignore the numerical if not statistical stress. A few significant figures may have been sufficient in the past, but, in an epoch of explosive population pressures in industrial cities, Balzac demands, as if he were a scientist surveying the entire field, that "multitude d'existence"[41] which would summarize the masses of human beings pressing into the once exclusive universe of fiction. Paris, *la ruche,* wants a new concrete universal articulating principles of ruthless addition.

But there are other differences. The typical literary character of the past was intuitively "conceived," while the new writer "composes" his type "par la réunion des traits de plusieurs caractères homogènes";[42] the modern novelist, Balzac implies, follows the methodological example of the natural scientist by closely observing a multitude of individuals, isolating their common traits, separating them from the individual case, and concentrating them in a new model inclusive of all the individuals of the group, or class. More important, Balzac believes that the traditional type, most convincingly emerging from the novels of Scott, often implied "toute une philosophie," or "une face de la vie";[43] and I suspect that it is not impossible to link these suggestions to the traditional type concept of the European romantic tradition. In characterizing Scott's outstanding characters as incarnations of principles of thought, Balzac comes close to Schelling, who defined types (e.g. Faust or Hamlet) as figures of mythical relevance,[44] or to Charles

39. *Comédie Humaine, 1,* 6, 13.

40. "Vorwort zur ersten Auflage," *Die Ritter vom Geiste,* ed. Reinhold Gensel (Berlin, 1912) , *1,* 42.

41. *Comédie Humaine, 1,* 13.

42. Ibid., pp. 6, 7.

43. Ibid., p. 12.

44. On the question, cf. René Wellek, "The Concept of Realism in Literary Scholarship," p. 242.

Nodier, who asserted, a few years before Balzac's "Avant-Propos," that a type presented "le signe représentatif d'une conception, d'une création, d'une idée." [45] Within a romantic context, Balzac anticipates Victor Hugo, who was to say in his semireligious book on Shakespeare (1864) that a type was "un mythe à face humaine," or Hippolyte Taine, who set out to construct an entire hierarchy of types according to the permanence rather than the historicity of human concerns which they represented (Siegfried and Roland are higher types than those of Dutch painting which are *types sains mais encore imparfaits*).[46] I think Balzac was aware of a divergence: traditional types as defined by romantic writers embody myths, ideas, essences, principles, tendencies, forces, and powers and greatly strain the narrow human form in which they are forced to fit. These traditional types symbolize supra-human, overpowering forces of existence, while a scientific type (as suggested by the methodological traditions of zoology and comparative anatomy) summarizes recurrent human characteristics in a model reminiscent of many individual lives. Traditional, or romantic, types incarnate ontological energies of fate and failure; the new, or scientific, type is concerned with the representation of the many by the one.

Yet there is another element at least implied in the concept of the scientific type which may have been highly attractive to Balzac and other writers of the mid-century. Erich Auerbach has shown that an intense awareness of time emerges from the transformations of the French Revolution and the Napoleonic Wars, and he suggested that German philosophy, nourished by Vico's visions, firmly articulated a corresponding theory of historical change. I wonder whether Balzac and his disciples did not feel particularly fascinated by zoological discussions concerning primeval and secondary types, because these scientific concepts offered their own kind of historicism, confirmed in practice by the rapid metamorphosis of the French political and social structure; ever since Buffon's *Histoire naturelle* (1749–89), introduced by a substantial chapter on terrestrial changes and their impact on organic life,

45. *Œuvres de Charles Nodier* (Paris, 1882), 5, 49.

46. Hugo, *Shakespeare* (Paris, 1864), p. 299; Taine, *De l'idéal dans l'art* (Paris, 1867), pp. 121–23.

the question of a progressive transformation as a principle of organic life constantly challenged zoologists and comparative anatomists. In his study, *De l'influence des circonstances extérieurs sur les êtres organisés* (1833), Geoffroy St.-Hilaire deplored that the "outside" world of things which influenced animality had not been studied closely, and he recommended to future generations that they explore the organic formations in their relationship with the environment (*le monde ambiant*) or rather "les circonstances convenables d'espace, de temps, et de lieu." [47] In his "Avant-Propos," Balzac fully accepted Geoffroy St.-Hilaire's "historicist" view of developing animality and, pushing the analogy, transformed it into a historicism of humanity. He repeated the zoologist's key formulation, *il n'y a qu'un animal*,[48] in his own text, and in his first version of the "Avant-Propos" he even added a parallel, *il n'y a qu'un homme*,[49] but later decided to delete this formulation because of its explosive social implications. His theory implies that the original form of man, which is comparable to the first *dessein* of animality, develops in time into different kinds of people to be represented, in fiction, by striking figures or types. The very principle of this concept of the type rests on the zoological assumption that the original *dessein* is "individualized" by a continuing pressure in which the forces of time and *les milieux* combine. One immediately suspects that *les milieux,* which to the scientific mind connote the two spheres of water and air (at least in French zoology of the 1820s and 1830s), assume a far richer and variegated meaning when Balzac changes zoological into sociological relevance and speaks of man "dans les milieux où son action se déploie"; [50] the zoological dual turns into a sociological plural of infinite potentialities. From man-the-model evolves in time a number of secondary forms as varied as the kinds of animals, and since these secondary forms are, by their process of formation, intimately related to history and locality, the literary types which

47. Geoffroy St.-Hilaire, *De l'influence des circonstances extérieurs sur les êtres organisés* (Paris, 1833), pp. 26, 27.

48. *Comédie Humaine, 1,* 4. Balzac quotes from Geoffroy St.-Hilaire, *Fragment sur la nature,* p. 27.

49. Herbert J. Hunt, *Balzac's 'Comédie Humaine'* (London, 1959), p. 275 n.

50. *Comédie Humaine, 1,* 4.

reflect these secondary forms in fiction differ profoundly from the grand if abstract types of narrative tradition. History separates them from one another: traditional types as incarnation of ideas transcend history, while scientific types that reflect human "conditions" of a social kind owe their particular character to shaping time. I do not wish to press the point too far because it is inherent in the structure rather than in a complete definition of Balzac's argument. It was, after all, Hippolyte Taine, and not Balzac, who mercilessly attempted to impose a scientific theory on a Hegelian idea of the world, and while Balzac continued combining his interest in *milieu* with an almost mystical idea of correspondences (the environment expresses man as much as man implies the environment), Taine reformulated Geoffroy St.-Hilaire's trinity of *espace, temps,* and *lieux* (1833) as *race, moment,* and *milieu* (1863) and was hailed by the intellectuals of the sixties who did not recall the pioneering ideas of the zoologists as thinkers of insight and originality.

There is a final distinction involved which emerges from the concrete examples Balzac offers on the first pages of the "Avant-Propos." The traditional types form a distinguished company in which the heroic, the expansive, the sensitive, and the forceful predominate: Daphnis and Chloë, Roland, Amadis, Panurge, Don Quixote, Manon Lescaut, Clarissa, Lovelace, Robinson Crusoe, Gil Blas, Ossian, Julie d'Éstanges, Uncle Tobias, Werther, René, Corinne, Adolphe, Paul and Virginie, Jeanie Dean, Claverhouse, Ivanhoe, Manfred, Mignon.[51] Balzac, however, does not hesitate to contrast these great incarnations of principles (be they heroic or grotesque) with a double asyndeton in which a number of professions and kinds of animals, sociological and zoological types, are linked. There are as many varieties of life in society, Balzac asserts, as among animals (or rather *mammifères*), and he dryly enumerates the figures of "un soldat, un ouvrier, un administrateur, un avocat, un oisif, un savant, un homme d'État, un commerçant, un marin, un poète, un pauvre, un prêtre," which in turn differ as markedly from each other as "le loup, le lion, l'âne, le corbeau, le requin, le veau marin, la brebis, etc." [52] I almost believe that

51. Ibid., p. 4.
52. Ibid.

Balzac secretly suggests a little emblematical joke by pairing the soldier and the wolf, the worker and the lion, or the scholar and the unarticulated *veau marin*. The important point is, however, that Balzac confronts embodiments of ideas with less than heroic "conditions" in the sense in which Diderot once defined different modes of human life as shaped by social and economic functions; and in the contrast of the two kinds of types (Roland vs. the merchant) an older, perhaps more selective view of the world clashes with the new, more inclusive *histoire de mœurs* which discovers all those people to whom literature had not yet granted space in which to exist.

Balzac's friend Félix Davin, as well as Balzac's liberal disciples of the following generation, were aware of the implications of a type concept emerging from close observation of social experience in an age of multitudes and masses. They eagerly interpreted these implications as something new, diverging from literary tradition, and politically relevant; after the revolution of 1848, the political and social implications predominated. I think we should read Félix Davin's "Introduction" [53] to *Études Philosophiques* as an answer to Charles Nodier, who, ignoring Balzac, had asserted in his essays that Walter Scott owed his immense popularity to the richness of his narrative universe as well as to the abundance and the originality *de ses types*.[54] To Balzac, such ideas constituted an intensely personal challenge. If he wanted to compete with Scott (and nothing did he desire more), he had to do it by offering his competing types, and it was Félix Davin's gallant task to demonstrate that he had successfully created types different from or superior to those of Walter Scott.

Anticipating Balzac's later statements in the "Avant-Propos," Davin elevated Balzac above Scott by implying that Balzac's middle-class types had much more relevance to the contemporary reader than Scott's old-fashioned universe of great passions. Davin suggested, as did Balzac, that Scott had happily created "types larges et saillants," of overwhelming powers, and expressive of entire historical epochs; Balzac's achievement, however, was far from being inferior because he had discovered the importance of "les

53. Louvenjoul, *Histoire des œuvres*, pp. 194–207.
54. *Œuvres de Charles Nodier, 5,* 63.

types secondaires" (a term oddly reminiscent of Geoffroy St.-Hilaire[55]) or those more modest and everyday figures representative of a more middling kind of passion (*passion du moyen ordre*) hidden in the recurrent rhythms of contemporary civilization.[56] Indeed, it was Balzac's essential achievement to have looked under the cover of deceptive conformity and to have found, close to the placid familial hearth, interesting and "new" characters of unusual interest. The important point is that Davin relates these two kinds of types—Scott's "primary" and Balzac's "secondary" concept—to degrees of reality. The grand old type of *passions majeures* has lost much of its relevance because it involved bizarre exceptions (evidently far beyond the reader's potential experience), while Balzac's more modest secondary figures had a higher degree of immediate vitality because they involved those *infortunes réelles* which anybody among contemporary readers might suffer.[57] Scott belongs, Davin implies, to an old-fashioned "histoire en toge," which concentrated on the grand and distant; Balzac, however, emerges among the more recent historians, who, while dealing with *détails et . . . petits faits,* explore the more basic fabric of existence and succeed in writing that *histoire de mœurs* which, as Balzac himself confirmed in the "Avant-Propos," encompassed the vicissitudes of all humanity rather than those of a few outstanding and select individuals.[58] "Les héros doivent être des généralités,"[59] Balzac remarked in his *Lettres sur la littérature* (1840) and thus confirmed, in his own way, his friends' gallant apologies of the more "democratic" secondary type.

Félix Davin's apology, which stresses Balzac's discovery of the humble and civil types of daily life, was in a few years contradicted by Hector Castille, who, in his well-known polemical letter of October 4, 1846, firmly excluded Balzac from "l'école réaliste."[60]

55. Geoffroy St.-Hilaire, "Considérations sur les pièces de la tête osseuse des animaux vertébrés," p. 199.

56. Louvenjoul, *Histoire des œuvres,* p. 199.

57. Ibid.

58. Ibid.

59. "Lettres sur la littérature," in *Œuvres Completes,* ed. M. Bouteron and Henri Longnon (Paris, 1940), *40, 271–95.*

60. Louvenjoul, *Histoire des œuvres,* pp. 362–68.

Castille believed that Balzac had discovered reality in detailed pre-
sentations of the human environment, but as far as his characters
were concerned, "adieu le vrai pur." [61] Castille preferred to see
only one group of figures (individualized types like Vautrin) and
ignored the typified individuals (like César Birotteau) ; he complained that Balzac's monstrous characters lacked "une physio-
nomie réaliste" [62] because they were not as general as those of
Lesage and others. By speaking of the general, he clearly referred
to those ordinary and everyday figures which Balzac, just four
years earlier, had "scientifically" concatenated with his catalog of
animal kinds: even Castille's examples (*abbés, voleurs, filous,
comédiens, poètes, grands seigneurs*) [63] were not far removed
from Balzac's typical professions (*soldat, ouvrier, administrateur,
avocat,* and so on) [64] or Diderot's "conditions" (*l'homme de
lettres, le philosophe, le commerçant, le juge, l'avocat, le politique,
le citoyen, le magistrat, le financier, le grand seigneur, l'inten-
dant*) .[65] But Castille's misreading of Balzac's ideas (which totally
ignores his scientific concerns as formulated in the "Avant-Propos"
and elsewhere) succinctly defined an issue that was to predominate for at least two generations: the "general" character, or the
representative if unexceptional figure, again emerged as a norm of
realistic fiction corresponding to the everyday soberness and "objective" precision of Dutch painting.

After the revolution of 1848 a new generation of critics and
writers emerged, which happily seized upon the social and political implications of Balzac's new concept of the type and related it
to the triumphant art of realism. Contrary to Hector Castille's
opinions (1846), the younger critics insisted on linking Balzac
with Courbet and the newly appreciated Dutch artists; a canon of
norms became established in which Courbet, *l'art flamande*, Balzac, and *réalisme* constituted central orientations. Courbet's friend
and apologist Champfleury praised Balzac as the true heir to the
French scientists, and in the writings of Champfleury's allies and

61. Ibid., p. 367.
62. Ibid.
63. Ibid., p. 368.
64. *Comédie Humaine, 1*, 4.
65. "Entretiens sur le Fils Naturel," ed. Pléiade (Paris, 1957), p. 1288.

younger followers a social interpretation of Balzac was relentlessly
advanced; the traditional image of the realist Balzac became fully
established within ten years after the revolution and was confirmed by Taine's influential essay (1864). Armand Baschet's
Honoré de Balzac: Essai sur l'homme et l'œuvre (1851), for
which "le confrère" Champfleury wrote an important postscript,
constituted a massive attempt to demonstrate Balzac's realism and
to disparage the opinions of traditional or romantic critics. If
Sainte-Beuve had not yet grasped recent artistic transformations,
Baschet believed, it was because he had lost contact with contemporary life: "M. Sainte-Beuve ne voit rien et ne sait rien que par
les livres, et quand il se met à la fenêtre deux fois le mois pour
croire encore au monde, c'est beaucoup." [66] Baschet not only
dealt with all the fashionable *topoi* of his moment (Dutch painting, milieu, Paris city-life), but he also supported his arguments
by discussing the new types which Balzac had created. Baschet was
fully aware that, in the everyday language of his decade, the term
"type" referred to "personnages bizarres, des physiognomies gro-
tesques et des natures étonnantes"; unfortunately, he remarked,
people had a habit of obfuscating the legitimate meaning of the
word, confusing the implications of an "expression technique,"
and identifying Balzac's type with "l'idéal." [67] But Baschet was
not satisfied with a neat, if abstract, separation of the traditional
idéal and Balzac's type; he knew Balzac's practice and admitted
that some of Balzac's social types strangely shared certain qualitative elements with traditional or "ideal" characters: they were far
too exceptional, or "original," to represent a mere average. Baschet resolutely tried to account for the tension of social "typical-
ity" and narrative "originality" by the pressure of conformist
society; in a world in which everybody has to make so many social
concessions to his neighbor one individual tends to look like another and the type which concentrates the most intense qualities
shared by everyone cannot help being a truly striking figure. To
Baschet, Balzac's type (in contrast to the traditional *idéal*) constituted "la personification réelle d'un genre parvenu à sa plus

66. Armand Baschet, *Honoré de Balzac: Essai sur l'homme et l'œuvre*
(Paris, 1851), p. 97.
67. Ibid., p. 196.

haute puissance," [68] and few of Baschet's successors have suggested a more perceptive way to discuss a concept concerned with social kinds and yet operative as a fictional technique.

In the critical essays of Champfleury's younger disciples who explicated their beliefs in the short-lived periodical *Réalisme* (1856–57), Baschet's concern with the essential aesthetic issues of Balzac's practice as a novelist gave way to unrestrained political reinterpretations; the social meaning of Balzac's scientific concept of the type (which now turns into a weapon of liberal partisans) supersedes and, in its almost naked isolation, destroys all other implications. In Balzac's "Avant-Propos" the older type (e.g. Roland) lives side by side with the more contemporary figures of managers and shopkeepers; in the theoretical explications of the younger generation social types, which are rightly seen in connection with Diderot's "conditions," counteract the claims of the traditional heroes of fiction who are felt to be ancien régime. The type is enthroned where the hero once reigned. In one of the more important essays in *Réalisme* (December 15, 1856) Henri Thulié revealed the concept of the social type in its ideological alliance with fighting liberalism when he declared that the young writer (whose task it is to deal with the problem of the greatest number) should substitute for the distant heroes of yore new types emerging from a world of declining social hierarchies: "il prend pour héros le type qu'il a vu, qu'il comprend et à quelque classe qu'appartienne ce type. . . . Il n'a pas de haut et de bas en littérature, il y a des hommes." [69] Thulié goes so far as to suggest a way of creating, or rather discovering, types which distinctly differ from the suggestions of Balzac and his scientific predecessors. While Geoffroy St.-Hilaire was occasionally not averse to admitting that the concept of the type had almost overpowered him in a shock of intuition when he looked at the wealth of the Royal Ornithological Collection and Balzac had implied a process of "composition" based on analysis and synthesis, Thulié suggested that the writer find in the world of his actual experience a real individual who would most aptly represent others of his kind. He believed, in some contrast to

68. Ibid., p. 197.
69. Quoted in H. U. Forest, " 'Réalisme,' Journal de Duranty," *Modern Philology, 24* (1926–27), 464.

other writers publishing in *Réalisme,* that it was possible to discover who *was* "le type du bourgeois, de l'homme du monde, de
l'épicier, du notaire, du bottier"; once the writer had discovered
his man, he had (anticipating Zola by one generation) closely to
study his life and describe him in detail: "en décrivant un homme
on en décrit dix mille." [70]

I cannot help feeling that Henri Thulié combines, in his notion
of discovering the social type on the streets of Paris, the passions of
an avid lepidopterist and those of a citizen concerned with representative elections: the writer, hunting his specimen, discovers his
man-as-type and places him in his literary *Chambre des Députés*
in which he represents "les allures, les idées, les préjugés des
différents bottiers, épiciers, etc., qu'il a vu précédemment." [71]
Armand Baschet (1851) was still concerned with the aesthetic
issues of the social type, but in a society suddenly deprived on
December 10, 1852, of its newly won liberal institutions, Henri
Thulié (1856) and his friends came close to transforming Balzac's
concept of the scientific type, conceived as an instrument of social
analysis, into a deputy of the restive *épiciers.*

On January 2, 1865, Sainte-Beuve complained in his *Nouveaux
Lundis* about the confusing ubiquity of the term "type": "un assez
vilain mot" [72] used by nearly everybody. Perhaps he should have
admitted that it was necessary for ordered discourse in many intellectual disciplines: we must be able to mediate somehow between
matter and shape, the many and the few. The history of the term
illustrates many of the metaphorical tendencies of literary criticism constantly looking beyond itself: originally relating to Greek
morphology, "type" was seized upon by the Church Fathers and
Christian theologians of the fourth century A.D. and, after almost
fourteen hundred years, secularized (as was the ubiquitous term
"symbol") by philosophers, scientists, and literary critics. German
thinkers of romantic temper (never too distant from the *Pfarr-
haus*) retained some of its metaphysical vitality inherited from
theology and transmitted it to their French counterparts; in the

70. Ibid., p. 471.
71. Ibid.
72. Sainte-Beuve, *Nouveaux Lundis* (Paris, 1863–70), *9,* 245–46.

meantime, French zoologists and their German colleagues, above all Vic d'Azyr (1774) and Johann Heinrich Merck (1786), returned to the morphological implications of the term in order to articulate a vision of organic life in which certain "forms" or "structures" were representative of a number of similarly organized animals, and Geoffroy St.-Hilaire made the concept the key to a "historicist" interpretation of the world. In Balzac's "Avant-Propos" (1846) the two traditions confront each other. Balzac preserves the "romantic" idea because it was useful in the past of literature, but for the future he postulates a new concept modeled on scientific precedents. I would suggest that the two concepts differ in at least five elements: the traditional type (often defined by the Romantics) strikes me as "selective," intuitively conceived, symbolic of supra-human forces and energies, largely a-historical, and suggesting the grand and distant; Balzac's scientific type emerges as concerned with "pluralities," composed in a sober process of analysis and synthesis, representative of many human individuals of the analogous kind, basically historical, and suggesting the modest and humble. Almost inevitably, Balzac's scientific concept was used by some of his liberal contemporaries and the new generation emerging after the revolution of 1848. Balzac himself never used the term "réalisme" (his substitute was "éclectisme"), but Félix Davin explicitly discussed the issues inherent in a social concept of the type, and Armand Baschet as well as Henri Thulié (together with other collaborators of *Réalisme*) elaborated on the essential functions of the concept and integrated it into a growing theory of realism.

It is strange to see Georg Lukács (who among the critics of our time most brilliantly defends the cause of nineteenth-century realism as great art) reverse, for Hegelian reasons, the opinions of Balzac's contemporaries and liberal followers. Lukács tries to separate Balzac's "valid" realism from Zola's problematical naturalism [73] by ascribing different concepts of the type to the older and the younger writer; curiously enough, Balzac emerges as the master of the traditional *personnage typique*, symbolizing vital forces, while Zola merely composes scientific types representing

73. Cf. Georg Lukács, *Balzac und der französische Realismus* (East Berlin, 1952).

statistical averages. Balzac creates great types in which the universal and the individual organically coalesce in a synthesis; the naturalists, however, construct figures of a gray statistical core (*eine graue, statistische Mitte*).[74] Lukács, I think, radically simplifies Balzac's views by relegating his concept of the social type to Zola's decadent naturalism, and his definition of the Balzacian type (to be an example to future socialist writers) comes very close to Hector Castille's characterization of the monstrous *démon de la fantasie*.[75] A paradox is involved: the Hegelian philosopher constantly stresses his unhesitating social commitment but glosses over Balzac's scientific concept of the type, which incisively strengthened a socially more inclusive literature, giving voice to multitudes speechless in the dark. Philosophical interpretation does not inevitably coincide with the rich evidence of literary history.

74. Ibid., p. 95 (these essays were written in 1940).
75. Louvenjoul, *Histoire des œuvres,* p. 368.

Herbert Dieckmann

Reflections on the Use of Rococo as a Period Concept

It is not my intention to discuss the origin and history of the term "Rococo," nor shall I attempt to define the nature or essence of "Rococo" either as a collective term for a period of cultural history or as a recurring expression of a certain way of viewing the world or "feeling" it. My purpose in this inquiry is more specific: I wish to examine the application of the term "Rococo" as a key to the understanding of the eighteenth century, its use as a general denominator for the "spirit" of this period as manifested in the arts, in literature, as well as in thought. The difficulties encountered by such an application will lead to the question: can a coherent pattern of the various currents which constitute the eighteenth century be found in another way?

The limited scope of this paper corresponds to the factual character of its starting point. My inquiry was not prompted by works on Rococo or definitions of it, but by my bewilderment in seeing that paintings, sculptures, and drawings of the eighteenth century are classified indiscriminately as expressions of the Rococo, the Age of Enlightenment, and the Age of Reason. The underlying assumption of this usage seems to be that the three terms can be used interchangeably. A similar reflection crossed my mind during a visit, in 1958, to the magnificent exposition, *Europäisches Rokoko, Kunst und Kultur des 18. Jahrhunderts*, organized in Munich under the high auspices of the *Europarat*. Here *Rokoko*, as the title already indicates, was considered to be the specific character of eighteenth-century art and culture; the first large and long room of the exhibit contained, in the words of the catalogue, "Dokumente des Geisteslebens, der Wissenschaft und Technik." This indeed corresponded to what one would expect of the Age of

419

Reason, but what was its relationship to Rococo, illustrated in other rooms by works of the fine arts, art objects, furniture, designs of parks and gardens, representations of various forms of entertainment of the period? And how, in turn, were these representative of Enlightenment and Reason? There was no answer to these questions either in the exhibit itself or in the introductory articles of the learned and informative catalog.[1] As a matter of fact, the author of one of these articles, Professor Hans Sedlmayer, warned against the identification of a period with an artistic style and pointed out that several art forms of the period under consideration show no trace of Rococo style.[2] To this word of caution one may add that some art historians distinguish between several forms of Rococo, not only according to periods but also to specific art forms: the decorative Rococo is said to differ from that of painting, and both to differ from the Rococo of church architecture, where again court Rococo occupies a special place. My personal experience has been that a visit to the church of *Kloster Schäftlarn* and to the Wallfahrtskirche *Die Wies,* both not far from Munich, both Rococo churches, and both markedly different from each other, amply demonstrates the justification of these distinctions and would put to no small discomfort those who maintain the idea of Rococo as a unified concept and who identify formal characteristics with mental attitudes and modes of feeling.

The presence of "Dokumente des Geisteslebens, der Wissenschaft und Technik" in a Rococo exhibit conflicted also with the widespread and convincing view that the Rococo style comes to an end toward the middle of the eighteenth century and is replaced by neoclassicism and a return to classical antiquity. Classicism and neoclassicism have often been identified with rationalism in art history. It was thus fitting that most of the "Dokumente" had been selected from the second part of the eighteenth century, but how could they be representative of Rococo?

This initial bewilderment, caused by the impossibility of reconciling visual evidence with historical classifications, increased as I began studying the arguments which have been set forth in de-

---

1. *Europäisches Rokoko, Kunst und Kultur des 18. Jahrhunderts* (München, Verlag Hermann Rinn, 1958).
2. See the article, "Das Gesamtkunstwerk," p. 29.

fense of the use of Rococo as a period concept for either the first part of the eighteenth century or the entire Age of Enlightenment.

I have taken the liberty of evoking some personal reminiscences because they were the starting point of my inquiry and proved to be very fruitful. Since the practice of applying the term "Rococo" to the style of a period originated in art history, and since those who extend it to works of literature and philosophy take their point of departure from art historians and frequently refer to architecture and paintings, it is both necessary and helpful to remind oneself of these origins and to consult again and again the visible, clear, and distinct examples of Rococo style. If, on the other hand, we set out from general definitions or from a period concept of Rococo, we shall lose ourselves in a speculative labyrinth.

Before examining the way in which the term "Rococo" came to be applied and has been applied to the eighteenth century, we shall point out some of the reasons for this application. As long as the division of literary and intellectual history by centuries and the designation of the period between 1700 and 1800 as *Aufklärung*, Age of Enlightenment or Age of Reason were taken for granted, no problem arose about the unity and coherence of the eighteenth century or its antecedents in the seventeenth and its anticipation of currents of the nineteenth century. To be sure, there were precursors, late-comers, and isolated cases, but they did not seem to disturb the system of classification; one could at the same time belong to one's century and maintain ideas that challenged it. This happy state of things was disturbed and finally destroyed by the discovery of various inconsistencies both in the traditional conception of the eighteenth century and in the nature of the century itself. The term "enlightenment" which stresses philosophical, social, and political ideas proved to be too narrow to encompass the literary works of the period. A great number of these works are playful and intellectually superficial, some are overtly erotic and lascivious, and all differ considerably from the sober concern of reason. So do many aspects of the social life of the period, though it was in the salons that many of the ideas developed. In several representative works of the eighteenth century, this trifling literary form was judged to be opposed to the serious content. It is this often observed contrast which later was called the dichotomy between Rococo and Enlightenment.

The general denominator of "Century of Reason" seemed also to be inconsistent with the currents of irrationalism, feeling, and "sensibilité," currents which in the second half of the eighteenth century were said to be so powerful as to constitute an early form of Romanticism. As these currents were studied closely, the Age of Enlightenment lost more and more of its original consistency and became in some measure a prelude to the early nineteenth century. As far as works of art and literature and their theories were concerned, the eighteenth century was divided into a period which continued the classical and one which preceded the Romantic age. And if the century was viewed in its social structure, which was said by some to determine all ideas as well as the forms of expression, it was split into a first part in which the aristocratic society and its values lingered on and a second part in which the bourgeoisie came progressively into its own. The Age of Enlightenment thus dissolved into a transience, a movement between a past that was on its way out and a future that was in the making.

This loss of unity and consistency deprived the eighteenth century of a distinctive feature which would give it a proper place in the periodization of the history of literature and the arts; a link was missing in the sequence of Renaissance, Classicism, Baroque, and, further on, Romanticism, Realism, and Naturalism. As a result a new period concept was needed that would fill the gap and restore the unity which the century had previously found in the idea of *Aufklärung*.

The choice of Rococo as a means to reestablish continuity and identify the proper character of the eighteenth century, a choice made by several historians of literature and of ideas, seems to have been influenced by the striking success which the introduction and establishment of Baroque as a period concept has been enjoying. Rococo is clearly related to Baroque and has been considered by many art historians and historians of culture as a Baroque restrained, refined, and intellectualized by Classicism. The sequence Baroque-Classicism-Rococo (or Classicism-Baroque-Rococo) offered a welcome solution for the desire to establish historical processes; the three movements could also be made to interact according to the pattern of contrast and historical "dialectics." Moreover, Rococo, like Baroque, originally was a collective term for stylistic features and thus seemed to lend itself well to the attempt to draw together the arts, the literature and the general culture of the century. Since these had been disregarded or underrated by the predominant concern for *thought* in the concept of Age of Enlightenment, it seemed advisable to seek the unity of the century by starting not with ideas, but with formal characteristics and with themes, which, if interpreted as an expression of ways of feeling and of "mental attitudes," would give insight into the spirit of the century and thus facilitate the transition to the ideas. To some extent this attempt corresponds to the desire (already existing in the eighteenth century) to replace the periodization of history according to centuries or to rulers by a history of cultural periods or cultural movements, which would encompass several countries as well as man's various activities and forms of existence. The very title of the Munich exhibit and the range of objects put together as an illustration of that title were a striking example of the search for unity in broad cultural periods. It is significant that the author of *Die Kultur der Renaissance in Italien,* Jakob Burckhardt, already used Rococo as a term designating partly a general trend and partly a period.[3] His association of Rococo with decadence (a decadence brought about by the predominance of a purely decorative principle and the ensuing destruction of architectural order) has had several revivals until recently, though the specific reason for his judgment has been generally modified and his name has rarely been mentioned. Last but not least, the choice of Rococo as a unifying period concept was also determined by the trend toward synthesis which is inherent in Rococo art, a trend which can be seen in the blending of the three arts (architecture, sculpture, painting) and by the pervasive influence which Rococo as the art of the *intérieur* and of decoration exerted upon the shaping of the *ambiente* in which the cultivated society of the period lived. Rococo themes or Rococo forms are present everywhere, in the furniture, hangings, porcelain, objects of daily use, and garments—in one word, in the taste and, less directly, in the

3. E.g. Jakob Burckhardt, *Gesamtausgabe, 1,* 116.

manners, habits, as well as the very forms of social entertainment. Some of these have left their trace also in literature and music.

It is thus the dissatisfaction with the practice of classifying literary, artistic, and intellectual history by centuries, with the choice of Age of Enlightenment as common denominator for the eighteenth century in its totality and with the subsequent divisions of the eighteenth century into different currents, which has played a major role in the choice of Rococo as a period concept. Understandable as such a choice is, it not only leads in my opinion to serious contradictions but also destroys the relative usefulness of the term. In order to justify this contention, I shall examine the thought processes by which Rococo as a period concept designating a coherent pattern of literature, the arts, thought, and social forms in the eighteenth century was formed. My method is not that used in historical surveys where definitions of a period concept, as we find them in books and articles of various authors, are briefly summarized and characterized in chronological order. Such a study would not only go far beyond the limits of the present inquiry, but would also defeat its purpose, which is that of an analysis of the factors that constitute the period concept Rococo and of the methods applied in the process. To these remarks on procedure I may add that the historical survey type of study rarely does justice to the individual authors with whom it deals. Their ideas are reduced to a few categorical statements which the authors themselves often modify and even contradict in the course of their demonstrations. An inquiry which is limited to the genesis of a concept will—it is hoped—be more objective and systematic.

Two factors have played a major role in the formation of Rococo as a period concept: transfer of meaning and generalization. At first certain formal characteristics of architecture, above all, interior architecture and their tectonic function, are interpreted as an expression of modes of thought and feeling; the same interpretation is then applied to these characteristics when they appear in other representative arts. In their totality, the formal features are said to constitute a specific style, called Rococo, which is opposed to a preceding style and is evaluated, with regard to it, either negatively or positively. In the first case, it is called a style of decadence, of ornamentation or decoration which destroys the principles of structure; in the second, Rococo is called a welcome contrast to and relief from monumentality, strictness, regularity, and rational clarity. Occasionally *motifs* or *themes* are added to the *formal* features and are so closely associated with them that all three, taken together, are said to denote the same style of Rococo.

This enlargement of the meaning of style is carried even further when the decisive step is taken to consider Rococo as the expression-form of a cultural period and the manifestation of a Zeitgeist,[4] a Zeitgeist that is often conceived as an active principle. Whether or not the idea of spontaneous activity is explicitly stated, we have here a form of hypostatization, in the sense that a number of data derived from observations of works of art and literature as well as from the habits and manners of society are combined into one concept which, as it were, constitutes their totality, and that this totality is not only conceived as essence but also has the characteristics of a person. A historical force, Rococo is said to create forms, themes, attitudes, modes of taste in a variety of domains which it pervades. Once this concept is formed, it permits relating all the various data and their particular meanings to each other and endowing them with the new significance of the totality. Rococo has become a collective concept and at once an interpretive, inventive principle.

The different steps which we have enumerated are now coordinated: the time limits of Rococo are established and its specific features are compared with those of the preceding and the following periods. The existence of the movement in different countries is examined. Not only the formal characteristics and the motifs or themes, which originally pertained to the representative arts, are extended to literature, to the thought and the social life of the period, but also their interpretation as expressions of ideas, feelings, and "attitudes."

The difficulties, complexities, and contradictions that result from this generalization of the term "Rococo" can best be demonstrated by a few examples. We are going to enumerate the various statements that have been made, beginning with those on the relationship between Rococo and Classicism in the representative arts:

4. The term "style" no longer designates definable formal characteristics but expresses a totality.

Rococo is considered to be opposed to the classicism of the seventeenth century. As in the case of the older confrontation of Classicism and Romanticism, the antithesis between *formal* characteristics as well as *themes* in the two movements is extended to one between their nature or essence. Subsequently new criteria are derived from this general antithesis; those said to be characteristic of one period are often simply antonyms of those of the other. Rococo is considered to be the predominant feature of the first half of the eighteenth century, whereas Classicism is that of the second.

These classifications are at odds with the theory that Rococo developed out of Baroque, that it is a Baroque refined by Classicism, and with the theory that Rococo blends with Classicism in a number of cases. The latter theory, the only one which recognizes that Classicism is a recurrent and variable factor in the eighteenth century, is stated only with regard to principles of architecture and decoration.

The contradictions, which arise when the relationship between Classicism and Rococo is formulated in terms of antithetical principles and contrasting periods, are even more striking when these classifications are transferred from the representative arts to literature, where forms and themes that can be called Rococo vary not only with regard to chronology, but also with regard to genres and authors, and where Classicism is similarly diversified and intermittent. No less serious than the neglect of the genres is that of the poetic theories, which are of prime importance in the confrontation of schools and movements in the arts.

We encounter the same type of conflicting pronouncements on the relationship between Rococo and Enlightenment: Rococo and Enlightenment are said to coincide (in its generality this is no more than the recognition of a historical fact). Rococo is called the dominant character of the first part of the eighteenth century, whereas Enlightenment is that of the second (a historically false statement). The two are considered to exist side by side either throughout the century or during a certain time. This coexistence is formulated in various ways: Rococo is the artistic and literary equivalent, the aesthetic counterpart of the Enlightenment; Rococo represents the "life" (in the social sense or in the general

sense) of the period; Enlightenment represents the thought
(phrases which are patterned upon the distinction between two
modes of the same substance; the latter is moreover not defined).
Finally, Rococo is conceived of as merely a form of expression or a
way of thinking; in the latter case it designates the skeptical,
witty, ironic, mundane, and brilliant mind, the detached, playful,
practical wisdom or, in a negative evaluation, the shallow phi-
losophizing of the eighteenth century.

It is apparent from the second group of conflicting pronouncements that the inconsistencies which arise when Rococo is transformed into a period concept are even more difficult to reconcile
when one attempts to relate Rococo and the Enlightenment. The
problem of the link between formal characteristics and ideas is in
all cases a complex one, and it cannot be solved by combining or
contrasting philosophical, psychological, social, and stylistic characteristics. The attempt to connect Rococo and intellectual history
shows moreover that the transformation of an architectural term
into the spirit of a period has the paradoxical result of destroying
the specific historical character of the period concept, for Rococo
becomes a recurrent trait of the human mind. Before we turn to
the last stage of this development where Rococo becomes a be-
wildering mixture of period concept and typological concept, we
shall briefly deal with the opinion that Rococo serves as a concealment of eighteenth-century thought.

We have seen that in the interpretation of Rococo as the counterpart of Enlightenment or as the literary equivalent of philo-
sophic and social ideas, the nature of the correspondence remains
vague. In its interpretation as mask and concealment, on the contrary, a real relationship is established, for it is claimed that the
elimination of the grave issues of man's existence is covered up,
and that the undermining of a centuries-old tradition of metaphysics, theology, religion, tradition, order, and hierarchy is ele-
gantly glossed over. Rococo as the outer form of eighteenth-
century thought is thus no longer ornament and playful or
gracious appearance but expresses a tension, is part of a tension,
and affects the thought as much as it is affected by it. The origin of
this tension is to be found in the dichotomies, contradictions, and
dilemmas from which the period suffered. This verdict is strik-

ingly reflected in the use which the representatives of this view
make of antithetical or contrasting epithets which serve to express
the peculiar character of eighteenth-century life, art, and literature. If we add to these accusations the evaluation of Rococo as
decadence and as the triumph of playful ornamentation over solid
and clear architectural principles, we have, I think, most of the
elements out of which the above-mentioned interpretation of
Rococo has been formed.

Let us observe first that this interpretation repeats a number of
arguments from a long tradition of hostile judgments on the
Enlightenment and that some of the charges are already to be
found verbatim in eighteenth-century attacks against the "phi-
losophes." Only the combination of the various accusations, in an
overall philosophical view of the *Aufklärung* as a unified epoch, is
new. This means, however, that most of the criticisms have been
borrowed from writings in which the notion of Rococo either does
not exist or plays a minor role. A representative listing of the
arguments used in the interpretation of Rococo as mask and concealment will illustrate both the nature of the indictment and its
derivation: Rococo being the art of the configuration of the surface disguises the lack of profound, searching thoughts and of
heartfelt emotions; it also indicates that transcendence is rejected;
the light, frivolous, trifling character of Rococo masks a metaphysical vacuum; its abstractness is an escape from harsh and
sordid reality, from the contradictions that eventually led to the
revolution; a gay and sprightly comedy hides spiritual anarchy;
uneasiness over the polarity between nature and civilization is re-
lieved by the *bergeries;* the evasive look on Rococo portraits reflects the uncertainty which results from the refusal to face essential issues; the predilection for paradox and for the correlation of
incongruent statements manifest the divided nature of the period
and the conflict between man's faculties; aggressive, intellectual
destructiveness makes itself acceptable in the form of *esprit;*
playful eroticism in delicate paintings and drawings, in charming
tales covers up the perversion of the senses and the heart; the
setting of this subterfuge is the intimate milieu of Rococo interior
architecture. We notice in these criteria again that the original
sense of Rococo (a set of distinctive formal features) is almost

completely forgotten and that only some of the *themes* of Rococo painting and literature have been retained. The starting point for the characterization is not an objective description of features which constitute the style of a definite period, but the moral, psychological, social, and cultural meaning which has been given to Rococo forms, motifs, and style. Rococo serves as a common denominator for a number of observations and judgments— mostly negative and drawn from various sources—on the philosophy, art, literature, and society of the *Aufklärung*. One of the most dangerous effects of this method to construct the entity of a period is that its arbitrary assumptions, exaggerations, and confused generalities will undermine the very notion of a cultural movement and of a period having definite characteristics. When tension and contrasts are declared to be the cause of Rococo style and the key to its interpretation, these terms not only become absurd but also blind us to the fact that they would be valid and meaningful if applied to specific cases and in combination with other factors.

The role of Rococo in an eighteenth century conceived as a period of contradictions and dilemmas has also been evaluated in a manner which is diametrically opposed to the one stressing concealment. Rococo is defined as the art of combining polarities, either by establishing an equilibrium through style or by expressing the very tension and stressing the contrasts. In the latter case, Rococo is considered to be the art which leaves issues open and presents a challenge. Though a formal principle of this kind and many of the detailed observations which have been made about it are valid for several works of the eighteenth century, they could equally well be applied to works of other periods and thus do not constitute the essence of Rococo art in particular. As far as Rococo society is concerned (the milieu out of which such an art must have grown and to which it is addressed), it would seem to me that this society's astonishing capacity to be pleased with itself, that its delight to see itself reflected not only in mirrors and artistic representations, but also in nature (the park and garden evoking a variety of emotions) and in the depiction of the animal world, are hardly compatible with an art that stresses contrasts and presents the challenge of open issues.

The successive stages in the transfer of meaning of Rococo criteria and the process of generalization, which we have been examining thus far, can also be observed in the interpretation of Rococo as expression of an attitude toward life. In this last form to be mentioned here, we find the paradoxical feature that the historical boundaries of the period concept are maintained as well as transcended, that Rococo is understood to be at the same time the dominant feature of the eighteenth century (or part thereof) and one of the constant forms of representative types of feeling and thinking which reoccur throughout history. This twofold aspect is explained either by the theory that Rococo is an undercurrent which comes into its own in the eighteenth century, or that an individual author anticipates a state of mind which later becomes general and predominant. Examples of Rococo as Weltanschauung and mental attitude are found, it is said, in the "esprit libertin" and the "esprit gaulois," i.e. in the spirit of independence, irreverence, and playfulness, in joyful egoism, in the refusal to be "engagé," in a penchant for the irregular and the frivolous, in hedonism, and in a predilection for imagination, fantasy, the arabesque, and the unreal—all traits opposed to the classical, rational, or "roman" spirit, to strictness, hierarchy, and linear order. We need not go into further details; at this level of generalization, the term "Rococo" has dissolved.

The contradictions which arise out of the use of Rococo as a period concept and the inadequacy of the term when it dominates the interpretation of the artistic and intellectual history of the eighteenth century would seem to make it advisable to discard the term altogether. This would, however, mean that the indiscriminate, all-embracing use of Rococo has blinded us to the historical reality of Rococo as a cultural movement. Rococo coexists with other currents in the eighteenth century and is at certain times with certain authors an important factor. It is this relative but real and significant role of Rococo which we should recognize and try to determine. As the preceding analysis will have shown, the main prerequisite for this task is that we be wary of generalization and of the transfer and mixing of criteria. The danger of generalization can be avoided if we remember that the phenomenon Rococo does not necessarily occur at the same time in different countries and is not necessarily present in all of the arts as well as in the thought and social life; that it is combined with other elements and that it may be limited to only one domain or period of intellectual and artistic activity. The dangers inherent in the transfer and combination of criteria are more complex and numerous. We can do here no more than indicate some fundamental distinctions which are necessary in order to free the mind for the clear perception of the phenomenon Rococo and for an unprejudiced study of its manifestations. As far as themes are concerned, the transfer of criteria from one art to the other and their identification with Rococo presents few difficulties; the transfer should be based on factual observation and a careful description of those themes which by the frequency of their occurrence prove to be representative of a general current. Examples can be found in subjects of landscape in painting, literature, decorations and in settings for philosophical works; in mythological scenes where, characteristically, the *minor* deities, an idyllic character, eroticism, and elegance prevail; in the great significance given to the *intérieur* and the intimate, though we should separate the Rococo features (marked by gracefulness, luxury, refinement) from those of the peasant, the bouregois, and the sentimental *intérieur*. Less specific and hence more difficult to define is the treatment of the time theme; still, we notice a marked interest in the fugitive moment, the transient and the sudden; the latter is related to the great role of the *surprise* in eighteenth-century art and thought.

The connections established between different arts and their interpretation as Rococo can also be shown in the increased significance of certain genres and techniques of presentation, as, for example, in the predilection for minor and familiar genres—even when the author deals with serious subjects—for brief and succinct forms and the miniature, all of which are brought to a high point of artistic perfection; in the preference for rapid sketching as opposed to careful, detailed objective presentation; in the playful handling of plot, themes, and characters.

With the last criteria, we have already touched upon the difficult and complex issue of the transfer of formal characteristics from one art to another and of the interpretation of these formal characteristics, an issue which seems to me to constitute the crux of any general usage of Rococo. Formal characteristics in architecture and furniture cannot be applied directly to works of literature. Only in the use of color—not a formal characteristic in the proper sense—may there exist a close parallel, if, for example, it can be shown that a poet or novelist prefers either the Rococo color scheme or the use of in-between shades, of, as it were, transient colors. It has been observed, for example, that Watteau's colors cannot be "defined" in the traditional way, that one color blends into the other. On the other hand, no close parallel does exist, if a critic calls the characterization and description in a novel, a tale, or a poem "shaded," "tinted," or "toned down," pastel-colored or iridescent. He uses a *metaphor* for his *impression*.

As far as strictly formal criteria are concerned, we must be heedful that they are in every transfer taken as symbols or manifestations of feelings and thoughts. It is this interpretation and not the formal feature itself which is found again in the forms or features of another art, or, a fortiori, in a way of thinking. Moreover the first stage of interpretation is, as the examples discussed previously in this paper show, often influenced by traits derived from domains other than the one from which the formal characteristics have been chosen, so that the mind moves in a vicious circle of comparisons. If, for instance, the linear perspective, the contrast of the vertical and horizontal, of weight and support are concealed in Rococo architecture, if the tectonic structure is meant to be seen from a distance as a total *pictorial* effect, we may safely, I trust, interpret this as the expression of a different feeling for space, of a wish to communicate the sensation of weightlessness, of being suspended, of almost autonomous rhythm (not including, however, a movement of transcendence) ; we also may find in other arts analogous forms and symbols (as e.g. meter, rhyme, cadence, syntactical pattern) expressing or eliciting the same feelings, but when we say that the architectural features are an expression of a general tendency to evade reality, to play over essential, decisive issues and to dissimulate—a tendency also evident in the attitude of the aristocratic society toward social and political questions— then we interpret artistic and aesthetic criteria in psychological and sociological terms which are determined by what they are supposed to illustrate. The stylistic features lose their specific meaning, their autonomy, and their significance which they have in the history of architectural forms.

The use of "playful" may serve as another example: the decorative and ornamental patterns of Rococo are considered to express playfulness; the fact that they are often combined with gay, reveling, or capricious *putti* probably has strengthened this impression; we find in literary works forms which evoke similar feelings and the same may be said of the desultory, variegated, capricious, or trifling way in which ideas are often developed and set forth by eighteenth-century authors. On the other hand, the means by which the impression of playfulness is achieved change considerably in the different arts and in philosophical writings. It will also be impossible to distinguish on formal grounds playfulness which expresses nothing but play from playfulness which serves the purpose of instruction or disguise. Stylistic devices are easily imitated and lose by the process of imitation their original meaning. We thus cannot define Rococo in general as an art of ornamentation which manifests itself *identically* in different domains, nor can we equate ornament with playfulness. Even less can we define playfulness as the essence or spirit of Rococo, for in doing so we extend the metaphoric process beyond formal and structural analogies, some of which, even when used too directly, remain at least plausible. Now ornamentation is taken as a penchant for graceful but trifling superficiality, shallowness of mind and heart, restlessness and escape, a refusal to accept binding feelings and forceful emotions. We notice here again the conversion of social and ethical criteria into aesthetic criteria in the very interpretation of formal features. One of the most conspicuous and dangerous examples of this practice can be seen in the use of taste and so-called style as a uniform norm of Rococo: fashion, conventions, decorum are combined to make up a dominant or representative period style which then is identified with the literary, artistic, or even intellectual style. The attempts to define the style of even one author have shown that its variability according to genres and periods does not permit any standardization and that it is a fallacy to identify the taste as it is expressed in an author's opinions and judgments with the taste that is expressed in an author's works.

It does not seem necessary to extend these observations on the

dangers inherent in the transfer of criteria; we would observe in
additional cases the same metaphorical process studied thus far.
What matters in the present context is the process itself, for I believe that we cannot recognize and accurately describe the specific
features of Rococo without being fully conscious of the changes of
significance which we impose upon them. To be conscious of it
does not mean that we should avoid using analogy or parallelism
in a comparative study of themes, forms, and structure of works of
literature and of the representative arts, but that we should control the transfer of these criteria from one domain to the other.
The idea that these criteria are representative of a unified cultural
movement called Rococo has to remain strictly hypothetical. In its
verification historical factors, genres, and the different media of
artistic representation will have to play a major role. On the other
hand, the fact that individual features identified as being characteristic of Rococo can also be found in works of a different
period does not invalidate their significance, provided that we do
not consider them to express the essence of a *Zeitbegriff* Rococo.
We must accept as premise, I think, that Rococo is in the eighteenth century a cultural movement among others, coexisting with
others, even in the case of an individual author, in order to regain
our freedom with regard to the identification of certain features as
being representative of Rococo. It will then also be recognized
that it is not the single feature which is characteristic of a period,
but the combination of several.

To conclude: the usefulness of Rococo in the study of eighteenth-century *literature* and *art* is limited but real; as far as the
thought of the eighteenth century is concerned, it cannot evidently
remain outside such an important cultural movement. The difficulties that confront us in our attempts to ascertain Rococo elements in the domain of ideas are, however, so great that a direct
approach to the problem seems impossible. Even if we avoid falling
back on the contradictory and vague notion of the spirit or "style"
of Rococo, from which the Rococo of ideas has been generally deduced, there remains the fact that we cannot in the case of
eighteenth-century thought start from forms, colors, or structures
(these terms taken in a broad sense, comprising the arts as well as
literature and language) but only from the interpretation of their

meaning. I also think that the notion of Rococo cannot serve in this case as a regulative principle, which, as instrument of an *ars inveniendi,* would permit us to draw together the hitherto dispersed and seemingly disparate phenomena of a period. We have to remind ourselves here first of Kant's wise distinction between "konstitutiv" and "regulativ": the latter principle cannot determine, let alone constitute, empirical investigation and knowledge; it cannot anticipate what is given in the object of our inquiry. Moreover, the notion of Rococo carries with it definite characteristics which destroy the necessarily abstract and general character of a principle of coherence. It would thus seem advisable to take as point of departure key concepts common to several domains of knowledge and methods or ways of thinking, concepts which were applied by representative minds of the eighteenth century to problems in different fields of investigation. Our choice should not be determined in any way by our conception of Rococo. Only after the key concepts and the methods have been studied in these fields and their similarities as well as differences have been established could they be compared to themes and to principles (the latter to be derived from the interpretation of forms and structure) of Rococo. It is to be expected that we shall find only rarely close parallels and that analogy and conjecture will play the major role in the rapprochements.

An investigation of this kind would not only permit us to understand more precisely than before the semantic range of Rococo as one of the important currents of the eighteenth century, but would also satisfy what seems to me to have been the major reason for the transformation of an architectural characteristic into a general "Formprinzip" and period concept, namely the wish to find coherent patterns and specific characteristics for a century that has become a grotesque mixture of post-Classicism, Pre-Romanticism, Rococo, and Enlightenment, a century where every movement seems to be derivative and out of time, for even Rococo is said to be only a refined, last-stage Baroque and the Enlightenment nothing but a broad application of the free thought, rationalism, and empiricism of the sixteenth and seventeenth centuries. It does not seem farfetched to recognize in some applications of these classifications another example of hostile and destructive criticism of the Enlightenment, a criticism which tries to deprive it of a character of its own.

The task of establishing coherent patterns is greatly facilitated by the eighteenth-century authors themselves, for rarely has a more deliberate effort been made to relate the different domains of man's activity to each other. This effort extended also to the field of aesthetics, and it is above all here that we can find themes and principles which are common to literature, art, and the thought of the eighteenth century, with regard not only to their general relationship but also to the specific and limited question of Rococo. It is impossible to deal briefly with such an extensive topic; I simply wished to point out the necessity of a study which, in addition to the methodological observations set forth here, should precede the use of Rococo as a key to eighteenth-century art and thought.

A. Bartlett Giamatti

Proteus Unbound:
Some Versions of the
Sea God in the Renaissance

Proteus, the sonne of Oceanus and Tethys, called of the
paynimes the god of the sea whom Homere nameth to
be the herde man of the fisshes called Phocae, and also
a prophete, notwithstandynge he would not geue aun-
swere but beyng costrained by Ulisses. He also tourned
himselfe into sundrie figures. Sometime like a bull, an
other time like a terrible serpente. . . . In verie deede
he was kynge of Aegypte in the time of Priamus kynge
of Troy. Of him came the proverbe, PROTEO MUTA-
BILIOR, more changeable than Proteus, applied to him
that in his acts or words is unstable.
        Sir Thomas Elyot, Bibliotheca Eliotae [1]

In 1518, the humanist and physician Ambrose Leo wrote Erasmus
and compared him to Pythagoras and Proteus, the latter who "in
varias formas mutasse sese, cum libuisset." The comparison is apt
because, says Leo to his friend, first you are in France, then you
appear in Germany, then in Italy, in England, in France again,

---

1. Ed. Thomas Cooper (1559). Cooper, in his own *Thesaurus Linguae*
Romanae & Britannicae (London, 1565), follows Elyot's account of Proteus
verbatim. For the tradition of Proteus as King of Egypt, see the good study
of Spenser by Thomas Roche, Jr., *The Kindly Flame* (Princeton, 1964), pp.
152–55. Unless otherwise noted, all references to Greek and Latin authors
and all translations from Greek refer to the appropriate volume in the Loeb
Classical Library.

437

and then "de Gallo in Germania transiisti." Leo quickly warms to
his conceit: truly, he says, you change from poet to theologian,
from theologian to cynic philosopher, and from cynic to orator:
"quae mirae metamorphoses Protei illius solius videbantur." Now
possessed by the spirit of his figure, Leo cannot resist one more
variation: "Vidimus enim innumeros libros tuos impressos, quibus
memoratas vel hominis vel ingenii personas et formas variasti . . .
non vt vnus idemque sententiarum magnarum autor fores, sed
tanquam tres quatuorue autores illarum essent." In a genial reply
from Louvain, Eramus protests he has never been other than he is
("Nec vnquam alius fui quam sum") and pointedly compares himself with Ulysses instead.[2] Perhaps Erasmus remembered, as his
correspondent had not, that in his *Enchiridion* (1503) Proteus had
figured the evil passions of man.

For an examination of Proteus in the Renaissance, two interesting themes emerge from Leo's homage to the great humanist and
from Erasmus' evasion: first, that it was natural to signify man's
potential for learning and virtue and, importantly, his artistic or
literary capacities under the figure of Proteus; and second, that of
all the interpretations of the shape-changer, some were by no
means benign.

Other uses of Proteus in the Renaissance's image of man appear
in a variety of thinkers. For instance, while in Louvain in 1518,
Erasmus met the young Spanish humanist Juan Luis Vives, and
shortly thereafter, Vives wrote his very suggestive *Fabula de
homine*. To celebrate man, Vives tells of his playing various roles
in the great theater of the world. Man assumes the guise first of
plants, then many animals, and finally appears as himself—"prudent, just, faithful, kindly, friendly"—he who lives in cities,
creates and upholds laws, cares for the well-being of his fellow
citizens, and is "finally in every way a political and social being."
The gods, astonished, proclaim him "multiform Proteus, the son
of the Ocean"; and when he first impersonates them, and then
Jupiter, father of all, so that one cannot distinguish creator from

2. Letter dated 19 July, no. 854 in *Opus Epistolarum Des. Erasmi
Roterodami*, ed. P. S. Allen, H. M. Allen, and H. W. Garrod (Oxford,
1906–58), *3, 353*; also letter dated 15 October, *3, 402*.

creature, man is elevated to a place equal to the gods, a "brotherly guest or fellow citizen." [3]

In this Renaissance amalgam of classical and Christian, the figure of Proteus is crucial to the fable. Not only is Proteus appropriate to figure the multiple glories of man, but man's Protean ability to adapt and to act many roles is the source of the power that enables him to assume the burdens of civilization, to create cities on earth and win citizenship among the immortals. Man is not Protean because he is civilized; he is civilized because he is Protean, and the role of civic Proteus is central to the Renaissance's view of man in society.

Written after meeting Erasmus, Vives' fable owes much, of course, to Pico della Mirandola's famous *Oratio De Hominis Dignitate*. According to Pico, God gave man the central place in the universe, whence—unfettered—he may by his own free will choose whatever his nature will be. "Tu, nullis angustiis coercitus, pro tuo arbitrio, in cuius manu te posui, tibi illam praefinies. Medium te mundi posui, ut circumspiceres inde quicquid est in mundo." [4] Man is given to be what he desires ("cui datum id habere quod optat, id essere quod velit") . Pico first compares him to the chameleon and then, following his Hermetic texts, to Proteus. For it was man, Pico says, who was symbolized by Proteus in the mysteries, and after examining the transformations found in Hebrew, Greek, and Islamic texts, Pico cites a Chaldaean saying which he translates thus: "idest homo varie ac multiformis et desultoriae naturae animal." [5] Why emphasize man as a creature

3. Text from the translation by Nancy Lenkeith in *The Renaissance Philosophy of Man,* ed. E. Cassirer, P. O. Kristeller, and J. H. Randall, Jr. (Chicago, 1948) , pp. 389, 392.

4. I cite the *De Hominis Dignitate Heptaplus De Ente et Uno,* ed. E. Garin (Firenze, 1942) , p. 106.

5. "Quis hunc nostrum chamaeleonta non admiretur?" (*De Hominis,* p. 106). The Chaldaean saying, p. 108. As Edgar Wind notes in his brilliant chapter "Pan and Proteus" in *Pagan Mysteries in the Renaissance* (New Haven, 1958) , p. 158, Ficino uses the same argument. The chameleon was commonly associated with Proteus; cf. Erasmus, *Epitome Adagiorum* (Amsterdam, 1650) , s.v. "Chameleonte Mutabilior" and "Proteo Mutabilior." Subsequent references to the *Adages* (1500) will be to the third or Aldine

varied, multiform, and inconstant? Because, he says, we must always remember the necessity to choose correctly, to be (and he quotes the 82nd Psalm) angels and not beasts.

As the *Oratio* unfolds, Pico becomes what he has described. For as he ranges through all human thought, he becomes a Proteus, a man with no native image but many appearances.[6] He says he is proud to be tied to no school, to no single doctrine, and to have known all forms of thought.[7] It is a superb boast, fulfilling the promise of Protean man set forth at the outset and revealing the way in which, through the forms of the Many, Pico is able to arrive at the One.[8]

Finally, as so often happens in the shimmering, shifting world of the Neoplatonic quest for unity, the subject and the object collapse into one another. This transference occurs at the end of the *Oratio,* as the material assumes its own Protean characteristics.

> Quod volui dixisse ut cognoscatur quis mihi labor, quae fuerit difficultas, ex affectatis aenigmatum syrpis, ex fabularum latebris latitantes eruere secretae philosophiae sensus, nulla praesertim in re tam gravi tam abscondita inexplorataque adiuto aliorum interpretum opera et diligentia.[9]

---

edition (Venice, 1508) or *Desiderii Erasmus Operum Omnium* (Leiden, 1703–06).

6. *De Hominis,* p. 108.

7. Ibid., pp. 138–40.

8. Wind, *Pagan Mysteries,* p. 158, cites Pico in "one of the Orphic *Conclusiones:* 'He who cannot attract Pan, approaches Proteus in vain' "; he continues: "The advice to seek for the hidden Pan in the ever-changing Proteus refers to the principle of 'the whole in the part,' of the One inherent in the Many." Associated with this quest for truth under disguises was the Silenus Alcibiades which derives from Plato's *Symposium,* 215, where Alcibiades compares Socrates to the statuettes of Silenus. See Erasmus' *Adagia,* s.v. "Silenus Alcibiades," *Opera Omnia,* 2, 770o–82c, esp. 770d, and Wind, *Pagan Mysteries,* p. 179. In the *Enchiridion* (trans. R. Himelick [Bloomington, 1965]), Erasmus says: "the Holy Scriptures, like the Silenus of Alcibiades, conceal their real divinity beneath a surface that is crude and almost laughable" (p. 105). Jacob Cats called a book of emblems *Silenus Alcibiades sive Proteus* (1618); cf. on this and the role of emblem books, Wind, p. 137.

9. *De Hominis,* p. 162.

The image of Proteus, he who contains the truth under strange guises, now informs not only the knower but also what must be known.

If the figures of the chameleon and Proteus lead Ficino and Pico to the One behind the Many, over a century later the image of Proteus, submerged in the oceanic language of the *Essais,* would lead Montaigne to find the Many in the One: "chacque homme porte la forme entiere de l'humaine condition" (III.ii) .[10] Protean is the image for life: "La vie est un mouvement inegal, irregulier et multiforme" (III.iii) , and for the best spirits: "Les plus belles ames sont celles qui ont plus de variété et de soupplesse" (III.iii) .[11] And it is the image for himself, in whom Montaigne finds the Protean quality of all human existence, with the result that he can only record the minute by minute change, the "metamorphoses" (III.ii) of growing old.

> Je peints le passage. . . . Je pourray tantost changer, non de fortune seulement, mais aussi d'intention. C'est un contrerolle de divers et mutables accidens et d'imaginations irresoluës et, quand il y eschet, contraires; soit que je sois autre moymesme, soit que je saisisse les subjects par autres circonstances et considerations. (III.ii) [12]

In such an undertaking, contradictions are inevitable, particularly because as in travel, so in all things: "la seule variété me paye, et la possession de la diversité, au moins si aucune chose me paye" (III.ix) .[13] As life is his changeable element, so Montaigne is— one feels perforce—Protean in response; and if he is, so, in a celebrated passage, is man: "Certes, c'est un subject merveilleusement vain, divers et ondoyant, que l'homme. Il est malaisé d'y fonder jugement constant et uniforme" (I.i) .[14]

As in Pico, so here the Protean character of the investigator is also the primary characteristic of the object under investigation.

10. My text is the *Essais,* ed. M. Rat, Classiques Garnier (2 vols. Paris, 1962) , *2, 222*. This quotation is from "Du Repentir."

11. "De Trois Commerces," *Essais, 2, 238, 237.*

12. "Du Repentir," ibid., pp. 237, 222.

13. "De La Vanité," ibid., p. 431.

14. "Par Divers Moyen On Arrive A Pareille Fin," ibid., *1, 5.*

But a different note is sounded in that "vain." The Florentine glory of man is here qualified, as all is qualified in Montaigne. The Protean language—man immersed in the ocean of life, an ocean of flux inhabiting man—carries an edge of melancholy, a sense of fatigue, the promise of futility. Now the limitless potential is also a curse. If man is Proteus, capable of all shapes, unfettered, as Pico has said, by any dogma—"Une seule corde ne m'arreste jamais assis" (III.ix) [15]—then he is also at the mercy of vanity and emptiness. None of us, Montaigne implies, Solon included, is exempt from the futility which attends this endless and necessary mutability.

The promise of humanism is proving false in the humanists' own terms. Where Pico or Vives had promised through Proteus angelic stature, an insight into single truth under multiple guises, a universe to command and enjoy, Montaigne knows that undulating diversity can also end in sheer waste: "Il n'en est une seule si vuide et necessiteuse que toy, qui embrasses l'univers"; and continuing, as if in reply to Pico's Protean knower and to Vives' Protean actor with his civic gifts, Montaigne can say of man: "tu es le scrutateur sans connoissance, le magistrat sans jurisdiction, et, après tout, le badin de la farce" (III.ix) .[16]

Let us glance at one final Protean version of the human personality in the Renaissance. Robert Burton devotes the first part of his massive *The Anatomy of Melancholy* (1621) to the kinds, causes, and forms of melancholy, and at one point he finds Hippocrates and Galen proposing fear and sorrow as the disease's most frequent causes. But Diocles and Hercules de Saxonîa disagree, says Burton—the latter particularly:

> Four kinds he excepts, fanatical persons such as were *Cassandra, Manto, Nicostrata, Mopsus, Proteus, the Sybils,* whom Aristotle confesseth to have been deeply melancholy. . . . Demoniacal persons, & such as speak strange languages, are of this rank; some Poets; such as laugh always and think themselves King, Cardinals, &c.   (I.iii, Mem. I, Sub. II) [17]

15. "De La Vanité," ibid., 2, 431; for Solon below, see p. 433.
16. Ibid., p. 446.
17. *The Anatomy of Melancholy*, ed. A. R. Shilleto, intro. A. H. Bullen (London, Bohn's Standard Library, 1920) , *1*, 443.

Here Proteus takes on a darker hue, that of the black bile which, according to Aristotle, afflicted "all men who are outstanding in philosophy, poetry or the arts" (*Problems,* 953a). Melancholia, whether of the poet, lunatic, or lover, was a distinguished disease to have; but what is most interesting is that here Proteus, considered in his role as seer, is included with the "demoniacal persons" and their use of language and with the poets. As we shall see, Proteus will play those roles too.

From our brief glance at Renaissance versions of the self, two points emerge. First, the emphasis on Proteus, like the view of man, is never the same. Obviously the age's sense of man's ambiguous personality is admirably figured in that creature classical poets invariably called "ambiguus." [18] Second, implicit in all the roles Proteus would play in Renaissance literature would be Pico's view of him as a symbol for man's enormous potentiality. Indeed, this attitude, combined with the widespread idea that Proteus was, in Sir Thomas Browne's words, "the Symbole of the first matter," will survive into the nineteenth century; there in the second part of *Faust* Goethe will use Proteus as the vehicle for Homunculus in his quest for form and life.[19]

18. Cf. Silius Italicus, *Punica,* VII.436; Valerius Flaccus, *Argonautica,* II.318; Ovid, *Metamorphoses,* II.9. In Orphic theology, all the gods are "dei ambigui," that is, as Wind (*Pagan Mysteries,* p. 161) says, they are "animated by a law of self-contrariety" and, later (p. 162), they are seen "both as inciters and as moderators." A better description of Proteus and of his roles could not be found.

19. *Faust,* II.iii.8152–487; cf. Shelley's "The Proteus Shape of Nature as It Slept," *Triumph of Life,* 271. For Proteus as a natural philosopher, see below, p. 447. For Browne, see *The Gardens of Cyprus,* in *Works,* ed. G. Keynes (New ed. Chicago, 1964), *1,* 225. I am indebted to Michael O'Loughlin for this reference. Francis Bacon, in *The Wisdom of the Ancients* (XIII) states that "the person of Proteus denotes matter, the oldest of all things, after God Himself" (*The Moral and Historical Works* . . . , ed. J. Devey [London, Bohn's Standard Library, 1854], p. 227); see also Andrea Alciati s.v. emblem clxxxii in *Omnia Andrea Alciati V.C. Emblemata* (Antwerp, 1581), p. 633. Bacon's source was obviously the great work of Natalis Comes (Natale Conti), *Mythologiae sive Explicationis Fabularum* (1551), VIII.8. See the edition I cite throughout, Hanoviae (1619), pp. 850–51. See also the very influential work of Carolo Stephanus (Charles Estienne), *Dictionarum Historicum, Geographicum, Poeticum* (Geneva, 1652), col. 1677. First published in 1553, I cite the Geneva edition throughout.

Besides the variations on Proteus as limitless man or as artist, an equally popular idea, our inquiry into Renaissance man has revealed another version of Proteus crucial to Renaissance literature. This is Proteus the lawgiver, or the civic Proteus of Vives; and because Proteus is nothing if not ambiguous, civic Proteus implies his opposite, Proteus the lawbreaker. This last form of Proteus is found in various guises everywhere—in the figure of the evil seer and the deceitful actor, both versions of the figure of the artist, as well as in his major role as violator of sexual norms and destroyer of cities and communal concord. Often Proteus will play several of these roles at once, hiding a malignant intention beneath a benign exterior. Thus he appealed to the Renaissance for many reasons, but above all two: because he could reconcile all differences and opposites, and because he embodied the principle of illusion as a mask for reality, appearance at once concealing and leading to vital or to deadly truths.

The time has come to make our move and to try to bind him. It will not be easy. Even the Middle Ages, where opinion on a given issue was often unanimous, was divided on Proteus. In the ninth century, Theodulph of Orleans could assure his readers that Proteus meant Truth, while the *Roman de la Rose,* in Chaucer's version, associates him with "gile ne tresoun." In his spirit, the Renaissance will embrace both these and many other extremes. Proteus will appear before us successively in his guises of artist, lawbreaker, and lawgiver.[20]

20. For Theodulph, see "De Libris quos legere solebam," in the *Patrologia Latina,* ed. J.-P. Migne, *105,* 331–32. Theodulph's statement is part of the long Christian tradition of seeing truth under the veil of fiction. Cf. Boccaccio, *Genealogie Deorum Gentilium Libri,* XIV.7, in the translation of Books XIV and XV by C. G. Osgood, *Boccaccio on Poetry* (Princeton, 1930), p. 157, n. 8, where the concept is traced from Augustine to Milton; cf. Erasmus on Silenus Alcibiades and Holy Scripture, above, n. 8. On Proteus and how to "temperare la fizzione poetica et ornare le cose sacre con le profane . . ." in his *De Partu Virginis,* see Jacopo Sannazaro's letter of 13 April 1521 in *Opere Volgari,* ed. A. Mauro (Bari, 1961), p. 373. Near the beginning of his *Davideis,* Abraham Cowley promises "T'unbind the charms that in slight *Fables* lie,/ And teach that *Truth* is truest *Poesie"* (ll. 41–42 in *Poems,* ed. A. R. Waller [Cambridge, 1905], p. 243) —the image is a Christian reversal of Proteus, now unbinding, not fettering, to grasp the truth.

To understand Proteus properly in his various roles as artist, it is necessary to see him first in his traditional role as seer or *vates*. This role originates in Homer where, in *Odyssey* IV (360–570), Menelaus tells how, on the advice of Proteus' daughter Idomethea, he tried to bind the god who appeared successively as a lion, snake, leopard, boar, water, and fire. (These became his standard shapes, as in Ovid, *Metamorphoses*, VIII.732–37.) Once bound, Proteus told him to honor the gods and then recounted the fates of Ajax, Agamemnon, Odysseus, and Menelaus himself.

Virgil's treatment of Proteus in *Georgic* IV was no less influential. There Cyrene advises woeful Aristaeus to consult the seer— "Est in Carpathio Neptuni gurgite vates/Caeruleus Proteus" (387–88) [21]—for he, like Yeats' bird, can sing of things past, passing and to come: "novit namque omnia vates,/quae sint, quae fuerint, quae mox ventura trahantur" (392–93). This episode including the prophecy ends the *Georgics* and establishes Proteus for later times as the ancient seer par excellence.[22]

The Renaissance constantly emphasized the prophetic powers of Proteus. Thus Boccaccio can begin his account in the *Genealogie* (VII.ix), "Proteus marinus deus, et insignis, ut, aiunt, vates," and then cite the Fourth *Georgic* verbatim. Erasmus stresses Proteus as seer in the *Adagia*, as do Cooper in his edition of Elyot's *Bibliotheca*, Alciati in his famous book of emblems, and writers like Comes, Cartari, Bacon, and Ross in their explications of mythology.[23] There is a good reason for this interest in the seer, for

---

For Chaucer, see *Romaunt*, 6319–22 in *Works*, ed. F. R. Robinson (2d ed. Cambridge, Mass., 1957), p. 624.

21. The epithet "blue" earlier occurs in Silius Italicus, *Punica*, VII.420, at the beginning of Proteus' long prophecy on the fate of Italy; cf. "blue Proteus" in Ben Jonson, *Volpone*, III.vii.153 (discussed below), and Shelley, *Prometheus Bound*, III.ii.24.

22. See also Lucan, *Pharsalia*, X.511 ff. Thetis, who prophesied to Achilles, *Iliad*, XVIII.34–147, is also a sea creature allied with Proteus' vatic powers. Cf. Plato, *Republic*, 2, 381d. In Ovid, *Metamorphoses*, XI.224, Proteus foresees a great son for Thetis; she then (249–65) changes shapes to escape Proteus.

23. For Boccaccio, VII.9, I use the Scrittori d'Italia edition of the *Genealogie Deorum Gentilium*, ed. V. Romano (Bari, 1951), *1*, 343; Erasmus,

in the Renaissance, the *vates* was also—as he would be for the Romantics—a general figure for the poet.

There is no need to stress this well-known idea. In his *Genealogie* (XIV.viii) Boccaccio follows Isidore of Seville and others in distinguishing between Moses and the prophets, who composed under the impulse of the Holy Ghost, and the secular poets. These last were impelled by a (Platonic) "vi mentis," an energy or power of the mind, and are therefore called *vates*.[24] Although there would be further refinements, Sir Philip Sidney sums up prevailing opinion in his *An Apology for Poetry* while reviewing terms for the poet:

> Among the Romans a Poet was called *vates*, which is as much a Diviner, Fore-seer, or Prophet . . . so heavenly a title did that excellent people bestow upon this hart-ravishing knowledge.

Later in speaking of the third and best kind of poet ("which most properly do imitate to teach and delight"), Sidney extends the term and makes it general:

> These be they that, as the first and most noble sorte, may be justly termed *Vates*, so these are waited on in the excellen-[te]st languages and best vnderstandings, with the fore described name of Poets.[25]

As the casualness of Don Quixote's comment to the Barber implies (II.i), this notion was the common property of all who thought or wrote about poetry in the Renaissance.

Adagia (1508), pp. 130–31, and in *Opera Omnia*, 2, 473b–74a; see the epigraph to this essay from the third edition of Elyot's *Bibliotheca*, ed. Cooper; Alciati, *Emblemata*, pp. 629–30; Comes, *Mythologiae*, p. 854; Vincenzo Cartari, *Le Imagini, con la Spositione de i Dei degli Antichi* (1556), for which I use the revised and corrected edition (Lyon, 1581), p. 214; Bacon, *Wisdom of the Ancients* (XIII), p. 227; Alexander Ross, *Mystagogus Poeticus or The Muses Interpreter* (London, 1647), p. 191.

24. See Osgood, *Boccaccio*, pp. xxxviii and 46, n. 23, for source in Isidore and ancients; p. xlii for idea in Alberto Mussato.

25. Text in *Elizabethan Critical Essays*, ed. G. G. Smith (Oxford, 1904), *1*, 154, 159.

If Proteus was considered a prophet and *vates* was the common term for a poet, it is easy to see how the Renaissance could conceive of Proteus as a figure for the poet. In Sidney's celebrated description of the poet's nature, which occurs between his two statements on the poet as *vates,* we see the forging of this link:

> Onely the Poet, disdayning to be tied to any such subjection, lifted up with the vigor of his owne inuention, dooth growe in effect another nature, in making things either better than Nature bringeth forth, or, quite a newe, formes such as neuer were in Nature . . . so as hee goeth hand in hand with Nature, not inclosed within the narrow warrant of her guifts, but freely ranging onely within the Zodiack of his owne wit.[26]

The Protean implications reside in the humanist idea of man free to grasp the universe with his mind, in the exalted status of the poet and his superior powers, attributes implicit in the vatic powers of Proteus and often attributed to him,[27] and finally in the language itself. For the poet, able to teach and delight, is like Proteus unfettered—"disdayning to be tied to any such subjection"—freely creating his version of things, constantly growing ". . . another nature."

This brave notion of the Protean writer who knows many things and can assume various forms through and of expression is one we have met before. It was explicit in Leo's encomium of Erasmus' multiple literary talents; it was implicit in Pico's and even Montaigne's vision of their writing and knowing selves as Protean; it was hinted by Burton's inclusion of Proteus (and other seers) with the poets. Finally it is stated clearly by Comes in his account of Proteus:

> Alii, inter quos fuit Antigonus Carystius in Diction, Proteum virum sapientissimum fuisse tradiderunt, qui multa de naturali philosophia scripserit, de plantis, de lapidibus, de natura ferarum, di mutatione mutua elementorum.

26. Ibid., p. 156.
27. For instance, wisdom was commonly attributed to Proteus; see Ross, *Mystagogus Poeticus,* p. 191, after Comes, *Mythologiae,* p. 854.

Later, under the name of Proteus, Edmund Waller can laud both a poet and his plays:

> The sundry Postures of thy Copious Muse
> Who wou'd express, a thousand Tongues must use;
> Whose Fate's no less peculiar than thy Art,
> For as thou cou'dst all Characters impart,
> So none cou'd render thine, who still escap'st
> Like Proteus in variety of Shapes:
> Who was, nor this, nor that, but all we find
> And all we can imagine in Mankind.
>
> ("Upon Ben Jonson")

Proteus as a figure for the writer's plenitude and grasp of all experience would survive to the nineteenth century, where a French novelist fighting the wars of realism will say: "L'idéal pour un romancier impersonnel est d'être un protée, souple, changeant, multiforme, tout à la fois victime et bourreau, juge et accusé." [28]

While it is true that classical literature offers no direct precedent for identifying Proteus and the poet, to the Renaissance mind ranging the zodiac of its wit the fact that Virgil's *vates* in *Georgic* IV tells Aristaeus the story of the archetypal poet Orpheus must have been suggestive. [29] And certainly one figure of the poet

28. Comes, *Mythologiae*, p. 854. *Poems* (9th ed. London, 1712), p. 99; I am indebted again to Michael O'Loughlin for this reference. Champfleury (Jules Husson, dit Fleury, 1821–89), cited by René Wellek, *A History of Modern Criticism* (New Haven and London, 1965), *4*, 473, in n. 14 to p. 2. In "The Poet" Emerson describes the poet as "the man without impediment, who sees and handles what others dream of, traverses the whole scale of experience" (*Essays: Second Series* [New York, John W. Lovell Co., n.d.], p. 8). Emerson's language suggests a Proteus and sounds like Keats' notion of "*Negative Capability*, that is when man is capable of being in uncertainties, Mysteries, doubts, without any irritable reaching after fact & reason." Here too the language for the poet is reminiscent of Proteus. See letter of 27 December 1817 to George and Tom Keats, in *The Letters of John Keats*, ed. H. E. Rollins (Cambridge, Mass., 1958), *1*, 193.

29. It is interesting that Silius Italicus, *Punica*, VII, says Proteus knows "arcana deum" (424) and so the prophet will begin far back in order to reveal the future (436–37); this knowledge of the gods and this method of telling are very similar to what Silius says of himself at the opening of the epic (I. 17–20).

Bacon, *Wisdom of the Ancients* (XIII), also calls Proteus "the revealer

in classical literature was associated in the Renaissance with Proteus. That was the shepherd poet, the singer of pastoral. From Homer on, Proteus had been the keeper of the sea creatures. A reference to him justifying the shepherd's calling in Theocritus (VIII.52) and a simile comparing him to a shepherd in *Georgic* IV (433–36) must have validated Proteus' pastoral credentials, for they were certainly in order for Comes, who grandly saw him as a type of the "populorum pastores." To Spenser, he was simply the

> shepheard of the seas of yore
> [Who] hath the charge of Neptunes might heard.
> (*Faerie Queene,* III.viii.30) .[30]

The fact that Proteus was a shepherd by itself did not necessarily link him with the poet-shepherd of pastoral. That final connection was made by the Renaissance poet uniquely suited to appreciate and exploit Proteus' marine duties. I refer, of course, to Jacopo Sannazaro, creator, he claimed, of the piscatory eclogue.[31] In his *Ecloga* I *(Phyllis)* , Sannazaro calls Proteus "divino pectore vates" (88) and thus echoes Virgil's *Eclogue* VI, "divino carmine pastor" (67) .[32] This is most interesting because of *what* is being echoed. Virgil's phrase occurs in a passage on poetry (64–73) and refers to Linus, who with Orpheus, Musaeus, and Arion was con-

---

and interpreter of all antiquity, and secrets of every kind." This admirably describes Bacon's own role; see his *Preface,* especially the end (pp. 227, 203) .

30. Comes, *Mythologiae,* p. 852. Milton's *Elegia Tertia,* 26, and *Epitaphium Damonis,* 99, refer conventionally to Proteus as herdsman under the sea, while Marlowe (*Dido, Queen of Carthage,* I.i.76–77) has followed Horace (*Odes,* I.ii.7) in a bizarre vision of water flooding the land and Proteus driving his herd in treetops. Horace never has much good to say for Proteus: cf. *Epistles,* I.i.90, and *Satires,* II.iii.71. Spenser is attracted by neither Proteus (called "unlovely," *Faerie Queene,* IV.xi.2) nor his charges: "his heard/Of stinking seales and porcpisces" (*Colin Clouts Come Home Againe,* 248–49) . I cite Spenser from *The Complete Poetical Works . . . ,* ed. R. E. N. Dodge (Boston, 1936) .

31. Sannazaro's pioneering claim ignores, as W. P. Mustard has indicated, "certain of the Idyls of Theocritus (VI, XI, XXI) an author whom Sannazaro knew very well." See Mustard's edition, *The Piscatory Eclogues of Jacopo Sannazaro* (Baltimore, 1914) , p. 14.

32. *Eclogues,* ed. Mustard, p. 78; cf: Tasso's Proteus as "sacro marin pastore," in *Intermedio* I to the *Aminta* in *Opere,* ed. Bruno Maier (Milano, 1963) , *1,* 206.

sidered in antiquity and the Renaissance as one of the fathers of
poetry. Thus Sannazaro's Proteus, "the seer divinely inspired,"
refers specifically to the great poet-"shepherd of immortal song."
But the possibilities of Proteus as pastoral poet are still not
exhausted for Sannazaro, who seems to take Proteus' shepherding
for granted. For who is singing of Linus in Virgil's Sixth *Eclogue?*
It is the god Silenus who, says Virgil, had to be caught when asleep
by Chromis and Mnasyllos and fettered with his own garlands
(15–19) else he would not sing. Silenus, already identified in the
Renaissance with Proteus because both embodied truth under
strange exteriors, here bears a striking resemblance to the sea god
who would not prophesy until bound.

Sannazaro exploits these possibilities to their fullest in his
Ecloga IV *(Proteus)*, where Silenus' song of creation becomes
Proteus' celebration of the Bay of Naples and its environs and
where all of Virgil's *Eclogue* VI is imitated down to its smallest
detail. Sannazaro even widens his scope in this poem to include by
allusion other Virgilian singers and his own previous references to
Proteus as a poet.[33] Proteus is now so completely a poet for
Sannazaro that in a *canzone* he will have Proteus simply arise from
the sea, immutable no less ("più non si cangia di sua propria
forma"), and sing the praises of a nameless lady like any other self-
respecting *cinquecento* versifier.[34]

When Comes alludes to Proteus' marvelous power with words
—"Alii dixerunt fuisse virum dicendi peritum, qui facile pos-
set in quosius animorum motus homines impellare"[35]—he is
only generalizing on the tradition we have traced. The concept of
Proteus as poet, whether as a result of his role as *vates* or as
shepherd, has been a benign one. He has shared and embodied the
exalted status of the poet as the free imitator of nature and maker
of forms, as the diviner of secrets and the possessor of valuable
truths. With Proteus, however, ambiguity is the norm, and the

33. See *Eclogues*, ed. Mustard, p. 84 f. Sannazaro's line on Proteus' song:
"laetus cantabat ad auras" (29) echoes Virgil, *Eclogue* I.56: "canet frondatur
ad auras," as well as Virgil, *Eclogue* VI.31 ff.: "Namque canebat" (see
Mustard, p. 85). At line 23, Sannazaro's "divino carmine" echoes his own
comment on Proteus in his *Eclogue* I.88 and Virgil's on Linus in *Eclogue*
VI.67, both cited above in the text.

34. I.xi in *Opere Volgari*, ed. Mauro, p. 143.

35. Comes, *Mythologiae*, p. 854.

other, darker side of Proteus' power with words is an important dimension in his role in Renaissance literature.

In the Renaissance, the power to manipulate words carried awesome responsibilities. As words could create, imitate, and ennoble, they could also falsify and deceive, projecting illusions which bore no necessary relation to actuality. Furthermore, words were notoriously unstable, in this way a true image of human affairs, which were also seen as constantly in flux. Words as a medium for illusion and as unstable, the image of mutability, found their proper counterpart in Proteus, who was archetypally both deceitful in his various disguises and the very quintessence of change. Therefore, Proteus' various roles as a manipulator of words must be seen as they were colored by the deceptive and mutable possibilities inherent in him and in language.

The link between the darker elements in Proteus and in words is magic. As Proteus' role as *vates* had allied him with the beneficent figure of the poet, it also associated him with the often sinister *magus* or magician. In his *Oratio*, Pico had distinguished two kinds of magic. He referred to both kinds as "artes" but says one is the most deceitful of arts, the other the best; one makes man a slave of evil powers, the other makes him their lord and master. Finally, one damns, the other saves:

> Ob hoc praecipue quod illa hominem, Dei hostibus mancipans, avocat a Dco, haec in eam operum Dei admirationem excitat, quam propensa caritas, fides ac spes, certissime consequuntur.[36]

Though Proteus is nowhere explicitly mentioned in this discussion of magic and its practicioners, he was certainly widely regarded as a *magus,* as both Tasso and Milton attest, and as one possessing certain (magic) arts. Perhaps echoing the reference in Virgil when Proteus begins to change shape—"ille suae contra non immemor artis" (*Georgic* IV. 440), Comes says that "Alii crediderunt per magicas artes Proteum in praedictas formas se mutasse."[37]

36. *De Hominis,* pp. 148–54.

37. Tasso, *Rime,* "Come sia Proteo o mago," in *Opere,* ed. Maier, *1,* 391; cf. also p. 500. Milton refers to the *"Carpathian* wizard's hook" in *Comus,* 872. Comes, p. 854. Boccaccio, *Genealogie,* XIV.6; XIV.7 (see Osgood,

Though there is nothing necessarily sinister in the imputation of magical power to Proteus, the potential for evil is there. Again Sannazaro exploits the possibilities. In the sixth eclogue of the *Arcadia,* the shepherd Serrano laments the passing of the Golden Age and demonstrates the depravity of the present by telling how a shepherd came to his door, tricked him into injuring himself, stole two kids and two goats, and then had the effrontery to boast of his crime before spitting three times and disappearing. "Questo è Proteo," says the much-abused Serrano, and though the passage again identifies Proteus with the shepherd, here he is no singer. Rather he is a perfidious magician, as Serrano's catalog of his tormentor's luggage proves:

> Erbe e pietre mostrose e sughi palidi,
> ossa di morte e di sepolcri polvere,
> magichi versi assai possenti e validi
> portava indosso, che 'l facean risovere
> in vento, in acqua, in picciol rubo o félice;
> tanto si può per arte il mondo involvere.
>
> (46–51) [38]

Here the "arte" is indeed that of the evil *magus,* though Sannazaro's polished, languid verses make Proteus sound more like a Neapolitan Puck. The most interesting trick in his bag are those "magichi versi assai possenti e validi," for they begin to reveal the link between Proteus and a long tradition concerned specifically with his ability to manipulate and distort words. From this tradition, the dark side of the benign poet will emerge.

Plato first equates Proteus with devious manipulators of words in the *Euthydemus.* There Socrates says of the two Sophists

---

Boccaccio, pp. 39, 40, and passim; notions of craft are also at issue: p. 158, n. 16), refers constantly to poetry as an art, and he also devotes a section (XIV.16; Osgood, pp. 76–78) to combating the pejorative designation of the poet as "seductor" or enchanter of men's minds. Osgood, p. 176, n. 6, shows how Boccaccio used the same word which was applied to Christ, Matt. 27:63. The (ancient, Platonic) objection Boccaccio was fighting, however, is related to the potential for evil in the poet's power which we have been discussing, and the idea achieved currency simply in Boccaccio's widely read condemnation of it.

38. *Opere Volgari,* ed. Mauro, pp. 43–44.

Euthydemus and his brother Dionysodorus: "They do not care to give us a serious demonstration, but, like the Egyptian wizard, Proteus, they take different forms and deceive us by their enchantments" (288c).[39] Proteus' wizardry is specifically the source of deceit and, through the Sophists, his magical powers are associated with the misuse of words. The same point is made at the end of the *Euthyphro*. Euthyphro's circularity on the question of piety finally exasperates Socrates, who asks:

> And when you say this, can you wonder at your words not standing firm, but walking away? Will you accuse me of being the Daedalus who makes them walk away, not perceiving that there is another and far greater artist than Daedalus who makes things that go round in a circle, and he is yourself.
> (15c)

and he then compares Euthyphro specifically with Proteus (15d). Through association with the great and cunning artist Daedalus and the unintentionally sophistic Euthyphro, Proteus is firmly implicated in the walking words—language as it serves ends other than the truth.

In their accounts of Proteus, Renaissance mythographers were not slow to echo and to elaborate on these Platonic hints.[40] In the meantime, another classical source confirmed Proteus' association with sinister, magical manipulation of words. In Petronius' *Saty-*

39. *Euthydemus*, 288c. Earlier Socrates described the pair as possessing such "skill in the war of words, that they can refute any proposition whether true or false" (272b). I cite Plato throughout from the four-volume *The Dialogues of Plato*, trans. B. Jowett (4th ed. rev. Oxford, 1953).

40. Abraham Fraunce, in *The third part of the Countess of Pembrokes Iuychurch* (London, 1592), says: "Plato *compareth him to the wrangling of brabling sophisters: and some there be that hereby understand, the truth of things obscured by so many deceauable appearences*" (cited in Roche, *Kindly Flame*, p. 159). Alciati, *Emblemata*, "Plerique vatem faciunt, alii Oratorem, vel Sophistam" (p. 634); and Stephanus, *Dictionarum*, "Plato in Euthydemo exponit de fallaciis quibus sophistae in disputando utuntur" (col. 1677). Without reference to Plato, Sir Thomas More compares a sophistic theologian to Proteus in his long letter to Martin Dorp defending Erasmus. See his letter of 21 October 1515, in *St. Thomas More: Selected Letters*, ed. E. F. Rogers, Yale Edition, Modernized Series (New Haven and London, 1961), p. 31.

ricon, the witch Oenothea praises the power of words after her own fashion. "Tantum dicta valent," she says, for a virgin can calm the fiery spirit of a bull:

>   Phoebeia Circe
> carminibus magicis socios mutavit Ulixis,
> Proteus esse solet quicquid libet. His ego callens
> artibus Idaeos fructives in gurgite sistam
> et rursus fluvios in summo vertice ponam.[41]

Oenothea's power to pervert nature, Circe's to change men, and Proteus' to shape himself are all evidently the result of demonic powers exercised through language.

Fully as interesting for the Renaissance as Proteus' ability to make words control and distort things is his association here with Circe, an association which parallels the way he was linked with Silenus in benign roles. For once Proteus falls within Circe's orbit, he is allied with a figure who exercised an enormous fascination for Renaissance poets, as Ariosto's Alcina, Tasso's Armida, Spenser's Acrasia, and others testify, and his own demonic potential is strengthened by the association.[42] Tasso, for instance, sees the link between Circe and Proteus in his *Gerusalemme Liberata.* At Armida's first appearance in the Christian camp, she manages "e far con gli atti dolci e co 'l bel viso/più che con lo arti lor Circe o Medea" (IV.86), while later, "Tentò ella mill'arti, e in mille form/quasi Proteo novel gli apparve inanti" (V.63).[43] In both cases, whether Armida is seen as Circe or Proteus, her "arti" are at issue, those deceitful arts which Pico had said could estrange man forever from God.

41. Text from Loeb Classical Library's *Petronius* (and Seneca, *Apocolocyntosis*), p. 302. Compare Oenothea's ability to disturb nature with Proteus in Horace, *Odes,* I.ii.7.

42. Circe represented the most dangerous impulses to self-destruction in the human soul while she masqueraded as the fulfillment of every man's deepest desires. For Circe, see A. B. Giamatti, *The Earthly Paradise and the Renaissance Epic* (Princeton, 1966), passim, and, for a different emphasis on her as an agent of illusion, the excellent unpublished dissertation of Richard Saéz, "The Redemptive Circe: Illusion and The Beneficence of Evil in Tasso, Milton and Calderón" (Yale University, 1967).

43. Text from *Torquato Tasso Poesie e Prose,* ed. S. A. Nulli (Milano, 1955).

Thus parallel to the tradition of Proteus as *vates* and poet is a tradition of Proteus as *magus* and sinister manipulator of words. The two traditions support one another, providing reciprocal tension and balance, for each depends on the other for the reservoir of ambiguity that gives Proteus, and language, the potency to adapt and to signify. The mutual dependence, or interpenetration, of the demonic and the divine elements in Proteus tells us something about the Renaissance and its view of language. Even more is said about the Renaissance itself when we notice that the demonic Proteus, the potential for chaos, falsity, and death, predominates.

In 1675 *Proteus Redivivus: Or the Art of Wheedling, or Insinuation* appeared in London, a cynical and entertaining book which pretends to teach the young how to succeed in society while it poses as an exposé of the vices of the times. In adopting the figure of Proteus, the author makes a serious point which bears directly on those dark powers of Proteus to manipulate words. The art of wheedling is defined as the

> *Art of Insinuation,* or Dissimulation, compounded of mental reservation, seeming patience and humility, (Self-obliging) civility, and a more than common affability, all which club to please, and consequently to gain by *conversation,*

and shortly the author observes that the

> *Protei* of this loose age can turn themselves into any shape, so that the *conversion* of the form will produce any profit or advantage.[44]

I have italicized "conversation" and "conversion" because these words, sharing a common root in the Latin "convertere," to turn

44. *Proteus Redivivus,* pp. 3, 5. The title page tells us the book was "Collected and Methodized by the Author of the First Part of the English Rogue." This would be Richard Head (1637?–1686?), whose *English Rogue, described in the Life of Meriton Latroon. Being a Compleat History of the Most Eminent Cheats,* appeared in 1665. For Head's other writings, some in collaboration with Francis Kirkman, see *The Cambridge Bibliography Of English Literature,* 2, 176–77, 529–30, 930. Head's labors were not only Protean but Herculean.

or to transform,[45] reveal how the changeable nature of language was associated with Proteus and with the power he had, which was to deceive. Words change, like Proteus; he is able to deceive by changing, and one of the ways he does it is by manipulating words. Thus he is an image for the demon in language and for the user of language for demonic purposes.

Such comments may seem to read too much into the bantering tone of the *Proteus Redivivus,* but the demonic powers in and of language and their association with Proteus had already been seriously noted and explored in English literature by the end of the sixteenth century. We have only to turn and note the uses of language in *Doctor Faustus* and *The Faerie Queene.*

Faustus knew well that there were times when one must

> Be silent then, for danger is in words.
>
> (V.i.25) [46]

But long ago he had succumbed to their power:

> Valdes, sweet Valdes, and Cornelius,
> Know that your words have won me at the last
> To practice magic and concealed arts.
>
> (I.i.101–03)

The magical properties in language make Faustus a great magician; after his first Latin incantation, Mephistophilis appears. Faustus' first words to him, however, are:

45. "Conversation," meaning familiar discourse (16th c.) as well as intercourse, acquaintance, or mode of living (17th c.), from OF *conversacion, -tion,* from L. *conversatio (n)* (conduct, frequent use or abode), from *conversārī,* a middle use of *conversāre,* to turn around, from *con + versāre,* a frequent form of *(con) vertere,* to turn or to transform. "Convert," from OF *convertir,* from L. *convertere.* See the *OED* and *The Oxford Dictionary of English Etymology,* ed. C. T. Onions and others (Oxford, 1966), s.v. "convert," "conversation," and, for the latter, "converse." It is also interesting to note that the epithet "ambiguus," traditionally used by classical poets for Proteus (see above, n. 18) maintains the sense of turning, being formed on *ambi* (around) and *ago,-ere* (to go).

46. My text is *The Complete Plays of Christopher Marlowe,* ed. Irving Ribner (New York, 1963).

I charge thee to return and change thy shape,

. . .

Go, and return an old Franciscan friar;
That holy shape becomes a devil best.

(I.iii.23–26)

Mephistophilis leaves, shortly to return at Faustus' command, and the *magus* is pleased the devil is so "pliant" (29). The humor here masks something more serious. Faustus thinks he has unlocked the demon by language, that his words can control the devil's shapes, but the terrible irony is that Faustus has also unlocked the demon *in* language—a demon who, like Proteus, can change shapes. Throughout the play, while Faustus thinks he shapes his own future with his magical words, the words are actually shaping the destiny of his soul. When Mephistophilis provides Faustus with words, Faustus believes he will have power over all men:

Hold; take this book; peruse it thoroughly . . .
Pronounce this thrice devoutly to thyself,
And men in harness shall appear to thee,
Ready to execute what thou command'st.

(II.ii.157, 161–63)

Like Pico's evil *magus*, however, upon whom the play is in a sense a gloss, Faustus is really the slave of the power he commands and is finally estranged from God.

Lucifer himself even gives Faustus a book:

view it thoroughly, and thou shalt turn
Thyself into what shape thou wilt

(II.iii.168–69)

as Marlowe, in a profound insight into conversation implying conversion, identifies the Protean character of the *magus* with the demonic force in words. Words have their origin in that Word which was God, and whoever tampers with this divine gift by assuming demonic powers will be assumed by those powers and will have his form altered by the demon in the words. Marlowe's irony derives from the fact that, for all his learning, Faustus is ignorant in the matter of salvation.

Spenser's Archimago, however, is no such innocent. This great wizard, explicitly identified with Proteus, knows precisely what he is doing or thinks he knows. Through him we gain even deeper insight into the demonic Protean power of words and the dangers, even for the *magus,* of using them. Archimago's powers are displayed in the first canto of *The Faerie Queene.* His "pleasing wordes" (35) lure the Red Cross Knight and Una to his house to pass the night. Once they have retired, he consults "his magick bookes and artes of sundrie kindes" (36), chooses a "few wordes most horrible, (Let none them read)" (37), and out of "deepe darkness dredd" (38) conjures two false sprights, one who descends to the Cave of Sleep for "a fit false dreame" (43), the other whom Archimago fashions into a false image of Una to deceive the Knight. But even after Red Cross has been divided from his lady, Archimago vows to work Una further harm:

> He then devines himselfe how to disguise:
> For by his mighty science he could take
> As many formes and shapes in seeming wise,
> As ever Proteus to himself could make:
> Sometime a fowle, sometime a fish in lake,
> Now like a foxe, now like a dragon fell.

> (I.ii.10)

This passage looks back to the whole tradition of the *magus* and Proteus' associations with him, and Spenser will later apply the imagery of Proteus again to his magician (I.xii.35;II.i.1). However, this episode will yield more.

As we know, the poet bade none read the "verses" Archimago originally framed (I.i.37) in order to summon the false sprights from the deep. There seems a hint here of the forces in language which the poet, creating this dream world of the poem, knows better than to tamper with—nightmare forces, which only Archimago, false creator or poet of darkness, whose muse is "Great Gorgon, prince of darknes and dead night" (37), can handle. Yet even Archimago is subject to terror, for at the end of the stanza identifying him with Proteus, we learn:

That of himselfe he ofte for feare would quake,
And oft would flie away. O who can tell
The hidden powre of herbes, and might of magicke spel?

(I.ii.10)

A good question, which is answered by the whole poem where the forces here out of control are constantly subjected to that ceremonious control of the poet and the good government, within and without, of the various heroes. But the power in language and those powers unleashed by language demand constant vigilance and can never be totally checked, just as in *The Faerie Queene* there are potent, demonic forces which can never be entirely curbed—the forces represented by Duessa and Malbecco, for instance, both expelled from society but neither extinguished; the powers of the Dragon, who can never be killed; of the Blatant Beast, who cannot be tied down; of Archimago himself, who disappears from sight but who, we assume, continues to roam the world; or, finally, of Despair, a central figure in the poem, whose own medium is words (I.ix.48, 53) and who cannot die until the Last Day, when all will be at peace.

We seem to have digressed, but, like our poet, with a purpose. That was to suggest that Spenser was profoundly aware of forces in human nature which would be a constant danger to man, that these forces lurked in that power which distinguished man from beasts—language—and that one could see the beginnings of Spenser's development of this theme in the Protean figure of Archimago, a type of the poet who could appeal to but not control the Protean potency in and of words.

There is one final exploitation of Proteus as poet and *magus* in alliance with the potential of language, and that occurs in *The Dunciad* of Alexander Pope. Here Proteus figures those poets and writers whose words corrupt. These writers corrupt, however, not because, like Faustus or Archimago, they appeal to the demonic forces in language. Rather these men have no sense of the divine origins of language or of the proper use of words to create and civilize. Thus through their ignorance their words invariably destroy, creating monsters instead of the proper image of man and spreading chaos instead of light.

Near the beginning of Book I, we read that from the Cave of Poverty and Poetry,

> Hence Bards, like Proteus long in vain ty'd down,
> Escape in Monsters, and amaze the town.
>
> (I.37–38) [47]

Were there any ambiguity about the identification of the targets of Pope's lash, it was dispelled in Warburton's note. There, after citing Ovid (*Metamorphoses* VIII. 730–34) on Proteus' changes into a boar, a snake, a bull, and a stone, Warburton says "Neither Palaephatus, Phurnutus, nor Heraclides" can elucidate this mysterious myth. With that jab at scholarship, he then provides some of his own:

> If I be not deceived in a part of learning which has so long exercised my pen, by *Proteus* must certainly be meant a hacknied Town scribler; and by his Transformations, the various disguises such a one assumes, to elude the pursuit of his irreconcilable enemy, the Bailiff. Proteus is represented as one bred of the mud and Slime of Ægypt, the original soil of Arts and Letters: And what is a Town-scribler, but a creature made up of the excrements of luxurious Science? By the change then into a *Boar* is meant his character of a *furious and dirty Party-writer*; the *Snake* signifies a *Libeller*; and the *Horns of the Bull*, the *Dilemmas* of a *Polemical Answerer*. These are the three great parts he acts under; and when he has completed his circle, he sinks back again, as the last change into a *Stone* denotes, into his natural state of immoveable Stupidity.

The effect of these Protean hacks is to "amaze the town," that is, by their writing to introduce into the human community a kind of confusion which finally reduces the city to chaotic wilderness. However, the poison seen as introduced into the City, either in

47. Text in *The Dunciad*, ed. James Sutherland (Twickenham ed. London, 1943), 5, 272–73. It is interesting to note that these lines were added to the final edition of 1743 (Sutherland's B text, which I cite). Compare the version of 1728 (A) in Sutherland, p. 64. For Warburton's note, cited in part below, see p. 272.

this couplet or in the processive movements to the Temple of Dulness in the poem as a whole, is but an analogue to the poisoning of the mind, seat of the city within and source of the power with which to civilize without. Here the reference to the Protean bards as Monsters finds its true meaning, for as their misuse of language fills the city with monstrous shapes, so these perversions are but reflections of what their ignorance has already done to them. The Queen explains it to Dulness:

> Son; what thou seek'st is in thee! Look, and find
> Each Monster meets his likeness in thy mind.
>
> (III. 251–52)

The Protean perversion of shapes becomes not only an emanation from but a symbol for the perverted imagination which, misusing the power originally in the Word, spreads horror and chaos instead of order and light.[48]

The final echo of Proteus occurs at the commencement of the decay in civil order, Silenus announces to the Queen that her "Magus" (IV.516) will preside: "With that, a WIZARD OLD his *Cup* extends" (517). "Here beginneth," Warburton explains, "the celebration of the *greater mysteries* of the Goddess" where, under the influence of the wizard's libation, "each of the Initiated . . . putteth on a *new Nature.*" Proteus had been called the "*Carpathian* wizard" by Milton in *Comus* (872), the same work in which Milton also referred to the "charmed cup" of Circe (50–51). And here a *magus,* with Proteus' (and Circe's) power to change shapes, presides over the final dissolution, a dissolution not only of all human forms but of all human and divine ties, hierarchies, order. For as Pope's and Warburton's note glosses the end of the line:

> The *Cup of Self-Love* . . . causes a total oblivion of the
> obligations of Friendship, or Honour, and of the Service of
> God or our Country; all sacrificed to Vain-glory, Court wor-

48. For other monsters, see I.81, 106. After writing this, I found my sense of Proteus' function confirmed and enlarged in the study of A. Kernan, "*The Dunciad* and the Plot of Satire," reprinted in *Essential Articles for the Study of Alexander Pope,* ed. M. Mack (Hamden, Conn., 1964), pp. 726–38, where the shapeless, disordering powers of Dulness are discussed.

ship, or yet meaner considerations of Lucre and brutal Pleasures.[49]

The monstrous Protean perversion of language will usher in the
kingdom of the "uncreating word" (IV.654) and the black arts of
the *magus* create the "Universal Darkness" (656) whence they
come.

At the outset of our binding of Proteus, I claimed he had
various guises under the general mask of the artist. And besides
the ambiguous conception of him as *vates*-poet, which only concealed his darker role as *magus* and demonic manipulator of
words, the Renaissance also distinguished Proteus the actor, a role
which will reveal him essentially as a seducer. From that version,
we will easily see the origins of Pope's use of Proteus as a force
hostile to civilization, for the deceiver leads naturally to the
lawbreaker.

The general idea of Proteus as a deceiver is a basic element in
all accounts of the god. In Homer, for instance, Idomethea deceives her father by telling Menelaus his secret; Menelaus disguises
himself in a sealskin; Proteus tries to deceive Menelaus by changing shape. The specific image of the actor stems from this general
theme, though as in the version of Proteus the poet, there can be
wide variations in emphasis. In Vives' *Fabula,* for instance, Protean man was explicitly conceived as an actor, and this ability to
mimic and adapt won him a seat of honor among the gods. Marlowe could also use Proteus positively to praise the great Edward
Alleyn:

> Whom we may rank with—doing no one wrong—
> Proteus for shapes and Roscius for a tongue,
> So could he speak, so vary.
> (*The Jew of Malta,* Prologue to the Stage, 9–11)

Others would speak of Proteus as actor or performer neutrally,
with neither sinister nor beneficent implications. As Lucian, in a

49. *The Dunciad,* ed. Sutherland, p. 393. Cibber and others had been
referred to as wizards at III.265 ff. It is generally agreed that the Wizard
figures Walpole.

passage noted by Renaissance mythographers, did in his dialogue
on *The Dance:*

> For it seems to me that the ancient myth about Proteus the
> Egyptian means nothing else than that he was a dancer, an
> imitative fellow, able to shape himself and change himself
> into anything, so that he could imitate even the liquidity of
> water and the sharpness of fire in the liveliness of his move-
> ments.

In the same neutral vein, Tasso ingeniously uses Proteus as an
actor by introducing him as the scene-changer in the interludes
written for *Aminta.*[50]

But as before, the associations of Proteus with deception and
evil predominate, and again Plato provides the ultimate impetus.
Now we turn to the *Ion,* where the (self-confessed) best rhapsode
in Hellas has also admitted he is the best general. Socrates accuses
him of deception (541e), as the typical Platonic technique of making the dialogue enact what it discusses unfolds. The rhapsode,
earlier associated with the actor and poet as links in the chain
whereby God "sways the souls of men in any direction which he
pleases" (536), now practices the deception of avoiding Socrates'
logic and his own promises. As before with the Sophists, Socrates is
annoyed:

> You literally assume as many forms as Proteus, twisting and
> turning up and down, until at last you slip away from me in
> the disguise of a general, in order that you may escape exhibit-
> ing your Homeric lore.   (542)

In the Renaissance, the sinister implications of Proteus the actor
are exploited, naturally enough, in the drama. Indeed, two recent
discussions of sixteenth- and seventeenth-century drama have
begun with the figure of Proteus, emphasizing his importance for

50. Text in Loeb Classical Library's *Lucian,* trans. Harmon, *5,* 231–33.
See Erasmus, *Adagia,* p. 130, and *Opera Omnia, 2,* 473b; Comes, *Mythologiae,*
p. 852; Alciati, *Emblemata,* p. 634; Stephanus, *Dictionarum,* col. 1677. Sir
John Davies, in his splendid "Orchestra, or a poem of Dancing," 561–67,
has also remembered his Lucian. For Tasso, see *Opere,* ed. Maier, *1,* 205–06,
and editor's n.

the controlling ideas of deceitful appearances in a world of flux.[51] Shakespeare uses the deceptive Protean actor to adumbrate an even broader theme in the culmination of the Duke of Gloucester's soliloquy in *III Henry VI:*

> Why, I can smile, and murder whiles I smile,
> And cry "Content" to that which grieves my heart,
> And wet my cheeks with artificial tears,
> And frame my face to all occasions.
> I'll drown more sailors than the mermaid shall;
> I'll slay more gazers than the basilisk;
> I'll play the orator as well as Nestor,
> Deceive more slyly than Ulysses could,
> And, like a Sinon, take another Troy.
> I can add colors to the Chameleon,
> Change shapes with Proteus for advantages,
> And set the murderous Machiavel to school.
>   (III.ii.182–93) [52]

All of which, as Richard III, he accomplishes. There is no need to dwell upon Gloucester-Richard's Protean abilities as an actor or upon the role his own shape and deformity play in the motivation for his various roles. We might only note that here Proteus the actor shares billing with Sinon and Machiavel, an association which foreshadows the uncivil powers of Proteus—of Proteus as he was in Pope—the poisoner of the body politic.

---

51. Jean Rousset, in his *La Littérature de l'age Baroque en France* (Paris, 1953), links Circe, as we have, with Proteus—"il est sa propre Circé, comme Circé fait du monde un immense Protée. Le magicien de soi-même et la magicienne d'autrui étaient destinés à s'associer pour donner figure à l'un des mythes de l'epoque: l'homme multiforme dans un monde en métamorphose" (p. 22). Stephen Orgel, in *The Jonsonian Masque* (Cambridge, Mass., 1965), opens by discussing *The Mask of Proteus and The Adamantine Rock*, presented at Gray's Inn, Shrovetide, 1595 (see edition by W. W. Greg, *Gesta Grayorum, 1688* [Oxford, Malone Society Reprints, 1914]). Like Rousset Orgel believes that Proteus was "the mythological representative of two central themes of the literature of the age: the dangers of inconstancy and the deceptiveness of appearances" (p. 10).

52. My text throughout is *The Complete Works of Shakespeare,* ed. G. L. Kittredge (Boston, Ginn and Co., 1936).

This hint of the actor as lawbreaker points to Ben Jonson and *Volpone,* where we are also introduced to Proteus' lustful qualities. Deception and lust are linked. Proteus breaks civil laws because he violates natural or sexual ones.

Volpone is a play permeated by the spirit of Proteus. Here, as Pope has it, the monstrous shapes of Protean master and man truly amaze the town. The satiric thrust partially derives from the fact that Volpone, concerned because

> I have no wife, no parent, child, allie,
> To give my substance to.
>
> (I.i.73–74) [53]

has no real substance at all, only forms. But while he is the master of all shapes in this world-as-bestiary, the real Protean genius is Mosca. He is able to deceive even Volpone for a time, and his ability to change shapes is finally unattached to considerations of money or sex or even power. It is the sheer disinterested joy of the artist, employing his native talent with superb skill.

> But your fine, elegant rascall, that can rise,
> And stoope (almost together) like an arrow;
> Shoot through the aire, as nimbly as a starre;
> Turne short, as doth a swallow; and be here,
> And there, and here, and yonder, all at once;
> Present to any humour, all occasion;
> And change a visor, swifter, than a thought!
> This is the creature, had the art borne with him;
> Toiles not to learne it, but doth practise it
> Out of most excellent nature.
>
> (III.i.23–32)

Here in Mosca's cold, and later Volpone's much warmer, reveling, we come to the core of the play where, as Alvin Kernan has indicated, the idea of acting is not only allied with deception but also— as it was in Vives, for instance—with man's unlimited potential. Jonson's irony, of course, depends upon our recognition that here the "art" inherent in "most excellent nature" creates only the un-

53. Text, with *v* normalized to *u,* from *Works,* ed. C. H. Herford and P. and E. Simpson (Oxford, 1925–52), *5;* commentary in *9.*

natural and finally ranges man among the beasts and not the angels.[54]

It is Volpone who explicitly mentions Proteus when he tells Celia that before

> I would have left my practice, for thy love,
> In varying figures, I would have contended
> With the blue PROTEUS.
>
> (III.vii.151–53)

He then offers to contend on the spot. In his seduction of Celia, he promises the delicacies of all the world and the entertainment of his household—all while

> We, in changed shapes, act OVIDS Tales,
> Thou, like EUROPA now, and I like JOVE,
> Then I like MARS, and thou like ERYCINE,
> So, of the rest, till we have quite run through
> And weary'd all the fables of the gods.
>
> (III.vii.221–25)

He expatiates on "more moderne formes" (226) and after a brave catalog of Celia's transformations, he promises: "And I will meet thee, in as many shapes" (233). The language of Proteus limns the limits of man's desires and reveals the terrible emptiness of Volpone, whose appetite can never be satisfied. His marvelous words are impotent, though he claims he is not (260–61). Volpone, who will never again soar so high, ends finally bereft of any "substance" (V.xii.119) he had left and "crampt with irons" (123) in the hospital of the *Incurabili*—a Proteus at last tied down by the state to become in truth what he had feigned.

Again Proteus the actor or deceiver has threatened the orderly processes of the human community. However in Volpone, he has added a new role to his repertoire, that of a figure of powerful sexual lust. There is some classical precedent for this role of libidinous Proteus. For besides the classical sources for Volpone's boast to weary all the fables of the gods, Lucian in *On Sacrifices* com-

---

54. See Kernan's introduction, to which I am indebted, to his edition of *Volpone*, The Yale Ben Jonson (New Haven, 1962), pp. 11 ff. Kernan specifically adduces Pico, pp. 14–15.

pares amorous Zeus, who inspired all the fables, specifically with Proteus.[55] Certainly, if like Burton one associated Proteus with melancholy, Aristotle's comment in the *Problems* (953b) that "the melancholic are usually lustful" would have been provocative. So would Protean Silenus' promise in Virgil's *Eclogue* VI (25–26) to sing a song for the shepherds but to give the nymph Aegle another kind of reward. These various hints as well as Marlowe's lines in *Hero and Leander* describing the carvings on Venus' temple all underline Volpone's Protean sexuality:

> Wherein was Proteus carv'd, and o'rehead
> A livelie vine of greene sea agget spread . . .
> There might you see the gods in sundrie shapes,
> Committing headdie ryots, incest, rapes.
>
> (I.137–38, 143–44) [56]

Proteus also had a well-established reputation for lust and passion among other types of Renaissance writers. Boccaccio said Proteus' various forms signified the passions which torment men; Alciati cited Clement of Alexandria who compares Proteus "ad cupiditatem animi humani in varias sese mutantem formas"; and Erasmus in his vastly popular *Enchiridion,* in a passage we referred to at the outset, says that when "vehementibus perturbationibus aestuat animus," you must use every resource to bind this Proteus with chains: "Quid autem tam Proteus, quam adfectus & cupiditates stultorum, quae cum eas nunc in belluinam libidinem, nunc in iram ferinam, nunc in venenatam invidiam, nunc in alia atque alia vitiorum portenta trahunt." [57] Finally, Proteus' reputation for sinister sexuality was only confirmed through his association with a figure like Circe. And if we

55. Herford and Simpson, eds., *Works, 9,* 720, cite Martial, X.v.17; for Lucian, see Loeb edition, *3,* 161.

56. Text in *Minor Elizabethan Epics,* ed. E. S. Donno (New York and London, 1963), p. 53; see through l. 156. Marlowe is looking back at the carvings on the palace of the sun, where Proteus is mentioned, in Ovid, *Metamorphoses,* II.9.

57. Boccaccio, *Genealogie,* VII.9: "Formas ver, quas sum sumere consuetum aiunt, et abicere, eas existimo passiones, quibus aguntur homines" (ed. Romano, *1,* 344) ; Alciati, *Emblemata,* p. 633; Erasmus, *Opera Omnia, 5,* 18c–d.

wonder why Erasmus, in his *Adagia,* would link Proteus and Vertumnus, the reason is manifest when we read in Ovid (*Metamorphoses,* XIV.628–771) of how Vertumnus seduced Pomona by assuming a disguise. Cartari will even describe Vertumnus as a figure for changeable human thought—a common designation for Proteus.[58]

The version of lustful Proteus is linked to the greater role of Proteus lawbreaker. This tradition, already mentioned in Shakespeare's *Richard III,* in *Volpone,* and *The Dunciad,* sees Proteus as uncivil, the violator of social and communal norms and wellbeing. In *Orlando Furioso,* Ariosto will use both the smaller and the larger roles. There the sea god's lust explicitly ruins a society.

As usual with Ariosto, the episode begins in a previous episode, and one must go back to Angelica to understand Proteus. In canto VIII, stanzas 29 ff., she is fleeing from Europe, and an old hermit, who has befriended her for reasons of his own, despairs of keeping pace. So he enchants her horse which, after a detour in the sea, brings her back to the hermit amid rocks and fearsome caves (37). The old man assaults her and she, "sdegnosetta," pushes him over with one hand, not forgetting to blush her famous blush (47). The resourceful hermit then drugs her by spraying a potion in her eyes, and she is his. But, as stanzas 49 and 50 make wickedly clear, all to no avail. Thus far we have burlesque in the assaults of the old magician, who is impotent; next comes the serious story of Proteus, who is not.[59]

Ariosto now disgresses to tell the ancient history of the inhabitants of Ebuda (one of the Hebrides) and their beautiful princess who one day on the beach was raped by Proteus (52). The rape is narrated swiftly and casually in two lines, as if this were standard behavior for Proteus, while the murder of the princess and her

58. Cartari, *Imagini,* p. 225; Erasmus, *Adagia,* p. 130; Milton, *Paradise Lost,* IX.393–95, used the deceitful and sensual implications of this story in treating Eve and her seduction by Satan (see Giamatti, *Earthly Paradise,* pp. 327 ff.). The name Vertumnus is derived from *verto,-ere,* to turn or to transform, the same root discussed in relation to Proteus. See above, n. 45.

59. The hermit is called a magician in VIII.67 and X.94. This fact, his age, and the marine locale serve to parody Proteus as they anticipate him. Text from *Orlando Furioso,* ed. Nicola Zingarelli (6th ed. Milano, 1959).

child by the men of her enraged and brutal father occupies a
stanza. The language now becomes crucial:

> Proteo marin, che pasce il fiero armento
> Di Nettuno che l'onda tutta regge,
> Sente de la sua donna aspro tormento
> E per grand'ira, rompe ordine e legge;
> Sí che a mandare in terra non è lento
> L'orche e le foche, e tutto il marin gregge,
> Che distruggon non sol pecore e buoi,
> Ma ville e borghi, e li cultori suoi:
>
> (54)

> E spesso vanno alle città murate,
> E d'ogn'intorno lor mettono assedio.
> Notte e dí stanno le persone armate,
> Con gran timore, e dispiacevol tedio;
> Tutte hanno le campagne abbandonate.
>
> (55)

From Proteus' rape comes the slaughter of a girl by her father, and
after that follow violations of other laws: first, the "ordine e legge"
of nature governing the habitat and behavior of the sea creatures,
and second, the assault of nature on nature—as the sea creatures
attack the oxen and sheep—and then nature on the farms and
their "cultori" and finally on the walled cities. We have worked
up the scale of being and inland to the centers of civilization.

From the sexual lawlessness and civil discord comes, inevitably,
more of the same. The oracle consulted by the islanders advises
offering girls to Proteus in appeasement for the dead princess
(56), and as these human sacrifices are bound to a rock, the monstrous orc consumes them (57). On Ebuda, this is the "empia
legge antica" (58) —the new law which long ago resulted from the
rupture of the old. Thus, Angelica—"in braccio al santo padre"
(61)—is found by a party searching for new victims, for the
people have long since become obsessed and depraved, "sì barbare
. . . e sì villane" (62). And after Angelica is exposed (67) and
the story resumed when Ruggiero comes to her rescue (X.93), the
barbarism and incivility of the islanders is continually stressed

(X.93, 95). This whole episode culminates in canto XI when Orlando finally kills the orc and the sea runs with blood while all the sea creatures lament terribly (44–45). The people, terrified of Proteus and his "ira insana" (46), assault rather than welcome their benefactor, and Orlando is forced to kill a number of the "gente pazza" (50). Finally the human community which decayed within so long ago is destroyed without as a party of Irish land and kill all the islanders and raze their cities' walls. In the meantime, Orlando, defender of another city, Paris, walks away.

Throughout the episodes involving Proteus and Ebuda, Ariosto's sense of the marvelous never falters. But noticeably absent is his habitual ironic preoccupation with the discrepancy between illusion and reality, perhaps because the incidents involving Proteus are part of a more somber theme in the poem, the insanity which is caused by love and, finally, the insanity which is love. This madness, afflicting the islanders and Proteus in different forms, finally will overwhelm Orlando himself, and in all cases Angelica, or, as in Canto VIII, her surrogate the princess, is the cause. However, we might also suggest that the Proteus episodes lack Ariosto's customary irony because that is what the episodes are about: they deal with that loss of balance, of perspective, of proportion—irony in its largest sense—without which men are doomed and which men seemed forever doomed to lack. "Grand' ira" (VIII.54), "ira insana" (XI.46), says the poet of Proteus, for Proteus, casual, brutal, and assured, is our key to the incipient frenzy and overmastering destructive power in us all. While as a lesson teaching what those forces can do, the sexual barbarism of Proteus has caused the death of a city.[60]

At this point, it is fair to say that the incivility of Proteus, Proteus as lawbreaker, has been implicit in all the darker hues on all

60. Spenser, *Faerie Queene,* III.viii.29 ff., tells the story of Proteus' rescue and attempted rape of Florimell. There is some humor in Proteus' assault and Ariosto (*Orlando Furioso,* VIII.29 ff.) is obviously being used, but the "civil" concerns of the Italian are not part of Spenser's purpose. For a full discussion of sources, see the Variorum edition, ed. E. Greenlaw and others (Baltimore, 1932–49; index, 1957), 3 269–72; for good critical commentary, see Roche, *Kindly Flame,* pp. 158–62.

the spectra—whether in Proteus as poet (as in *The Dunciad*) or as actor (as in *Volpone*) or as sinister rapist (as in the *Orlando Furioso*). As we have come to expect, however, a given version of Proteus always implies its opposite, and there is also the civic Proteus, the figure of concord, not discord, the maker of civilization, not death and destruction. More than once we have mentioned Vives' *Fabula,* deriving from Pico's *Oratio,* where Protean man was a builder of cities, a giver of laws, "in every way a political and social being." [61] The most striking versions of the civic Proteus in the Renaissance, however, are found in its most influential mythographer and its greatest poet. Differing and unrelated as these versions are, they demonstrate that Comes and Shakespeare could see the Proteus figure as containing all and the Protean spirit as a force for good.

In his long account of Proteus, Comes saw him as the original principle of all things; as a wise man and author of works on natural philosophy; as a *vates* and as one who practiced magic arts (these two are distinguished); as a man whose words could move the souls of men; and finally as the "populorum pastores," the type of the prince who considered the health as well as the comfort of his people.

I think, says Comes finally, that Proteus is a wise man *(virum prudentem)* who draws men into concord and warm friendship and soothes souls, who heals the differences arising among them and teaches them to adapt to the human condition. For, Comes continues, who does not know there is no greater thing, "vel in administratione ciuitatum, vel quotidiana consuetudine," than to accommodate the spirit to changing situations and to changes in human affairs?

> oportet igitur virum prudentem, quoniam non omnes ijsdem studiis delectanur aut capiuntur, per varias formas se in nominem amicitiam ingerere, ac varias uti rationibus in civitatum administrationibus, quoniam alij eventus clementiam, alii severitatem iudicis requirunt.

Thus the Renaissance principle of tolerance, of amending oneself to the necessities of life, of adapting oneself to one's sense of the

61. *Renaissance Philosophy,* p. 389.

contingencies in things, underlies the proper government of the city of man. And Proteus, whose various forms signify the wise man's ability to influence men for the good, is a proper figure for this principle of flexible civility.

But the fable does not only pertain to friendship and civil administration, Comes says. Above all it relates "ad universam humanae vitae rationem," which consists neither in gorging oneself nor in living austerely. Rather the proper time for things must be recognized: "sed utriusque rei tempora sunt cognoscenda." Comes concludes that to him the fable means no more than what the oracle said:

> Ne quid nimis: cum omnis omnium rerum salus & constantia in mediocritate, moderationeque sit collocata,

Nothing in excess, for the health and constancy of all things consists of mediocrity and moderation in all things: The ethical life underlies the civic life, as in a powerful exordium to his readers Comes transmits the essentials of the humanistic wisdom drawn from the ancients. And Proteus, the man whose friendship, prudence, and civic sense are figured by his ability to adapt to the demands of life and the needs of man, is the symbol for it all.[62]

Our final consideration of Proteus will be as one of the two main characters in Shakespeare's *The Two Gentlemen of Verona*. Indeed, we may ask why Shakespeare chose the name at all, for it appears in none of the play's sources.[63] The usual answer—that this is a comedy of true and false friendship and love where Valentine figures faithfulness and Proteus, inconstancy—is not adequate, for it ignores both the full possibilities in the name and Shakespeare's exploitation of them. In *Two Gentlemen of Verona*, Proteus plays all the roles we have examined, and Shakespeare extends the spirit of Proteus in order to supersede the

---

62. Comes, *Mythologiae*, pp. 854–55. See also Ross, *Mystagogus Poeticus*, pp. 191 ff.

63. See *Narrative and Dramatic Sources of Shakespeare*, ed. G. Bullough (London and New York, 1957), *I*, 203–11 (intro.), 212–66 (texts of sources).

figure of Proteus. At least, the figure is superseded as it contains sinister elements. Finally, even the purged figure is redeemed by the spirit.

In the play's Protean world, where love has "metamorphis'd" both Proteus and Valentine (I.i.66, II.i.32) and "deform'd" Valentine's Silvia (II.i.70), Proteus easily plays all his traditional roles. The "subtile, perju'd, false, disloyal man," as Silvia calls him in IV.ii.95, is an actor or deceiver throughout. He is also an artist in III.ii.51–87, where he is compared to a weaver and a sculptor, and where he acts, on Sir Thurio's behalf, as a poet and a stage director. As before he was a figure for language, here in the balcony scene he is allied with the instability of music (IV.ii.54–72). And he is still the traditional manipulator of language in IV.ii. 120–34 as he, Silvia, and Julia (disguised as a boy—another form of deformation) talk about the ambiguities of illusion and reality, "shadow" and "substance," their puns demonstrating and embodying those ambiguities. Finally, Proteus is throughout a corrupter and a would-be seducer; he is even willing, as he was in Ariosto, Spenser, and Jonson, to be a rapist (V.iv.55–58). His reference to his own "augury" in IV.iv.73 even recalls the traditional role as Proteus, *vates*.

In Act V, the banished Valentine is in a wood outside Milan, the chief of a band of outlaws. He is worried that his men "make their wills their law" and that it is difficult "to keep them from uncivil outrages" (iv.14,17). When he sees Proteus assault Silvia, who has come to find him, Valentine cries, "Ruffian! let go that rude, uncivil touch" (60) and the deeper issue of law and lawlessness—civility in its widest sense—begins to develop. After sharply rebuking Proteus, Valentine forgives him and then—gives him Silvia (77–83). This episode, a scandal to commentators, was once adduced as proof Shakespeare was not the only begetter of *Two Gentlemen of Verona* [64] and is usually justified by the conventions of male friendship. But it seems clear that what is at work

64. Arthur Quiller-Couch and J. Dover Wilson in their Cambridge edition of the play (Cambridge, 1921) were forcibly struck, but not dumb; for their detection of other hands, see their introduction, pp. xiii–xix, and notes to V.iv, pp. 102–04.

here is simply the spirit of Proteus; for now the play begins to supersede the figure while developing the spirit—the spirit of Proteus in Comes' terms of concord and amendment.

Men are first reconciled with themselves: Julia reveals her true nature and identity; Proteus seemingly sees his falsity (108–12). Men are then reconciled with each other, as Valentine, embodying the spirit of adaptability, friendship, and healing, invites Proteus and Julia: "Come, come, a hand from either. . . . 'Twere pity two such friends should be long foes" (116–18). "Bear witness, heaven, I have my wish forever" (119), says Proteus, and by implying constancy ceases to be Proteus. He never speaks again.

The Protean spirit, however, continues to work its good. Sir Thurio now reverses himself and renounces his claim to Silvia, thus causing the Duke to turn on him, a conversion which reconciles the Duke with Valentine, in whom he recognizes "unrivall'd merit" (144). And now the Protean spirit of lawgiving completely surpasses lawbreaking, as Valentine asks for his outlaws the same recognition of inner worth he has received.

> Forgive them what they have committed here
> And let them be recall'd from their exile.
> They are reformed, civil, full of good. (154–56)

The deformations of Proteus and Protean love are now "reformed" on the widest scale by the Protean spirit embodied in Valentine. Men find themselves and each other, the outlaws are included in the new law, the forest is reconciled with the city, and "civil" restoration is effected within and without.

Nothing is beyond the healing spirit. "Come Proteus," says Valentine,

> 'Tis your penance but to hear
> The story of your loves discovered.
> That done, our day of marriage shall be yours;
> One feast, one house, one mutual happiness. (170–73)

Valentine will "discover" or reveal the final shape of Proteus himself, and with that reformation the civilizing spirit will have reclaimed the purged figure of this society's greatest outlaw. In the rituals of marriage and feast, those ceremonies of social harmony, and in the house, very symbol of the city, the Protean spirit of reconciliation will reside. In drawing the spirit of concord from the figure of discord, the play has reversed itself and is revealed as an example of what it is about.

Mutability, lawlessness, baseness, constancy, civility, gentility: in addition to his traditional roles, Proteus as figure and spirit has signified them all. There is no more inclusive vision of the versions of Proteus in the Renaissance, no clearer depiction of his dangers and redeeming possibilities.

In the last decade of the sixteenth century, those redeeming possibilities—the spirit of Proteus to unite and to civilize—extended beyond the romantic comedy of Shakespeare. In *The Faerie Queene,* when Medway relents and will marry Thames,

> both agreed that this their bridale feast
> Should for the gods in Proteus house be made. (IV.xi.9)

And so they go, in grand and spacious order, all the gods and waters great and small. The bride, with flowers scattered in her hair, upon her head "A chaplet of sundry flowers . . . wore" (76), while he, "a coronet . . . In which were many towres and castels set" (27), a crown like Cybele's, symbol of the city, Troynovant. This great myth of the most ceremonious of all Renaissance poets marries all—male and female, art and nature, the city and the garden worlds—through the pageant in Proteus' house. And perhaps after all the versions, this should be the final one, the last thought to have of Proteus: like the Renaissance poet, entertaining the very stuff of creation, presiding over the most civilizing of ceremonies, while participating in and controlling a world of ceaseless change.

Claudio Guillén

Second Thoughts on Currents and Periods

To explore the idea of literary history may very well be the main theoretical task that confronts the student of literature today. Where criticism is concerned, no one will deny that the work of theorists in recent years has been spectacular and influential. The most subtle command of terms and methods can be encountered in the writings of countless scholar-critics. Metaphors have been applied to the concept of metaphor, symbols to the symbol, and myths to myth. But the situation is different in the area of literary history. In contrast, its scope, particularly the understanding of its own terms and methods, seems limited or relatively stationary. One of the features of the present moment in literary studies is this odd imbalance between a fast-growing body of practical criticism, well grounded in theory, and the ability to translate individual insights into persuasive historical constructions on the basis also of adequate theory.

A great deal of useful thinking has been devoted to interrelationships. First of all, between literature and general history—the history, one might say, of non-art. Despite the abusive or rather the one-sided character of certain exercises in formal analysis, the relevance of various aspects of the history of societies and civilizations to the illumination of literary texts has been widely recognized and demonstrated during the last twenty or thirty years. Most often, however, these connections are not a contribution to literary history. They involve, on the one hand, the poetic text in its supra-temporal dimension (as it emerged initially from the flow of historical time), and, on the other, the history of non-art. These contacts usually subsume, or tend merely to predict, a history *of* literature itself, an attempt to recapture and interpret the process of literature in historical time.

The mutual dependence of criticism, theory, and literary history, which has been a cornerstone of René Wellek's teaching and writing,[1] is of course the condition, or the indicator, of the imbalance I am commenting upon. And the study of the relationships between literary criticism and literary history is likely to remain an ungrateful task as long as our conception of the latter is so much more obscure and less robust than that of the former.

Let us take the metaphor of "current," for example, which, as applied to literature, is frequent and harmless enough. Like many of the terms composing the vocabulary of literary history, we use it easily and most often without second thoughts. One associates it readily with some sort of dynamic or continuous process, more or less akin to the notion of development. "But the concept of the development of a series of work of art," Professor Wellek has remarked, "seems an extraordinarily difficult one." [2] Upon scrutiny, the notion of current, like the entire conceptual framework of literary history, perhaps, poses serious problems too, which the following pages intend only to identify.

One might begin by observing that the idea of "literary current" appears to complement that of "literary period." This alliance seems to be more than empirical. There is, as it were, a limit in each of the concepts that calls for complementation by the other (or by the dimension that it represents). At first glance, they could respond or correspond to the two principal aspirations that H.-I. Marrou, in his recent summary for the *Encyclopédie de la Pléiade,* thinks are essential for historians: *reconstitution d'un devenir* and *récupération de valeurs.*[3] Literary currents would reconstruct past processes of change, while literary periods would imply values revisited. Our initial hypothesis might then be: currents are diachrony, and periods synchrony.

1. Cf. "Literary Theory, Criticism, and History," in René Wellek, *Concepts of Criticism* (New Haven and London, 1963), pp. 1–20, items B4, B6, B54, and C12 of the bibliography at the end of the same book; and Chaps. 4 and 19 of René Wellek and Austin Warren, *Theory of Literature* (3d ed. New York, 1956).

2. Wellek and Warren, p. 255.

3. Cf. H.-I. Marrou, "Comment comprendre le métier d'historien," in *L'Histoire et ses méthodes,* ed. C. Samaran (Paris, 1961), pp. 1475, 1481.

But one discovers immediately the difficulties that such a scheme raises. Do literary periods generally fail to be dynamic or diachronic, and, if so, is this understood? Is it possible that in the particular branch of history that is literary history, a process of change or of becoming should exclude the recapturing of values, such as those that are present in the literary works themselves? How can this experience of values based on artistic structures be, on the other hand, a sensitive instrument for the apprehension of time? Are periods and currents but different methods for the conceptual grasp of an identical chronology? If history, as Lucien Febvre said, is the science of man in time, how can any reflection on literary history find pride in independence from diachrony?

It would be impractical to review here the complex question of periodization as it has been understood by various modern schools of historiography. But I can bear witness to the shock of the literary critic when he first approaches the subject and realizes that it is common among general historians to think of epochs and eras and periods with stunning freedom and open-mindedness or even with a degree of skepticism. I know no better example of the critical position towards periods than Huizinga's deservedly famous essay on the idea of the Renaissance.[4] Somewhat less boldly, it is frequent among historians of non-art to use period terms as a temporal backdrop of neutral, conventional content—almost as a simple chronology or quantifying device—to which more interesting constructions can be referred, or to consider them as necessarily provisional, biased, or pedagogical. I need only recall, among the lively discussions in which German historians took part, the debate between Karl Heussi (who had challenged the notion of a generally valid periodization) and Georg von Below in the early 1920s,[5] and, in our day, the remarkably flexible and creative atti-

4. Cf. J. Huizinga, "Het probleem der Renaissance" (1920), reprinted in *Tien Studiën* (Haarlem, 1926) and in *Verzamelde Werken* (Haarlem, 1949), *4*; I have read it in *Wege der Kulturgeschichte*, trans. W. Kaegi (München, 1930).

5. Cf. K. Heussi, *Altertum, Mittelalter und Neuzeit in der Kirchengeschichte. Ein Beitrag zum Problem der historischen Periodisierung* (Tübingen, 1921), and G. von Below, *Ueber historische Periodisierungen* (Berlin, 1925), as well as the earlier "Ueber historische Periodisierungen," *Archiv für Politik und Geschichte, 4* (1925), 1–29, 170–214; and the review by P.

tude of Fernand Braudel and his collaborators toward the never-ending organization of the past—"le bornage, toujours à reprendre, du temps perdu." [6]

The fact that literary historians, on the contrary, often defend a broad and also stationary pattern of periodization is rather puzzling. The reasons that come to mind are very basic, and they can only be sketched here in summary fashion. A literary work of art, as we know, is a response to experience, and it cannot be grasped properly in social or historical terms without reference to that experience. It is also a construction, in the final analysis, of a structure transcending, or emerging from, the flow of time which had surrounded the response, This is the difficult, self-denying historicity with which the literary scholar has to deal. When an economic historian, on the other hand, isolates a list of prices, a balance of payments, or an index of production, he is defining events firmly embedded in temporal change except insofar as he is able to place them in a significant whole. The individual fact must be integrated by the historian into a structure or inserted into a larger pattern of facts, such as an economic cycle. No single economic event can coincide possibly with the cycle, the *conjoncture,* or any similar economic period concept. The single events and the total pattern are fundamentally different.

In contrast, the literary historian is structuring structures. His starting point is charged already with significance. Were we to turn to the modern, yet basically theological, vocabulary of those structuralist discusisons, in the manner of Claude Lévi-Strauss and Roland Barthes, where single events are deemed "contingent" and only the larger pattern is gifted with significance, one would immediately need to recall that in the world of art the situation is quite the opposite: nothing is less contingent than the individual phenomenon (the work of art) or less necessary than the overall concept.[7] It is useless to isolate, at any rate, any radical difference

---

Joachimsen, *Historische Zeitschrift,* *134* (1926), 369–73. Cf. also W. Schneider, *Wesen und Formen der Epoche* (München, 1926).

6. F. Braudel, "Qu'est-ce que le XVIe siècle?", *Annales E.S.C., 8* (1953), 73.

7. In *La pensée sauvage* (Paris, 1962), p. 37, C. Lévi-Strauss states that the work of art functions half-way "entre l'ordre de la structure et l'ordre de

in kind between the literary scholar's reflections on the style of an individual work and his thoughts on the style of a group of works. The economic historian proceeds from event to structure while remaining time-bound. The literary historian moves from one structure to another while maintaining all the way an ambiguous attitude toward historical time.

The group of works which was just mentioned as the object of a literary scholar's thoughts can also be regarded as characteristic of a certain *period.* In this case, the literary historian may develop broad generalizations about a series of works associated with a period without abandoning the level of stylistics or without returning for an instant to the flow of historical becoming. He has made the transition from the work to the series and from the series to the period concept, that is to say, from criticism to so-called literary history, without reentering history. I am not saying that I condone this, but stylistics *can* entertain the illusion of history by simply proceeding from the work to the series. René Wellek and Austin Warren, in the final chapter of the *Theory of Literature,* dealing with literary history, stress that the individual work of art is not an instance of a class or a type but a part of the period concept and of its process of definition. Nevertheless, literary norms, standards, styles, will tend to form static clusters. They do not, like economic cycles, periodize change in the first place. It is not uncommon for a critic to confuse his typology of stylistic responses with the time-section to which they responded and to conclude that his style *is* a period or a concept fully coincident with it. As the critic can become a historian without modifying his principal aim—literary structures—it seems natural that he should develop in the process an inclination for the kind of period concept that is as solid and as timeless as his definition of a style.

For this he can hardly be blamed. His task is particularly arduous. Universals based on artistic structures are not readily reconciled with history. It may be that no generalization concerning a group of works can possibly provide us with a dynamic organization of historical change comparable, say, to economic cycles,

---

l'évènement"; cf. also p. 99; and R. Barthes, *Critique et vérité* (Paris, 1966), p. 51.

unless it focuses on a subject that does not, unlike style, transcend
time in the first place. The difficulty may reside not merely in relating art to the history of non-art, or structures to events, but in
studying literary structures—particularly collective ones, shared
by entire generations of writers—*as* events.

We are all familiar with a conception of literary epochs that is
less monolithic. The tendency to stiffen or to congeal has been
rather less conspicuous recently than the dynamic and problematic
consideration of, for example, the Baroque—in studies that are
intent on not losing sight of the contradictions in literary history
and of the flow of historical time itself. In 1961, to mention but
one instance, Jean Rousset summarized his experience as a critic of
the Baroque in such words as these:

> Bien entendu, nous devons être conscients qu'il s'agit d'une
> espèce de grille, construite par nous, historiens du XXe siè-
> cle, non par les artistes du XVIIe. On évitera de confondre la
> grille et les artistes, le schéma interprétatif et les œuvres
> soumises à l'interprétation. Les catégories ne sont qu'un
> moyen d'investigation de ces faits que sont les œuvres, on les
> considérera même comme des hypothèses de travail et des
> instruments d'expérience, comparables à des échafaudages
> qui perdent leur utilité une fois la construction édifiée.[8]

The period concept serves here to interpret a style which reached
its peak during a certain section of time. But this dominant style
in no way coincides with all the valuable artistic works of the
moment. Homogeneity is neither the goal nor the premise of such
a critical position, for, as Rousset also makes clear, "en l'histoire
de l'art comme en histoire littéraire, c'est la diversité des ten-
dances qui frappe autant que les similitudes, et les résistances au
Baroque presque autant que les consentements." It will not do to
underestimate the "dominated" style, any more than a true critic
will neglect a minor poem. There is no simple equivalence between Baroque and seventeenth century: "Si le principe baroque

8. J. Rousset, "La définition du terme 'baroque,'" in *Actes du IIIe
Congrès de l'Association Internationale de Littérature Comparée* ('S-Graven-
hage, 1962), p. 167.

est peut-être le plus actif, occupant dans l'époque une position centrale, il y a toutes sortes de courants parallèles ou latéraux, toutes sortes de solutions individuelles possibles; et les grands artistes sont précisément ceux qui réussissent des solutions singulières." [9]

Rousset's approach recalls those interpretations, too substantial to be reviewed here, that succeed in making room for both Classicism and Baroque, or even Mannerism, Classicism, and Baroque, within the *same* section of time. I am reminded, for example, of E. B. O. Borgerhoff and Lowry Nelson, Jr., V.-L. Tapié, and Pierre Francastel on the subject of the seventeenth century.[10] Or of Huizinga's refusal to consider the Renaissance as more than one aspect of the culture of the sixteenth century.[11] Or of Ortega y Gasset's insistence on the interplay of generations in history, where the—I think—arguable theory of generations had the advantage of bringing out the extent to which any historical situation, if only we try and visualize it as a "today," is a "drama," a "dynamic system" of attractions, polarities, and polemics.[12] The earlier notion of period as harmony or singleness of style, so characteristic, of course, of *Geistesgeschichte,* yields in these cases to an emphasis on competition and confrontation, in other words, on dialectics.

The dialectics of literary history tend to blend, naturally, with those of general history. Literary controversies will evoke class struggles and, beyond these, recall the economic and political fabric of societies. While the static or synchronic conception of periods depends usually on coherent styles, the dynamic or diachronic view draws upon social tensions. Time, besides, is involved again. Insofar as we restore the polemics of time past, we are likely to rejoin the perspective of time passing. The system of genera-

9. Ibid., pp. 173, 174.

10. Cf. E. B. O. Borgerhoff, "Mannerism and Baroque: A Simple Plea," *Comparative Literature,* 5 (1963), 323–31; L. Nelson, Jr., *Baroque Lyric Poetry* (New Haven and London, 1961), p. 166; V.-L. Tapié, *Baroque et Classique* (Paris, 1957); and P. Francastel, "Baroque et Classicisme: histoire ou typologie des civilisations," *Annales E.S.C., 14* (1959), 142–51.

11. Cf. J. Huizinga, *Wege der Kulturgeschichte,* p. 119.

12. Cf. J. Ortega y Gasset, *En torno a Galileo* (1933), in *Obras Completas* (6th ed. Madrid, 1964), *5,* 40.

tions propounded by Ortega needed a trajectory of events, a series of triumphs and reversals. Francastel, who practices with admirable tact the joint study of painting and society, does not surprise us when he likewise demands a diachronic idea of the Baroque: "Le Baroque ne s'est pas défini entièrement au départ. Ce n'est pas une formule qu'on applique. C'est un bilan que nous dressons après épuisement d'une veine longtemps créatrice." [13]

But these views raise a number of difficulties that can only be handled with respect to an appropriate conceptual framework for periodization. However briefly, it will be necessary to pose here one or two of the questions that are basic for an understanding of the subject. The first, unavoidably, concerns method. By this I mean a method for relating period concepts to single works of art. It has long been assumed that the idea of a Baroque or a Romantic period was reached by means of induction. In practice it appears that this often was not the case, although one is not surprised to find a prevailing loyalty to "facts" in a field—literary history— where the integrity of a fact like *Macbeth* can hardly be denied or regarded as an assumption of some kind. It is, however, the relationship between the single work of art and a period that is often seen as dependent, in Jean Rousset's previously quoted words, on "hypothèses de travail." I need not recall here the reservations with which modern logic discusses inductive procedures. More importantly for us here, contemporary developments in linguistics and anthropology have shown that generalizations in the humanities and in the social sciences are attained most effectively not by the pretended reasonableness of an inductive approach to facts, but rather, as in the natural sciences, by the choice of certain rules in order to explain certain results, or, as this is often termed now, by establishing hypothetical "models of description," which are later referred to all empirical instances at hand.[14] In practice, periods sometimes have been hypothetical models of description of the dominant values of a time-section in artistic history. But it is not uncharacteristic of the literary critic, so proud of the fine edge of his sensibilities, that he should neglect in theory his familiarity

13. Francastel, p. 146.
14. Cf. Barthes, *Critique et vérité*, p. 58; M. Barbut, "Sur le mot et le concept de 'modèle,'" *Annales E.S.C., 18* (1963), 383–86.

with the kind of speculative daring that Ortega portrayed so well thirty years ago:

> Para des-cubrir la realidad es preciso que retiremos por un momento los hechos de en torno nuestro y nos quedemos solos con nuestra mente. Entonces, por nuestra propia cuenta y riesgo, imaginamos una realidad, fabricamos una realidad imaginaria, puro invento nuestro; luego, siguiendo en la soledad de nuestro íntimo imaginar, hallamos qué aspecto, qué figuras visibles, en suma, qué hechos produciría esa realidad imaginaria. Entonces es cuando salimos de nuestra soledad imaginativa, de nuestra mente pura y aislada, y comparamos esos hechos que la realidad imaginada por nosotros produciría con los hechos efectivos que nos rodean.[15]

There are, of course, differences between the general mode of thought that Ortega refers to and the scientific use of descriptive models by Noam Chomsky in *Syntactic Structures* or by Claude Lévi-Strauss in a number of his studies. Chomsky tests logical or mechanical analogues for the complex *process* of language generation. In Lévi-Strauss, the model signifies not so much the terms of the subject to be interpreted as the structural *relations* between them, and, as a result, not only a real but a potential subject.[16] To what extent such procedures have actually been used in periodization, or could be used, is a question that can only be posed here, though I would add that there seems to be some promise in Umberto Eco's study of models in terms of transactional psychology.[17]

The "system of literary norms, standards, and conventions" [18] that, according to René Wellek, is the core of a period does not have to be isolated then only or exclusively by the direct contemplation of single works and a passage from the particular to the general. An alternate conception posits a number of generalities founded not only on facts but on hypotheses, i.e. on structures and

---

15. *En torno a Galileo*, p. 16.

16. Cf., for example, Lévi-Strauss, *Le Totémisme aujourd'hui* (Paris, 1961), p. 23.

17. Cf. U. Eco, "Modelli e strutture," *Il Verri*, No. 20 (1966), 11–28.

18. Wellek and Warren, p. 265.

assumptions deriving to a large degree from the observer. Corrections and connections are then made, in the opposite direction, between generals and particulars. My point here is that no system of norms, standards, or conventions is merely given to us. A *system* of this kind proceeds from the questions that we choose to direct to the single works; from the theory of genres which we decide, either consciously or in routine fashion, to accept; from our attitude toward the appropriate poetics; and so on. Historians and philosophers of history normally recognize today that there is no such thing as a ready-made subject matter of history. It exists only insofar as the historians have selected it and shaped it for us. Objectivity in history, it has always seemed to me, is as much a misnomer or a *petitio principii* as "realism" in the novel. The same certainly applies to the order of *literary* history (perhaps also to poetics and certain general categories of criticism, our outstanding contemporary "model" being Northrup Frye's *Anatomy of Criticism*). At any rate, the isolation of a period concept must rely on the previous choice of pertinent criteria. It is only a *certain* set of criteria that makes it at all possible to distinguish between the Middle Ages and the Renaissance in the history of literature. As H. P. H. Teesing makes clear in his valuable book, the unity of a period is inseparable from that of the examples we have chosen to interpret.[19] Any periodization, while sufficiently "objective" or "real," is partial and does not preclude, as we shall see later, other principles of organization of historical time. In each case a certain objectivity resides in the coherence between the criteria initially picked and the facts to which they are supposed to apply.

A mere discussion of method has taken us fairly far afield, but the question of the relationship between periods and historical time must also be looked into. It might be useful, as a start, to recall the ideas of Bogumil Jasinowski in a suggestive 1937 article on the logical foundations of history. In Jasinowski's view, periods are not entirely discrete entities. They do not exclude one another like objects existing simultaneously in space or like the parts resulting from the division of a single entity. They are different

19. Cf. H. P. H. Teesing, *Das Problem der Perioden in der Literaturgeschichte* (Groningen, 1948), Chap. 1.

moments in a temporal continuum: "Les époques consécutives ne s'excluent donc pas, comme s'excluent les membres d'une division en classes, car les unités périodologiques ne sont pas fondées sur la disjonction des caractères et ne relèvent pas du principe de contradiction dont toute la discrimination dans le domaine du discontinu (*entia discreta* d'une classification) reste inséparable."[20] It is not only because "transitions" occur between one period and another, as is often said, or because one gradually gives way to another for a limited interval that periods cannot be placed simply side by side or juxtaposed. Within the continuous flow of a culture, there are no islands, but only qualitative differences. For example, in the history of Spain, according to Américo Castro's interpretation, what is most important periodologically is the break between culture and culture at the time of the Islamic invasions of the eighth century, and on a certain level all subsequent periods overlap totally. Jasinowski's own example is Dante, whom he regards not only as the heir of Virgil and the climax of the Middle Ages, but as the beginning of the Renaissance. Huizinga once stressed the fact that medieval culture runs into or beneath the Reformation of the sixteenth century and even recommended that the Middle Ages and the Renaissance be considered not only as severed by a vertical line but as flowing horizontally together.[21]

Periods do happen *after* one another—but the meaning of "after" is not fixed. How much *diversity* does temporal succession imply? Do we tend to visualize it spatially, like a separation, a complete break? If "after" connotes difference, it denotes above all succession and perhaps even continuity. The question, then, with regard to Jasinowski's view, is whether a period can adapt itself to the trajectory of time as intimately as such a view assumes. In other words, the distinction between an absolute and a relative periodization is not a matter only of logical stress—as if I, for ex-

20. B. Jasinowski, "Sur les fondements logiques de l'histoire," in *Travaux du IXe Congrés International de Philosophie* (Paris, 1937), p. 44.

21. Cf. "Het probleem der Renaissance," in *Verzamelde Werken, 4,* 257: "Liep ónder de Renaissance de middeleeuwsche cultuur inderdaad door in de Hervorming, dan was de grenslijn tusschen Middeleeuwen en Renaissance niet alleen verticaal te trekken, maar nog horizontaal bovendien"; and in *Wege der Kulturgeschichte,* p. 119.

ample, were saying, focus on the dominant features of a period, and differences will come out sharply; stress, on the other hand, dialectics, keep in mind the "dominated" traits, and, since these traits are likely to recur in another period, you will get a combination of differences and similarities. Jasinowski's concern was with *temporal,* as against spatial, typologies and with their peculiar nature. Our basic concern should be with the extent to which periods are supposed to reflect becoming or to parallel the course of time. To understand the degree of their diachrony, to measure their proximity to time, is to be in a position to know what "after" and "before" mean in this area of discourse. In fact, every period concept gives away something, loses something, on the level of diachrony, but the degree of the loss in each case is very important.

In the last chapter of *La pensée sauvage,* Claude Lévi-Strauss brings up the same question, that is to say, the distinction between time as continuity and time as succession of discontinuous parts, in the following terms:

> Le codage chronologique dissimule une nature beaucoup plus complexe qu'on ne l'imagine, quand on conçoit les dates de l'histoire sous la forme d'une simple série linéaire. En premier lieu, une date dénote un *moment* dans une succession: d_2 est après d_1, avant d_3; de ce point de vue, la date fait seulement fonction de nombre ordinal. Mais chaque date est aussi un nombre cardinal, et, en tant que tel, exprime une *distance* par rapport aux dates les plus voisines.[22]

The problem is whether history can recapture the process of change in men and societies, that is, whether it is able to render or reflect *becoming* so genuinely, so much "from within," that it offers a particularly intimate and faithful knowledge of human existence. But, Lévi-Strauss points out, time is one thing, and chronology, which is a "code," a patterned approach to time, is another. All historical narrative is anchored in chronology, in the quantified code. Chronology is composed of a number of classes, each instance of which refers basically to another member of the *same* class: 1685 has meaning with regard only to 1610, 1648, 1715,

22. *La pensée sauvage,* p. 342.

and other members of that class; the same applies to the class seventeenth century, second century, and so on, or to the class January 18, September 24, and so on. Thus, the vaunted reconstitution of becoming takes the form not of an uninterrupted and homogeneous series but of the constant leap from one order to another:

> Il n'est donc pas seulement illusoire, mais contradictoire, de concevoir le devenir historique comme un déroulement continu, commençant par une préhistoire codée en dizaines ou en centaines de millénaires, se poursuivant à l'échelle des millénaires à partir du 4e ou du 3e, et continuant ensuite sous la forme d'une histoire séculaire entrelardée, au gré de chaque auteur, de tranches d'histoire annuelle au sein du siècle, ou journalière au sein de l'année, sinon même horaire au sein d'une journée. Toutes ces dates ne forment pas une série: elles relèvent d'espèces différentes. . . . Les évènements qui sont significatifs pour un code ne le restent plus pour un autre. Codés dans le système de la préhistoire, les épisodes les plus fameux de l'histoire moderne et contemporaine cessent d'être pertinents; sauf peut-être, (et encore nous n'en savons rien) certains aspects massifs de l'évolution démographique envisagée à l'échelle du globe, l'invention de la machine à vapeur, celle de l'électricité et celle de l'énergie nucléaire.[23]

My comment on these words will be twofold. They lead us, in the first place, to visualize more clearly the distance existing between period concepts and the flow of events to which they refer. It is obvious that periods do not compose a class of chronology (though the frequent need to equate them with centuries—particularly in Italy—indicates a tendency to confuse them with chronological classes), not only because they can last a century, or three centuries, or thirty years, or a millennium and therefore, according to Lévi-Strauss, would not, as chronology, make sense vis-à-vis one another, but because they do not respond to quantification at all. A system of periodization is a *criticism* of becoming. It attempts to make time intelligible or meaningful by creating an order, a par-

23. Ibid., p. 344.

allel level, that is more or less removed from temporality itself. As I suggested earlier, and a structuralist might agree, it acts like a series of temporal "models." The historical presentation of events in their detailed trajectory (*histoire évenementielle*) alludes to chronology as to a fundamental framework for narrative. In this sense, it is twice-removed from time. A period concept, thrice-removed, looks back to both chronology and the tale of events in order to work out its own structural goals. We should therefore expect periods most often to form a series of discontinuous parts, as separate from one another as cardinal numbers are. Periods existing somewhere between the order of chronology and that of an a-temporal typology, between diachrony and synchrony, are thus a good example of "le caractère discontinu et classificatoire de la connaissance historique," [24] though only more so than the chronological classes that Lévi-Strauss was talking about.

It seems to me, secondly, that Lévi-Strauss has not recognized on this occasion the functional advantages of that very leap from one class of chronology to another that is so characteristic of historical writing, and the extent to which this reflects a human being's experience of historical time. It is enough to imagine such leaps (or indeed to read the admirable paragraph that Lévi-Strauss writes about them) for one to see how near they come to that flow of becoming intimately rebuilt from within, which *La pensée sauvage* was willing to concede to history. And why is this so? The obvious must first be recalled: history is necessarily selective and constructive. That it must surrender a certain portion of a topic, of its concrete abundance, in order to make it intelligible, is a predicament on which the historical disciplines claim no monopoly. Levi-Strauss knows full well that after a social scientist's subject has been analyzed in its individual richness, a second step forces him to move away and measure the distance between his subject and the intellectual means that he has at his disposal (cf. *La pensée sauvage*, pp. 334–35). This being granted, one can only admire the extraordinary wealth and complexity of chronology as an approach to time, on the one hand, and, on the other, the appropriateness of switching from one level of chronology to another—say, from brief sections of time like hours to huge ex-

24. Ibid., p. 345.

panses like millennia—while being forced to *speak* of one class at once. Although it is certainly true that, as Lévi-Strauss explains, a century followed by an hour and a week do not compose a series, it is also reasonable to presume that none of the series to which each belongs is ever "interrupted," that is to say, that these codes or structures are such that they are potentially available at any moment; the levels of the weeks, of the days, of the centuries, *can* go on, *can* flow by, simultaneously, whenever we choose to imagine them jointly, and it is only a matter of intellectual montage that persuades us to refer *explicitly* to one and then to another. In fact, though one level of chronology may be uppermost in one's conscious mind at a given moment, one is also dimly aware of the others and constantly led to reshuffle this tacit hierarchy of chronological classes. Everything happens as if there were not simply *one* flow of time to which *various* classes of chronology refer, but a multiplicity of both code and coded subject, signifying and signified. What the richness, the variety, even the contradictions or the absurdity of chronology reflect so well is precisely the diversity and the multivalence of time as experienced by persons and groups. And I think that this is extraordinarily important for periodization from the point of view of diachrony and historical becoming.

Personally speaking, for example, and only with a slight measure of exaggeration, I realize as I am writing these lines that I can experience this moment in my life, after an effort of consciousness, as embracing simultaneously various levels of chronology and of history. I can recognize the late hour of the day at which I am writing, the heat and the late phase of a summer, the start of a new week, the imminence of a new academic year as distinct from a normal year or a fiscal year, the proximity of a birthday or of middle age, or, in a more periodological sense, a period of accelerated social change, another of very slow political development, the persistence of a long history of European nationalism, the beginning of real contacts between East and West, a certain rhythm in the process of contemporary music reminiscent of that in painting thirty years ago, and another rhythm in painting and poetry, and still another in sculpture, as well as the technological age that Lévi-Strauss stresses in the quotation above, going back to the industrial revolution and the dawn of that "electronic" or "tactile" era of which Marshall McLuhan is the inspired prophet. In Spain, I can imagine that a day could come, a day of extreme political convulsion, during which I for a single *hour* might witness the end of a historical millennium. Chronological classes and periods mingle and cross in my most immediate awareness of change. In other words, the variety of both renders faithfully the multiplicity of temporal processes that surround the life of men and societies and that historians are called upon to recapture. And there is nothing a posteriori about Jasinowski's remark that Dante (though this would not have been Dante's vocabulary) was the heir of Virgil, the culmination of the Middle Ages, and the beginning of the Renaissance.

This is of course a problem that would require, as a foundation for further study, a historical and practical survey of past schemes of periodization and of how they differ from one history of literature to another. I will only offer a sketch, in closing this section, of the two limit-concepts, the two poles, toward either of which any such scheme is likely to have tended. At one end, the emphasis is on discontinuous structures. These structures of norms and values are static *enough* to be comparable to "dwelling places" (Américo Castro's *moradas vitales*) in history. The historian "settles" his imagination in a portion of the past, after having traversed, as it were, time backward and moved into a period where, as in a safe haven, time no longer flows visibly. Intervals, smaller units, contradictions that might draw one nearer to becoming, are overlooked. At this pole, the sense of "before" and "after" as qualitative distinctions is very strong. Basically, by singling out the predominant traits of a period, we subsume change and understress continuity. Time is used as the condition or the support for a certain kind of otherness, and the period emerges from it in order to gain full significance. In other words, though this form of periodization, like any other, seeks an organization of past historical time, it does so by providing us with eternal "presents" in the past. Highly structured and intelligible in terms of values, these period concepts, from our point of view, are instances of pseudo-diachrony (as they do not render processes of becoming) and of pseudo-synchrony (insofar as they cover many years at once and do not really intersect time). They reflect the antinomies of chronology of which Lévi-Strauss wrote: "pour autant que l'histoire aspire à la signification, elle se condamne à choisir des régions, des époques, des groupes d'hommes et des individus dans ces groupes, et à les faire ressortir, comme des figures discontinues, sur un continu juste bon à servir de toile de fond." [25]

The outstanding and most influential example of a period concept as an axiomatic cosmos is probably Jakob Burckhardt's idea of the Renaissance. While Michelet, and other predecessors, had associated the Renaissance with the Enlightenment and the concept of progress with emphasis on dynamic development, Burckhardt would *isolate* it and view it as a cultural ideal sui generis.[26] The purest examples of static periodization can be found in *Geistesgeschichte,* whose roots are a romantic belief in the homogeneous spirit of ages and a love of local color in time, which are like a synchronic counterpart of the diachronic myth of national character. Concerning this pole or limit-concept, finally, I should like to touch upon two topics that might be worthy of further consideration. One is a Marxist comment, taking into account the prevalence of periodization in the nineteenth century and the thought of Marx in such writings as the postscript to the second edition of *Das Kapital:* [27] periods, one might say, domesticate historical change and insert revolutions into a reassuring pattern; the dialectical stress on history as ceaseless change through negation frightens the bourgeois class and threatens the stability which they wish

25. Ibid., p. 341.

26. Cf. Huizinga, *Wege der Kulturgeschichte,* p. 104.

27. Cf. K. Marx and F. Engels, *Werke* (Berlin, 1962), 23, 27: "In ihrer rationellen Gestalt ist sie [die Dialektik] dem Bürgertum und seinen doktrinären Wortführern ein Aergernis und ein Greuel, weil sie in dem positiven Verständnis des Bestehenden zugleich auch das Verständnis seiner Negation, seines notwendigen Untergangs einschliesst, jede gewordne Form im Flusse der Bewegung, also auch nach ihrer vergänglichen Seite auffasst, sie durch nichts imponieren lässt, ihrem Wesen nach kritisch und revolutionär ist." Cf. F. Martini, *Deutsche Literatur im bürgerlichen Realismus, 1848–1898* (Stuttgart, 1962), p. 15: "Das bürgerliche Bewusstsein . . . suchte, gegenüber der bewegten Zeitlichkeit des Lebens und seinen Veränderungen, das Humane als etwas Zeitloses zu bewahren."

for themselves and which they also value in the life of past epochs. Secondly, I have not discussed the ways in which a system of periodization can assume a philosophy of history: either explicitly— whenever there predominates, above all, the concept of history as coherent development [28]—or unconsciously. This is a dimension that would require a historical survey of our subject. But a minimal form of such a philosophy might be this: the meaning of a period justifies those components that otherwise might offer some resistance to design; each part, each detail of a period "spreads out" and rejoins the meaning of the whole; a single event, such as a literary movement, alone and by itself could appear contingent or accidental; but if it falls under a period concept, it did not just happen, and it has its place in a larger pattern; even when it pretends to delay an explanation, a periodized history offers a constant vindication of itself.

At the opposite end, a dynamic periodology is often found among reformers and liberal personalities, such as Georg Brandes, whom I will discuss presently, and generally in the twentieth century, so conscious of its own experience of accelerated change. Yet Francesco de Sanctis wrote during the nineteenth century the history of a national literature that is hailed by all today as the masterpiece of the genre, while seeking to re-create the development of literature without any serious reliance on a conventional scheme of literary epochs: "Al nostro scopo" in his own words —"è più utile seguire il cammino del pensiero e della forma nel suo sviluppo, senza violare le grandi divisioni cronologiche, ma senza cercare una precisione di date che ci farebbe sciupare il tempo in congetture e supposizioni di poco interesse." [29] Turning to recent years, I will mention only two studies in which periods are presented and understood through a constant preoccupation with duration and change. In 1957 Michael Seidlmayer published

28. Cf. E. Cione, *Dal de Sanctis al Novecento* (Milan, 1945), Chap. 8, "Il periodizzamento storico ed i concetti funzionali."

29. F. de Sanctis, *Storia della letteratura italiana*, ed. B. Croce (Bari, 1939), *1*, 107. Cf. also G. Getto, *Storia delle storie letterarie* (Milan, 1942), p. 32: "Il De Sanctis rifugge in effetti da ogni catalogazione di epoche definite, e tenta invece di render dinamica la storia letteraria segnando, più che le divisioni, i passaggi."

a book, *Weltbild und Kultur Deutschlands im Mittelalter,* where the medieval period is not depicted as the most unanimous and homogeneous in the history of Europe. Seidlmayer, instead, portrays a restless and vital world, charged with tensions and energies. The "unity" of the Middle Ages was not simply destroyed by conflicting forces after a certain date. It was always questionable. Underlying stresses, strains, and contradictions—between Empire and Papacy, between monasticism and the secular spirit in education or in the knightly life—were at work as early as the ninth century.[30] The slow emancipation of earthly attributes from a clerical design is compared by Seidlmayer to a mighty process of breathing in and breathing out, where the breathing organ was the religious system. With these tensions in mind, he is able to distinguish between four sub-periods, all dynamically defined.[31] My second example deals with an epoch, the second half of the nineteenth century, where the unorthodox, the deviant, the individual are expected to play a central role. In an admirable history, *Deutsche Literatur im bürgerlichen Realismus, 1848–1898,* published in 1962, Fritz Martini refuses to impose an artificial unity, either stylistically or historically, on a period characterized by a sense of crisis. During those decades of change and inquiry German literature presented a series of different strata (*Schichten*). Although the concept of "bourgeois realism" is used as an organizing principle for the book, Martini does not claim that it is a period style, a diffuse aesthetic presence: "die folgende Darstellung wird dieser These das Bild einer vielsichtigen, widerspruchsvollen, wandlungs- und krisenreichen Zeit entgegenstellen, in der, auch und gerade in der Dichtung, antinomische, subjektivistische und zentrifugale Tendenzen überwiegen." [32] The problem is not one of logic but of critical pertinence and tact. The capacity to "see" one's own time is a gift that certain German authors of "bourgeois realism" have in common with a Flaubert, but also with Marx and Nietzsche, their contemporaries. The best work of

30. Cf. M. Seidlmayer, *Weltbild und Kultur Deutschlands im Mittelalter* (Darmstadt, 1957), p. 12. (There is an English translation in the series "Studies in Medieval History," edited by G. Barraclough.)

31. Cf. ibid., p. 19.

32. Cf. Martini, pp. 4, 13, and 3.

the narrators in the group, from Stifter to Meyer, discloses consistently the nineteenth-century writer's ability to challenge both social and artistic conventions and to draw strength from a solitary, relentless dialogue with the epoch in which he lives.

> The course of history can be likened to the flow of a great stream as it runs down to the ocean. There are places where the swift current will break its force against hidden rocks. When the winter snows have melted the river may burst its dikes and flood the countryside. During the summer drought the flow can be sluggish and great sand bars will appear above the surface. But also over long distances the river will flow peacefully and majestically toward an unknown sea.[33]

The words are familiar, the simile has endless possibilities, and the passage appears in a book called *Historical Change*. Jorge Luis Borges holds that, though metaphors are potentially infinite, only a few have shown that they are enduringly significant, like the pairing of dreams and death, stars and eyes, women and flowers, old age and the setting of the sun, time and water.[34] Time and water, time and the river, have alluded together to the destinies of individual men, but also—Heraclitus spoke for all philosophers, and the death of Jorge Manrique's father was the death of all fathers—to the eternity, the faith or the mutability of all men. In a collective way also, the metaphor, fatally enough, had to qualify history during the history-conscious nineteenth century and to assume many forms. That of "current" has been frequent in literary history. We have already seen, in an earlier quotation, that Jean Rousset used it in the midst of a discussion of the Baroque period ("si le principe baroque est le plus actif, occupant dans l'époque une position centrale, il y a toutes sortes de courants parallèles ou latéraux"), and this compensating function is rather characteristic of the term. In a brief essay on Romanticism, Benedetto Croce speaks of *correnti* in a similar frame of mind:

33. L. Einstein, *Historical Change* (Cambridge, Mass., 1946), p. 6.
34. Cf. J. L. Borges, "La metáfora," in *Historia de la eternidad* (4th ed. Buenos Aires, 1966), p. 71. The point is made by Borges often, also in fictional form: cf. "La busca de Averroes," in *El Aleph* (6th ed. Buenos Aires, 1966), p. 98.

Ma poiché "romanticismo" non è semplice equivalente della partizione cronologica "prima metà del secolo decimonono," né della partizione etnica "civiltà germanica," tanto vero che in quello stesso limite di tempo e in quello stesso limite nazionale si distinguono correnti romantiche e correnti non romantiche, correnti dominanti e correnti d'opposizione, e si parla di un romanticismo francese e di uno italiano, e anche di un preromanticismo e di un protoromanticismo;—giova determinare quali fatti e quali disposizioni spirituali si richiamino o si dovrebbero richiamare alla memoria con quella parola.[35]

Usually the metaphor, though it may have completely "faded," is rather complex and can be subdivided into "undercurrents," "cross-currents," and so forth. Some argue, we read in Lewis Einstein, that historical change is caused by the clash of opposites or "cross-currents."[36] In a mood of landscape description, Georg Brandes explored the literal level of the term, concerning the southern end of the Lake of Geneva: "The spot is one of the loveliest in the world. Pass the island and cross another bridge and you see the Rhone rush, impetuous and foaming white, out of the lake. A few steps further and you can see its white stream joined by the grey slow waters of the Arve. The rivers flow side by side, each retaining its colour."[37] In contrast with such combinations and clashes, or because of them, others prefer to single out "main currents," "major currents," and the like. One recalls that currents and rivers have a direction—or a goal, or even a purpose—and that one of the meanings for "current" in the *Oxford English Dictionary* is "course or progress in a definite direction: tendency, tenor, drift (of opinions, writings, etc.)."[38] Thus, Marcel Raymond, writing about the period of French poetry that was to be

35. B. Croce, "Le definizioni del Romanticismo" (1906), in *Problemi di Estetica* (5th. ed. Bari, 1954), p. 293.

36. Einstein, p. 3.

37. G. Brandes, *Main Currents in Nineteenth Century Literature* (London and New York, 1906), *1*, 17.

38. *The Oxford English Dictionary* (1961 ed.), *2*, 1270. An example is given from Locke, *Toleration* (1692): "in your first paper, as the whole current of it would make one believe . . . etc."

the subject of *De Baudelaire au Surréalisme*, could state: "il est nécessaire de considérer les choses dans leur durée, et en profondeur, pour apercevoir le courant majeur qui anime la poésie, l'idée qui s'incarne en elle, souvent à l'insu des poètes, et qui commande son développement"; even as Cleanth Brooks, a comparable critic of the modern poetic tradition, would offer this comment on one of the meanings of the word: "we can speak of *the* tradition, whereby we mean the essential line of development coming to us out of the past, the main current as distinguished from the accidental or the peripheral." [39]

T. S. Eliot, in "Tradition and the Individual Talent," had made clear at one point that he did not really have in mind "the *whole* of the literature of Europe from Homer," but, rather, only what (most untraditionally) *he* thought was the best in it: "The poet must be very conscious"—he wrote—"of the main current, which does not at all flow invariably through the most distinguished reputations." [40] It would subsequently become possible to speak of "traditions" as if they were "main currents" and vice versa. A tradition thus signifies a main current to which a very real value is attached. This is a complex question that cannot be discussed here, though it is interesting to notice in passing the dogmatism that lurks in diachrony as it does in synchrony. A stress on historical becoming does not imply by far an absence of belief. Traditions isolate continuities and unify the timeless in time, as period concepts do within the limits of a section of history. Yet period concepts are historical in a way that traditions are not. Tradition connotes history but does not denote it. Traditionalists, like some aristocrats, would rather praise than investigate the past. Or to make my point more clearly: whenever I speak of the "tradition of X," I formulate my awareness not exactly *of* a historical continuity but, rather, of the mere *fact that it exists*. I color the present with a legitimacy rooted in the past. Thus, literary

39. M. Raymond, "Les étapes récentes de la poésie française" [Second International Congress of Literary History, Amsterdam, 1935], *Bulletin of the International Committee of Historical Sciences, 9* (1937), 385; C. Brooks, "Tradition," in *Dictionary of Literature*, ed. J. Shipley (New York, 1953), p. 418.

40. T. S. Eliot, "Tradition and the Individual Talent" (1917), in *Selected Essays, 1917–1932* (New York, 1932), p. 5.

traditions are present-oriented, synchrony-oriented. They are only vaguely, or sentimentally, diachronic.

Because the notion of main currents is selective, it lends itself to the abuses of ideologists such as V. L. Parrington in his *Main Currents in American Thought* (1927–30), whose principal concern was political, sociological, extra-literary. These are the pitfalls, to which I shall return later, of a metaphor that is commodious indeed: it suggests continuity; change, too, or increase; and, within such change, the clashes of different elements, the rhythm of diminution and growth. It also implies, very easily, development, evolution, plan. My purpose, however, is to underline here the usefulness of a term that has been advantageous and may become more so in the future.

The notion of literary currents is frankly diachronic, dynamic, open-ended, and suggestive of relations with historical and social developments. I need not dwell on its diachronic aspect. I have already mentioned, à propos of a very similar kind of period, that this factor is often linked with the image of history-in-the-making, of the evolution of society by means of an understanding, as in Ortega and Francastel, of contradictions, alternatives, confrontations. This coloring is present in even as old-fashioned a book as Frederick E. Pierce's *Currents and Eddies in the Romantic Generation* (1918).[41] Clearly what matters most here is the plural "currents" and the vision of their simultaneous process, their coexistence in time, within a single section of history, a single period. Finally, there is the aspect that I have been calling "dynamic." I have in mind those historians who call forth a picture of the vitality of man, of his capacity for creation and progress. For them, the diachrony of "currents"—or of kindred terms—is complemented by an awareness of the continuity of man's artistic and intellectual achievement. Writing simply as a humanist and a literary historian, the great Polish scholar Ladislas Folkierski once

41. Published in New Haven in 1918. Pierce describes the different literary camps, the cleavages, the polemics, the interplay of various movements, i.e. the picture from the point of view of the original readers of Romantic and non-Romantic poetry. He writes about "The Eddy around Bristol," the "Spanish current" (Southey, Landor, Byron, Mrs. Felicia Hemans), the relationship between the different social strata of the reading public and the literature that was available to them (Chap. 2, p. 93, etc.).

complained that literary periods were unpersuasive abstractions and that it would be preferable to develop different concepts that might be more amenable to the flow of cultural history:

> Laissons à nouveau couler le flot ininterrompu de la vitalité européenne depuis l'Occitanie jusqu'à Pétrarque et Desportes, depuis Arnaut Daniel jusqu'à Marini, depuis Joachim de Flore jusqu'aux rêves millénaires de certains illuminés du XVIIe et du XVIIIe siècles. . . . Il est à présumer, dès maintenant, que de la sorte on n'aboutirait guère à des coupures brusques qui veulent arrêter sur une année ou même sur un quart de siècle tel mouvement puissant, tel flot de la pensée européenne, mais que bien plutôt on arriverait à noter la courbe d'une vague plus ou moins rythmée avec ses flux et ses reflux, ses hauts et ses bas.[42]

It is difficult to speak fairly of Georg Brandes. Though some may have overrated him as a literary critic, others may also have underestimated him as a literary historian. The history of criticism can be, of course, a melancholy discipline unless one approaches the critics of the past with some of the sympathy, or even of the empathy, that we willingly grant poets and novelists when we first begin to read them. The practical judgments of these critics will seem today, more often than not, obsolete and mistaken, but there are three other aspects of their achievement that one cannot neglect: their quality as writers; the nature of their method; and their ability as historians, that is to say, as builders of large compositions. In the case of Brandes, even for those readers who have no Danish, the lucid, burning intensity of his writing is such that it tolerates translation. The point of view, particularly in the *Main Currents in Nineteenth Century Literature,* is that of the liberal reformer and believer in scientific progress—a position common enough in the nineteenth century or even in our own. In Italy, for example, one recalls the histories of Italian literature by P. Emiliani Giudici (1844) and Luigi Settembrini (1866–72),

42. L. Folkierski, "Renaissance et Romantisme ou les sables mouvants dans l'histoire littéraire" [Second International Congress of Literary History, Amsterdam, 1935], *Bulletin of the International Committee of Historical Sciences,* 9 (1937), 333 and 332.

with their emphasis on the old battle between Guelphs and Ghibellines.[43] Among historians, a Michelet in France or a Lelewel in Poland and of course many others are not often reproached with defending the idea of progress or the concept of freedom. Yet on the part of Brandes this is sometimes considered naïve or obnoxious. Finally, the *Main Currents* and some of the later books as well evidence a vigorous capacity for historical construction—our principal interest here. We must grant Brandes, writes René Wellek, "an original, effervescent sensibility, an insight into psychology, and a power of marshalling currents or movements, which, as he knew very well, is an art." [44]

Professor Wellek explains that Brandes, in the six-volume work originally entitled *Hovedstrømninger i det 19de Aarhundredes Litteratur* (1872–90), is actually writing a history of national minds in the romantic sense.[45] This is certainly an important part of his achievement. Brandes himself promises his readers, in starting, a history of the "psychology" or the "soul" of Europe during the first half of the nineteenth century. In fact, he presents them with an eclectic combination of approaches. He doubtless enjoys formulating his ideas on national character, particularly in the fourth volume on England and Ireland. In the same volume, too, he stresses more than once the notion of period. Just as often, however, Brandes singles out international Romantic themes, like childhood, incest, or suicide, or a particular idea of poetry, or an international "current" like the revival of the ballad after Bürger and Sir Walter Scott.[46] And his real gift, as René Wellek also points out, may be for portraiture, à la Sainte-Beuve, and there are numerous chapters where writers, like Friedrich Schlegel, are treated biographically. Brandes is even capable of textual commentary, as in the pages on Heine and, particularly, the bravura passage on the translations of Shakespeare by August Wilhelm Schlegel, which he studies genetically.[47] Nevertheless, despite such differences, what holds the entire work together is above all

43. Cf. Getto, pp. 233, 290, etc.

44. René Wellek, *A History of Modern Criticism: 1750–1950* (New Haven and London, 1965), p. 368. Chapter 16 is devoted to Brandes.

45. Cf. Ibid., p. 358.

46. Cf. Brandes, *Main Currents, 4,* Chap. 2 (also, *1,* 135, or *2,* Chap. 8); *4,* Chap. 1; and *4,* pp. 3 ff.

47. Cf. Brandes, *2,* Chap. 3.

the image of literature-in-the-making, of work in progress—the whole powerful stream of events that imparts a common impulse and movement to all instants and all components in the narrative. That Brandes is actually dealing with *events* and telling a story is corroborated by the fluency of his pure narrative writing, as in the sequence on the Irish rebellions against English rule.[48]

The "currents," then, are made up mostly of single portraits and critical pieces and of the unifying effect of an overall historical élan. The subject is the period 1800–48, but Brandes perceives it dynamically as a great movement—essentially, as a passage from the constructive forces of the Enlightenment, through the French Revolution, the decades of reaction, the setbacks of 1848, to the synthesis of liberalism and the scientific advances of the second half of the century. His strategy is the study of a succession of representative writers. By treating one writer at a time, as exemplified usually by a single book, which often emerges as a type (*Corinne, Adolphe, Obermann, Werther, Lucinde,* and so on), he is able to stress the linear nature of the currents at hand. It is not an exhaustive but a highly selective history (even as he reduces himself to France, England, and Germany, with the addition of frequent digressions on Denmark, but almost no references to Italy, Russia, and Spain), though so broad-ranging that the total effect is that of a flow along a few fundamental lines.[49]

Fortunately, though the currents may augur an identical goal in the future, they can, at any moment in the narrative, confront each other and clash. This is made possible by the dialectics of progress and reaction. Brandes' individual analyses are often surprising and far from one-sided, not because a doctrinaire mind is being tempered by tact, but because his interest in the dynamics of history elicits the contradictions of the past. The principal paradox is that the nineteenth century had upset the eighteenth while perfecting the ideals of the Enlightenment. Romanticism overthrew neoclassicism while returning to Rousseau; and similar oppositions, of course, had filled the eighteenth century itself: "Frenchmen had instituted a Republic and overturned Christianity"—Brandes writes—"before it occurred to them to dispute

48. Cf. ibid., *4*, Chap. 12.
49. On these points, cf. Wellek, *A History of Criticism, 4,* Chap. 16.

the authority of Boileau." One might say, in the terms of this
paper, that Brandes is aware of the superposition of periods or of
the fact that they are not discrete entities. These contradictions
have effects of varying scope. The literature of exile, for example,
typically shows a dual character ("whatever the nature of the
compound, a double current is discernible in emigrant literature"), and Brandes underlines the dualism of individual writers
like Novalis or Benjamin Constant ("no truth, he was accustomed
to observe, is complete unless it includes its antithesis. He succeeded in completing many truths") or even of single works such
as Chateaubriand's *René* or Kierkegaard's *Enten-Eller*.[50]

Harry Levin has appropriately remarked that a book for Georg
Brandes is a force, a "continuing force," and, within the causal relation existing between literature and society, a cause rather than
an effect.[51] Obsessed with the need for forward movement,
Brandes admires those literary works that are vital enough to be
new, that is, to start anew, as each generation must on the basis of
its own vitality and capacity for creation. Madame de Staël's *De
l'Allemagne,* he says, was epoch-making "because, not accidentally
but on principle, it broke with all antiquated literary traditions
and indicated new sources of life." (Unfortunately, he was not able
to recognize the novelty of Novalis or Hölderlin, for whose sensibilities he had no understanding.) Brandes the battler, the militant critic, was *engagé* in the past exactly as if it were the present.
He practiced in criticism the commitment that he sought and
appreciated in literature: "for a nation has a literature in order
that its horizon may be widened and its theories of life confronted
with life." [52]

The character of such an *engagement* is inseparable from
Brandes' position on our topic, i.e. his subordination of periods to
currents. Brandes, I recalled earlier, studies the passage from the
Enlightenment to the first half of the nineteenth century. He is
also profoundly aware of the relationship between that time and
his own. Brandes could very well have regarded the first half of the
nineteenth century *as a period* and then, in counterposition to it,

50. Brandes, *1*, 31, 4, 71; cf. *2*, 188; *1*, 39.
51. Cf. H. Levin, *The Gates of Horn* (New York, 1963), pp. 13, 14.
52. Brandes, *1*, 107, 101.

individualized *his own* as well. This is precisely what certain historians of the first half of the century had done vis-à-vis both (and simultaneously) the Renaissance and the eighteenth century, which immediately preceded theirs.[53] This had been made possible by the French Revolution and the collapse of the previous political and social systems. Brandes (and it would be interesting to compare his views with those of other literary historians writing in the 1870s and 1880s about the beginning of the century, like Faguet and De Sanctis) could have individualized his period and the preceding one if only he had been able to rejoice over the failure of the 1848 liberal revolution and to consider it a cleavage as substantial as that of the French Revolution. He preferred, instead, to regard the nineteenth as a single, dynamic, unfinished movement emerging from the eighteenth, marked by tensions and ambiguities from the start and still fighting an indecisive battle. He thus preserved his feelings of solidarity with the spirit of the Revolution, and his hopes that Scandinavia might yet take its proper place or play a larger role in the general liberation of Europe from reaction, hypocrisy, and cant.

Brandes writes somewhere that the horses in Fouqué's *Zauberring* are the only creatures in the book whose psychology the author has fully mastered. Yet despite his bias, and even with regard to writers he did not esteem or failed to understand, Brandes lacks spite and maintains a sort of serenity. Perhaps this was due to the fact that his century had known so many setbacks and that he received at first so little recognition in Copenhagen. He was not a utopian and did not expect the realization of his ideals in his own day. In fact, he judged it indispensable, like Unamuno (who shared his fire and discovered Kierkegaard through him), to shock and irritate his contemporaries.[54] As a person, he simply was the opposite of the man that Taine advised him to be in a letter of July 23, 1873, after having read the *Main Currents:* "Permettez-moi de vous conseiller, en un sujet si brûlant, l'attitude du spectateur abstrait: vos coups seront d'autant plus perçants que vous

53. On this point, cf. Jasinowski, pp. 42–43.

54. Cf. M. de Unamuno, "Ibsen y Kierkegaard" (1907), in *Ensayos* (Madrid, 1951), 2, 415 (I am grateful to Juan Marichal for this reference); cf. Brandes, *4,* 124.

paraîtrez au-dessus de toute polémique; il faut partir de ce principe que vos adversaires n'existent pas, ou mieux encore, que votre domicile est dans un autre planète." [55] But Brandes, so committed to his planet, had never gotten over the impression he had received as a youth from reading the *Ethics* of Spinoza, which he recounts in his memoirs: "A love of humanity came over me, and watered and fertilized the fields of my inner world which had been lying fallow, and this love of humanity vented itself in a vast compassion." [56] In later years, Spinoza would be replaced by Darwin and, still later, by Nietzsche, and Brandes would continue to suffer, as Oskar Seidlin explains, from the conflict between his vitalism, his philosophy of the individual will, and his scientific positivism.[57] Yet it seems that at all moments Brandes was inspired by a religious or a metaphysical need, despite his doubts concerning a God, and that his feelings of solidarity with other men, harsh though their expressions could be, his awareness of continuity if only within an earthly order, and his desire to participate in the main historical currents of his century responded to such a profound need. How can one bear being simply nailed to life—"cloué à la vie"—he asked his good friend Georges Noufflard in a letter of April 1875; and his advice to Noufflard was: "il faut regarder la chose individuelle d'une manière symbolique, la chérir, y voir une image du grand tout et s'y attacher le plus sérieusement que l'on peut. Ainsi on peut dire avec une certaine raison que l'on a participé à la grande vie, n'ayant vécu qu'un court temps dans un espace circonscrit." [58]

In my discussion of periods and currents, a number of the points that I have touched upon obviously brought to mind some of the subjects that fall under the jurisdiction of the philosophy of history. This is an affinity that I can only recall in passing, not because of any lack of space, but because of a matter of method and

55. *Correspondance de Georg Brandes,* ed. P. Krüger (Copenhagen, 1952), *1,* 13.

56. Brandes, *Reminiscences of My Childhood and Youth* (New York, 1906), p. 102.

57. Cf. O. Seidlin, "Georg Brandes, 1842–1927," *Journal of the History of Ideas, 3* (1942), 428.

58. *Correspondance de Georg Brandes, 1,* 75.

of priorities. Let us grant that any instrument, any term, any metaphor for the interpretation of literary diachrony begs, echoes, or assumes a philosophy of history. Do literary currents, for example, imply some version of evolution or development? The fulfillment of a law or a purpose? Literary currents would have to be associated with a linear, hence basically Judeo-Christian, view of history. But as a nineteenth-century term, despite these theologies, a current is normally open-ended and inconclusive. It seems that most of us can agree on a minimal notion of continuity as being basic to the historical existence of literature and characteristic of its nature.[59] Consequently, it seems difficult to yield to any historical pessimism in our field, to the melancholy, for example, with which anthropologists view the slow death of the savage mind. The Brazils and the New Guineas, the Ashantes and the Nambukwaras, of the poetry of the past will long remain available, with the immediate freshness of poetry, in our libraries. But how are we to conceive of the additions and accretions of time?

One could continue, though in a more rigorous fashion, in this vein. But the matter that I am considering is whether one should. The idea of literary history, to which this essay alludes, would require the application to the literary field (and this may be a principal task of comparative literature) of recent gains and accomplishments in the philosophy of history. But it is also true that a philosophy of the history *of literature* must perforce build on its own premises and learn from its own investigations. It should, first of all, study and understand itself. It is easy enough to speak of "development," of "unity," of "national literature," without serious intent, and some sort of cathartic liberation from routine and *idées reçues* would be most welcome in this area. But it is also a facile procedure to automatically adapt to literary studies a set of systematic ideas from general history, politics, economics, or science. It cannot be *assumed* that a philosophy of literary history will coincide in all essentials with an overall philosophy of history. It also cannot be supposed that it will *not*. For the moment, one can demand that literary studies, in order to make such confrontations possible in the future, look after their own affairs with a fair measure of independence.

59. On the idea of continuity in history, cf. K. Löwith's discussion of Jakob Burckhardt in *Meaning in History* (Chicago, 1957), pp. 21–22.

Toward this end, the growing dialogue today between American or Western European critics and the historians of Eastern Europe should be particularly fruitful for all concerned. One must doubtless be grateful to Georg Lukács and his more intelligent followers for asking the great questions, for discussing themes and opening vistas to which too many Western critics are indifferent. Marxism, in this sense, has brought about the beginning of a rapprochement between literary studies and the philosophy of history. To these difficult and important problems, however, Marxists often offer ready-made solutions. It is curious that some should be so slow with the questions, and others so fast with the answers. It is to be hoped that many will pursue the philosophy of literary history in a spirit of both caution and freedom from preconceptions.

In this essay I have discussed some of the difficulties raised by periodization, especially with regard to diachrony and the organization of historical time. My purpose was not to further any form of nominalism, of surrender to flux and mutability, of indifference to generalizations.[60] An attitude of that kind would be, as it were, "colonial," for it really would mean that in practice one would rely, for reference and clarity, on the periodological *points de repère* laid down by others. But I also have tried to single out those forms of periodization that provide us not only with an access to styles and values, but with a sensitive and genuine vision of history, and hence can serve as foundations for an idea of literary history.

I was led by the discussion of a paragraph from Lévi-Strauss to support a multiple-level characterization that would accommodate the realization that men apparently live in more than one "period" at once. I went on to say that there is not simply one current of time to which various classes of chronology and periodization refer, but a multiplicity of both code and coded object, signifying and signified. Our vocabulary presents some problems here, of course, and it would be necessary to define more fully one's terms. Let us accept for the moment that we do not mean by period here

60. Cf. Wölfflin, *Kunstgeschichtliche Grundbegriffe*, as quoted by Teesing, p. 38: "Alles ist Uebergang, und wer die Geschichte als ein unendliches Fliessen betrachtet, dem ist schwer zu entgegnen. Fuer uns ist eine Forderung intellektueller Selbsterhaltung, die Unbegrenztheit des Geschehens nach ein paar Zielpunkten zu ordnen."

simply a time-section. We mean a critical concept that is *applicable* to a section of historical time and to its dominant structures and values. Now, my hypothesis is that a section of historical time should not be understood as a single entity, a bloc, a unity, but as a plural number of temporal currents, temporal levels, rhythms or sequences, running, like the Arve and the Rhone which Georg Brandes so enthusiastically described, simultaneously and side by side. If we conceive of the diachronic object of periodization as being multiple in the first place, it is then not so arduous to accept the idea of multiple periodization either in terms of dynamic periods or, preferably, of literary currents (or other similar terms).

We took notice that the seventeenth century has already been studied most convincingly not as a Baroque *period* but as a blending of Baroque, Classical, and Mannerist "currents." I have repeatedly recalled Johan Huizinga's suggestion that the Renaissance should also not be approached as a monolith—the only possible solution to that tiresome riddle. It seems obvious, as a final example, that the literature of the turn of the last century should not be interpreted as a single Symbolist period, but as a strong Symbolist current in poetry, in aesthetics, in the novel, coincident and diachronically contemporaneous with a continuing realistic or naturalistic vein in the novel, various forms of decadentism, aestheticism, or *art nouveau*, the final stages of certain Romantic styles, such as the political "poetry of ideas," the final phases of the Parnasse, a brief interval of neoclassic or idyllic poetry, and the first emergence of experiments that would ultimately flow into surrealism and other avant-garde movements of the twenties—each of these currents having its own rhythm, speed, intensity, and particular life span. It is only in these terms, certainly, that one can approach periodologically the work of poets writing, like Rubén Darío, far from Paris, and the situation of authors of the next time-section, so as not to overestimate the participation in an exclusive "Symbolist heritage" of post-World War I poets like Lorca, Ungaretti, or Montale.

Thus, the example of De Sanctis and of a growing number of contemporary critics has made quite clear the nature of a workable alternative to periodization and the division of literary history into separate temporal units. This alternative, I think, is promising enough. It relies on the use of a simple, non-interpretative chronology (in Italy, *il Trecento, il Quattrocento,* and so on [61]). And it stresses essentially the confrontations, within such a chronology, of a multiplicity of movements, currents, and temporal processes. "Qu'on se place en 1558 ou en l'an de grâce 1958," writes Fernand Braudel, "il s'agit, pour qui veut saisir le monde, de définir une hiérarchie de forces, de *courants,* de mouvements particuliers, puis de ressaisir une constellation d'ensemble." [62]

61. Sometimes what is supposed to be pure chronology becomes colored with significance, as in Italy, where a derogatory meaning was attached for many years to *Seicento* and *secentismo*—Alfieri's "il Seicento delirava": cf. V. Santoli, *Fra Germania e Italia* (Florence, 1962), p. 274.

62. Braudel, "Histoire et Sciences sociales: La longue durée," *Annales E.S.C., 13* (July–Dec. 1958), 735. There are obvious affinities between my position in this essay on the problem of periodization and Braudel's extraordinarily interesting and important "dialectique de la durée," of which I was not aware originally, and which I plan to discuss leisurely in another article. Cf. also Braudel, "Qu'est-ce que le XVIe siècle, *"Annales E.S.C., 8* (1953), 69–73, and "Pour une Histoire sérielle: Séville et l'Atlantique (1504–1650)," *Annales E.S.C., 18* (1963), 541–53.

Edith Kern

The Romance of Novel/Novella

The *Oxford English Dictionary* defines the term "novel" as
follows:

> a) (Chiefly in *pl.*) One of the tales or short stories contained
> in such works as the *Decameron* of Boccaccio, the *Hempta-*
> *meron* of Marguerite of Valois, etc.; a short story of this type.
> b) A fictitious prose narrative or tale of considerable length
> (now usually one long enough to fill one or more volumes),
> in which characters and actions representative of the real life
> of past or present times are portrayed in a plot of more or less
> complexity.

Confronted with these two meanings for the same word—meanings almost mutually exclusive at that—English, as languages are
wont to do, has tried to find a way out of its dilemma. It has in this
case almost entirely suppressed the meaning given under "a." Although this meaning represents the earlier one, it has today
mainly historical significance, having been replaced in current
usage by "short story" and "tale." "Novel" has become the generic
term for all long fictitious prose narratives. Even retroactively, it
has usurped the place of "romance," which now designates only a
particular kind of long narrative, although it was once applicable
to all of them. "Romance" has been supplanted by "novel" to such
an extent that modern critics unflinchingly speak of chivalric and
picaresque "novels" where earlier critics would have used the term
"romance." [1] This total acceptance of the secondary meaning of
"novel" at the expense of the original one and the subsequent
ousting of "romance" from its usual place cannot be explained as a
mere coincidence or as the arbitrary choice of certain critics. Both

1. See *OED*, "romance."

reflect a complex development in European literature and, above all, a flux and reflux of ideas from one country to another.

Romance

Of the two terms "romance" is the older. As a literary term it is of French origin and goes back to the beginnings of French literature, although it established itself in England mainly during the sixteenth and seventeenth centuries. In the form of *roman,* it remains in France the equivalent of English "novel." Its origin was known to French critics as early as the seventeenth century. They knew that *roman* had been used at first to designate all that was spoken or written in the *linguae latinae filiae,* that is, in any of the languages which developed from Latin and which we have come to designate as Romance languages. *Romance* is a corruption of the Latin adverb *romanice,* which described the speech of the Romans after it had undergone admixtures and deviations in the various provinces. The adverb was used mainly to distinguish this manner of speaking from the Latin used by the Church, the Law, and men of letters. Then, changing its status from that of an adverb to that of a noun, *romans, romanz, romance,* or *roman* came to designate any of the vulgar languages—regardless of whether that language was spoken in France or Spain, for instance.[2] But in addition to distinguishing the local vulgar speech from the official Latin, it also came to designate—in each of these countries—that particular genre of literature which its people favored and cultivated.

It has been shown that, for a while, two meanings existed side by side in those countries. In Spain, for instance, where the ballad developed as the most prominent national genre, one may find among thirteenth-century books such titles as *Estoria del romanz del infant Garcia,* where *romanz* is used in the sense of "vulgar language."[3] At the same time, one will encounter the word used

2. Huet, *De L'Origine des Romans,* in *Œuvres Complétes de Madame de la Fayette* (Paris, 1825), *1,* 52; Charles Sorel, *De la Connaissance des bons livres* (Paris, 1671), pp. 149–50; Ludwig Pfandl, "Das spanische Wort 'romance,'" *Investigaciones Linguisticas,* 2 (1934), 242–53; Leo Spitzer, "Petite rectification à l'article de M. Pfandl 'La Palabra española *romance,'"* *Investigaciones Linguisticas, 3* (1935), 203–07.

3. Pfandl, p. 243.

as a generic term for songs of all kinds composed in that language. Then, by the middle of the fifteenth century, the term came to designate exclusively—as it still does today—that ballad form of literature.[4] In France, where during the Middle Ages the long narrative in prose or verse became the favorite literary expression, *roman* eventually became the term specifically attached to it. Indeed, together with the genre which it designated, it gained immense popularity and spread far beyond the borders of its country of origin.

Speaking of these *vieux romans* in 1646, the French critic Chapelain did not boast when he described their impact on Italian literature:

> Il y a trois cents ans que Boccace a parlé de Lancelot, de Tristan et de Gallehaut des îles lointaines, comme des héros célébrés par les écrivains du temps passé. Il y en a près de trois cent cinquante que le Pétrarque a parlé d'eux et de leurs aventures comme de songes et de rêveries. Plus de trente ans avant lui, le Dante allègue Lancelot comme ayant donné sujet à un événement tragique.[5]

(The *événement tragique* is, of course, the story of Paolo and Francesca who had become lovers upon reading *Lancelot* and whom Dante had immortalized in his *Inferno*.) Huet's famous study *De l'Origine des Romans* (1671) also confirms both the French provenance and the international popularity of the genre that had become known as *roman*. He can even cite as his spokesman the sixteenth-century Italian critic Giraldi who, in discussing the *romanzi* of his compatriots Boiardo and Ariosto, averred that this kind of writing had its origin in France, went from there to Spain, and was finally adopted by the Italians.[6] (What he does not mention is the success of these Italian *romanzi* which, in turn, left their mark upon European literature, including that of France and England.)

While the treatises of Chapelain and Huet vouch for the antiquity of genre and term, they underline at the same time their con-

---

4. Ibid., pp. 244–45.

5. Jean Chapelain, "De la lecture des Vieux Romans," *Opuscules Critiques* (Paris, 1936), p. 212.

6. Huet, p. 53.

tinuity from the Middle Ages to the seventeenth century. In addition, however, these treatises reveal clearly their authors' awareness of certain changes that the genre had undergone at the time
of their writing. When Chapelain speaks of *vieux romans,* he obviously implies that there are others which should be considered
modern and which he considers better. Although he finds much
praise for the author of *Lancelot,* he also accuses him of having
been barbaric and having written for barbaric readers during
barbaric times. "He did not know," Chapelain maintains, "how to
organize a work; how to arrange it according to the rules so as to
create a harmonious relationship between its parts; or how to
bring its events to a climax and then resolve all." [7] Huet concurs
that the *troubadours* or *trouverres* of Provence were *les princes de
la romancerie,* that they were amazingly successful, and that some
of the many *romans* in prose and verse which they wrote were still
read in the seventeenth century. But he also felt that these works
bore the marks of their ignorance and that D'Urfé was the first
"qui les tira de la barbarie et les remit dans les règles dans son
incomparable Astrée, l'ouvrage le plus ingénieux et le plus poli
qui eût jamais paru dans ce genre." [8] In his opinion the French
roman had since reached incomparable heights of art and elegance.

Thus the changes these critics were conscious of are those which
took place with regard to form and *bienséance.* They clearly
prefer the manners of their contemporaries, the *précieux* and the
honnêtes gens, to those of their forebears. Concerning the form of
the *roman,* they must have liked the influences exerted upon it, on
the one hand, by the Italian *romanzo* and, on the other, by Heliodorus' *Theagenes and Chariclea.* Tasso, by comparing the Italian
romanzo to an epic, had defended its beginning in medias res.
Heliodorus' romance, which had come to be known and regarded
as a model, had encouraged the same approach, and had inspired
many of the highly fashionable, romantic stories which usually
started with a shipwreck of the lovers who were perpetually separated but ultimately reunited.

Huet's definition of *roman* is naturally derived from these

7. Chapelain, p. 221 (my translation).
8. Huet, pp. 67, 68–72.

seventeenth-century samples of the genre which he so greatly admired. In contrast to the Italian *romanzo,* he considered the French *roman* a prose genre. Yet, by defining the *roman* as an epic in prose—the epic being a genre held in high esteem by Aristotle—he gave it the respectability which it had lacked during most of the seventeenth century. According to Huet then, "ce que l'on appelle proprement *romans,* sont des fictions d'aventures amoureuses, écrites en prose avec art, pour le plaisir et l'instruction des lecteurs." [9] Since the popularity of seventeenth-century French *romans* was such that they filled the libraries of multitudes of ladies of leisure, not only in France but also in England and the entire continent, it is not in the least surprising that the definition of English romance (then the equivalent of French *roman*) is almost identical with that of Huet. It was thought of as a long "fictitious narrative in prose." The *Oxford English Dictionary* adds appropriately that the immediate source was apparently F. *roman,* and it implies moreover that the genre was particularly prevalent in England during the sixteenth and seventeenth centuries.[10]

Novel

Unlike *roman, novella* cannot be traced back as a literary term to the beginnings of Romance and especially French literature. Most etymological dictionaries will inform us that *novella* is a vulgar Latin word and represents the plural neuter of the adjective *novellus,* meaning "news." It has also been advanced that the Italian word *novella* acquired the meaning of "noteworthy saying" or "speech." But whatever its previous meaning, in the fourteenth century the word established itself in Italy as a literary term. In the *Proemio* to his *Decameron,* Boccaccio introduced his tales as *novelle* (pl. of *novella*), and, when in the course of the following centuries his work was translated and imitated in France, Spain, Germany, and England, the term was accepted together with the genre and attached itself firmly to it.

Nor was the origin of the term easily forgotten. In Spain, for in-

9. Ibid., p. 2.
10. *OED,* "romance."

stance, it was still strongly felt even after Cervantes had published his *Novelas ejemplares*. In the early sixteenth century, Juan de Valdés declared *novela* and *novelar* specifically as Italianisms which he would like to see adopted in Spain.[11] The Spanish translators of the many editions of the *Decameron* retained the Italianized spelling *novellas*. Tirso de Molina considered it necessary to explain that the short stories he had inserted in his *Cigarrales de Toledo* were not stolen from the Italians.[12] Indeed, one of the interlocutors in Suárez de Figueroa's *Pasajero*, published four years after Cervantes' *Novelas ejemplares*, admits to the Doctor that he has never heard the term *novela*.[13] In England "novél" was stressed for some time on the last syllable in the Italian manner, and it retained this stress in Scotland until the nineteenth century. Only in France, where the *nouvelles* of Marguerite de Navarre soon came to vie in popularity with those of Boccaccio, were genre and term easily assimilated. (It is noteworthy, however, that the spirit of the *Heptaméron* is courtly rather than bourgeois, corresponding to the *novelle* which Boccaccio inserted in his *romanzi* rather than those of the *Decameron*.)

Following the pattern of either the *Decameron* or the *Heptaméron, novelle* or *nouvelles* appeared at first in collections that were linked together by a more or less tenuous framework or as inserts in longer romances. Thus the word established itself at first mainly in its plural form: It., *novelle;* Fr., *nouvelles;* Sp., *novelas;* Eng., "novels." Not even in Spain where the singular is used today—as it is in English—to designate all long prose narratives, whether of recent or ancient date, did the term occur in this sense or form. The long Spanish narratives presented themselves rather as *versos y prosa* (pastorals) ; *historia, estoria,* or *corónica* (chivalric novels, which thereby made claim to historical authenticity); or simply as *libro* or *libro de entretenimiento*.[14] Thus in spite of the fame gained by some *novella* collections, the individual *novella* was considered a minor genre, until the triumph of Cer-

11. Werner Krauss, "Novela-Novelle-Roman," *Zeitschrift für romanische Philologie, 60* (1940), 19. Reprinted in *Studien und Aufsätze* (Berlin, Rütten & Loening, 1959) .

12. Ibid., pp. 19–20.

13. Christóbal Suárez de Figueroa, *El Pasajero* (Madrid, 1617), p. 55.

14. Krauss, pp. 17–20, 25.

vantes' *Novelas ejemplares* prepared for it a new and more independent existence. Full individual status was to be reached by word and genre temporarily in France, but permanently only in England and Spain more than a century after Cervantes' work.

It has been shown that Cervantes could avail himself of the Spanish tradition of the *ejemplo* when he wrote his *Novelas.* Yet he was justified in his claim that he was the first to have "novelado en lengua castellana." [15] He was the first, moreover, to lengthen the Italian *novella* and provide it thereby with greater significance. When Figueroa differentiated in 1617 between the *novelas al uso,* that is, the small tales already known to Spanish readers, and the *novelas tomadas con el rigor que se debe,* that is, the genre created by Cervantes, he not only praised the latter but also envisioned them as stories capable of some length and philosophical weight.[16] But what Cervantes achieved above all in his *novelas* was to assimilate to his own more philosophical probings Boccaccio's art of story-telling and tolerant acceptance of human nature. Boccaccio had insisted in his *Proemio* that the *casi d'amore* told in his *novelle* might have happened in modern times as well as in antiquity, and he had defended in his *Conclusione* the author's right to speak of ordinary objects and problems of life, as long as he clothed them in *onesti vocaboli.* In his *Don Quijote* and his *Novelas ejemplares,* Cervantes also wrote about simple men and women, not about heroes and heroines or ladies and lords of society, and Werner Krauss perceptively defined his attitude as a "conscious rejection of the values and relationships of the ruling society." [17] It is in this respect in particular that the spirit of Boccaccio and that of Cervantes are happily in agreement. This was felt already by Cervantes' contemporaries. Lope de Vega found the manner of the *Novelas ejemplares* humbler than that of his own prose narratives: "es grande la diferencia y mas humilde el modo." While praising Cervantes' achievement, he could not refrain from wishing that such *novelas* had been written by "hombres científicos, ó por lo menos grandes cortesanos." [18] Avellaneda, the intrepid intruder and author of a second part of the *Don Quijote,*

15. Ibid.
16. Figueroa, p. 55.
17. Ibid., p. 21.
18. Lope de Vega, "Novelas," *Biblioteca Autores Españoles* (*BAE*), *38.*

showed greater insight when he called Cervantes' work "casi una comedia" (using the term, of course, in the prevalent meaning of a genre dealing with ordinary people in ordinary circumstances where magic and the marvelous happen only when the human mind fails to see things as they are) .[19]

Cervantes' impact in France was immediate and powerful. As early as 1627, Sorel's *Berger extravagant* proved his indebtedness to the *Don Quijote,* and his even earlier *Nouvelles françaises* (1623) are usually considered an attempt to adapt the *Novelas ejemplares,* known and translated in France almost immediately upon their publication.[20] Even Cervantes' Spanish imitators were soon welcomed in France, so that the year 1628 saw a collection entitled *Nouvelles tirées des plus célèbres auteurs espagnols,* and Scarron was enabled in his *Roman comique* (1651) to include four *novelas* of María Zayas.

What particularly impressed French authors with regard to Cervantes' *Novelas* was their *vraisemblance,* the fact that they seemed to be true to life. Camus praised them for that reason in 1628, and Scarron admiringly stated in his *Roman comique* that the Spaniards knew "de faire de petites histoires qu'ils appellent Nouvelles, qui sont bien plus à notre usage et plus à la portée de l'humanité que ces héros de l'Antiquité qui sont quelquefois incommodes à force d'être honnêtes gens." [21] In the discussion of the genre preceding the actual text of Segrais' *Nouvelles françoises* (1656) , Spanish writers of *nouvelles* were commended for having given their heroes ordinary Spanish names instead of the outlandish names found in French romances of the time. On the grounds of *vraisemblance,* Segrais even attacked the custom of imposing contemporary French manners upon the heroes of antiquity who peopled the fashionable *romans.*[22] (His attack was, of course, to be amusingly elaborated by Boileau in his *Héros de Roman.*)

19. Alonso Fernandez de Avellaneda, "Prólogo" of his *Don Quijote de la Mancha, BAE, 18,* 2 (Avellaneda is the pseudonym of an author whose real name is unknown) .

20. Antoine Adam, *Histoire de la Littérature française au XVIIe* (Paris, Domat, 1948–56) , *4,* 140–41.

21. Ibid., 2, 140.

22. Jean Regnaud de Segrais, *Les Nouvelles françoises ou les divertissemens de la Princesse Aurélie* (Paris, 1722) , *1,* 21–23.

Pleading likewise for a more broadly human approach, he expressed the view that ordinary people and what happened to them might profitably be made the subject matter of *romans,* inasmuch as these were supposed to instruct and divert. "Qu'est-il besoin que les exemples qu'on propose, soient tous de Rois et d'Empereurs, comme ils le sont dans tous les Romans?" he asked.[23] Implicit in such observations and in the praise of the Spaniards is the ever-growing dissatisfaction with the long *romans* of the times, with their lack of *vraisemblance* and their stylized characters that were removed from human reality.

Soon, however, the tone of French criticism was to reflect the fact that writers had adopted and adapted the new form of the *nouvelle.* Sorel still gives credit to its Italian and Spanish progenitors in his *Bibliothèque françoise* (1664), but he claims at the same time that French taste refined the genre and made it conform to the rules of *bienséance.* Through the impetus of the *nouvelle,* on the other hand, French fiction came closer to *vraisemblance,* imitation of nature, and truth—ideals as yet undefined and perhaps undefinable [24]—so that French *nouvelles* resembled more and more "histoires véritables de quelques incidents particuliers des hommes." Truth became, in fact, so dominant a preoccupation in France that Sorel wished the word *nouvelle* would actually coincide with its original meaning of "news." [25] He explicitly declared himself an admirer of Madame de la Fayette's *Princesse de Montpensier* (1662) because it adhered to history.

Under the impact of such thinking, French fiction began to appear in so historical a guise and works of history, in turn, in so romanticized a form that it became hard to differentiate between the two.[26] As a consequence, the word *histoire,* which in French means both "history" and "story," can be found in the titles of

23. Ibid., p. 24.

24. See René Wellek, *A History of Modern Criticism, 1750–1950* (New Haven, Yale University Press, 1955), *1,* 13–21, 113 ff. Also René Bray, *La Formation de la Doctrine classique en France,* (Paris, Nizet 1951), Chap. 5.

25. Sorel, pp. 149–50; Maurice Magendie, *Le Roman Français au XVIIe siècle de l' Astrée au Grand Cyrus* (Geneva, Droz, 1932), pp. 152–57.

26. Cf. Frederick C. Green, "The Critic of the 17th Century and His Attitude Towards the French Novel," *Modern Philology, 24* (1926–27), 285–95.

many works of the period.[27] But it would be wrong, it seems to
me, to conclude from this alone that *histoire* was seriously vying as
a designation with *roman*—as was done by S. Paul Jones on the
basis of the list of French prose fiction which he compiled for the
eighteenth century.[28] Even a perusal of lists of earlier prose fiction yields only a few titles which contain the term *roman,*
whereas the all-inclusive *histoire* can be found since the Middle
Ages.[29] Moreover, if we consider the fact that even nineteenth-
and twentieth-century writers of fiction rarely entitle their works
roman, we come to realize that such generic terms seldom occur in
titles, even if they are firmly established as designations.

What is of greater interest, therefore, concerning the relationship *roman–nouvelle* in France is the fact that Madame de Villedieu, who was soon to cultivate a pseudo-historical type of fiction,
began to refer to her works as *nouvelle.* When, in outspoken opposition to the writers of long *romans,* she asked her readers' indul-
gence for having omitted all that was miraculous or marvelous
from her *Cléonice* (1669) because she was writing of "une aven-
ture de nos derniers siècles," she pleaded precisely for the kind of
prose writing Segrais had defined as *nouvelle.* "Le Roman," he
had written, "écrit ces choses comme la bienséance le veut et à la
manière du Poëte; mais . . . la Nouvelle doit un peu davantage
tenir de l'Histoire et s'attacher plutôt à donner les images des
choses comme d'ordinaire nous les voyons arriver, que comme
notre imagination se les figure."[30] As Segrais had proposed,
Madame de Villedieu emphasized the ordinary human rather than
the heroic qualities of her characters, maintaining that she was not
concerned with the fate of thrones and nations but rather with experiences of truly human dimensions. If her protagonist were attacked by twenty men on horseback and defended by only four,
she would, she asserted, simply make him surrender, "comme s'il

27. Georges May, "Histoire et Roman au XVIIe et XVIIIe siècles," *Revue
d'Histoire Littéraire de la France,* 55 (1955), 155–76, 165.

28. S. Paul Jones, *French Prose Fiction 1700–1750* (New York, 1939), p. xv.

29. A. W. Wurzbach, *Geschichte des französischen Romans* (Heidelberg,
1912), Bibliography; Ralph C. Williams, *Bibliography of the 17th Century
Novel in France* (New York, Century, 1931).

30. Segrais, pp. 165–66.

n'était point le héros de ma nouvelle." [31] Moreover, as this very quotation indicates, she not only adopted Segrais' conception of *nouvelle,* but actually—like him—used the term in the singular rather than the plural.

It was largely due to Madame de Villedieu's work that *nouvelle*—as genre and designation—steadily gained in popularity in the 1670s in France. The long *romans*—"trop longs," according to Sorel—had been considered annoying for some time. In his *Dictionnaire,* Bayle credits Madame de Villedieu with "s'étant fait un nouveau goût de narrations romanesques" and with having been successful in making the "petites historiettes galantes" fashionable. With what seems almost a sigh of relief, he observes that, as a result, "elle fit tomber ces longs et vastes récits d'aventures héroïques, guerrières et amoureuses, qui avaient fait gagner tant d'argent aux imprimeurs de Cassandre, de Cléopâtre, de Cyrus et de Clélie, etc." [32] When Sorel had compared *roman* and *nouvelle,* he had found the latter more rigid and lucid in its structure: "Le dessein en est assez agréable; on n'y a pas tant de peine qu' à comprendre et à retenir une longue suite d'aventures meslées ensemble." [33] And these were the same qualities for which the Abbé de Charnes later praised *La Princesse de Clèves* and which prompted him to classify the work neither as *poème épique, tragédie,* or *roman* but rather "une histoire suivie, & qui représente les choses de la manière qu'elles se passent dans le cours ordinaire du monde." [34]

Nouvelle vs. *Roman*

One might assume that the decline of the long *roman* and the emergence of the long *nouvelle* would have caused the demise of the older term in favor of the new one. Reality, however, took a different course. The term *roman* persisted. Even Madame de

---

31. Cited by Moses Ratner, *Theory and Criticism of the Novel in France: From L'Astrée to 1750* (New York, New York University Press, 1938), p. 67. See also Segrais, n. 22.

32. Pierre Bayle, *Dictionnaire Historique et Critique* (Paris, 1820), p. 165. First published in 1699.

33. Sorel, p. 165.

34. Ratner, p. 42. See also Sorel, p. 123.

Villedieu did not always refer to her works as *nouvelle* but sometimes called them *petit roman*.[35] Bayle, in commending her for the change she had wrought in the prose narrative, speaks of her as a writer known for her *romans*. Huet ignored the term "nouvelle" and entitled his famous treatise *De l'Origine des Romans*. Indeed, the French *roman* proved to be capable of adjusting itself to the new taste. New editions of the *Astrée* and *Théagènes et Chariclée*, which were published in the early eighteenth century, were shorn of all that was miraculous and seemingly superfluous and rearranged by their editors in chronological order. Following the lead of the *nouvelle*, the *roman* also ceased to emulate the form of the prose epic and no longer had to begin in medias res. "Ayant observé l'ordre des temps, j'ai disposé les événements entre eux comme ils sont arrivés," wrote the editor of the new *Théagènes et Chariclée*.[36] In this rapprochement of the two genres it was the element of *galanterie* that temporarily won out as compared to the element of "comedy" inherent in Boccaccio as well as Cervantes. Sorel regretfully recorded the contempt in which were held "les bons livres comiques" which he had particularly appreciated as being "Tableaux naturels de la Vie humaine" and whose protagonists he had preferred to the "Heros de masquarade" of the heroic romances with their "aventures chimériques." But in the eighteenth century protagonists similar to his own Francion or to those of the *Roman comique* were to reappear in France in the works of Lesage and Marivaux.[37] If *nouvelle* thus never supplanted *roman*, this was because of the adaptability and all-inclusiveness of the older term.

Romance vs. Novel

In England, criticism concerning the prose narrative echoed largely what French critics—especially Segrais and Sorel—had observed with regard to *roman* and *nouvelle*. Madame de Villedieu's theories and practice also made themselves felt. The French lengthening of the *nouvelles* was reflected in the English novels so

35. Bruce A. Morrissette, *The Life and Works of Marie-Catherine Desjardins (Madame de Villedieu) 1632–1683* (St. Louis, Washington University Press, 1947), p. 86.

36. Cited by Ratner, p. 43.

37. Sorel, p. 158. See also Ratner, p. 64.

that they were eventually published separately and no longer merely in collections. Attempts were made parallel to those in France—to differentiate between "romance" and "novel": for some time, both terms were used side by side—seemingly as equivalents; finally a decision was made in favor of "novel." "Romance," either because—as term and genre foreign to England—it lacked the flexibility of French *roman,* or because England was not bound to the term by tradition, never acquired the all-inclusiveness of *roman.* The meaning which English associated with "romance" remained that of a long French or Italian narrative in verse or prose whose characters or events were removed from ordinary life. The term "novel," on the other hand, proved capable of semantic change and came to designate, more and more, narratives concerned with those human elements traditionally associated with comedy.

In the sixteenth century, "novel" had had almost exclusively the meaning of short story. The *OED* attests for 1566: "In these histories (which by another terme I call Nouelles) he described the liues . . . of great princes (Painter *Pal. Pleas.* Ded.) ." In the seventeenth and eighteenth centuries, the word maintained itself in that sense and was used mainly in the plural:

> 1621 Burton *Anat. Mel IV.*II.ii (1624) 230 Such as the old womene tolde Psyche in Apuleius, Bocace Nouells, and the rest; 1674 Evelyn *Mem.* (1857) III. 245 Marguerite of Valois . . . whose novels are equal to those of the witty Boccaccio; 1697 Dryden *Æneid* Ded., Ess. (Ker) II. 155 The trifling novels, which Ariosto, and others, have inserted in their poems; 1700—*Pref. Fables* ibid. 248 Boccace . . wrote novels in prose, and many works in verse.

But by 1834 the word had definitely undergone a semantic change. For the *OED* records: "Motley *Corr.* (1889) I.iii. 35 Tieck's novels (which last are a set of exquisite little tales, novels in the original meaning of the word) ." The writer was obviously cognizant of the fact that "novel" had lost the meaning of short story.

This change, then, took place in the course of the seventeenth and eighteenth centuries. The earliest evidence of "novel" in the sense of a fictitious prose narrative of considerable length is attested by the *OED* for the year 1643: "Milton *Divorce* I.vi.Wks.

1851 IV. 33 This is no mere amatorious novel." By 1693, a novel is clearly thought of as a publication of book length. The *OED* quotes from *Humours Town* 24: "She seats herself with some Novel or Play, in a very solitary posture." In 1867, needless to say, a novel is specifically referred to as a volume: "Trollope *Chron. Barset* I. xxxv. 311: [He] sat down over the fire with the volume of a novel" (*OED*).

By the end of the seventeenth century, "romance" and "novel" were used in England side by side and compared in a manner somewhat reminiscent of that of Sorel. As early as 1691, Congreve found them to differ in such a way that "Romances are generally composed of the Constant Loves and invincible Courages of Hero's, Heroin's, Kings and Queens, Mortals of the first Rank, and so forth; . . . Novels are of a more familiar nature; Come near us, and represent to us Intrigues in practice." [38] But often the terms were used interchangeably. In *A Letter Concerning Enthusiasm* (1708), Shaftesbury blames romance and novel alike for arousing the passions of young and old. In his *Advice to an Author* (1710) he censures the tastes of readers who prefer a "romance or novel, to an *Iliad*." [39] For the year 1711, the *OED* adduces an analogous passage from the *Spectator*: "I am afraid thy brains are a little disordered with Romances and Novels. (Steele, *Spect.* No. 254)." A passage from Chesterfield's *Letters* (1774) reflects what French critics had stated decades earlier, namely that "A Novel is a kind of abbreviation of a Romance" (I.130, *OED*).

Although Bayle's *Dictionnaire* and Huet's *Traité* had been translated in 1710 and 1715 respectively, they did not provide English critics with a clear distinction between the two terms. The country's preoccupation with morality and its concern for truth and *vraisemblance,* however, prompted writers to distance themselves from romance.[40] Emulating Madame de Villedieu, they assured their readers that they presented them with facts rather

38. William Congreve, *Incognita: or Love and Duty Reconcil'd*, Preface (1691).

39. Both in Anthony Earl of Shaftesbury, *Characteristicks of Men, Manners, Opinions, Times* (5th ed. Birmingham, 1773), pp. 40, 41.

40. Joseph Bunn Heidler, *The History, From 1700 to 1800, of English Criticism of Prose Fiction,* Illinois University Studies in Language and Literature, 13 (1928), passim.

than fiction. Richardson, in fact, rejected both romance and novel and wanted to create a "new species of writing." He insisted in his Preface to the sequel of *Pamela* (1741) that the letters it contained avoided "all romantic flights, improbable surprises, and irrational machinery." [41] He claimed that they were written "to Nature," and that it was his desire to get away from the "improbable and marvelous with which novels generally abound." [42]

When Fielding defined the prose narrative a year later, he designated it neither as romance nor as novel but emulated the French critics who had likened it to an epic poem. Only ten years earlier (1732), Dubos had published his *Réflections critiques sur la Poésie et sur la Peinture,* wherein he referred to Fénelon's *Télémaque* as an epic in prose.[43] It seems that Fielding also remembered the association of prose narrative with comedy which, implicitly and explicitly, had been established by Cervantes, Sorel, and Scarron. Fielding, who greatly admired the *Don Quijote,* referred to it in his Preface to his sister's *David Simple* as having been written in prose by a "comick writer." We may recall here his own definition of the comic epic poem in prose: "Now a comic romance," he wrote in his Preface to *Joseph Andrews,*

> is a comic epic poem in prose: differing from comedy as the serious epic from tragedy: its action being more extended and comprehensive; containing a much larger circle of incidents, and introducing a greater variety of characters. It differs from the serious romance in its fable and action in this: that as in the one these are grave and solemn, so in the other they are light and ridiculous; it differs in its characters, by introducing persons of inferior rank, and consequently of inferior manners, whereas the grave romance sets the highest before us; lastly in its sentiments and diction, by preserving the ludicrous instead of the sublime.[44]

Segrais and Sorel come to mind with their discussions of the *nouvelle* and the *romans comiques.* But there are also echoes of a

41. Samuel Richardson, *Pamela* (London, 1955), 2.

42. Cited by Heidler, pp. 51–52.

43. Jean-Baptiste Dubos, *Réflections critiques sur la Poésie et sur la Peinture* (Utrecht, 1732).

44. Henry Fielding, *Joseph Andrews,* in *Works* (London, 1882), *4,* x.

traditional definition of comedy which had only recently been re-
stated by Dubos. The subject matter of comedy, Dubos had
written,

> doit être pris entre les événemens ordinaires, & . . . ses
> personnages doivent ressembler par toutes sortes d'endroits au
> peuple pour qui l'on la compose. La Comédie n'a pas besoin
> d'élever ses personnages favoris sur des piedestaux, puisque
> son but principal n'est point de les faire admirer . . . . La
> Comédie ne sçauroit donc rendre le ridicule de ses person-
> nages trop sensible aux spectateurs.[45]

Fielding's differentiation between the serious and the comic
romance—so reminiscent of Congreve's and earlier French discussions of romance versus novel—made it obvious that these were
two genres which had to be designated in two different ways. The
terms "romance" and "novel" were so readily at hand and must
have so easily imposed themselves that Smollet actually used
"novel" to designate Fielding's work. "The genius of Cervantes,"
Smollet was to write in his *History of England* in 1757, "was trans-
fused into the novels of Fielding, who painted the characters, and
ridiculed the follies of life, with equal strength, humour, and
propriety." [46] Two elements in this statement interest us in particular: the use of the term "novel" and the reference to Cervantes. For, in 1748, Smollet had still employed "romance" in a
similar context. He had stated in his Preface to *Roderick Random*
that Cervantes had converted "romance" to purposes far more useful and entertaining. The shift from "romance" to "novel" seems
to be indicative of a general trend.

Shift to Novel

In subsequent years critics continued to strive for a clear distinction between "romance" and "novel." Though Hugh Blair, in
1783, speaks of the "insignificant class of writings, known by the
name of Romances and Novels" as if they were exactly the same

45. Dubos, pp. 86–87.
46. Tobias Smollet, *The History of England* (1757), reprinted in part as
*The History of England From the Revolution in 1688 to the Death of
George II* (London, 1811), pp. 414–15.

thing, he credits the "ingenious Cervantes" with having exploded the "Chivalry Romance." He notes with satisfaction that the "magnificent Heroic Romances" of France "dwindled down to the familiar Novel." Even if "these novels, both in France and England, during the age of Lewis XIV. and Charles II. were in general of a trifling nature," Blair finds that "a degree of reformation" has since been "introduced into the spirit of Novel Writing"; and that "imitations of life and character have been made their principal object" as well as "interesting situations, such as may actually occur in life." [47] He particularly singles out for their quality the novels of Lesage and Marivaux. Though he considers English novelists of his time inferior to the French, he gives honorable mention to Defoe, Richardson, and Fielding.

In *The Progress of the Romance,* published in 1785, Clara Reeve emulates earlier French critics as she draws a "line of distinction" between romance and novel. She declares the romance to be "an heroic fable which treats of fabulous persons and things" and the novel to be "a picture of real life and manners, and of the times in which it is written"; the romance a description in "lofty and elevated language" of "what never happened nor is likely to happen"; the novel "a familiar relation of such things, as pass every day before our eyes, such as may happen to our friend, or to ourselves." [48] Romances, according to her, ceased to be fashionable in England by 1752, and novels began to take their place. She also implies that the popularity of the term declined together with the form of writing to which it was attached. She registers amazement at people who still refer to eighteenth-century prose narratives, for instance those of Marivaux and Crébillon, as "romances" and concludes with some resignation that the two terms are still being confused and mistaken for each other. [49]

Moore's *View of the Commencement and Progress of Romance* (1791) quite justifies her conclusion. Although the author clearly distinguishes between two kinds of prose fiction, he speaks of the

47. Hugh Blair, *Lectures on Rhetoric and Belles Lettres* (London, 1783), 2, 303, 307, 308.
48. Clara Reeve, *The Progress of Romance* (*1785*) (New York, Facsimile Text Society, 1930), Pt. 1, pp. 6–7.
49. Ibid., Pt. 2, pp. 7, 31, 131; Pt. 1, pp. 111, 131.

romances of La Calprenède and Scudéry, on the one hand, and of
the "modern romance or novel," on the other, without clearly
opting for one or the other designation. He finds the modern
romance or novel close in spirit to the tales of Boccaccio and
Chaucer, describing "domestic life and the real manners of the
age," and not unlike the *Don Quijote* of Cervantes. Moore specifically considers the work of Cervantes the "model of the species
of romance which has since been adopted by Lesage, Marivaux,
Rousseau, Richardson, Fielding, Smollet, and so many others." [50]
In spite of its failure to employ the term "novel" in its newly
acquired meaning, Moore's work contributed to the definition of
the genre to which the term became more and more firmly attached. Moore also confirmed its link with the tradition of Boccaccio and Cervantes.

The "new romance" or "novel" is linked, in fact, so frequently
and persistently with the *Don Quijote* that one is tempted to attribute the final victory of "novel" over "romance" in England to
Spanish *novela,* in its current meaning, which designates precisely
a long prose narrative. But this would be entirely wrong. For
novela occurs in this meaning only toward the end of the eighteenth century. As late as 1732, Mayans Siscar refers to the *Don
Quijote* simply as a "género de Narración fabulosa" and as "fic-
ción entretenida." According to Krauss, the work is designated
only in 1789, in Cadalsos' *Cartas Marruecas,* as "una novela
immortal." [51] Krauss holds Spanish critics responsible for this use
of *novela,* which previously had been employed to designate only
short stories. Criticism needed, he explains, a term as all-inclusive
as French *roman.* Spanish *romance*—although it had briefly been
used as an equivalent for Italian *romanzo* (novel)—could not
fulfill this function, since tradition had established it as the generic term for ballad. The dilemma of Spanish critics is evident.
But Krauss' argument does not account for their choice of *novela,*
since the literature of Spain did not witness the steady growth of
novela-short story to *novela*-long story which we observed both in
France and England. If Spanish critics chose to expand the mean-

50. John Moore, *A View of the Commencement and Progress of Romance,*
in *Works,* ed. Robert Anderson (1820) , 5, 49, 50, 53, 54.
51. Cited by Krauss, p. 28.

ing of the term, they did so more likely under the impact of English criticism which had come more and more to associate the *Don Quijote* with the novel. The semantic change of Spanish *novela* seems to reflect the development of English "novel" rather than vice versa—a view supported by the growing influence of English letters in Spain during the eighteenth and nineteenth centuries.[52]

When Scott speaks, in his review of Jane Austen's *Emma* in 1815, of a new style of novel which had arisen within the last fifteen or twenty years, he attests to the extent to which both term and genre had been accepted in England by the end of the eighteenth and the beginning of the nineteenth centuries. He refers to the novel in general as the "legitimate child of romance" and to *Emma* in particular as belonging "to a class of fictions which has arisen almost in our own times, and which draws the characters and incidents introduced more immediately from the current of ordinary life than was permitted by the former rules of the novel." As for the characters in Jane Austen's world of fiction, Scott observed that "the author of Emma confines herself chiefly to the middling classes of society" and that "her most distinguished characters do not rise greatly above well-bred country gentlemen and ladies; and those which are sketched with most originality and precision, belong to a class rather below that standard." [53]

It is, therefore, when the novel is felt to be most genuinely English (by 1871, England was considered the birthplace of the modern novel—*Spectator,* Apr. 22, 484—*OED*) that it is also most strongly a part of that universal literary tradition concerned with the common man: the tradition of comedy which embraces Boccaccio, Cervantes, Marivaux, Lesage, as well as Richardson, Fielding, Smollet, and Jane Austen. Aldo Scaglione has rightly credited Boccaccio with having restored "in one sense at least, Humanism, in the broadest philosophical implications of the term . . . : namely as an open, unprejudiced appreciation of all that is human

52. Cf. A. Valbuena Prat, *Historia de la literatura Española* (Barcelona, Gili, 1960) , 2, 627 ff.

53. "Art. IX. *Emma; A Novel. By the Author of Sense and Sensibility, Pride and Prejudice,* etc. 3 vols. 12 mo. London. 1815," *The Quarterly Review* (in the number of October 1815, which appeared March 1816), pp. 189, 193.

inasmuch as it is part of human nature, however good or bad ethically, right or wrong rationally it might be." [54] Scaglione sees as the basis for this humanism Terence's utterance "homo sum, humani nihil a me alienum puto." Hence Boccaccio's assertion in the *Decameron* that he felt free to speak of all things created as long as he could do so with art. Such humanism is the realm of comedy in the traditional sense of the word. The tragic poet, as Beattie stated in 1776, "imitates characters more exalted." But "Comedy, whether Dramatic or Narrative (. . . perhaps the *Comic Epopee* is a more proper term), must seldom deviate from the ordinary course of human affairs, because it exhibits the manners of real, and even of familiar life." [55] "Poetry . . . to please, must be natural." If French *roman* could maintain itself against all sorts of odds, this was perhaps because the concept had embraced, from its very beginnings, this "humanistic" spirit. Already in the *Roman de la Rose* it had united the stylized refinement of de Lorris with the naturalist humanism of de Meung, of which even Boccaccio may have felt the impact. [56] Even when it boasted of abandoning this humanism during the seventeenth century, it never fully succeeded in doing so because of such writers as Scarron, Segrais, and Furetière who in their turn inspired the Marivauxes and Lesages of later generations. English "romance" lacked this spirit, since it came to be known mainly as the designation of the "vastes récits d'aventures héroiques, guerrières et amoureuses" of seventeenth-century France. When England opted for "novel" at the expense of "romance," it showed, therefore, preference not only for a literary term but also for the naturalist humanism—humanism in the broadest philosophical implication of the term—of de Meung, Boccaccio, Cervantes, Marivaux, and Fielding.

54. Aldo D. Scaglione, *Nature and Love in the Middle Ages* (Berkeley and Los Angeles, University of California Press, 1963), p. 101.

55. James Beattie, *Essays on Poetry and Music as They Affect the Mind* (Edinburgh, 1776), pp. 380 ff., 373.

56. Edith Kern, "The Gardens in the *Decameron* Cornice," *PMLA*, 66 (1951), 505–23. See also Scaglione, pp. 110 ff.

Agostino Lombardo

Shakespeare and Italian Criticism

"Chacius, Spenns, Drayton, Shakespier, Johnson, Bemont comico, Flesher comico"—in this list of confused and mangled names we find the first mention of Shakespeare in Italian writing. The author was probably that brilliant and versatile essayist, Lorenzo Magalotti, to whom Piero Rebora very convincingly attributes the account, in 1667, of a journey to England.[1] The account, indeed, gives such an interesting description of life in Restoration London as to make us regret the complete absence of any allusion to the Shakespearean performances which Magalotti surely must have attended, as he did others of a more frivolous nature (for example, the three spectacles "given in London for the lowest orders. Wrestling, bull and bear baiting, and cock-fighting, on all of which great wagers are laid"). Instead we have nothing except that poor name, and it is already a great deal if we consider that not even this can be found in the writings of other travelers and men of letters from whom we might have expected it. An example of this is Gregorio Leti with his *Teatro Brittanico* (sic) (1683), where the title is used in a metaphoric sense and applied to England in general (even though he does note the *magnificentissimi* theaters of London, which, "for that which concerns the scenes of the comedies, the ability of the players, the invention and design and all things else, surpass the other theaters of Europe"). A similar case is Apostolo Zeno, whose melodrama *Ambleto* (1705) goes directly to the source of Saxo Gramaticus, in complete ignorance of the Shakespeare play.[2] Even a half-century after the account of

1. See *Interpretazioni Anglo-Italiane* (Bari, 1961).

2. For a good analysis, see Lacy Collison-Morley's still useful *Shakespeare in Italy* (Stratford-upon-Avon, 1916).

Magalotti, there is the Florentine doctor Antonio Cocchi, who was in London in 1722–23 and learned English well enough to write part of his diaries in the language and deal competently with English philosophy and literature—and yet of Shakespeare he too gives only the name.

It is in these years, however, that certain men of culture began to lay the basis for a less superficial knowledge. The Paduan abbé, Antonio Conti, scientist, philosopher, and scholar, after going to England between 1715 and 1727, not only began to translate English poetry (including the *Rape of the Lock*) but also wrote a tragedy, *Cesare* (1726), which to some extent seems to reflect a reading of Shakespeare's *Julius Caesar* (as well as of the tragedies by the Duke of Buckingham, *Caesar* and *Brutus*). At the same time, he repeats the English and French judgments that were to prevail in Italy for many decades, writing, as a good classicist, that *"Sasper* is the Corneille of the English, but much more irregular than Corneille, though like him pregnant with grand ideas and noble sentiments." In his own tragedy Conti does, in fact, try to compose a work as "regular" as possible, also owing to the influence of Addison's *Cato,* which he praised enthusiastically. Like Conti, and in the same period, another abbé, Paolo Rolli, is concerned with Shakespeare; but, partly because of his excellent knowledge of English (he lived in London from 1715 to 1744), he reveals a greater understanding of Shakespeare's work and a greater independence of judgment. So it is that in 1729, introducing his celebrated translation of *Paradise Lost,* he says that Shakespeare "elevated the English theater to insuperable sublimity with his tragedies"; he manages to guess at the problem of interpolations, anticipates Romantic attitudes by comparing Shakespeare to Dante, and underlines the importance of the histories:

> This wondrous genius . . . wrote certain tragedies which I would call historical, since they represent historical happenings concerning the illustrious kings and nobles of his nation: and in these the events and the characters that participate are so vivid and so poetically expressed with most fitting style as not to be bettered. An example which I could wish followed in other nations.

Finally, it is to Rolli that we owe, in 1739, what is almost certainly the first Italian translation of a passage from Shakespeare ("To be or not to be").

Both this translation and these critical judgments also derive from a desire to take issue with Voltaire. Voltaire, indeed, in Italy as in the rest of Europe, represents an essential stage in the "fortune" of the dramatist. On the one hand, with his influence and authority, Voltaire confirms the importance of Shakespeare's work; on the other hand, he lays down the limits within which criticism is to move until the advent of Romanticism. Certain comments contained in the *Essay on Epic Poetry* (published in English in 1727 during Voltaire's stay in England, 1726–28) and above all the eighteenth of the *Lettres Philosophiques* (published in French in 1734, but in English in 1733 under the title *Letters concerning the English Nation*) are in fact at the base of nearly all eighteenth-century criticism of Shakespeare, which, in turn, always refers back to Voltaire ("Shakespeare boasted of a strong, fruitful genius: he was natural and sublime, but had not so much as a single spark of good Taste, or knew one Rule of the Drama . . . there are beautiful, noble and dreadful scenes in this writer's monstrous farces, to which the name of tragedy is given"). With all the many reservations and qualifications natural to eighteenth-century taste, Voltaire has, in these years, a genuine admiration for Shakespeare, and though he frequently inveighs against his irregularities and "absurdities," and especially against the mingling of comic and tragic, he does not fail to define, in a famous passage, his peculiar greatness:

> One would think that the English had been hitherto formed to produce irregular beauties only. The shining monsters of Shakespeare give infinitely more delight than the judicious images of the Moderns. Hitherto the poetical genius of the English resembles a tufted tree planted by the hand of Nature, that throws out a thousand branches at random, and spreads unequally, but with great vigour. It dies if you attempt to force its nature, and to lop and dress it in the same manner as the trees of the garden of Marly.

But with time, as René Wellek points out, "Voltaire's opinion of

Shakespeare grew more unfavorable"; [3] in 1776 his letter to the French Academy recognized the genius of Shakespeare but accused him of obscenity and vulgarity, ridiculed him, and called him "gille de village," while in another letter to the Academy in 1778 Shakespeare is described, in words which will be ironically adopted by Manzoni, as a barbarian not devoid of genius, whose dramas can please only in London or in Canada.

Voltaire, however, had discovered the greatness and at the same time the "monstrousness" of Shakespeare not only for the French, but also for the Italians, who follow in his footsteps and, in the wake of his judgments, begin to form their own. An obsequious follower of Voltaire is Luigi Riccoboni (the actor Lelio, resident in France) with his *Réflexions historiques et critiques* of 1734 (published in 1740). Francesco Algarotti, a friend of Voltaire, praises his *César* in a letter of 1735, affirming that "in this tragedy Voltaire takes to imitating the severity of the English theatre, and in particular Shakespeare, in whom it is rightly said there are both numberless errors and inimitable thoughts." Francesco Saverio Quadrio, in his *Della Storia e della Ragione d'ogni Poesia* (1743), literally repeats the major passages of Voltaire, defining Shakespeare as a poet gifted with "a genius . . . full of fecundity and strength" but with "no knowledge of the just rules"; and Carlo Denina in his *Discorso sopra le vicende della letteratura* (1761) makes the same affirmation when he writes that, whereas "he was sovereignly gifted with sublime genius, with great fire, with a most fertile imagination, and with all the natural qualities for the making of a great poet," he was nonetheless "completely in the dark as to the rules of the theater." The same attitudes are revealed by Saverio Bettinelli, who refers to Shakespeare in *Lettere Inglesi* (1766) and elsewhere, emphasizing his "rough and bestial ignorance of history and manners" as well as the bad taste that ruins his high poetic qualities:

> I say with you, dear Sir,
> That *Scespir* is an author
> Admirable, immortal,

3. See the chapter dedicated to Voltaire in the first volume of Professor Wellek's admirable *History of Modern Criticism: 1750–1950* (New Haven and London, 1955). All the volumes that have appeared so far are indeed extremely useful for our subject.

> Divine, original,
> A great tragedian; but then,
> What can be said of such a taste
> And what can be thought of you?

Finally, in *Dialoghi sopra il Teatro Moderno* (1788) he inveighs against the "vulgar" scenes of *Hamlet, Antony and Cleopatra,* and *Julius Caesar*. On *Julius Caesar* we also have the comments of Melchiorre Cesarotti, who, despite his famous translation of Ossian, dear to the Romantics, remains firmly bound to neoclassical theories. While appreciating the "enthusiasm and fire" of Shakespeare's style in the *Ragionamento sopra il Cesare* (1762), he gives him "no merit, either for invention, or for regularity and artifice of plot," preferring to *Julius Caesar* not only the *César* of Voltaire, but also the *Cesare* of Conti. One can point to a long list of similar judgments, from Francesco Milizia's *Trattato completo, formale e materiale del Teatro* (1773) to certain letters and works by Agostino Paradisi, Stefano Arteaga, Vincenzo Marenco, Aurelio Bertòla, Luigi Richeri, and others. The frequent disapproval of Shakespeare's "horror" finds expression in a letter (1775) of Giambattista Roberti, who calls him "sanguinary." In *Storia Critica de' Teatri Antichi e Moderni* (1777) Pietro Napoli-Signorelli gives a synthesis of what the period considers the major defects of Shakespeare's art: "neglect of the unities, yoking of the lowest comedy to the most sublime tragedy, introduction of the marvellous." Finally there is the celebrated work of the Spanish Jesuit, Giovanni Andrès, *Dell 'origine, progressi e stato attuale d'ogni letteratura* (1785), where the positive element still present in the other critics is completely lacking: "But whatever his adorers may say, I cannot find in the work of Shakespeare those beauties which they extol, nor, even should they really exist, would I think it fitting counsel or well-spent toil to search them out amid so much dross."

We must indeed agree with Arturo Graf when he stresses the difficulties met by Shakespeare's work in its Italian progress.[4] And yet we can say with him:

4. In his *L'Anglomania e l'influsso inglese in Italia nel secolo XVIII* (Turin, 1911).

with French tragedy triumphant on our stage; with our native tragedy enslaved to French imitation; opposed by a backward and stubborn tradition with timid or ineffective attempts at reform; sentimental drama prevailing; Arcadia persisting: in these circumstances was the work of William Shakespeare to enter our country and, overcoming aversions and fears, obtain recognition and applause.

While, in fact, at least in the more acute followers of Voltaire we still find those positive elements recognized by Voltaire himself, other critics, like Rolli previously, show a clearer perception of the values of Shakespeare's art. Although, as Croce justly observes, Vico was, in the eighteenth century, the best qualified to understand Shakespeare fully, he has left us nothing that testifies to his knowledge of the dramatist.[5] Metastasio, however, though he does not speak of the poet directly, probably knew of him, at least through the French translations of La Place, whose *Théatre Anglois* (1746–49) is most important for the propagation of Shakespearean drama in Europe. Metastasio's acquaintance with Shakespeare can be deduced from a letter in 1754 to Ranieri de' Calzabigi, stating that he has tried to take account of "the progress of the theater in England," and also from his arguments against the unities (published posthumously in his *Estratto dell'Arte Poetica di Aristotele*). The unities are also attacked, of course, by Carlo Goldoni, who, moreover, names Shakespeare explicitly in *Il Filosofo Inglese* and *I Malcontenti* (1754), where the character of Grisologo (ridiculing Chiari) is an imitator of *Sachespir*. In a letter to John Murray introducing *I Malcontenti* he writes:

> My enterprise depends on your approval: you have indeed a refined taste for Comedy, learned from the best Authors, and precisely those of England who have such enlightened comic strength. I myself, though ignorant of the language, aided by the best translations, have studied to profit, with the most serious observation, from such worthy Masters, and all that politic and moral force which I have scattered through my writings, is the result of studied imitation of the English originals. Your celebrated Shakespeare, not less venerated in British

5. See Croce's *La Filosofia di G. B. Vico* (Bari, 1911).

Theaters than in foreign nations, has perfectly united in himself the Comic and the Tragic faculties. He is at the head of
numberless English Authors who have honored the stage and
are today preferred above all others. Indeed, in his works are
to be found such artifice in the plot, such truth in the characters, such force in the sentiments, as to serve as a school for
whoever wishes to undertake such an arduous career. He has
not observed in his works that scrupulous unity of time and
place which confines the fantasy of Poets . . . the English
and the Spanish . . . have freed themselves from the injuri-
ous yoke.

After discussing the unities at length, Goldoni concludes the letter
affirming that in *I Malcontenti* he has introduced an imitator of
Shakespeare "to render public my veneration towards such a
worthy Author, and to bring his name before those who perchance
do not already know it."

Goldoni, as he himself admits, knew Shakespeare through
French translations (those of La Place), and the same is true of
the other Venetians, from Carlo Gozzi to the journalists of the
period, especially Antonio Piazza.[6] They were also introduced to
Shakespeare by the *Lettres sur les Anglois et les François* (1745)
of Abbé Le Blanc and later by Martin Sherlock's *Letters of an
English Traveller,* published in French in 1779 and in English in
1780. But even though to the *Théatre* of La Place were added the
Shakespearean adaptations of Ducis from 1769 on, the time was
ripe for the first Italian versions.[7] And so, in 1756, we have the
Giulio Cesare of Domenico Valentini. It is difficult to say whether
this prose translation is done from the English text or not, but,
being the first, it is, nonetheless, of notable importance. This is especially true because Valentini, in his introduction, proves to be
an acute and courageous critic, especially when, discussing the
"rules," he grasps the intrinsic necessity of Shakespearean "irregularity":

6. See the excellent book by Rosa Maria Colombo, *Lo Spectator e i
giornali veneziani del Settecento* (Bari, 1966).

7. For which see Anna Maria Crinò's *Le Traduzioni di Shakespeare in
Italia nel Settecento* (Rome, 1950).

> The rules laid down by Aristotle, Horace, and other critics
> whom I know not whether to call severe or superstitious, are
> ample enough for mediocre talents; but for an imagination so
> strong, so rapid, so lively as that of Shakespeare they appeared
> too narrow, and had he retained himself within those narrow
> limits we would certainly be deprived of great beauties.

This affirmation is so new and fruitful that it is not surprising that
in 1762, Valentini is brutally attacked by Francesco Antonio
Zaccaria.

But neither the translation nor the critical comments of Valentini would have been enough to accelerate the progress of Shakespeare in Italy had it not been for the appearance in the critical
arena of that vigorous and brilliant scholar, Giuseppe Baretti. The
first mention of Shakespeare in his works comes fairly late, the
second year of his first stay in England, when, in *A Dissertation
upon the Italian Poetry* (1753; written in English) , he attacks the
opinions of Voltaire on epic poetry and places Shakespeare among
the great figures of world literature. He speaks of Shakespeare at
greater length in 1757 (*A Dissertation upon the Italian Tongue*),
comparing him to Metastasio, and in 1760 in the preface to that
English-Italian Dictionary which was for more than a century a
model of its kind, where he speaks of "the elevation, the daring,
and the impetuous and noble fury" of Shakespeare and Milton.
Shakespeare is also certainly among the protagonists of the *Frusta
Letteraria,* the review he began to produce in 1763 on his return
from England. Here there is much on Addison, Pope, and Samuel
Johnson, his master and friend, but there are also important passages on Shakespeare. Replying to Carlo Denina, whose opinion of
Shakespeare is quoted above, he reproves him for having spoken
"of the English Shakespeare as one might speak of a Chiari" and
then bursts out in a vehement and impassioned defense of Shakespeare:

> But let Signor Denina be convinced, despite all the letters *sur
> les anglois* and *sur les anglais* he has read, and despite his pro-
> found veneration for the theatrical laws issued by the tremen-
> dous tribunals of France, let him be convinced, I say, that
> Shakespeare is a poet, and in tragedy and comedy fit to stand

alone before all the Corneilles, all the Racines, and all the Molières of Gaul. I have heard them myself, those famous theatrical laws; but I know, on the other hand, that *Romeo and Juliet, Othello, Hamlet, King Lear, The Tempest, The Death of Caesar* and other Shakespeare plays have been performed for a hundred-and-fifty years in the theaters of London, which are anything but puppet-shows . . . . Now let Signor Denina teach me some fine rule, drawn from the letters *sur les anglois,* or from those *sur les anglais,* which shall serve better than those used by Shakespeare to make people crowd the theaters days after day, year after year, century after century . . . . May I tell you something in confidence, Signor Denina? Shakespeare, like Ariosto, is one of those transcendental poets "whose genius soars beyond the reach of art." I see from your Discourse that you already understand a little English, and so I shall not do you the injustice of translating these few words. I would rather exhort you to study that language better than you have been able to do so far, before passing judgment on the English, and above all on Shakespeare and Milton.

This passage is indeed a perfect example of how contact with Shakespeare can bring a personality in many ways conservative to positions of ardent innovation—the same had happened in England with Samuel Johnson, an authentic representative of classicism and yet, in his Shakespearean criticism, a precursor of Romantic interpretations.

From Johnson, in fact, derives much of that *Discours sur Shakespeare et sur Monsieur de Voltaire* (1778), which Baretti wrote after returning to England in 1777–78, and which is not only his most important work of Shakespearean criticism but the first serious and extensive critical study of Shakespeare in Italy. Some scholars have tended to underestimate the influence of Johnson, whose edition of Shakespeare, with the fundamental *Preface,* had appeared in 1765; but the evidence is undeniable. Baretti called assiduously on the great Doctor, participated in his admirable conversation, shared with him a close and mutual friendship, and admired him more than any other English writer of the time. It is not surprising therefore that the *Discours* is permeated with John-

sonian ideas; the dispute with Voltaire is in itself Johnsonian and
the most significant statements are taken almost literally from the
Preface. The famous discussion about the unities will serve as an
example. Here an imaginary questioner condemns the absurdity of
Shakespeare's practice and asks whether it is possible, in a few
hours, to make credible events lasting years or to render probable
great changes of place before the eyes of an audience that does not
move from the theater; Baretti replies:

> Comment donc ceux qui savent d'être à Paris et dans la salle
> de la Comédie, peuvent'ils se donner le change et croire qu'ils
> sont à Rome, à Memphis ou à Samarcande? Comment peuvent-
> ils voir, de leurs yeux, que c'est la mademoiselle Vestris et le
> sieur Lekain, et croire néanmoins que l'une est Agrippine ou
> Lucrèce, et l'autre Tarquin ou Tibère? . . . Qu'importe que
> le consul Marcantoine se tienne à Rome pendant toute la pièce,
> ou qu'il parte au second acte pour le Méxique, s'embarque au
> troisième pour Péterbourg, fasse une escapade à Pondicheri
> dans le quatrième, et aille au cinquième se faire capucin en
> Irlande, pourvu que le poète ait l'adresse de nous faire savoir
> où Marcantoine est, aussitôt qu'il paraît, et les raisons qui le
> réduisent pas-à-pas à quitter le consulat et se faire capucin?
> Faut-il de plus grands efforts d'imagination pour aller d'un
> pays à l'autre, que de se tenir ferme dans Rome durant tous
> les cinq actes, quand on sait d'être à Paris, que l'acteur ne
> bouge du Capitole ou qu'l courre de pays en pays jusqu'à Cork
> ou à Dublin?

And to the new question, "où est l'illusion pendant tout ce
temps?", Baretti replies again with Johnsonian words: "L'illusion,
messieurs? Je viens de vous dire qu'aucun d'entre vous n'est
sujet à la moindre illusion dans votre cas . . . personne ne va
voir jouer *Cinna, Britannicus, Hamlet, Macbeth* . . . pour se
procurer le plaisir d'une illusion qu'il serait impossible d'obtenir.
Chacun y va pour s'amuser d'une représentation." These and other
passages of the *Discours* (for example, on the character of Falstaff)
are, without any doubt, paraphrases of Johnson's *Preface,* and their
originality lies not in the content but in Baretti's polemical stance,
in his liveliness, in his fantasy, in the hearty vigor with which he

defends his author. On the other hand, if it is already important that Baretti presents and elaborates Johnsonian ideas, it should also be noted that some parts of the *Discours* not only are completely original but also show acute and frequent insights into Shakespeare's art. Among these are the comments on Voltaire's method of translating Shakespeare, the discussion of certain characters, especially Caliban, the comparison between the Ghost in *Hamlet* and the specter of Ninus in Voltaire, and the polemic against some Italian writers, against the hated Goldoni, and against Arcadia. One remembers particularly the passage where, having affirmed that Shakespeare cannot be translated into French, Baretti continues:

> Shakespeare ne savait latin, ni grec, ni autre langue. Il n'avait devers soi qu'une profonde connaissance de la nature humaine, un de ces génies, si rares partout, qu'on appelle "génies d'invention," et par dessus cela une imagination toute de feu. Avec ces trois qualités, Shakespeare sut former, à l'age de trente-deux ans, un langage quelquefois bas et plein d'affectation, mais plus souvent compact, énergique, violent, d'où sort une poésie qui enlève l'âme quand il le veut . . . . La langue française . . . est trop chatiée, trop scrupuleuse, trop dédaigneuse, pour rendre Shakespeare . . . . Il est plus libre dans le choix de ses expressions que le vent sur l'océan, pour le dire à sa manière.

On the whole, therefore, the *Discours* represents a milestone for Shakespearean criticism in Italy: from it emerges a portrait of Shakespeare with much clearer outlines than the rough sketch of previous years. And there emerges also that new concept of the liberty of art and of the artist which is to be fully affirmed by the Romantics and in which the "discovery" of Shakespeare plays an important part.

The Shakespearean activity of Alessandro Verri moves in the same direction. Already in the years of the Accademia dei Pugni and of *Il Caffè* (1764–65) the name of Shakespeare circulated among the editors of the Milanese review, so sensitive to the influence of English culture (as can be seen, among other things, from the Shakespeare passages written in the notebook of the

Cremonese Giambattista Biffi) . After a journey to Paris and London in 1776–77, Alessandro Verri, having learned English, began to take a serious interest in Shakespeare, with the result that from him we have the first Italian translations since that of Valentini— *Hamlet* (1769–77) and *Othello* (1777) .[8] These are prose versions, not without errors owing partly to the editions used by Verri; but they are nonetheless of considerable importance both for their pioneering nature and for the faithfulness and intelligence of the translation. The notes are of particular interest, being not only philological but also critical. The substance of them also can be found in the many letters sent by Alessandro to his brother Pietro—letters that represent by no means a negligible chapter of Shakespearean criticism, as the following extracts may demonstrate:

> I see that Voltaire either does not know the language or desires . . . to ridicule Shakespeare. But wrongly so, because with all his extravagances he is a great man . . . . To judge him properly and with full knowledge of the facts, one must confess that he is a sovereign poet and that his noble moments, which are many, represent the highest point of poetry, and even his defects have a certain strangeness and wonder indicating an extraordinary genius . . . . The Moor of Venice is beautiful, most beautiful, divine, copied directly and at first impulse from the effects of Nature. These are real passions and this is their strength . . . . In short, he is an author full of defects, but in whom every kind of poetry can find treasures, as in a rich mine of every style and every passion. This author shows the true path of Nature, and after reading him, one finds the heroes of the French theater artificial . . . . He is the true painter of Nature; the others are mannered, he paints with the naked model before his eyes . . . . Everything in Shakespeare is free, original, and strange; the new words and the daring phrases make the Academy of Inscriptions sigh, and since

8. They are still unpublished. For reproduction of extracts and for a detailed analysis, see Silvana Colognesi's article "Shakespeare e Alessandro Verri," in *ACME,* University of Milan (maggio-dicembre 1963) ; see also Crinò.

there is no other example of a writer who has broken these chains, the first who dares to do so appears a monster.

Not only Alessandro but also Pietro Verri is struck by Shakespeare, and some of his letters constitute precious evidence of the reactions of a man of Illuminist culture to the works of an author in whom there are so many elements dear to the Romantics:

> I hold very dear the translation you have sent me of a scene from *Hamlet*. I find there a quite particular force and energy: dark colors which have their full effect; nothing exaggerated, but everything taken from Nature; most interesting sentiments, but true to the human heart . . . . He is unique in his manner of conceiving objects . . . . I have read The Moor of Venice . . . . One sees the original man, who has no model before him, passion taken to the height and portrayed exactly, a manner energetic to the highest degree that puts before you thoughts of blood . . . . I have read Caesar . . . . He never makes his characters shamelessly clear, there is always a mist . . . . I do not accuse the works of Corneille, Racine, or Voltaire, no, they move me, they instruct me, they arouse me to virtue; but they have the improbability of a painting in decisive and primary colors, whereas Nature always presents its objects in half-tones.

Unfortunately, the opinions of Alessandro and Pietro Verri were limited to a private circle and lacked the influence they deserved. It should be noted, however, that Alessandro Verri also contributes to the establishment of close relations between Shakespeare and Italian culture with his own creative work. In the *Notti Romane* we have Shakespearean touches together with much more frequent echoes of the English pre-Romantics and Ossian. More important are the two attempts at drama in 1778, *Pentea* and *La Congiura di Milano (Galeazzo)* ; in the latter work particularly, it is not merely a question of echoes and derivations (mainly from *Julius Caesar*) but also of dramatic techniques. Verri respects the unity of time, but not that of place, and inserts in the action a series of spectacular expedients clearly derived from his Shakespearean experience. The choice of a subject from national history is also Shakespearean.

The need for a more direct and detailed knowledge of Shakespeare, to which Alessandro Verri responds, is typical of the last
years of the eighteenth century. There was further Shakespearean
influence through the translations of Le Tourneur, which began
to appear in 1776, and through the first performances of *Hamlet* (1774) and *Romeo and Juliet* (1778) in the adaptations
of Ducis (these also translated and published). All this led to the
request for an Italian version, and in 1798 Giustina Renier
Michiel, probably encouraged by Cesarotti, published the first
volume of *Opere drammatiche di Shakespeare volgarizzate da una
Dama Veneta*. This volume contained *Othello* and was to be followed in the same year by *Macbeth* and in 1800 by *Coriolanus*.
The result, if not particularly inspired, is certainly useful, not
least for the biographical and critical material given, drawn not
only from Le Tourneur but from Pope, Addison, Warburton,
Richardson, and above all Johnson. Like Verri, other men of
letters came into contact with Shakespeare. Some were essentially
minor figures, such as Alessandro Pepoli or Lorenzo Pignotti, who
in 1779 wrote a poem in praise of Shakespeare (and of Mrs.
Montagu's *Essay*, to be translated in 1828) entitled *The Tomb of
Shakespeare*:

> This man was great indeed because
> The servile yoke of art could never bind
> His tireless and defiant
> Impatient wings . . . .

But the list also contains some of the major names in Italian literature. Vittorio Alfieri, as he tells us in his autobiography, was so
struck by his reading of Shakespeare that in 1775 he decided to
break off, both because it happened to be a French translation and
because "the more I was pleased by that author (all whose defects
I could distinguish well enough) the more I wanted to avoid
him." He had indeed already written and then destroyed a drama
called *Romeo e Giulietta*. Shakespearean reminiscences, however,
can be found in *Filippo* and even in works like *Saul* which are, in
intention, quite the opposite of Shakespeare. Cesarotti is aware of
this when he urges Alfieri not to let himself be influenced too
much by the English dramatist. And so is Ranieri de' Calzabigi

when, in a letter prefixed to the 1806 edition of Alfieri's tragedies, he compares the two. First, he gives examples of Shakespearean translation (from *Richard III* and *Romeo and Juliet*) and then, after affirming that this "English Aeschylus . . . scared with his own unaided strength . . . Produced monsters, but originals," he states that Alfieri "for his energy, brevity and pride must be likened to Shakespeare more than to anyone else." The comparison however is condemned by Carmignani in his *Dissertazione critica sulle tragedie di V. Alfieri* (1806): "to compare Alfieri with Shakespeare is to link things essentially contrary, it is a comparison between works of art and works of nature." Shakespeare is also known to Ippolito Pindemonte, whose Prologue to *Arminio* contrasts Shakespeare, "dear son of Nature," with Addison, nourished instead by "art." In 1812, however, in three discourses on the theater, he attacks Shakespeare severely and takes issue with the Romantics: "If taste—as is admitted—does not abound in Shakespeare's brain, and if his tragedies cannot serve as an example— which is not denied,—then I conclude, contrary to the general opinion, that he had no real genius." Giovanni Pindemonte, Ippolito's brother, also shows some signs of Shakespearean influence in his work. This is even truer of Vincenzo Monti who comes to Shakespeare fairly early, in 1779–80, both through performances which impressed him deeply and through Sherlock's *Letters of an English Traveller*. He speaks of Shakespeare frequently: in 1780, in a letter to Vanetti, he dwells at length on some passages from *Romeo and Juliet,* and in a letter of 1825 he rates his own enthusiasm for Shakespeare even higher than that of the Romantics. As evidence of this enthusiasm there are traces of Shakespeare in Monti's own work, from *Aristodemo* to *Galeotto Manfredi,* from *Caio Gracco* to the *Bardo della Selva Nera.*[9]

Ugo Foscolo, in his dramatic works, appears less directly influenced by Shakespeare (with the possible exception of *Ricciarda*), but the contacts are no less interesting for this. In 1796, in his "Plan of Studies," Shakespeare is among the tragedians selected for particular attention, together with Sophocles, Voltaire, and Alfieri. In 1798, in his "Defence" of Monti, he appeals to *Julius*

9. On this see the lively book by S. A. Nulli, *Shakespeare in Italia* (Milan, 1918).

Caesar as to an undisputed exemplar in the argument, while the *Ultime Lettere di Jacopo Ortis* (1802) shows us a Jacopo in the steps of *Werther* with a Romantic enthusiasm for Shakespeare: "Homer, Dante and Shakespeare, the masters of all superhuman minds, have possessed my imagination and inflamed my heart: I have bathed their verses with burning tears, and I have adored their divine shades as if I could see them seated on the lofty peaks that dominate the universe." After moving to England in 1816, Foscolo speaks even more of Shakespeare, often together with Dante. Here, from the *Discorso sul testo della Divina Commedia,* is a character sketch of Juliet: "In the heart of Juliet timidity, simplicity, and all the virginal graces instead of cooling conspire to inflame in a moment the impulsiveness and generosity of love." We also find a comment on Shakespeare and the unities: "The unities are not in the least scorned by the English, who do not think they should be completely violated, unless sometime it should please Nature to create another Shakespeare or unless fortune should bring back a century not unlike that in which his tragedies were performed. Today it is the actors who mutilate them." Most important are some passages from the article *Della nuova scuola drammatica in Italia* (1826) where, though Shakespeare is used as a polemic weapon against the historical drama of the Romantics, there are observations which show better than anything else Foscolo's critical insight and genuine Romantic sensibility.

> Shakespeare himself, in the tragedies drawn from English history, achieved success and rendered them interesting through the importance which the audience naturally attached to national traditions, through the exactness with which he drew the real characters of past princes, through the variety of incident and character that he introduced, through his knowledge of human nature, and above all through the luminous and constant fire that his heart and imagination inspired in his verses . . . .
>
> . . . But in *Othello, Hamlet* and *Macbeth,* where he was bound to history only as far as served his purpose, the characters are his own invention and therefore more original and also more true because to their creation contributed the whole of human nature . . . .

. . . His genius infused into the shadows of his mind form and life and potent spirit and all the illusions of reality: and if one considers well his play *The Tempest,* it would seem that he even had the privilege of creating from nothing . . . .

. . . In *Othello* he adopted a semi-barbarian hero because in this state of society the virtues are genuinely simple, bold and generous, and the passions profound, impatient and vehement: while the age, the candor, the confiding soul and the love of the Venetian heroine, who sacrifices everything for such a man and finds death, provide a contrast with the character of the husband that arouses at every moment pity and terror, but neither hatred for Othello nor scorn for Desdemona; all our aversion is concentrated on the character of Iago, to whom, nonetheless, we are compelled to give some part of our admiration for the slow, profound art, efficacious and almost superhuman, with which he matures and accomplishes his infernal treason.

Foscolo expresses these opinions in 1826 when the Italian debate over Romanticism had already died down. But it is precisely to this debate that we must return, because in Italy, as in the rest of Europe, the Romantic battle was largely fought in the name of Shakespeare. This is due, above all, to the identification of Romantic poetry with Shakespearean drama brought about in Germany and France. Indeed, it would be impossible to carry this discussion further without reference to some foreign works that influenced profoundly Italian culture and its attitude toward Shakespeare. Of Goethe there is not only *Werther* but the first part of *Wilhelm Meister* (translated in 1809) , where the interpretation of Hamlet offers to the Romantic sensibility an image in which it recognizes many of its own features. In addition to the writings of Lessing, Herder, and Friedrich Schlegel, one must remember that *Course of Dramatic Literature* by August Wilhelm Schlegel, which, translated by Gherardini in 1817, is at the base of all successive critical opinions. This is not surprising if we consider that Schlegel's work gave a mass of information about Shakespeare and the Elizabethan drama and analyzed the whole of Shakespeare's work in detail and often with great critical insight, despite

the "bardolatry" typical of Romantic criticism. The most significant fact, however, is that we have here an image of Shakespeare
that includes all the components of Romanticism, from liberty of
form to exaltation of art and the artist, from aspiration toward the
infinite to unrest and melancholy, from religious anguish to the
fervor of feelings and passions.

We should not neglect, among other works, *De la littérature du
midi de l'Europe* (1813) by Sismondo de' Sismondi and especially *De la littérature* (1800) and *De l'Allemagne* (1813) of
Madame de Staël. The latter is particularly important as the
author of the article "On the Manner and Utility of Translations," which, in January 1816, appeared in the *Biblioteca Italiana*
and opened the debate on Romanticism. Although many passages
translated from Shakespeare had appeared in *Saggi di Eloquenza
Estratti dal Teatro di Shakespeare* (1811), and although in the
same year Michele Leoni published his version of *Julius Caesar,* to
be followed in 1819 by *Le Tragedie di Shakespeare,* Madame de
Staël puts Shakespeare among those authors in need of translation:

> If letters are enriched by the translation of poems, the trans-
> lation of drama would be of much greater utility; because the
> theater is, as it were, the magistrate of literature. Shakespeare,
> translated with lively resemblance by Schlegel, has been per-
> formed in the theaters of Germany as if Shakespeare and
> Schiller were fellow-citizens.

The same ideas are stressed by Giovanni Berchet in his *Lettera
Semiseria di Grisostomo* (1816), the real manifesto of the Romantic movement in Italy, where we read that "Homer, Shakespeare, Calderón, Camœns, Racine and Schiller are for me Italians
just as much as Dante, Ariosto and Alfieri"; further on he says
ironically:

> But God above! that Shakespeare is mad beyond all bounds;
> he transfers men onto the stage just as they are; human life
> just as it is; he lets the hero talk with the gravedigger, the
> prince with the ruffian; things that are only allowed to real
> heroes and not those of the stage. And instead of inflaming the
> soul with fine and politic discourses, with arguments for and

against in the manner of our advocates, he puts before you virtues and vices in action: all of which diminishes the interest and leaves you cold.

In fact, all the writings that contribute to the debate on Romanticism deal, directly or indirectly, with Shakespeare—as can be seen from the ample anthology edited by Egidio Bellorini.[10] In a second article Madame de Staël praises the Shakespearean enterprise of Michele Leoni but speaks of it as an absolute exception in Italy:

> The whole of Europe knows by heart the celebrated authors of past centuries, but Italy is still afflicted by the conspicuous sloth that weighs on its present literature. If only some merit at least were given to those who seek to overcome it! A Florentine scholar has made a deep study of English literature, and has undertaken a translation of the whole of Shakespeare because—incredible as it may seem—there is still no Italian translation of this great man. He translates Milton once again and among the English poets has made a choice of the finest odes to render in the language of his fellow-citizens. But does he obtain for this the encouragement and esteem that his labors deserve?

Shakespeare and the Romantic drama are, on the contrary, attacked by Carlo Giuseppe Londonio, whose words take us back to Voltaire:

> our taste and opinions are too far removed from the taste and opinions of other nations to permit the adoption on our stage of certain tragedies without unity of time, place, or action, in which the most sublime thoughts are mixed with gross scurrilities, angels with demons, miracles with magic, where one is now offended by the statement of dangerous principles and then uplifted by the majestic ceremonies of our religion, where the most profane verses are followed by the Dies Irae, where, at last, after a murder, the curtain falls to the song of Alleluia.

Carlo Botta takes up an essentially negative position, though he still affirms that Shakespeare is "a great poet, indeed very great

10. *Discussioni e Polemiche sul Romanticismo, 1816–1826* (Bari, 1943).

. . . because he could move supremely the affections." Among
others, we have the author of an article in *Corriere delle Dame*
who, in reply to Madame de Staël, seems to sum up the opinions
of the anti-Romantics:

> As for Shakespeare, Madame must allow that we cannot all be
> blindly and entirely of her opinion; since, though we willingly
> confess that in the dramas of this author there are many beau-
> ties, and that, *considering the times* in which he wrote and *the
> people* for whom he wrote, he was a good writer, we cannot
> agree with those who would exalt him a little too much, when
> we see the enormous monstrosities of his dramas, the serious
> errors of chronology, certain rather too-English phrases in the
> mouths of characters who are not such, certain manners and
> speeches full of scurrility, the enormous changes of scene from
> one country to another, the duration of many of the dramas
> which cover years and years, the neglect or ignorance of all, or
> almost all the dramatic rules, the barbarities and atrocities in
> which they abound,—things, which, though they may please
> the English and Madame, cannot but arouse the indignation
> of our sensitive hearts.

Even Giovanni Gherardini, the translator of Schlegel, turns out to
be less sensitive to the art of Shakespeare than we might expect:
polemicizing with the German critic, he writes:

> Herr Schlegel . . . regrets not to see followed that manner of
> poetry, judged by him the only perfect and fitting for our time,
> I mean the manner of Shakespeare. Now Shakespeare, I repeat,
> is a great poet, sublime, extraordinary; whoever has read and
> considered him well, if he has any sense, should understand
> this much; but this does not alter the fact that the form of
> his dramas is bizarre and that enormous defects are to be
> found in them, things not to be tolerated by a nation which
> is heir to the taste of those immortal masters who taught the
> world the true rules of all the arts.

One could mention many other critics for whom a condemnation
of Shakespeare meant a defense of classical principles. It should be
noted, however, that in these years the most important criticism

follows Schlegel in exalting Shakespeare and taking him as a model. A few examples, among the many possible, should be enough to serve our purpose here. First of all we have Silvio Pellico, an assiduous reader of the dramatist as can be seen from his own *Francesca da Rimini* (1815). In an 1818 issue of the *Conciliatore* he writes: "If Shakespeare's *Othello,* with its many characters and without unity of place or time, can still arouse pity and terror, it is a true and genuine tragedy just as much as if it produced the same effects with three characters and all the venerable unities." In the *Conciliatore* in 1819 Ermes Visconti publishes his famous *Dialogo sulle Unità Drammatiche di Luogo e di Tempo.* Here, though we find again the arguments of Johnson, Baretti, and Schlegel in defense of Shakespeare's "irregularity," there are also some acute passages in which irregularity is considered as a necessary form of the drama.

> You will choose the catastrophe: you will present Macbeth torn by remorse for the past and fear of the future: the zeal of the defenders of the just cause; you will make someone recount the previous crimes; you will portray Lady Macbeth who feigns tranquillity and security and reveals the secret of her conscience as she walks in her sleep. But will you thus have told the story of the passion of Macbeth and Lady Macbeth? Will you have shown how a man can harden himself to commit a crime? Will you have painted the exultant and at the same time melancholy ferocity of ambition when it exceeds the sense of justice? It is true that you will have chosen the finest moment, that is the last stage of remorse; but a great part of the beauty will have been lost, because the beauty of this last stage depends to a large extent on the fact that it comes after the others; it depends on the law of continuity in the sentiments of the human soul. And to inform the spectator of previous events will you not be obliged to turn to the artifice of narrative soliloquies written expressly to inform him? In Shakespeare everything is action, natural action. Be honest, my friend; agree with me that the unity of time and place is a drawback. Indeed, what has been said of time is valid also for place. In short, you must agree that if an action falls naturally

in twenty-four hours, the tragedy should represent twenty-
four hours, as in *Philoctetes;* but if it does not fall naturally in
twenty-four hours, let the tragedy represent many days or
whatever time is necessary. If it happens naturally in one
place, very well; if not, do it in many.

Finally there is the opinion of Niccolò Tommaseo, who in 1825
writes in the *Nuovo Ricoglitore* that the "sources" from which
authors like Sophocles and Shakespeare draw and which make
them "one spirit" consist in "treating with wisdom things close to
their own hearts, to their own ideas, to their own needs," "in scorn-
ing the mythological vanities that make us dote after eighteen centuries," "in not speaking of a love which they did not feel . . .
not portraying objects which they did not know . . . not disgrac-
ing poetry with rhetorical nonsense, with pedantic imitations,
with ridiculous questions of language and with the detestable fury
of factions."

These words of Tommaseo are a clear indication of what elements the influence of Shakespeare introduces not only into the
theater but into the literary awareness of the time. They come
from an article on the *Adelchi* of Manzoni; in fact, in this period
many of the essays and articles dealing with Shakespeare, such as
those of Acerbi, Zaiotti, and Montani, are inspired by *Adelchi*
(1822) and *Il Conte di Carmagnola* (1820) (while others, also by
Acerbi, Pellico, Pezzi, and Di Breme derive from the growing
popularity of Byron). This is not surprising if we remember that,
with the exception of Pellico's *Francesca da Rimini,* it was in the
tragedies of Manzoni that Italian Romanticism found the drama it
had been seeking so eagerly. Moreover, these tragedies were born
of an aesthetic and moral meditation in which the Shakespearean
experience played a fundamental part. The relations between
Manzoni and Shakespeare have been given due importance by
many scholars—Bertani, Galletti, Bellezza, Carducci, Mazzoni,
Nulli, Lacy Collison-Morley, and, recently, Silvana Colognesi and
Giovanni Getto.[11] They have pointed out the many passages in
the tragedies and also in the *Promessi Sposi* where the reading of

11. Silvana Colognesi, "Shakespeare e Manzoni," in *ACME,* University of
Milan (settembre-dicembre 1964). Giovanni Getto, "Manzoni e Shakespeare,"
in *Lettere Italiane* (aprile–giugno 1967).

Shakespeare has left its mark, they have stressed the open admiration of Manzoni for Shakespeare, and they have noted the importance of Shakespeare in directing Manzoni toward an art that is, on one hand, romantically free from the "rules" and, on the other, turned toward a representation that working through history arrives at the truth. What can and should be added here is that, precisely because the connection with Shakespeare is deeply ingrained in the rich and complex nature of Manzoni's work, his observations not only have an independent critical value but constitute the climax of all previous Italian critical research. (This remains true despite the fact that he knew no English and read Shakespeare most importantly in the translations of Le Tourneur, whose preface, together with the writings of Schlegel and Madame de Staël, he considered among his guides to the understanding of the dramatist.) And so we have the preface to *Il Conte di Carmagnola*. In it the name of Shakespeare is never mentioned, but the arguments of Manzoni derive, nonetheless, from a reading of Shakespeare and his commentators, and the condemnation of the "rules" is an implicit defense not only of Romantic but of Shakespearean drama. A few extracts should be enough to confirm this:

> The unity of place and the so-called unity of time are not rules based on the logic of art, nor are they intrinsic to the nature of the dramatic poem; they have come from a misunderstood authority and from arbitrary principles . . . . When there came those who, careless of authority, asked the reason for these rules, the upholders of them could find only one; that is since the spectator is actually present at the representation of an action, it becomes incredible for him that the various parts of this action should happen in different places and that it should last for a long period of time, when he knows that he has not moved and has spent only a few hours in watching it. This argument is evidently based on a false supposition that the spectator is there as a part of the action, whereas he is, so to say, an extrinsic mind that contemplates it. Credibility should be born in him not from the relation between the action and his present state, but from the relations that the various parts of the action have between themselves. When one

considers that the spectator is outside the action, the argument
in favor of the unities vanishes . . . . Finally these rules fore-
stall many beauties and create many improprieties . . . . And
all this is so evident from the slightest consideration of some
English and German tragedies, that the very upholders of the
rules are obliged to admit it. They confess that the inobserv-
ance of the real limits of time and place leave the field free for
an imitation, varied and strong in a very different way; they
do not deny the beauties obtained at the expense of the rules;
but they affirm that we must renounce these beauties, since to
obtain them we have to fall to the unbelievable.

The connection with Shakespeare becomes absolutely explicit in
the famous *Lettre à M. Chauvet sur l'unité de temps et de lieu
dans la tragédie* (published in 1823) . Here we have not only a
new and energetic defense of Romantic drama but a lengthy and
intelligent discussion of Shakespeare. One remembers, for example, the fine comparison between *Othello* and Voltaire's *Zaïre,*
considered as typifying two contrasting concepts of drama:

La force croissante d'une passion jalouse dans un caractère
violent, l'adresse malheureuse de cette passion à interpreter en
sa faveur, si on peut le dire, les incidents les plus naturels, les
actions les plus simples, les paroles les plus innocentes, l'habil-
eté épouvantable d'un traître à faire naître et à nourrir le
soupçon dans une âme offensée, la puissance infernale qu'un
scélérat de sang-froid exerce ainsi sur un naturel ardent et gé-
néreux; voilà quelques-unes des terribles leçons qui naissent de
la tragédie d'Othello: mais que nous apprend l'action de
Zaïre? que les incidents de la vie peuvent se combiner parfois
d'une manière si étrange, qu'une expression équivoque, in-
sérée par hasard dans une lettre qui a manqué son adresse ne
vienne à occasioner les plus grands crimes et les derniers mal-
heurs? À la bonne heure . . . ce qu'il y a, dans Zaïre, de vrai,
de touchant, de poétique, est dû au beau talent de Voltaire; ce
qu'il y a dans son plan de forcé et de factice me semble devoir
être attribué en grande partie, à la containte de la règle des
deux unités.

The tone of this passage is indeed typical of the best European
Romantic criticism; the discussion of the rules has nothing auto-
matic about it and is accompanied by a penetrating and impassioned analysis of the psychological movement of the characters. As
examples of this one could note the passage on Iago and the discussion of the mixture of comic and tragic, which in Shakespeare is
not a necessary consequence of the violation of the rules but
derives from the fact that he "had observed this mixture in reality." Finally we have the long analysis of *Richard II,* intended to
demonstrate the intrinsic necessity of spatial and temporal liberty:

> Richard délibère, avec les amis qui lui restent, sur ce qu'il doit
> faire, et c'est ici que le caractère de ce roi commence à prendre
> un développement si naturel et si inattendu. Le spectateur
> avait déjà fait connaissance avec cet étonnant personnage et se
> flattait de l'avoir pénétré; mais il y avait en lui quelque chose
> de secret et de profond qui n'avait point paru dans la pros-
> périté, et que l'infortune seule pouvait faire éclater. Le fond
> du caractère est le même; c'est toujours l'orgueil, c'est toujours
> la plus haute idée de sa dignité: mais ce même orgueil qui,
> lorsqu'il était accompagné de puissance, se manifestait par la
> légèreté, par l'impatience de tout obstacle, par une irreflexion
> qui ne lui permettait pas même de soupçonner que tout pou-
> voir humain a ses juges et ses bornes; cet orgueil, une fois privé
> de force, est devenu grave et sérieux, solennel et mesuré. Ce
> qui soutient Richard, c'est une conscience inaltérable de sa
> grandeur, c'est la certitude que nul événement humain n'a pu
> la détruire, puisque rien ne peut faire qu'il ne soit né et qu'il
> n'aît été roi. Les jouissances du pouvoir lui ont échappé; mais
> l'idée de sa vocation au rang suprême lui reste: dans ce qu'il
> est, il persiste à honorer ce qu'il fut; et ce respect obstiné pour
> un titre que personne ne lui reconnait plus, ôte au sentiment
> de son infortune tout ce qui pourrait l'humilier ou l'abattre.
> Les idées, les émotions par lesquelles cette révolution du
> caractère de Richard se manifeste dans la tragédie de Shake-
> speare sont d'une grande originalité, de la poésie la plus

relevée, et même très touchantes. Mais ce tableau historique
de l'âme de Richard et des événements qui la modifient em-
brasse nécessairement plus de vingt heures.

How many reflections on Shakespeare lie behind these works is
shown even better by the *Materiali Estetici*, only partly transcribed in the Preface to *Carmagnola* and in the *Lettre* and published for the first time by Bonghi in 1887 (*Opere Inedite o Rare*).
One notes particularly the passage where Manzoni speaks of

> a tragedy that, starting from the interest that the great events
> of history arouse in us, and from the desire that they leave in
> us to know or imagine the hidden sentiments and considera-
> tions, etc., that these events caused and with which they devel-
> oped—a desire that history cannot and does not wish to satisfy
> —invents indeed these sentiments in the most lifelike mov-
> ing or instructive way.

And Manzoni affirms that "the practice of this dramatic ideal can
be seen taken to the highest degree in many tragedies of Shakespeare." Further on we have a passage written in preparation for
the *Lettre*:

> The dramas of Shakespeare can serve as an example of narra-
> tive thread. Familiar events and arguments are useful in trag-
> edy because, among other things, many passions could not be
> brought to a climax except by means of these things. For
> example, how far the jealousy of Othello surpasses that of
> Orosmane! And one of the reasons is that the poet has used
> means which, to a common critic, might seem of a comic na-
> ture because of their familiarity. The handkerchief is essential
> in Shakespeare's tragedy.

This observation prefigures the concept of Shakespeare as a conscious artist which underlies the whole of Manzoni's criticism and
which, though learned from Schlegel, is one of his major contributions to understanding the dramatist:

> One hears . . . it said every day that Shakespeare is an un-
> polished and undisciplined genius, who, without rules and
> without premeditated intention, flows here and there, meet-

ing occasionally with some extraordinary beauty. This oft-repeated opinion has been confuted expressly and at length by Herr Schlegel. This confutation seems to me to destroy the opinion totally.

The *Materiali Estetici* indeed offers an explicit declaration of the exalted place Shakespeare occupies in the moral and artistic world of Manzoni:

> Demonstrate that Bossuet, Nicole and Rousseau, just as they were mistaken in considering the works of the French theater immoral, were mistaken also in believing that the theater is essentially immoral. This error comes partly from ignorance of the English theater, and partly perhaps from not being able to imagine that the things of the theater could be treated in a way different from that followed by the French, in whom they found art taken to the highest degree in every aspect except that of morality. Touch on this point, that moral perfection is the perfection of art, and that therefore Shakespeare surpasses the others because he is more moral. The deeper one goes into the heart, the more one finds the eternal principles of virtue . . . . The representation of deep sorrows and indeterminate terrors is substantially moral because it leaves impressions that draw us nearer to virtue. When a man in his imagination leaves the familiar field of common things and circumstances with which he is accustomed to struggle, and finds himself in the infinite region of possible evils, he feels his own weakness, the cheerful thoughts of vigor and defense abandon him, and he thinks that, in such a condition, virtue alone and an upright conscience and the help of God can give succor to the mind. Let everyone ask himself, after the reading of a Shakespeare tragedy, whether he does not feel a similar effect in his soul.

In 1828 the Reverend Charles Swan, the English translator of the *Promessi Sposi*, reproached Manzoni for referring in the novel to Shakespeare as "a barbarian not devoid of genius." Swan had, of course, failed to understand the irony of the allusion, and it is not surprising that Manzoni's letter of reply contains further evidence of his admiration for the dramatist and a clarification of his opinions on Shakespeare's art:

> My dear sir, do you remember that stage character, who, after being scolded and beaten by his jealous wife, rejoices in those reproaches and blesses those blows which are evidence of love? Now imagine that this, or something like it, is my feeling in seeing you angry with me in defense of my Shakespeare; since, although I do not know a word of English and am therefore acquainted with the great poet only through translation, yet I admire him so warmly that I almost suffer if others claim to do so more than myself. In days past when I used to get more heated about poetry and poets than I do nowadays, I can hardly tell you how angry I was made by those scornful and rash statements of Voltaire and his disciples about Shakespeare. And perhaps even more than the injurious phrases, I was annoyed by that strange way of praising him, saying that in the midst of a series of extravagances he occasionally comes out with a flash of genius: as if the voice of genius which in those passages raises, as it were, a shout, were not the same that speaks elsewhere; as if the same power which is there revealed in such an extraordinary way, did not show itself, with less impetus but with marvellous continuity, in the portrayal of so many and such varied passions, in the language of so many characters and situations, so human and so poetic, so unexpected and so natural; as if the same power did not appear in the selection, conduct and progression of events and passions, in the order, so careless in appearance and so consequent in reality that one hardly knows whether to attribute it to a wondrous instinct or a wondrous artifice: or rather there is, extraordinarily, something of one and something of the other, etcetera, etcetera. And it was precisely against this attitude of Voltaire (about which others before me have spoken better than I ever could) that my ironic phrase was intended: since you understood it literally, I am not surprised that scandalized you so much.

Manzoni's constant admiration and understanding of Shakespeare and his assumption of the dramatist as a model and ideal of art are certainly among the major causes of the extraordinary success which, after the initial difficulties, Shakespeare finally met in Italy. The "victory" of Romanticism and of Manzoni is also in fact the "victory" of Shakespeare. As a result we have a succession of translations: the *Macbeth* of Giuseppe Niccolini (1830), the *Romeo and Juliet* of Gaetano Barbieri (1831), who left also an unpublished version of *Othello*, the various plays translated by Giunio Bazzoni and Giacomo Sormani (1830–31), the versions of *Othello* and *Macbeth* by Virginio Soncini and those of *Julius Caesar, Othello,* and *Coriolanus* (1829, 1830, 1834) by Ignazio Valletta, down to the first complete prose translation by Carlo Rusconi (1839). The first complete verse translation is that of Giulio Carcano who began in 1839 with some scenes from *King Lear* and continued with *Teatro Scelto* (1843) and three volumes of Shakespeare plays in 1857, until finally the complete works appeared between 1875 and 1882. Another result of Manzoni's example is the increasing evidence of Shakespeare's influence on the dramatists of the period, Silvio Pellico, Carlo Tebaldi Fores, G. B. de Cristoforis, Cesare della Valle (author of a *Giulietta e Romeo* in 1826), Carlo Marenco, and Edoardo Fabbri. The most important of these minor figures is perhaps Giovanni Battista Niccolini, in whose works, as in those of the other dramatists, allusions to Shakespeare are frequent—the more so in that they result not only from the influence of Manzoni, but also from that of Victor Hugo, whose preface to *Cromwell* (1827) was especially important for the diffusion of Shakespearean drama in Europe, as important as Stendhal's *Racine et Shakespeare* (1823). Shakespeare became increasingly staged in Italy, first in the adaptations of Ducis mentioned above, and even in the form of ballet (especially by the famous Viganò), but later, as Italian translations gradually became available, in less approximative versions. From the tentative interpretations of Francesco Menichelli and Antonio Morrocchesi, the first Italian Hamlets, we come to the much more convincing efforts of Alemanno Morelli, who acted Hamlet in 1850, and particularly those of Ernesto Rossi and Tommaso Salvini. All this is remarkable if we consider that in mid-century the great Gustavo Modena failed to complete a Milanese performance of *Othello*. Nor, of course, can we neglect the great contribution of Giuseppe

Verdi. Shakespeare has indeed exercised a constant attraction on our operatic composers, from Rossini and Bellini to Zandonai, Malipiero, and Castelnuovo Tedesco; but in the case of Verdi there is a relationship not unlike that between Shakespeare and Manzoni, a contact, that is, which could not be more stimulating and creative. "Ah Shakespeare, Shakespeare! . . . the great master of the human heart," we read in a letter; and elsewhere:

> There may seem to be a contradiction in these three words: *invent the truth,* but ask Papa about it. Papa may perhaps have met with some Falstaff, but he will hardly have found a villain as villainous as Iago, and never, never, angels like Cordelia, Imogen, Desdemona, etc., etc., and yet they are so true.

We need only read his correspondence with Somma, Carcano, and Arrigo Boito, librettists of the Shakespearean operas, to understand how the superb artistic result derives in part from a constant, admiring, and impassioned study of the dramatist.

Shakespeare therefore penetrates the literary consciousness in many ways, and, with Verdi, the popular consciousness as well. In this situation, given also the interest in English literature that accompanies the vast success of Scott and Byron, it is only natural that, besides Manzoni, other writers and critics should contribute to the critical understanding of Shakespeare.[12] Leopardi, whose temperament and critical genius could have led him to understand better than most certain aspects of Shakespeare's art, unfortunately limits himself to occasional vague references; but less casual observations can be found not only in the writers, dramatists, and translators already mentioned, but also in Guerrazzi, Gioberti, Carlo Cattaneo, Giovita Scalvini, and, supported by a far from superficial knowledge of English literature, in Giacinto Battaglia's *Mosaico, Saggi diversi di critica drammatica* (1845) and Giuseppe Pecchio's *Storia critica della poesia inglese* (4 vols. 1833–35). But the most significant figure is probably Giuseppe Mazzini with his essay *Della Fatalità considerata come elemento drammatico* (1836). Although he looks forward to a "drama of the future," a "drama of Providence," a "social drama, highly reli-

12. See Muoni's useful *I drammi di Shakespeare e la critica romantica italiana* (Florence, 1908).

gious and highly instructive, vaster in scale and intention than the drama of Shakespeare by as much as the thought of Humanity towers over that of the individual," nonetheless his comments on Shakespeare contain the finest insights of European Romantic criticism. For example, on the individual element in Shakespearean drama, he writes:

> The drama of Shakespeare is the drama of the *Individual*. The individual is everything for him, and in the art of portraying a character with a few touches perhaps only Dante, Tacitus and Michelangelo are his rivals. He does not portray at length: he succeeds in a single impulse; he does not evoke: he creates. Shakespeare's men have life and motion as if they came out of the hands of God: a life both single and varied, complex and harmonious. They do not symbolize an absolute ideal type; they do not profane the divine work by representing the creature in fragments . . . the secret of a life, the interpretation of a character sometimes flash on one who observes attentively from the slightest revelation, in a phrase, in a saying unnoticed by the many.

On the presence of "necessity":

> The "I" reigns in the plays of Shakespeare with all its modifications, with all its mysteries, with all the apparent irregularities of which the conscience is capable. But it does not reign supreme. In the plays of Shakespeare, as in the Middle Ages, a mysterious power governs the destinies of the individual . . . . Necessity, which he found rooted in the times, wanders invisible through his plays, magically introduced, whether by art or instinct I do not know: I know that its reflection touches the brow of Othello like that of Macbeth, the bitter skepticism of Hamlet not less than the light ironic banter of Mercutio . . . . It generally inspires in the characters of Shakespeare those reflections on the nothingness of human things and the futility of life which recur so frequently and which leave a bitter taste of delusion in the young souls who approach the works of the Genius as the sanctuary from which to draw inspiration and advice for the years of manhood.

On the difference between the characters of Aeschylus and those
of Shakespeare:

> The characters of Shakespeare, like those of Aeschylus, are
> fated. Necessity broods in the shade over them all and poisons
> their ideas, their hopes, their very joy, with an undefinable,
> inexplicable sense of distress, like remorse for an unpardoned
> fault. But in Aeschylus the individual is fated at birth . . . .
> In Shakespeare—and this is a real advance—liberty lives: a day
> perhaps, an hour, has subdued a life to necessity, but in that
> day, in that hour, the man was free and the arbiter of his fu-
> ture . . . . In the doctrine that emerges from the plays of
> Shakespeare, the creature is responsible for his own actions.

And it is along the lines laid down by Mazzini and Manzoni, as
well as by Hegel and the German Romantics, that we have the
Shakespearean work of our greatest nineteenth-century critic,
Francesco De Sanctis, who, although he did not know English (he
read Shakespeare in the translations of Rusconi) and although he
lacked a wide knowledge of English literature, nonetheless contributed in a decisive way to Italian and European criticism of the
dramatist.[13] This contribution is already clear from the lessons
held in Naples in 1846–47, which Croce published first in the
Shakespearean number of *La Critica* (1919) and then in F. De
Sanctis, *Teoria e Storia della Letteratura* (2 vols. Bari, 1926).
Here the methodological basis is laid for a critical examination
"free from so many futile questions, from so many judgments born
of particular and arbitrary principles," liberated from neoclassical
prejudices, but also from Romantic ones; we have the suggestion
of a Shakespeare who "though feeling the sublimity of the ideal
represents the whole of reality," who is the Hegelian poet of the
"idea," but of an idea incarnate, rendered absolute reality:

> Shakespeare then unites with an immense reality immense
> truth and poetry. It seems to me that among poets, as among
> philosophers, there are some who have diligent patience in
> registering and classifying phenomena and others who rise
> to the highest abstractions, leaving behind the external world

13. See, for a detailed analysis, Agostino Lombardo, "De Sanctis e Shakespeare," *English Miscellany*, No. 7 (Rome, 1956) .

and reality . . . . The greatest poet is he who unites the two forces: like Shakespeare, like Dante . . . . As in nature one can hardly separate form and idea, so in his poetry, where all is individualized.

De Sanctis passes, in the lessons, to a detailed examination of a number of plays, from *A Midsummer Night's Dream,* in which is portrayed, as we read, the "first form of life" and which he feels is "perhaps the only play of Shakespeare in which the serious and profound aspect of life does not appear," to *As You Like It,* where on the one hand we have "a serene, innocent and angelic life," but on the other "in the distance there is outlined the real world with its passions, its anguish, its remorse." *The Tempest* is considered as an example of the poetry of fantasy and leads him to more general considerations on the truth that even fantastic poetry can communicate:

Nor should this truth be understood in a narrow way, as if in those images one had to find an abstract idea, whose truth makes them acceptable. This is the error of Schlegel who, in Shakespeare's plays sees only abstract ideas presented through those actions and those characters. To pretend reality in the images means constricting poetry to the laws of verisimilitude: now it is not in the reality, but in the truth of poetry that one must believe: not that the thing represented really exists, but that the idea represented is true: those images are forms, and one cannot impose faith in mere forms taken by themselves. In other words, the truth which one seeks in these forms must correspond to some aspect of human and inward life, of that life which the poet has the duty, not of understanding, but of representing in its mystery. And this capacity of conveying life through imaginary phantasms Shakespeare possessed in the highest degree, not only in those plays we have mentioned and where it dominates, but also in the others where it appears from time to time in figures sometimes terrible, sometimes serene and sometimes comic, not in the main part of the play, but in detail and incident.

It is clear that these comments go well beyond the particular problem that occasions them and concern the general concept of

art. This, moreover, happens constantly when De Sanctis writes on
Shakespeare, who, more than any other poet, seems to arouse him
to critical meditation, confronting him with a subject unusually
rich and complex in its problems.

Of particular importance in the long analysis of *Romeo and
Juliet* is the interpretation of the play as a tragedy of youth:

> The two young people, not yet detached from the images and
> amusements of childhood, and still ignorant of sorrow, are
> precipitated into a world they do not understand, experience
> sorrow for the first time, become victims of their dreams. This
> is the magnificent theme, magnificently carried out by Shake-
> speare.

There is also a very acute comment on the "coincidence" that supposedly dominates the work: it is true, says De Sanctis, that the
misfortunes of the two young people "come not from men, but
from the course of things themselves, which leads the two lovers to
catastrophe and crushes them"; nevertheless, he continues:

> Coincidence is coincidence for the common mind; for poets it
> is the mysterious link between human actions, the process fol-
> lowing a first step that is mistaken and dangerous. Think how
> Juliet and Romeo are, think of their passion, of their inex-
> perience, of their illusions; can you be surprised that the
> course of human events overwhelms and crushes them?

This is a highly important passage, indicating how De Sanctis saw
clearly the completely "modern" nature of Shakespeare's art, and
how he could recognize it even in a play where it was not easy to
avoid the danger of attributing the catastrophe to an external
force.

The discussion of *Romeo and Juliet* is the most meticulous
Shakespearean analysis that De Sanctis has left us, and it is certainly unfortunate that in the Neapolitan lessons equal penetration was not applied to the great tragedies, where the treatment is
too summary not to leave the reader unsatisfied. This, however,
does not exclude flashes of insight, such as the observation that

> if in the tragedies of other authors character is an extraordi-
> nary direction of the human faculties in an extraordinary

moment of life, in Shakespeare it is the whole education and the whole life considered in its different stages; and from the man, from the simple common man one sees emerging the hero, but not to such an extent that there does not remain even in the hero the weakness of the man.

Further on there is a new rejection of the unities:

How was it possible to question whether in these tragedies there is or is not unity of time and place and whether it is good or bad that it should or should not be there? Here there is unity of character; and if other writers have busied themselves with the unities, it is because they did not, like Shakespeare, rise to this superior unity.

Finally, there is the contraposition between modern and ancient tragedy:

In the five tragedies . . . the whole of life, all the epochs of civilization are represented; the most grim and the most tender things that can be imagined, the most barbaric and the most delicate. A vast and astonishing understanding, equaled only by the mental energy of the poet, who thus stands beside Aeschylus and Dante who conceived figures such as Prometheus and Capaneus. But between the figures of ancient and modern heroes there is a profound difference. The ancient heroes felt themselves crushed by a superior force, and, when they could not show it in action, their greatness revealed itself in suffering, in *pati fortia*, in scorn and defiance: hence derives that calm, that immobility, that silence of these ancient heroic figures: conscious of their greatness they await destiny with head held high. But the modern heroes struggle and fight. Macbeth, abandoned by everything, collects his strength and fights as a man . . . . From this one sees the difference between the ancient tragedy and that of Shakespeare, which is the tragedy of the modern hero, of the hero who acts.

Coming at the beginning of his critical career, these Neapolitan lessons largely determine the later development of De Sanctis. So much so that it does not seem mistaken to attribute to this Shakespearean study the passage of De Sanctis from what he called "the sickness of the ideal" to the fertile concept of "the ideal immersed in reality," and we can affirm with Croce that Shakespeare is, from the start, "the great poet of his critical ideal." As a result, while Shakespeare seems the touchstone of many later judgments, the critic returns to him repeatedly. For example, the essay on Schiller in *Saggi Critici* (1866) :

> The meaning of life begins to reveal itself in Shakespeare: the miraculous disappears; Destiny is man . . . . In English drama it is man who dominates in all the ardor of his passions and in all the power of his will . . . . There is a quality of genius which touches the divine and which I would almost call the immensity. Dante, Shakespeare, Ariosto and Goethe are omnipotent men who live with their imagination in that infinite space which frightens us.

If we look at the other essays, at the series of lessons, at the *Storia della Letterature Italiana* (1870–71), at the writings on Dante, we note how Shakespeare is still present in the mind of De Sanctis, and how he judges Italian authors and their characters in the light of the work and characters of Shakespeare (and the Shakespearean characters are thus in their turn illuminated). An example from an essay on Dante should suffice:

> the journey through the three realms, Hell, Purgatory and Heaven, makes it possible to embrace all the varieties of man. And so Dante sowed the seed that from Shakespeare and Calderon to Leopardi and Manzoni all later poets cultivated . . . . The tragedy of the ancients is that of Sophocles; that of the moderns, the drama of Shakespeare: and Dante indeed had already treated art in this way, making the gluttony of Ciacco follow the love of Francesca . . . . If we wish to find anything comparable to Francesca we must look for it in Shakespeare, in Byron, in Goethe, in foreign literatures, the first and immortal type being Francesca . . . . It is sad to think of it, but easy to understand for one who knows our history: the man of Dante, the type of Farinata, the stuff from which the characters of Shakespeare emerged, has remained a unique and sole example in our poetry.

This last is a memorable phrase, prefiguring the statement in the *Storia:* "These great figures . . . await the artist who will take them by the hand and throw them into the tumult of life and make them dramatic beings. And the artist was Shakespeare." Dante and Shakespeare are indeed, for De Sanctis, the two great protagonists of literary history and Shakespeare brings to fulfillment the work that Dante, his greatest precursor, had begun.

In this assumption by De Sanctis of Shakespeare as an artistic ideal there are certain dangers, such as that of considering literature, romantically, in the light of drama and seeking in the characters of Dante and Manzoni the features of Hamlet, Macbeth, or Richard III. In this Shakespeare of De Sanctis, however, romantically elevated to a model of poetry, there is also something that goes beyond Romanticism to reach a new, realistic way of understanding poetry and life itself. In addition, in the more limited field of Shakespearean criticism De Sanctis indicated a new direction with his concept of a Shakespeare not abstract but concrete, a Shakespeare whose "ideal" is "immersed in reality" just as the dramatist is immersed in history. With Croce this new direction was to prove particularly fertile in its developments. However, before Croce and his essay of 1919, Italian Shakespearean criticism went through a phase in which the truly notable volume of work did not correspond to equally notable results.

It is not that the reputation of Shakespeare declined. On the contrary, performances became ever more frequent and to the actors already mentioned must be added the names of Giovanni Emanuel, Ermete Novelli, Adelaide Ristori, Eleonora Duse, and, later on, Ermete Zacconi and Ruggero Ruggeri. The operas of Verdi made the dramatist and his characters still more popular, and in 1858 there was even a play about Shakespeare by L. Gualtieri. At the same time there was an increase in the number of translations. Besides the complete translations by Rusconi and Carcano there are versions of single plays by O. Garberini, P. Santi, and A. Maffei and finally in 1911 a new and unsuccessful attempt at a complete verse translation by Diego Angeli. At the end of the nineteenth century and the beginning of the twentieth we have the first attempts at the sonnets by A. Oliveri (1890), L.

De Marchi (1891), E. Sanfelice (1898), and L. Darchini (1908). These translations, together with an increasing knowledge of English, made Shakespeare part of the common heritage of Italian culture. From Dossi to Prati, from Carducci to Zanella, from Pascoli to D'Annunzio, to name only the most important figures in a list that should include them all, there is not a writer who fails to allude to Shakespeare or to use his characters as already universally recognized symbols. But the interest of these writers, though general, is no longer animated by that direct creative adhesion to Shakespeare's art which characterized the Romantics, and the contemporary tendencies, naturalistic, neoclassical, or aesthetic, could approach Shakespeare only as a simple though fundamental cultural element. At the most we have that limited sympathy which led to an insistence on *Hamlet* interpreted in a decadent key. For these reasons, perhaps, Shakespearean criticism did not progress with the energy one might have hoped. There was, of course, a considerable amount of work on Shakespeare—discussions of single plays, especially *Hamlet* and *Romeo and Juliet;* discussions of biographical or pseudo-biographical problems, such as the Baconian question; and attempts to offer a general interpretation of the poet, such as Federico Garlanda's thoroughly rhetorical *Guglielmo Shakespeare: il poeta e l'uomo* (Rome, 1900). Nevertheless, one can hardly disagree with Croce, who lists them in an excellent bibliography in the Shakespearean number of *La Critica* (May–July 1919), when he remarks that a history "of the contribution of Italian criticism to the study of Shakespeare" in this period "could scarcely take any other form than that of a bibliography, of a catalog of volumes, memoirs and articles, of which very few have made any progress in the problems of Shakespearean interpretation." Among the "few," however, we should note the works of those critics who, in the steps of Pecchio, approached Shakespeare with a sound knowledge of English literature, not so much Nencioni and Camerini, who were little concerned with Shakespeare, as Giuseppe Chiarini (*Studi Shakespeariani,* 1897) and A. R. Levi (*Storia della letteratura inglese dalle origini al tempo presente,* 1898–1901), who lay the basis for a more historically sound study of Shakespeare. Nor should we neglect certain positive results of the "historic method" applied to Shakespeare, that is, the study on the one hand of his Italian sources and on the other of his influence in Italy. Thus we have the work of Segrè, D'Ovidio, Zumbini, Neri, and, later, Natali, Mazzoni, Galletti, and other historians of Italian literature, culminating in the more ample studies, already noted, of Graf, who wrote frequently of Shakespeare, and Nulli.

In 1919 Croce also deals with the "fortune" and sources of Shakespeare in Italy, both with the bibliography and with a study of the influence on Shakespeare of the *commedia dell 'arte*. But it is, of course, with his critical essay [14] that Croce makes a direct and highly significant contribution to Shakespearean criticism, in addition to the indirect contribution provided by his whole work. The essay deserves a detailed analysis, but to indicate its importance it should be enough to note some of its salient passages.[15] First of all there is the long methodological introduction in which Croce, following the lines laid down by De Sanctis, denounces the errors of "biographism," "sociologism," "exclamative" and "imaginistic" criticism, and the "aesthetic criticism" of the philologists. One should then note his definition of Shakespeare as a "cosmic poet" like Ariosto, because:

> in him there does not dominate any particular feeling or order of feelings: one cannot call him a love poet like Petrarch, or sorrowful and despairing like Leopardi, or heroic as we say of Homer . . . . Nor is he a poet one might say of ideals, religious, ethical, political or social . . . . Shakespeare did not cherish ideals of any kind, much less political ideals; and although he portrays political struggles magnificently, he always goes beyond their specific character and object, reaching through them to the only thing that attracts him profoundly: life . . . . The poet is not beyond conflicting emotions, attraction and disgust, love and hate, hope and despair, joy and sorrow; but he is beyond what is unilateral in each of them. He takes them all to himself, not to suffer them or to shed tears of blood upon them, but to form of them a single world, the

14. Later published in *Ariosto, Shakespeare, Corneille* (Bari, 1920) and in *Shakespeare,* ed. G. N. G. Orsini (Bari, 1948) .

15. See Agostino Lombardo, "La letteratura inglese nella critica di Benedetto Croce," in *Rivista di Letterature Moderne,* No. 12 (1955) .

Shakespearean world, which is the world of these unsolved conflicts.

Another fundamental moment in the essay is when Croce, once more developing and consolidating the premises of De Sanctis, places Shakespeare at the heart of his time and culture:

> Shakespeare is truly . . . a man of the Renaissance, of that age which, with its wars between great states, with its voyages, with its trade, with its philosophies, with its religious struggles, with its natural science, with its poems and paintings and joyous architecture, had given full evidence to earthly life, no longer allowing it to fade, pale and disperse before the rays of another alien world, as had happened in the long centuries of the Middle Ages. But he does not belong to the happy, rejoicing, paganizing Renaissance, which is only one small aspect of that great movement, so much as to the other Renaissance, animated by new needs, by new religious urges, by the search for new philosophical tendencies, tormented by skepticism, shot through with intuitions of the future.

We should also stress the insight revealed in the many analyses of individual plays; for example, the definition of *A Midsummer Night's Dream* as "the quintessence of the love comedy" or the comment on the histories which contains one of Croce's most original and convincing theories. The histories seem to him to be animated by an "interest in practical action," that is,

> in the action carefully followed in its expedients and in its boldness, in the obstacles it meets with, in the defeats, in the triumphs, in the varying attitudes of the temperaments and characters of men. This interest, finding its most fitting material in political and warlike struggles, turned naturally to history, and to that history which was nearest to the mind and culture of the poet, of his people, and of his time: English history and Roman.

We also have the discussion of the Roman plays and of some of the great tragedies, particularly *Macbeth,* where Croce sees the action of "characters who are, at the same time, more than individuals, eternal positions of the human soul," and where there is not only "the tragedy of the gain or loss of a throne or some other earthly object, but . . . the gain or loss of the soul itself, the struggle fought in the heart of things between good and evil." On *King Lear* there is the excellent characterization of Cordelia:

> Cordelia is not the symbol or allegory of abstract goodness, but she is permeated by goodness: she represents a need of purity, tenderness and adoration which has projected its image both unreal and real, poetically real. Cordelia is Goodness itself in its primal source, limpid and shining in its overflow: moral beauty and therefore both reserved and courageous, modest and dignified, ready to disdain conflicts when they cannot serve, but equally ready, when necessary, to fight with spirit; goodness real and achieved, not merely softness, meekness and indulgence. Words have been so misused by deceivers that she has almost renounced this inadequate means: she is silent when speech would be in vain or when it would put her own truth on the same level as the lies of others . . . . And since goodness is also understanding intelligence, she understands and pardons and lovingly assists her old father, unjust and inconsiderate toward her. And since, even in opposition and struggle, goodness cannot take the form of blind passion, and since, even in its intolerance of evil, it is permeated by a severe resignation to the law that governs the universe and which thus entrusts it with its highest office, Cordelia does not inveigh against the wickedness of her sisters when she learns of the outlawed and abused King Lear, but immediately calms herself to patience and sorrow. As the gentleman who sees her at that moment comments:

> > You have seen
> > Sunshine and rain at once; her smiles and tears
> > Were like a better way . . .

The discussion of *Othello* also is very acute, especially in its further development of the interpretation of Iago:

> Iago is not evil committed for a dream of greatness, nor yet evil for the selfish satisfaction of his own desires, but evil for evil's sake, performed almost for an artistic need, in order to realize his own being and feel it as powerful, dominating and de-

structive, even in the subordinate social condition in which it is placed. Certainly, Iago, in his speeches, wishes to convince one, or convince himself, that he is aiming only at "his particular end," as Guicciardini would have said . . . . But the truth is that he promotes no material advantage for himself; for this the way chosen was unnecessary and it produces no such result. Still less is he moved by an urge to avenge offenses and injustices suffered, as he sometimes says and would have one believe or tries to believe himself. What his acts reveal is wickedness as an end in itself, born of a turbid desire to prove himself superior to the world and to deceive it and to make it dance by pulling on the strings of his own mental combinations, and, with a single movement, to send it down to ruin.

Finally, we shall give all the importance deserved to the development of the concept, derived from Schlegel and Manzoni, of Shakespeare as a "conscious" artist—a concept which leads Croce to define Shakespeare as "classical."

Even by his admirers he is usually denied the classical sense, according to a partial and outworn idea of the classical as consisting in certain exterior regularities; but classical he was, as a force secure in itself, without strain, proceeding without starts and paroxysms, carrying in itself its own moderation and serenity; and likewise he possessed taste, the taste proper to genius and commensurate with genius, for genius without taste is an abstraction of the theorists. The various passages in which he happens by chance to theorize about art show that he had meditated deeply on the activity that he practiced. In some famous lines from *A Midsummer Night's Dream* he makes Theseus say that

The poet's eye, in a fine frenzy rolling,
Doth glance from heaven to earth, from earth to heaven;
And as imagination bodies forth
The forms of things unknown, the poet's pen
Turns them to shapes, and gives to airy nothing
A local habitation and a name.
Such tricks hath strong imagination
That, if it would but apprehend some joy,

> It comprehends some bringer of that joy;
> Or in the night, imagining some fear,
> How easy is a bush supposed a bear.

That is, he shows himself conscious of the creative power of poetry, which derives from the emotions and converts them into forms in which it encloses the aerial sentiment. But in another no less celebrated passage from *Hamlet* he emphasizes the other aspect of artistic creation, universality and therefore calmness and harmony; for what Hamlet, in his advice to the Players, recommends above all is moderation: "for in the very torrent, tempest, and as I may say whirlwind of your passion, you must acquire and beget a temperance that may give it smoothness." To consider Shakespeare as the representative of an art of furious and disordered outburst, as has been done so often, is to say the opposite of the truth.

Apart from a certain harshness toward previous criticism and toward philology, deriving, as always, from a necessary polemic, what one regrets in Croce's limpid and stimulating essay is the lack of a real study of Shakespeare's language or of the relations between Shakespeare and the general context of English literary and dramatic culture. These defects can be largely attributed to limits in linguistic and literary knowledge, limits that may be greater in other critics but are nonetheless present even in Croce. These are precisely the limits that will be overcome by Italian Shakespearean criticism in the period following Croce's essay, and in particular after the Second World War. In the general revival of studies, connected in so many ways with Croce and his deprovincializing of our culture, Italian studies of English language and literature gradually lose all traces of casual or amateur work and through the university and personal research acquire an individual dignity and vitality. The pioneering and therefore isolated work of Pecchio, Giuseppe Chiarini, and A. R. Levi is carried forward by scholars, teachers, and critics such as F. Olivero, C. Foligno, P. Bardi, S. Policardi, P. Rebora, G. S. Gargàno, Cino Chiarini, C. Formichi, A. De Lorenzo, V. Piccoli, and A. Farinelli. These writers, with differing approaches and differing results, carry out efficient research in the world of English culture so that their Shakespearean contributions have a less precarious literary and linguistic basis.[16] The work becomes even more intense and prolific in the immediate postwar period when Mario Praz begins his tireless activity. Although Praz has been less concerned with Shakespeare than with other writers and periods, his direct contribution is nonetheless significant. Apart from his research into the sources and occasional Shakespearean articles, one thinks especially of some of his translations and editions (*Troilus and Cressida, Measure for Measure*), of the series of translations edited for the "Sansoniana Straniera" and later collected in *Teatro* (Florence, 1943–47) and in *Shakespeare: Tutte Le Opere* (Florence, 1964), and of the ample Shakespeare chapter in *Storia della Letteratura Inglese* (Florence, 1960; first ed., 1937). His studies of Anglo-Italian relations in the Renaissance period concern essential aspects of Shakespeare's art,[17] and the work on Donne, Crashaw, and the seventeenth century illuminates both the language and feeling of Shakespeare. Nevertheless, it can be said that the stimulus given by Praz to English studies makes his indirect contribution even more important. As a result of this stimulus Italian Shakespearean criticism can now rely not only on the scholarly, critical, and historical work of English-speaking nations, but also on the vast researches carried out in Italy on almost all periods of English literature, and in particular on those more directly relevant to Shakespeare—medieval and Renaissance drama (G. Baldini, B. Cellini, A. Lombardo), Renaissance culture (S. Baldi, G. N. G. Orsini), Elizabethan drama (G. Baldini, B. Cellini, N. D'Agostino, M. Pagnini, G. Pellegrini, A. Obertello, S. Rosati, A. Zanco), and seventeenth-century literature (E. Chinol, V. Gabrieli, C. Izzo, G. Melchiori, M. Pagnini, G. Pellegrini, S. Rosati, V. Sanna). These researches, which naturally continue to develop in profundity and extent, have allowed Italian criticism to approach all the various aspects of

16. For these contributions, apart from the bibliographical note of Croce, one should refer to the bibliography compiled by Beatrice Niccolai in *Bollettino degli Studi Inglesi in Italia*, Nos. 1, 2, 3 (Florence, 1936); for later works there are no complete bibliographies, but useful guidance can be found in G. Baldini's *Le Tragedie di Shakespeare* (Turin, 1957) and in various histories of literature, especially by Praz, Zanco, and Izzo.

17. Now collected in *Machiavelli in Inghilterra* (Florence, 1962; first ed., 1941).

Shakespeare studies. The "fortune" of Shakespeare in Italy has been treated by A. M. Crinò, A. Lombardo, and P. Rebora, but it should be noted that a full awareness of the intrinsic rather than extrinsic relations between Shakespeare and Italian culture has also been shown by scholars of Italian literature. There has also been philological and textual research (G. Baldini, B. Cellini, G. Melchiori, G. Ramello, S. Gerevini), analysis of Shakespearean language (A. Lombardo, S. Rosati), and critical study of particular periods (F. Ferrara, A. Guidi) and single plays, such as S. Rosati's study of *King Lear, Il Giro della Ruota* (Florence, 1958), which is a fine example of how Italian criticism, making use of English critical tools but inserting them in its own cultural context, can produce results of genuine significance.

This new critical seriousness and intensity has, of course, not failed to influence the whole relation between Shakespeare and Italian culture. As it has greatly reduced and certainly redimensioned certain critical adventures which are, to say the least, eccentric, so it has gradually helped to raise the standard of translations. (In this the new English critical editions have been a decisive factor.) As a result, from the translation of Diego Angeli mentioned above or the partial and not completely successful version of A. Muccioli (1922), we have been able to pass to good translations of single plays (G. Celenza, A. Obertello, and the translators of *Teatro*, edited by Praz) and of the complete works. Among the latter, apart from the *Teatro* of Praz, is the verse translation of Vincenzo Errante (1946–49) and finally, as a worthy celebration of the Shakespearean year, the prose version of the complete works by Gabriele Baldini (Milan, 1964). Baldini's version is notable for the accuracy and intelligence of the text, as one might expect from the Italian critic who, to date, has dedicated himself to Shakespeare with the greatest energy and zeal.[18] Baldini has the added merit of including the poems and the sonnets. In this century the sonnets have indeed already appeared in partial or complete translations by P. Padulli, P. Rebora, G. Ungaretti, A. Rossi, F. Politi, A. Guidi, A. De Stefani, G. Melchiori, and E. Montale

18. See also *Il dramma elisabettiano* (Milan, 1962), *Manualetto shakespeariano* (Turin, 1964), and *La Fortuna di Shakespeare* (2 vols. Milan, 1965).

and in a recent complete and annotated critical edition by
Melchiori (Bari, 1964) . One should also note Benvenuto Cellini's
monograph study, *Vita e Arte nei Sonetti di Shakespeare* (Rome,
1943) . From Baldini we pass to versions intended for the theater,
such as those of E. Montale, L. Squarzina, G. Guerrieri, and, above
all, the complete translation of C. V. Lodovici. These, though not
without questionable solutions, also reflect a new critical and philological awareness. The same can be said of the performances,
which, through the work of actors like Renzo Ricci, Memo Benassi,
Vittorio Gassman, Salvo Randone, Gianni Santuccio, and Giorgio
Albertazzi and producers such as Visconti, Squarzina, Strehler,
Guerrieri and Zeffirelli, and through a more direct contact with the
Shakespearean tradition of the English theater, have reached a
genuinely high standard of textual intelligence. Similar progress
can be seen in theater criticism, which deserves more attention
than we can afford to give it here. We should, however, at least
mention some of the more important figures in this century:
Renato Simoni, Piero Gobetti, Silvio d'Amico, Ermanno Contini,
E. F. Palmieri, Nicola Chiaromonte, Sandro De Feo, Raul Radice,
and the younger critics, Roberto Rebora, Roberto De Monticelli,
and Renzo Tian; they have carried out a lively and stimulating
activity, not less valuable in that it derives from an immediate
contact with the performance. Indeed, in this way they have been
of valid help to literary criticism in its efforts to understand those
"theatrical" aspects of Shakespeare so finely illustrated by Granville-Barker and so necessary for the full appreciation of an art
born in the theater and intended for it. It should be noted in passing that Granville-Barker has been partially translated and a start
has been made in the translation of the major English critics.

This reciprocal influence and communication between literary
criticism and theatrical experience constitutes, in fact, one of the
clearest signs of the maturity of Italian culture in its contact with
Shakespeare. But this maturity is also witnessed and made possible
by the increasing interest in Shakespeare shown by our major
writers and poets. Riccardo Bacchelli has not only written a *Hamlet* (1918) which is both a commentary on Shakespeare and an
original work but, in the various editions of this play and in other

articles and essays, has contributed observations of acute insight. In 1923, for example, he writes of the Shakespearean imagination:

> Shakespeare obstinately despairs of ever being able to cease imagining, he is overwhelmed and persecuted by the imagination, a faculty which has its negative aspect; and he never mentions the poet except to deride and insult him with a furious shrug of the shoulders. His work closes with a magical figuration; he has suffered all his life from his inability to throw Prospero's staff into the sea. His characters, like Brutus in the tent, need very little to turn against themselves and their neighbor with that unmistakable accent, dull, furious and muffled, like Romeo against the Mantuan apothecary. Perhaps they all know that the life they live, being purely imaginary, has been too cheaply bought . . . . But Shakespeare understood this imaginary and fictitious world as if it were actual and true. His unprecedented expressive power had the word for everybody, and in this act he is dominant, predominant, omnipotent. His language is his own and yet of all kinds, courtly, popular, delicate, trivial, brutal, refined, patriotic, exotic: it includes the most speculative gothic subtleties of an exasperated absoluteness, and the most cultured and measured artificial refinements of the Renaissance. If he cannot dispense with the imagination, there is nothing he cannot say to the poet.

Bacchelli's interpretation of *Macbeth* (1960) catches perfectly the internal movement of a tragedy that is too often considered static:

> There is something in him that does not become obscured or confused in that "tale told by an idiot, full of sound and fury, signifying nothing" which is what life seems to him. What does not become obscured or confused, but rather burns bright and dazzling, is his own stubborn lucidity as a damned man, his ferocious determination. Here Goethe is right when he says that even the rhetorical figures in Shakespeare are bound to action.
>
> The story of Macbeth, therefore, is one of perdition, dreadful and terrifying, but still heroic and tragic; human life and

cosmic existence may be the meaningless tale of an idiot, not so his life which is hopelessly logical and lucid, obstinate and inevitable, the story of a conscious and voluntary downfall, not of an unconscious and passive decay as in the criminals of Dostoyevsky.

Like Bacchelli, Eugenio Montale also has constant contact with Shakespeare through reading and study, a contact which is revealed in a number of articles and above all in his fine translation of *Hamlet* and some splendid pages of the *Quaderno di Traduzioni* (1948). Here is a version of Sonnet 22 where there seems to be a perfect fusion between his own personal modes and those of Shakespeare:

Allo speechio, ancor giovane mi credo
ché giovinezza e te siete una cosa.
Ma se una ruga sul tuo volto io veda
saprò che anche per te morte non posa.
Quella beltà che ti ravvolge è ancora
parvenza del mio cuore che nel tuo
alberga—e il tuo nel mio—; e come allora
decidere chi è il vecchio di noi due?
Poni in serbo il tuo cuore, ed io lo stesso
farò di me: del tuo così zelante
come fida nutrice in veglia presso
la cuna che ogni morbo stia distante.
        Spento il mio cuore, invano il tuo riprendere
        vorresti: chi l'ha avuto non lo rende.

And this is his version of Sonnet 33:

Spesso, a lusingar vette, vidi splendere
sovranamente l'occhio del mattino,
e baciar d'oro verdi prati, accendere
pallidi rivi d'alchimie divine.
Poi vili fumi alzarsi, intorbidata
d'un tratto quella celestiale fronte,
e fuggendo a occidente il desolato
mondo, l'astro celare il viso e l'onta.

Anch'io sul far del giorno ebbi il mio sole
e il suo trionfo mi brillò sul ciglio:
ma, ahimè, poté restarvi un'ora sola,
rapito dalle nubi in cui s'impiglia.
      Pur non ne ho sdegno: bene può un terrestre
      sole abbuiarsi, se è così il celeste.

To reveal something more of Shakespeare's infinite power of suggestion it may be interesting to read a version of the same sonnet by another major Italian poet, Giuseppe Ungaretti:

Ho veduto più d'un mattino in gloria
Con lo sguardo sovrano le vette lusingare,
Baciare d'aureo viso i verdi prati,
Colorire con alchimia celeste i rivi pallidi,
E poi a vili nuvole permettere
Di fluttuargli sul celestiale volto
Con osceni fumi sottraendolo all'universo orbato
Mentre verso ponente non visto scompariva, con la sua disgrazia.
Uguale l'astro mio brillò di primo giorno
Trionfando splendido sulla mia fronte;
Ma, ah! non fu mio che per un'ora sola,
E già le nuvole del nostro grado l'hanno a me mascherato.
    Non l'ha in disdegno tuttavia il mio amore;
    Astri terreni possono macchiarsi se il sole del cielo si macchia.

The stylistic solutions are very different, and each poet has stamped his version with the seal of his own temperament and his own personal research; and yet both of them succeed in keeping intact the essence of the Shakespeare poem owing above all to the faithfulness and one might say the humility with which they approach their author. From *Quaranta Sonetti,* translated by Ungaretti and prefaced by some very acute critical comment, is the very successful version of Sonnet 72:

Quel tempo in me vedere puoi dell'anno
Quando o già niuna foglia, o rara gialla in sospeso, rimane
Ai rami che affrontando il freddo tremano,
Cori spogliati rovinati dove gli uccelli cantarono, dolci.
Della giornata vedi in me il crepuscolo

Che dopo sera all'ovest si dilegua
Portato a gradi via da notte buia
Che pari a morte tutto suggella nel riposo.
In me tu vedi d'un fuoco la fiamma
Che sopra le ceneri della sua gioventù vacilla
Come in letto di morte dove dovrà spirare,
Consumata da ciò che la nutrì.
   Te ne avvedi e il tuo amore va facendosi più forte
   Nell'amare quel bene che tra breve dovrai lasciare.

To these poets we should add the name of Salvatore Quasimodo, whose concern with Shakespeare is certainly no less serious. On the one hand he frequently writes of Shakespeare in his dense theatrical notes; on the other he is lovingly engaged in the work of translation, often obtaining excellent results.

With this reference to three major contemporary Italian poets it seems fitting to end our review of the "fortune" of Shakespeare in Italy. One might also say that through the mediation of Brecht, Beckett, and even Pirandello, who must have turned to Shakespeare for some of his theatrical inventions and for his dramatic language, especially in its tragicomic dimension, Shakespeare still offers new creative stimulus to dramatists. With this in mind, it does not seem too much to affirm that, almost three centuries after Magalotti, Shakespeare has become, as the Romantics hoped—but more completely and profoundly than during Romanticism—our "fellow-citizen," a living and active part of our culture.

Translated by Anthony Mortimer

G. N. G. Orsini

Coleridge's Manuscript Treatise on Logic

One of René Wellek's earliest pieces of research was the masterly *Kant in England, 1793–1838* (1931), in which he was the first to give, among other things, a critical analysis of Coleridge's MS. *Treatise on Logic,* now in the British Museum. The attention of scholars had been called to this work in 1929 by Miss A. D. Snyder, who accomplished first-rate pioneer work on the subject, but who was not sufficiently acquainted with the philosophical background to see the whole significance of the *Logic.* Wellek went fully into that, and to this date his is the most penetrating study of the *Logic,* although there have since been a number of important contributions to its study.[1] Some account will here be given of the *Logic* in the light of these studies and of a fresh examination of the MS.

The MS. itself is bound into two very unequal volumes, the first of only 90 folios and the second of 460 folios, according to the numbering of the British Museum. As regards its date, Miss Snyder in her book noted that its paper is "watermarked variously 1823 and 1827" (pp. 67–68), and indeed folios 1, 5, and 7 are

1. Bibliography (in chronological order): A. D. Snyder, *Coleridge on Logic and Learning* (New Haven, 1929); J. M. Muirhead, *Coleridge as a Philosopher* (London, 1930); R. Wellek, *Kant in England, 1793–1838* (Princeton, 1931); E. Winkelmann, *Coleridge und die Kantische Philosophie* (Leipzig, 1933; *Palaestra,* 184); O. Barfield, *Romanticism Comes of Age* (London, 1944); E. Chinol, *Il pensiero di S. T. Coleridge* (Venezia, 1953). Furthermore, K. Coburn, ed., *The Philosophical Lectures of S. T. Coleridge* (New York, 1949), has some quotations from the *Logic,* e.g. p. 415, n. 21.

In addition, I use the abbreviation *BL* for the Shawcross edition of the *Biographia Literaria* (1907; reprint of 1949), and I quote from Coleridge's *Shakespearean Criticism,* ed. T. M. Raysor (1930).

1823 and 1, 36, and 38 are 1827. Miss Snyder supposed that "the MS was in part at least dictated to members of the philosophical 'class' that Coleridge conducted during the winter of 1822–23" (p. 71), on which further details will be found in her book. She also argued reasonably that, since the class was held in 1822–23 and some of the watermarks are dated 1827, the MS. as we have it is "a second copy, rather than the original taken down directly from dictation" (p. 72). There is also a well-known letter of Coleridge's to Thomas Allsop, 26 December 1822, which contains a general description of the contents of the *Logic* (see Chinol, p. 50). So, unless other evidence is forthcoming, the date of the *Logic* may be assumed to be 1822–23.

The MS. is written in at least two hands, belonging to two amanuenses. It also bears some notes attributed to Coleridge's philosophical disciple, Joseph Henry Green, who owned the MS. for a number of years, and many corrections and observations in pencil by another owner of the MS., C. A. Ward (*1*, 1), who bought it in 1892 for 18 shillings (*2*, 1). Many of his corrections are useful in establishing the text.

On the whole the MS. is written in a large and legible hand, with little or no textual difficulties, except some minor gaps and imperfections. The gaps are usually short and occur where the amanuensis did not catch a word or two, particularly if it was a Greek word or phrase. Most of the latter gaps have been filled in in ink by someone who knew Greek. The sheets are written on one side only, the verso usually remaining blank. But repeatedly long supplementary notes were inserted in the verso, sometimes running to two or three pages, as in the important discussion of "function" (*2*, 40^v–41^v).

The MS. is divided rather unevenly into chapters, most of them unnumbered. A list of them was made, apparently by Green (see pencil note on list), on a separate sheet now bound in the book (*1*, 3) and containing the titles of sixteen chapters. This list has been reproduced in translation by Chinol (p. 49). Actually there are seventeen chapters, for Green missed a fourteenth "chapter" not numbered in the MS. but occupying twenty pages (*2*, 347–67) and entitled "Of the ways and means by which the mind arrives at mathematical evidence." It was lumped by Green with the preceding chapter, also "on mathematical evidence." The divisions of topics between chapters are not too clearly maintained. This list of contents, revised, is given in the Appendix.

The MS. was first owned by Green who, after Coleridge's death in 1834, long debated with himself whether he should publish it. Finally, in accordance with his "sound discretion," he decided against publication (Snyder, pp. 66–67). The MS. then passed through the hands of other owners, one of whom made "persistent attempts" in the nineteenth century to get it published but failed (Snyder, p. 67). In 1899 it became the property of the British Museum, where it was classified as Egerton MS. 2825 and 2826, and there it lay until 1929, when Miss Snyder published a detailed account of it, together with a number of extracts, which however do not exhaust the interest of the subject. Other studies followed rapidly: in 1930 Muirhead discussed the relevance of the MS. to later logical investigations (pp. 60–88) and connected it with other unpublished works by Coleridge. In 1931 Wellek made a shrewd analysis and a sharp criticism of it in his book on Kant. In 1933 Winkelmann utilized Snyder's extracts and some other MS. notes. Later, Barfield noted important ideas in it (pp. 154–58), and Chinol made a serious study of it, stressing the Kantian element. At long last, a complete edition of it is now being prepared by Professor Robin Jackson of Victoria College, Toronto.

It is a pity the work has not been published earlier, for, in spite of some foreseeable shortcomings, it possesses remarkable qualities. It is Coleridge's most sustained effort in the field of pure philosophy; it is more comprehensive than any of his published works in this field; and it fills many gaps between them, thus achieving something more like a system than most people expect of Coleridge. It contains a number of brilliant illustrations, devised by Coleridge himself, of its abstruse topics. It also contains abundant references to the works of Kant, including some works not elsewhere referred to, as well as quotations from other writers (notably Moses Mendelssohn) of whom there is not much trace elsewhere in Coleridge's published works: these quotations were noted by Miss Snyder. There are repetitions from his published works, particularly the passages from Schelling incorporated in Chapter XII of the *Biographia Literaria,* and some anticipations of works yet to come, as the illustration borrowed from Mendelssohn (2, 138–40), which reappears in the Appendix to *Church and State* of 1830 (p. 231).

Since it is by Coleridge, the work is also rambling and digressive, somewhat repetitious and redundant, not very clear in arrangement and at times somewhat inconsistent. Yet it is fuller and more satisfactory than any of his published philosophical works. It does not break down in the middle and then turn off in another direction, as does the *Biographia Literaria,* but proceeds continuously with its main topic until the end. The end itself is abrupt, and the work appears to be unfinished; but I shall try to show that it is not substantially so.

We have seen that the book is rather unequally divided into chapters, which in itself is not a very important matter. A division which goes deeper, and which will lead us straight into the core of the book, is that of the fundamental parts of the subject, i.e. the three divisions of Logic as Canon, Logic as Organon, and Logic as Criterion, which are mentioned in the already cited letter to Allsop (Chinol, p. 50). The first is "a Canon or form, to which all legitimate constructions of the Understanding must correspond"; the second is "an organ for discovery" of new truths; and the third is "a test for the discovery of Truth" (2, 4). In other words, the first concerns the forms of arguments, such as the syllogism; the second concerns the methods for the discovery of fresh facts and laws; and the third is the method for checking conclusions. These divisions are not too satisfactory, but Coleridge found them in his text (Kant) and adopted them, at least in part.

"Canon" includes what Coleridge calls "pure and simple Logic," or what we would call traditional logic, and of course excludes the other two divisions. In other places, however, Coleridge appears to discuss topics belonging to the other divisions, so that it seemed to Miss Snyder that the treatise as we have it is actually divided into those three parts, Canon, Organon, and Criterion. She subdivided her exposition accordingly, but she acknowledged that "Coleridge is not consistent in the use of the term," i.e. "Logic" (p. 81, n. 16). On the other hand, Chinol, relying on the above quoted passages (2, 4) and others, argues that the *Logic* includes only the Canon or "pure and simple Logic" and does not include the other two parts (p. 55).

Since the MS. was never given a final revision by its author, we may expect some inconsistencies in it. Coleridge may well have intended to limit it to the Canon, as Chinol argues, and yet occasionally glanced at topics which belonged to the other divisions. In effect, the *Logic* includes a number of discussions which go beyond any of the divisions of logic and belong to the domain of epistemology and metaphysics. Toward the end, the book enters into a detailed exposition of Kant's "Analysis of the Sensibility and of the Understanding" in the *Critique of Pure Reason*.

This fact has been duly noted by previous students of the work. But what about the third and most important part of the *Critique*, the Dialectic, in which Kant argues powerfully that pure Reason cannot reach ultimate truth, or as he called it, the realm of *noumena?* Did Coleridge take any notice of it? To some it seems that Coleridge merely set it aside without taking any notice of it (e.g. Winkelmann, pp. 175 and 246–47). But in the *Logic* we find a clear statement of the central doctrine of the Dialectic, namely the Antinomies of pure Reason:

> When from two premises, both of which are affirmed with equal right by the understanding, the understanding itself can arrive at two contradictory conclusions, the only possible solution of the difficulty is found in assuming that the understanding has been applying its own forms and functions, or those which it has borrowed from the sense, to objects that do not fall under its cognizance, as for instance the understanding applies the forms of time and space, of quantity, quality and relation to the Idea of the Supreme Being, or of things [in] themselves contradistinguished from phenomena. (2, 190^v)

This was quoted by Miss Snyder (p. 119), but she did not note the reference to Kant. However, for Kant the Antinomies affect pure Reason, while for Coleridge they affect only the Understanding, not the Reason; hence, in a note written earlier, he could speak of "the Kantean [sic] supposed Antinomies of Reason"

(*Philosophical Lectures,* p. 425). Coleridge thus did not ignore the Kantian doctrine of the Antinomies but adapted it to his own ends. Whether this adaptation is philosophically sound is of course another question.[2]

More valuable, perhaps, is the doctrine of "productive unity" which Coleridge develops in several passages (2, 381–82, 389–90, and 417–19), and which was noted by Wellek (p. 120) and strongly stressed by Barfield. Coleridge here makes a distinction between two kinds of unity, original and derivative. The latter is produced by the coming together of separate and preexistent parts, as "a watch for instance" (2, 417). Original unity instead preexists to the parts that compose it. Since it preexists to its parts, it may be assumed to have produced them and so is both antecedent and productive.

Now the Kantian origin of this doctrine should be noted. A preexistent unity is precisely what Kant ascribed to Ideas. "An Idea," he says in his *Logic*,[3] "cannot be obtained by composition, for in it the whole is before the part." In Kantian terminology, this unity is a priori, and the mental act which effects it is an a priori synthesis, i.e. one of the most important concepts of Kantian and post-Kantian speculation. Coleridge has grasped it, but he does not carry it to the lengths that the post-Kantians go in their absolute idealism. As he puts it in a note, productive unity is

> distinguished from a whole as elsewhere I have proposed to use the term *Form* as the technical antithesis of *shape*. As *Form = forma formans* [stands] to *shape = forma formata,* so the productive unity = *Totum suas ipsius partes constituens* [stands] to the whole (mass aggregate) = *Totum a partibus constitutum.* The former is the same with the Leibnizian monad and the Entelechy of Aristotle. (2, 381ᵛ–82ᵛ)

The importance of this discussion for aesthetics is that the distinction between productive unity and mass aggregate is parallel to

2. I propose to deal more fully with the relations of Coleridge to Kant in a forthcoming book.

3. Kant, *Logik,* Chap. 1, par. 3; see the 1800 edition (the one used by Coleridge), p. 140, and cf. Richardson's translation (1836), p. 128.

that between organic form and mechanical form, which plays such an important part in Shakespeare criticism.[4]

There are passages in the *Logic* in which Coleridge sums up the idealistic position of the post-Kantians in terse, striking arguments, like the following:

> The mind affirms firstly its own reality. Secondly, that this reality is a unity. Thirdly, that it has the power of communicating this unity, and lastly, that all reality for the mind is derived from its own reality, and in proportion to the unity which is its form. (2, 63)

But after having followed the idealistic argument so far and expressed it so vigorously, Coleridge turns back and returns to orthodox theism. The argument he presents here is not perfectly clear, but it might perhaps be summarized as follows. Self-consciousness, or the mind as absolute identity of being and knowing, is not ultimate. It "supposes reflection and reflection an act antecedent thereto." Therefore "we have inquired for something more and higher than this self-consciousness" (2, 68). This presumably means that self-consciousness implies some previous act of the mind cognizing some object or some previous experience, and this would pave the way for the mind's successive awareness of itself as the subject of experience. Then it could be argued that this previous act or acts imply the existence of the mind making those acts, so that the actual existence of mind, or its being, precedes its self-awareness. Now once it is admitted that Being absolutely precedes Thought, then Idealism, which affirms the identity of the two, is rejected. An idealist like Schelling, however, would probably have had an answer to this argument, i.e. that this "previousness," this "before" and "after," is psychological and not logical.

The vacillation which is observable in these pages is the same in substance as the one found in Chapter XII of the *Biographia Literaria*: a vacillation obscurely expressed between the idealistic formula "*sum qua sum*, I am because I affirm myself to be" and the theistic formula "*sum quia in Deo sum* or I am because I am

4. See my paper, "Coleridge and Schlegel Reconsidered," *Comparative Literature, 16* (1964), 97–118.

in God" (2, 75; cf. *BL, 1,* 183, Thesis VI) . He repeats in the *Logic*
the footnote already published in the *Biographia* (*BL, 1,* 184 n.)
on the distinction between the "conditional finite I" and the
"absolute I am, and likewise the inherence of the former in the
latter in whom we live and move and have our being" (2, 75ᵛ) ,
and so on, as in the *Biographia.* In other words, the Absolute is
God and not the mind. Coleridge is safely back in the theistic fold.

Among the topics discussed in the *Logic* is language. Not only
was Coleridge well aware of the close relationship between
thought and speech, the idea and the word, but he was also deeply
interested in the subject in all its aspects and continually reverts to
it. He insists upon the necessity of technical terms of philosophy
(*1,* 87 f.; 2, 378–81, and so on) , and he defends their use against
the often repeated request that he should use "common language." The latter is good for ordinary communication but not for
logic; however, the logician must always define his technical terms
and also warn the reader every time he deviates from common
usage (2, 129) . Words alone are never the causes of bad thinking
or of logical confusion, but "the pre-existence of such confusion"
causes "their own existence as equivocations" (2, 159) .

This deep interest in language is of course related to Coleridge's
own magnificent capacity for verbal expression. Every reader of
his prose knows how meticulous he can be in the use of synonyms
and antonyms, and how often he refers to the principles of "philosophical grammar." The *Logic* begins with a discussion of this
very subject and includes a rather fanciful attempt to derive all
the parts of speech from a few general categories. Still more fanciful but quite in keeping with the tendencies of German meta-
physicians are some of the suggested etymologies, such as that of
"cogitans," from *"cogito"* and *"ens"* (2, 68) . Coleridge also shows
here his love of the German language, already manifest in other
works—nowhere perhaps so strongly as in the Shakespeare lectures
of 1811, where he says that the German language "is incomparable
in its metaphysical and psychological force" (Raysor, 2, 119) . In
the *Logic* he also makes use of etymology: "The 'definition of the
term Judgment' . . . is most happily expressed in the Teutonic
language by *Urtheil* and the Judgment itself or the judicial faculty

Urtheilskraft, that is, the power of resolving a thing into its primary and original or constituent parts" (*2, 61*).

This is remarkable, because the same philosophical pun is made by Hegel repeatedly: e.g. in the *Encyclopaedia,* par. 166, and in the *Logik* of 1812,[5] the latter a book that Coleridge owned and annotated (but not on this point). The copy, which once belonged to Joseph Henry Green, Coleridge's disciple, is now in the British Museum, C.43.a.13. Since Coleridge seems to have taken very little notice of Hegel, it would be interesting to find another reference to Hegel in his writings. Unfortunately, the pun is already in Schelling (*Werke, 3, 507*), from whom it is more likely that Coleridge got it.

Another way in which Coleridge shows his admiration for German is his attempt to create new English words modeled on German ones, for instance "Inhold" for *"Inhalt"* (*2, 125*) or "allcommon" for *"allgemein"* (instead of "general"): "if I might borrow a more expressive and more English form from our sister language, the German, the allcommon (*allgemein*)" (*2, 382*). In this connection it may be of interest to call attention to another verbal creation by Coleridge, not generally known: in an attempt to find an English equivalent for *Anschauung,* or intuition,[6] Coleridge coined the term "aspicience," which is to be found in Additional MS. 34,225, fol. 144[r].

However, Coleridge's concept of language in the *Logic* remains strictly intellectualistic; for instance, he says: "words are themselves the earliest products of the abstracting power" and "all language originates in reflection" (*1, 24; 2, 388*). This is probably natural in the logical context of the book; but it is also possible that Coleridge was not aware of the other view, found among German philosophers and critics, which considers language not the product of the logical faculty but of the intuitional faculty—that particularizing faculty sometimes called *"Anschauung,"* a term

5. "Das Urtheil ist die Diremption des Begriffs durch sich selbst . . . . Es ist insofern die ursprüngliche Theilung des ursprünglich Einen" (*Logik* [1812], 2, 74).

6. For the aesthetic importance of the term "intuition," cf. *BL, 1,* 109, and 2, 230.

which as we have seen was considered important by Coleridge. As Miss Coburn notes, "I have found no evidence that Coleridge read Herder on the origin of language, and K. W. von Humboldt's work appeared two years after Coleridge's death" (*Philosophical Lectures*, p. 416).

In conclusion, Coleridge in his *Logic* raised a building largely made up of Kantian bricks but held together with Coleridgean mortar and designed after a Coleridgean pattern. Its goal was ultimate truth, which Kant in the *Critique of Pure Reason* thought inaccessible, but which the post-Kantian idealists thought within reach. However, in spite of strong leanings toward absolute idealism, Coleridge in the end always returned to the fold of orthodox theism. But the attempt to reconcile idealism with theism and to build a traditional metaphysic on a transcendentalist foundation was made by Coleridge honestly and wholeheartedly, as it has been attempted since by other thinkers.

The *Logic* also has several secondary merits. First of all, as René Wellek puts it:

> as an exposition of Kant, the *Logic* ranks high indeed and shows a far better insight into Kant than most of Coleridge's contemporaries could boast of and a much more precise knowledge of Kant's actual teachings than one would have expected from the loose phraseology of some of Coleridge's more popular writings. (*Kant in England*, pp. 121–22)

The *Logic* also provides a foundation for Coleridge's other philosophical writings, both published and unpublished, and fills a gap in his general argument. It fulfills its titular purpose by being essentially a treatise on the functions and processes of the Understanding, to which Coleridge, following Kant, limits the sphere of logic. When he had covered nearly all the functions that Kant assigned to the Understanding, the book comes to an end. True, there are further developments in the *Critique* which Coleridge omits, such as the doctrines of the Schemata and of the Principles of the Understanding. Coleridge was not ignorant of them, since he referred to them in *The Friend*, but in the *Logic* he stops short of them. There is also no formal conclusion or epilogue. Coleridge apparently had said all he had to say on the Understanding, and there the book ends.

Even if it were unfinished, it is deplorable that the work should have remained so long unpublished. The condition in which it was left also arouses regret that a mind like Coleridge's, whose capacity for philosophical speculation and grasp of transcendentalism does not appear to have been potentially inferior to, say, that of a Schelling, should have suffered from misfortunes and shortcomings to the extent of being unable to write a single complete philosophical treatise and then bring it to light, while Schelling was able to compose and publish a number of striking philosophical treatises and so make a much deeper philosophical impact on the world.

The Contents of Coleridge's *Logic*

The titles of the chapters are given below as in the "Green" list (*1, 3*), but the numbering of the last four chapters has been corrected. Quotation marks indicate that the title is identical to that in the text; otherwise the words are Green's.

7. "Judicial Logic" is Coleridge's term for Kant's "Transcendental Logic" (see 2, 210, 212).

E. N. Tigerstedt

The Problem of Progress in Literature in Classical Antiquity

The problem of progress in literature is as old as literature itself.[1] Ever since there have been poets, there have been men who wanted them simply to repeat the old songs, and also men who wanted them to sing a new—and therefore better—song. The poets themselves have been torn between a desire to create something new and unheard—the *carmina non prius audita* of Horace—and a fear that they could add nothing to the achievement of their predecessors. Yet every true poet is a secret or open believer in progress as meaning a change for the better insofar as he believes in his own creative power, even if he confesses, nay, boasts that he is only a small link in a great chain: *Doch Homeride zu sein, auch nur als letzter, ist schön.*[2] There is much pride in this humility.

Ab Jove principium! And Jove in European literature means Homer. The Homeric bard does not hesitate to stress his originality. "I am self-taught," says Phemius, and he adds that the god has planted in his mind all sorts of tales.[3] Thus, he is indebted to no mortal man.

1. There seems to be no monograph or any special treatment of this subject. There is, of course, much that is pertinent to it in books which treat of progress in general, esp. in J. B. Bury's old but not superseded *The Idea of Progress* (London, 1920). Frederick J. Teggart and George H. Hildebrand, *The Idea of Progress* (Berkeley and Los Angeles, 1949) is a convenient collection of texts in translation. Some remarks on this topic can be found in Ladislaus Madyda, *De arte poëtica post Aristotelem exculta quaestiones selectae,* Archiwum filologiczne, 22 (Kraków, 1948), pp. 147 ff.

2. Goethe, *Elegien: Hermann und Dorothea.*

3. *Odyssey* XXII.347; cf. Giuliana Lanata, *Poetica Pre-Platonica* (Firenze, 1963), pp. 12 ff. Miss Lanata's anthology contains much material of interest for our subject, together with a copious commentary and bibliography.

This proud confession of independence and originality recurs often in old Greek poetry. Pindar refuses to follow the beaten path; he knows a shorter road[4] and exhorts us to praise the flowers of songs that are new.[5] Nor is he unaware of the resistance which meets everything new: "for any one to find something new and submit it to a touchstone for assay is perilous." [6]

But Pindar can also take pride in following the paths of the ancients.[7] His immense self-esteem is balanced by his strong attachment to tradition as well as by his deep piety. His poetry is due to his natural talents ($\phi\upsilon\dot{\alpha}$),[8] but it is at the same time the heavenly gift of the Muses. Even so, Pindar would never have subscribed to the humility, sincere or feigned, which Bacchylides professed: "Now as of old, one poet learns from another, for it is not easy to find words which never have been pronounced." [9] It is the confession of a *poeta minor,* writing in a genre and a style soon to be exhausted, for, with Pindar and Bacchylides, the great choric lyric of Greece comes to an end.

If more of ancient Greek lyrical poetry had been preserved, no doubt we should have many utterances in the vein of Pindar, and some perhaps in the vein of Bacchylides. One thing which must have laid heavily upon the minds of poets was the fact that the first Greek poet was also the greatest. The overwhelming fame and authority of Homer, upheld and propagated by the schools, must have caused irritation and envy in later poets and aroused their opposition. Pindar himself cannot suppress his resentment at the ease with which "sweet-worded Homer" fooled the minds of men, for there is "something august" in his lies.[10] Pindar's attitude toward Homer seems here as ambiguous as Plato's a hundred years later.

On the other hand, the indebtedness of all later poets to Homer was confessed by Aeschylus, saying that his tragedies were "large

4. *Pyth.* IV.247–48. On Pindar's conception of poetry, see Sir Maurice Bowra, *Pindar* (Oxford, 1964) , pp. 1 ff.

5. *Olymp.* IX.47–49; cf. *Olymp.* III. 4–6, *Isthm.* V.63, and fr. 70b Snell. See Bowra, pp. 194 ff.

6. *Nem.* VIII.20–22.

7. *Nem.* VI.55–56.

8. *Olymp.* II.86. Cf. *Olymp.* IX.100.

9. Bacchylides fr. 5 Snell.

10. *Nem.* VII.20ff.; cf. Bowra, pp. 70 ff.

cuts taken from Homer's mighty dinner." [11] Usually, Aeschylus'
words are taken as a homage to Homer, but it is possible to interpret them as a declaration of independence, as a statement of the
difference between the concentrated technique of tragedy and the
loose technique of epic.[12] In any case, the Greek poets of these
centuries did not feel unduly oppressed by their predecessors, not
even by the greatest of them.

True, epic poetry languished and decayed, but other genres
flourished all the more, and new genres were created, for example,
tragedy and comedy. In these genres, Homer can never have been
regarded as a deadly danger to what might be called "progress,"
though there was no word for it.[13] Change and novelty were more
and more in demand and were more and more supplied. The age
of the Ionian philosophers was followed by the age of the Persian
War, and this in turn by the age of the Sophists. Soon, there was
nothing old which could not be challenged, nothing new which
could not be tried.

The center of this cultural revolution was Athens, which astonished and frightened the rest of Greece with her "lust for innova-
tions" ($\nu\epsilon\omega\tau\epsilon\rho\sigma\pi\sigma\iota\iota a$).[14] Thucydides, who tells us this, also
makes the reflection that "in politics as in art ($\tau\epsilon\chi\nu\eta$), the new
must always prevail." [15] Thucydides is speaking of technics, craftsmanship, not of "art" in our sense (though $\tau\epsilon\chi\nu\eta$ could include
the fine arts), but his own work testifies to the victory of the new
over the old. Many enraged battles must have been fought between "ancients" and "moderns" in Athenian literature of the
fifth century B.C. But, except for the plays of Aristophanes, only
faint echoes have reached us.

Aristophanes is famous as an anti-modernist.[16] Yet in his own

11. Athenaeus, *Dipnosophistae*, VIII.347E. Cf. Lanata, p. 141 n.

12. See Lanata, p. 141 n.

13. $\epsilon\pi\iota\delta\sigma\sigma\iota s$ may mean a change for the worse as well as for the better;
$\pi\rho\sigma\chi\omega\rho\eta\sigma\iota s$ is very late.

14. Thucydides, I.102, 3; cf. I.70, 1.

15. Thucydides I.71, 3. This is said by the Corinthian ambassadors to
Sparta, but we cannot well doubt that it expresses Thucydides' own
opinion.

16. The vast literature on Aristophanes' aesthetical opinion cannot here
be indicated; see Albin Lesky, *Geschichte der griechischen Literatur* (2d ed.
Bern, 1963), pp. 464 ff.

art, he proudly claims to be an innovator and criticizes his predecessors and rivals, especially Cratinus.[17] He can even accuse his public of being deaf to the new tunes.[18] But outside comedy, he has little use for novelty. We should, however, not forget that Aristophanes' plays are late, darkened by the approaching great catastrophe. He is already looking back to a glorious past, compared to which the present is but "decline and fall." Therefore, Euripides is to Aristophanes the representative of political, moral, and poetical degeneration. Against him, Aristophanes in the *Frogs* (405 B.C., a year before the fall of Athens) extolls old Aeschylus, not only as the better poet, but also and especially as the better patriot, the man who fought at Marathon.[19]

This attitude prevails in fourth-century Athens, which dreams of recapturing the glories of the past. The orators, e.g. Isocrates and Demosthenes, speak wistfully of the mighty deeds of the forefathers, proclaiming them as models for the present generation.[20] As in politics, so in literature. In spite of vigorous productivity, there is a feeling of weariness and exhaustion, at least in some fields. The theater is dominated by the great dramatic poets of the last century, for Euripides is now put on the same level as Aeschylus and Sophocles. The decree of Lycurgus (ca. 330 B.C.), which consecrated the already established custom of performing their works together with works of living poets, was the official confirmation of their status as classics, whose very words were sacred.[21]

However, the greatest Athenian writer of the fourth century had no admiration for the political or literary glories of the past. To Plato, Athenian history since Themistocles was a sorry story of errors and crimes. And dramatic poetry was to him the worst, most dangerous kind of poetry. Being a Greek city, Plato's ideal city must have poetry, if only hymns to the gods and poems in praise of virtuous citizens. Even those poems must be closely supervised and rigorously censured, however, as Plato tells us in the *Laws*.

17. *Clouds* v. 518–62 and *Knights* v. 507–50.
18. *Clouds* v. 535 ff.
19. *Frogs* v. 1296.
20. See my *The Legend of Sparta in Classical Antiquity*, *1* (Stockholm, 1965), pp. 180 ff.
21. See A. E. Haigh, *The Attic Theatre* (3d ed. by A. W. Pickard-Cambridge, Oxford, 1907), pp. 71 ff.

This control of poetry aims not only at suppressing all sorts of religious, moral, or political heresies, but at eradicating the very spirit of novelty and change, in which Plato sees the greatest danger to his city. All change is perilous, unless from the bad to the good—and humanity mostly changes for the worse. Plato's political and therefore also artistic ideal is immobility. He speaks with high praise of the Egyptians, who for over ten thousand years have kept their "musike" (poetry, music, and dance) unaltered, in contrast to the fickleness of the Greeks.[22]

In order to make the inhabitants of his ideal city—the second-best one—as much like the Egyptians as possible, Plato demanded a survey even of the children's games.

> For when the program of game is prescribed and secures that the same children always play the same games and delight in the same way and under the same conditions, it allows the real and serious laws also to remain undisturbed; but when these games vary and suffer innovations, amongst other constant alterations the children are always shifting their fancy from one game to another, so that neither in respect of their own bodily gestures nor in respect of their equipment have they any fixed and acknowledged standard of propriety and impropriety; but the man they hold in special honour is he who is always innovating or introducing some novel device in the matter of form or colour or something of the sort: whereas it would be perfectly true to say that a state can have no worse pest than a man of that description, since he privily alters the characters of the young, and causes them to contemn what is old and esteem what is new.[23]

In this way, the devil of modernism is driven out of the very young—whom Plato distrusts deeply [24]—before it has seduced the rest of the citizens. This is indeed misoneism with a vengeance. But Plato's anti-modernism carries small hope for even the oldest and most venerable poetry, because to him all Greek poetry from

22. *Laws* II.656D.
23. *Laws* VII. 797B–C; cf. 798B–C. I quote from the translation by R. G. Bury in *The Loeb Classical Library*.
24. *Laws* VII.808D–E.

Homer on is suspect, if not downright evil. On this point, Plato the reactionary suddenly changes, as so often, into Plato the revolutionary.

Plato's attitude toward poetry was determined by the political aims of his philosophy, and all attempts to construct a Platonic aesthetics or poetics are therefore doomed to failure. As a philosopher, Plato was not interested in poetry as poetry. This, on the contrary, is not true of his greatest disciple. In the *Poetics* of Aristotle, we find at last the first—or, let us cautiously say, the first preserved—real treatment of progress in literature.[25] It occurs in the famous, still hotly debated description of the evolution of tragedy. After speaking of its origins, Aristotle says: "Tragedy then gradually evolved as men developed each element that came to light and after going through many changes, it stopped when it had found its natural form" (ἐπαύσατο, ἐπεὶ ἔσχε τὴν αὑτῆς φύσιν).[26]

It has often and rightly been pointed out that this conception of progress postulates a fixed goal, an ideal of tragedy, which somehow is realized through the vicissitudes of literary history. Once the goal is reached and the ideal is realized, however, progress as such comes to an end: it stops. Further changes can only be either unimportant variations or deteriorations.

Aristotle, evidently, does not share Plato's love of immobility, but neither does he profess a belief in limitless progress. There is, indeed, "progress in literature," namely development of different, well-separated literary forms or genres (εἴδη), each with its predetermined goal, beyond which it cannot go without destroying itself.[27] Some recent scholars assert that Aristotle regarded trag-

25. Most books on the *Poetics* do not treat this subject, but see William K. Wimsatt and Cleanth Brooks, *A Short History of Literary Criticism* (New York, 1957), pp. 28 ff., and esp. the fundamental remarks by Albin Lesky, "Wesenszüge der attischen Klassik," *Gesammelte Schriften* (Bern, 1966), pp. 452 ff.

26. *Poetics* 1449a15. In this and later quotations, I use the translation by W. Hamilton Fyfe in *The Loeb Classical Library*, but with occasional corrections. The authoritative text is now that by Rudolf Kassel (Oxford, 1965).

27. Professor Wimsatt seems to regard the concept of literary genres as post-Aristotelian (Wimsatt and Brooks, p. 36). But this concept is inherent in Greek literature from the very beginning (cf. Lesky). The existence of

edy as having evolved out of epic, which would have been "a phase in the genesis of tragedy."[28] In their opinion, Aristotle believed in the possibility of transformation of one literary genre into another. But Aristotle says nothing about such a transformation. Indeed, he finds the tragedy a later and better (κρείττων) genre than the epic.[29] There is, for him, in the literary world—as in the biological—a hierarchy of genres, lower and higher. There is a "ladder" of forms. But no single form ever changes into another form, for that would be "transformism," in which Aristotle—contrary to post-Darwinian man—did not believe.[30] To him, literary history as well as natural history was the story of the birth, evolution, and decay of intransformable organic forms, each represented by many individuals.[31]

Our judgment of any single literary work would therefore depend upon what stage of development of its genre it represents. Clearly, maturity is not to be expected from the first work in any genre. Perfection comes late. For this reason, probably, Aristotle thought that Homer had many predecessors, though he knew of no older Greek poet and hesitated to say whether Homer knew the laws of epic from instinct (φύσις) or from art (τέχνη),[32] the latter being the sum of theoretical knowledge and practical skill inherited from his predecessors.

---

separate genres was to Aristotle an indisputable fact which needed no proof, as appears from the casual mention of the εἴδη in the first sentence of the *Poetics* (cf. Madyda, pp. 146 ff.). See also the important paper by Johannes Stroux, "Die Anschauungen vom Klassischen im Altertum," *Das Problem des Klassischen und die Antike,* ed. Werner Jaeger, (2d ed. Stuttgart, 1961), pp. 3 ff.

28. Wimsatt and Brooks, p. 35; cf. Gerald F. Else, *Aristotle's Poetics* (Leiden, 1957), p. 204: "Tragedy represents a further point along a common line of development." I am not quite sure whether Professor Else really believes that in Aristotle's opinion epic was transformed into tragedy, for there is a certain ambiguity in this and the following statements of his.

29. *Poetics* 1462b14.

30. See Louis Robin, *Aristote* (Paris, 1944), p. 178, and Ingemar Düring, *Aristoteles* (Heidelberg, 1966), pp. 528 ff.

31. On the biological origin of Aristotle's concept of literary evolution, see T. B. L. Webster *Art and Literature in Fourth Century Athens* (London, 1955), pp. 54 ff.

32. *Poetics* 1488b28 ff., 1451a23 f.

But our decision can scarcely be made *before* the genre in question has developed its inherent possibilities. How can we judge a work, unless we know by what ideal it should be judged? And how can we know that ideal, unless it is fully realized? Aristotle's own definition of tragedy and his description of its evolution take this for granted.[33] The Aristotelian critic is like Friedrich Schlegel's historian: "ein rückwärtsgekehrter Prophet." [34]

As a matter of fact, the *Poetics* deals with two literary genres of which one—epic—was obviously finished,[35] and the other—tragedy—had its great period behind it. It is therefore not astonishing that practically all the authors quoted in the *Poetics* belong to earlier times. There is scarcely one real contemporary among them, though Aristotle may have known some of them in his youth.[36]

It is improbable that this retrospective character of the *Poetics* would be much altered if we could read the now-lost second book, though it seems that Aristotle disliked the licentiousness of the Old Comedy and therefore would have preferred the contemporary Middle Comedy (he did not live to see Menander) .[37] Nor is this retrospective character really challenged by such concessions to novelty as the praise of Agathon's *Antheus,* where the plot as well as the persons were invented by the author [38] contrary to the usual practice of tragic poets, for this practice is not included in the Aristotelian definition of tragedy and could therefore be disobeyed without imperiling the genre.

The question whether Aristotle would have accepted the rise of

33. *Poetics* 1449a7 ff. Aristotle, indeed, says that "to consider whether tragedy is fully developed by now in all its parts or not . . . is another question," but what follows shows that he answers this question in the affirmative; cf. Augusto Rostagni's edition of the *Poetics* (Torino, 1945) , pp. 22 ff. On this point as on many others, I am unable to accept the interpretation given by Professor Else.

34. Friedrich Schlegel, *Prosaische Jugendschriften,* ed. J. Minor (Vienna, 1885) , 2, 215 (Athenäumfragment 80) .

35. Cf. the complaints of Choerilus of Samus in the prologue to his epic on the Persian war (fr. 1 Kinkel) .

36. The difficulty is that some of the poets quoted are known only from the *Poetics* and others are of uncertain date.

37. See Else, pp. 105, 309 ff.

38. *Poetics* 1451b19 ff.; cf. Else, pp. 318 ff.

new, hitherto unknown literary genres cannot be answered with certainty, though the *Poetics* does not exclude the possibility, insofar as Aristotle seems to regard the prose-mimi of Sophron and Xenarchus and the Socratic dialogues as a new genre.[39]

Even so, the literary cosmos of the *Poetics* is a static one. Aristotle is not interested in the future of literature; he writes not for would-be poets but for his fellow philosophers at the Peripatos. To be sure, he does not hesitate to pronounce very firm judgments upon poets and their works. At the very beginning of the *Poetics,* he promises to deal with "the way in which the plot must be constructed if the poem is to be a success." [40] That is a theoretical conclusion, however, not practical advice. In reality, the *Poetics* cares as little for the future as the *Politics*. Both deal with things as they are or have been.

But then Aristotle is not deeply interested in any future. Of all great thinkers, he perhaps is the one who most lacks a vision of the future. Change, indeed, there is in his world, at least in the sublunary world, the world of man. But this change means no real novelty, only variation—death and rebirth in an eternal circle.[41] Human civilization has passed through innumerable such circles and will forever pass. "Each art and science has often been developed as far as possible and has again perished." [42]

This is the famous cyclical cosmology which seems to have been accepted by most ancient philosophers.[43] It certainly was by Plato, but this did not abate his zeal for reforming humanity. Indeed, the very vastness of the cycles made it perfectly possible for anyone to be an optimist or a progressivist in regard to his own time, if he

---

39. *Poetics* 1447b9 ff.; cf. Else, pp. 41 ff.

40. *Poetics* 1447a9–10.

41. See Werner Jaeger, *Aristotle* (Oxford, 1948), pp. 388 ff. and, for a different point of view, Düring, pp. 352 ff.

42. *Metaphysics* XII.8 (1074b10–13); cf. Sir David Ross, *Aristotle's Metaphysics* (Oxford, 1924), 2, 396.

43. Of the extensive literature on this subject, I will only quote some recent works: Charles Mugler, *Deux thèmes de la cosmologie grecque* (Paris, 1953); W. K. C. Guthrie, *In the Beginning* (Ithaca, N.Y., 1957); and Rodolfo Mondolfo, *La comprensione del soggetto umano nell' antichità classica* (Florence, 1958), pp. 575–739. See also Mircea Eliade, *Le mythe de l'éternel retour* (Paris, 1949).

believed that it belonged to the rising part of a cycle.[44] The
Sophists are often regarded—on rather doubtful evidence—as
prophets of progress,[45] but a belief in the future of, let us say,
Periclean Athens would have been as compatible with a cyclical
cosmology as a nineteenth-century liberal's belief in progress with
the Second Law of Thermodynamics. A destruction which lies in
the far future has no reality to most men. To Aristotle it had, because of his intense intellectualism, which finds its supreme goal
in pure, eternal, unchanging Thought.

Aristotle's most famous pupil conquered Asia, and another
pupil, Demetrius of Phalerum, helped to found the great Alexandrine library. A new age began, very different from that of
Aristotle—the Hellenistic age. In the big centers of the new civilization, there was no place for that nostalgia for the past which
had characterized fourth-century Athens. Was not the present
greater than any past? What mythological heroes could compare
with the godlike Alexander and his soldiers?

The self-confident and triumphant mood of the first Hellenistic
century—so manifest in its art—did not necessarily imply contempt of the past, at least not in literature. On the contrary, the
great resources of the new states made it possible for the first time
to study the history of Greek literature exhaustively and systematically. Never before and never since has there been such a collection of Greek books as in the Alexandrine library. Never before

44. Eliade's statement (p. 197) that in a cyclical system the present always
constitutes decay in comparison to earlier periods has no general validity;
see Guthrie, pp. 78 ff., and Eric A. Havelock, *The Liberal Temper in Greek
Politics* (2d ed. New Haven, 1964), p. 405.

45. On the progressivism of the Sophists, see, e.g., W. Usxhull-Gyllenband,
Griechische Kulturentstehungslehren (Lipsic, 1924); Wilhelm Nestle, *Vom
Mythos zum Logos* (2d ed. Leipzig, 1942), pp. 282 ff.; Guthrie, pp. 80 ff.;
and Mondolfo, *a.a.*, pp. 647 ff. Sigfried Lauffer, in *Der antike Fortschritts-
gedanke* (Actes du XIème Congrès International de Philosophie, 12 [Paris,
1953], pp. 37–44), states that the cyclical cosmology was inherited from the
Ancient East, but that classical antiquity believed in progress—a statement
which simply does not correspond to the facts. Even the more cautious
argument in Havelock's book (see esp. pp. 52 ff.) seems too hypothetical.
On the other hand, the sweeping statements of Heinrich Dörrie, in *Entwicklung* (Reallexikon für Antike und Christentum, 5 [1962], cols. 476–504), are
even more misleading in the opposite direction.

and never since has Greek literature, in the widest sense of the word, been subjected to such a penetrating analysis.[46]

This study of the past was inspired by reverence and love. The Hellenistic scholars, especially the great Alexandrians, from Zenodotus to Aristarchus, were stout defenders of the old masters. As the most ancient and famous of them, Homer was also the most reviled. Zoïlus earned his perennial infamy by writing "A Whip for Homer" ('Ομηρομάστιξ).[47] Attacks on Homer's art—not only on his morals—appear much earlier, in Xenophanes and Protagoras,[48] against whom Aristotle strongly defended the Divine (θεσπέσιος) Poet.[49] By now, however, the great change in literary style and taste made many readers and critics very sensitive to Homer's shortcomings. To their modern and delicate taste, the old Ionian poet seemed naïve, artless, and crude. In the *scholia* to the Homeric poems, we find traces of these attacks, together with the scholars' refutations of them—if need be, by striking out Homeric verses which sinned against decorum (τὸ πρέπον). For the scholars too were children of their age and would not allow Homer to express himself in a manner unworthy of a classic.[50]

46. On Hellenistic literary opinion and criticism, see Ulrich von Wilamowitz-Moellendorff, *Hellenistische Dichtung in der Zeit des Kallimachos, 1* (Berlin, 1924), pp. 91ff., and Felix Jacoby, *Die griechische Moderne,* Kleine philologische Schriften, 2 (Berlin, 1961), pp. 285–300. Cf. also G. M. A. Grube, *The Greek and Roman Critics* (London, 1965), pp. 122 ff., and Rudolf Pfeiffer, *The Future of Studies in the Field of Hellenistic Poetry,* in his *Ausgewählte Schriften* (Munich, 1960), pp. 148 ff.

47. See Ulrich Friedländer, *De Zoilo aliisque Homeri obtrectatoribus* (Diss. Königsberg, 1895).

48. *Xenophanes* fr. 28 Diels-Kranz; *Protagoras* test. 29 Untersteiner.

49. *Poetics* 1465b15 ff. Aristotle wrote a now-lost treatise, Απορήματα 'Ομηρικά, in which he defended Homer. See Franz and Henrietta Apfel, "Homeric Criticism in the Fourth Century B.C.," *Transactions and Proceedings of the American Philological Association* (1938), pp. 245–58, and H. Hintenlang, *Untersuchungen zu den Homer-Aporien des Aristoteles* (Diss. Heidelberg, 1961.

50. Little has been written on the aesthetical criticism of Homer in classical antiquity as compared to the vast amount of literature on the philological criticism. The main sources are the *scholia* in the *Codex Venetus A,* now to be edited by Hartmuth Erbse. Rudolf Griesing, *Die ästhetischen Anschauungen der alten Homererklärer dargestellt nach den Homerscholien* (Diss. Tübingen, 1913), deals only with the composition of the Homeric

This defense of the past, however sincere, did not mean that the past should be regarded as a model. The great poets, even Homer, were to be admired and studied, but not imitated. Their very greatness made it impossible to follow in their steps. The poets of the present age had another task: to create a poetry of their own, different from but not inferior to earlier poetry.

Thus one could outline the program of many Hellenistic critics and poets as it emerges from the fragmentary remnants of their writings. The Atticizing proscription of most Hellenistic literature has made it difficult to form an adequate idea of Hellenistic criticism, though Egyptian papyri have lessened our ignorance. But even such an outstanding figure as Callimachus is only partly known.

This is especially regrettable, as the little we know of Callimachus' literary opinions shows that he was a pronounced modernist.[51] His profound knowledge of literary history, manifested in the *Pinakes,* the monumental inventory of Greek literature, convinced him of the futility of imitation and imitators. As a poet, he shuns the beaten track and refuses to drink from the common well.[52] Others—like Apollonius of Rhodes—may imitate Homer; *he* knows that he is no "Thunderer." [53] This humility should not be taken too seriously: [54] Callimachus is well aware of his own worth and does not hesitate to proclaim it.[55] He is not Homer, but he is Callimachus.

Callimachus was a leader of opinion and must have had many

---

poems. Limited also is the subject of Adolf Clausing, *Kritik und Exegese der Homerischen Gleichnisse im Altertum* (Diss. Freiburg i. B., 1913). The best treatment is still Karl Lehrs' classic work *De Aristarchi Studiis Homericis* (3d ed. Leipzig, 1882); cf. also G. C. Cobet, ΑΠΡΕΠΗ *apud Homerum pravo Alexandrinorum iudicio,* Miscellanea critica (Leiden, 1876), pp. 225–29.

51. Callimachus' literary opinions have often been discussed by scholars; see the latest monographs by Walter Wimmel, *Kallimachus in Rom,* Hermes. Einzelschriften, 16 (Wiesbaden, 1960), and Egon Eichgrün, *Kallimachos und Apollonios Rhodos* (Diss. Berlin, 1961).

52. Callimachus, *Epigram XXVIII;* cf. fr. 1 Pfeiffer (*Against the Telchines*) and the end of the *Hymn to Apollo.*

53. Callimachus fr. 1, 20 Pfeiffer.

54. As Grube seems to do (p. 126).

55. In *Against the Telchines* as well as in the *Hymn to Apollo.*

followers among Hellenistic authors and critics.[56] But their writings have nearly all disappeared, wiped out by the triumphant reaction of Atticism, the only really victorious literary reaction in Europe.[57] We know neither its origins nor its originators, but in the first century B.C. it was already conquering literature and—above all—education, as we can infer from Cicero's self-defense in the *Brutus* and the *Orator* (46 B.C.) and from the somewhat later treatises of Dionysius of Halicarnassus.

From that time on, to study literature meant to study the great old writers from Homer to Demosthenes, and to write meant to write like them, especially the Attic prose writers of the fifth and fourth centuries. Literary Greek became more and more an artificial language—not dead, but living a secluded and secondhand life, carefully separated from everyday speech and rigorously controlled by schoolmasters, grammarians, and critics. Glossaries, manuals, and anthologies helped young and old to acquire the difficult art of mastering a language which every year became more remote.

Atticism appealed, of course, only to the small educated minority, and it met with hard resistance. A sensible man like Plutarch disliked its excesses, and a witty man like Lucian poked fun at its absurdities. The schools, however, assured its rule, and both Plutarch and Lucian were Atticists. Until the fall of Constantinople in 1453 A.D., there would never be a lack of Greeks who tried to write like Demosthenes and sometimes succeeded in deceiving their contemporaries, though not modern scholars.

The triumph of Atticism established a literary orthodoxy which strongly denied any possiblity of progress. Greek literature was now conceived as a rigidly organized hierarchy of styles and genres, each with its appropriate rules and acknowledged masters, above all of whom reigned The Poet (Homer) and The Orator

56. See Theocritus' attack upon the modern imitators of Homer, *Idylls* VII.45–48.

57. In spite of its great historical importance, Atticism has been little studied since Wilamowitz' famous paper *Attizismus und Asianismus* (Hermes, 1900); see also his survey in *Geschichte der griechischen Literatur,* Die Kultur der Gegenwart, I:VIII (3d ed. Berlin, 1912), pp. 219 ff., and W. Kroll, *Rhetorik,* Real-Encyclopädie, Suppl. VII (Stuttgart, 1940), cols. 1105 ff. Lesky's treatment of it in his otherwise excellent history is inadequate.

(Demosthenes). Lists were made of "canonical" authors in different genres, implying that these and no others were worthy of being read: the Nine lyricists, the Three tragedians, the Three comedians, the Ten orators, and so on.[58]

The pedagogical purpose of these lists was obvious, and Atticism was, to a high degree, the work of schoolmasters. To them, literature was study and imitation of the great writers of the past. The way to success and fame was along the beaten track which Callimachus refused to follow. Even such an unconventional spirit as the unknown author of *On the Sublime* takes this for granted: the only road which leads to sublimity is "zealous imitation of the great prosewriters and poets of the past," and he condemns severely the craze for novelty.[59] The perhaps greatest luminary of Atticism, Aelius Aristides, acquired immortal fame by imitating not only the style but the subject of Demosthenes' speeches, in his own speeches on Greek politics in the fourth century B.C.—about five hundred years before his own time.

All Atticists were, fortunately, not so rigorous as Aristides, and even he succumbed to the temptation of treating modern subjects, though always in the Attic of Demosthenes. But what originality there is in Greek literature after the victory of Atticism owes its existence to a happy inconsequence—for the consequence of Atticism is frozen immobility, an eternal imitation of models and masters.

With imitations of Greek models Roman literature begins, the first work of which is Livius Andronicus' translation of the *Odyssey*. *Graecia capta ferum victorem cepit*. From then on, however, this imitation was not free from emulation and rivalry. Ennius, the first forger of Latin hexameters, believed that Homer's soul had taken its abode in him: he was "the new Homer" and his *Annals* the new *Iliad*.[60] His contemporaries and the following

---

58. See L. Radermacher, *Kanon*, Real-Encyclopädie, X (Stuttgart, 1919), cols. 1873 ff., and E. R. Curtius, *Europäische Literatur und lateinisches Mittelalter* (2nd ed. Bonn, 1954), pp. 253 ff. The now current term κάνωνες was never used in this sense in classical antiquity; see Herbert Opel, ΚΑΝΩΝ, Philologus, Suppl. XXX:4 (Leipzig, 1937), p. 47.

59. *On the Sublime* XIII.2. See, on rhetorical μίμησις, Kroll, cols. 1113 ff.

60. Horace, *Epist.* II.1, 50, a quotation from Lucilius.

generations accepted this claim. Cicero still admired him, and Lucretius called him "our Ennius, who first bore down from pleasant Helicon the wreath of deathless leaves, to win bright fame among the tribes of Italian people." [61]

Lucretius is well aware of the Greek masters and rivals, but he finds it possible to match and even to surpass them. Every Roman poet of those times had to believe in progress, because only thus could he believe in himself. True, the difficulties in his way were formidable, and despair was always lurking. The greatest masters of Latin poetry confessed to it. In his epistle *Ad Pisones,* Horace bitterly exclaims:

> Grais ingenium, Grais dedit ore rotundo
> Musa loqui, praeter laudem nullius avaris.[62]

And in ever-quoted verses, Virgil in his great epic solemnly warns the Romans that to abandon themselves to arts and sciences is the privilege of other peoples.[63] But the very splendor of these verses testifies against the poet, and seemingly humble renouncement ill conceals an immense pride. The Romans should not be artists and scientists because their duty is to rule nations! Horace, too, has something of the same ambiguity common to many educated Romans: the wonderful Greek civilization with all its beauties was not quite manly, not quite serious.[64]

But if you wanted to be a poet, as good as, nay, better than the Greeks, you had to study them. The only way to surpass them was to imitate them. As Horace and every other Roman poet knew:

> vos exemplaria Graeca
> nocturna versate manu, versate diurna.[65]

Through imitation to originality—this eternal paradox of European classicism was first discovered and expressed by the Romans.

61. *De rerum natura* I.117–19. I quote from the translation of Cyril Bailey (Oxford, 1947).

62. *Ad Pisones* 323–24.

63. *Aeneis* VI.847–53.

64. *Epist.* II.1, 93–96. I follow the interpretation of Eduard Fraenkel, *Horace* (Oxford, 1957), p. 390, as against that of C. O. Brink, *Horace on Poetry* (Cambridge, 1963), pp. 196 ff. See also Carl Becker, *Das Spätwerk des Horaz* (Göttingen, 1963), p. 222.

65. *Ad Pisones* 268–69; cf. Becker, pp. 102 ff.

When Horace wrote those lines, however, he found before him another less forbidding but more annoying hindrance: the admiration of his contemporaries for older Roman poets, coupled with a conceited contempt for modern poetry such as his own. On this point, Horace was a firm and consistent modernist. In the epistle *To Augustus*, he satirizes the antiquarian predilection for the oldest monuments of the Latin language and the snobbish delight in archaic authors, down to Livius Andronicus himself, a painful memory. But the value of a poem, Horace contends, has nothing to do with its age. If the Greeks had shared the opinions of today, there would have been no old literature to admire.[66] In the *Ad Pisones*, Horace returns to the subject when he claims the poet's right to coin a new word for a new thing. Why should Horace and Virgil not use the same liberty as Plautus, Ennius, or Cato before them? Language changes like everything else in this world; words blossom and wither like flowers, subjected to the demands of utility.[67]

The necessity for self-defense probably made Horace sound more modernistic than he really was. As highly critical of older Latin literature as he was, his relation to Greek literature is marked by deep admiration. The models whom he chooses for imitation are not his feeble contemporaries, not even the Alexandrian poets so dear to Catullus and the other *neoterici*, but the great lyric poets of the high classical age—Archilochus, Alcaeus, Sappho, and Pindar. In the poem which closes his greatest achievement, the first three books of the *Carmina*, he mentions as his sole claim to immortality that he was the first to adopt Aeolian song to Italian verses.[68] And in the introductory poem, he expresses his hopes that Maecenas will assign him to the lyric poets [69]—we may add, as the tenth.

Certainly, the imitation of which Horace boasts is not a slavish

66. *Epist.* II.1, 18–92; cf. Fraenkel, pp. 387 ff., and Brink, pp. 193 ff. Horace had already criticized the archaists in *Sat.* I.10; cf. Brink, pp. 165 ff., and Becker, p. 239.

67. *Ad Pisones* 45–73; cf. Richard Heinze, *Q. Horatius Flaccus Briefe,* ed. A. Kiessling and R. Heinze (5th ed. Berlin, 1957), pp. 296 ff.

68. *Carmina* III.30, 13–14.

69. *Carmina* I.1, 35–36; cf. Fraenkel, p. 232.

one. In the epistle to Maecenas in which he airs his disappoint-
ment at the reception of the *Carmina,* he fulminates against the
servum pecus of imitators and proudly declares that he has walked
untrodden paths and has not feared to alter his models, in the
same way as the old Greeks altered theirs.[70] For he is well aware of
the difference between them—e.g. Pindar—and himself.[71] For his
own imitators, Horace has only contempt.

Horace's utterances show his preoccupation with the Greeks but
also his desire to separate himself from them. Even in his imitation
of them, he remains a Roman; he remains Horace: he feels the
whole weight of the literary tradition, but he is not crushed by it.
He is an heir, not an epigone.

On this point, he is representative of his age, the Augustan age,
when Roman literature at last felt itself not only the rival, but the
equal of Greek literature—the equal, and perhaps even superior.
Some years before, young Propertius had written of the yet unpublished *Aeneid:* "yield, Greek poets! something greater than
the *Iliad* is being born." [72]

The Greeks who did not learn Latin—save for exceptions, like
Plutarch—continued to regard Roman writers as clumsy imitators.[73] To the Romans themselves, the great Augustan authors,
together with some from the last period of the Republic—Terence, Sallust, Caesar, and above all Cicero—quickly became classics, read and expounded in the schools, edited and annotated by
scholars. In Quintilian's *Institutio Oratoria,* written at the end of
the first century A.D., the Augustans are praised as the great masters and models, who compare favorably with the Greeks.[74] Quintilian is a good patriot who rarely concedes that Greeks can be
superior to Romans, as, for instance, in comedy. In other fields,
however, the Romans do not yield to the Greeks, not even in epic,
in which Virgil may be second to Homer, but only just. In elo-

70. *Epist.* I.19, 19–34; cf. *Sat.* I.10, 17–19. See also Fraenkel, pp. 341 ff.;
Brink, pp. 179 ff.; and Becker, pp. 82 ff.

71. *Carmina* IV.2; cf. Fraenkel, pp. 435 ff.

72. *Elegies* II.34, 65–66.

73. See, e.g., Strabo, *Geographica* VII.19 (C 166).

74. Quintilian's literary opinions are to be found mainly in the tenth
book of the *Institutio Oratoria.* The quotations are from the translation of
H. E. Butler in *The Loeb Classical Library.*

quence Rome possesses the marvelous and unique genius of Cicero, whose name is regarded by posterity "not as a name of a man
but as the name of eloquence itself." [75]

Quintilian is usually regarded as "a conscious classicist and admirer of the writers of the golden age," [76] hostile to archaic, pre-
classic authors like Ennius and to modern writers like Seneca.[77]
His classicism and anti-modernism should not be exaggerated,
however. He does, indeed, stress the necessity for studying the
great writers of the past and warns his young readers from lightly
pronouncing judgment upon them, but he follows his survey of
literary models with a long chapter in which he severely condemns
mere imitation of them.[78] "What would have happened," he asks,
"in the days when models were not, if men had decided to do and
to think of nothing that they did not know already? The answer is
obvious: nothing then would have been discovered. Why, then, is
it a crime for us to discover something new?" If no Roman had
done more than his predecessors, we would still be left with the
poems of Livius Andronicus and the Annals of the Pontiffs.

> Cast your eyes over the whole of history; you will find that no
> art has remained just as it was when it was discovered, nor
> came to a standstill at its very birth, unless indeed we are
> ready to pass special condemnation on our own generation on
> the ground that no further development is possible; and it is
> undoubtedly true that no development is possible for those
> who restrict themselves to imitation.[79]

We see that Quintilian's classicism does not exclude a belief in the
possibility, nay, the necessity of progress in literature. He criticizes such a modern writer as Seneca, but not for being modern,
and he does not admire the ancients for being ancient.[80] His posi-

75. *Institutio Oratoria* X.1, 99–100, 85–86, 105–14.

76. Grube, p. 300; see also George Kennedy, "An Estimate of Quintilian," *American Journal of Philology* (1962), pp. 130–46.

77. *Institutio Oratoria* X.1, 88, 125–31.

78. Ibid., X.1, 26; X.2. Curiously enough, Grube in his long résumé of the
Institutio passes over this chapter in silence. Kennedy's remarks on it are
misleading.

79. Quintilian's argument is applied to art in Philostratus Jr.'s *Imagines*,
Prooemium.

80. Ibid., X.1, 43, and VI.5, 21 ff.

tion resembles Horace's, though he is not a creative poet in a great literary age but a critic and educator in a later, post-classical age, trying hard to keep a just balance between the admirers of the present age—men like the impetuous Aper in Tacitus' *Dialogue on Orators*—and the admirers of bygone days—men like Tacitus' Messalla.[81] But for all his modernism, Aper is an admirer of Horace and Virgil,[82] and for all his classicism, Messalla does not want to go back further than Cicero.[83] This testifies to the strength of the "Augustan orthodoxy."

This literary establishment had, like its Greek counterpart, its detractors and rebels. True, the Latin modernism of the first century A.D., whose greatest representative was Seneca, quickly disappeared; in Greece, Atticism made a real modernism impossible. But the other extreme, archaism, was an ever-present danger. In Greece, there were readers who preferred the Sophists of the fifth century to the Attic writers of the fourth, and authors who wrote in the long defunct Ionic of Herodotus and Democritus or in the Aeolic of Alcaeus and Sappho. In Rome, the archaists, odious to Horace and Quintilian, triumphed in the second century with Fronto, the teacher of Marcus Aurelius, his pupil Aulus Gellius, and Apuleius, who went back to pre-Ciceronian Latinity in a paradoxical attempt to vindicate their originality which, in contrast to the ruling classicism, could be called modernism and indeed was felt as such.[84]

Archaism was for a long time fashionable, but it never succeeded in capturing the inner citadel of the establishment, the schools. There, classicism kept its sway, and Virgil, Cicero, Horace, and the other Augustans continued to be the canonical authors, to

81. Scholars have often drawn the parallel between the *Institutio* and the *Dialogus;* see, e.g., Sir Ronald Syme, *Tacitus, 1* (Oxford, 1958), 114 ff., and Clarence W. Mendell, *Tacitus* (New Haven, 1957), pp. 21 ff., 71 ff. My interpretation of Tacitus' attitude in the *Dialogus* agrees more with Mendell's than with Syme's.

82. *Dialogus de oratoribus* 20.

83. Ibid., 25.

84. On modernism and archaism in Greek and Roman literature, see Eduard Norden's classical work *Die Antike Kunstprosa, 1* (5th ed. Stuttgart, 1958), but cf. the corrections given by René Marache, *La critique littéraire de la langue latine et le développement du goût archaïssant au IIe siècle de notre ère* (Diss. Paris, 1952).

whom only some authors of the first century A.D. were added; Juvenal was the last.[85] While some despised Virgil for being too old-fashioned and others despised him for being too modern, most felt for him the piety which inspired Statius to close his *Thebaid* with a humble prayer that his poem might live, not to rival the divine *Aeneid*, but to follow piously in its footsteps.[86] When Rome succumbed to the barbarians, it was these authors whom the last Roman aristocrats strived to save from the deluge.[87]

In the latter days of classical antiquity, we would not expect to find believers in progress. Already Tacitus and the author of *On the Sublime* [88] had pointed out the decline of eloquence and ascribed it to the decline of political liberty. The latter writer even quotes an unnamed philosopher's opinion that "really sublime and transcendent natures are no longer, or, only very rarely, now produced." Before Tacitus and "Longinus," Seneca the Rhetor had complained of the evil law that decay swiftly follows upon an acme—in this case, the Ciceronian age of eloquence.[89] His contemporary, the historian Velleius Paterculus, applied the scheme —progress, culmination, regress—to the history of Greek and Roman literature and art down to his own time.[90]

Of course, such gloomy views of the present were in themselves nothing new. Long ago, Hesiod had complained of living in an age worse than all earlier ones, and his complaints have been repeated by many later writers. This is as it should be, for the *laudator temporis acti* is always with us. But it would be quite misleading to say that "the general view of Greek (or Roman) philosophers

85. See H.-J. Marrou, *Histoire de l'éducation dans l'antiquité classique* (3d ed. Paris, 1955), pp. 373 ff. and Norden, *1*, 348.

86. *Thebaid* XII.816–17; cf. Karl Büchner, *P. Vergilius Maro,* Real-Encyclopädie, II:8 (Stuttgart, 1958), cols. 1463 ff.

87. See Norden, *2*, 577 ff., and F. Klingner, "Vom Geistesleben im Rom des ausgehenden Altertums," *Römische Geisteswelt* (3d ed. Munich, 1956), pp. 475 ff.

88. *Dialogus de oratoribus* 36–40; *On the Sublime* 49; cf. the commentary by D. A. Russell, *Longinus: On the Sublime* (Oxford, 1965), pp. 185 ff.

89. *Controversiae* I praef 7; cf. Norden, *1*, 245 ff. A parallel from Greek literature is in Cicero, *Brutus* 37; cf. Norden, *1*, 127 ff.

90. *Historia Romana* I.16 f.; cf. Norden, *1*, 245, and A. Dihle, *Velleius Paterculus,* Real-Encyclopädie II:15, col. 645, who both point out that the source of this interesting passage is unknown.

(or writers) was that they were living in a period of inevitable degeneration and decay." [91] Some believed this, but by no means all. Certainly it was not the general feeling in the self-confident Greek and Roman civilization of the first centuries A.D. which boasted of the *felicitas saeculi* [92] and its new-won youth.[93]

Such declarations were repeated even in later and less fortunate times, after the great crisis in the middle of the third century. But the officially manifested faith in the *Roma aeterna* was more than counterbalanced by a deep consciousness of living in an aging world, *mundus senescens*, where man and the whole universe degenerate and decay.[94] In such a world, progress can only mean a further step downward to chaos and annihilation.

91. Bury, p. 9.

92. See, e.g., Tacitus, *Agricola* 3 and the *senatus-consulta* of Hosidius and Volusius (42–46 and 56 A.D.) in *Textes de Droit Romain,* ed. P. F. Girard (5th ed. Paris, 1923), pp. 132 ff.; cf. Marache, p. 68.

93. Florus, *Epitome* I.4–8. The comparison of the different periods of Roman history to the different ages of man ought to lead to pessimism, as it evidently did in some work by Seneca (the Rhetor or the Philosopher) quoted by Lactantius, *Div. Instit.* VII.15, 14–16, in Vopiscus' "Life of Carus" in the *Historia Augusta,* and in Ammianus Marcellinus, *Historiae* XIV.6, 4. Cf. Martin Schanz, *Geschichte der römischen Literatur, 3* (3rd ed. Munich, 1922), pp. 71 ff.; Carlo Tibiletti, *Il proemio di Floro, Seneca il Retore e Tertulliano* (Convivium, 1959), pp. 334–42; and R. Häussler, *Vom Ursprung und Wandel des Lebensaltervergleichs* (Hermes, 1964), pp. 313–41.

94. See the texts collected and quoted by Johannes Geffcken, *Stimmungen im untergehenden Weströmerreich,* Neue Jahrbücher für das Klassische Altertum (1920), pp. 256–69; Walther Rehm, *Der Untergang Roms im abendländischen Denken,* Das Erbe der Alten, 18 (Leipzig, 1930), pp. 18 ff., 144 ff.; Franz Christ, *Die römische Weltherrschaft in der antiken Dichtung,* Tübinger Beiträge zur klassischen Altertumswissenschaft, 36 (Stuttgart, 1938), pp. 70 ff., 198 ff.; Helmut Werner, *Der Untergang Roms,* Forschungen zur Kirchen- und Geistesgeschichte, 17 (Stuttgart, 1939); and Häussler, *Vom Ursprung und Wandel.* One of the most interesting utterances occurs in St. Cyprian's *Ad Demetrianum 3–4,* Corpus Scriptorum Ecclesiasticorum Latinorum, III:1 (Vienna, 1878), pp. 352 ff. See also the general remarks by F. Vittinghoff, "Zum geschichtlichen Selbstverständnis der Spätantike," *Historische Zeitschrift, 198* (1964), 529–74.

Contributors

F. W. Bateson, Reader in English, Christ Church, Oxford

Cleanth Brooks, Gray Professor of Rhetoric, Yale University

Calvin S. Brown, Alumni Foundation Distinguished Professor of Comparative Literature, University of Georgia

Peter Demetz, Professor of German and Comparative Literature, Yale University

Herbert Dieckmann, Professor of French and Comparative Literature, Cornell University

Victor Erlich, Bensinger Professor of Russian Literature, Yale University

Ralph Freedman, Professor of English and Comparative Literature, Princeton University

A. Bartlett Giamatti, Associate Professor of English, Yale University

Thomas Greene, Professor of English and Comparative Literature, Yale University

Claudio Guillén, Professor of Spanish and Comparative Literature, University of California, San Diego

Thomas R. Hart, Professor of Spanish and Comparative Literature, University of Oregon

Geoffrey H. Hartman, Professor of English and Comparative Literature, Yale University

Helmut Hatzfeld, Professor of Romance Languages, Catholic University of America

Heinrich Henel, Sterling Professor of German, Yale University

Robert Louis Jackson, Professor of Russian Literature, Yale University

Edith Kern, Professor of French, University of Washington

Harry Levin, Irving Babbitt Professor of Comparative Literature, Harvard University

Edgar Lohner, Professor of German, Stanford University

Agostino Lombardo, Professor of English Literature, University of Rome

Herman Meyer, Professor of German, University of Amsterdam

Lowry Nelson, Jr., Associate Professor of Comparative Literature, Yale University

Stephen G. Nichols, Jr., Professor of French and Comparative Literature, Dartmouth College

G. N. G. Orsini, Professor of Comparative Literature, University of Wisconsin

E. N. Tigerstedt, Professor of General Literature, University of Stockholm

W. K. Wimsatt, Ford Professor of English, Yale University

Eléonore M. Zimmermann, Associate Professor of French and German, University of Rochester